Sex & Gender
An Introduction

Sex & Gender
An Introduction

Second Edition

Hilary M. Lips
Radford University

Mayfield Publishing Company
Mountain View, California
London • Toronto

Library of Congress Cataloging-in-Publication Data
Lips, Hilary M.
    Sex & gender : an introduction / Hilary M. Lips.—2nd ed.
        p.   cm.
    Includes bibliographical references and indexes.
    ISBN   1-55934-090-8
    1. Sex role. 2. Sex differences (Psychology) I. Title.
·II. Title: Sex and gender.
HQ1075.L58 1992
305.3—dc20   92-20228
                                              CIP

Manufactured in the United States of America

10 9 8 7 6 5 4 3 2 1

Mayfield Publishing Company
1240 Villa Street
Mountain View, California 94041

Sponsoring editor, Franklin C. Graham; production editor, Sondra Glider;
manuscript editor, Carol Dondrea; manufacturing manager, Martha Branch;
photo researcher, Melissa Kreischer; illustrator, Laslow Meszoly; text designer,
Victoria Vandeventer; production artist, Jean Mailander.

The text was set in 10/12 Galliard Roman by TBH/Typecast, Inc., and printed
on 50# Finch Opaque by Malloy Lithographing, Inc.

Art, photograph, and text credits appear on a continuation of the copyright
page, p. 482.

For Jennifer, Hilary, and Leif
In the trust that your talents and strengths,
unfettered by notions of femininity and masculinity,
will shape what you choose and seek

Contents

Preface

The division of the human race into females and males has, in many ways, assumed an importance that overshadows other divisions. From culture to culture, the male–female distinction has been assigned meanings and significance that have implications for work, family, leisure, ritual—virtually all aspects of social life. Yet it is only within fairly recent history that we have begun to stand back from and question the meaning that cultures have placed on femaleness and maleness, femininity and masculinity. It is this process of questioning that both leads to and is nourished by the study of sex and gender.

The study of the differences and similarities between women and men is compelling because of both its personal and its political implications. Since they are emphasized so strongly in our culture, issues of femininity and masculinity can be important aspects of individual identity and self-concept. But such issues go far beyond questions of personal self-awareness; feminist scholarship over the last two decades has made it increasingly apparent that beliefs about the differences and similarities between women and men are both rooted in and help to perpetuate particular social and political arrangements. To appreciate both the personal and political dimensions of gender, it is useful to examine what we know and do not know about the similarities and differences between women and men, where that knowledge comes from, and how that knowledge may itself be shaped and limited by cultural perceptions of femininity and masculinity. It is to precisely this type of examination that this book is dedicated.

Any one person's attempt to summarize a body of knowledge must necessarily reflect her own values and biases; this book is no exception to that rule. As a feminist social psychologist, I came to the writing of this book with a conviction that many of the differences in the ways that female and male human beings behave can be traced to such social factors as stereotyping, self-fulfilling prophecy, conformity to social pressure, expectancy effects, and different socialization practices for the two genders. Furthermore, although I believe that empirical research—research that tests theories against observable facts—is one of the best tools for unmasking and discrediting false assumptions and inaccurate stereotypes about sex and gender, I am also well aware that researchers shape their own truths to some extent and that the biases built into the research process itself affect investigators' findings and can perpetuate faulty theories and sexist interpretations of data. Thus, this book emphasizes empirical research, but takes a critical approach to that research.

Knowledge is gathered and opinions formed in a social context. Early research on male–female differences took place in a context in which, for instance, it was often taken for granted that women's chief purpose in life was to bear children, and that men were naturally better suited than women to take on public roles outside the family. Had I written this book 25 years ago, it would have been difficult to find and include a substantial amount of research that examined the social underpinnings of gender roles or challenged the assumption that sex differences in temperament were the inevitable outcome of the anatomical and physiological differences between females and males. It is largely under the impetus provided by the feminist movement that social scientists have begun to consider gender as something that is socially constructed rather than biologically inevitable. Yet our present social context continues to limit the study and understanding of sex and gender, and important gaps remain in the information that is available. Two of these gaps have been particularly noticeable to me as I compiled information for this book. The first is the small proportion of research on sex and gender that focuses on, or even includes, perspectives other than those of white, middle-class females and males. Since most of the research is based in universities, and universities have been much more accessible to this group than to any other, this gap is hardly cause for surprise, but it is cause for concern. If we shape our "feminine" or "masculine" behavior largely in response to social cues and social pressure, then it stands to reason that, to the extent that different groups emphasize or are subjected to different patterns of social cues and social pressure, femininity or masculinity in those groups will be associated with different experiences and behavior. For example, while some commonalities certainly exist, the female experience may differ in important ways for African-American women, Asian-American women, and European-American women in the United States; the male experience may differ in important ways for Native American men or for men of Indo-Pakistani or European descent in Canada. Where possible in this book I have tried to include information that broadens the perspective on gender beyond that of white middle-class culture. Such inclusiveness has been a little easier in this second edition because of a burgeoning emphasis on diversity in feminist scholarship. However, information on every group for every topic is not always readily available.

A second gap in the knowledge base about sex and gender stems from a tendency on the part of social scientists to ignore the experience of anyone who is not heterosexual. Thus, research on the development of sexual feelings and relationships, and research on couples and families, has until recently all but ignored the experience of lesbians and gay men. Although gaps still remain in this area, some excellent studies now exist. I have tried to include this perspective wherever information is available.

The book is divided into three parts. The first, "Myths, Theories, and Research," focuses on the stereotypes of femininity and masculinity and on the ways that theory and research in psychology and the other social sciences have been influenced by and have impacted on these stereotypes. The second, "Behavior and Experience: Female–Male Similarities and Differences," pits the gender stereotypes against the research evidence. It examines the evidence for male–female similarities and differences in a wide range of domains, from aggression to altruism, from mathematical performance to sexuality, from the experience of reproduction to mental and physical health. Throughout this section, the emphasis is on evaluating the evidence for gender differences and, where differences appear, on trying to understand the reasons for them. The third section, "Sex and Gender in Social Relationships," examines the reciprocal links between gender roles and the structure of relationships in the social world, from friendships to families, from work relationships to politics and law. This section stresses the position of individuals in their social context; feminine and masculine gender roles are not simply sets of qualities developed by individuals, they are part of the rules of a social system in which these individuals live. Built into that system is a hierarchy in which males, in general, have more power than females. The power difference cannot be ignored, and it is not easy for an individual to break away from it or to change it. Its consequences can be very negative for women; there are negative side effects for men as well. An understanding of the way that gender as an aspect of social relationships is a reflection of a status hierarchy in which males outrank females leads back to an understanding of why gender stereotypes are the way they are, thus completing the circle that was begun in the first chapter of the book.

New to this second edition, besides a greater emphasis on diversity and a general updating of findings, are discussions of a variety of issues that were omitted or touched on only briefly in the first edition. Chapter 1 now includes a discussion of the intersection of gender stereotypes with social class and sexual orientation. Chapter 2 includes an expanded section on Karen Horney and new sections on social interaction process theories of gender and on perspectives on "difference." Chapter 5 covers new correlational research on male aggression and hormones. The discussion of gender and mathematics and science in Chapter 6 is expanded. The chapter on sexuality, Chapter 7, gives more attention to several issues: sexually transmitted diseases, rape on college campuses, new reproductive technologies. Gender-related political issues in the funding of health research and in the diagnosis of mental illness are covered in Chapter 9. Chapter 10 provides a more extensive discussion of gender-related issues in self-esteem in early adolescence. The coverage of marital violence has been increased, in Chapter 11 and elsewhere in the book. Many new findings on gender and workplace issues appear in Chapter 13. Chapter 14 includes more information on gender and criminal victimization.

Many people have provided me with help and encouragement in the writing of this book. I thank the following people for insightful comments and suggestions on all or part of the manuscript or proposal for the first edition: Katherine Schultz, Dena Davidson, Nina Colwill, Jane Prather, Rhona Steinberg, Jeanne Kohl, Jeanne Maracek, Anne Peplau, and Ann Costain. Nina Colwill, my coauthor for Chapter 13 ("Issues in the Workplace"), provided welcome expertise and inspiration on many occasions. A book that she and I coauthored more than a decade ago, *The Psychology of Sex Differences*, provided some of the groundwork for this one, and I am indebted to her for some of the ideas that have been carried over from that earlier work to this. For this second edition, I extend my circle of thanks to include the following reviewers: Judy Rollins Bohannon, East Carolina University; Claire Etaugh, Bradley University; Lisa Judd, Winona State University; Faye D. Plascak-Craig, Marian College; Gwendolyn T. Sorrell, Texas Tech University; Michael R. Stevenson, Ball State University; Gail A. Thoen, University of Minnesota; Mary Roth Walsh, Harvard University. I am grateful to Frank Graham, my sponsoring editor at Mayfield, for his support, suggestions, and encouragement through both editions. In the editing and production of this second edition, I have much appreciated the careful help of Carol Dondrea, Sondra Glider, Melissa Kreischer, Jean Mailander, and Pam Trainer. My colleagues at the Center for Gender Studies gave me much needed moral and intellectual support as I worked through this edition. In particular, I thank Jerri Frantzve, Jeri Carter, Susan Freedman, and Al Harris for helping me to keep my sense of humor. My students in the Psychology Department also deserve thanks for sharing their ideas with me and keeping me on my toes. Finally, I am deeply indebted to Wayne Andrew for his patience and care, and for help in a multitude of ways large and small.

1
Masculinity & Femininity: Myths & Stereotypes

Jazz musician Billy Tipton lived life as a man, developed a thriving public career, married, adopted three sons, and spent a lifetime playing piano and saxophone in nightclubs. In death, at age 74, Billy Tipton was revealed to be a woman. In life, Tipton's secret was kept from everyone but his spouse, who said that Tipton had taken on a male identity to remove barriers to a musical career. Tipton's sons, as well as his former musician colleagues, were surprised and shocked to learn that he was female. "I'm just lost," said one son. "He'll always be Dad, but I think that he should have left something behind for us, something that would have explained the truth" (Jazzman, 1989, p. 3A).

Ms. magazine carried a story about an "electronic imposter" (Van Gelder, 1985). This individual, a man, had presented himself as a woman on one of the large computer communication networks, and had interacted for months with other users of the network under this assumed identity. When his deception was unmasked, the man's electronic "penpals" were furious and hurt, not only because he had lied to them, but also because they felt they had been tricked into relating to him in ways that they would not have done had they known he was male.

These stories are two of many possible illustrations of the force with which the dimension "male–female" affects our perceptions of and reactions to other people. The discovery that someone with whom we have interacted is female when we supposed her to be male, or male when we supposed him to be female, is upsetting. Even when communicating by means of words typed onto a screen, it is unnerving to be uncertain of the sex of the person on the other end of the conversation. The labels *female* and *male* carry powerful associations about what to expect from the person to whom they are applied. We use the information the labels provide to guide our behavior toward other people and to interpret their behavior toward us. We also use the label applied to ourselves to create guidelines for our own activities. Not sure whether you believe this? Ask yourself the following questions: If I heard footsteps behind me in a lonely, dark alley, would I care whether they were those of a man or a woman? If I were boarding a transatlantic flight and found that the pilot was a woman, would I feel a touch of extra anxiety? If a bright, articulate male friend decided to postpone finishing university in order to get married and raise children, would I be more surprised than if a bright, articulate female friend made the same decision? more disapproving? If you can give an unhesitating "no" to all of these questions, it is just possible that you have evaded the effects of the stereotyping on the basis of sex that is prevalent in North American society. Most of us, however, have not.

Sex stereotypes are socially shared beliefs that certain qualities can be assigned to individuals, based on their membership in the female or male half of the human race. Stereotyping of individuals can proceed on the basis of race, age, religion, height, social class, or any other distinction that can be used to divide people into groups. Sex stereotyping, though, has the relatively unique aspect of being based on a distinction that divides human beings into two groups: Everyone is categorized as either male or female. A result of this situation seems to be that many of our sex stereotypes are based on the notion of opposites. Indeed, our custom of referring to "the opposite sex" in discussions of female–male relationships springs from this tradition. In various cultures the nature of the opposites has been specified. In some, the male principle has been represented by the sun, the female by the moon; the male by rationality and logic, the female by emotion and intuition; the male by light and clarity, the female by darkness, mystery, and magic. Some researchers now suggest that the notion of the two sexes as opposites, and of femininity and masculinity as two opposing poles on a continuum, may be one of the basic organizing principles that human beings have learned to use when thinking about gender (Deaux & Lewis, 1984; Foushee, Helmreich, & Spence, 1979). It is not necessarily natural to think of women and men as opposites, however. Historians have noted that in Western culture the "opposites" tradition succeeded an equally strong "hierarchical" one in which women and men were considered to be similar, with women less advanced than men along the same continuum of perfection (Laqueur, 1990).

An implication of the stereotyping of two groups as polar opposites is that any movement away from the stereotype of one group is, by definition, a movement toward that of the other group. In this framework, for instance, a man who acts less rational than the male stereotype is seen as not only less masculine but more feminine; a woman who acts less emotional than the female stereotype is viewed as not only less feminine but more masculine. Thus it is that, for example, women doing competent intellectual work have been told "you think like a man," and men showing reluctance to enter dangerous situations have been taunted with the epithet "old woman."

Another implication of the opposing stereotypes of masculinity and femininity is the notion that women and men should be separate from each other in a variety of contexts. A lone male or female in the midst of a group of the other sex is often made to feel like an invader or is obviously excluded, and individuals may scrupulously avoid situations they feel are geared for the other sex. The ludicrous lengths to which such avoidance may be carried was demonstrated in an old episode of the television show "Candid Camera." The crew labeled two adjacent telephone booths with the signs Men and Women, placed a man in the "men's" booth, and waited to see what would happen as male passersby came along wanting to make a phone call. Remarkably, men ignored the obviously empty "women's" phone booth and paced around impatiently waiting for their turn to use the one labeled Men. Such is the power of the notion that women and men must be wary of trespassing on each other's turf!

Another example that reflects both the arbitrariness of gender stereotypes and the phobia about violating them is provided by Tonkinson (1974), writing about the Aboriginal people of Australia. He tells of encountering a group of rural Aboriginal men who had been given some used clothing by a white station owner traveling through the area: "When our patrol arrived at the spot, the men in the group were wearing not only the trousers they had been given, but also the dresses. Our Aboriginal guide was quite embarrassed and quickly informed the men of their mistake; within seconds they discarded the female attire" (p. 104). To these men, who had not grown up with Western European customs, wearing dresses seemed just as appropriate as wearing pants—*until* the dresses were labeled as "for women."

The Social Context of Stereotypes

Stereotypes about women and men, like stereotypes about ethnic, racial, religious, or other groups, do not exist in a social vacuum. To understand why stereotypes persist in a particular form, it is necessary to know something about the social relations between the groups in question. In the case of women and men, there is in many cultures, including our own, a long history of a hierarchical relationship between the groups: Men have held more social power than women; men have been dominant and women subordinate (for comprehensive overviews of power and gender, see Lipman-Blumen, 1984, and Lips, 1991). One function of stereotypes is to bolster the status quo, so it is not surprising that dominant groups are stereotypically credited with more competence and intelligence than are subordinate groups, and that groups with low social power are more likely to be stereotyped as emotional and incompetent than are their higher power counterparts. This pattern, which can be seen in the stereotypes for blacks and whites in the United States, and for francophone and anglophone Canadians, is also evident in stereotypic beliefs about women and men. Indeed, stereotypes are often perpetuated simply *because* they justify prejudice against a subordinate group.

Stereotyping and prejudice involve dynamic processes, not just static collections of beliefs and evaluations. People who lack power and who are victims of prejudice actually develop qualities that are due to the prejudice and serve, in a self-fulfilling way, to reinforce it (Allport, 1954). They may, for instance, identify with the dominant group and accept that group's negative evaluation of their own group. Thus, for example, a woman may say that she does not like other women, and that she finds men more interesting than women. In the discussion of stereotyping that follows, and indeed for the remainder of this book, it is important to remember that the behaviors and traits attributed to women and men have been observed in particular social contexts—contexts in which men have, in many ways, held greater social power than have women.

Since stereotypic views of females and males are dynamic and depend on social context, sex stereotypes and ideals of femininity and masculinity are likely to vary somewhat across social/cultural groups and historical periods. For a white woman in the American south of the 1950s, femininity might mean emphasizing one's frailty and forswearing smoking on the street (King, 1985). For an African-American urban woman in the United States of the 1990s, the notions of acceptably "feminine" behavior might be quite different. For a contemporary middle-class Japanese man in Tokyo, masculinity might involve working an intense 80-hour week without complaint, rarely taking vacations, and squeezing in time with his family when he can (Makihara, 1991). For his North American counterpart, however, masculinity might imply having the leisure and means to do things with his family. Thus, there is not a *single* stereotype of masculinity or of femininity. Rather, these constructs are somewhat specific to time and place; they are continually being reworked, and their boundaries renegotiated. Moveable though the boundaries are in theory, however, we often experience them as daunting in our own culture, time, and place; we sense that transgressing them may involve negative reactions from others.

Sex or Gender: More Than a Question of Terminology?

In the past, the words *sex* and *gender* have often been used interchangeably. They will not be used interchangeably in this book, however, because many psychologists, stimulated by an appeal from Rhoda Unger (1979), have adopted more precise definitions of the two terms. *Sex* is used to refer to a person's biological maleness or femaleness, *gender* to the nonphysiological aspects of being female or male—the cultural expectations for femininity and masculinity. The distinction is a useful one because it keeps us focused on the fact that many female–male differences in behavior or experience do not spring naturally or automatically from biological differences between the sexes. However, no clean, absolute separation of *sex* and *gender* is possible. Cultural expectations for women and men (gender) are not separable from observations about women's and men's physical bodies (sex). Thus, cultural constructions of gender include sex, in some sense. Conversely, history illustrates that even the most obvious biological "facts" about sex are susceptible to misperception and misinterpretation when they violate investigators' assumptions about gender. For example, the distinguished anatomist Herophilus of Alexandria, working under the assumption that women were essentially unperfected men, "saw" in his dissections of human bodies that women had testes with seminal ducts that connected to the neck of the bladder, just as men did (Laqueur, 1990). What he saw were ovaries and Fallopian tubes—which clearly do *not* connect to the bladder. However, his expectation that women and men should be anatomically similar guided his perceptions, encouraging him to see similarities even where the evidence favored differences. Thus, our understanding of biological sex differences is likely to be shaped by our culture's notions of gender. Sex and gender, then, are overlapping constructs that differ in emphasis. In this book, *gender* is used as the more inclusive term; *sex* is reserved for discussions of more narrowly biological aspects of femaleness and maleness.

For the following discussion of stereotypes, the sex–gender distinction offers the clear advantage of being able to separate femaleness from femininity, maleness from masculinity. It allows us, for example, to contemplate the idea that a woman can deviate from cultural notions of femininity (gender) without having any impact on her femaleness (sex).

"Sugar and Spice" or "Snakes and Snails": The Content of Gender Stereotypes

Personality Traits

Aggressive. Sensitive. Cries easily. Ambitious. Which of the preceding adjectives would you say are typically associated with men? With women? It is on questions such as this that much of our knowledge of the content of gender stereotypes is based.

More than a decade ago, two researchers asked students at an American university to categorize 300 adjectives as being typically associated with women or men (Williams & Bennett, 1975). Seventy-five percent of the students agreed on 30 adjectives describing women and 33 describing men. These adjectives are shown in Table 1.1. They are not atypical of the findings of research on gender stereotypes. Researchers in Canada (Edwards & Williams, 1980) and Britain (Burns, 1977) have found similar if not identical patterns, and a study of gender stereotyping in thirty countries has shown considerable cross-cultural uniformity in these descriptions (Williams & Best, 1982). Some cross-cultural differences do exist, however. Block (1973) found that American students, both male and female, were more likely than their counterparts in England, Sweden, Denmark, Finland, and Norway to endorse agentic (instrumental, forceful) adjectives such as adventurous, assertive, and ambitious in their description of both the masculine and feminine ideals, while Lii and Wong (1982) found American students more likely than Chinese students to use agentic and competent attributes to describe the feminine stereotype. It must be remembered, however, that such findings describe the extent to which people in various parts of the world *know* the male and female stereotypes, not necessarily the extent to which they actually believe them to be true.

Although the existence of both female and male stereotypes can be demonstrated, the male stereotype seems to be the more rigidly defined of the two. When 400 undergraduates were asked to use lists of trait and appearance adjectives to describe personal (How do you personally see males?), social (How does society view males?) and ideal (How do you see the ideal male?) views of males and females, all three perspectives on males were more stereotypic than the comparable perspectives on females (Hort, Fagot, & Leinbach, 1990).

In trying to describe the themes inherent in gender stereotypes, psychologists have relied on a dichotomy first proposed by two family sociologists: instrumentality vs. expressiveness (Parsons & Bales, 1955). The masculine stereotype is said to be

Table 1.1 Adjectives stereotypically associated with
women and men (based on Williams & Bennett, 1975)

Women

Affected	Feminine	Prudish
Affectionate	Fickle	Rattlebrained
Appreciative	Flirtatious	Sensitive
Attractive	Frivolous	Sentimental
Charming	Fussy	Softhearted
Complaining	Gentle	Sophisticated
Dependent	High-strung	Submissive
Dreamy	Meek	Talkative
Emotional	Mild	Weak
Excitable	Nagging	Whiny

Men

Adventurous	Disorderly	Realistic
Aggressive	Dominant	Robust
Ambitious	Enterprising	Self-confident
Assertive	Forceful	Severe
Autocratic	Handsome	Stable
Boastful	Independent	Steady
Coarse	Jolly	Stern
Confident	Logical	Strong
Courageous	Loud	Tough
Cruel	Masculine	Unemotional
Daring	Rational	Unexcitable

characterized by expectations of instrumentality: an orientation toward action, accomplishment, leadership. The feminine stereotype, on the other hand, combines attributes that add up to expressiveness: an orientation to emotion and relationships. Congruent with this pattern are the findings of Broverman, Vogel, Broverman, Clarkson, and Rosenkrantz (1972) and McKee and Sherriffs (1957), who noted that the most highly valued male-stereotyped traits formed a "competency" cluster, while the most highly valued female-stereotyped traits formed a "warmth-expressiveness" cluster. Although this dichotomy focuses only on positive qualities and fails to capture completely the stereotypic beliefs about female–male differences (for example, the masculine traits "loud" and "disorderly" do not really seem to depict instrumentality, while the feminine traits "weak" and "whiny" bear no obvious relation to expressiveness), it does help to provide a framework for studying these stereotypes. But how is such study carried out? What do researchers really mean when they claim to have delineated the existence of a certain stereotype about a particular group among members of a particular population?

Measuring Stereotypes

Researchers using a question like the one at the beginning of this section may end up with findings that overestimate the strength of stereotypes and underestimate the overlap in the popular perceptions of females and males. The question comes with a built-in assumption that each adjective may be classified as more typical of either women or men. People answering such a question are thus subtly encouraged to provide stereotypic answers, and the results may provide an exaggerated view of the stereotypes. Moreover, respondents in these studies have usually been asked to indicate whether certain traits are "typically associated" with women or men, not whether they personally believe that a particular set of adjectives actually reflects what women and men are like. Finally, a fact often overlooked in discussions of stereotypes is that the average ratings obtained for males and females in these studies, although significantly different from each other, do not usually represent opposite extremes. For instance, on a 10-point scale ranging from passive (1) to active (10), males might be rated at 7.2 and females at 6.1. Indeed, the mean ratings of males and females on such scales rarely fall on opposite sides of the midpoint (Spence, Helmreich, & Stapp, 1974).

Researchers using different methods to assess stereotypes have found less evidence for their pervasiveness or for their bipolarity. When measures are used that allow respondents to describe males and females on the basis of overlapping as well as differentiating characteristics, subjects indicate that the "most feminine" and "most masculine" persons they can imagine possess many of the same desirable traits (Jenkin & Vroegh, 1969).

Stereotypes are more than catalogues of adjectives, and researchers now recognize that, for example, some "masculine" adjectives are considered more representative of the category *Men* than others are. Studies using a method that allows participants to rate the degree to which traits characterize both the typical woman and the typical man suggest a tendency for the clusters of traits seen to characterize each to overlap (De Lisi & Soundranayagam, 1990). Such studies, based on the idea that gender stereotypes represent natural language categories composed of "core" (prototypical) traits (the clearest examples of each category) surrounded by peripheral traits (those less strongly associated with each category), find that the "core" traits for women belong to a niceness/nurturance dimension, while those for men belong to a potency/power dimension. Overlap between the two categories is seen in that core adjectives for one gender tend to fall in the periphery for the other gender. One intriguing finding is that female respondents add to the niceness/nurturance qualities that constitute the female core a second group of adjectives: capable, competent, dependable, intelligent, responsible. Male respondents do not include these adjectives in the female core; rather, they tend to add attractive, good-looking, sexy, and soft (De Lisi & Soundranayagam, 1990).

Beyond Personality Traits: The Many Faces of Gender Stereotypes

If you had to choose the qualities that most clearly make people seem "feminine" or "masculine" to you, would you focus on personality traits? Or might you concentrate instead on other things about the person: physical appearance, perhaps, or certain behaviors, occupation, sexual preference? In recent years, researchers have come to realize that gender stereotypes are multifaceted, encompassing a variety of expectations about how people will look, act, think, and feel. Moreover, it is becoming apparent that there is more than a single "typical" male and female; rather, many people hold sets of stereotypes about different "types" of males and females.

Kay Deaux and Laurie Lewis (1983) showed that a number of separate components of gender stereotypes can be identified: traits, role behaviors, occupations, and physical appearance—each of which has a masculine and a feminine version. Their research suggests that people see these components as able to vary independently to some extent. For example, a person could have a very masculine appearance but not necessarily be in a masculine occupation or show a lot of masculine personality traits. However, they have also demonstrated that information about one component influences people's assumptions about the others, in the absence of conflicting information (Deaux & Lewis, 1984). For a hypothetical person, they gave subjects a sex label (male or female) and information about specific role behaviors (masculine, feminine, or mixed) and asked the subjects to estimate the likelihood that the person possessed particular masculine and feminine traits, pursued particular male- or female-associated occupations, and was heterosexual or homosexual. For example, subjects in the female/feminine role condition were given the following description: "A woman has been described in terms of the following characteristics and behaviors: source of emotional support, manages the house, takes care of children, responsible for decorating the house. Consider these characteristics carefully and think about what type of woman this would be." When subjects did think about it, they concluded that this woman was more likely to show feminine traits such as emotionality, gentleness, and understanding of others and to be in a feminine occupation such as occupational therapist or elementary school teacher than to show masculine traits or be in a masculine occupation. They also indicated a high probability that the woman was heterosexual. In general, the subjects apparently relied more heavily on the information they were given about role behaviors than on the male–female labels to estimate the probability of masculine or feminine traits or occupations. A person described in terms of the masculine role behaviors—head of household, financial provider, a leader, and responsible for household repairs—was judged much more likely to possess masculine traits such as independent, active, and competitive, and to be in male-associated occupations such as truck driver, insurance agent, or urban planner than was a person described in terms of female role behaviors, regardless of whether the person was labeled female or male. Also noteworthy is the finding that role behavior that is counterstereotypic for an individual's biological sex is linked to speculation that the person is homosexual. When feminine role behaviors were described for a hypothetical man, the estimated probability of homosexuality reached 40 percent. It is clear that gender stereotypes and stereotypes about homosexuality are linked, despite the lack of evidence that a person's sexual preference is related to gender role behavior.

In a follow-up experiment, these researchers found that physical appearance cues (masculine: tall, strong, sturdy, broad-shouldered; feminine: soft voice, dainty, graceful, soft) always outweighed sex labels when subjects were making inferences about a hypothetical person's traits, occupation, or role behaviors. Other researchers have subsequently found that the masculinity or femininity of facial appearance can have an impact on judgments about a person's sexual orientation: Individuals with feminine male faces and masculine female faces were more likely than others to be judged as homosexual (Dunkle & Francis, 1990). Indeed, it is quite likely that appearance is a core aspect of gender stereotyping, judging by the level of dismay that greets deviations from "appropriate" feminine and masculine physiques. It is instructive to note that a common reaction to female bodybuilders, for example, is not to marvel at their achievement of a muscular body but to bemoan their lack of feminine appearance. In the women's bodybuilding championship depicted in the documentary film *Pumping Iron II,* the woman with the biggest, most well defined muscles was given low scores because she "didn't look like a woman," despite one judge's argument that penalizing a contestant for having muscles that were too big was akin to telling a female skiier that she would be disqualified if she went too fast! It is becoming clear that people's ideas about gender are composed of several dimensions and that specific information about a person's characteristics can be more important in setting expectations about that person than is the knowledge that she or he is female or male.

The research just described underscores another important point: Despite our tendency to think of females and males as opposites, stereotyping by sex is not an all-or-nothing affair. Clearly, respondents do not believe that *only* males can be aggressive, drive trucks, or act as leaders, or that *only* females can be nurturant, have soft voices, and be elementary school teachers. Rather, the stereotypes are an expression of the perceived *probability* that a person will have certain qualities, given that she or he is female or male. Table 1.2 shows the probability judgments that subjects made about whether men and women would have particular characteristics. The table shows that, although a higher probability is given to the possession of stereotypic characteristics by men and women, there is always some acknowledged probability that each characteristic could be displayed by an individual of either sex.

One final note on the complexity of gender stereotypes: Not only do they seem to be made up of different components, but they also seem to be organized in terms of specific *types* of men and women (Ashmore, Del Boca, & Wohlers, 1986; Six & Eckes, 1991). Researchers find that respondents can quite easily list several types of

Table 1.2 Probability judgments of male and female stereotypic characteristics (adapted from Deaux, 1984b)

Characteristic	*Judgment*[a]	
	Men	*Women*
Trait		
Independent	.78	.58
Competitive	.82	.64
Warm	.76	.77
Emotional	.56	.84
Role behavior		
Financial provider	.83	.47
Takes initiative with opposite sex	.82	.54
Takes care of children	.50	.85
Cooks meals	.42	.83
Physical characteristic		
Muscular	.64	.36
Deep voice	.73	.30
Graceful	.45	.68
Small-boned	.39	.62

[a]Subjects' estimate of the probability that the average person of either sex would possess a characteristic.

women and men, along with descriptions that differentiate among the types. Sample types of males obtained from respondents in one study included the career man (well-dressed, self-confident, calculating, materialistic, eloquent), and the softy (sympathetic, can show weakness, sensitive, unconventional, frank), along with such others as the egoist, the intellectual, the macho type, the cool type, and the playboy. Female types included the feminist (self-confident, cunning, intolerant, doesn't show feelings) and the housewife (unattractive, "good girl," obsequious, selfless, no interests of her own), along with such others as the society lady, the maternal type, the vamp, and the secretary (Six & Eckes, 1991).

Different and Unequal?
The Evaluative Aspects of Gender Stereotypes

Although stereotypes imply only beliefs about group differences and are not necessarily accompanied by positive or negative judgments about the groups in question, there is some evidence that such evaluative judgments *do* accompany gender stereotypes.

The negative evaluation of persons or their activities because they belong to a particular group is known as prejudice, and the brand of prejudice that is based on a person's sexual category is called sexism. By definition, sexism can be used against either females or males; both women and men can be judged harshly, not taken seriously, or be deprived of opportunities *because* they are women or *because* they are men.

The evidence that sexism plays a role in reactions to and treatment of women is long-standing and comprehensive. It can be found even within the rather prosaic literature on stereotyping just discussed. More of the qualities stereotypically assigned to males than females are rated as "positive" qualities (Broverman et al., 1972) and masculine traits are considered more desirable than feminine traits (Rosenkrantz, Vogel, Bee, Broverman, & Broverman, 1968). One need not, however, be familiar with the psychological research literature to detect evidence of sexism either in our history or in our everyday lives. The length and bitterness of the struggle for women's suffrage in so many countries, the necessity for Canadian women in the 1920s to go to court to have women declared "persons" under the law,[1] and the continuing controversy over issues such as equal pay for work of equal value, and equal access to work, bear strong testimony to the pervasiveness of sexism in the treatment of women.

Does all this mean, however, that people *don't like* women as much as men? Not necessarily. In fact, recently researchers have found that women are evaluated more favorably than men—perhaps because women are stereotyped as more likely to be helpful, gentle, and understanding (Eagly, Mladinic, & Otto, 1991). But being liked apparently does not necessarily translate into being respected or being treated fairly.

What of sexism in the treatment of men? Although men are privileged over women in many respects, they can also be the victims of sexist assumptions. Sexism

---

[1] In 1927, a group of prominent Canadian feminists petitioned Parliament for an interpretation of a clause in the Constitution that referred to the eligibility of "persons" for appointments to the Senate. The Supreme Court of Canada ruled that women were not to be considered as persons under this clause, and so did not qualify for Senate appointments. This decision was reversed by Britain's Privy Council in 1929—an event that is still celebrated by Canadian feminists on "Persons Day" in October.

cuts both ways; for example, the other side of the prejudiced attitude that bars women from combat positions in the military is the attitude that it is somehow less upsetting to have male soldiers killed than to have female soldiers killed. Small but active organizations of men have identified ways in which stereotypic expectations of men can result in negative consequences for them. Men's organizations—both liberal, feminist (e.g., National Organization for Changing Men) and conservative, masculinist (e.g., National Congress for Men)—note that the stereotype of men as tough, unemotional, and aggressive can result in harsh treatment of men and in male alienation. They cite, albeit from differing perspectives, society's lack of support for fathering, the expectation that men will do the fighting and dying in wartime, and ways in which the protector and provider roles have damaged and dehumanized men (Franklin, 1988).

With respect to the evaluation of men, some research suggests that men may be more rigid than women in their insistence on stereotypical masculinity. Male college students describe the "ideal" man in more stereotypic terms than do female students (Hort, Fagot, & Leinbach, 1990). Moreover, when female college students were given the opportunity to "listen in" on scripted interviews in which the male interviewees portrayed either traditional masculine or nontraditional, androgynous roles, they consistently rated the nontraditional male more favorably (more appropriate, likable, moral, adaptive, conscientious, tactful, reliable, and less conventional, conceited, and jealous) than his traditional counterpart (Cramer, Dragna, Cupp, & Stewart, 1991).

Sexism in the Evaluation of Work

One of the most obvious manifestations of sexism directed against women is in the undervaluing of their work. In a now classic study, Goldberg (1968) gave college women articles to evaluate that were supposedly written by a woman or a man. The same article was rated more favorably when attributed to a man than to a woman, leading Goldberg to suggest that women were prejudiced against other women. Similar research carried out more recently by Paludi and Strayer (1985) indicates that a pro-male bias can still be found, in both men and women, in reactions to written work. They asked 300 women and men to evaluate an article that was supposedly written by a man, a woman, an author with a sexually ambiguous name, or an anonymous author. The articles used were chosen to represent areas of stereotypically masculine expertise (politics), stereotypically feminine expertise (the psychology of women), or a neutral field (education). Raters judged the articles, even in the feminine and neutral fields, to be better written, more insightful, more persuasive, and higher in overall quality when they were told they were written by a man. Moreover, when presented with the "neutral" article attributed to either an anonymous author or to one whose name was sexually ambiguous, most respondents thought that the author was a man—and rated the article more favorably than did those few who assumed the author was a woman. Such a tendency to evaluate men's work more favorably than women's is not always found; however, when differences in evaluation are found they tend to favor men (Top, 1991). An anti-female bias is most likely to occur in domains that are stereotypically masculine.

Other research suggests that prejudice against women keeps them out of certain jobs or confined to the lower rungs of the promotion ladder. A review of experimental studies of the impact of gender and qualifications on hiring recommendations shows that, while the effect is not always found, males tend to be preferred over females (Olian, Schwab, & Haberfeld, 1988). For example, studies have demonstrated that, when confronted with male and female applicants with equivalent qualifications, respondents favored the male over the female applicants for positions in university-level psychology teaching (Fidell, 1970), management (Rosen & Jerdee, 1974), newswriting (Etaugh & Kasley, 1981), furniture store management (Dipboye, Fromkin, & Wiback, 1975), life insurance (Heneman, 1977), sports photography (Heilman, Martell, & Simon, 1988), and accounting (Zickmund, Hitt, & Pickens, 1978). In addition to unfavorable judgments of performance, women receive other negative evaluations with respect to their competence: Their success is often devalued by being explained as "luck," and competent women are sometimes described as "unfeminine" and as less likable than competent men (Lott, 1985).

Clearly, the stereotypes about women as a group pave the way for the inference that women will not perform as well as men in a variety of arenas. Such an inference can be countered, however, by specific information about a job applicant—information that preempts stereotypic characterization. A review of available studies shows that, when specific, unambiguous information of direct relevance to job performance is presented about applicants, it tends to undermine discrimination against women (Tosi & Einbender, 1985).

Perhaps the reason for discrimination against women is not simply bias against women, but bias against people behaving, or trying to behave, in ways incongruent with gender stereotypes. After all, all of the activities just mentioned, from writing articles to accounting, demand professional, competent, instrumental behavior—a type of behavior that forms part of the masculine stereotype. If the job or task in question required more expressive than instrumental qualities or was classified as more suitable for a woman than a man, would men be the victims of discrimination? Some research suggests that they would. Professional personnel consultants judging the suitability of applicants for two male sex–typed jobs (automobile sales person, hardware shipping and receiving clerk), two female sex–typed jobs (telephone operator, receptionist) and two neutral jobs (motel desk clerk, darkroom assistant) judged male and female applicants as more suitable for their respective sex-typed occupations and showed no significant preference for male or female applicants on the neutral jobs (Cash, Gillen, & Burns, 1977). Kalin, Stoppard, and Burt (1980) found similar results using a greater number and variety of sex-typed occupations. Thus, there is some evidence that discrimination against either women or men may be based on the perception that they are behaving in ways that do not fit gender expectations. But where do these expectations come from? Alice Eagly and Valerie Steffen (1984) have shown that they come, in part, from the very way women and men are distributed into social roles. We seem to be caught in a vicious circle: We expect women and men to be different because we observe that they tend to do different things, and this very expectation then leads us to react negatively to those whose behavior does not match our original observations.

Can competence in a "gender-inappropriate" endeavor ever work to one's advantage? Some researchers argue that persons presented as very competent in a field that is extremely unusual for their gender can be *overevaluated*. Thus, in one study, females identified as finalists in a football photography contest (a strongly male sex–typed field) were judged as more competent than male finalists in the same contest, but a similar overevaluation of females did not occur in the more moderately male sex–typed field of tennis photography (Heilman et al., 1988). In a similar vein, raters awarded the highest presentation marks, among two female and two male speakers, to a man who spoke on a strongly female sex–typed topic: "sex bias in the counseling of women" (Gilbert, Lee, & Chiddix, 1981). It appears that, at least under some conditions, women who are good at "men's" work and men who are good at "women's" work are the beneficiaries of more positive evaluations than are their more traditional counterparts. What is going on here? Researchers speculate that when behavior contrasts so sharply with stereotypical expectations that it exceeds a critical threshold, it creates a boomerang effect (Weber & Crocker, 1983). The individual is characterized as an exception who does not fit the stereotype, or as a member of a "subtype" of the larger group ("career woman"? "sensitive man"?) whose qualities are different from those of the larger group. These individuals may be given positive evaluations simply *because* their good performance is so surprising for their gender—gender bias works *for* them instead of against them.

Unfortunately for people entering nontraditional jobs, they cannot usually count on this *positive* effect of gender bias. Such an effect occurs, at least with respect to women, under very specific conditions: Information about high performance ability must be present, and the job in question must be very atypical for a woman to pursue (Heilman et al., 1988). When these conditions are not met, gender bias works against, not for, women pursuing nontraditional occupations.

One of the clearest illustrations that the prejudice against women involves something more than their perceived suitability to do particular work is the fact that occupations undergoing a transition from being dominated by men to being dominated by women lose status, sometimes drastically. When secretarial positions were held mainly by men, they were reasonably high-status positions, whose occupants had reasonable chances for advancement (Davies, 1975). Now that virtually all secretaries are women, the job is low-status and often a dead end. A similar pattern has been noted for bank tellers (Prather, 1971) and teachers (Oppenheimer, 1970). In a laboratory demonstration of this phenomenon, Touhey (1974) gave subjects descriptions of five high-status professions: architect, college professor, lawyer, physician, and scientist. On the information sheet describing each profession, half the subjects were told that the percentage of women in the profession was expected to remain stable and low for the next twenty-five to thirty years, while the other half were told that the percentage of women would increase dramatically over the same time period. When they were told to expect an increasing proportion of women within the professions, subjects consistently rated them lower in prestige.

Worry over the potential decline in personal or institutional status associated with an increase in the number of women may explain some aspects of men's resistance to such an increase. Such resistance has been documented in cases ranging from private golf clubs (e.g., MacLean, 1991) to state universities (e.g., Greene, 1987; Henderson & Baker, 1990). For example, at the University of North Carolina, concern over the fact that female students had become a majority led some trustees to propose changing the weights for admission criteria to restore the male majority (Greene, 1987).

It is safe to conclude that although both women and men are subject to the restrictions of gender stereotypes, the masculine stereotype is viewed more favorably. Moreover, while members of either sex may suffer discrimination based on views that their gender renders them unsuitable for a task or position, women are the targets of more discrimination in this respect than men. Not only are almost all of the high-status jobs defined as more suitable for men, but high-status jobs that become female-dominated quickly lose their prestige.

Gender and Other Stereotypes: Race, Class, Age, Appearance, Sexual Orientation, Disability

When someone completing a questionnaire to measure male–female stereotyping is asked about the "typical" woman or man, what kind of person do you suppose comes to that individual's mind? An elderly black woman? A middle-aged Native American man confined to a wheelchair? A young woman who has trouble finding stylish clothing because she weighs two hundred pounds? Most likely, the image is influenced by the person's tendency to define "typical" with reference to himself or herself and to the people most visible in the environment. Probably, as Landrine (1985) suggests, research participants cannot imagine a woman (or man) "without attributing a race, a social class, an age, and even a degree of physical attractiveness to the stimulus" (p. 66). The image, at least among the North American college students whose responses have formed much of the basis for research on gender stereotypes, is likely to be of someone who is relatively young, white, able-bodied, neither too fat nor too thin, neither too short nor too tall, and of average physical attractiveness. Thus, our studies of the stereotypes that accompany gender are most likely limited by their reliance on generalizations that systematically exclude such groups as old people, blacks, Chicanos, native peoples, Asians, disabled people, fat people, lesbians and gay men, and people whose appearance diverges markedly from the norm. It is also likely that, in holding to gender stereotypes based on the so-called typical man or woman, our society creates added difficulties for individuals already victimized by racism, ageism, an intolerance of difference, or society's obsession with attractiveness and thinness.

Gender Stereotypes and Race

Only in recent years have researchers tried to understand the workings of racism and sexism by comparing the experiences of different gender–race groups. It has been noted, for example, that the forms of racism directed at black women and black men may differ, and that sexism may be expressed toward and experienced by a woman differently as a function of her race (Smith & Stewart, 1983). An examination of gender stereotypes cannot ignore the way race and gender stereotypes interact, or the ways in which different racial groups may differ in the images and ideals they hold for femininity and masculinity.

Femininity. In an attempt to determine whether the often-reported stereotype of women is actually just a stereotype of middle-class white women, Landrine (1985) asked undergraduates to describe the stereotype of each of four groups of women—black and white middle-class women, and black and white lower-class women—based on a list of 23 adjectives. She found that, although the stereotypes differed significantly by both race and social class, with white women and middle-class women being described in ways most similar to the dominant culture's traditional stereotypes of women, all four groups were rated in ways consistent with this feminine stereotype. White women were described more often than black women by the most stereotypical terms: dependent, emotional, and passive. However, both groups were rated similarly on many other adjectives: ambitious, competent, intelligent, self-confident, and hostile, for example. The findings suggest that race and social class are implicit in what have been described as gender stereotypes, but that, to some extent, there is a set of expectations for women that transcends these variables.

According to the stereotypes held by the dominant white society, black women may be judged as less "feminine" than white women (O'Leary, 1977). The history of black women in the United States makes it clear that they have not, as a group, been conditioned toward the helpless, delicate, even frail image of femininity so often cultivated in their white counterparts. As slaves, women were expected to endure back-breaking physical labor and hardships, and were denied the security in their marital lives that white women took for granted (Hooks, 1981). Angela Davis (1981) notes that, under slavery, black women constructed a definition of womanhood that included "hard work, perseverance and self-reliance, a legacy of tenacity, resistance and an insistence on sexual equality" (p. 29). One view within the black community is that "blacks have withstood the long line of abuses perpetrated against them ever since their arrival in this country mainly because of the black woman's fortitude, inner wisdom, and sheer ability to survive" (Terrelonge, 1989, p. 556). Indeed, there appears to be a persistent stereotype of black women in the social science literature that encompasses strength, self-reliance, and a strong achievement orientation (Epstein, 1973; Fleming, 1983a), and Fleming (1983b) has documented the existence of a "black matriarchy" theory among social scientists suggesting that black women are more dominant, assertive, and self-reliant than black males. While such a stereotype may appear positive at first glance, the narrow labeling of black women's strengths as "matriarchal" represents a refusal to conceptualize strong women in anything but a family context. Moreover, there has been a tendency to blame black women's strong, assertive behavior for some of the problems experienced by black men—a tendency that surely reflects stereotypic notions about what kinds of behavior are "proper" for women. Fleming and others (e.g., Dugger, 1991; Staples, 1978) argue that the black matriarchy theory is a myth based largely on flawed or misleading evidence. Fleming suggests that this particular stereotype may have arisen from the fact that "their long history of instrumentality in the service of family functioning may well have built in black women an air of self-reliance that arouses further stereotyping among those (largely white) social scientists more accustomed to white traditional norms for women" (Fleming, 1983a, p. 43).

In contrast to black women, Chicanas have traditionally faced an ideal of femininity that glorified motherhood, subservience, and long-suffering endurance (Garcia, 1991). A woman was supposed to gain fulfillment by loving and supporting her husband and nurturing her children, and her place was unquestionably in the home (Astrachan, 1989). Historically, this ideal was fostered by the Catholic church, which played a large role in the colonization of what is now Mexico and the American southwest. The church taught women to venerate the Virgin Mary and to emulate her by being silent, submissive, altruistic, and self-denying (Almquist, 1989). In recent years, however, Mexican-American women have taken on new roles. Their rates of participation in the labor force now resemble those of Anglos. In addition, a vocal Chicana feminist movement has emerged (Garcia, 1991). This movement, reflecting the values of Mexican-American culture, has incorporated a positive valuing rather than a rejection of the roles of wife and mother along with the acceptance of broader roles for women (Mason, 1980).

One of the reasons for race-related differences in gender-role attitudes is that members of different racial groups frequently live in different social conditions. For example, in the United States, black women have been more likely than white women to have to work for economic reasons; thus, working for wages has been a normative aspect of womanhood. For white women, however (and perhaps even more for Chicana women, who have only recently joined the labor force in such large numbers), the movement into paid work is more likely to provoke a questioning of traditional views of gender, since it represents a break with past traditions (Dugger, 1991).

Masculinity.   The interaction of masculinity stereotypes with race is similarly complex. Black, white, and Chicano males in the United States, for example, hold and face differing, though overlapping, images of what it means to be masculine. The differences probably stem as much or more from variations in the social structural conditions currently facing the three groups than from their differing cultural heritage (Baca Zinn, 1989).

For example, the status of black males in American society has been in flux for the last several decades. Long after legal racial segregation ended, the effects of racism were still extremely obvious in the white society's treatment of black men. Black men were, in fact, often referred to *not* as men, but as "boys." Some writers have argued that it was not until the advent of the Black Power Movement in the late 1960s that adult black males were recognized as *men* by most of American society (Franklin, 1984; Poussaint, 1982). As a group, black males currently live a hazardous existence as they try to maintain the competitive, success-oriented, aggressive aspects of masculinity in the face of discrimination and a lack of economic opportunities to pursue the "protector/provider" role. The result, according to some authors, is the channeling of attempts to be masculine into a cluster of behaviors that emphasize physical toughness, violence, and risk-taking, especially among *young* black men (Franklin, 1984). A tragic result is that the death rate from violence is frighteningly high in this group. Homicide is the leading cause of death among young American black men.

Richard Majors (1989) writes of the "Cool Pose"—a cultural signature adopted by many black males as a mechanism for survival and social competence. A set of poses and postures displays elements of control, toughness, and detachment that symbolize strength, pride, and a refusal to show hurt or weakness—especially to outsiders. According to Majors, "coolness" is also displayed through the "expressive life style." The style is manifested in creative, even flamboyant, performances in arenas ranging from the street, to the basketball court, to the pulpit: performances that say "you can't copy me." The Cool Pose, an aggressive assertion of masculinity, guards these males' pride and dignity, but may be costly to relationships when it blocks the expression of emotions or needs.

Chicano men have also developed a tradition that places strong importance on masculinity—expressed in an ideology of male dominance often labeled "machismo." Although some have argued that machismo is a myth used to negatively stereotype

Chicanos and rationalize their lack of success in the dominant society, there seems little doubt that a male-dominant ideology of masculinity has played an important role in relations between Chicanos and Chicanas (Garcia, 1991). The core aspect of machismo is men's dominance over women. The stereotypical macho male expects to be considered the head of his household and demands deference and respect from his wife and children. He may feel strongly that his wife's place is in the home and that his manhood is demonstrated by the number of children he has (Astrachan, 1989). A Chicano man may behave in an aggressive, macho way partly as "a conscious rejection of the dominant society's definition of Mexicans as passive, lazy, and indifferent" (Baca Zinn, 1989, p. 95). Yet, machismo appears to be, in its own way, a public pose. Researchers find that actual decision making in Chicano families is as likely to be egalitarian as male-dominant and that Chicano fathers are nurturant and expressive rather than distant and authoritarian with their young children. Even in egalitarian families, however, patriarchal ideology is strong, as expressed in statements that the father is the head of the house, the boss, the one in charge (Baca Zinn, 1989). Baca Zinn suggests that patriarchal ideology is associated with family solidarity and that perhaps "the father's authority is strongly upheld because family solidarity is important in a society that excludes and subordinates Chicanos" (p. 95).

It is possible that, in a society that values masculinity over femininity, gender may take on a special significance for men of color and other men who have little access to socially valued roles. They may emphasize and act out the toughness and dominance aspects of masculinity, both as a defense against putdowns from the larger society and because "being male is one sure way to acquire status when other roles are systematically denied" (Baca Zinn, 1989, p. 94).

Stereotyping Within Groups. Studies of gender stereotyping and gender-role attitudes within racial groups other than whites show mixed results. A review of research on black gender roles finds some studies in which blacks are more egalitarian in their gender-role attitudes than are whites, some in which the opposite is found, and some in which gender attitudes among blacks do not fit neatly into the egalitarian/ traditional distinction that has been useful for whites (Hatchett & Quick, 1983). O'Leary and Harrison (1975), comparing the gender stereotypes of black and white women and men, found that blacks endorsed fewer items that discriminated between the sexes than whites did, and that black respondents were less likely than whites to devalue females on stereotypic grounds. White subjects of both sexes rated the white woman more negatively than the black woman was rated by black subjects. Romer and Cherry (1980), studying black, Italian, and Jewish children, found that black children described male and female roles as similar in expressiveness. When a sample of black and white male and female university students were asked to rate various qualities as characteristic of their "ideal man," the black males placed significantly higher emphasis on aggressiveness than did the other groups (Cazenave & Leon, 1987). Black males also ranked highest among the groups in their rating of being comfortable with children as an ideal male quality, while white females ranked highest among the groups in their rating of warmth and gentleness as essential characteristics of an ideal man. In a comparison of the gender-role attitudes of American black and white women, Dugger (1991) found that black women more often rejected culturally dominant views of the female role—for example, they were more likely than their white counterparts to indicate that they noticed sex discrimination; supported the women's movement; admired intelligent, outspoken women; and accepted nontraditional family structures. On the other hand, these black women were *more* likely than white women to accept that girls and boys should be brought up to be feminine and masculine, respectively.

Gender Stereotypes and Social Class

In a television advertisement for plastic wrap, a male chef—obviously very refined, very "cultured"—is shown debating what brand of wrap to use for his creation. In the background, a pudgy man in coveralls and a dirty face waits to take the package. The chef asks, appalled, "Is he going to *touch* it?," then hurriedly decides, presumably to avoid contamination of his food, to use the advertised brand of wrap.

In this example, the two men are stereotyped according to social class: one (the chef—clearly portrayed as middle-class) is apparently educated, intelligent, sensitive, and has an appreciation of the finer things in life; the other (the man in coveralls—presumably a working-class man) is portrayed as dumb and dirty. The pro-middle-class bias is obvious, as is the observation that the notion of masculinity embodied in the two portrayals is quite different.

Social class is measured through socioeconomic indicators such as education, income, and occupation. The stereotypes applied to women and men differ somewhat according to their perceived social class. For example, one study found that, among middle-class college students, the stereotype of lower-class women was significantly higher than that of middle-class women for the traits confused, dirty, hostile, illogical, impulsive, incoherent, inconsiderate, irresponsible, and superstitious (Landrine, 1985). Working-class males, in the view of many middle-class social scientists, have been stereotyped as exemplars of old-fashioned, defiant, aggressive masculinity (Ehrenreich, 1983).

Members of different social classes may differ in their notions of masculinity and femininity. Rubin (1976) argues that professional men, with more access to status and prestige outside the home, are more able than working-class men to assume a less authoritarian role within the family. Astrachan (1989) suggests, however, that the apparent differences between middle-class and working-class men may be partly just a matter of honesty:

> Blue-collar men feel the contradiction between their physical power and their place at the bottom of the male hierarchy, and they are more obvious than men in other classes about their need to treat women as underlings to compensate. They are more honest, or quicker to voice their anger and their fear, about changes in the balance of power and in sex roles, at work and at home. (p. 63)

Finally, Ehrenreich (1983) warns that

> patterns of working-class behavior may be formed, in part, in response to middle-class behavior and observation. . . . The middle-class 'gaze' . . . can be an uncomfortable one—associated, in lower classes, with workplace supervision and negative judgments by teachers and other authorities. What appears to be

a lack of 'interpersonal skills' can be a withdrawal from middle-class discourse; what looks like residual 'physical aggression' can be actual and ongoing hostility; and . . . 'working-class male chauvinism' might be an expression of class, rather than gender, antagonism. (p. 135)

Because people can move between social classes, it is easier to understand group differences if social class is considered a dynamic variable rather than a static category (Cazenave, 1984). Such a perspective allows researchers to recognize, for example, that what may appear at first to be racial differences are probably attributable to social class. For example, one study of black and white American men's conception of the "ideal man" found differences between the white and black middle-class samples. The black sample placed more emphasis on, among other things, being aggressive and competitive, being successful at work, protecting one's family, and self-confidence (Cazenave, 1984). The researcher notes that, while many of the white men in the sample had been born into the middle class and were thus likely to take its advantages for granted, many of the black men were first-generation middle-class and so still felt a sense of struggling to "make it." He argues that "in the quest for upward mobility, middle-class blacks may embrace traditional gender-role prescriptions, which more established and secure middle-class whites feel secure in relinquishing" (Cazenave & Leon, 1987, p. 246).

In a similar vein, a study of the well-being of employed professional and managerial women found that women from working-class families had received far less financial and informational support from their families in the transition from high school to college than had those from middle-class families (Cannon, Higginbotham, & Leung, 1991). Because the typical black woman volunteer for the study had been raised in a working-class family and the typical white woman volunteer had been raised in a middle-class family, it would have appeared simply that black families gave less support to their daughters than did white families, if the researchers had not attended to the social class background of the women.

Gender Stereotypes and Age

The stereotypes of femininity and masculinity seem to apply most strongly to the young. There is scattered evidence that, as they age, both women and men describe themselves in less stereotypic terms (Cooper & Guttmann, 1987; Farrell & Rosenberg, 1981; Feldman, Biringen, & Nash, 1981). Older men rate older women as more active, involved, hardy, and stable than themselves (Kahana & Kahana, 1970). There are some indications that women become more powerful as they move into older adulthood (Friedman, 1987; Helson & Mitchell, 1990). Some investigators note that men at mid-life appear more interested in close relationships and are less caught up in competition and achievement strivings than are younger men (Moreland, 1980). There is, however, little evidence that self-reported investment in male or female role behavior changes between young adulthood and mid-life (Carlson & Videka-Sherman, 1990).

Perhaps gender stereotypes become less pronounced for older people because age stereotypes replace them. One of the widely accepted stereotypes about the elderly is that they are no longer interested in sexuality (Kay & Neelley, 1982). But sexuality is one of the major underpinnings of social expectations about gender. One of the main reasons for a man to be masculine is to be sexually attractive to women, and vice versa. If sexuality becomes irrelevant, so, in a sense, do masculinity and femininity. Although studies show that sexuality is *not*, in fact, irrelevant to older people (e.g., Masters & Johnson, 1966), perhaps one accidentally beneficial consequence of the myth is that it is a partial release from the restrictions of gender stereotypes.

On the other hand, many writers have noted a "double standard" of aging that places older women at a disadvantage with respect to older men (Bell, 1989). Because, in contemporary North American society, so much of a woman's worth tends to be defined in terms of her physical attractiveness to men, the aging woman may find that, along with her "femininity," she is losing her value as a person. The changes in physical appearance that accompany aging, while often considered acceptable or even "distinguished" in men, move women farther and farther from current definitions of female beauty. One study found that ratings of an individual's attractiveness decreased with age when the individual was a woman, but not when the individual was a man (Mathes, Brennan, Haugen, & Rice, 1985). For women, who often have few other sources of power and prestige than their attractiveness, these changes can signify a slide into decreasing social worth. Older men, who are less likely to have to rely on their appearance for power and prestige, may have wider access to sources of social worth— through occupational achievement, money, and even relationships with younger women.

Research suggests that women who abandon the strict constraints of gender stereotypes to make nontraditional choices while they are young may find themselves better equipped than their more traditional counterparts to handle old age. Among 70-year-old women, work-centered mothers showed higher life satisfaction than women who were more exclusively family-focused (Maas & Kuypers, 1974), and, among women in their sixties, the most feminine women were the most critical of themselves (Lowenthal, Thurnher, Chiriboga, & Associates, 1975).

Appearance

Psychologists have become increasingly aware that physical appearance is a critical aspect of stereotyping (McArthur, 1982). In terms of gender stereotypes, physical appearance may have strong implications for how masculine or feminine a person is thought to be. Many a tall, broad-shouldered woman has slouched and crouched through life in a vain effort to appear petite and thus "feminine," and many a short man has quietly cursed his diminutive stature because it seemed to detract from his ability to project a "masculine" image.

Although physical appearance is important to both males and females, beauty is generally defined as a peculiarly feminine attribute, and preoccupation with one's appearance is seen as part of the feminine stereotype (Rodin, Silberstein, & Striegel-Moore, 1985). In an exploration of the concept of femininity, Susan Brownmiller (1984) illustrates the powerful role played by physical appearance in cultural definitions of femininity. In various times and places, aspects of the female anatomy have become supposed signals of how feminine and how sexual a woman is. For example, she notes the way that others react to a young woman's breast development: "Parents and relatives mark their appearance as a landmark event, schoolmates take notice, girlfriends compare, boys zero in; later a husband, a lover, a baby expect a proprietary share. No other part of the human anatomy has such semipublic, intensely private status" (pp. 40–41). Why all the fuss? Brownmiller argues that breasts are used as a prime cue to a woman's sexuality. She notes the myth that a flat-chested woman is nonsexual and that a woman with large breasts is flaunting her sexuality and seeking attention. Small wonder that women sometimes become intensely self-conscious about this part of their anatomy!

Stereotypical masculinity, too, is reflected in physical appearance, particularly in strength and muscularity. Men, like women, are not immune to concerns about how their bodies will be judged—but, perhaps because concern with one's appearance is supposed to be a feminine quality, it seems less acceptable for them to talk about it. Nonetheless, muscles are equated with masculinity, and entrepreneurs have made fortunes playing on men's insecurity about their bodies. Bernarr Macfadden, originator of the physical culture movement, warned men that they must choose "whether you shall be a strong virile animal . . . or a miserable little crawling worm" (quoted in Glassner, 1989), and Charles Atlas enticed thousands of men into his exercise program in the 1950s with the promise: "I manufacture weaklings into MEN."

Recent studies show that up to 95 percent of men express dissatisfaction with some aspect of their bodies, most frequently with their chest, weight, and waist (Mishkind, Rodin, Silberstein, & Striegel-Moore, 1987). The overwhelming majority of men studied say they would prefer to be of well-proportioned, average build rather than thin or fat. Most say that their ideal would be a muscular mesomorphic body—characterized by well-developed chest and arm muscles, broad shoulders, and a narrow waist (Tucker, 1982). Thinning hair is also a source of much anxiety for many men (Franzoi, Anderson, & Frommelt, 1990).

Perhaps no aspect of appearance is the cause of more grief in our own society right now than weight. Dieting has become a North American obsession, with an estimated 52 million adults in the United States either dieting or contemplating a diet at any one time (Bayrd, 1978). Being fat is a subject of special concern to women. Thinness is a major aspect of the definition of attractiveness, and attractiveness increases perceived femininity (Cash, Gillen, & Burns, 1977; Gillen & Sherman, 1980). In a sample of black American adult women, body weight was inversely related to body image satisfaction (V. G. Thomas, 1989). When Canadian female university students were asked what kinds of activities or situations would make them feel less feminine, by far the most frequently checked item was "being overweight," which was endorsed by more than 50 percent of the sample (Lips, 1986a). So highly charged is the issue of weight for women that, according to Hatfield and Sprecher (cited in Rodin et al., 1985), women respondents in the early Kinsey surveys of sexual practices were more embarrassed when asked their weight than when asked "How often do you masturbate?" or "Have you ever had a homosexual affair?"

Research shows that physical attractiveness is a more central part of the self-concept for women than for men (Lerner & Karabenick, 1974; Lerner, Orlos, & Knapp, 1976). Moreover, a test of a sample of college undergraduates indicated that weight and body shape, although important to men, were the *central* determinants of women's perception of their physical attractiveness (Rodin & Striegel-Moore, 1984). Women are less satisfied with their bodies than are men; college women report a greater discrepancy between their actual and ideal body image than do men (Fallon & Rozin,

1985). And women have good reason to be concerned about their weight and shape—obesity seems to trigger more negative evaluations for women than for men. Researchers who showed silhouettes of fat and thin women and men to hundreds of passersby at a summer fair found that fat men were rated significantly less negatively than were fat women, while thin women were rated less negatively than their male counterparts (Spigelman & Schultz, 1981). Furthermore, women who are "in the market" for a male partner receive a consistent message that appearance, especially thinness, is a crucial selling point. Males placing "personal" advertisements for dating relationships in singles magazines and newspapers are more likely than women to emphasize the desired partner's physical appearance (Davis, 1990; Smith, Waldorf, & Trembath, 1990) and are far more likely than females (33.6 percent vs. 2.2 percent) to specify that they are looking for someone who is thin (Smith et al., 1990).

There is some evidence that even among women who have rejected many of the traditional norms of femininity, the obsession with slenderness continues to exert a powerful force. Women who value nontraditional roles for women prefer a smaller, thinner female body shape, and associate a larger, rounder form with the "wife and mother" stereotype (Beck, Ward-Hull, & McLear, 1976).

Gender Stereotypes and Sexual Orientation

As just noted, gender stereotypes are linked with social notions of sexuality: A "feminine" woman is supposed to be attractive to men, a "masculine" man is thought to be desirable to women. A major aspect of the stereotypes surrounding individuals who are homosexual in orientation is that they do not fit the accepted stereotypes for their own gender. According to the dubious logic of stereotypes, a really feminine woman would not be sexually attracted to other women; a "real" man would not be sexually attracted to other men. Thus, in a reversal of gender stereotypes, lesbians are often characterized as masculine, and gay men are described as feminine. We have already seen that facial and other physical features that are stereotyped as feminine are linked, when found in males, with attributions of homosexuality, as are masculine features when found in females.

Lesbian and gay male relationships are also stereotyped, often as mimicking heterosexual relationships. For instance, one widely held (and inaccurate) view of lesbian couples is that one member of the couple must be a "butch" and the other a "femme," in order to imitate male–female relationships (Weitz, 1989).

The stereotyping of lesbians and gay men is linked with anti-homosexual prejudice. Perhaps because the masculine role is more highly valued by society, and gay males are seen to be deviating from that role, such prejudice is usually more obvious in relation to gay men than to lesbians (Morin & Garfinkle, 1978; Herek, 1988).

Gender and Disability

Although the general stereotype of persons with disabilities involves victimization, helplessness, dependence, social isolation, and suffering (Seifert, 1979), this stereotype seems to be moderated by the gender of the person with the disability. For women, who are already stereotyped as more passive and dependent than men, the disability stereotype can reinforce the image of dependence (Fine, 1991; Fine & Asch, 1981). Indeed, newly disabled women are far more likely than their male counterparts to be advised by their physicians to retire from paid employment (Russell, 1985; Thurer, 1982), and less likely than their male counterparts to find a job post-disability (Fine, 1991). For men, on the other hand, the dependence on others that many disabilities enforce is perceived as a threat to their masculine image.

Physical attractiveness is another area in which gender and disability stereotypes interact. We have already noted that physical attractiveness is more central to femininity than to masculinity; it is also apparent that a woman who is visibly disabled, even if not disfigured in any way, falls short of the cultural ideal of beauty. Here, for example, is the reaction of a former executive of the Miss Universe contest to the notion of a paraplegic woman as a contestant: "Her participation in a beauty contest would be like having a blind man compete in a shooting match" (Matthews, 1985, p. 49). However, 1987 saw the first entry of a wheelchair-bound woman, Maria Serrao, in a major American beauty contest ("Paralyzed woman," 1987).

The stereotypic expectations about femininity that many women find oppressive may be experienced as more complex by disabled women. For example, the automatic expectation that a woman will have children may be greeted with resentment by a woman who has no physical barriers to such a choice, but a woman with a disability that interferes with this choice may resent the automatic expectation that she will *not* have children. Similarly, although many women object strongly to the casual sexual harassment they encounter on the street, some disabled women may object just as strongly to the assumption that they are not "harassable" (Fine, 1991).

Like the elderly, persons with disabilities are often stereotyped as asexual (Rousso, 1986; Thurer, 1982). However, even the slowly growing public awareness that disability does not imply a lack of sexual needs or interest has been channelled by gender stereotypes that say that sex is more important to men than to women. Much more has been studied and written on the subject of sexuality among disabled men than among disabled women. When the stereotypes about women's "weaker" sexual needs are combined with stereotypes about disability, the results can be ludicrous. Fine (1991) tells the story of a newly disabled woman who, when she asked her physician whether her disability would preclude a satisfying sex life, was "reassured" that her vagina would be tight enough to satisfy any man!

Statistics indicate that the popular presumption that disabled women are asexual does not protect them from sexual assault. In fact, disabled women may be more likely than other women to be sexually assaulted (Moglia, 1986). Children of both sexes are at high risk for sexual abuse if they are disabled, because they are often less able to get away from an abuser and/or unable to communicate to others about what is happening (Moglia, 1986). During both childhood and adulthood, females with disabilities are more likely than their nondisabled counterparts to experience sexual or physical abuse. In one small-scale study, 67 percent of disabled women, as compared to 34 percent of nondisabled women, reported that they had been physically abused or battered as children (Doucette, 1986).

Gender stereotypes are pervasive, interacting with other stereotypes to shape social perceptions of persons of various races, ages, abilities, and appearances. Gender stereotyping both grows out of and reinforces the social relations between women and men and, as seen in the following section, does so in ways that are both complex and subtle.

The Process of Stereotyping

Despite the pervasiveness of gender stereotyping, almost everyone can, if given a good reason to do so, summon up example after example of people, personalities, and actions that do not fit the stereotypes. Yet, in the face of counterexamples, the stereotypes persist. A good example is the notion that the "typical" North American family consists of a woman staying at home with the children and a man going out to engage in paid employment to support the family. In fact, less than half of the families on the continent now fit this traditional model, but mothers of young children who stay in the labor market are still regarded as anomalies by many people.

Why do stereotypes persist to such an extent in the face of lack of support or even countervailing evidence? To answer this question, it is necessary to look beyond the content of specific stereotypes to the process of stereotyping itself. In recent years, psychologists have focused on two approaches in attempts to understand and describe how stereotyping works: information processing and self-fulfilling prophecy.

Stereotypes and Information Processing

Psychologists now think of stereotypes not simply as sets of beliefs about specific groups of people, but as knowledge structures that guide the way individuals process information: what they notice, what they remember, what kinds of information they seek out, and how they explain and make sense of what they see (Hamilton, 1979). These knowledge structures, often called *schemas,* act as self-perpetuating channels or filters of information, guiding the individual to pay attention to information that fits the schema or stereotype and to ignore or explain away things that don't fit. Such schemas are useful in that they allow for more efficient handling of the vast amount of information to which most of us are exposed, but, inevitably, they produce and perpetuate blind spots. Thus, for example, research participants' search for information to explain an automobile accident of which they are given a vague description can apparently be guided by their schemas for young and elderly men respectively. Participants told that the driver of the car was an elderly man tend to ask for information about the man's health and eyesight, while those told the driver was a young man request information about whether he was speeding or drinking (Carver & de la Garza, 1984).

This example illustrates how stereotypes can perpetuate themselves by orienting the individual toward information that confirms the stereotype and away from information that is irrelevant or disconfirming. Women and men whose behavior is at odds with prevailing gender stereotypes are often startled by the apparent inventiveness observers use in linking this behavior to "normal" roles for their sex. For instance, one woman was bemused to discover that the men in the gym where she was working out with weights in an effort to develop her strength and fitness were convinced that what she was really trying to develop was her bust. And a man who had chosen to stay home with his young daughter while his wife worked outside the home was dismayed one day at the playground to overhear two mothers of other children speculating that the reason he was caring for his daughter was that his wife was dead. Such apparently creative explanations are probably the result of stereotype-guided information processing that makes it difficult or impossible for the observer, without a conscious effort, to use incoming information in ways that are not in accord with preexisting gender stereotypes. Behavior that appears to disconfirm the stereotype, if it is noticed at all, is attributed to external forces (as in the assumption that the man would not be caring for his daughter if his wife were alive) or to internal motives that can be subsumed under the stereotype (as in the assumption that the woman in the gym was striving for sexiness rather than strength). Thus, stereotypes guide the individual to interpret information in ways that keep stereotypes intact—even in the face of contradictory evidence.

But not all of the evidence *is* contradictory. In fact, social psychologists have begun to show that the cognitive aspects of stereotyping are helped along considerably by a social-behavioral phenomenon known as self-fulfilling prophecy. In many cases, people sense others' expectations of them and, in the interests of smooth interactions, act in such a way as to fulfill those expectations.

Self-Presentation and Self-Fulfilling Prophecy

It has been noted that male–female differences are more likely to be observed in interactive situations than in less social, individualistic ones (Deaux, 1977; Maccoby, 1990). The explanation for this finding may reside in people's sensitivity to the expectations of others. For example, Darley and Fazio (1980) have described the way in which social interaction might result in behavior that confirms the expectations of the participants: The perceiver holds a particular expectancy for the target person's behavior and acts in accordance with that expectancy, the target person interprets the perceiver's actions and responds accordingly, and the perceiver uses the target's response to confirm or reevaluate the original expectancy. If the target's action is very discrepant from the original perception, the perceiver may attribute it to situational constraints or may even end the interaction to avoid taking in information that is counter to expectancies.

Thus, the implicit pressure on the target to play out the expected role is very strong; failure to do so may result in "bungled" or strained interaction. Moreover, if there is a motivation to be liked or approved of by the other participant, there are even stronger reasons to conform to that person's expectations. Some researchers, for instance, have shown that women will present themselves in a more or less stereotypically feminine manner depending on their beliefs about how a male job interviewer or potential date with whom they are interacting views women (von Baeyer, Sherk, & Zanna, 1981; Zanna & Pack, 1975). Similarly, Fried and Major (1980) found that males adjusted the way they presented themselves according to what they believed an attractive female partner would prefer.

Other aspects of the situation may also affect the likelihood of a self-fulfilling prophecy: the strength of the social desirability cues provided by the situation in which the interaction takes place, whether the situation is public or private, the target person's concern with looking good and/or with being true to herself or himself, the strength and certainty of the perceiver's expectancy, the power of the perceiver over the target (Deaux & Major, 1987).

A good demonstration of the way people adopt gender-role behaviors in response to the implied expectations of others was provided in laboratory research by Berna Skrypnek and Mark Snyder (1982). They asked individual male research participants to divide a series of tasks between themselves and a partner. The partners were located in separate rooms and communicated only by means of a signal system. In each case, the hidden partner was a woman, but some of the men were led to believe that their partner was male. The men who thought that their partner was female divided the tasks in a more gender-stereotyped way than those who thought the partner was male. Moreover, when the female partners, unaware of what the men had been told about them, were subsequently given the opportunity to choose tasks, they themselves chose more feminine-stereotyped tasks when paired with a man who had been expecting a female partner. All of this happened without the participants ever seeing or talking to each other.

A factor that may play a large part in the expectancy-confirmation sequences for gender roles is physical appearance (Deaux, 1984b). A person's appearance is a powerful influence on the initial impressions and expectations that others form of her or him. Thus, a person who looks the part of the masculine stereotype—tall, strong, sturdy, broad-shouldered—may, before having done or said anything, be the object of a set of perceiver expectancies for masculine role behavior, and may find him- or herself falling into step with them. Indeed, big, strong-looking men and petite, fragile-looking women may have more trouble than anyone else in trying to break out of the confines of gender-role expectations.

Stereotyping and the Media

Even preschool children are familiar enough with gender stereotypes to believe that "boys don't play with dolls" and "mommies can't be pilots." By adulthood, people are aware of a whole range of subtle and not-so-subtle facets of the different sets of expectations for women and men. How is such knowledge of the stereotypes transmitted from one generation to the next, or to a newcomer to the culture? We will delve into the theories of gender-role socialization in the next chapter, but, for now, let us look briefly at the cultural factors that help to signal and maintain different expectations about women and men—expectations that, in turn, set in motion the self-fulfilling prophecies that are such an important aspect of gender stereotyping.

Most of the major institutions in society—education, religion, business, politics—contribute strongly to gender stereotyping in ways that will be discussed in later chapters. Their impact is often distilled through the mass media. Indeed, outside of the direct influence of family and peers, probably no factor has as pervasive an impact on ideas about gender (or anything else!) as the mass media. Television teaches gender stereotypes (Atwood, Zahn, & Weber, 1986); in fact, research shows that the more television children and teenagers watch, the more they subscribe to male–female stereotypes (Eron, Huesmann, Brice, Fischer, & Mermelstein, 1983; Sternglanz & Serbin, 1974; Morgan, 1982). This finding is not surprising, given the content of television programs. Content-analysis studies have illustrated that central characters are much more often male than female, that male characters are more active than females, and that characters are frequently portrayed engaging in stereotypical behaviors and occupations (Sternglanz & Serbin, 1974; Mayes & Valentine, 1979). Furthermore, subtle and not-so-subtle sex-discriminatory behaviors are modeled for children on television. One study of male–female behavior as portrayed on the ten programs most popular among a sample of eighth-graders found that men in these programs manifested avoidance and exclusion with respect to women, by distancing themselves from women more than from one another and more than the women distanced themselves from men (Lott, 1989).

Nor is gender stereotyping limited to children's programming. Commercials, both child- and adult-oriented, and prime-time shows display a similar pattern. A study of British television commercials showed that women were more likely than men to be portrayed in dependent roles, to be shown as product users, and to be shown in a home setting using domestic products (Manstead & McCulloch, 1981). Moreover, the message that a woman must be attractive to be acceptable is loud and clear in network television commercials. One study of 4294 commercials showed that statements about attractiveness most commonly occurred with female performers and male voice-overs (Downs & Harrison, 1985).

While TV viewers are less likely now than they were a few years ago to see ads portraying housewives as dippy creatures who care about nothing except a "whiter than white" wash, or are mortified when someone discovers "ring around the collar" on their husbands' shirts, subtle sexism is still present (Thompson, 1985). A large-scale study of the portrayal of the sexes in the Canadian media found that women still lag far behind men in their overall portrayal on television and radio (Makin, 1986). The study showed that men comprised 86 to 88 percent of the radio announcers, about 70 percent of the program staff on television news and public affairs shows, and 79 percent of those interviewed on such shows. In advertisements, women were twice as likely as men to appear scantily clad, were more likely to be portrayed as consumers than as salespersons or experts, and were less than half as likely as men to be portrayed as holding paid employment.

In the United States, a study of the portrayal of women on prime-time network television showed that, despite the recent arrival of such TV heroines as "Murphy Brown" and "Designing Women," the proportion of women in prime-time shows has changed little since the 1950s (Davis, 1990). In this study, about 65 percent of the characters in prime-time were male, 35 percent were female. Differences in the ways females and males were portrayed were also striking: Males were far more likely than females to be included in action-adventure shows, and to be of indeterminate marital and parental status, while females were far more likely than males to be shown in provocative dress (nightwear, underwear, swimsuits, tight clothing) and to be blonde or red-haired.

All over North America companies with advertising campaigns perceived as sexist have been the targets of protest. The changes engendered by protest may well have positive effects. Jennings (Walstedt), Geis, and Brown (1980) showed that women who watched counterstereotypic TV commercials showed more self-confidence and less conformity to group pressures in later situations. These authors have also argued that television commercials can act as "achievement scripts" for women, providing women with models of achievement behavior (Geis et al., 1984).

A relatively new form of mass media entertainment, the rock video, provides another powerful avenue for the transmission of gender stereotypes (Brown, 1985). Many such videos are far more blatant in their sexual stereotyping than are current television programming and commercials, often portraying women as aloof seductresses and men as angry, macho conquerors or brooding, rejected introverts. The words of the rock songs that accompany these visual presentations frequently reinforce the sexist message. A content analysis of videos shown on MTV and other television music channels showed that young white males appeared in these videos twice as often as females, that whites appeared four times as frequently as nonwhites, and that most of the videos contained both violent acts and sexual imagery (Sherman & Dominick, 1986). One study of California high schoolers found that these adolescents watched music videos for an average of two hours per day (Sun & Lull, 1986). Given the repetitive nature of the exposure and the compelling quality of the music video presentation, it would be surprising if such videos did not have a strong effect on viewers. Some effects have been demonstrated: Violent videos have been found to foster a greater acceptance of stereotypical beliefs about rape among both male (Peterson & Pfost, 1989) and female (Barbarino, 1991) viewers.

Television and music are not the only media that help in the promotion of gender stereotypes. Print media, from elementary school textbooks to newspaper comic pages, often elaborate and strengthen the messages about what women and men are supposed to be like. Studies of elementary school textbooks used in the 1970s found that male characters repeatedly outnumbered females, that female characters were overwhelmingly portrayed as working only within the home, and that boys were portrayed as having active adventures while girls watched and waited (Key, 1975; Kolbe & LaVoie, 1981). Has the situation changed appreciably in the intervening decades? More recent studies show that, despite some more equitable treatment of males and females, textbooks continue to be male-focused (Hahn & Blankenship, 1983; Light et al., 1989; Pursell & Stewart, 1990).

Print advertising also has shown little recent improvement in nonstereotyped depiction of the sexes. Magazine readers are still confronted with pictures of remote, authoritative men and sexy, submissive women in ads for everything from cigarettes to cars. Even ads that incorporate the image of the "new" strong or competent woman often manage to undercut that image in the same breath. For instance, ads for sporting goods depicting women athletes tend to portray them as sexy rather than strong (Tyler & Phillips, 1984), and a Maidenform ad shows a female physician making hospital rounds in a lab coat that is open to display her elegant underwear!

Even the comic pages of newspapers show a preponderance of male characters (Chavez, 1985), but some of the older, sexist comic strips are beginning to be balanced by ones that poke fun at sexist assumptions and at our attempts to liberate ourselves from them. Lois of "Hi and Lois" now holds a job selling real estate; "Adam," the househusband, copes humorously with everything from the tribulations of housework to jealousy over his wife's business trips; and "Cathy" struggles, usually unsuccessfully, to reconcile her aspirations for success, status, and a liberated lifestyle with her desire for more traditional romance and her "typically feminine" insecurities about her appearance and her competence. Although there is still no shortage of sexist jokes in the comic pages, perhaps humor is serving as one vehicle to encourage, in small ways, the reexamination of gender stereotypes.

There is little doubt that our culture is filled with messages telling us how we should be and how we should behave in order to be adequate or proper women and men. There is also little doubt that these messages have an effect on us—that we believe what we are told. Our ideas about gender are intimately bound up with our culture and change along with it, despite the fact that, most of the time, humans have clung to the idea that the female and male roles prescribed for that particular historical period are the inevitable result of innate, natural differences. The myth that women and men are simply "doing what comes naturally" when they behave according to accepted gender roles has even influenced the researchers who have studied male–female differences, as seen in the following section.

Gender Stereotypes and the Research Process

In an early article on "the fantasy life of the male psychologist," Naomi Weisstein (1971) sounded a stinging challenge for psychologists interested in discovering the truth about human behavior to examine their own discipline for sexism. In a few pungent pages, she produced example after glaring example of cases in which researchers had accepted without question the notion that observed male–female differences in behavior were the inevitable result of natural, inborn differences in inclination or temperament. She railed against what she saw as the general failure of psychologists to consider the social context as an important contributor to gender differences, and against the tendency to consider "natural" or "normal" any behavior that fit easily into gender stereotypes. Her analysis points to a factor with which all students of behavior should still be concerned: It is all too easy to be uncritical of research questions, findings, and interpretations that fit one's own preconceptions.

The history of psychology shows that it has indeed been far too easy to frame research questions and to interpret findings in ways that were consistent with gender stereotypes. For instance, at one period, a vast amount of research energy was expended to study the possible existence of a "maternal instinct" in women, while the possibility of a "paternal instinct" in men was ignored. As well, countless studies of achievement motivation were carried out on boys and men before anyone thought of seriously studying the motive in women. But perhaps the most clear-cut example of the biasing effects of gender stereotypes on the research process can be found in the history of psychology's attempts to measure femininity and masculinity.

Psychology and the Measurement of Masculinity and Femininity: A Comedy of Errors

Psychology, along with the larger culture, has held historically to the implicit assumption that adherence to gender stereotypes is normal and desirable: that women should be feminine and men masculine. This assumption has shaped psychological conceptions of masculinity–femininity (M–F) and attempts to measure it. In particular, it has, until recently, trapped psychologists in the idea that masculinity and femininity must be thought of as the opposing poles of a single dimension.

The notion that such apparently intangible concepts as masculinity and femininity could be measured first became prominent through the work of Lewis Terman and his one-time student and colleague, Catherine Cox Miles. Convinced that the "real" mental differences between the sexes were in nonintellectual mental traits, they created the 456-item Attitude Interest Analysis Survey (AIAS) (1936) to tap the differences. This test and its authors' attempts to validate it are described at length by Miriam Lewin (1984), and the following owes much to her account.

The AIAS, like most of the tests that followed it, was based, not on coherent theories about the "essence" of masculinity or femininity, but on statistically typical sex differences in the way respondents answered particular questions. Large numbers of items were given to a sample of junior high and high school students. Items on which girls and boys tended, on the average, to answer differently were included in the test; those that showed no sex differences were dropped. In its final form, the test consisted of items for which the typical male and female were expected to choose different response alternatives. People taking the test received Femininity (F) points for all answers corresponding to the typical female choice and Masculinity (M) points for all answers corresponding to the typical male choice. To obtain the total M–F score, the F score was subtracted from the M score.

It is interesting to note the kinds of answers that produced high Femininity and Masculinity scores, respectively, using this method. On the information subtest, Femininity points were achieved through ignorance, such as indicating that Goliath was killed by Cain or that the earth turns once on its axis every 12 hours, while Masculinity points were gained by giving the correct answers. On the emotional and ethical attitudes subtest, femininity was associated with greater anger at seeing others treated unfairly; masculinity, on the other hand, was connected with anger at "being disturbed when you want to work." On forced-choice items, boys indicated they preferred to "command others" and to do "uninteresting work with a large income," while girls preferred to "persuade others" and do "interesting work with a small income"—so Masculinity points were assigned to the former and Femininity points to the latter. Femininity points were also achieved by indicating a dislike for "people with loud voices," "argumentative people," and "bald-headed men" or a liking for "very forgiving people," "washing dishes," and "being alone"; Masculinity points were given for reporting a dislike of "tall women," "mannish women," "thin women," or "women cleverer than you"! In retrospect, it is quite clear that the items included in the test, based as they were on gender differences in the self-reports of American junior high and high school students, simply reflected the gender stereotypes of a particular group in a particular time and place. What self-respecting junior high school girl of that era, knowing full well how ladies were supposed to behave, would admit, for example, that she liked to "command others"? What young boy could face his peers after an admission that he liked women cleverer than himself? The meanings assigned to femininity and masculinity using this test, then, are not at all universal, but reflect a particularly American (white? middle-class? urban?) pre-World War II set of biases. Had a similar test been developed using a sample of rural Mexican adolescents or of elderly Chinese office workers, the items associated with masculinity and femininity might have been quite different.

Terman and Miles found masculinity–femininity ratings to be less reliable than those of almost any other personality trait. Moreover, they were unable to show that their test scores correlated with any other criteria of masculinity and femininity. For example, in keeping with the then-prevalent assumption that feminine women were weak and masculine men were strong, the researchers correlated masculinity–femininity scores on the AIAS with the self-rated health ("robust" to "frail") of 533 adults. Alas, the robust men scored as slightly less masculine than the others, and the frail women were not conclusively more feminine. Other research was equally discouraging. The idea that a highly masculine husband and a highly feminine wife should make the happiest couple was tested and found wanting. Ratings of a person's attractiveness to or interest in the other sex showed no relationship with M–F scores. The researchers were undaunted, however, because they believed that by basing the test on observed sex differences in their original sample, they had ensured it was a valid test of masculinity and femininity. Their confidence in the test was not shaken even by the discovery that both women and men were very good at faking their scores to make themselves look masculine or feminine when instructed to do so.

Terman and Miles were not the only psychologists to become mired in imprecision while trying to define and measure M–F. Constantinople (1973), reviewing the literature on M–F measurement, searched in vain for a definition of the two terms that went beyond the idea of "whatever distinguishes males from females." Lewin (1984) describes the series of erroneous assumptions that underlies the AIAS and most subsequent M–F tests up to the 1970s. Among these are the notion that M–F is a static trait that does not change from an early age (hence the use of school children as a criterion group for developing the test), the idea that homosexual men and feminine women will give equivalent responses (the femininity dimension of the M–F scale of well-known personality test, the MMPI, was "validated" on 13 gay men!), and the belief that the gender norms of mid-twentieth century America are universal and fixed rather than linked to changing social, economic, and political conditions.

Researchers currently developing or working with measures of femininity and masculinity are less likely to make these assumptions. In fact, they tend to view such tests not so much as measures of fixed personality traits, but rather as indicators of gender-relevant aspects of a person's self-concept or of the degree to which a person's self-image conforms to sex-role stereotypes (Lewin, 1984). Their approach has changed in another way: They have abandoned the assumption that femininity and masculinity are at opposing ends of the same continuum, and have accepted the possibility of androgyny.

Androgyny

Earlier, we noted the tradition of considering the sexes as opposites—of conceptualizing masculinity and femininity as extreme poles of the same dimension. We have also seen how researchers developing measures of femininity and masculinity adopted this assumption without questioning it, designing tests to accommodate it so that, by definition, a low masculinity score automatically meant high femininity, and vice versa. But there is another tradition in human thinking about sex and gender: the idea that femininity and masculinity are two complementary halves of a single whole, each one needed to complete the other. According to this tradition, not only do women and men need each other, but each individual can achieve wholeness only by developing both the feminine and masculine aspects of herself or himself. This notion is a basic aspect of the ancient Chinese philosophy of Taoism, where the male and female principles, yin and yang, are thought to be the archetypal poles of nature. The two poles are creatively interdependent, each one giving rise to the other. To achieve wholeness and peace, the individual must completely transcend the duality and opposition of the two principles and perceive their underlying unity (Bazin & Freeman, 1974).

Many myths of the origin of the sexes contain elements of this tradition—for example, the biblical account of the creation of Eve from Adam's rib, the Hindu myth of the separation of the Supreme Self into male and female, and Plato's story of Zeus's decision to cut all beings in two. Much mythology and literature contains themes of striving to reunite the two halves—male and female—into a being or state of androgyny (see Heilbrun, 1973, for an overview of this literature). *Androgyny,* deriving from the union of the Greek terms "andro" for man and "gyne" for woman, refers to the psychological merging of the masculine and feminine principles. An androgynous person, by this definition, is one who has reconciled femininity and masculinity within herself or himself, who has both feminine and masculine qualities.

An examination of the procedures used to score traditional M–F tests is sufficient to show that, if there is such a thing as an androgynous person, these tests could not identify that person. An androgynous individual would have substantial feminine *and* masculine qualities and so should score high on both masculinity and femininity on an M–F test. But the design of these tests makes such a score impossible: One cannot score high on femininity without scoring low on masculinity, and vice versa. An androgynous person would end up looking like a zero on an M–F test—as someone who was neither like men nor like women—instead of looking like someone who was like both men and women.

Psychologist Sandra Bem was the first to design a test that would allow an individual to score as androgynous. The Bem Sex Role Inventory (BSRI; Bem, 1974) treats femininity and masculinity as two separate, independent dimensions, so that a respondent can score high on both, low on both, or high on one and low on the other. This change was a significant one, not just for conceptual reasons, but because masculinity and femininity are such highly charged concepts. On the BSRI, a male who admits to some feminine qualities need not fear for his masculinity score, for instance, and people of both sexes who show a mixture of "feminine" and "masculine" traits are classified as androgynous, not maladjusted or deviant.

Besides its treatment of femininity and masculinity as two separate dimensions, the BSRI also differs from traditional M–F tests in another way. Items for the masculinity and femininity scales were developed, not by using the old approach of picking the items on which males and females answered differently, but by picking the items that a pool of male and female respondents rated as most desirable "for an American man or woman." Twenty items rated as highly desirable for men were selected for the masculinity scale, and twenty items rated highly desirable for women formed the femininity scale. Another twenty neutral items were chosen for the social desirability scale. People taking the test are asked to indicate on a 7-point scale how well each of the adjectives describes them. Based on their responses, they can be classified in one of four ways: Masculine (high on masculinity, low on femininity), Feminine (high on femininity, low on masculinity), Androgynous (high on both femininity and masculinity), or Undifferentiated (low on both femininity and masculinity). Using the test with samples of California college students, Bem found that about one-third of the subjects scored as "sex-typed" (Feminine females and Masculine males), one-third scored as Androgynous, and fewer than 10 percent scored as "cross-sex-typed" (Masculine females and Feminine males). Other researchers have also now developed scales that allow for the measurement of psychological androgyny, such as the Personal Attributes Questionnaire (Spence, Helmreich, & Stapp, 1974) and the PRF Andro scale (Berzins, Welling, & Wetter, 1975). Like the original Terman and Miles (1936) scale, all of these scales reflect the particular biases of the samples (usually middle-class American college students) on which they were developed.

While abandoning the notion that femininity and masculinity were two ends of a bipolar continuum and incorporating the idea of androgyny into psychological tests of gender have been important steps, they have not solved all the problems inherent in trying to measure masculinity and femininity. Several issues in designing the tests remain unsolved: the assumption that femininity and masculinity are unidimensional constructs rather than constellations of several dimensions, the difficulty of scaling the test items so that each one is "worth" the same amount of masculinity or femininity, and the problem of sex specificity—the possibility that a given item may count more heavily toward self-perceived femininity or masculinity for one sex than for the other (Colwill & Lips, 1978). Underlying all the problems, however, is one major theme: Psychologists are still not sure what they are trying to measure. Masculinity and femininity are still defined only as the two sets of qualities that distinguish males from females, and since these distinctions vary a great deal across time and place, trying to devise standard criteria with which to assess them appears to be a hopeless task. People's perceptions of masculinity and femininity appear to be far more complex than implied by the collection of items on these scales (Spence & Sawin, 1985). To further complicate matters, it appears that when ordinary people are asked to describe what femininity or masculinity means to them, their answers bear little resemblance to the items on the most widely used psychological tests (Lips, 1986a; Myers & Gonda, 1982). Psychologists are left with a dilemma: On the one hand, masculinity and femininity are such slippery concepts that it seems fruitless to waste any more time trying to measure them; on the other hand, it is clear that they are experienced by people as important concepts against which to measure themselves and others. Popular conceptions of femininity and masculinity are complex and multidimensional and probably cannot be represented adequately by single scores on a personality test.

Gender Schema

Some researchers have recently begun to treat masculinity and femininity not just as personality characteristics, but as gender schemas (Bem, 1981) or masculine and feminine self-schemas (Markus, Crane, Bernstein, & Siladi, 1982), cognitive structures that guide the processing of incoming information about the self. According to these approaches, a person who has a strong gender schema or self-schema for femininity or masculinity would tend spontaneously to organize incoming information about herself or himself around the notion of gender rather than around some other notion, such as age or nationality, for which no strong schema was present. An individual who is "gender schematic" would simply be more ready than someone who is "gender aschematic" to process information about the self in terms of gender. He or she would, for example, be more likely to remember things relevant to gender than things relevant to nationality, and to make faster, easier, and more confident decisions about the applicability to herself or himself of gender-related than nationality-related traits. As Bem (1985) suggests, highly masculine or feminine individuals may differ from others "not in their *ability* to organize information on the basis of gender but in their *threshold* for doing so spontaneously" (p. 197). Bem's own research and that of others (summarized in Bem, 1985) provides some support for this idea. Interestingly, research suggests that a person need not be sex-typed to be gender schematic; for example, a woman who does not describe herself in stereotypically feminine ways may still process information readily in terms of gender, perhaps because she is interested in gender for academic or political reasons (Freedman, 1991). It has been argued that, when interacting with and forming initial impressions of others, people activate their gender schemas more quickly than schemas based on less easily observable attributes (Deaux & Major, 1987). When it comes to processing information about the *self*, however, research suggests that strongly gender schematic persons are rare, and that stereotypical femininity and masculinity are not central to the self-concepts of most individuals (Signorella & Frieze, 1989).

Gender schema theory provides one useful perspective on femininity and masculinity because it helps to explain how people with very diverse repertoires of traits and behaviors might all think of themselves as feminine or masculine. Thus, for example, traits that do not fit easily into cultural definitions of one's gender might be acknowledged but considered unimportant. This theory further suggests that by adjusting their notions of what qualities are relevant to gender, people may adapt to changing cultural expectations for women and men without suffering damage to their belief in their own femininity or masculinity. Moreover, as will be seen in the next chapter, gender schema theory provides some interesting ideas about the process by which children learn to be masculine or feminine.

Disarming the Stereotypes: Approaches to Empowerment

Recent approaches to gender in psychology have often rested on the desire to free people from the constraints of stereotypes based on biological sex. The freedom to be or behave in a particular way without worrying about whether or not one is being "appropriately masculine" or "feminine enough" allows individuals to seek out their own strengths, to use their energy where it will do the most good. Making gender stereotypes less rigid and inclusive of fewer aspects of behavior, then, should be empowering for both women and men—a way of increasing their sense of effectiveness and self-actualization. As well, the process should unleash new sources of human energy for societies, adding to a collective sense of power and accomplishment. Finally, the dismantling of gender stereotypes may, by removing the justification for segregation of society's institutions and occupations by sex, ultimately help to reduce the power imbalance between women and men and foster an era of greater equality.

Are the new approaches to gender in psychology really having this empowering effect? The answer is controversial. Many people have argued that the concept of psychological androgyny, while initially liberating, has now become simply another prescription against which people must measure themselves (e.g., Bem, 1985; Pyke, 1980). Now people can feel inadequate not only because they are not masculine enough or feminine enough, but also because they are not androgynous enough! Even more seriously, since androgyny is built on the concepts of femininity and masculinity, it continues to impart a sense that these are real entities rather than cultural constructions, and it can never transcend them. Thus, androgyny, while pushing back the limitations imposed by a bipolar conception of masculinity–femininity, contains its own built-in limitations.

The gender schema approach may ultimately prove more useful because it focuses attention on the extent to which cultures and individuals use gender as an organizing principle. A gender schema can be made smaller; that is, the number of things to which the gender dichotomy is considered relevant could conceivably be reduced to the small group associated with biological sex differences. In a culture that had achieved such a reduction in the scope of the gender schema, people would waste little time or energy worrying about their masculinity or femininity, trying to prove it or live up to it or change it. Gender distinctions would be acknowledged but not emphasized, and would not be used as a basis for deciding most things. Such a society is envisioned by one of the main promoters of gender schema theory, Sandra Bem (1985).

Is Bem's vision an impossible one? It is too early to say. One thing is likely, though: The attempt to create that scenario is itself an exercise in empowerment.

Summary

The labeling of an individual as female or male has a powerful impact on others' perceptions of and reactions to that individual. Stereotypically, we expect different behaviors, personal qualities, and physical appearance from women and men. When we categorize people by sex (their biological femaleness or maleness), we tend to assume that we have also categorized them by gender (the set of cultural expectations for femininity and masculinity) although on many dimensions there is no necessary relationship between biological sex and cultural expectations for women and men.

Our conceptions of femininity and masculinity are framed in the language of opposites. Men are thought to be competent and independent; women to be expressive and affiliative. Such gender stereotypes are more than just a random collection of groundless beliefs about women and men. Rather, they represent cultural constructions of femininity and masculinity, sometimes based tenuously on physical differences, that serve as underpinnings for the social relations between women and men, as groups and as individuals. However, human beings have often failed, and still do, to recognize the extent to which gender stereotypes are products of the social context in which they exist, how resistant they are to disconfirmation, and how easily they can act as self-fulfilling prophecies. We react negatively to individuals who violate the stereotypes, as if they were acting in an "unnatural" way, when, in fact, they are simply violating cultural norms. The history of attempts by psychologists to measure femininity and masculinity reveals all too clearly that psychology as a discipline has not been exempt from gender stereotyping or from the mistaken belief that observed differences between the sexes automatically represent the natural state of affairs.

In recent years, psychologists have emphasized new concepts—androgyny and gender schema—in an effort to deal with issues of masculinity and femininity without invoking the stereotypic notion of the "opposite sexes." These attempts have been only partially successful, but they have provided frameworks for new thinking about sex and gender.

For Additional Reading

Cruikshank, Julie, in collaboration with Angela Sidney, Kitty Smith, and Annie Ned. (1991). *Life lived like a story: Life stories of three Yukon Native elders*. Lincoln: University of Nebraska Press. Three Native women born at the turn of the century in the southern Yukon Territory tell their stories in their own words.

Gilmore, David G. (1990). *Manhood in the making: Cultural concepts of masculinity*. New Haven, CT: Yale University Press. A cross-cultural examination of what it means to "be a man" in societies around the world.

Hooks, Bell. (1989). *Talking back: Thinking feminist, thinking black*. Boston: South End Press. A writer discusses, in a personal and powerful way, the experience and meaning of being Black and female in a culture that privileges those who are white and male.

King, F. (1985). *Confessions of a failed southern lady*. New York: St. Martin's Press. The autobiographical account of a young woman's conflicts with southern notions of femininity.

Mairs, Nancy. (1990). *Carnal acts*. New York: HarperCollins. A woman writes eloquently about her own life, including the paradoxes and difficulties that accompany disability.

2
Theoretical Perspectives on Sex & Gender

During the latter part of the nineteenth century, the idea flourished that educating women in the same way as men was dangerous and damaging. The danger supposedly arose from the energy needs of women's reproductive processes: menstruation and preparation for childbearing. Physicians theorized that the womb exercised a dominating influence over a woman's personality and ability, almost as if the "Almighty, in creating the female sex, had taken the uterus and built a woman around it" (physician quoted in Smith-Rosenberg & Rosenberg, 1976, p. 56). Women who, during puberty, used up too much precious energy on the brain function required for advanced education would enfeeble their bodies, ruining their health and crippling their capacity to bear children. These dire warnings, sounded most prominently by Dr. Edward Clarke (1873), were based on a theory of thermodynamics: All physical systems, including the human body, followed the principle of conservation of energy, so that force expended in one function would be unavailable to any other. Men, whose passage into puberty supposedly did not place such a heavy strain on their bodies, could safely turn their energies to demanding intellectual tasks without endangering their physical well-being.

Clearly, in this example, the acceptance of two theoretical assumptions—the domination of female personality by the uterus and the principle of conservation of energy—had a profound impact on popular and scientific thinking about the differences between women and men. In the history of the study of sex and gender, the role played by theory has been substantial. But what exactly is a theory? Basically, it is a set of ideas about how and why things happen. In the realm of science, where psychology is situated, the role of a theory is to guide research: to generate hypotheses (propositions) that can be tested against observed reality. For example, if one subscribed to the theory that women's personality was dominated by the uterus, one should be able to think of some testable hypotheses—things that should occur if the theory were true and should not occur if it were false—and then test them. Such testing might involve comparing women who had borne children with those who had not, or comparing groups of same-age women who had or had not undergone hysterectomies.

Given this example, it is easy to see how the acceptance of a particular theory can have a major impact on the kind of research that gets done: what questions are asked, what issues are investigated or ignored, what findings are considered important or trivial. It is also easy to see that a theory that did not lend itself to being checked against reality in some way might linger in people's imagination for a long time without being either proven or disproven and laid to rest, particularly if it had some popular appeal. A requirement for a good and useful theory, then, is that it be subject to verification.

The history of the study of sex and gender provides many examples of a problem that always besets the scientific process: Theories that fit well with the accepted assumptions at a particular time and place tend to receive a lot of attention and generate research, while those that seem to be at odds with accepted notions are frequently ignored. Indeed, we scientists are such creatures of our culture that our theories often incorporate as presuppositions untested aspects of the "conventional wisdom" of our time and place. Thus, for example, the basic cultural notion that men were intellectually superior to women was frequently accepted as a given by psychologists, who then set out to construct theories to explain *why* this was so. In the words of the eminent psychologist William James (1890), "It is astonishing what havoc is wrought in psychology by admitting at the outset apparently innocent suppositions that nevertheless contain a flaw" (p. 224).

Before anyone had ever heard of psychology, theories about gender were being offered by the early philosophers. Within these early theories lies an idea that influenced psychology for years afterward: woman as incomplete man.

The idea of equality between the sexes can be found in the early writings of the Greek philosopher Plato, who described women and men as having the same nature and worth and deserving the same education and legal treatment. This idea fades out in his later writings, however, in which female weakness and inferiority are used as justification for assigning different social roles to men and women (Dickason, 1976). Later, in the writings of Aristotle, the idea of feminine inferiority and "incompleteness" was developed in detail. Aristotle claimed that the female state was an "ordinary" deformity and that a woman was, in some respects, a defective man (Whitbeck, 1976). Female inferiority lay in the fact that women supposedly had less "soul heat" than men, and so could not process their menstrual blood to what he deemed the "final stage," semen. Women's inability to produce semen meant that, in the process of conception, they could contribute nothing but formative material to the embryo, and made no genetic contribution to its distinctive character.

The Aristotelian notion that women were inferior because of a shortage of intrinsic heat received a later expression in the work of Juan Huarte, a sixteenth-century Spanish writer expounding on individual intellectual differences. He argued that the testicles were responsible for maintaining the "heat and dryness" characteristic of the male principle. Since "dryness of spirit" was necessary for intelligence, and since the testicles maintained this quality, obviously men, who had testicles, were more intelligent than women, who did not (Shields, 1975).

Theories that viewed women as lesser beings than men—because of their inability to produce enough heat to process body fluids into semen—did not view women as *opposites* to men. Women and men were thought to be similar, but differently developed. In fact, proponents of these theories often argued that women and men had similar bodies: There were many early medical references, for instance, to the male uterus, to female testicles, and to the "fact" that the female reproductive organs were the same as the male's—only "inside out," with the scrotum equivalent to the uterus, the penis to the cervix and vagina (Laqueur, 1990). Laqueur quotes a bit of popular verse from the early nineteenth century:

> . . . though they of different sexes be,
> Yet on the whole they are the same as we,
> For those that have the strictest searchers been,
> Find women are but men turned outside in. (p. 4)

The second-century anatomist Galen used the simile of the eyes of a mole to describe female genitalia. As he explained it, the eyes of the mole appear the same as those of other animals, except that they do not open and thus do not allow the animal to see. The mole's eyes remain closed, as if the animal were still in the uterus. Similarly, the female's genitalia remain unopened and undeveloped after birth, as if still in the womb, while the male's project outward and develop fully (Laqueur, 1990).

The "woman as defective man" motif affected theories of gender, inside and outside of psychology, for centuries, appearing in the writings of men from Thomas Aquinas to Sigmund Freud (de Beauvoir, 1952). The strength of the idea is not surprising, given that these theorists, encountering women mainly in subordinate positions, developed their theories to explain and justify what seemed to them a natural and inevitable situation. However, by the nineteenth century, the hierarchical approach to male–female differences had been supplanted to some extent by the "opposites" approach, an approach that treated the two sexes as irreconcilably different. Echoes of both approaches can be found in psychological theories of gender.

Six general types of theories have emerged in psychology to explain the differences and similarities between human males and females. The first type, *psychoanalytic/ identification theories,* focus on personality development. The second set, *social structural theories,* concern social structures and culture, concentrating on how intergroup relations between women and men are linked to gender roles and stereotypes. The third category, *sociobiology,* attempts to explain gender issues with reference to the evolution of the human species. All three of these theoretical approaches put a heavy emphasis on the origins of gender, focusing on *why* the sexes may differ. The next three approaches, *social learning, cognitive development, social interaction process theories,* focus more heavily on *how* gender differences occur, stressing the processes through which males and females may be led to adopt different or similar ways of behaving.

Psychoanalytic/Identification Theories

Sigmund Freud

Sigmund Freud was the father of psychoanalytic theory—perhaps the first theory of human personality to assign a central role to sexuality. His writings and the controversies they have generated fill volumes, and have had a profound impact on ideas about male–female differences. Reaction to his work on gender has ranged from assertions that he has done more than anyone else to set back the cause of women (Figes, 1970) to praise for his brilliant analysis of a patriarchal society (Mitchell, 1974).

Freud's theory was predicated on the idea that the human mind, like an iceberg that floats with only a small tip showing above the surface of the water, is only partially available to our awareness. This part of the mind available to awareness, referred to as the region of *consciousness,* contains the thoughts and feelings people know they have; the much larger part, the unconscious, contains the unacceptable urges, passions, ideas, and feelings that people cannot acknowledge. The contents of the *unconscious* can be explored only indirectly through dreams, free association, symptoms, mistakes (now sometimes called "Freudian slips") or other "leaks" of the unconscious into conscious awareness. The unconscious was the cornerstone of Freudian theory, for he felt that the motives hidden in the unconscious are often the driving force behind conscious thoughts and deeds. The notion of the unconscious is also what makes this theory difficult to verify or disprove, however, since, by definition, the contents of the unconscious cannot be investigated with traditional objective methods for assessing people's thoughts and feelings.

Freud proposed that the personality is composed of three structures—id, ego, and superego—and that a person's behavior is produced by the interaction among these systems (Freud, 1960). In his theory, the *id,* consisting of the individual's biological heritage, including sexual and aggressive instincts, provides a reservoir of psychic energy that powers the other two systems. A nonrational system, it operates strictly on the pleasure principle: Uncomfortable tension must be discharged and needs satisfied. The *ego,* on the other hand, is a rational system that works on the reality principle: Discharge of tension or satisfaction of needs should be prevented until an appropriate situation is found. This second system handles transactions between an individual's subjective needs and the objective world of reality, thus helping to keep her or him out of trouble and ensure survival. Finally, the *superego* acts as the moral aspect of the personality, striving for perfection rather than pleasure, and persuading the ego to substitute moralistic goals for realistic ones. The superego, also nonrational, was described by Freud as the internal representative of society's values and ideals as taught to the child by parents and enforced by rewards and punishments. The three systems should be balanced in an individual's personality, and dominance of the personality by one of them can cause problems. A very strong id, combined with a weak ego and superego, creates a person who is impulsive, hedonistic, and unfettered by the demands of conscience; an overdeveloped superego produces one who is inhibited from most forms of self-expression by the crippling fear of imperfection.

Personality development occurs in a series of five "psychosexual stages." In each stage, strong pleasurable feelings, attributed by Freud to the satisfaction of sexual instincts, are associated with particular body zones. In the *oral* stage, during the first year of life, pleasure is centered in the mouth and sucking. During the second year, the child passes through the *anal* stage, in which pleasure is linked to defecation. Next comes the *phallic* stage, in which erotic pleasure is obtained from the penis for boys and the clitoris for girls. This is followed by the *latency* phase, in which erotic impulses are repressed until just before puberty. Puberty ushers in the *genital* stage, that of mature sexuality.

According to Freud, it is during the phallic stage, which lasts from about age 3 to age 6, that the development of boys and girls diverges. This divergence, and consequent formation of appropriate masculine or feminine identification, is precipitated by the development and resolution of the *Oedipus complex*, a system of feelings named by Freud for the mythical Greek character who unwittingly killed his own father and married his own mother.

Boys at this stage develop an intense attachment for the mother and a desire to possess her sexually. The boy begins to see his father as a rival—a competitor for the mother's affections—and he wishes to replace him. Unable to acknowledge his strong negative feelings toward his father, the boy unconsciously projects the feelings onto the father, thus coming to believe that his father sees *him* as a rival. He then fears what his father may do to him, and the fear that begins to haunt him is that of castration. Why a fear of castration? This is the phallic stage, the stage at which the penis is the source of a great deal of pleasure and pride for the little boy. It is a time when he has discovered masturbation, and perhaps has been threatened by his parents that if he doesn't stop, they will "cut it off." Most importantly, according to Freud, it is a time when he discovers with chagrin that not everybody has a penis. His first glimpse of a naked girl or woman leaves him shocked and perturbed because it gives reality to his parents' threats and his own fears: Some people have apparently already been castrated! So intense does his fear become that he is literally forced to resolve the Oedipus complex in order to allay the fear. He achieves this end by identifying with his father (accepting his father as a model and incorporating many features of his father's personality into his own) and crushing his desire for his mother. Freud believed that boys emerged from the Oedipus complex with either a contempt for or fear of women, based on the danger associated with attraction to the mother.

For a girl, the road to feminine identification begins, according to Freud, when she first notices that boys have something she does not: a penis. The realization produces what Freud labeled "penis envy":

> She has seen it and knows she is without it and wants to have it. . . . The hope of someday obtaining a penis in spite of everything and so of becoming like a man may persist to an incredibly late age and may become a motive for the strangest and otherwise unaccountable actions. Or again, a process may

> set in which might be described as a "denial" . . . a girl may
> refuse to accept the fact of being castrated, may harden herself in
> the conviction that she *does* possess a penis and may subse-
> quently be compelled to behave as though she were a man.
> (Freud, 1925/1974, pp. 31–32)

Seeing herself to be lacking such an important organ, the girl develops a sense of inferiority and contempt for her own sex. Gradually, her penis envy becomes a more general attitude of jealousy. She blames her mother, her original love object, for her lack of a penis and starts to withdraw her affection from her. She tries to suppress the tendency to masturbate, since her clitoris is so inferior to the boy's penis. Her penis envy eventually leads her to enter the female version of the Oedipus complex (called the *Electra complex,* after the mythical Greek personage who urged her brother to slay their mother, who had murdered their father): "She gives up her wish for a penis and puts in place of it a wish for a child: and *with this purpose in view* she takes her father as a love object. Her mother becomes the object of her jealousy" (Freud, 1925/1974, p. 34). Gradually, she realizes that she can never possess her father. By facing this frustration she accepts the link between pain and pleasure that is inherent in the female role, and becomes masochistic. Grudgingly, she reestablishes her feminine identification with her mother and concentrates on becoming an attractive love object so that she will be adored by some other man. Sexual attractiveness becomes her primary source of self-esteem and identity.

Females, unlike males, do not have a powerful fear motivation to resolve the Oedipus complex. For them, after all, the worst has already happened: They have been castrated. Freud felt that, in their case, the complex was slowly abandoned or repressed, rather than smashed, as it was for boys. For boys, the necessity to destroy the Oedipus complex results in the formation of a strong superego; for girls, the more gradual abandonment of the complex makes strong superego development less necessary.

Thus, the different courses followed by boys and girls in forming and resolving the Oedipus complex have far-reaching consequences in Freudian theory for the development of psychological gender differences. Among males, the result of resolution is masculine identification, contempt for or fear of women, and a strong superego. Among females, the upshot of the complex is feminine identification, a sense of inferiority, contempt for other women, a tendency toward jealousy, a rejection of clitoral sexuality, masochism, a wish for a child, an obsession with sexual attractiveness, and a weaker superego.

Two of Freud's conclusions in particular arouse the indignation of modern women. The first is his idea that the rejection of clitoral sexuality was a normal part of female development. Freud believed that the suppression of sexual activity focused on the clitoris was necessary for the emergence of true feminine (vaginal) sexuality. In psychoanalytic theory, the clitoral orgasm was considered immature and not truly satisfying; a "real woman" found satisfaction only in vaginal orgasms achieved during intercourse. This element of Freudian doctrine is puzzling in light of the complete lack of evidence that erotic sensitivity was transferred from the clitoris to the vagina during women's maturation. Nineteenth-century medical books made it abundantly clear that the clitoris had far more nerve endings than did the vagina, and Freud, as a doctor, could hardly have been unaware of this. So powerful was his theory's hold on the popular imagination, however, that scientists "forgot" what had been well known to doctors and to ordinary women and men for centuries—that the female orgasm is almost entirely clitoral (Laqueur, 1990). When researchers in the second half of the twentieth century "discovered" what seventeenth-century women would have thought to be common knowledge—that the clitoris has as many nerve endings as the penis and that all female orgasms originate there (see Chapter 7), many women who had been suffering guilt and inadequacy over their inability to have "proper" vaginal orgasms suddenly realized they'd been "had." Resentment still simmers against Freudian-based psychiatry for its complicity in orienting women toward denial rather than trust of their own experience of sexuality.

The second Freudian concept that has rankled in women is penis envy. Freud suggested that since the pressure to resolve the Oedipus complex is weak in women, it may happen that no resolution is achieved. In this event, his theory indicates, the adult woman will be a neurotic victim of penis envy. She may try to be masculine, become resentful and jealous of men, and reject the feminine fulfillment of pregnancy—all the while completely unaware that it is her unconscious wish for a penis that is making her so cranky! If women take offense at this aspect of the theory, it is little wonder, for it implies that any woman who is not satisfied with her socially defined feminine role is neurotic and psychosexually immature. Freud himself was not above using the penis envy concept as a weapon against female psychoanalysts who broke ranks and criticized his theory: "We shall not be very surprised if a woman analyst who has not been sufficiently convinced of her own desire for a penis also fails to assign an adequate importance to that factor in her patients" (quoted in Garrison, 1981).

Because Freudian theory acknowledged the importance and pervasiveness of sexual feelings and desires—experiences that were largely denied or minimized in the Victorian era in which he worked—it opened the door for consideration of some hitherto undiscussed sexual behaviors. In one such case, incest, the door was opened slightly, then hastily closed. In another, homosexuality, some light was allowed to shine on a subject that had been shrouded in disapproval.

Many of Freud's women patients told him that they had been "seduced" by their fathers. At first, Freud believed these accounts, and attributed the women's neurotic symptoms to repressed horror over the incest. Later, however, he began to feel uneasy about the large numbers of his female patients who claimed to have been sexually molested by their fathers and male relatives. Refusing to accept the possibility that daughters were sexually victimized with such high frequency, he asserted in his public writings that the women's accounts (and their symptoms) were based on fantasies rather than real occurrences. In fact, he came to describe the fantasy of being seduced by the father as the expression of the Oedipus complex in women.

Unbelievable though it may have seemed to Freud, evidence suggests that most of his women patients were telling the truth. The occurrences of traumatic seduction were, in many cases, confirmed by the seducer or other reliable witnesses (Sulloway, 1979). In the present day, surveys have placed the occurrence of father–daughter incest at between 1.3 and 4.5 percent and the occurrence of child sexual abuse in general at between 19 and 38 percent (Finkelhor, 1979; Russell, 1983a). Moreover, documentation of the widespread character of sexual abuse of girls is not new, and was apparently available to Freud and known to him through medical colleagues in Paris. Some of his unpublished letters seem to suggest that, long after he had publicly discounted the truth of his patients' seduction stories, he continued to believe that, at least some of the time, the stories were true (Masson, 1984). The damage done by Freud's public refusal to believe his female patients is incalculable. Victims of incest who seek help still encounter disbelief, or the charge that the incident was an outcome of their own unconscious incestuous wishes (Rush, 1980).

Freud's legacy with respect to homosexuality was more positive. He argued that neither masculinity and femininity nor heterosexuality and homosexuality were polar opposites; rather, every individual displayed a mixture of these qualities. As he wrote to a woman concerned about her son's homosexuality:

> Homosexuality is assuredly no advantage, but it is nothing to be ashamed of, no vice, no degradation; it cannot be classified as an illness; we consider it to be a variation of the sexual function. . . . Many highly respectable individuals of ancient and modern times have been homosexuals, several of the greatest men among them. . . . It is a great injustice to persecute homosexuality as a crime—and a cruelty too. . . .
>
> What analysis can do for your son runs in a different line. If he is unhappy, neurotic, torn by conflicts, inhibited in his social life, analysis may bring him harmony, peace of mind, full efficiency, whether he remains homosexual or gets changed. (Freud, 1961, pp. 419–420)

Freud's theory opened new possibilities for debate in the whole area of sexuality and gender. And a debate is exactly what happened. One current of controversy has challenged the phallocentrism of Freudian theory, arguing for a more "gynocentric" approach. A second area of argument has revolved around the issue of male gender-role identity.

Karen Horney

Almost from the first, some critics felt that Freud, in looking at psychosexual development from the male point of view, had developed a theory that overemphasized the role played by the penis and anxiety over losing or not having it, in the development of both sexes. An early proponent of this viewpoint was Karen Horney, a member of Freud's circle, with a reputation as one of the foremost training analysts in Europe. She questioned the idea that women look on their bodies as inferior, and argued that masculine narcissism is the only basis for the assumption that one-half of the human race is automatically discontented with the sex assigned to it. Although accepting the possibility of penis envy in girls and castration anxiety in boys, she noted that males are also envious of females:

> From the biological point of view, woman has in motherhood, or in the capacity for motherhood, a quite indisputable and by no means negligible superiority. This is most clearly reflected in the unconscious of the male psyche in the boy's intense envy of motherhood. We are familiar with this envy as such, but it has hardly received due consideration as a dynamic

factor. When one begins, as I did, to analyze men only after
fairly long experience of analyzing women, one receives a most
surprising impression of the intensity of this envy of pregnancy,
childbirth, and motherhood, as well as of the breasts and the act
of suckling. (Horney, 1926/1973, p. 10)

Horney also believed that the rejection of the female role in girls is mainly caused,
not by envy of the penis, but by an unconscious fear of vaginal injury through penetra-
tion, aroused by guilt over masturbation. Thus, she proposed that a girl's psychosexual
development centers around her own anatomy rather than that of the male. Furthermore, she argued, the rejection of the feminine role is partially a response to a society
that views women as inadequate and inferior and gives them few opportunities outside
the home. Thus, she became one of the first psychoanalysts to draw attention to the
possibilities for interaction between cultural and inner dynamic forces in the shaping
of the personality. Although both she and her views were rejected in orthodox Freudian circles, her work had considerable impact, and she herself became respected, rich,
and famous, despite the controversy she created (Garrison, 1981).

Whereas Freudian theory can be labeled "phallocentric"—centered on the male
penis—the perspective taken by Horney and a group of other psychoanalysts has been
labeled "gynocentric"—centered on the female womb (Stockard & Johnson, 1979).
This latter approach emphasizes the importance for personality development of both
boys' and girls' pre-Oedipal relationship with the mother, and links male dominance
of women to that early mother–child tie. The bases proposed for the link are unconscious fear and envy of the mother and the necessity for boys but not girls to switch
their identification from the mother to the father.

Horney suggested that the strength of men's desire to achieve and create is an overcompensation for their unconscious sense of inferiority in the creative process of reproduction. Furthermore, she proposed, the masculine tendency to depreciate women
is also an outcome of this unconscious envy, rather than of the recognition that the
female lacks a penis. On this point she was echoed by Melanie Klein (1932/1960), who
asserted that boys' pride in and emphasis on the penis compensates for feelings of anxiety, envy, and inferiority regarding the mother.

Although Horney's critique of Freud reclaimed the primacy of women's own bodies, rather than envy of the male body, in their psychological development, it was as
limited as Freud's approach in its fatalistic reliance on anatomy and instincts to explain
personality. In her later work, Horney rejected the notion that human behavior
springs from instinctual drives (sex, aggression), and developed instead the notion that
behavior is a product of experience in its cultural context (Westkott, 1986). She postulated that human beings are guided by needs for safety (inner security) and satisfaction,
and that a child's social environment determines whether these needs can be met easily
or whether the child must develop a neurotic "solution," such as dependency, to the
anxiety and hostility that arise from an insecure environment.

According to Horney's (1939) theory, the environment presents two potential dangers to the young child: devaluation (parents' lack of respect for the child as unique,
worthwhile) and sexualization (a sexual approach to the child, an emotional "hot-
house" atmosphere). She argued that the clinging to one parent and jealousy toward
the other that characterized what Freud had called the Oedipus complex was actually

a child's anxious response to the abuse of parental power: sexualizing, devaluing treatment of the child (Westkott, 1986).

It is clear from Horney's writings that she felt that the cultural pattern of preference for sons over daughters made girls more vulnerable than boys to devaluation and the development of a sense of inferiority. She noted as well the pervasive cultural tendency for families to treat girls as if their sexuality was the most important aspect of their identity. Thus, although theoretically applicable to both boys and girls, the experiences of devaluation and sexualization were more likely, in a society that valued males over females, to characterize the childhood of girls than of boys. Girls might, then, be more likely than boys to develop neurotic personalities characterized by the submissiveness and self-directed hostility that develops in response to parental devaluation. However, this gender difference is based, not in anything biological, but in a culture that values one sex more than the other.

Feminism and Psychoanalytic Theory

During the last two decades, much theorizing has been done about the aspect of development virtually ignored by Freud and highlighted in Horney's early writings: the early bond between mother and child. Writing in the gynocentric tradition of Karen Horney, Melanie Klein, and other early analysts, Dorothy Dinnerstein (1976) argued that society allows men to hold the power outside the mother–child relationship precisely because the power held by the mother over the infant is so awesome. The relationship produces in both men and women, Dinnerstein says, a fear of female power and authority. In the process of growing up, the individual flees from the power of the mother and finds it easier to accept male than female authority. Men end up with a particular fear of becoming overly dependent on women, whereas women carry with them throughout their lives a sense of inadequacy because they can never live up to the magically powerful mother image they experienced as infants. The result is a society that accepts and encourages male dominance.

Sociologist Nancy Chodorow (1978), taking a similar perspective about the overwhelming effect of the mother–child relationship, has argued that exclusively female mothering produces men and women with very different emotional needs. Women, having been parented by an adult with whom they could identify, try unsuccessfully to reexperience this sense of unity in their sexual relationships with men.

> But families organized around women's mothering and male dominance create incompatibilities in women's and men's relational needs. In particular, relationships to men are unlikely to provide for women satisfaction of the relational needs that their mothering by women and the social organization of gender have produced. The less men participate in the domestic sphere, and especially in parenting, the more this will be the case. (p. 199)

Furthermore, Chodorow (1989) notes, family arrangements in which women do the primary caretaking produce different problems for males and females. Contrary to Freud, whose analysis of the Oedipal trauma emphasized the difficulties faced by girls in forming a positive gender identity, Chodorow argues, it is boys who face the most problems in initially forming their identity as males. Because of the early, close attachment between mother and child,

> Underlying, or built into, core male gender identity is an early, non-verbal, unconscious, almost somatic sense of primary oneness with the mother, an underlying sense of femaleness that continually, usually unnoticeably, but sometimes insistently, challenges and undermines the sense of maleness. (p. 109)

Because boys form an initial identification with the mother, forming a masculine identity is a negative process that involves separation and denial. Males must form their gender identity by defining themselves as "*not* women." For girls, such drastic separation is not necessary. However, girls develop difficulties with identity later; these center around the problems of identifying with "a negatively valued gender category, and an ambivalently experienced maternal figure, whose mothering and femininity, often conflictual for the mother herself, are accessible, but devalued" (pp. 110–111).

Why is feminine identity negatively valued? Chodorow (1989) explains that men devalue it in their flight from it. Moreover, because men have more power than women, they have been able to "define maleness as that which is basically human, and to define women as not-men" (p. 111).

Chodorow notes, however, that human family arrangements are not invariant, but change in response to the economic organization of society. The arrangement that emphasizes women's mothering and male dominance, then, is not an inevitable aspect of human social organization.

The attention paid to the mother–child relationship in the gynocentric branch of psychoanalytic theory makes it quite different from orthodox Freudian theory, in which the father–child relationship is the crucial one. An interesting implication that both Dinnerstein and Chodorow have drawn from their theoretical work is that society would be better off with a family system in which parenting was more equally shared between women and men. Such sharing of roles would presumably reduce the internalization of a perception of mothers as "all-powerful," paving the way for more egalitarian and intimate relationships between adult women and men.

Male Sex-Role Identity

Chodorow's description of the difficulties associated with masculine identity echoes the ideas of other theorists who have been specifically concerned with the male role. The idea that "sex-typing," or gender-role acquisition, was based on early identification with the appropriate parent, led some theorists on a quest for the explanation of "masculinity problems." In contrast to Freud, who felt that girls encountered the most difficulties on the road to proper gender identification, these later theorists argued that boys faced greater obstacles. Pleck (1981) describes the historical context that led to a special concern with masculinity: the disqualification of large numbers of American males as mentally or physically unfit for the draft in World Wars I and II, the incidence of emotional breakdowns among men in battle, the erosion of the male breadwinner role through the Great Depression and women's wartime entry into the labor force, and such incidences of "hypermasculinity" as wartime aggression and the rise of juvenile delinquency.

In trying to explain such "failures" of masculinity, theorists looked again to notions of identification, and focused on the same critical issue identified by Chodorow: boys, like girls, initially identify with the mother. Thus, they reasoned, males have more difficulty than females in forming the appropriate gender-role identity, and overcoming their initial feminine identification is a central problem in males' psychological development.

Why should identification with the appropriate gender role be especially difficult for boys? First, the boy must *switch* identifications from his mother to his father, something the girl does not have to do. Second, the father is so much less available than the mother as a model that the boy may have trouble knowing precisely what being masculine entails.

The potential difficulties inherent in the failure to form "proper" masculine identification were thought to be twofold: Men might be "sissified" or feminized, or men might become hypermasculine, in overcompensation for their unconscious feminine identification. In the first category lay fears that boys who did not form a proper masculine identification would become homosexual—fears based on the then-current stereotype that male homosexuality was equivalent, in personality terms, to femininity. In the second category lay fears of male violence deriving from men's needs to disengage from inner feminine identification. The greater the underlying feeling of weakness, supposedly, the more a man would act out aggressively to prove masculinity.

The theory had some interesting political implications. It appeared to justify the view of male homosexuality as a failure in psychological development, and so provided ammunition for attempts to cure it and to suppress it as an open lifestyle. The theory was also used extensively to explain the problems faced by black American men. Both Pettigrew (1964) and Moynihan (1967), in volumes that received widespread attention, attributed many of black males' difficulties in American society to their frustrated masculinity, caused by father-absent, mother-dominated homes. Against the background of the Vietnam War, Moynihan recommended military service as a way for black youths to develop a sense of masculinity in "a world away from women, a world run by strong men of unquestioned authority" (1967, p. 42). The recommendation, expedient in the context of a war that needed manpower, reflects a biased view that male dominance is "natural," as well as an alarming willingness to sacrifice young black men on the altar of masculinity.

Developments in research and changes in public attitudes have created some new perspectives on male sex-role identity. Some theorists now argue that the difficulties males face with respect to masculinity have more to do with role expectations than with identity conflicts. Pleck (1981), in his *Sex-Role Strain* paradigm for understanding the social construction of masculinity, argues that the very behavior *expected* of males (for example, aggression, emotional constriction) can be dysfunctional, causing problems for males even when they conform to their masculine role. Furthermore, he notes, gender roles are contradictory and inconsistent, so it is difficult not to violate them (witness the simultaneous demands on modern men to be both sensitive and tough). He notes that "sex-role strain" may be especially important for men, since violating gender roles often has more severe consequences for males than for females.

Pleck's analysis alerts us to the difference between masculine identity and masculine role. One of the most important outcomes of the debates over the difficulties associated with masculinity has been just that: an increased awareness of the distinctions among gender identity, gender role, and sexual orientation.

Gender Identity, Gender Role, and Sexual Orientation: Distinct Issues

The "identification" theories just described make few explicit distinctions among gender identity, gender role, and sexual orientation. All three are considered aspects of identification with the same-sex parent. Researchers now acknowledge, however, that the three issues are conceptually separate and, in fact, not necessarily correlated. *Gender identity* is defined as the individual's private experience of the self as female or male—a powerful aspect of the self-concept that is formed early in childhood and, in most adults, extremely resistant to change. Only a tiny percentage of people form a gender identity that is incongruent with their biological sex when no physiological abnormalities are present. *Gender role* refers to the set of behaviors socially defined as appropriate for one's sex. The degree to which an individual conforms to the prescribed gender role is often referred to as her or his sex-typing (Spence & Sawin, 1985). It is now quite clear that an individual can refuse to conform to society's gender-role prescriptions without experiencing any conflict about underlying gender identity; for example, a man can reject the masculine stereotype of aggressiveness and toughness without experiencing any serious doubts about whether he is actually male. Finally, *sexual orientation* refers to an individual's preference for sexual partners of the same or other sex. A person with a heterosexual orientation is attracted to partners of the other sex; one with a homosexual orientation is attracted to partners of the same sex. Despite the early theorists' equation of male homosexuality with femininity, sexual orientation does not necessarily correlate with either gender identity or gender role. For example, a woman who is sexually attracted to other women usually has no conflict or uncertainty about whether she is indeed female, and she may or may not adhere to aspects of the traditional feminine gender role (see Chapter 7 for an extended discussion of sexual orientation). Theories of gender developed subsequent to the psychoanalytic/identification theories tend to draw clearer lines between gender identity and gender roles than does the psychoanalytic approach, and sexual orientation is often treated as a separate issue.

The debate over the merits of the psychoanalytic/identification approaches to gender contains the seeds of another, quite different type of viewpoint: one that emphasizes social structure and culture as important determinants of the way females and males develop. As some of Freud's critics noted, the observations that he made about parent–child relationships and sexuality were embedded in a particular culture that emphasized male dominance and had a particular, rigid set of ideas about male and female sexuality. Horney's ideas too were developed in the context of a society that had strong norms about female–male relationships, a society in which a cult of domesticity for women flourished and men and women were expected to occupy different, complementary spheres. The more recent theories of Chodorow and Dinnerstein have also not escaped the influence of their cultural context. As Nancy Chodorow (1989) commented after interviewing a number of the women who were pioneers in the psychoanalytic movement in the 1930s,

> I began to realize how much my perceptual and analytic categories had been shaped by my coming of age in the women's movement and my immersion in the recent literature of gender theory. Only with this recognition, that the salience and meaning of gender were products of one's time and place, could I come to understand gender within the fabric of my interviewees' lives. (p. 217)

What if the cultural context that is treated as background in psychoanalytic theory were moved to the foreground? The following theoretical approach, instead of focusing on anatomy and early parent–child relationships in the search for an understanding of gender, concentrates on the culture in which these things exist.

Social Structure/Cultural Theories of Gender

While psychologists have often focused on identification theories as explanations for the development and maintenance of gender roles, the social structural approach has long been popular among sociologists and anthropologists. Such an approach stresses not the mechanisms through which children develop gender identity or acquire gender roles, but the overarching social arrangements that define and support gender. In other words, instead of focusing on how little boys acquire the notion that it is especially important for them to be tough and competent, and how little girls learn that it is especially important for them to be pretty and nice, it focuses on *why* society supports their learning of this message.

Power and Status

Many theorists now argue that most of the differences between the feminine and masculine gender roles come about because of the greater power and status accorded to males than to females in most societies. The work of Dorothy Dinnerstein and Nancy Chodorow, discussed earlier, exemplifies one branch of the "power and status" approach to understanding gender. Researchers in a number of areas have demonstrated that "typical" gender differences hold only or most strongly when the sexes are in the common male dominant–female subordinate relationship and that much so-called "feminine" behavior is actually powerless behavior (Lips, 1991). These findings lead to the hypothesis that if women and men were accorded equal status in society, many of the differences in behavior that we attribute to gender would disappear. While this idea will come up at many points in later chapters, we look briefly now at some examples of how power–status differences can be confused with or can affect gender differences.

Nonverbal Communication. Nancy Henley (1973, 1977; Henley & Freeman, 1989) has argued persuasively that the differences in nonverbal communication between women and men parallel those between less powerful and more powerful people. For example, people tend to "touch downward" in a status hierarchy: It is considered more appropriate for a higher status person to touch a lower status person than vice versa. Similarly, men are more likely to touch women than vice versa (Henley, 1973; Major, 1981). Also, both women and subordinates are characterized by controlled, circumspect nonverbal behavior, while men and people in authority are characterized by expansive behavior. Weitz (1976) showed that the nonverbal behaviors of women in interaction with men were significantly related to the males' scores on dominance and affiliation measures. Nonverbally, women were more submissive with dominant male partners and more dominant with submissive male partners. Men showed no evidence of making such adjustments, nor did women when interacting with other women. Weitz suggests that women are specifically attuned to men's nonverbal behavior because women are so frequently subordinate in status to men.

The idea that "masculine" and "feminine" nonverbal behaviors are reflections of status differences suggests that similar nonverbal asymmetries might be found between other groups (racial, ethnic, cultural) that differ in status. This possibility is discussed by Henley and LaFrance (1984), who predict that any group that is seen as inferior to another will tend, in relation to that other group, to be more submissive, more readable, and more sensitive to others' nonverbal behavior, as well as more accommodating and adaptive to those nonverbal behaviors. This idea is reinforced by reports that blacks in the United States are more nonverbally sensitive than whites, to whom they have a history of subordination (Gitter, Black, & Mostofsky, 1972), and by other findings that nonverbal sensitivity is linked to authority rather than gender (Snodgrass, 1985).

Women in Organizations. Rosabeth Moss Kanter's (1975, 1976) pioneering research on women in the workplace began as an attempt to discover the gender differences that would explain the stereotype that women make poorer leaders than men. Her conclusion was that people in token or dead-end positions, whether women or men, showed poor leadership and success skills: rigidity and hostility toward outsiders and powerful superiors, and more concern with socializing than with career advancement. It was the nature of the position, rather than the gender of the person occupying the position, that was linked to these behaviors. The problem was that many more women than men were stuck in such positions.

> I could find nothing about women in my own research, and that of others that was not equally true of men in some situations. For example, some women do have low job aspirations, but so do men who are in positions of blocked opportunity. Some women managers are too interfering and coercive, but so are men who have limited power and responsibility in their organizations. Some women in professional careers behave in stereotyped ways and tend to regard others of their sex with disdain, but so do men who are tokens—the only member of their group at work. (Kanter, 1976, p. 56)

Thus, Kanter concluded, many of the apparent gender differences in leadership and organizational behavior have no necessary relationship with gender. Instead, they could be traced to the social structure: women's more precarious positions in organizations and their lack of power relative to men.

"Rape-Prone" vs. "Rape-Free" Societies. Gender differences in rape and sexual assault are also linked to power differences. One gender difference to which people often point as an example of the inevitability of a "war" between the sexes is in sexual aggressiveness. In its ultimate form, rape, sexual aggressiveness does differentiate the sexes: men rape, women, by and large, do not. Yet even this difference is attenuated or magnified by the power relations between women and men in a given society. Sanday (1981b), after a study of 186 societies, concluded that those in which rape was prevalent were characterized by interpersonal violence, male dominance, and separation of the sexes, while those in which rape was a relatively rare occurrence were societies in which male and female qualities were equally valued.

The Division of Labor

If power and status differences between women and men do exist, where do these differences come from? The nonverbal communication and the organizational behavior examples just discussed suggest that one key to the status differences between the sexes is that they do different kinds of work: Women are the secretaries, men are the executives; women are the lab technicians, men are the scientists; men are the hunters and warriors, women stay home with the children. Anthropologists have been embroiled for years in controversies over whether the sexual division of labor is a cause or a consequence of the status differences between women and men; most likely, the process is a kind of vicious circle. It should be noted, however, that the way in which work is divided between women and men in our own society practically guarantees that women will have less control over economic resources than men do. Men's greater control over economic resources, achieved through better jobs with higher salaries and through more continuous participation in the paid labor force, creates the expectation that women (and children) will depend on men for support. Under this set of expectations, which is communicated to children long before they understand the economic realities on which it is based, it is little wonder that girls and boys, women and men, tend to make choices that emphasize different aspects of their skills, aspirations, and preferences. These choices lead males and females into different types of work, and the cycle repeats itself. Whatever its source, the division of labor by sex and the parallel male–female difference in control over resources contribute to gender differences in behavior.

Not all social scientists emphasize culture as the driving force behind the construction of gender, however. As the following section describes, some theorists argue that the "why" of female–male differences can be found in biology.

Evolutionary Theories of Gender

One set of theories about differences between women and men has stressed—not parent–child interactions, cultural understandings, or social structure—but possible genetic bases for behavioral differences between the sexes. According to this approach, the power differences between the sexes are not the result of learning and culture, but the natural and inevitable outcome of our genetic heritage. Such theories were popular in North America around the turn of the century, and have recently gained visibility again.

Functionalism

The functionalist school of psychology was concerned with how an organism's behavior and consciousness were functional for its survival (Shields, 1975). Men and women, it was thought, had different and complementary functions for the survival of the human race, and had probably evolved somewhat differently in order to fulfill these functions. Psychologists using this theoretical approach came up with generalizations about sex differences in temperament that had implications for a wide range of behaviors. Perhaps the most well known of these generalizations is the notion of a "maternal instinct" in women. Many functionalists held that women had evolved with an inborn emotional tendency toward nurturance—a tendency that could be triggered by contact with a helpless infant. Because the biological tasks of pregnancy, childbirth, and lactation are fulfilled by women, these theorists reasoned, the presence of a "maternal instinct" in women but not in men made evolutionary sense. The behavioral differences thought to result from the differential presence of such an instinct, however, went far beyond those directed specifically toward infants. Spencer (1891, cited in Shields, 1975), for example, felt that women devote most of their energy to preparation for pregnancy and lactation, with the result that there is little energy left over for the development of other qualities. His ideas, along with those of Clarke (1873), were used to justify the exclusion of women from higher education, as discussed at the beginning of this chapter. Edward Thorndike (1914, cited in Shields, 1975), an eminent American psychologist, contended that a number of instincts were relevant to the female reproductive role. He described, for example, a nursing instinct manifested in a strong tendency to nurture others. This instinct, he suggested, is the source of women's general moral superiority to men. He also felt that women have an instinctive tendency to submit to mastery by men. Thus, Thorndike conceived of women as naturally both more nurturant and more submissive than men—a viewpoint that has gathered little empirical support but that lingers on in many people's assumptions about male–female differences.

Sociobiology

In recent years, we have seen the emergence of sweeping claims about male–female differences by proponents of a new school of human sociobiology. Their analysis rests on an assumption, often labeled "reductionism," that behavior can best be explained by examining the lowest levels of organization (that is, genes rather than whole organisms, individuals rather than societies). Human sociobiology rests on the notion that, in the interests of the survival of their own particular genes, women and men have, across successive generations, evolved different strategies of sexual selection and reproduction: Men, who can produce millions of sperm with relatively little investment of energy, have evolved with an innate tendency to fertilize as many women as possible in order to maximize the chances that their own genes will survive, while women, for whom reproduction (both the production of eggs and the gestation of embryos) involves a greater and more time-consuming commitment, have evolved with a tendency to be sexually selective, choosing only the best mates and trying to trick them into monogamy.

As Ruth Hubbard (1990) notes, the assumption of greater investment by females in producing eggs and gestating embryos than by males in producing sperm is difficult to verify. How does one quantify the amount of energy involved in the production of a lifetime of seminal fluid and sperm, for instance? Moreover, there is no evidence to support the idea that stronger and more powerful men have more children than do weaker ones. Yet sociobiology claims that underneath our cultural trappings lie genetically based human universals: sexual aggressivity among men, a sexual division of labor that assigns childcare to women, and an innate desire for sexual variety among men but not women. Moreover, the proponents of this theory argue, the genetic basis of these social patterns makes them more or less inescapable. Acceptance of such a viewpoint would imply that the push for changes in certain aspects of gender roles is doomed to failure.

It is perhaps precisely *because* the new school of sociobiology offers such a direct challenge to feminist views about human possibilities that it has received so much press. So far, the theory rests largely on inferences from nonhuman evidence, but its initial appearance of scientific respectability makes it a useful source of ammunition for proponents of the status quo and a red flag to people concerned with equality between the sexes. Although an ideal, objective scientific process would dictate a dispassionate and careful search for supporting and countervailing evidence before a theory was catapulted into the realm of public debate, such an ideal process has here, as historically in other areas of the scientific treatment of the woman–man issue, not been achieved.

Traditionally, the field of sociobiology has been concerned with the social behaviors and characteristics of animals. Researchers in this field have uncovered fascinating facts about the diversity and complexity of the social lives of different species, and have searched for links between social behavior and biology. In 1975, E. O. Wilson, an expert in the behavior of insects, wrote a controversial book in which he proposed the thesis that *all* social behavior, including human social behavior, has a biological basis. Wilson's version of sociobiology is based on the premise that human behaviors and many aspects of human social organization have evolved, like such physical characteristics as the thumb or the capacity to digest certain foods, through a process of adaptation through natural selection.

The claims of Wilsonian sociobiology are couched in the language of Darwin's (1871/1967) theory of evolution—a theory developed to explain the way that the physical characteristics of animals changed over successive generations to favor those that were most conducive to species survival. This theory postulates that a physical characteristic is adaptive if it contributes to the *maximum fitness* of the species, where "maximum fitness" means being able to reach sexual maturity and leave healthy descendants. Thus, for example, if a certain skin or fur coloration enables a particular type of animal to avoid being eaten by predators and thus to reach sexual maturity and to reproduce, the genes for that particular coloration are more likely to be passed on to the next generation than are the genes for alternative colorations. Over successive generations, then, the protective color will become increasingly common in that species, a process known as adaptation through natural selection.

Darwin's theory is concerned primarily with physical characteristics, however, not with social behaviors. Although behavior always reflects some inherent limits in physical capacity imposed by the genes (e.g., humans cannot fly), the idea that such complex human behaviors as competitiveness, the selection of sexual partners, or altruism are genetically encoded aspects of the human "biogram" (Wilson's shorthand for "biological program") that have evolved through Darwinian natural selection is a still dubious extrapolation of the theory. Why should the extension of evolutionary theory into the realm of human social behavior raise so many doubts? The reasons are both political and scientific.

From the political point of view, many people find Wilson's version of sociobiology unpalatable. The theory implies that such human social behaviors as war, rape, and racism are inevitable and that it is impossible to make fundamental changes in the relations between the sexes. It is not surprising, then, that people have sought arguments to counter or cast doubt on the theory. What is surprising, perhaps, is the ease with which such arguments are found.

Scientific arguments (e.g., Bleier, 1984; Fausto-Sterling, 1985) against human sociobiology tend to emphasize three themes: (1) the complete lack of evidence that any of the social behaviors in question are linked to any specific gene or configuration of genes; (2) the use of the circular logic that, if a behavior is maintained across generations it must be genetic, and, since it is genetic, it will inevitably continue to be maintained; and (3) the selective inclusion or omission of evidence based on animal behavior to bolster arguments for the genetic basis of human behavior.

Addressing the second point, the use of circular logic, Fausto-Sterling (1985) suggests that the apparent universality of a behavior is, in fact, no guarantee that it is genetic rather than learned. Her counterexamples include the story of a troop of Japanese macaques who came to feast on grain that had been spread on a sandy beach. Researchers observing the monkeys noted that, at first, they slowly picked out the food from the sand, grain by grain. Eventually, however, one young female monkey picked up a handful of sand and grain, carried it to the water, and threw it in. The sand sank and the food floated, enabling her to scoop it off the water. This new, efficient method of separating the sand from the grain was quickly learned by other members of the troop, and continues to be passed on to succeeding generations. Yet, as Fausto-Sterling notes, an outside observer, unaware of the history of the behavior, might guess from its apparent universality that it was genetically based.

Writing on the dangers of ignoring unwelcome animal data, Bleier (1984) lists a number of examples that run counter to the Wilsonian thesis that males are "programmed" for promiscuity while females are instinctively more domestic: the South American male rhea bird, which builds a nest and then tends about 50 eggs that are laid in it by several females; the female jacana bird, which lays eggs in the nests of several male birds, leaving each male to incubate the eggs and care for the young; the seabird pairs that take turns sitting on the nest while the partner goes out to sea in search of food; the emperor penguin father, which incubates the egg in a fold of skin over his feet. Further examples of the variety of behavior among animal species are provided by Hrdy (1981), whose extensive descriptions of relations between the sexes among different groups of primates illustrate that the pattern of male–female differences cited by some sociobiologists as "natural" is far from universal among these, our closest animal relatives.

In summary, the sociobiological notion that gender differences in behavior stem from different genetically based strategies evolved by females and males to maximize their reproductive fitness, has not been proven. If a genetic basis should be established for some of the behaviors in question, scientists have, at this point, no way of knowing whether their persistence is the result of random genetic events or of, as sociobiologists argue, adaptations for fitness maximization (Fausto-Sterling, 1985). This is not to say that there is no possible merit in a sociobiological approach to understanding human behavior; in fact, many researchers (e.g., Rushton, Russell, & Wells, 1984) are amassing data to explore various controversial possibilities of genetic components to human behavior. In many respects, however, the theory defies proof, and extravagant claims about the evolutionary basis of female-male differences are more reflective of the claimant's preference for a particular explanation than of any conclusive evidence for that explanation.

The three theoretical approaches discussed to this point have all focused on the reasons for gender differences. Psychoanalytic/identification theories locate the origins of the differences in anatomy and examine the early development of parent–child relationships. Social structural/cultural theories pinpoint culturally based power and status differences between females and males as the reason for gender differences in behavior. Evolutionary theories point to the genes as the cause for male–female differences. We turn now to three theoretical approaches that focus on the "how" rather than the "why" of gender differences and similarities: social learning, cognitive developmental, and social interaction process theories.

Social Learning Theory

Social learning theory (Bandura, 1977) suggests that the child develops both gender identity and gender role through a learning process that involves modeling, imitation, and reinforcement. The theory rests on the assumption that boys learn to be masculine and girls to be feminine because gender-role appropriate behavior is rewarded while gender-role inappropriate behavior is punished or ignored. Children learn which behaviors are gender-role appropriate by observing and imitating adult and peer models, as well as through trial and error in their own behavior. Social learning theory suggests that a child is most likely to imitate a model who is readily available and perceived as powerful, nurturant, and similar to the self (Mischel, 1970). According to this viewpoint, parental models, particularly the same-sex parent, are the most effective in influencing the child's behavior. The theory suggests that parents and other socializing agents map out gender roles for the child, and then the child is differentially reinforced for following the appropriate one. Children begin to be aware of the two gender roles as early as the first year of life (Del Boca & Ashmore, 1980; Lewis & Weinraub, 1979) and, as early as age 3, imitate same-sex models more than other-sex models (Bussey & Bandura, 1984).

As the child is repeatedly reminded that he is a boy or she is a girl and differentially reinforced for doing boy-things or girl-things, it gradually becomes rewarding for him to think of himself as a boy and for her to think of herself as a girl. Thus, through observation, imitation, and reinforcement, sex-typing or the formation of an appropriate gender role precedes and lays the groundwork for the establishment of gender identity.

David Lynn (1966) developed a theory of gender role and identity development that in some ways forms a bridge between the psychoanalytic and social learning approaches. While Lynn's theory uses the psychoanalytic concept identification to refer to an individual's internalization of the characteristics of a person or role, it also emphasizes the learning of behavior through observation, imitation, and reinforcement—the basic concepts of social learning theory.

Lynn's theory makes some of the same predictions about gender differences as Freud's does, although for different reasons. Both theories, for example, suggest that the male will follow the rules of his role more rigidly than the female will follow hers. Both also predict that both males and females will tend to devalue femininity. However, whereas Freud saw these results as a virtually inevitable aspect of human nature, Lynn's theory suggests that they are a direct result of the childrearing practices and social structure of our society. In this respect, his work anticipates the ideas of Dinnerstein (1976) and Chodorow (1978), described earlier in this chapter.

Lynn suggests, as did Freud, that the first typical human identification of both female and male infants is with the mother and that the male must shift from this early identification if masculine role identification is to be achieved. In contrast to Freud, however, Lynn emphasized the role of the cultural situation in this process. Since fathers spend so many fewer hours than mothers do with children, boys do not have as clear a model for masculinity as girls do for femininity. Thus, Lynn argues, "the father, as a model for the boy, is analogous to a map showing the major outline but lacking most details, whereas the mother, as a model for the girl, might be thought of as a detailed map" (p. 466).

According to Lynn, the boy attempting to be masculine is helped along not so much by modeling his father, who is often unavailable, but by following the stereotyped prescriptions of the masculine role spelled out by his mother and teachers. These socializing agents reward typical masculine behavior and punish behavioral indications of femininity. Gradually, the boy learns to identify, not with his father, but with the stereotyped masculine role. The girl, on the other hand, maintains an identification with her mother. In support of this notion, Lynn (1979) cites studies finding greater mother–daughter than father–son similarity.

Lynn postulates that the necessity for the boy to learn the masculine role in the relative absence of male models and through early and vague demands backed by punishment causes anxiety about gender-role behavior. Such anxiety causes the boy to adhere very rigidly to the rules of his role—a situation reminiscent of Freud's idea that males develop stronger superegos than do females. In fact, boys do seem more concerned than girls with playing the "right" gender role: Boys, for example, are more likely than girls to attend to same-sex models, to imitate same-sex models, and to reject behaviors and objects associated with the other sex (Bussey & Bandura, 1984; Bussey & Perry, 1982; Downs, 1983).

Because boys are so often punished for acting "girl-like," Lynn suggests, they develop a dislike of and contempt for females and femininity. Girls, who are not punished so early or so severely for "boyish" behavior, do not develop a similar degree of hostility toward males and masculinity. Thus, the male contempt for women, which Freud explained as a natural result of women's "inferior" anatomy, Lynn sees as stemming from our culture's process of male socialization. Similarly, Lynn, like Karen Horney, explains any tendency for women to feel inferior as due to cultural prejudice against them rather than to their sense of dismay over not possessing a penis.

People who have witnessed the extreme upset sometimes occasioned in parents by a young son's "feminine" behavior may well find Lynn's explanation of male gender anxiety appealing. One distraught mother came to her psychology professor panic-stricken because she had found her 3-year-old son playing with her cosmetics. Having found this little boy with lipstick on his face, she was terrified that he would "grow up to be a homosexual." One can only imagine the degree of anxiety and confusion that must have been engendered in this little boy by that encounter with his mother, so out of proportion to the seriousness of his "misbehavior" was the intensity of her reaction. Whatever the reason, boys are subject to more intense gender socialization pressure from parents than are girls (Maccoby & Jacklin, 1974), and they also exert this type of pressure on each other. Even among toddlers, boys are more likely than girls to be scolded by their same-sex peers for participating in other-sex activities (Fagot, 1985).

Social learning theory may appear, at first glance, to treat the child as a relatively passive learner, but the socialization process is much more complex and interactive than such a view implies. Children's influence on their parents' behavior may be just as strong as the reverse (Lewis & Rosenblum, 1974). For instance, an initially small difference between a female and male infant in response to comforting may gradually be magnified because it produces, through differential reinforcement of the parents for comforting behavior, differences in the degree of comforting the parents will provide the two infants. The different levels of comforting behavior directed toward the two infants will then cause greater differences between them, which will in turn cause the parents to treat the two even more differently, and so on. Some theorists have suggested that many aspects of gender roles may be learned through reciprocal role learning: learning one gender role through interacting with a person (e.g., a parent) playing the complementary one (Lamb, Owen, & Chase-Lansdale, 1979). The process works through subtle reinforcement: "Interaction proceeds most smoothly (i.e. positive reinforcement occurs) when the behavior of the daughter meshes smoothly with the masculine behavior of the father. This is most likely to occur when she behaves in a feminine manner" (Lamb et al., 1979, p. 94).

On the whole, there is a great deal of evidence that social learning plays a part in the learning of gender roles. For example, knowledge about gender stereotypes increases with age from preschool age to college (Del Boca & Ashmore, 1980; Leahy & Shirk, 1984) and the trend toward same-sex modeling increases during the same period (Bussey & Bandura, 1984). However, it is clear that social learning is, by itself, insufficient to explain the development of gender-roles and gender identity. In the first place, direct reinforcement does not play as strong a role as one might think. For example, parents do not treat their male and female children differently enough to account for gender-role differences (Maccoby & Jacklin, 1974), and young children are apparently impervious to reinforcement from certain sources, with boys responding more to male peers and females responding more to teachers and female peers (Fagot, 1985). In the second place, the importance of imitation in the learning of gender roles is not as clear-cut as the theory predicts. Children do not always select same-sex models to imitate (Maccoby & Jacklin, 1974; Raskin & Israel, 1981). However, the imitation process may be more complex than simply choosing a single model in a given situation. Research by Perry and Bussey (1979) indicates that children may observe the different frequencies with which males and females, in general, perform certain behaviors in given situations, and may then use these observations to construct abstract models of female-appropriate and male-appropriate behavior. Once a child has constructed these abstract models, he or she is more likely to imitate a particular same-sex person if that person usually behaves in ways that fit the child's model for sex-appropriate behavior. Thus, a girl might not imitate the behavior of a mother whom she sees as an atypical female, and a boy might imitate his father only when the father behaves in ways the boy sees as representative of males in general.

The modification of social learning theory presented by Perry and Bussey (1979) incorporates a view of the child as an active participant in the socialization process and implies that cognitive abilities are important in this process. In these ways, it blends social learning theory into the next major theoretical approach to gender: cognitive developmental theory.

Cognitive Developmental Theory

Cognitive developmental theory (Kohlberg, 1966; Kohlberg & Ullian, 1974) proposes that gender, like other concepts, cannot be learned until a child reaches a particular stage of intellectual development. Between the ages of 3 and 5, a child acquires "gender constancy"—an understanding that a person's gender is fixed and cannot be altered by a change in hairstyle, dress, or name. Before that age, according to Kohlberg, although a child may have learned that people can be categorized as either male or female, she or he may sometimes make errors in classifying the self or others and think that arbitrary changes in classification can occur (e.g., a little girl may say, "When I used to be a boy . . ."). Slabey and Frey (1975) describe the process of gender identity formation as having three stages: (1) an awareness that two sexes exist (attained around age 3), followed by (2) an understanding that gender does not change over time (stability), followed in turn by (3) an awareness that gender remains unchanged across situations and behaviors (constancy). The idea that children do not understand the permanence of gender categories until achieving a certain stage of cognitive development is rooted in Jean Piaget's (1954) theory that children's cognitive development occurs in stages, and that they do not have an understanding of physical constancy (e.g., constancy of mass or volume) before approximately ages 4 to 7.

According to the cognitive developmental approach, once the child has categorized herself or himself with some certainty as female or male, she or he will use this self-categorization as an organizing focus for attaching value to behaviors. The child will attach higher value to gender-appropriate behaviors, and thus will find the performance of gender-appropriate behaviors more reinforcing than gender-inappropriate behaviors. In other words, gender-appropriate behaviors acquire a meaning that makes them self-reinforcing for the child, while gender-inappropriate behaviors acquire negative connotations and are avoided. The little girl embraces "feminine" values; the little boy adopts "masculine" ones. At this stage, the child may identify with the same-sex parent, using the parent as one of many guides for establishing correct behavior for her or his gender category. Other models, such as peers, television, and stories, will also be used, and rewards and punishment meted out to the child will be used by her or him as additional cues to appropriate behavior.

Cognitive developmental theory portrays the child as actively searching for cues as to how to behave competently and correctly, rather than as being passively shaped by environmental forces. In the process of seeking out the correct way to behave, the child passes through a stage of great rigidity with respect to gender roles. Children aged 6 to 7 often have oversimplified, inflexible views of the two gender roles and adhere tenaciously to gender stereotypes. At this age, for example, a child may refuse to believe that women can be physicians or carpenters, even if the child's own mother holds one of these positions! It is as if the child at this stage is trying to solidify a sense of gender identity by renouncing any form of ambiguity. At a later age, secure in a gender identity, the child becomes less uncomfortable about occasional deviations from the appropriate gender role and less rigid about gender stereotypes.

Cognitive developmental theory receives support from a variety of studies that find that children, especially boys, value their own sex more highly (Bussey & Perry, 1982; Etaugh, Levine, & Mennella, 1984; Urberg, 1982). Also supportive of the theory is an accumulation of evidence that children increase their accuracy at gender differentiation and labeling from ages 2 to 5 years (Coker, 1984; Etaugh & Duits, 1990; Kuhn, Nash, & Brucken, 1978; Reis & Wright, 1982). Moreover, between the ages of 3 and 8, children show a progression in their views of gender stereotypes that is related to other measures of the children's cognitive flexibility (Coker, 1984; Leahy & Shirk, 1984); this same progression also has been found in other cultures (Munroe, Shimmin, & Munroe, 1984).

All is not roses for cognitive developmental theory, however; some research findings are inconsistent with the theory. Particularly contentious is the issue of *when* gender identity is established. As discussed in Chapter 5, Money and Ehrhardt's (1972) work suggests that some important aspects of gender identity are formed by the age of 2, since changing a child's assigned sex after that age proves difficult. Moreover, Martin and Halverson (1983) have shown that the age at which gender constancy is demonstrated depends on the type of test used; children responding to a real, as opposed to pretend, situation show signs of gender constancy as young as age 3.

While cognitive developmental theory indicates that sex-typing occurs as a result of gender identity formation, much sex-typing occurs *before* the age of gender constancy (Downs, 1983; Maccoby & Jacklin, 1974; Urberg, 1982), and preferences for gender-stereotyped toys and behaviors have been found among children who have not yet developed gender constancy (Bussey & Bandura, 1984; O'Keefe & Hyde, 1983). It has been suggested that social learning theory and cognitive developmental theory may account for two different aspects of the formation of gender role and gender identity: Early sex-typing may stem from differential reinforcement and observational learning, as social learning theory proposes, whereas the sex-typing that occurs after the child has achieved gender constancy may be due to deliberate same-sex modeling, in accordance with cognitive developmental theory (Basow, 1986).

Theories Integrating Social Learning and Cognitive Development Approaches

Although some support exists for the premises of both social learning and cognitive developmental theories, neither one of them appears able to explain fully the development and maintenance of gender roles and gender identity. New theoretical approaches that incorporate new research findings and integrate and extend these two classic theories are required. Several new approaches have been proposed in recent years, including gender schema theory (Bem, 1981, 1985), which was introduced in the previous chapter; "sex role as rule" theory (Constantinople, 1979); and gender roles as developmental pathways (Archer, 1984). Of these, gender schema theory has had the most impact to date.

Gender Schema Theory

As described in Chapter 1, a schema is a cognitive structure (or set of interrelated ideas) that guides and organizes the way an individual processes and makes sense of information. An individual person holds a variety of schemas, each one helping to structure information into categories that are important to him or her. A person might (or might not) have a schema with respect to age, to ethnicity, to gender, to particular occupations, and to proper vs. rude behavior. The schemas are used in evaluating and assimilating new information. Information that is relevant to a person and fits a schema held by that person is attended to and processed quickly, while information that does not relate to an existing schema is ignored. Thus, a person with a strong gender schema would spontaneously sort people, characteristics, and behaviors into masculine and feminine categories, regardless of their differences on other dimensions unrelated to gender. In the previous chapter, we saw how this type of gender-schematic processing could lead to the perpetuation of gender stereotypes. It can also be used, however, to explain how children are socialized into masculine and feminine roles.

Two cultural conditions explain the widespread reliance on gender schema for organizing information: (1) social ideology and customs construct a large number of associations between gender and other qualities, behaviors, concepts, and categories (e.g., there is a long list of behaviors considered feminine or masculine); and (2) society assigns great functional importance to gender distinction, using gender as a basis for many norms, taboos, group membership, and institutional arrangements (Bem, 1985). Thus, "gender has come to have cognitive primacy over many other social categories because the culture has made it so" (p. 212). Children are taught not only a large network of sex-related associations that can form the basis for a gender schema, but also the message that "the dichotomy between male and female has intensive and extensive relevance to virtually every domain of human experience" (p. 212).

Bem (1981, 1985) suggests that people differ in the degree to which they use the gender schema to process information about themselves and others, and she argues that strongly sex-typed individuals are those who have a strong tendency toward gender-schematic processing. Her theory states that individual differences in reliance on the gender schema stem from differences in the degree to which the gender dichotomy is emphasized during socialization. Research support for this aspect of the theory is not yet available; however, Bem (1985) has speculated on her theory's implications for parents trying to raise gender-aschematic children in a gender-schematic society. She suggests first that parents teach children about sex differences in a way that emphasizes the biological aspects and deemphasizes the cultural correlates of maleness and femaleness, thus providing the child with a much narrower and more precise network of associations on which to construct a gender schema. Thus, she argues that children should be taught that genitalia are the definitive attributes for distinguishing females from males, and that other attributes such as dress, occupation, or behavior are irrelevant.

Second, she suggests that parents provide alternative schemas for their children to use in interpreting the wider culture's large set of sex-related associations. In particular, she proposes that children be provided with an "individual differences schema" (a great deal more variability exists between individual members of a group than between most groups), a "cultural relativism schema" (different people believe different things), and, finally, when children are able to understand it, a "sexism schema" (an understanding of the history and process of sex discrimination). All of these alternative schemas should help the child to organize information about the cultural correlates of maleness and femaleness without incorporating them into a gender schema.

Bem provides an example of an outcome of her first suggestion:

> The liberation that comes from having an unambiguous genital definition of sex and the imprisonment that comes from not having such a definition are nicely illustrated by the story of what happened to our son Jeremy, then age four, the day he decided to wear barrettes to nursery school. Several times that day, another little boy told Jeremy that he, Jeremy, must be a girl because "only girls wear barrettes." After trying to explain to this child that "wearing barrettes doesn't matter" and that "being a boy means having a penis and testicles," Jeremy finally pulled down his pants as a way of making his point more convincingly. The other child was not impressed. He simply said, "Everybody has a penis; only girls wear barrettes." (p. 216)

Bem's theory is a provocative one that needs, and will inspire, more research. It builds on both cognitive developmental and social learning theories in that it portrays the child as both actively constructing gender categories and responsive to environmental cues, and it provides an interesting perspective on how the sociocultural context influences the acquisition of gender roles.

Sex Roles as Rules

Constantinople (1979) proposed a model of gender-role acquisition that bears some similarity to gender schema theory. The model presents the acquisition of gender roles as similar to the process of pattern recognition in vision and speech. The capacity to generate gender-role categories, according to this model, grows out of an interaction between the child's built-in ability to generalize, discriminate, and form categories of all kinds and the specific sex-related associations that pervade the environment. Like Bem, Constantinople suggests that children learn the distinctive features of the masculine and feminine categories through observation and direct teaching. The first step toward acquiring these categories is learning the labels associated with gender: boy, girl, mommy, daddy, man, woman. Words as distinctive features for gender are joined later by clothing, hairstyles, toys, and other cues that are differentially associated with boys and girls. Positive and negative reinforcement serve to focus the child's attention on relevant stimuli and to associate gender-related behaviors with positive or negative feelings. The child then combines these distinctive features into cognitive categories (or schemas), which are then used to evaluate new information and experience. The entire process is motivated both by the child's need for structure in his or her environment and by the child's desire to gain rewards and avoid pain.

Constantinople takes her model one step further and addresses the question of *how* the child combines information to form schemas concerning gender. In line with cognitive theories of pattern recognition, she suggests that gender-related schemas are developed through two types of information processing: *data-driven,* in which categories are formed through stimulus generalization and discrimination as the child encounters new information, and *concept-driven,* in which the child's processing of incoming information is guided by an already-formed expectancy. She suggests that the child's earliest attempts at handling gender-relevant information are data-driven, with the child making sense of new information by organizing it into categories. Once these categories have begun to take shape, however, the child can use them as expectancies in concept-driven processing of information. These expectancies or categories are revised when they lead to wrong predictions, and are expanded and refined as the child becomes capable of handling more complex concepts and is exposed to a broader social environment. Constantinople suggests that the major consolidation of gender-role categories occurs at the point cited by Kohlberg (1966) as the acquisition of stable gender identity.

Constantinople closes her discussion of gender-role acquisition with an intriguing question: If children were reared without any distinctive features for gender, except for the anatomical and physiological differences between the sexes, would these cues alone be sufficient for the child to develop a gender category? And, if so, would that category then be used to search for regularities in behavior and attitudes paralleling the anatomical differences? A direct test of these questions is virtually impossible, but cross-cultural research, and perhaps some systematic investigation of some of the childrearing strategies proposed by Bem (1985), may provide clues to the answer.

Gender Roles as Developmental Pathways

Archer (1984) suggests that, rather than seeking to explain the development of feminine and masculine roles as simply two variations produced by the same process (that is, both are produced by imitation and reinforcement, but boys and girls are reinforced for different things), feminine and masculine roles may be separate developmental pathways. In other words, the *process* of acquiring gender roles, not just the *content* of these roles, may differ for males and females. His discussion concentrates on four related dimensions of gender-role acquisition, which, he argues, may be fundamentally different for the two sexes: (1) rigidity or flexibility (the extent to which cross-gender-typed behavior is permitted), (2) simplicity or complexity (how elaborate the content of the gender role is, (3) internal consistency or inconsistency of the role requirements, and (4) the degree of continuity or discontinuity in role development. Archer assembles evidence to suggest that, in childhood, the masculine role is more rigid, complex, and inconsistent than the female role. Boys show sex-typed behavior earlier than girls and are more specifically discouraged from cross-gender activities (rigidity); more masculine than feminine stereotypic traits are known by both boys and girls (complexity); and, boys are more likely than girls to receive conflicting messages about what behavior is acceptable, such as the formal disapproval but informal approval of aggression (incon-sistency). He also reviews evidence to show that gender-role development involves different discontinuities at different ages in males and females. For example, at adoles-cence, the female begins to follow a more rigid set of rules than the more flexible ones of childhood (Katz, 1979). Her role becomes narrower and more inflexible, while the masculine role simultaneously becomes more flexible and varied. In another example, the birth of their first child to young couples is related to an increase in cross-gender behavior for the men and an increase in gender-typed behavior for the women, representing a shift *away* from the masculine role for men and a shift *toward* the femi-nine role for women (Nash & Feldman, 1981).

Archer's theory alerts us to the possibility, suggested by much of the current litera-ture on gender socialization, that females and males may not travel along completely parallel tracks in the development of their gender roles. Furthermore, his approach illustrates the usefulness of a lifespan approach to gender-role development. Further research is needed to investigate his suggestions.

Social Interaction Process Theories

While both social learning and cognitive developmental theories are "process" the-ories (that is, they focus on the mechanisms through which gender roles are acquired), they tend to emphasize the learning of behavior during childhood as a basis for lifelong gender roles. But is childhood learning the whole story when it comes to behaving "like a woman" or "like a man" in later life? Does a woman act feminine mainly because she was rewarded in childhood for doing girl-things and she internalized feminine val-ues? Or does the process continue beyond early learning of gender roles to encompass her choices and her interactions with others throughout her life? Some theoretical models of gender-related behavior have highlighted the processes that maintain con-tinuity in behavior once it is learned and that elicit such behavior in particular social contexts.

Continuities in Interactional Styles

Will an ill-tempered child grow up to be a grouchy adult? What determines whether a dependent child matures into a dependent adult? Does the gender of the child make a difference? Two aspects of the way an individual interacts with the social environment provide keys to answering these questions: *cumulative continuity* and *inter-actional continuity* (Caspi, Bem, & Elder, 1989).

Cumulative continuity is the process through which an individual, beginning in childhood, selects and creates environments that fit her or his preferred forms of behavior—and these selected environments, in turn, reinforce and sustain that behav-ior. A shy child, for example, may select environments where little social contact is required. Such environments will not push the child in the direction of becoming more gregarious; rather, they will sustain the child's shyness. The older the child gets, and the more independent from parentally chosen environments, the more influen-tial is this tendency to select environments that feel comfortable and that reinforce already-existing behavior patterns (Scarr, 1988). The process is truly cumulative, in that, over time, the choices have a "snowball" effect, reinforcing more and more strongly the original behavioral preferences.

Interactional continuity refers to the two-way transactions between the person and the social environment. The person's behavior elicits reactions from others, and those reactions promote continuity in the original behavior through reinforcement, confirmation of expectations, and confirmation of the person's self-concept. For example, an aggressive child expects others to be hostile, and so behaves in ways that trigger hostile reactions in others—confirming the child's expectations and making aggressive behavior still more likely in the future.

This continuity theory suggests that, if small initial temperamental differences exist between females and males, such differences might well be solidified and even magnified over the lifecourse as individuals choose compatible environments and elicit reactions from others. Some researchers *have* suggested that male and female infants differ on such dimensions as activity level and amount of crying. It is difficult to be certain that such differences exist at birth, since reactions to females and males differ from the first moments of the infant's encounter with the world. However, the theory implies that differences that exist for *any* reason can be maintained and amplified through interactional and cumulative continuity.

A particularly interesting aspect of this analysis for understanding gender-related behavior, however, is that the outcomes of these continuity-oriented processes depend on the degree to which the individual's preferred behavior fits the social expectations for females and males. For example, one study of individuals who reached adulthood during the 1940s shows that boys who were shy grew up to be men who were described as aloof, lacking social poise, and showing a reluctance to act. These men, compared to other men, were delayed in marrying, becoming fathers, and establishing stable careers—acting out, in general, a reluctance to enter new and unfamiliar social settings and role transitions (Caspi et al., 1989). An examination of the lifecourse of the shy men shows the "snowball" effect of early shyness: They tended to delay entering a stable career, which in turn lowered their overall achievement, which in turn decreased their occupational stability. The researchers suggest that these men's shyness slowed them down precisely because it did not fit with the role requirements for American men: taking the initiative during courtship, and being self-assertive at work.

In contrast to males, shy girls did not grow up to be adults who delayed marriage and parenthood. Although their shy interactional style seemed to endure, their descriptions were less negatively tinged than were those of the shy men—the shy women were described as quietly independent, intellectual, inner-directed. It appears that shyness, being more expected from females than from males, elicits more positive reactions from others, and thus does not inhibit females' social relationships in the same way that it inhibits men's. Similarly, shyness did not impact on the timing of marriage and parenthood for women because they did not have to take the initiative in courtship. Shyness did seem to affect women's working life, however: Shy women were much more likely than other women to have no employment history or to have left employment as soon as they were married or had a child. Shyness was obviously more compatible with the traditional expectations for females than with those for males. The importance of social context and of role expectations, even in the expression and life consequences of early personality dispositions, is clear here. Early shyness meant different things for the lives of the women than for the lives of the men. Had these individuals grown up in a time and place where shyness was acceptable for men and not for women, the results would have been very different.

An Interactive Model of Gender-Related Behavior

The models of gender differences that we have considered so far focus on how people acquire gender roles. They begin with childhood and show how various forces encourage some behavior and discourage others, eventually solidifying a repertoire of behaviors that fits expectations for the person's gender. This final model, proposed by Kay Deaux and Brenda Major (1987) does not look at long-term causes of gender-related behavior. Rather, it zeros in on the aspects of the immediate social situation that promote or inhibit behavior that is congruent with femininity or masculinity. In other words, its focus is on the *display* of gender-related behaviors rather than on their *acquisition*.

The interactive model is built on the proposition that an individual's gender-related behaviors in a given social interaction are influenced by what others expect, what the individual believes about herself or himself, and situational cues. The processes involved in this influence are expectancy confirmation (both "seeing" only what one expects to see, and self-fulfilling prophecy), and the individual's strategies to both confirm her or his self-view and present an acceptable image to others.

In the abstract, the model works as follows: Two people, a perceiver and a target, approach an interaction, each with a set of beliefs *about the target*. The perceiver's beliefs about the target are based on the gender category (female or male) of the target as well as on personal experience with that person. Beliefs related to the gender category of the target can be activated, or made especially salient, by certain occurrences or environmental conditions. These beliefs influence the perceiver's actions toward the target. The target, on the other hand, enters the situation with a set of beliefs about the self, particular aspects of which may be emphasized by the situation or by recent occurrences. The target interprets the actions of the perceiver, weighs possible alternatives, then takes actions that may either confirm or disconfirm the expectations of the perceiver. The course of the entire interaction is affected by certain modifying conditions: the social desirability of the behavior the perceiver expects from the target, the certainty with which that expectation is held and communicated, and the relative balance between the target's concerns with sustaining her or his self-concept and presenting a positive image.

An example of how the model predicts when the behavior of women and men will tend to be similar and when it will tend to differ is provided by Deaux and Major (1987) in Figure 2.1. In this example, the perceiver is Manager X, who supervises two entry-level managers, Joan and John. The situation is a performance appraisal exercise involving leadership of a small group.

We begin by summarizing an interaction sequence that
should maximize the likelihood that sex differences in leadership

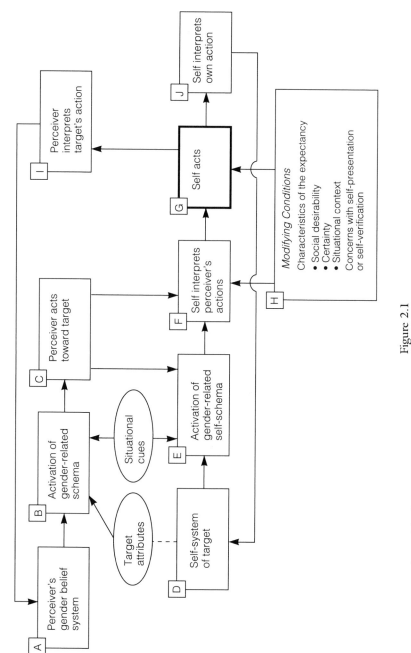

Figure 2.1

A model of social interaction for gender-related behavior (From "Putting Gender into Context: An Interactive Model of Gender-Related Behavior" by K. Deaux and B. Major, 1987, *Psychological Review*, *94* (3), p. 372.)

style will emerge. Manager X firmly believes that men and women have quite different characteristics, particularly in the area of leadership style (Box A). These beliefs are not only chronically accessible for Manager X but have been recently activated by an incident at work that highlighted differences between women and men (Box B). These beliefs prompt Manager X to convey quite different messages to Joan and John as to what is expected in the exercise (Box C). For example, Manager X hints to John that the group session is an opportunity for him to show his ability to take charge, but Manager X emphasizes the cooperative aspects of the group situation when talking to Joan.

To continue our maximal sex differences example, assume that Joan and John have quite different histories of leadership experience and quite different self-images as to their leadership abilities and preferred styles (Box D). Furthermore, the group context, because of past associations, activates different issues for the two managers, differences that are accentuated by the expectancy the manager has conveyed (Box E). Not surprisingly, John interprets the situation as an opportunity to show how well he can take charge, whereas Joan interprets the situation as an opportunity to show her cooperative talents (Box F). Joan and John then act quite differently in the group setting (Box G). This observable sex difference in behavior then feeds back to confirm the initial beliefs of Manager X (Box I) as well as the initial self-assessments of John and Joan (Box J). (p. 372)

Deaux and Major note that the same basic scenario would produce few male–female differences if Manager X did not view male and female leadership styles differently, Joan and John had equivalent beliefs about their own leadership styles and abilities, and nothing happened to trigger gender-related expectancies in either party. Furthermore, they point out, the situation would become more complicated if the manager's expectations were inconsistent with those of Joan and John—for instance, if Manager X believed that women and men manage very differently, but Joan and John had very similar self-conceptions and behavioral tendencies. In such cases, the modifying conditions in Box H must be considered. For instance, Joan and John would be more likely to behave differently, despite their similarity in self-concepts and behavioral dispositions, if the manager had a great deal of power and conveyed the expectations very clearly, and if their concern with presenting themselves in a positive light was stronger than their concern with behaving in a way consistent with their self-conceptions.

The models discussed earlier in the chapter postulate explanations for the stability of and differences in the behavior of women and men. The one presented by Deaux and Major provides a possible explanation for the flexibility and variability of gender-related behavior: why, even if they have learned well how to be "feminine," women do not always act that way and why, when the conditions are arranged a certain way, even the most predictably "macho" man will be unassertive and compliant. Both types of models are necessary for an understanding of gender-related behavior.

Perspectives on Difference

The theories discussed in this chapter address the issue of how and why female and male human beings might come to be different. Some of the theories, such as Freudian psychoanalytic theory and sociobiology, take female–male difference as a given and attempt to explain why it is inevitable. Others, such as social learning and social interaction process theories, emphasize the flexibility of cultural processes that produce differences, and show how different social environments might produce alternative patterns of male–female difference.

But should we be focusing so strongly on differences? Should we be, instead, accepting that gender differences, however produced, are minor, and search instead for the similarities between women and men? We have seen in this chapter that perspectives on gender differences have shifted dramatically over the centuries between a hierarchical one that looks at women and men as essentially similar though differently developed, and one that looks on the sexes as opposites. Missing, of course, is a perspective that views women and men as very similar and *equally* well developed.

Since both the hierarchical and the opposites views of gender differences have been used as "explanations" for female inferiority, a generation of feminist-oriented psychologists has, beginning in the 1970s, rejected the emphasis on female–male difference and focused instead on demonstrating that men and women are similar in their abilities, in their traits, and in their reactions to many situations (Jacklin & McBride, 1991). However, in recent years a tension has developed between this approach and another that reemphasizes the study of differences—this time from the viewpoint that the qualities distinguishing women from men are positive ones, not sources of inferiority (Kimball, 1991). The latter approach emphasizes the differences in females' and males' experiences and women's role in reproduction.

Which is the best approach? Neither. Both. If we focus on similarities at the expense of differences, we risk failing to understand the ways in which women and men experience the world differently. If we focus on differences at the expense of similarities, we risk a perpetuation of the notions of inferiority that a "male as norm" tradition has foisted on women. The tension between the two approaches may be necessary. Moreover, as Elizabeth Percival (1991) notes, that tension may help us to be conscious of both the similarities and differences *among* women and *among* men of different races, classes, ages, and sexual orientations. For example, just as women and men share many qualities and experiences that cut across gender lines but also are likely to have differing experiences, so women of different races, or men of different races, are also likely to share many qualities and experiences that cut across racial lines but also to have differing experiences. Although the pull to choose between emphasizing similarities or emphasizing differences is compelling, ignoring either approach is the most dangerous choice of all.

Summary

Six general types of theories address the origins, development, and maintenance of behavioral and personality differences and similarities between human males and females. The first, psychoanalytic/identification theories, emphasize individual personality development, placing particular importance on early parent–child relationships.

The second set of theories focuses on social structure and culture, emphasizing the role of social arrangements on the maintenance of gender roles and stereotypes. Power and status differences between women and men and the division of labor by sex have been pinpointed within this theoretical context as important factors in maintaining gender differences in behavior. The third set of theories proposes an evolutionary framework for the explanation of differences between human females and males, arguing that observed differences between the sexes have a genetic basis and have arisen through adaptation. The fourth and fifth approaches, social learning and cognitive developmental theory, place strong emphasis on the *processes* governing the development of gender identity and gender roles. Both theories focus on the role of the wider social environment and the child's understanding of it in developing gender identity, roles, attitudes, and stereotypes. Social learning theory emphasizes observation, imitation, and reinforcement, and conceptualizes the child as someone who acts in ways most likely to result in social reinforcement. Cognitive developmental theory stresses the child's active attempt to understand social rules and to be socially competent. More recent approaches—gender schema theory, "sex role as rule" theory, and the theory of gender roles as developmental pathways—integrate some of the principles of both social learning and cognitive development. The sixth approach, social interaction process theories, continues to focus on process but extends it to an explanation of behavior over the lifecourse. Within this approach, Deaux and Major's (1987) interaction process model focuses, not on distant or long-term factors, but on the specific conditions of particular social interactions that promote gender-differentiated or gender-similar behavior. Their model helps us to understand why gender-related behavior is flexible and variable and why, in the face of fairly consistent socialization pressures to be different, women and men still frequently behave similarly.

No theory discussed in this chapter has emerged as adequate to explain all aspects of gender although some, based on the evidence, seem to be more adequate than others. All are useful, however, in that their presence gives rise to questions that can be investigated and to ideas that can be debated. They provide, at least, a place to begin the analysis.

Much of the research described in the remainder of this book is based on these theories; the careful reader will find both support and contradiction for the various theoretical approaches. She or he will also find instances in which the adoption of a different theory would have led the researcher to frame questions differently and to measure different things. The message is that in research, as in the rest of life, the answers one gets depend partly on the questions one asks—so it behooves the student of the psychology of gender to understand where the questions come from! Of course, the answers a researcher gets also depend on *how* the questions are asked, a subject to which we turn in the next chapter.

For Additional Reading

Chodorow, Nancy. (1989). *Feminism and psychoanalytic theory*. New Haven, CT: Yale University Press. The author looks at the mother–child bond from a perspective that is both feminist and psychoanalytic.

Hare-Mustin, Rachel, & Maracek, Jeanne. (Eds.). (1990). *Making a difference: Psychology and the construction of gender.* New Haven, CT: Yale University Press. In a collection of essays, a group of psychologists explores the ways in which psychology has participated in the construction of socially accepted ideas about gender.

Westkott, Marcia. (1986). *The feminist legacy of Karen Horney.* New Haven, CT: Yale University Press. The author explores Karen Horney's insights, as well as some aspects of her life, and places them in relation to contemporary feminist theory.

3

Researching Sex & Gender: Exploring the Whys & Hows

$\mathbf{A}$t the turn of the century, Helen Thompson, a graduate student at the University of Chicago, embarked on an ambitious thesis project. She wanted to "obtain a complete and systematic statement of the psychological likenesses and differences of the sexes by the experimental method" [Thompson (Woolley), 1903]. Having reviewed the literature on sex differences in mental abilities, she was appalled by the inconsistencies and contradictions she found and believed that only a careful experimental investigation could produce the evidence needed to resolve the disputes about male–female psychological differences.

Thompson used 50 Chicago undergraduates, half of them male and half female, of the same age and background. She tested a variety of their motor skills and sensory abilities: auditory and visual reaction times, ability to hit a target, rapidity of finger movement, pain threshold, ability to discriminate heat and cold. It was the first time that anyone had systematically compared men and women on a wide variety of abilities measured in a controlled, laboratory setting.

Thompson found a striking *lack* of evidence for sex differences in mental abilities. Although men and women performed differently on some tests, the results did not conform to popular beliefs about the nature of sex differences. Women were not, for example, uniformly more sensitive than men; men did not show consistently higher motor performance than women. On the whole, it was the similarities rather than the differences between the sexes that were most impressive. These similarities could be readily seen when Thompson graphed her data. The distribution curve of scores on any particular test for the women in her sample overlapped almost completely with the distribution curve of the same scores for the men. Her research thus provided the first empirical basis on which to question the popular assumption, shared and promulgated by many scientists, that women's and men's different mental abilities fitted them for different social roles.

In the late 1950s, psychologist Evelyn Hooker administered clinical projective tests to groups of heterosexual and homosexual males (Hooker, 1957). She found, contrary to the stereotypic beliefs of the day, that the homosexual men were not more maladjusted than their heterosexual counterparts. Expert clinical judges could not distinguish between the test protocols of nonclinical homosexual and heterosexual men, nor were there any differences in adjustment ratings between the two groups. This research laid the groundwork for a change in the psychiatric labeling of homosexuality as an illness.

Helen Thompson's approach to the question of female–male differences in ability and Evelyn Hooker's investigation of the differences between men with homosexual and heterosexual orientations are classic illustrations of scientific psychology: the attempt to test ideas about human behavior against observable reality. Psychologists, like other scientists, are trained to be skeptical—to withhold their acceptance of theories or ideas until provided with evidence that the theories are correct. Although we enjoy spinning an elegant theory, we are taught that theory construction is only the first step in the scientific process; theories should be tested to see how well they fit the facts as we know them.

Much effort (and much of this chapter) is devoted to finding the right research methods: ways of testing theories against real-world data. However, even with the most careful methods, research is an imperfect process, unable to capture "pure" truth. Even when theories *seem* to fit the facts, we must still be cautious, asking ourselves three questions: (1) How well have we been able to *measure* reality? (e.g., if we do not notice a change in a person's attitude, does that mean that no change has occurred, or that our way of assessing change is not sensitive enough?); (2) How may we have altered, or even produced, the "facts" by studying them? (e.g., if a middle-class researcher finds working-class men to be hostile, is that hostility characteristic of working-class men or merely an attitude that is elicited by the presence of the researcher?); and (3) How are our own backgrounds and biases influencing what we notice and do not notice and how we "construct" reality? (e.g., in seventeenth-century Europe, the prevailing medical opinion was that a woman could not become pregnant through intercourse unless she experienced an orgasm. Counterexamples to this belief were simply not noticed by doctors or were explained away.) The necessity to ponder such questions does not mean that the research enterprise is useless, only that it exists in a constant tension between the search for unequivocal proof and the awareness that total certainty is simply not possible.

Given the limitations of research, what constitutes acceptable evidence in favor of or against a theory? In the realm of sex and gender, this question has been crucial. As seen in the previous chapters, the ease with which particular theories about sex and gender are accepted depends to a large extent on how well they fit with popular notions held about women and men by the culture. A theory that seems to challenge these notions will be subjected to more intense scrutiny and to higher standards of evidence than will one that seems to fit in with and justify them. And even research evidence that is conceded to be ironclad can be conveniently forgotten or overlooked when it goes against favored assumptions. Thus it is that Leta Hollingworth (1914) was moved in frustration to accuse her male colleagues in psychology of adopting a double standard of scientific proof, refusing to subject their assumptions about male–female differences to the same careful criticism as they devoted to other assumptions. Her exasperation is, from our current vantage point, quite understandable. Her own advisor, Edward Thorndike, held fast, in the absence of data, to the notion of a "maternal instinct" in women, long after he had abandoned other instincts as too vague and mentalistic. As this chapter will show, the problem noted by Hollingworth has not disappeared; the impact of biases about sex and gender continues to be felt on the design, conduct, interpretation, and acceptance of research.

Asking Questions About Female–Male Differences: What Evidence to Gather

Research on sex and gender tends to focus on two basic questions: (1) *What* differences exist between women and men? and (2) *Why* do these differences exist? Attempts to answer the first question bring the researcher face to face with a host of issues common to all attempts to compare naturally formed groups of people (e.g., racial groups, tall vs. short people). Attempts to answer the second question place the researcher on the shifting sands of the "nature vs. nurture" debate. Also, researchers' ability to answer the *why* question is limited by their degree of success in answering the *what* question. It makes little sense to pursue an explanation for a gender difference that has not been established with any degree of certainty.

Methods for Comparing the Sexes: What Differences and Similarities Exist?

A researcher who wants to collect evidence bearing on differences or similarities between males and females can use any of several approaches. She or he may, for instance, study a few individuals in depth, using a *case history* approach. This method allows the researcher to gather a lot of information and to delve deeply into complex issues that may be difficult to measure in large samples or with less in-depth attention to particular individuals. The case history method, sometimes used in clinical research, involves the gathering of many details about one or several individuals, usually through interviews. The information gathered is then used to support, develop, or refine a particular explanation of behavior. Freud, Horney, and other psychoanalysts relied on the case history approach to construct their theories, and it has frequently been argued that their own biases colored their interpretations of particular cases. The case history provides a richness of detail that can suggest ways of understanding very complex processes. However, the method offers little protection against the influence of researcher bias—a real disadvantage in the realm of sex and gender research, where biases are often strong and unacknowledged.

Another qualitative approach, the *phenomenological* method, is oriented toward understanding behavior from the perspective of the person being studied. Like the case history method, it is based on in-depth, subjective information collected in interviews. This method, however, demands that the researcher begin with no theoretical preconceptions and then proceed to construct a theory based on the information provided by the individuals being studied (e.g., see Fischer, 1984). In addition, the analysis is supposed to be precise enough, based on specific words and phrases in interview transcripts, that two independent researchers trained in the phenomenological method will reach the same interpretation when analyzing a particular interview. This ideal may sometimes be difficult to achieve, and the approach shares a problem with the case history method: When only a small number of people are studied, they may not be representative of the population to whom the researcher wishes to generalize.

Some approaches to phenomenological methodology, however (e.g., Andrew, 1985, 1986), can incorporate experimental variations without compromising the qualitative approach. Such methods allow for an inclusion of the investigator's standpoint as a variable to be studied as part of the research process. In addition, these methods allow the possibility of involving subjects as true participants—as conscious, intentional collaborators with the researcher—who, for instance, systematically respond to a particular research situation, provide reflections about their own responses, and respond to externally derived presentations of their responses (e.g., to a videotape or an observer's account). This type of research makes possible the study of processes such as increasing self-awareness, which can elude other methods. Also, it emphasizes the idea that the research enterprise cannot be separated from the persons or behaviors it examines. All of these factors are increasingly recognized as important to the development of a nonsexist psychology, as will be evident from later sections of this chapter.

Evidence may also be collected through *naturalistic observation*. For example, a researcher interested in comparing girls and boys on aggression might spend hours observing nursery school children at play, keeping track of the number and type of aggressive behaviors displayed by boys and girls. This method also has its share of problems. For one thing, it may be difficult to know how much the setting or the sample is responsible for the patterns observed. If boys are more aggressive than girls, how much is this difference a function of the particular nursery school environment or the particular group of children who attend that school? The pattern would have to be observed in a number of settings before it could be accepted as reliable.

The problem of researcher bias also comes up in naturalistic observation. Several studies have now shown, for example, that behavior by a child is rated differently by observers, depending on whether they think the child is female or male (Condry & Condry, 1976; Condry & Ross, 1985; Gurwitz & Dodge, 1975). Thus, Condry and Condry (1976), who showed subjects a videotape of an infant responding to emotionally arousing stimuli, found that subjects who thought the child was a boy rated an ambiguous negative reaction to one of the stimuli as anger, whereas those who thought the child was a girl rated the same response as fear. Such findings cast doubt on the ability of researchers to be unaffected by their own gender stereotypes when carrying out observational research.

Survey methods of data collection involve the use of a standardized questionnaire or interview to collect information from a large number of people. This type of investigation, if based on a large representative sample of respondents, may allow a researcher to make some general statements about female–male differences in responding to certain types of questions. However, interpretation is still difficult, since questionnaire and interview responses may be heavily influenced by respondents' desires to look good or to please the researcher, and by memory biases. Thus, for example, on a survey asking subjects to rate the relative importance in their lives of marriage and career, a male–female difference in responding may not reflect an actual difference in the importance placed by women and men on these two things. Rather, or in addition, it may reflect women's knowledge that they are expected to place more importance on marriage and men's knowledge that they are expected to place more importance on career. Finally, a limitation of survey research is that the results it produces are *correlational*. In other words, the method is capable of showing that two things are related to each other, or go together, but cannot show that either one caused the other. Thus, in the preceding example, the finding that females were more likely than males to rate marriage more important than career would simply mean that, for the sample studied, being female was associated with a greater likelihood of making that response. The researcher could not assume that being biologically female or male *caused* the difference in responding; sex might be related to some other, unmeasured variable that was the real cause of the difference. For instance, maybe the underlying reason for differences in the perceived importance of career is whether one's same-sex parent has had a satisfying career, and men's fathers may be more likely than are women's mothers to have done so.

The most controlled way to test the tenets of a theory is an *experiment*. In this methodology, the researcher directly manipulates (that is, sets at different levels) one variable, called the *independent variable*, while measuring its effects on another variable, the *dependent variable*. The researcher must control all other factors that might influence the dependent variable, so that the experimental conditions differ only in the level of the independent variable. This entails, for one thing, randomly assigning research participants to experimental conditions, so there are no systematic differences at the outset in the kinds of people assigned to each condition. It also entails manipulating the independent variable and measuring the dependent variables under identical circumstances for each level of the independent variable. If all these conditions are met, it should be possible to draw conclusions about a cause and effect relationship between the independent and dependent variables—to conclude that changes in the level of the independent variable *caused* changes in the dependent variable. Thus, if a researcher wanted to test the hypothesis that women who exercise during pregnancy experience fewer physical symptoms than do women who do not exercise, she or he might screen a group of women for health risks early in pregnancy, then randomly assign each of them to either an exercise group or a control group. The two groups would have to be handled identically except for the amount of exercise. Thus, for instance, both would receive the same amount of attention, would be under the same constraints to report to the researcher, and be given similar expectancies about the impact on their pregnancy of participation in the project. Various dependent variables, such as symptom reports and physiological measures, would be assessed, and the two groups compared on their scores. If the two groups differ significantly, it would be possible, provided proper procedures have been followed, to conclude that the amount of exercise had caused the difference. Lest this procedure sound too straightforward, it should be noted here that it is often extremely difficult or impractical to control all the necessary variables. In addition, researchers using the experimental method sometimes assume that they are controlling for all of the important variables when, in fact, there are crucial variables that they have inadvertently ignored. Thus, although the experimental method provides the most potential for controlled examination of the effects of particular variables, the researcher must be mindful of the possibility that in any given study such control may be more illusory than real.

The astute reader will have noticed that the discussion of the potential to assess cause and effect using the experimental method did not feature sex as an independent variable. This is because, even using the experimental method, it is not possible to prove that biological sex differences are the cause of differences in dependent variables. Why? First, it is impossible to manipulate sex—to randomly assign people to be females or males. Second, it is a hopeless task to disentangle biological sex from the many other variables (e.g., training, expectations) that are associated with it. Thus, two of the conditions for inferring cause and effect through the experimental method are not met: the manipulation of the independent variable and the control of extraneous variables. All data on sex differences, no matter what research method is used, are correlational data, and in that sense it is more accurate to speak of *sex-related* differences than of sex differences.

The Social Psychology of the Psychological Experiment

Many years ago, Rosenweig (1933), in a pioneering paper on the social psychology of the psychological experiment, mentioned sex as a "personal quality" of the experimenter that could introduce "errors of personality influence" into the laboratory. In other words, whether the experimenter was female or male might make a difference to experimental results simply because people react differently to men and women, and so it is one of those extraneous variables that should be controlled when not being deliberately used as an independent variable.

Rosenweig's point was largely lost on his contemporaries (Adair, 1973), but in recent years experimenter gender has become not only an accepted factor of consideration in research design but also an independent variable of interest in its own right. "Sex-of-experimenter effects," although still sometimes overlooked (Silverman, 1979), have been found in virtually every area of psychological research, from hypnosis (Johnson, Smith, Whatley, & DeVoge, 1973) to eyeblink conditioning (Gold, 1969). There are many complex effects: Some indications are that female experimenters tend to *disconfirm* their hypotheses, whereas male experimenters *confirm* theirs (Rosenthal, Persinger, Mulry, Vikan-Kline, & Grothe, 1964). It has also been suggested that male and female researchers each tend to design research in ways that favor the portrayal of their own gender (Eagly & Carli, 1981).

The social psychology of the psychological experiment is rife with other aspects that can interact with gender, causing artifactual findings. It has been found, for instance, that females are more likely than males to comply with the demand characteristics of an experimental situation (Rosenthal, 1966). Thus, reported male–female difference in a laboratory study about nurturance may really reflect the fact that women are more likely than men to respond to the demand characteristics of the experiment: to act nurturant, as they think the experimenter wants them to.

Since research on human behavior is, by its very nature, a social endeavor taking place in a particular social context, it would be unrealistic to expect the interactions between researcher and subject to be "uncontaminated" by the gender stereotypes and gender-related habits predominant in the surrounding culture. Psychologists studying female–male similarities and differences have gradually acknowledged this problem and taken measures to deal with it: by using male and female experimenters and subjects, by trying to minimize demand characteristics, and by trying to be aware of potential artifacts that would make gender differences appear to exist when they are not really present. However, although such precautions can move the interpretation of research in the direction of greater accuracy, they cannot eliminate the difficulties completely. Since the problems stem not only from the personal biases of individual researchers and research participants but also from widely accepted societal values and attitudes that may be all but invisible to most members of society, researchers should be conscious of the limitations of all research methods (Peplau & Conrad, 1989).

Differences and Distributions

Whenever a researcher collects quantitative data with a view to comparing two or more groups of individuals, whether the methodology used is a survey, an experiment, or naturalistic observation, he or she is faced with the problem of interpreting that data—deciding whether or not it reflects a real difference between the groups. Suppose, for example, a researcher asked a sample of girls and a sample of boys to complete a jig-saw puzzle, and measured the time it took each child to complete the task. How would the researcher use the data to determine whether girls and boys differ in their ability to complete such a puzzle quickly?

One fairly simple option for comparing the girls' and boys' performance would be to compare the average times taken by children in each group to complete the puzzle. If the boys took an average of five minutes and the girls an average of four and a half minutes, it would be tempting to conclude that girls were faster than boys at this kind of task. Such a conclusion would be premature, however, until the researcher had taken into account two important issues: the *distributions* of the boys' and girls' time scores, and the *statistical significance* of the difference in mean scores.

If the researcher drew a graph showing the number of children with each particular time score, as shown in Figure 3.1, the distribution of scores would probably look like a "normal" or bell-shaped curve. The highest part of the curve shows the scores most often attained, and represents the average score for the group. Children whose scores fall to the right of the highest point have performed above average, while those whose scores fall to the left have performed below average. If boys' and girls' scores were

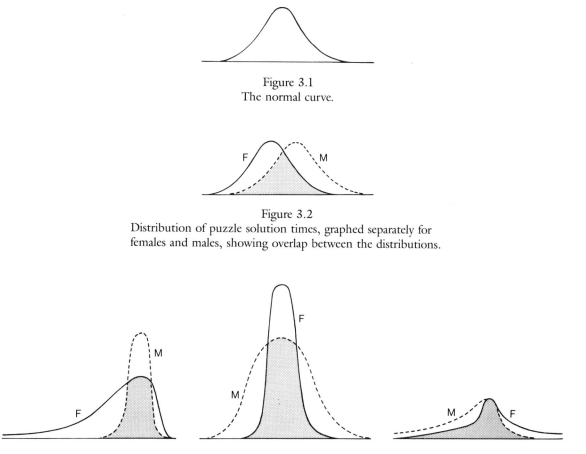

Figure 3.1
The normal curve.

Figure 3.2
Distribution of puzzle solution times, graphed separately for
females and males, showing overlap between the distributions.

Figure 3.3
Examples of different ways in which males and females could
achieve identical averages in puzzle solution times.

to be graphed separately, as shown in Figure 3.2, the researcher could learn a great deal
about how to interpret the 30-second average time difference between the two groups
by examining the degree and pattern of overlap between the two distributions. In fact,
even if no difference in average scores had been observed between the two groups, it
would have been useful to examine the distributions. As seen in Figure 3.3, the two
groups could have achieved identical averages in very different ways, and a difference
between samples in their amount of variability can be just as interesting as a difference
in their means. Thus, it is good practice for researchers to report on distribution overlap and variability as well as average differences when giving the results of studies that
compare females and males.

In many cases, reporting or trying to interpret mean differences between groups
without paying attention to the distribution of scores is misleading and encourages
unwarranted stereotyping. For instance, a commonly accepted generalization based on
a comparison of group average scores is that women are slower than men at mental

rotation tasks (see Chapter 6). Researchers who have examined the distributions of the mental rotation scores, however, note that the average woman is not slower at this task than is the average man. Rather, there appears to be a subgroup of women who are slower than the average man *or* the average woman (Favreau, 1991). Olga Favreau (1991) provides an excellent example of the difference in understanding to which focusing on averages or distributions can lead: When considering the perception of color, we could, based on averages, make the statement that women perceive color better than men do. However, more accurate information is provided by the statement that more men than women are color-blind.

When interpreting data, the researcher must also deal with the possibility that a particular finding can occur by accident. The 30-second average difference between the male and female samples in this study may be nothing more than a fluke. Maybe this sample of girls is especially quick for some reason or the boys are a slower than usual bunch. Scientists use statistical tests that take into account sample size and variability to calculate the probability that a particular result could occur by chance alone. By convention, if the probability of the result occurring by chance alone is less than 5 percent, the finding is accepted as *statistically significant*. Even with this information, however, some caution is in order. Not all statistically significant differences are socially significant or even meaningful. As Petersen and Wittig (1979) note, since the calculation of statistical significance is based partly on sample size, extremely large samples may reveal statistically significant results that are essentially meaningless. In a sample of 100,000 males and 100,000 females, an IQ difference of 0.02 point would be statistically significant despite the fact that the difference is too small to be reliably measured by an IQ test in the first place, and too tiny to have any practical implications even if it *could*.

Knowledge as Self-Reflexive

It is important to remember that, no matter what methods social scientists use to discover whether or not particular gender differences exist, their findings tend to have a transformative effect on the very situation under study. When researchers publish a finding that, for example, in dual-career couples, wives spend a lot more time doing housework than do husbands, the very dissemination of that information may eventually change the situation. Individual women, finding out that their situation is not unique, may become angry enough to insist that their partners take on more of the domestic duties. Individual men, seeing the documentation of the unequal distribution of household tasks, may change their own behavior out of a sense of fairness. Other men and women may respond differently, seeing the findings as confirmation that they are in step with the majority and become more committed to an uneven distribution of household labor. In either case, the knowledge gained by researchers who study human behavior is not independent of that behavior, but has an impact on it. By finding and reporting a gender difference, researchers can contribute to the magnitude and perceived importance of that difference.

By now it should be clear that attempts to establish the existence of particular differences or similarities between the sexes are complicated by a number of factors. The issues become even more complex when researchers confront the next question: *Why* do differences exist?

Why Do Gender Differences Exist:
Nature, Nurture, and the Interactionist Position

Is human behavior determined more by environment or heredity? This question has obsessed the field of psychology for decades, and no introductory psychology student escapes exposure to it. In the realm of sex and gender, the question becomes: Are female–male differences part of our human inheritance, or do we learn to be feminine and masculine by interacting with the environment in which we find ourselves?

There are dangers in the pat acceptance of either an extreme "nature" or an extreme "nurture" view. A one-sided emphasis on heredity can mean that a researcher will not look for socioenvironmental explanations for behavior that she or he observes. A rigid emphasis on environment, however, may blind a researcher to biological underpinnings of behavior, thus blocking the solution to certain problems. It is now clear that both approaches are too simplistic to explain the development of particular human behaviors. For example, postulating a genetic reason for a behavioral gender difference just because no other obvious explanation has been found contributes nothing to the solution of the mystery. As geneticists and medical researchers have now demonstrated, even knowing that a person carries a specific well-understood disease-linked genetic defect (e.g., for sickle-cell anemia), does not allow for accurate prediction of the course of the disease—what symptoms will develop and with what severity and timing (Fausto-Sterling, 1985). The course of the disease is influenced not only by the genetic defect, but also by the individual's environment. In the case of behavior, which is likely to be even more susceptible than physical symptoms to environmental influence, the postulation of an undiscovered genetic basis contributes little to our understanding.

Many scientists have argued that it is meaningless to consider either heredity or environment in the absence of the other or to treat their relationship as a simple additive one: Both are always important. Anastasi (1958) contends that the question to which researchers should address themselves is not *how much* of an individual's behavior is determined by heredity and environment, respectively, but *how*—in what ways—do genetics and environment work together to produce behavioral outcomes. This question implies that the presence of particular genetic or environmental components merely increases or decreases the probability of specified behavioral results; neither one may, in any fundamental sense, be considered more or less important. Both heredity and environment are always fully present and fully interacting with each other.

Even biologists are far from enamored of simple biological determinism. Fausto-Sterling (1985) argues for

> a more complex analysis in which an individual's capacities emerge from a web of interactions between the biological being and the social environment. Within this web, connecting threads move in both directions. Biology may in some manner condition behavior, but behavior in turn can alter one's physiology. (p. 8)

A clear example of such a reciprocal relationship between behavior and physiology is provided by Lowe (1983) in her analysis of male–female differences in strength and physical performance. She notes that the assumption that men are strong while women are weak has powerful consequences for the way women and men both view their bodies and try to shape them according to different standards of health and beauty. Even in infancy, parents exercise boys more than girls, and, as children develop, girls are channeled into more sedentary kinds of play than are boys, a pattern that continues into adulthood. Studies show, however, that when women break out of the "weak" stereotype, their bodies can change dramatically: When women and men begin training with weights, women increase their strength faster than men do, and the physical performance of American women athletes differs from that of their nonathletic female counterparts much more than that of men athletes differs from that of nonathletic men (Gerber, Felshin, Berlin, & Wyrick, 1974, Wilmore, 1974, 1975). When women become more active physically, not only their strength but also other physical attributes change. Percentage of body fat decreases, and bones become stronger and more dense. All of these findings lend support to the idea that social stereotypes can influence physical attributes by influencing behavior—an example of the interactionist position that how an individual turns out is a function of the joint effects of heredity and environment.

Further examples of heredity–environment interaction illustrate just how complex the relationship between "nature" and "nurture" can be. A growing body of research indicates that the physical structure of the adult brain is established through the interaction of the maturing child with its environment. Some studies, for instance, show that the prenatal environment can affect body type and appetite in adulthood. Maternal starvation during the early pregnancy may affect the part of the brain, the hypothalamus, concerned with regulating appetite. Children born to such starved mothers are more likely than others to experience obesity due to overeating (Ravelli, Stein, & Susser, 1976). Other research shows that infants' development of motor skills, once thought to follow a genetically programmed timetable, seems to be speeded up by direct teaching and practice in certain cultures—a result thought to be due to the strengthening of the neuronal pathways in the brain that govern these behaviors (Super, 1976). Both examples illustrate that the environment can, by influencing brain development, interact with biology in such intimate ways that the two are inseparable.

Biologist Ruth Hubbard (1990) coined the term *transformationism* to describe the way that biology and environment work together, with neither being more fundamental than the other to an organism's development. She argues, in concert with other scientists, that neither biology nor environment can be said to "determine" reactions to the other. Rather, at every level of development, the combination of biological and environmental factors transforms the organism so that it responds differently to other concurrent or subsequent biological or environmental influences:

> If a society puts half its children in dresses and skirts but
> warns them not to move in ways that reveal their underpants,
> while putting the other half in jeans and overalls and encourag-
> ing them to climb trees and play ball and other outdoor games;
> if later, during adolescence, the half that has worn trousers is
> exhorted to "eat like a growing boy," while the half in skirts is
> warned to watch its weight and not get fat; if the half in jeans
> trots around in sneakers or boots, while the half in skirts totters

> about on spike heels, then these two groups of people will be biologically as well as socially different. Their muscles will be different, as will their reflexes, posture, arms, legs and feet, hand–eye coordination, spatial perception, and so on. . . . There is no way to sort out the biological and social components that produce these differences, therefore no way to sort nature from nurture. (Hubbard, 1990, pp. 115–116)

Cross-cultural Research

In the quest to understand just how heredity and environment work together to influence such things as ability, behavior, personality, and appearance, researchers have often turned to cross-cultural comparisons. Examining other cultures helps to jolt us out of the assumption that the social and behavioral patterns of our own culture are somehow completely "natural" or that they represent the only normal kind of human organization. (On the other hand, as seen in the following section, bias can interfere with the way researchers from one culture see and interpret another, blinding them to certain crucial differences.) In the realm of sex and gender, the pioneer of cross-cultural research was anthropologist Margaret Mead (1935), whose research in New Guinea demonstrated that cultures could and did differ dramatically in their notions of masculinity and femininity. Mead noted that most human societies used the conspicuous categories of age and sex to structure expectations about people, "whether it be the convention of one Philippine tribe that no man can keep a secret, the Manus assumption that only men enjoy playing with babies, the Toda prescription of almost all domestic work as too sacred for women, or the Arapesh insistence that women's heads are stronger than men's" (p. xi). However, these sex-related assumptions did not follow the same pattern across all societies. Her book contrasted the Arapesh, a tribe in which both women and men were expected to be gentle, responsible and nurturant, with the Mundugumor, in which men and women both were individualistic, ruthless, aggressive, and nonnurturant, and the Tchambuli, a group wherein the women were raised to be dominant, impersonal, and in charge, while the men were less responsible and emotionally dependent. She concluded that

> If those temperamental attitudes which we have traditionally regarded as feminine—such as passivity, responsiveness, and a willingness to cherish children—can so easily be set up as the masculine pattern in one tribe, and in another be outlawed for the majority of women as well as for the majority of men, we no longer have any basis for regarding such aspects of behaviour as sex-linked. (pp. 279–280)

Mead's was the first, but not the last, word on cross-cultural differences in patterns of gender roles, and anthropologists continue to debate her specific conclusions as well as the universality of such aspects of gender role as higher male than female status. Her work, and that of her successors, alerts us to a wide variety of human behaviors that can vary as a result of different combinations of heredity and environment.

Animal Research

Research with nonhuman animals is another strategy that has been used to try to understand how biology and environment interact to produce certain behavioral outcomes. Because it is easier to control both the genetics (through breeding) and the environment of individual animals in a laboratory situation than it ever is to control such factors for humans, laboratory research with animals can investigate questions that are difficult or impossible to approach with humans. For example, it would be out of the question to inject pregnant humans with cross-sex hormones in order to observe effects on the behavior of their offspring, but such research can be done with animals. Similarly, we cannot isolate human infants at birth in order to observe the effects of a lack of socialization on sex-differentiated behaviors, but such a technique is sometimes used with animals. This type of research helps to generate ideas about what may be happening in human development to produce sex-related differences in behavior. However, since there are many differences between humans and even our closest animal relatives, the primates, it is dangerous to make direct generalizations from animal research to human behavior. We do not, for instance, know what cues are used by lower animals to differentiate between males and females and what steps they take to socialize their young and their peers into sex-appropriate behavior (Linton, 1971). It may be, for instance, that smell is a very important component in an animal's ability to differentiate between its male and female peers. If so, attempts to study the impact of sex hormones per se on animal behavior may be doomed to failure. Sex hormone treatments may disturb the "sex smell" sufficiently that animals that have received sex hormone treatments will be treated very differently by their peers than are those who have not received hormone injections. Thus, the impact of the sex hormones on behavior would be confounded with the impact of differential treatment. Even with animals, then, the separation of biological from environmental influences on behavior is not a simple matter. In addition, the use of animals as research subjects does not free researchers from ethical concerns, but raises a new series of ethical issues. For all of these reasons, animal research does not provide any easy answers in the nature–nurture debate.

Whether studying human beings or other animals, then, researchers must be mindful of the interaction between nature and nurture, between heredity and environment. The meaningful question is, as Anastasi (1958) argued, not "which one?" or "how much?" but "how?"—in what ways do our genetic heritages interact with the worlds in which we live to produce the complex packages we know as females and males?

Biases and Pitfalls: Problems Encountered in the Study of Sex and Gender

Although the idealistic view of science is that of an objective search for truth, conducted by unbiased researchers, the reality of the scientific endeavor seldom approaches the ideal. The research process cannot be completely objective or separate from the social context in which it occurs: The existence of a "value-free science" is now commonly recognized as a myth. A scientist cannot avoid being influenced by the assumptions and agendas, hidden or articulated, of the surrounding culture, and even researchers in fields such as chemistry and physics, which might seem at first glance to be immune to cultural influence, may overlook observations that seem incongruent with accepted theory. Objectivity may be an even more remote possibility in the social sciences, where the processes under study are directly and personally significant to the researcher. The study of sex and gender, which touches on an issue that is basic to self-perception and social relationships, is virtually impossible to approach in a completely unbiased way.

Studies of the values that researchers hold with respect to knowledge and the research process show that differences on these dimensions can be large. For example, Mary Ricketts' (1989) study of the theoretical orientations and values of North American feminist psychologists showed that members of this group tended to place more emphasis on external or social determinants of human behavior than on internal or biological determinants. Feminist psychologists also emphasized subjectivism (an interest in persons' experience and a belief that people construct their reality) over objectivism (an interest in persons' behavior and the belief that reality constructs the person). Within the sample of feminist psychologists, differences were found between heterosexual and lesbian feminists, with the latter group favoring a more subjectivist focus and a more externally oriented search for causes. By contrast, an earlier study (Krasner & Houts, 1984) indicated that senior psychologists, founders of the behavior modification movement, preferred a more objectivist orientation than did a comparison group of nonbehaviorist psychologists.

Although all researchers are bound to be influenced by personal and cultural values, anyone committed to finding things out through the process of research must *try* to be aware of her or his biases, to acknowledge them, and to eliminate the blind spots that they engender. The following section, which draws on several thorough examinations of sexism in research (Eichler, 1983; Favreau, 1977; McHugh, Koeske, & Frieze, 1981; Messing, 1983; Stark-Adamec & Kimball, 1984), details some of the aspects of the research process in which bias can be expressed. Armed with the knowledge of potential pitfalls, a researcher attempting to do nonsexist science has at least a fighting chance. However, most of the problems stem from biases that are not merely personal but cultural in nature; researchers must look not only to their own blind spots but to those of the entire scientific enterprise in which they work.

Choosing a Research Topic

Laboring under the inevitable constraints of time, energy, and motivation, a scientist can do only so much research during her or his career. How does she or he choose what questions to study and what to set aside? The decision is based not on the researcher's interest alone, but also on what topics are considered important by the researcher's employers, professional colleagues, and funding agencies. All of these factors are susceptible to bias. A researcher will not think to study the underlying causes of sexual harassment, for instance, if he or she is oblivious to its prevalence or is a participant in cultural assumptions that such behavior is merely an inevitable manifestation of sexual attraction between men and women who work together. Or, she or he may wish to study it but find that employers and colleagues dismiss it as a frivolous topic and that funding agencies are unwilling to provide support. In recent years, there has been a veritable explosion of research in psychology on topics relevant to sex and gender and to women's experience, as universities, professional associations, and granting agencies have bowed to pressure to legitimize such topics. Nevertheless, some researchers report that their work on gender or on women is not taken seriously as legitimate psychology.

Formulating the Research Question

The way a particular research question is articulated may have built-in biases that keep the investigator from finding results that cast doubt on his or her assumptions. If the investigator has not considered the possibility that males' and females' experience of a particular situation (e.g., feelings after acting aggressively against another person) may differ, the hypothesis she or he formulates may reflect this lack of awareness of gender as an important variable. The reverse is also true: Researchers may perpetuate sexist biases by using different concepts to describe the same activities for women and men, as when the term *maternal deprivation* is used in conjunction with the children of employed mothers, while the parallel term, *paternal deprivation,* is never used when discussing children of employed fathers (Eichler & Lapointe, 1985). Someone who frames a hypothesis about the impact of maternal deprivation on preschool children will not interpret anything he or she observes as being due to *paternal* deprivation, even though the children being studied may actually be more "deprived" of their father's than of their mother's presence.

Within the psychology of gender, a prevailing bias that has shaped many research questions has been the tendency to focus on personality and individual differences rather than on social conditions that differ for males and females. For example, researchers studying women's achievement have tended to search for personality differences between women and men that would explain why women appear to achieve less than men: women's lack of achievement motivation, fear of success, the "mommy track." Such a focus perpetuates the status quo (that is, stereotyping of women as not achievement-oriented and discrimination against them for positions that require a strong focus on achievement) by encouraging a tendency to blame women for their lack of achievement (Kahn & Yoder, 1989). An approach emphasizing social forces rather than personality characteristics might focus instead on the "glass ceiling" that many women report encountering in their attempts to move up to higher levels in their organizations. Clearly, researchers taking the preceding two approaches would find very different reasons for women's lack of achievement relative to men.

Research Design

We have already noted some potential pitfalls in design that can emerge from the social psychological aspects of the research process itself. A researcher must always specify, and counterbalance when appropriate, the sex of the experimenters and subjects. Further, she or he must be sure that the research context is similar for male and female subjects so that gender differences do not emerge as artifacts of the research situation. Thus, for instance, in a laboratory setting, if gender differences in conformity are found in response to persuasive statements made by a male confederate, confident conclusions about gender differences in conformity cannot be drawn since male and female subjects are operating under different social conditions. Males are being pressured by a same-sex peer, while females are being pressured by an other-sex peer. Similarly, a researcher attempting to compare the on-the-job behavior of female and male secretaries could not safely draw conclusions about sex-related or gender differences since the females would be occupying a traditional role in which women form the majority while the males would be holding a job considered unusual and surprising for their sex. Female and male secretaries, then, would be working under different kinds of constraints and social pressures, and to compare their behavior without taking these differences into consideration would be to invite inaccurate conclusions.

Another important aspect of research design is the choice of subjects or respondents. Who should be studied, and with whom should they be compared? A major point here is that the people to be studied should be representative of those about whom the researcher wishes to draw conclusions. Obvious though this point may seem, it has been common practice for researchers to study only one sex (usually males) while drawing conclusions about people in general (Prescott, 1978). An interesting case in point is a frequently cited effect in social psychology: the way that watching oneself on videotape affects one's judgments about the causes of one's own behavior. Research on men led to the conclusion that the videotape experience caused people to feel more like external observers of their own behavior, rather than like actors—people engaged in the behavior (Storms, 1973). Although this conclusion is often presented as one that holds for people in general, efforts to replicate it with female subjects have failed (Martin & Huang, 1984; Scott & Webster, 1984).

Another problem in subject selection occurs when researchers study people who are having difficulties with a normal process (e.g., menopause or the menstrual cycle), and the researchers then generalize their conclusions to all people who are experiencing that process. Thus, information gathered about a female patient may be generalized unthinkingly to females in general, and information about male homosexual patients may be wrongly assumed to characterize gay men (Stark-Adamec & Kimball, 1984). This type of overgeneralization is most likely to occur when the observations gleaned from the patients conform to stereotypes about the larger group.

One further issue must be considered in the choice of research samples: Does the choice of one sample rather than another reflect biased assumptions? If a researcher chooses to study mother–child interaction instead of parent–child interaction, is this because he or she implicitly assumes that the mother is the only parent whose interaction with the child really has any important impact? If a researcher asks only women but not men about their experience of role conflict between paid employment and family responsibilities, does this choice reflect a belief that only women experience such conflict? Although such sample choices often reflect practical considerations as much or more than biased assumptions, they may act to reinforce stereotypes that could be challenged (e.g., that women but not men are stressed by trying to maintain dual roles).

In order to put information about a particular group into perspective, it is necessary to make comparisons with other groups. Where no comparisons are made, information about the group being studied may be too easily assimilated into an existing stereotype. For instance, within a climate of opinion that says pregnancy is a time of emotional instability, the finding that 24 percent of a sample of pregnant women agreed with the statement that "I sometimes feel as if I am going to have a nervous breakdown" might easily be taken as supporting that opinion—unless, as was the case in the study in question, it was balanced by the finding that the comparison group (female university students) showed an agreement rate of 57 percent with the same item (Barclay & Barclay, 1976). When the symptoms reported by pregnant women are compared with those reported by their husbands, nonpregnant women, and husbands of nonpregnant women, the myth that pregnancy is a time of emotional instability receives little support (Lips, 1982a; 1985a).

Not only must researchers use comparison or contrast groups, they must choose such groups and examine the assumptions governing their choices with care. For example, when comparing males and females, it may not always be appropriate to equate the two groups for age, since the order of some activities across the lifespan differs for women and men (McHugh et al., 1981). Moreover, when discussing the results of cross-gender comparisons, a researcher trying to avoid sexism will avoid describing male behavior as the norm and female behavior as deviation from that norm (Stark-Adamec & Kimball, 1984).

A crucial part of the research design is the choice of dependent variables or measures. If a study is concerned with marital satisfaction, for instance, how will that satisfaction be defined and measured? Will each member of the couple be asked to rate their happiness on a scale from 1 to 10? Will they be watched to see how many arguments they have? Will mood ratings be taken? Will their neighbors be asked? Obviously, the measure of marital happiness chosen can affect the results of the study.

In comparing females and males on any variable, care must be taken that the measure used to tap that variable is truly equivalent for the two groups. This procedure has not always been followed. For instance, early research on achievement motivation used a test that featured all-male illustrations as cues to elicit achievement stories (McClelland, Atkinson, Clark, & Lowell, 1953). Such a choice no doubt reflected an assumption that achievement was more important in the lives of men than women, and it made the results of the research difficult to interpret. If women and men behaved differently, was it because they differed in their basic approaches to achievement, or simply because the test that *measured* achievement had a different effect on women and men? Another example of bias built into dependent measures comes from the history of conformity research (Weyant, 1979). Early studies tended to support the notion that women were more likely than men to conform to group judgments. However, when researchers are careful to use topics that are equally familiar to women and men, the gender differences in conformity weaken or disappear (Karabenick, 1983). Early investigators, who ignored the familiarity issue, were inadvertently using measures of conformity that were not equivalent for their female and male subjects; thus, in retrospect, their findings of apparent gender differences are not surprising.

Data Analysis and Interpretation

Looking for Differences.   Research on sex and gender is, like research in other areas of psychology, strongly oriented to examining the differences between groups. Differences between males and females are used as springboards for understanding the way that gender works. The problem with such a strong orientation toward differences, however, is that it leads researchers to look for evidence of differences and to ignore similarities. In analyzing data, researchers may focus on testing the difference between the mean scores of males and females while overlooking the pattern of overlap between them or the shapes of the score distributions. In reporting results, they may stress the areas in which differences were observed and give only passing mention, or no mention, to areas in which the two groups appeared to be similar. This orientation toward differences is frequently encouraged by the publication policies of scholarly journals: A finding of "no difference" is often considered uninformative and rejected for publication (Favreau, 1977). Thus, there are strong pressures in the direction of finding and reporting gender differences. The reader of the psychological literature must be mindful of the possibility that, for many studies that report male–female differences, there may be comparable studies gathering dust in file cabinets in which no differences were found.

Interpreting Differences.   Once differences are found and reported, the possibility that bias may influence the research process is still not over. In fact, some would argue that the largest scope for the expression of bias lies in the *interpretation* of findings. A prime pitfall here is making generalizations that are too broad: drawing conclusions about human beings from the study of other animals, about all human beings from the study of one sex, or about adult gender differences from the study of children. Many other problems are less easily recognized, however, including the differential evaluation of the behaviors of males and females, the use of androcentric (male-centered) norms to evaluate female behavior, ethnocentric (focused on one's own cultural group) assumptions to explain behaviors observed among members of other cultures, the viewing of human behavior "through the lens of heterosexual experience" (Brown, 1989, p. 447), the use of anthropomorphic (human-focused) language to describe animal behavior, and the automatic assumption that observed gender differences have biological causes.

Labels.   Similar behavior by male and female subjects may be labeled and evaluated differently by researchers—a situation that often originates in and perpetuates social stereotypes of the two sexes. The sexually active behavior of a female adolescent may be labeled "promiscuous," while that of a male adolescent is called "experimental" (Eichler & Lapointe, 1985). Where the two sexes show differences on a particular trait or skill, sexist biases may be reflected and perpetuated by the way the qualities in question are labeled. For example, some psychologists have demonstrated gender differences in the ability to recognize a pattern or shape embedded or hidden in a larger field and in the ability to focus on the overall field. The first of these abilities, long thought to be more common in males, has been labeled "field independence," while the second, often cited as more common in females, has been called "field dependence." As Spender (1980) notes, these labels tend to make the female-linked ability sound negative— women are "dependent" on the context, while men can transcend it. If the concepts had been labeled "context blindness" and "context awareness," however, the male-linked ability would have a negative connotation, while the female-linked one would sound more positive. Ideally, of course, the characteristics associated with either sex should not be arbitrarily devalued through the labeling process.

Androcentric Norms. In the interpretation of findings of gender differences, there is a tendency to use androcentric norms—to apply male behavior as the norm against which to measure females. This habit, while less blatant now than when Freud based all of feminine psychology on the female's lack of a penis, still underlies much of the discussion of gender differences that are observed by researchers. Thus, if women are found to be less ready than men to do "whatever it takes" to succeed in a career, a researcher may discuss the finding in terms of women's relative lack of ambition. It is less likely that, if men are found to be less ready than women to do "whatever it takes" to have time to spend with their children, researchers will discuss the finding in terms of men's relative lack of care and responsibility. In fact, even the very terms used to describe a number of desirable qualities and behaviors may be defined in ways that make masculine behavior normative: *achievement* is success outside the home, not within it; *responsibility* is taking charge of others, not taking care of them; *bravery* is facing battle, not facing childbirth.

Ethnocentrism. Whether as social scientists or casual observers, we often impose our own ethnocentric biases about male–female relations when interpreting data from other cultures. Thus, argue some feminist anthropologists, there has been a tendency to see evidence of male domination where little exists, to ignore evidence of parity between women and men in many hunter-gatherer societies (Leacock, 1983; Poewe, 1980), and to interpret observed behavior in ways that fit preconceived cultural notions about the two sexes. An example of the latter tendency has been the common assumption among anthropologists that, in societies where menstruating women were secluded, this seclusion was a restriction imposed by men on women and was experienced by women as an exclusion. More careful research now suggests that, at least in some societies, women see their menstrual seclusion as a positive time—a holiday from their normal duties (Eichler, 1980). Studying the customs of other cultures should open our eyes to new possibilities for female–male relationships, but only if the data collected are not unquestioningly interpreted to fit our own cultural preconceptions.

Heterosexism. Persons whose sexual orientation is heterosexual greatly outnumber those whose orientation is homosexual. Yet those with a homosexual orientation—lesbians and gay men—form a significant minority, whose experience is often relegated to invisibility by psychologists studying gender. Researchers may mean only heterosexual couples when they speak of "couples," only two-heterosexual-parent families when they speak of "families" (Brown, 1989). Heterosexual relationships are often used as the norm against which lesbian or gay male relationships are evaluated. However, the study of homosexual relationships is likely to provide many clues about what "works" in intimate relationships in general, and examining the experience of lesbians and gay men is likely to help researchers get a clearer view of the construction of gender by providing a different perspective. Such insights can be gained, however, only if researchers do not automatically assume that the standard for a functional intimate relationship is the heterosexual couple or that the experiences of lesbians and gay men are so different that they offer little to the understanding of the psychology of heterosexual women and men.

Anthropomorphism.   Although research with other animals can provide some clues about human behavior, we have already noted the dangers in careless generalizing from animals to humans. One factor that tends to perpetuate this type of carelessness is the use of anthropomorphic language (language that refers to human traits or behaviors) to describe animal data. This practice is common in some sociobiological writing, and it can make the researcher's understanding of an animal's motivation and behavior appear more complete than is actually the case. A widely cited example of this practice is Barash's (1979) use of the term *rape* to describe what appears to be a male's forcing of sexual advances on an unwilling female among a variety of species, including mallard ducks and even plants! Although the use of the word *rape* in such contexts may have an attention-getting function for the scientist, it does little to clarify what is indeed going on. How, for instance, does the researcher establish that a female flower or a female duck is "unwilling"? More seriously, how does this trivialization of the notion of rape, and the implication that, because it happens in nonhuman species it is a biological rather than social phenomenon, affect the view of rape among humans?

Another example of anthropomorphic, biased language used to describe animal behavior is the use of the word *harem* to describe primate groups comprising a single male and many females (Bleier, 1984). In human terms, a harem refers to a group of women that is virtually owned by a powerful male, whose members are economically and sexually dependent on him. The word carries these same connotations when used with primates, but careful observation shows them to be inaccurate in many cases. For many primate species, the solitary male member of the group holds a peripheral rather than central position, tolerated by the females mainly for his sexual function (Fedigan, 1982; Lancaster, 1975). Once again, the use of a term that has particular meanings in the human context creates confusion when applied to animal behavior, and lends unwarranted support to the notion that a particular social arrangement among humans has a biological basis.

Reliance on Biological Explanations to Fill Gaps.   A distressing tendency among researchers of sex and gender is to postulate biological bases for observed gender differences whenever other explanations are not obvious. Such hasty falling back on biological explanations to fill gaps in our understanding, even when the biological mechanisms that might be involved are not apparent, is something like attributing our observations to magic—"we don't know how it happens, so it must be magic (or hormones)"! Exactly this type of reasoning has sometimes emerged in the interpretation of gender differences in mathematics achievement. After their careful research on a large sample of mathematically talented children had shown that the girls in these samples performed somewhat less well than the boys, Benbow and Stanley (1980) concluded that the performance differences were due to superior male math ability, a superiority based at least partly in biology. Benbow later suggested that exposure in the womb to high levels of the male hormone testosterone, rather than gender differences in upbringing, were the key to males' better performance (Trotter, 1987). Her suggestion is based on her finding that extremely mathematically gifted youngsters are much more likely than their less gifted counterparts to be left-handed and on research that indicates a possible connection between left-handedness and prenatal exposure to testosterone The issue of gender differences in mathematics achievement will be discussed at length in Chapter 6, but for now it serves as a good example of the tendency to attribute gen-der differences to biology. The apparent assumption behind Benbow's conclusion is that researchers know all there is to know about social-environmental influences on the behavior in question, and have exhausted these possibilities before finally putting their faith in biology. There are two serious problems with this assumption, however. In the first place, although some socialization explanations have been tested by Benbow her-self and other researchers, psychologists are still a long way from a complete under-standing of all the subtle mechanisms of social-environmental influence, so it is extremely unlikely, in most cases, that all such possibilities have been ruled out. In the second place, as discussed earlier in the chapter, biology and environment work so closely together that it is virtually impossible to rule out one or the other altogether in the explanation of behavior. Although in the current example, as in other cases, researchers may eventually understand the ways that biology interacts with environ-ment to influence the gender–mathematics relationship, it is probably premature to attribute the differences with any certainty to hormonal influences.

Of course, there is little doubt that heredity plays a role in the distribution of some abilities and personality traits. Researchers have demonstrated, for instance, that the correlation between intelligence levels of identical twins, who share the same genes, is stronger than that between fraternal twins and other siblings (Bouchard, 1983), and that, within normal functioning families, mothers' IQ levels are better predictors of their children's IQ levels than are parenting styles and certain other environmental vari-ables (Scarr, 1991). Yet, the implications of such findings for gender (or for other group differences, such as race, class, or ethnicity) are far from clear. In the case of gender, in the first place, there is no evidence that particular abilities, such as mathematical ability, are more likely to be passed on genetically from parents to sons than to daughters (or vice versa). In the second place, even having the same level of ability is no guarantee that children from different groups will make the same choices or achieve similar levels of success. As discussed in the next chapter, for instance, longitudinal studies of high-IQ girls and boys have shown that gender rather than IQ has been the best predictor of what such "gifted" children accomplish in adult life. The differences in the opportu-nities and pressures presented to females and males by their environments ensure that similar ability levels do not predict the same outcomes for the two groups.

One additional problem with overreliance on biological explanations is faulty evolutionary theorizing. Researchers may be too quick to conclude that observed gen-der differences exist because they are adaptive for survival. As discussed in the previous chapter, it is difficult to prove that particular gender differences in humans offer evolu-tionary advantages. It is probably safe to assume that, *if* there is a genetic basis for a par-ticular difference, it is at least not maladaptive enough to have been selected out (Stark-Adamec & Kimball, 1984). However, it is important to consider all the possible reasons for an apparently stable difference, including environmental and social learning factors.

A strategy sometimes used to support an evolutionary interpretation of observed behavior is what Bleier (1984) calls "validation by prediction." Proponents of this approach use evolutionary theory to "predict" an already established fact; then, having demonstrated the validity of the theory by the correctness of the prediction, they freely apply the theory to interpret other observations. The problem with this approach, as Bleier demonstrates, is that, given any set of premises, a variety of logical predictions may follow. Starting from the sociobiological premise that women have a great biological investment in each pregnancy by virtue of their need to ensure the survival of their genes, for example, Bleier draws the following predictions, all of which, she notes, are at variance with the observed facts: a low incidence of postpartum depression in women, since depression interferes with optimum infant care; a high incidence of postpartum depression in fathers, due to deprivation of the spouse's attention; a low incidence of depression among women in general, since most of them are following their biological urge to produce children. All of the predictions follow logically from the sociobiological premise, but none are correct. The exercise is a good reminder of how incautious evolutionary theorizing can lead the researcher astray.

Popularization of Findings.   If the interpretation of data by researchers can be influenced by bias, the popularization of these interpretations tends to magnify the bias by oversimplifying the conclusions. Thus, in the example of gender differences in mathematics achievement discussed in the previous section, media coverage has made the attribution of gender differences to biology sound even more conclusive than the researchers probably intended. "Do Males Have a Math Gene?" asked a *Newsweek* headline (Williams & King, 1980); with more assurance, a Canadian paper headlined an article "Male Hormones Key to Math, Study Says" (Male hormones key to math, 1986).

The biases that emerge in media coverage of scientific results are partly due to the media's habit of distilling simple statements from complex facts. However, they often also reflect the biases of the writer and/or publication that provides the coverage. An obvious example is the headline given by *Playboy* magazine to an article on sociobiology: "Do Men Need to Cheat on Their Women? A New Science Says Yes" (Morris, 1978).

Although scientists cannot always be held responsible for the ways in which their work may be distorted or oversimplified in the popularization process, they should at least exercise care when making statements that might be taken to imply that there is scientific evidence justifying sex discrimination. Just as importantly, the consumer of the popular press should be sensitive to the presence of bias in the media reporting of research results. Readers should be mindful of the possibility that only the most sensational sounding findings are likely to be reported and that coverage may reflect editorial bias, the distillation of the most dramatic conclusions from a more complex set of findings, and the stripping away of hedges and qualifications provided by the scientist.

Science, Androcentrism, and Misogyny

There is much to suggest that science has served as a source of justifications for the status quo with respect to women and men, that its theories have been shaped by misogyny (hatred of women) and instrumental in promoting and maintaining male dominance over women, that it has been for most of history a male-centered institution (Bleier, 1984; Harding, 1986; Keller, 1985). Science has influenced women's lives without allowing women a voice in the process; its findings have often ignored or distorted women's experience. The science of psychology specifically has been accused of furnishing support for stereotypic beliefs about women and men—beliefs that, in turn, supported patriarchal ideology and political, legal, and economic inequalities between the sexes (Parlee, 1975; Weisstein, 1971). Could it be that the seeking out and eradication of specific sources of bias, as described in the preceding section, is merely a hopelessly superficial approach to a much larger problem—the problem that science as an institution is so shaped by masculine values and dominated by men that the bulk of it can never have anything but an androcentric orientation?

Many feminist scientists would feel constrained to answer a qualified no to this question; after all, if one is to continue to do scientific research, one cannot accept total pessimism about the endeavor (Peplau & Conrad, 1989). Yet there is a growing realization that science as an institution will not be easily overhauled by egalitarian or feminist concerns, that the whole scientific enterprise—its accepted way of doing things, its values, its areas of focus—have been shaped by generations of mostly masculine input, and that its rewards are still reserved mainly for men.

Values

Science is popularly held to be "value-free," but an examination of scientific institutions and processes shows this assumption to be false. Science revolves around values of objectivity, prediction, and control. Several writers have highlighted the separation and control-oriented themes in the scientific endeavor: The ultimate object is the conquest of and control over nature (Keller, 1985; Leiss, 1974). "Man" is considered to be separate from and destined to dominate the natural world. Interestingly, the term *man* rather than *humanity* is probably the more accurate term in this context, both because nature is characterized as feminine (e.g., mother nature) and because women have historically been excluded from participation in science. Even in the social sciences, where the main focus of study is not some aspect of nature distinct from the human species but human behavior itself, women have often been treated as somehow separate from the mainstream of human activity, deviants from the male norm. From Aristotle's notion of "woman as defective man," through the Freudian explanation of most of feminine behavior as a reaction to the lack of a penis, to the current insistence that "work" means paid employment and that "productivity" excludes unpaid household labor, social science has revealed a consistent proclivity to use men as the norm and to define women as "different."

Participants

Science has traditionally been a male activity and it continues to be, despite recent increases in women's participation. In 1987 in the United States, women, compromising a majority of undergraduate students, earned only 15.2 percent of the undergraduate degrees in engineering, 16.1 percent of the degrees in physics, 46.4 percent of those conferred in mathematics, and 34.6 percent of those awarded in computer science. Female underrepresentation becomes more severe at the graduate level; for instance, women earned only 17.4 percent of the doctorates in mathematics and 6.9 percent of those in engineering in 1987 (National Center for Education Statistics, 1989). African-American and Hispanic women, showing the double disadvantage of being female and members of racial minorities, are underrepresented relative to African-American and Hispanic men, who are already underrepresented relative to Caucasian men.

Among Ph.D.'s awarded in engineering in 1987, for example, the ratio of Caucasian men to Caucasian women was 8.8 to 1, the ratio of African-American men to African-American women was 8.7 to 1, and the ratio of Hispanic men to Hispanic women was 21.7 to 1. In absolute numbers, only 3 African-American women and 3 Hispanic women, as compared with 170 Caucasian women, were awarded doctorates in engineering in 1987. Women make up about 4 percent of the engineering work force and 27 percent of employed scientists (Lane, 1988).

Women are moving into the social sciences in larger numbers. Forty-five percent of employed psychologists in the United States are women (Lane, 1988). Fifty-seven percent of American students in recent graduating classes in psychology are women (Vetter & Babco, 1984); in Canada, women obtain 73 percent of the undergraduate degrees in psychology, 68 percent of those in sociology, and 37 percent of those in political science (Abella, 1984). Yet training for research and access to research facilities and positions requires an advanced degree. In the early 1980s women earned only 32 percent of the doctoral degrees awarded in *all* fields in the United States (Vetter & Babco, 1984) and 24 percent of those awarded in Canada (Abella, 1984).

Relatively few women have risen to prominence or have become influential policymakers within the realm of science (Bruer, 1983). Of the approximately 500 Nobel Prizes that have been awarded to scientists, only 10 were to women (and two of these ten were to the *same* woman: Marie Curie). Women form a very small minority of the membership of the National Academy of Sciences. Their minority status has been further underscored by the Academy's practice of awarding them a membership scroll inscribed with the message that this particular woman is being honored for "his" accomplishments and that "he" is now entitled to membership in the Academy (Gornick, 1990).

The image of the research scientist continues to be a masculine one, albeit not always a particularly complimentary one. Observers have noted that the stereotypic media portrayal of a scientist is of a neurotic man in a lab coat, often too obsessed with his experiments to be interested in the outside world (Fausto-Sterling & English, 1986), a man who is all intellect and no feelings, cold and asexual (Keller, 1985). Such an image reflects the meshing of stereotypes about gender with stereotypes about science. Science is for rational, intellectual men, not for irrational, emotional women. Small wonder that women have difficulty seeing themselves as scientists!

Psychology as a field has come some distance from the era in which such eminent research psychologists as Helen Thompson Woolley and Leta Hollingworth faced extraordinary difficulty in obtaining professional positions simply because they were women. Women with doctoral degrees in psychology are still less likely to hold tenured faculty positions than are their male colleagues, however (Weston, 1986). In addition, some of this field's apparent progress in accommodating women is due to the so-called "hard" and "soft" divisions within psychology. The "hard-soft" distinction is here, as in other arenas, a code that is often interpreted as "masculine–feminine." Women are more likely to end up in the "soft" areas of psychology, such as child and clinical, while men are more likely to be in the "hard" areas of neuropsychology, and cognitive and perceptual processes (Ostertag & McNamara, 1991; Ricks, Pyke, Ames, Parry, & Duncan, 1980). The hard–soft distinction is basically meaningless, in that the intellectual effort and rigor required to understand and do good research is no less in the "soft" than in the "hard" areas. The function served by the distinction is to perpetuate an implicit bias in favor of the importance of the "hard" branches of science and to serve as a subtle reminder that such branches are masculine (Keller, 1985).

The claim is sometimes made that, if there were more women in science, science itself would be different, perhaps fundamentally so (Keller, 1985). However, as long as the women in a particular scientific field remain a small minority, the likelihood is that it is they rather than science that will be changed by their participation. Women entering the fields of science and technology have been compared to immigrants in a new country; after working so hard to gain admission and establish themselves, it is unlikely that they will be severely critical of their new milieu (Franklin, 1985). If women enter a field in large numbers, on the other hand, they can have a noticeable impact on the discipline. In psychology, where relatively large numbers of women have entered the field, the effect of women's increasing participation has been dramatic on at least one dimension: the topics addressed by psychological research. Major psychological journals now carry significantly more articles dealing with gender and with issues specifically related to women. Entire journals concerned with such topics have been established. Guidelines for the conduct of nonsexist research have been published by both the American and Canadian Psychological Associations (McHugh et al., 1981; Stark-Adamec & Kimball, 1984), and conscious efforts are made to include women on editorial boards. Yet problems remain. There is still a tendency to "ghettoize" research on women and on gender, as if such topics could be split off into a subdiscipline; and debates rage about the appropriateness of taking a feminist approach—one explicitly oriented to understanding and improving the situation of women—to the study of human behavior. Women and men trying to do nonsexist psychological research or practice, or to work from an explicitly feminist perspective, must still confront the question of how to help develop a psychology that has shed its old androcentric bias.

A Transformational Psychology of Gender?

Michele Wittig (1985) has argued that psychology as a whole needs to shift perspectives, away from the old notion that behavior and our understanding of it can be separated from each other and from the social context in which they occur. Rather, psychologists must acknowledge that their research methods, their theories, and even judgments about the validity of their theories are influenced by their historical, personal, social, and cultural milieu. Such an acknowledgment inevitably brings those engaged in the research enterprise face to face with the tension that characterizes all attempts by psychologists to gather information about human behavior: the tension between trying to be sensitive to the effects of the social context and trying to transcend them. In studying the psychology of gender, then, researchers must continually be aware that their own notions of gender, what aspects of it should be studied, and how it should be studied are all influenced by their personal values and social milieu. That awareness should not paralyze them in their attempts to understand the psychology of gender; rather, it should force them to use research methods that include an examination of the context of behavior, that allow the complexity of multiple causes for behavior to emerge, that allow for the possibility that the very attempt to study a behavior may change it.

If researchers of the psychology of gender reject the idea that they are separate from the process they are trying to study, Wittig argues, they can achieve resolution to some of the dilemmas facing the psychology of gender. For example, she suggests that a careful study of "what is" need not imply the change-neutral, purely intellectual exercise associated with traditional ideas about an objective, detached science—that a psychology of gender can be change-oriented and emancipatory without becoming trapped in ideology: "Constructing what could be requires knowledge of what is . . . propositions in the psychology of gender are both an attempt to understand the functioning of gender in the world as it is and an articulation of what could be" (p. 804). Careful scholarship need not preclude advocacy; rather, advocacy can contribute to scholarship by influencing the content of theory and the choices of topics and methods of study, while scholarship acts as a check on the claims made by advocacy. Wittig argues that a "transformational psychology of gender" is oriented not only toward change in the world beyond psychology, but also toward a transformation of the discipline itself from within—into a nonsexist psychology. Such a psychology is not yet a reality, but, as discussed in this chapter, the self-critical processes necessary to the transformation are being vigorously undertaken.

Summary

There are a variety of research methods for gathering information about sex- and gender-related aspects of human behavior, yet no one method is adequate to the task. Phenomenological, observational, survey, and experimental methods can all shed some light on the links among sex, gender, and behavior, but none of them allow the researcher to conclude with certainty that biological sex differences cause behavioral differences. Since biological sex cannot be manipulated, and since it is always confounded with a variety of social-environmental variables, sex difference research is always correlational, and it is more accurate to speak of sex-related differences than of sex differences. Moreover, it is becoming clear that biological and environmental factors ("nature" and "nurture") have such closely linked, reciprocal roles in human development that it is usually meaningless to try to isolate either biology or the environment as the sole cause of an observed female–male difference.

Problems of bias abound in the research on sex and gender. Cultural stereotypes about masculinity and femininity impact on the research at many levels and stages, from the choice of the research topic, to the research instruments, to the behavior of the experimenter, to the language and concepts used in the interpretation of findings. There is a pervasive tendency to look for differences rather than similarities between females and males, not only because of stereotyped preconceptions by the researchers, but also because findings of differences are more likely to be published than findings of similarities.

The entire enterprise of scientific research, as currently constructed, cannot help but reflect an androcentric approach, since it has been developed in a culture dominated by masculine values and most of the participants in the scientific enterprise have been men. A transformation is underway, however, fueled by feminist concerns and by the entry of increasing numbers of women into the scientific professions. This change is beginning to be felt in psychology, where increasing attention is being paid to research on gender and on topics of special concern to women, and where many traditional assumptions about the research process are being critiqued. Although we do not yet have a psychology free of sexism, we are more conscious of the potential pitfalls in researching sex and gender; we are moving away from a psychology that unwittingly helped to perpetuate masculine and feminine stereotypes and the power imbalances between women and men.

For Additional Reading

Edwards, Carol, & Whiting, Beatrice. (1987). *Children of different worlds*. Cambridge, MA: Harvard University Press. The authors describe the variations in gender roles across many cultures.

Hubbard, Ruth. (1990). *The politics of women's biology*. New Brunswick, NJ: Rutgers University Press. A professor of biology examines the ways in which the assumptions made by researchers have shaped the scientific investigations and findings about human nature, sexuality, and female–male differences.

Tavris, Carol. (1992). *The mismeasure of woman*. New York: Simon & Schuster. The author illustrates the pitfalls inherent in traditional social scientific assumptions that treat male behavior as a standard against which female behavior should be measured.

4

Worlds Apart?
Gender Differences in Social Behavior
& Experience

On March 14, 1990, Susan Butcher storms into Nome, Alaska, recording her fourth victory in five years in the 1158-mile Iditarod Trail Dog Sled Race. As in previous years, people make much of the fact that she is female; her victory is somehow more surprising because of her sex. Similarly, when Julie Croteau begins to play baseball for St. Mary's in 1988, more attention is paid to the fact that she is the first *woman* to play college baseball than to her record. And when a young professional puts career ambitions on hold to care for a new baby or follow a spouse to a new job in a distant city, it causes considerably more comment if that young professional is a man than if she is a woman.

Expectations for women and men are still so different in some domains that observers are surprised, even shocked, when an individual woman or man "crosses the line" to behave in a way that is thought normative for the other group. Women and men are, in fact, often described as "opposite sexes." How different are we really? A look around North America quickly shows that, in terms of how we spend our time, women and men are very different indeed: Women do most of the housework, men play most of the football, women do most of the typing, men run most of the corporations, women do most of the childcare, men commit most of the violent crimes. Small wonder if the casual observer were to conclude that human males and females differ dramatically in abilities, motivation, and temperament.

As illustrated in previous chapters, however, an observed gender difference in behavior can often be shown to result from a complex interaction between characteristics of the individuals involved and characteristics of the social environment. The observation that men commit more violent crimes than women cannot automatically be interpreted as proof that males are always and under all conditions more aggressive than females; the fact that women do most of the childcare does not itself prove that women are generally more nurturant than men. This chapter overviews the research evidence for the existence of gender differences in several areas of social behavior: aggression, influenceability, dominance, nurturance, empathy, and altruism. These particular behavioral areas are chosen partly because they are all aspects of the qualities stereotypically assigned to women and men in our society. Men are supposedly more aggressive, dominant, and independent of influence than are women; women are believed to be more nurturant, empathetic, and altruistic than are men. Perhaps because each of these qualities is stereotypically either feminine or masculine, they have been the focus of a good deal of research aimed at exploring gender differences. Our overview of this research will show, however, that, while large gender differences sometimes exist in the probabilities that people will perform particular behaviors, sweeping statements about general differences, such as "women are more altruistic than men," are usually difficult to justify.

"Heavy-Duty" Strategies for Comparing the Sexes: Longitudinal Studies and Meta-Analysis

When trying to uncover evidence that can be used to evaluate claims of very general male–female differences in behavior, researchers have two techniques that both add to and incorporate the arsenal of methods described in the previous chapter. The first, the *longitudinal study*, involves following the same research participants over an extended period of time, usually years, and obtaining data from them repeatedly during that time. Such a strategy allows the researcher to find out the age at which particular gender differences first appear, and to assess their stability over time. This information is important; apparent gender differences may arise because one sex is developmentally ahead of the other during a particular age range, or because one sex runs into a unique set of cultural constraints at a certain age. Longitudinal research can also identify variables that predict later differences in behavior *within* gender groups; such variables may turn out to be much better predictors of later behavior than gender itself. The second technique, *meta-analysis,* involves using statistical methods to combine the findings of a large number of different studies of the same behavior in order to evaluate the overall pattern of findings. This approach, adopted only within this decade by investigators studying gender differences, allows the researcher to begin to make sense of a collection of contradictory findings.

Longitudinal Studies

Perhaps the most famous longitudinal study in psychology was Terman's (1925) "gifted children" research. Beginning in 1922, Terman selected over 1000 preschool and elementary schoolchildren and 300 high school students, all of whom had intelligence test scores (IQs) of 140 or more. For more than half a century, Terman and, after his death, other psychologists maintained contact with these people and monitored their achievements (Oden, 1968; Terman & Oden, 1947, 1959). It was a gigantic undertaking, and one that provided a wealth of information about the extent to which high tested intelligence in schoolchildren predicts achievement in a variety of domains across the lifespan. Interestingly, although the project was not conceived with the idea of examining gender differences, its findings in this area have been very telling: High IQ was a much better predictor of achievement for males than for females. Very bright boys were likely to go on to chalk up accomplishments in the arts, science, literature, business, or public affairs as adults; very bright girls were considerably less likely to do so. More than two-thirds of the girls with IQs of 170 or more became housewives or office workers in adulthood. Follow-up studies show that many of them devoted their lives to supporting their husbands' careers or to childrearing (Tomlinson-Keasey, 1990).

The questionnaire responses of some of these high-IQ women in later life often reflect a sense of failure or lack of confidence in their abilities:

> You might be interested to know that if I ever had a good mind, it has been lost in the shuffle. I seem to have stagnated and I am aware that I'm not using any capacity that I have to the fullest; however, don't give up hope, maybe I'll make you proud yet.

> As I grow older, I am more and more surprised at the thought that I was ever considered a gifted child. I realize that I am slightly more intelligent than the average, but only slightly.

> I have not used my gifts and regret this very much. Also I believe IQs change and mine dropped considerably. I'm no longer very competent in any area. My children all turned out well but not due to me, rather to a strict father who allowed no nonsense.

> (Tomlinson-Keasey, 1990, pp. 229–230)

Being male or female, then, was a far better predictor of recognized achievement in adulthood than was intelligence. Those women who were able to transcend gender-role expectations in their educational and occupational pursuits, however, maintained intellectual levels similar to those of the men. Occupation, not gender, accounted best for IQ changes over the lifespan (Bayley & Oden, 1955). Interestingly, when this study is described in textbooks, the issue of gender is rarely raised, and the predictability of achievement from IQ is discussed as if it held for all subjects. The study does not explain the gender difference, but it serves a crucial function by demonstrating two points: (1) the gender difference in adult achievement is clearly not due to an earlier difference in intelligence, and (2) gender is eclipsed by occupation as an explanatory variable for adult changes in IQ.

Block (1973) used data from the longitudinal archives of the Institute for Human Development to examine the relationship between family background and sex-typing. She was able to demonstrate that, among those who were highly socialized (that is, whose personality test scores indicated that they had internalized social standards), adults who scored as highly appropriately sex-typed on the California Personality Inventory had grown up in family contexts of clear and conventional gender roles, while those who scored as low-sex-appropriate came from families in which parents had offered more complex role models. In addition, her data suggested that, for men, high socialization was associated with androgyny—a mixture of such "feminine" traits as nurturance and warmth with traditionally "masculine" qualities. In contrast, for women, high socialization seemed to be linked with a reinforcement of the most conservative aspects of the traditional feminine role: passivity and dependence.

The latter two studies were designed to link variables measured during childhood with other variables measured in adulthood. A longitudinal study that took a more fine-grained approach is the Stanford Longitudinal Study (e.g., Maccoby, Snow, & Jacklin, 1984; Martin, Maccoby, & Jacklin, 1981; Snow, Jacklin, & Maccoby, 1981). This study has followed three cohorts of children from birth through the preschool years, gathering data at frequent intervals on a long list of child behaviors and aspects of parent–child interaction. The researchers began by collecting information about hormone levels at birth for each child, then went on to measure such things as tactile sensitivity, muscle strength, sociability, timidity, and parental responsiveness. Findings have been and continue to be published at intervals; among the most interesting is that, for many variables, birth order seems to account for as much or more variability as does sex (e.g., Snow et al., 1981). Also intriguing are findings that offer support for earlier indications (e.g., Baumrind, 1979; Block, 1973) that similar socialization practices may have different effects for girls and boys. The Stanford researchers examined the relationship between mother's responsiveness to a child at 9 months of age and the child's willingness, 9 months later, to interrupt the mother's conversation with another adult (Martin et al., 1981). They found that mothers' nonintrusiveness (their tendency to avoid interrupting the child when she or he was playing successfully alone) had different correlates for girls and boys. Boys whose mothers had been nonintrusive at 9 months tended to play independently at 18 months; girls whose mothers had been nonintrusive were more likely than other girls to seek proximity and attention from their mothers when observed 9 months later. The reason for the difference is unclear; it is likely that parenting style interacts with other variables—environmental, biological, or both—to produce different outcomes for the two sexes. What *is* clear is that careful studies of the same individuals over time are necessary in order to understand whether, how, and why males and females develop differently.

One final reason for doing longitudinal research is to examine the historical aspects of gender differences. Anastasi (1981) suggests that researchers replicate their studies on subjects who have been socialized under the different cultural conditions created by different historical periods (e.g., compare 30-year-olds tested in 1950 with 30-year-olds tested in 1980). Such comparisons would allow for an examination of the impact of cultural change on gender differences. Ideally, she argues, research comparing males and females would follow a *cross-sequential* method: incorporating cross-sectional comparisons of different age groups tested at one time period, longitudinal comparisons of the same individuals tested repeatedly over time, and time-lag comparisons of same-age samples at different time periods.

Unfortunately, the resources required to conduct long-term research projects are hard to find, and few large-scale longitudinal studies have been done. This chapter's discussion of the relationship between gender and social behavior relies largely on short-term and cross-sectional research.

Meta-Analysis

Efforts to draw conclusions about the existence of gender differences in a particular behavior have always involved collating the results of many studies of that behavior. Thus, if someone wanted to determine whether there were gender differences in nurturance, for example, he or she would gather all the studies that examined nurturant behavior in males and females, and would look at the overall pattern of results. Suppose that 70 percent of the studies showed that females behaved in a more nurturant way than males, 10 percent showed males to be more nurturant, and the remaining 20 percent showed no gender differences. Faced with this pattern, the researcher might well conclude that gender differences in nurturance were fairly well established, and that females were, in general, more nurturant than males. A number of painstaking literature reviews of this type have been carried out, perhaps the most frequently cited of which is Maccoby and Jacklin's (1974) *The Psychology of Sex Differences*. Maccoby and Jacklin, in a mammoth undertaking, reviewed the psychological literature relating gender to a large number of behavioral domains. They concluded that there were only four areas in which female–male differences were well established: aggression, spatial ability, verbal ability, and quantitative ability—although they reserved judgment about a number of others.

In recent years, there has been a recognition that this approach has some serious limitations. Although the studies included in a review may vary greatly in quality and on dimensions such as the variability in the sample and the size of the difference found, all are simply tabulated together and given equal weight. The now popular technique of meta-analysis allows for a more sophisticated appraisal of the overall picture that is created when a large number of studies are examined (Beaman, 1991). Using this technique, all four "well-established" gender differences cited by Maccoby and Jacklin (1974) have been challenged or qualified (see this chapter for results of a meta-analysis of aggression studies, and Chapter 6 for information on meta-analyses of studies in the three ability areas.)

Meta-analysis begins with a concerted attempt by the researcher to gather a well-defined, complete set of studies of the behavior in question. She or he must be careful to find and include well-done but unpublished studies, such as theses and studies that went unpublished because they found no gender differences. Then, using the means and standard deviations for males and females reported in each article, the researcher calculates the *effect size* for each study. There are two commonly used measures of effect size: (1) the proportion of variation in the mixed (male + female) population that can be accounted for by gender differences, and (2) the distance, in standard deviation units, between the means for males and females. Once the researcher has determined the effect-size for each study in the collection, she or he can calculate the average effect size across all the studies in order to draw conclusions about the robustness and importance of the gender difference in question. The effect sizes may also be compared across studies that used different kinds of dependent variables, different ages of subjects, male vs. female experimenters, and other variations that could possibly influence the size of the gender difference obtained. Other types of meta-analysis combine probability levels for effects found in the studies sampled; still others use techniques to pool the data for the various studies. The effect-size analysis has, however, been the most popular among investigators of gender differences.

The following example of meta-analysis provides a good illustration of the kind of information the technique can provide. Eaton and Enns (1986) gathered 127 studies of male–female differences in human motor activity level (defined as the individual's customary level of energy expenditure through movement). Although there has been a widespread belief that males have a higher motor activity level than females, reviewers of the literature, including Maccoby and Jacklin (1974), have found the results too mixed to be conclusive. If females and males do differ in activity level, the difference might have some interesting implications: for example, more active infants receive more attention from their caretakers, so if males are generally more active they may be eliciting different kinds of caretaker behavior than females. Such a difference in caretaker behavior might be the basis for other behavioral differences between female and male infants. Thus, Eaton and Enns attempted to use meta-analysis to determine whether and to what extent a gender difference in human motor activity level exists.

When Eaton and Enns (1986) calculated the effect size for the gender differences reported in the 127 studies, they found that the average difference between the male and female mean activity level scores was just under one-half of a standard deviation. Furthermore, the proportion of total population variance in activity level that could be accounted for by gender was about 5 percent. That means that 95 percent of the variability in activity level could be attributed to either variation *within* gender groups or experimental error (random fluctuations, measurement error).

The finding that only 5 percent of the variance in the activity level of mixed-sex populations could be explained by gender differences appears, at first glance, to argue that male–female differences in activity level are too small to be important. However, many of the group differences or experimental effects reported in psychological research are of this magnitude (Eagly & Wood, 1991). Moreover, as Eaton and Enns (1986) note, small differences in means can translate into large differences in the proportions of males and females at the extremes of a given behavior. (As noted in the previous chapter, however, the implications of a difference in means depends on the shapes of the distributions of scores for the two groups. If the distributions of scores for males and females are both normal and have similar variances, differences in means will translate into differences at the extremes; otherwise, they may not.) The presence of different proportions of females and males at the extremes of activity level may cause the females and males to be differentially included in diagnostic categories such as "hyperactive." Moreover, it has been argued that, in coding information, human beings are particularly sensitive to the frequency with which something occurs (Hasher & Zacks, 1984). Eaton and Enns (1986) argue that despite the small number of people of either sex whose activity level reaches an extreme threshold, the difference in the proportions of males and females who show especially high activity levels will tend to be readily noted and remembered by observers, who will use the information to define or reinforce their gender stereotypes. Thus, a teacher who has, over several years of working with children, encountered four boys and one girl who could be characterized as "hyperactive," may find it easy to subscribe to the belief that boys are more active than girls, even though, among the hundreds of normally active other children the teacher has taught, no striking gender differences in activity level appear. In this way, a gender difference that is noticeable only at the extremes of a behavioral distribution can form the basis for a much broader gender stereotype.

Meta-analysis is so far the most useful tool researchers have found for aggregating the results of many studies of a particular male–female difference. It can provide information about the average size of the effect of gender on a particular behavior, and can tell the researcher what other variables, such as age or situational effects, may be mediating the effect of gender. Yet one final caution is in order: The results of a meta-analysis are only as good as its sample of studies. If a complete sample of studies is not included, or if the studies included have inaccurate results due to bias or sloppy data collection, the meta-analysis is worth little. Also, if the sample of studies used is overrepresentative of biased situations (e.g., if most of the experimenters in the sample are male, or if most of the measures used are biased in favor of females), the results of the meta-analysis will reflect a similar bias (Eagly & Carli, 1981).

Gender Differences in Social Behavior: A Sampling of Current Findings

Having explored the techniques available for determining the presence of gender differences, we turn to an examination of what these techniques have found in the realm of social behavior. For each of several kinds of social behavior, we examine the evidence for the reliable presence and magnitude of female–male differences. Where differences are found to exist, evidence concerning the reasons for these differences is reviewed. Similar examinations of evidence for gender differences in other domains, such as intellectual abilities, achievement, communication, intimacy, sexuality, and morality, will be presented in later chapters.

Aggression

In many societies, including our own, male aggression is tolerated and expected more than female aggression. Instances of serious male aggression against other men or against women are tragically common. In Washington, D.C., three young men beat and kill a 65-year-old man whose car collides with theirs—apparently merely because he is inebriated and verbally belligerent (Driver, 65, beaten, slain, 1991). In Kenya, a group of young men at a church boarding school attack the women's dormitory, beating and raping all the women they can lay their hands on. Seventy-one women have been raped and nineteen young women are dead at the end of the rampage, which the head of the school characterizes as "a joke turned nasty" (School rapes, 1991). It is difficult to imagine these situations with women as the aggressors. Is that because males really are more aggressive than females, or do they simply commit more "spectacular" acts of aggression? Do males have stronger aggressive drives than females do, or have they simply not been taught as carefully as females that they must control those drives?

Maccoby and Jacklin (1974) concluded from their extensive review that greater male than female aggressiveness was a well-established finding. The difference occurred for both physical and verbal aggression, and was found across a variety of cultures. It appeared by between ages 2 and 3, and continued through the college years, after which there was little information available. A decade later, Hyde (1984b) used meta-analysis to evaluate the size of the gender difference and to examine developmental aspects of it. She found that gender differences were not large, even though they were well established. Gender accounted for an average of 5 percent of the variance in aggression found in the combined-sex populations of the 75 studies in her sample, with the male mean being about one-half a standard deviation higher than that of the females. Thus, within-gender variation in aggression appears to be considerably larger than between-sex variation. The size of the gender difference tended to be larger for younger than for older subjects: for subjects under the age of 6, gender accounted for 7 percent of the variance in aggression, while for college students, gender accounted for only 1 percent. The interpretability of the latter finding is made difficult, however, by the fact that aggression was generally measured differently for preschool children and college students. For preschoolers, physical or verbal aggressive behaviors were often measured, while for college students, aggression tended to be measured by willingness to shock another individual. Hyde also found that gender differences tended to be larger in naturalistic, correlational studies than in experimental studies, and in earlier (1966–1973) than later (1978–1981) studies. The smaller differences in later studies may be due to changes in gender socialization patterns, changes in perceptions by experimenters or other observers, or an increased likelihood of publication of "no difference" findings after Maccoby and Jacklin's (1974) review.

Hyde (1984) also noted that larger gender differences were found when aggression was measured by direct observation, projective methods, or peer reports than when measured by self-reports, parent, or teacher reports. Such a finding may point to observer bias in the noticing and reporting of aggression. Observers, influenced by gender stereotypes, might be more likely to notice aggressive behavior in males than females. One study suggests, however, that observer bias may be working in the reverse direction: toward the minimization of observed male aggression and the exaggeration of observed female aggression. Condry and Ross (1985) showed college students a videotape of two children playing roughly in the snow. The children's actual gender was disguised by their snowsuits, and the researchers varied the gender labels for each child. Observers who thought they were watching a boy acting aggressively against another boy rated the behavior as significantly less aggressive than those who thought they were watching a boy acting aggressively against a girl or a girl acting aggressively against either a boy or a girl. Apparently, the observers tended to discount the aggressiveness of an interaction when two boys were engaged in it, and to inflate the aggressiveness of the same interaction when it involved a girl. The authors argue that such an observer bias would work to minimize observed gender differences in aggression, and speculate that the existing literature may therefore underestimate the magnitude of male–female differences. It is difficult, then, to be sure of the magnitude of gender differences in aggression. Nevertheless, it appears that, where such differences are found, it is more likely to be males than females who are more aggressive.

Another meta-analysis of female–male differences in aggression suggests that such differences are largest in situations where expectations for women and men differ most strongly (Eagly & Steffen, 1986). The researchers asked college students to imagine the aggressive behavior detailed in each of the studies included in the meta-analysis and to rate the harmful consequences of the act, the anxiety or guilt they themselves would feel in performing it, how much danger they would face in performing the act, and the likelihood that the average man or woman would perform the act. The results showed that, not only were women more likely than men to rate the aggressive acts as harmful, potentially guilt-inducing, and likely to be dangerous to the performer, but also that the raters believed the average man was more likely than the average woman to perform these aggressive behaviors. Significantly, the size of the gender-differentiated beliefs and norms among these college students was positively related to the size of the behavioral gender difference in aggression found in the studies. For studies of aggression using behaviors where expectations and norms for women and men were most different according to the raters, the greatest female–male differences in aggressive behavior were found.

When are males most likely to behave aggressively against females? According to one laboratory study, the chances of such aggression are increased when a man performs poorly on a masculine task in the presence of a woman, and the woman criticizes his performance (Richardson, Leonard, Taylor, & Hammock, 1985).

Along with overall differences in level of aggression, there is some evidence that females and males differ in their most common forms of aggression. When school-age children behave aggressively, boys may be more likely to show physical aggression, while girls may be more likely to show verbal aggression (Feshbach, 1970). Indeed, some studies (e.g., Archer & Westeman, 1981) have found higher levels of verbal aggression among girls than boys, but the preponderance of evidence is that, even for verbal aggression, male levels are generally higher. The consensus among reviewers is that male–female differences in aggression are largest and most consistent for physical aggression (Hyde, 1984b; Maccoby & Jacklin, 1974). One possible qualification to this conclusion is that much of the apparent difference may stem from extremely aggressive behavior by a few boys. Such a finding was reported by Archer and Westeman (1981); it may have gone unnoticed in other studies.

There are other qualifications to the general finding of greater male than female aggression. When boys and girls are similarly rewarded for aggressive behaviors, girls are as aggressive as boys (Bandura, 1973). Gender differences are more likely to occur in studies where the subjects are not angered or provoked (Baron, 1977; Frodi, Macaulay, & Thome, 1977; White, 1983). Certain aggressive cues, such as weapons, may be linked to more instigation to act aggressively in men than women. Also, there is evidence that women have more anxiety about aggressive feelings than men, and that they feel more anxious after being aggressive than men do (Frodi et al., 1977). In situations where aggression anxiety is reduced, either through strong justification for the aggression or confidence that aggression will be an effective strategy, women's likelihood of aggression may rise. For instance, Hokanson and his colleagues (Hokanson & Edelman, 1966; Hokanson, Willers, & Koropsak, 1968) found that males' physiological arousal decreased dramatically after they were allowed to give electric shocks to someone who had insulted them. Females showed no such "relief response" following aggression; in fact, their arousal decreased following a friendly response toward their insulter. However, the researchers were able to teach the relief response for aggression to the female subjects simply by changing their reinforcement history: rewarding aggressive responses with nonshock trials and shocking subjects if they made a friendly response.

There are some serious limitations to the psychological literature on gender differences in aggression. Most of the studies have been carried out on populations that are the most easily accessible to researchers: preschool and schoolchildren, and college students. There are practically no studies of adults older than college age. Moreover, the measures of aggression used in controlled studies have, of necessity, been artificial and limited. When real-life is considered, the pattern of greater male than female aggression appears more clear-cut. Men commit far more of the violent crimes than women do (Gove, 1985; *Social Trends*, 1984), and far more wives than husbands are driven from their homes or live in fear because of a violently abusive spouse (MacLeod, 1980; Walker, 1979, 1984). When these statistics are considered, it appears that, whatever the size of the average gender difference in aggression, the ratio of men to women at the upper extreme of the distribution is very high.

It seems fair to conclude that, among humans, males are somewhat more likely than females to respond aggressively in certain situations. Controversy continues to rage, however, about the reasons for this difference. As usual, the controversy centers on the roles played by biology and environment in the shaping of the gender difference. Some researchers (e.g., Maccoby & Jacklin, 1980) have argued that there may be a biological, probably hormonal, basis for greater male than female aggression, while others (e.g., Tieger, 1980) claim that the difference can be explained by social-environmental causes.

Possible social-psychological reasons for gender differences in aggression include the direct teaching of more aggressive behaviors to boys than girls, the rewarding of males more than females for aggressive behavior, the rewarding of girls more than boys for inhibiting aggressive behavior, and the presence of more male than female aggressive models. There is evidence that males are more rewarded by their peers than females are for aggressive behavior (Fagot & Hagan, 1985) and that aggression in females meets with disapproval, even in children. An interesting example of the social disapproval of female aggression is the negative reaction to women boxers (Archer & Lloyd, 1985). Aggressive models for males are provided in abundance in sports and in the popular media; physical aggression by females is much less frequently portrayed. Moreover, when aggression by women *is* portrayed in the media, as in the movie *Thelma and Louise*, it seems to be met with far more public outrage than portrayals of equivalent behavior by males. Taken together, the different socialization pressures for boys and girls could well lead to greater readiness by males to behave aggressively, and to a stronger inhibition by females against aggression.

At another level, power and status differences between females and males in their social environment are likely to support gender differences in aggression. To the extent that males are bigger, stronger, and better trained in aggressive techniques than are females, aggression is more likely to be an effective strategy for them. Furthermore, in situations where women are economically dependent on men—situations that are frequent in societies where men are given preferred access to resources such as education, employment, and income—men may find aggression a less risky strategy than women do, and so employ it more. Male aggression that is specifically directed against women is greater in cultures in which women have little economic or political power or authority (Sanday, 1981a). These power-related issues are discussed further in Chapters 11 and 12.

Some of the biological factors postulated as causes for the gender difference in aggression include the influence of the Y chromosome, the prenatal influence of male hormones *in utero* on the developing brain of the fetus, and the level of male hormones circulating in the mature individual's bloodstream. All of these factors will be examined in the following chapter, in the discussion of sexual differentiation. It is possible but unproven that one or more of these biological factors contributes to a predisposition for males to behave more aggressively than females, perhaps by building in a sensitivity to certain kinds of stimuli or by making certain aggression-related responses more rewarding (Hamburg & Lunde, 1966). However, the existence of such a predisposition would not lead inevitably to male–female differences in aggressive behavior; biological and social influences on behavior work in combination. Cross-cultural studies show that societies differ in the degree to which they encourage male aggression, and that gender-related differences in aggression reflect these cultural norms (e.g., Block, 1973; Mead, 1935). Societies in which there is a great deal of emphasis on warfare, aggressiveness and bravery tend to foster conditions in which women become property to be conquered or prizes to be won by male warriors. In certain forager societies, on the other hand, aggression and violence of all kinds are frowned upon. In such societies, gender differences in aggression appear to be minimal (O'Kelly & Carney, 1986). The expression of aggressive tendencies occurs through the individuals' interaction with their social and cultural environment.

Influenceability

There is little evidence to support the stereotype that women are generally more easily influenced, or more compliant, than men (Maccoby & Jacklin, 1974; Eagly & Wood, 1985). Although there is some evidence that little girls are more obedient to their parents than little boys are (e.g., Hetherington, Cox, & Cox, 1976; Smith & Daglish, 1977), there are also indications that little boys are more susceptible than their female counterparts to pressure from peers (Maccoby & Jacklin, 1974). Among adults, when gender differences are found, they are usually in the direction of greater female conformity. However, a meta-analysis of social influence studies, by Eagly and Carli (1981), indicates that the size of the difference is quite small, with male and female means about one-quarter of a standard deviation apart. Furthermore, their analysis indicates that findings of gender differences tend to be associated with particular situational variables. The difference is larger in laboratory studies when subjects are confronted with group pressure, and in studies where subjects know they are under observation. Male researchers are more likely to find gender differences in influenceability than are female researchers. Also, the small amount of evidence that is available suggests that race or ethnicity may be an important variable. In the United States, black females tend to be less easily influenced than their black male or white female counterparts (Adams, 1980, 1983).

Both sexes show less conformity when dealing with a topic or task that is familiar or gender-appropriate (Karabenick, 1983; Sistrunk & McDavid, 1971). However, although gender-biased topics may contribute artificially to findings of gender differences in particular studies, there is no evidence that the research in this area has an overall masculine content bias (Eagly & Carli, 1981). Thus, the general finding of modestly greater female than male influenceability in certain situations cannot be attributed solely to this bias.

One reason for the finding that females are slightly more influenceable than males under some circumstances may lie in gender roles. Research by Eagly, Wood and Fishbaugh (1981) suggests that at least some of the observed differences may occur not because women conform more but because men conform less when they are sujected to group pressure. It has usually been assumed that women more often than men change their opinions to coincide with those of a group in the interest of group harmony. However, these researchers showed that women's opinions tended to remain unchanged when confronted with a group. Rather it was the men's opinions that changed—in the direction of greater nonconformity. Eagly and her colleagues suggest that the sometimes observed gender difference in who can be influenced may stem, not from greater female compliance, but from male concern with not *appearing* influenceable. Males may tend to think of nonconformity or independence as "masculine," and thus tailor their behavior in that direction. Congruent with this explanation is the finding that conformity appears to vary with sex-typing. "Masculine" and "androgynous" individuals of both sexes tend to conform less than "feminine" individuals (Bem, 1975; Brehony & Geller, 1981).

Another explanation for gender differences in conformity in certain kinds of situations may be the status differences between women and men (Eagly, 1983; Eagly & Wood, 1982). Men are automatically ascribed higher status than women under many circumstances; they also tend to hold higher status positions (Lockheed, 1985; Lockheed & Hall, 1976). With higher status come expectations for greater influence, and these expectations may become self-fulfilling prophecies. Men are expected to exert more influence because of their higher status; thus, they act in influencing ways, while females, who are not expected to exert as much influence, act in conforming ways. The result is a status difference disguised as a gender difference.

Important to the evaluation of this body of research (and other research on gender) is Eagly and Carli's (1981) finding that greater female influenceability is significantly more likely to be found by male researchers. The finding cannot easily be explained as an effect of higher-status male experimenters or influencing agents, since group pressure studies commonly use same-sex groups and many conformity studies do not identify the influencing agent by sex. Rather, Eagly and Carli suggest that bias related to the sex of the researcher may enter the design in a number of ways: Researchers may choose topics that favor the interests and expertise of their own gender; they may unwittingly design settings and procedures that make subjects of their own sex more comfortable and self-confident and therefore less easily influenced. To find out about the generality of the tendency for male researchers to report more gender differences, Eagly and Carli compared their findings to those in a sample of studies collected by Hall (1978) on interpreting nonverbal communication. Where gender differences are found in the accuracy of interpreting nonverbal communication, they tend to favor females; however, the male researchers in Hall's sample were *less* likely than female researchers to find such gender differences. Eagly and Carli suggest, then, that there is no overall tendency for male researchers to find more gender differences; rather, both male and female researchers introduce bias in ways that make the portrayal of their own gender more favorable. If their suggestion is correct, the fact that the majority of researchers in psychology has been and continues to be male has serious implications for the view of women that has been generated by research.

Dominance

Dominance encompasses a wide range of behaviors that have to do with imposing one's will on others and controlling and influencing others' behavior. In our culture, males are stereotypically viewed as more dominant than females, and there is some truth to that stereotype, at least in certain situations. However, as was the case with aggression and conformity, it is difficult to disentangle the effects of gender on dominance behavior from the effects of status.

In mixed-sex groups or pairs, men tend to dominate the conversation, talking more than women, interrupting or ignoring women, and failing to pick up conversational topics raised by women (Eakins & Eakins, 1978; Krupnick, 1985; Lockheed & Hall, 1976; Spender, 1980; Zimmerman & West, 1975). Women speak more tentatively than men do when they are in mixed-sex pairs—and this strategy has a mixed payoff. Women who speak tentatively are more influential with men but less influential with women in such groups (Carli, 1990). Nonverbally, men signal dominance in these mixed-sex situations by expansive gestures, touching women, and control over physical space, while women are more likely to be circumspect and tense in their posture, to avoid touching, and to take up little space (Henley, 1977).

In initially leaderless groups of women and men, men are more likely than women to emerge as leaders, particularly if the groups are short-term or working on tasks that do not require much social interaction. However, women are slightly more likely than men to become social leaders (Eagly & Karau, 1991). When college women and men whose dominance has been measured with a personality test are placed in same-gender pairs, the high-dominant individual assumes leadership most of the time. However, in female–male pairs, the male partner is more likely to assume leadership, regardless of dominance score (Carbonell, 1984; Megargee, 1969; Nyquist & Spence, 1986). In male–female pairs where the woman is high-dominant and the man is low-dominant, the highest percentage of female leaders selected in any study is 50 percent (Fleischer & Chertkoff, 1986); where the man is high-dominant and the woman is low-dominant, the percentage of male leaders selected has averaged between 85 and 90 percent. When women and men are interacting together, then, men often act in more dominant ways than women do.

In same-sex groups, men show no more tendency to try to dominate the conversation than women do (Kimble, Yoshikawa, & Zehr, 1981). However, there may be some differences in dominance behavior between all-female and all-male groups. Aries (1976) found that all-male groups established a more stable dominance order over time and showed more instances of one member addressing the group as a whole than did all-female groups. Paikoff and Savin-Williams (1983) found that, among adolescents, female groups tended to be less structured, more cohesive, and show less evidence of linear dominance hierarchies than male groups. There is some evidence, then, that men may be more concerned than women with dominance, even in same-sex groups.

Some researchers have argued that gender differences in dominance are linked to gender differences in aggression, and may thus have a biological basis. However, aside from the problem that a biological basis for gender differences in aggression has not yet been established, many forms of dominance in human society do not involve aggression. Successful dominance in some situations may even involve an inhibition of aggression. It is more likely that status and role expectations govern dominance behavior. There is some evidence, for instance, that the more competence a person is seen as having in a particular situation, either by others or by herself or himself, the more leadership she or he will be able to assume. Lockheed and Hall (1976), postulating that men take on group leadership roles because, having automatic higher status than women, they get more respect and deference from the group from the beginning, devised a way to reduce the impact of these initial status differences. They provided females with task experience, in order to build task-specific expectations of competence, before putting them into mixed-sex groups to work on the task. This strategy had a dramatic impact: In mixed-sex groups, males were four to seven times more likely than females to emerge as leaders *unless* the females in the group had been given the opportunity to develop competence on the task ahead of time, in which case female ranking improved fairly dramatically. In groups where the female participants had been given, through experience, task-specific expectations of competence, females were more active than in other groups and a female was ranked either first or second in leadership-related behaviors in all groups.

Another example of the impact of perceived competence on dominance can be found in the relationship between leadership and the sex-typing of the group task. One study (Wentworth & Anderson, 1984) found that male undergraduates were more likely than their female counterparts to emerge as leaders when the group was working on a "masculine" (how to invest $10,000) or neutral (how to spend $10,000 on entertainment items) task; however, females took the leadership role for the "feminine" task (how a young woman should spend $10,000 on her wedding).

How does perceived competence or status translate into leadership or the ability to dominate a group? Apparently, group members behave quite differently toward those whom they view as having high or low status. Butler and Geis (1990), for instance, found that, when making equivalent contributions to group discussions, male leaders received more smiles and fewer frowns than female leaders. In fact, the more a female leader talked, the more unfavorable were the facial expressions directed toward her by other members of the group—male and female alike. The researchers attribute the differing reactions to perceptions by group members that females were violating role and status expectations by taking on leadership. Given the differing nonverbal reactions to female and male leadership attempts, it is likely that males find it easier than females to dominate or lead a group, but this may have little to do with gender differences in predisposition toward dominance.

The complexity of the relationship among status, social expectations, and dominance behavior is illustrated by research on how gender and race interact in helping to determine dominance behavior. Race, like sex, is considered by researchers to be a status characteristic—a characteristic that automatically influences the status ascribed to a person. While an individual's overall status is thought to be made up of a combination of all the status characteristics relevant to the person judging it, it seems to be more complex than a simple average (Adams, 1983). American research indicates that being black is associated with a lower status than being white, just as being female is associated with a lower status than being male. Black women, then, might be expected to have the lowest perceived status of the four possible sex–race combinations. In line with predictions about status and dominance behavior, black women would be expected to be less dominant than anyone else. This prediction is not supported, however. Black women are more likely than white women to assume leadership positions in all-female groups (Fenelon & Megargee, 1971), and a study of influence in dyads showed that black females were better than black males and white females at resisting challenges to their preferences (Adams, 1980). Black males, on the other hand, sustained fewer challenges from white than from black partners. Clearly, it is too simple to think of status as something that is unchanging across social contexts; the status accorded to being male or female, black or white, may vary according to the norms of the situation and the status characteristics of the person with whom the individual is interacting (Adams, 1983). On the whole, the interaction between gender and race in dominance situations suggests that gender differences in dominance may be largely socially produced and vulnerable to situational change. This research also illustrates the dangers of trying to understand gender differences by studying only members of a particular racial or cultural group.

The limitations of a narrow cultural perspective on gender differences are further highlighted by cross-cultural research on dominance. While leadership and dominance are behaviors that are often encouraged in American society, there are cultures, such as the Arapesh (Mead, 1935) and the Mbuti (Sanday, 1981a) that favor equality and discourage leadership and dominance hierarchies. In such groups, there tends to be more equality of power and less role differentiation between women and men. Among the Mbuti, for example, diversity of opinion may be expressed through discussion, and participation in such discussions is evenly divided between males and females of all adult-age levels. However, prolonged disagreement is labeled "noise," and is discouraged because it is considered offensive to the forest.

In still other societies, certain aspects of leadership and status are or have been assigned to women. For example, the constitution of the Iroquois, the North American Indian confederacy of six nations that was formed in the mid-fifteenth century, declared that women were the progenitors of the Nation, that descent of the people would run in the female line, and that the women would own the land and the soil (Sanday, 1981a). This principle acknowledged significant power for the women. For example, women of the Seneca, one of the Six Nations, controlled all cultivated tribal land, had the final say over the distribution of surplus food, and exercised strong influence, through their councils, over tribal decisions with respect to warfare and peace negotiations (Jensen, 1990). Other North American Indian groups, such as the Hopi and the Navajo, also have strong traditions of female power (Katz, 1977; O'Kelly & Carney, 1986). Part of the process of the colonization of Native Americans by invading Europeans was the undermining of this female power. Native Americans were increasingly pressured by missionaries and government officials to adopt the European values and practices of female subordination (Jensen, 1990). Research on gender differences in dominance might have produced quite different results in certain Native American than in European American groups at this time.

Nurturance

Women are so often seen in nurturant roles, not only as mothers caring for small children, but as nurses, childcare workers, and social workers, that it is easy to accept a stereotype that women are the more nurturant sex. This stereotype permeates the writings of professionals about women and about motherhood (Ruddick, 1989), and in North America is applied to white middle-class women (Rich, 1976), poor women (Belle, 1984), Chicana women (Mirande & Enriquez, 1979), and black women (McCray, 1980). In fact, as seen in earlier chapters, the idea that women had a maternal instinct, a built-in tendency to care for small children, was popular in psychology for a time. It is now understood, however, that greater female than male participation in the above nurturant activities cannot by itself be taken as an indication that women are "naturally" more nurturant than men; rather, the participation rates may reflect social pressure and the nature of the choices available to women and men.

Nurturance involves caring for and promoting the welfare of others. Many activities fall under this definition, from comforting a sick child to soothing the ruffled feathers of a tired, grumpy spouse, to mending a leaky roof so that one's family will be warm and dry. There is no evidence of a gender difference in nurturance that holds across all such activities. Even for responses to babies, where, stereotypically, one might expect the most clear-cut gender difference in favor of women, the research reveals a cloudy picture. The sexes do not differ in their physiological responses (heart rate, blood pressure, skin conductance) to an infant's cry, although females are more likely to report that the crying bothers them (Frodi & Lamb, 1978). Men can be as good as women are at feeding infants and at correctly identifying the meaning of a baby's cry. College males and females have been found to be equally good at discriminating among different kinds of baby cries (Parke, 1981), and fathers are as good as mothers at using infants' cues to guide their own caretaking behavior (Parke & Sawin, 1976). In the hospital, just after birth, and later at home, Parke and Sawin (1976) observed that fathers were as likely as mothers to hold, rock, talk to, and smile at their babies; and during bottle feeding, babies took just as much milk from their fathers as from their mothers. On the other hand, some studies show that boys are less responsive than girls are to an unfamiliar infant in a waiting-room situation (Feldman, Nash, & Cutrona, 1977), and that new mothers paid more attention than other adults did to a baby who was not their own (Feldman & Nash, 1978). In the latter case, however, more than a simple gender difference was observed: The new mothers were more responsive not only than men, but also than women who did not have children and women who were pregnant.

There seems little doubt that gender differences in nurturant behavior, where they are found, can be traced to stereotyping and social pressure. Cross-cultural research shows that girls and boys differ more in nurturance in those societies where girls are directly socialized more toward nurturance than boys are. In cultures where these differential socialization pressures are minimal—where, for instance, both girls and boys are expected to help with infant care—gender differences in nurturance are minimal as well (Whiting & Edwards, 1973). In our culture, differences in reactions to infants are more likely to show up in self-reports or in situations where participants know they are being observed and evaluated than in other situations (Berman, 1976, 1980). Also, it is masculine sex-typing, rather than being male, that seems to interfere with nurturant behavior. In one study, androgynous men were as responsive to a baby and to a kitten as were women, but masculine men were less responsive (Bem, Martyna, & Watson, 1976).

Although evidence for the impact of gender expectations on nurturant behavior is strong, researchers have not ruled out the possibility that biology plays a role, through prenatal hormones, in the development of some gender differences in nurturance. This research will be discussed in the following chapter. Once again, whatever potential differences may be provided for by biological factors would have to develop through the individual's interaction with her or his social and physical environment. Despite some interesting changes that have begun to take place in that environment, it is still less supportive of male than female nurturance.

Empathy

Empathy, the quality of being sensitive and responsive to the feelings of others, is often cited as a feminine characteristic. Women are said to have "woman's intuition," to be good at listening to people's problems, to be more easily swayed than men by emotional appeals. This stereotype has been echoed in decades of social and psychological theory about women, from Freud's notion of women's weak superego, to Parsons and Bales's instrumental-expressive distinction between male and female roles (Eisenberg & Lennon, 1983). When the evidence is examined however, this particular stereotype does not hold up very well.

A review of empathy research, using meta-analysis, showed that, where gender differences in empathy exist, they tend to favor females (Eisenberg & Lennon, 1983). However, such differences were found inconsistently and seemed to depend on the method used to measure empathy. When the measure used was self-report—subjects' responses to questionnaire items such as "I tend to get emotionally involved with a friend's problems"—females scored much higher than males on empathy. Every study in the sample showed a statistically significant difference, and the mean empathy score of the females was, on the average, almost a full standard deviation above that of the males. For other measures, however, the gender difference was considerably less clearcut. When subjects were asked to respond to emotional situations simulated in the lab or on videotape, most studies found no gender difference in reports of sympathy or concern or of feeling the same emotion as the story's protagonist. Measures of physiological response to another person's emotional distress also yielded no evidence of greater female than male sensitivity to others' feelings. When children's reactions to others' distress were observed unobtrusively, gender differences were not found; however, when children were explicitly questioned about their reactions, girls showed more nonverbal signs of empathy than boys did.

On the whole, the reviewers noted, the gender difference in empathy was most evident in studies where it was most obvious that empathy was being measured. Largest differences were found in studies using self-report or explicit questioning; no differences were found using physiological measures or unobtrusive observation. They suggest that the appearance of gender differences in empathy is largely influenced by the demand characteristics of the research situation—the cues to the participant about how to behave. Why should demand characteristics produce a gender difference instead of across-the-board increases in empathy responding? Females and males are quite likely to differ in how empathetic they would like to appear to others. Since empathy is a stereotypically feminine trait, it is not surprising that, when they know empathy is being measured, as in the case of the self-report studies, females produce more empathy responses than males do.

Further support for the influence of gender stereotypes on the gender difference in empathy can be found in research linking empathy to sex-typing. Self-reports of empathy are correlated positively with self-ratings of femininity and negatively with self-rated masculinity (Foushee, Davis, & Archer, 1979), and people who are sex-typed as masculine show fewer empathetic behaviors than androgynous or feminine individuals, when listening to a person describing personal problems (Bem et al., 1976).

One measure of empathy for which there is a fairly consistent finding of higher levels for females is sensitivity to nonverbal cues. Females seem to be moderately better than males at all ages at interpreting the meaning of auditory cues (such as tone of voice) and among adults, women are better than men at decoding visual cues such as facial expression, particularly when the nonverbal message is intentional (Eisenberg & Lennon, 1983; Hall, 1978, 1984; Rosenthal & DePaulo, 1979). Some investigators feel that women learn to refrain from "eavesdropping" on nonverbal cues that the sender cannot control. This pattern appears to strengthen from childhood to adulthood—a clue that it may be shaped through social learning.

Empathy for others' feelings in general, and sensitivity to nonverbal emotional cues in particular, probably relate to situational factors such as status and role. Rosenthal and his colleagues (Rosenthal, Archer, DiMatteo, Kowumaki, & Rogers, 1974) found that men who were training for or working in occupations that required nurturance or sensitivity were as good as women at decoding nonverbally expressed emotions. Whether this finding can be attributed to the effects of practice or to the self-selection of unusually sensitive men for such occupations is difficult to know. Women's greater sensitivity may be due to their lower status in many situations. People with subordinate status generally have to develop more sensitivity to others' feelings than high-status people do, as a matter of survival (Snodgrass, 1985). Lipman-Blumen (1984) has argued that "woman's intuition" is a skill developed by women to help them to predict and thus control or at least cope with the moods and behaviors of the more powerful men with whom they must interact. Of interest in this regard are findings of greater nonverbal sensitivity among blacks than whites in the United States (Gitter, Black, & Mostofsky, 1972).

Altruism

Consistent with the stereotype that females are more nurturant and empathetic is the notion that they have a stronger tendency than men to do things for others, to be helpful to people in need. This assumed gender difference has been widely studied, but results have proven inconsistent. Girls clearly have more of a reputation for altruistic behavior than boys do (Zarbatany, Hartmann, Gelfand, & Vinciguerra, 1985). However, when actual helping behavior is measured, females do not consistently come out ahead; in fact, differences are found more often in the direction of greater male than greater female helpfulness (Eagly & Crowley, 1986; Piliavin & Unger, 1985).

Researchers trying to make sense of apparently contradictory findings in this area have focused on the situational variables that distinguish settings in which males are more likely to help from those in which females tend to be more helpful (Eagly & Crowley, 1986). In general, they have found that men are more likely than women to help when some kind of active intervention is required, such as when a victim has apparently collapsed on the subway. The presence of an audience also accentuates the tendency for men, more than women, to be helpful to strangers—probably because an audience is a reminder of the norm that men are supposed to be chivalrous. The kind of activity required of the helper also makes a difference: Each sex, but especially males, is more likely to help when the activity required is gender-role appropriate. There is also evidence that characteristics of the person who needs help can be important. Some research has found that males are more likely to help females and females to help males, at least in nonthreatening situations (Bickman, 1974), while another investigation suggests that this pattern is magnified by how dependent the potential recipient appears to be (Wolfson, 1981). The latter pattern may hold only in relatively nonthreatening laboratory-type situations, however. In real-world situations, such as hitchhiking or stopping a stranger on the street at night, women may receive more help from both sexes, both because women are presumed to be frailer and more dependent than men and because both males and females may feel more suspicious and threatened when approached by a male than a female for help (Latane & Darley, 1970).

In summary, gender differences in helping behavior seem to be largely determined by situational factors; there is no overall tendency for either females or males to be helpful to others.

What Happened to the Differences?

This chapter's overview of research on gender differences in various aspects of social behavior suggests that, in most areas, these differences are small ones, and in many areas the findings are so inconsistent as to make it impossible to draw conclusions. If gender differences in social behavior are really so small and inconsistent, how is it that women and men end up leading such different lives? How is it that most bank managers are men and most tellers are women? that most single parents are women? that most of the world's nations have never had a female head of state? that so many more men than women play hockey, soccer, football? We are faced with the task of reconciling psychology's findings of small behavioral differences between the sexes with our observations that, in daily life, women and men often seem to differ dramatically in their concerns, their accomplishments, and the way they spend their time.

Several things can work to maximize the apparent difference between the findings of carefully controlled research in laboratory or classroom situations and casual observations in everyday life. Psychologists have designed their research to determine whether, all things being equal, females and males will differ in the way they respond to certain situations. They have tried, although not always with success, to ensure that conditions in their studies are equivalent for the males and females. But outside the laboratory, all things are seldom equal for males and females. Men and women face differing expectations, different pressures, different constraints. Thus, while psychological research has demonstrated that, for instance, women *can* be as aggressive as men and men *can* be as nurturant toward infants as women, it does not follow that, given current social conditions, they *will* be. One reason for the apparent discrepancy between some of the research findings and everyday life, then, is the difference between potential and actual behavior. Psychologists have often tried to control or minimize the impact of social context on the behavior they are studying. To the extent that they succeed in doing this, they may see gender differences that are smaller than those we observe in everyday life. In everyday life, however, two aspects of the social context are often confounded with being female or male: role expectations and status.

Role Expectations

We have seen that some of the largest gender differences appear in situations where people know they are being observed, and that self-reported behaviors often differ more than unobtrusively observed behaviors for women and men. According to a gender-role perspective, female–male differences in social behavior occur partly because people are responding to social norms about how women and men should behave and partly because, by playing their expected roles, women and men tend to develop different attitudes and skills (Eagly, 1987).

Clearly, gender-related behavior is influenced by people's ideas about how others want and expect them to behave. Aggression and dominance are prescribed behaviors for the masculine role; compliance, nurturance, and empathy for the feminine role. Role expectations extend beyond the general concepts of masculinity and femininity, however, to the more specific roles that are occupied with differential frequency by women and men: secretary, company president, wife, husband, mother, father, scientist, cab driver, and so on. Company presidents, more often than secretaries, are put in situations where they are expected to be dominant. The fact that most company presidents are men is both a result of and a perpetuation of the expectation that men are more dominant than women. Men are more likely than women to be promoted to this position because they are seen as having the capacity to be appropriately dominant; once in the position, a man confronts many situations where dominance is expected, so his behavior becomes more dominant. Thus, the demands of the roles in which people are more or less likely to find themselves because of their gender, act to reinforce gender-related behavior and gender stereotypes. When women and men are in similar occupational roles, however, as in studies of female and male managers, they respond to similar role pressures and their behavior tends to be similar (Eagly & Johnson, 1990).

It is noteworthy that most of the studies comparing females and males on social behavior have been done with children or university students—people who, although certainly subject to gender-role expectations, have not yet become heavily involved in the occupational or parental roles that reinforce these gender expectations.

Status

It is all but impossible for researchers to disentangle gender and status. In most situations, males are ascribed higher status than females, so when behavioral differences between the sexes are observed it is difficult to know whether to attribute them to gender or status. As noted earlier in this chapter, high-status people may find it easier and more appropriate than low-status people to act aggressively and dominantly; low-status people are more likely than high-status people to find themselves in situations where conformity and sensitivity are required.

In confronting this problem, researchers have often been at great pains to be aware of the effect of status in research on gender, to measure it, and to control for it, if possible. The latter is not always easy. For instance, in trying to construct stimuli in which a male and a female are each portrayed in role-appropriate but equally high-status jobs, researchers have been stymied by the impossibility of finding a really high-status job that is typically considered female-appropriate (Lips & Mayo, 1978). To make the issue even more complicated, the status ascribed to gender may be inconsistent with the status achieved in a particular occupation. A woman who holds a high-status position such as physician is likely to be pegged as a nurse by people who do not know her. Similarly, male nurses are often mistakenly taken as physicians. Such situations of status inconsistency add to the difficulty of investigating the relationship between gender and status.

To the extent that status differences between males and females are successfully controlled in research, the researcher may observe few gender differences. For example, the use of a speaking style that is filled with intensifiers, hedges, hesitations, and questioning intonations—often considered a "feminine" speaking style—is linked much more strongly to social power and status than to gender. Both females and males, when in low-status positions, are more likely than high-status individuals to use this speaking style (Erickson, Lund, Johnson, & O'Barr, 1978).

Since researchers generally try to control for status when comparing females and males, even though they are not usually completely successful, they probably observe smaller gender differences in the laboratory than others see in the outside world. A research participant coming into a psychologist's lab is removed from her or his normal social context, with all of its expectations. The researcher is careful to treat female and male subjects exactly the same way, to have them respond to identical stimuli. In the outside world, however, there are many dimensions on which males and females are probably *not* treated the same way. For example, a study of influence might expose males and females to a series of identical challenges to their opinions, to see whether one sex is more persuasible than the other. Using this method, the researcher may find minimal gender differences in persuasibility. Outside the lab, however, it is unlikely that people use exactly the same tactics to challenge the opinions of women and men. Instead, the status and role expectations associated with femininity and masculinity will produce, in many situations, different approaches to influencing women and men, and more noticeable gender differences in susceptibility to influence.

Choosing Behaviors to Study

Researchers find it most practical to study behaviors that can be defined clearly and measured precisely. This predilection usually leads them to focus on isolated behaviors rather than on complex processes or the expression of a behavioral disposition across a wide range of situations. For example, researchers studying nurturance may focus on parental reactions to a new infant during the first few weeks after birth. They may define nurturance as the amount of time the parent spends holding, touching, smiling at, or talking to the baby during the hours of observation. Yet nurturance is potentially a much broader concept. It could be thought of as including awareness of the infant's needs, the amount of one's attention focused on the child even when not interacting with it, the proportion of one's daily decisions and choices that are made with the child in mind, and so on. The latter aspects of nurturance would be much harder to measure than holding, touching, and smiling. If they *could* be measured, perhaps conclusions about gender differences in nurturance would be very different. It is important to remember that researchers' conclusions about sweeping categories of behavior such as nurturance and aggression are based on the measurement of isolated, easily measurable behaviors. This focus on easily measurable behaviors may be another factor responsible for the difference between research findings of small gender differences and casual observation of apparently larger differences on certain dimensions.

The Observer Bias Problem— Exaggeration of Small Differences

A final important reason for the apparent discrepancy between research findings and casual observation is the bias built into casual observation. As discussed in earlier chapters, people are strongly influenced in what they notice and remember by their stereotypes and schemas. Observations that fit into preexisting cognitive categories tend to be more easily incorporated than those that do not. Thus, if a person is a believer in the general stereotype that women are more altruistic than men, he or she will tend to notice and remember instances of women being helpful as confirmation of the stereotype, while discounting instances of selfish behavior by women and unselfish behavior by men as exceptions to the general rule.

There are many examples of such resistance to information that disconfirms one's stereotypes. The phenomenon was recently demonstrated with some force on television's "60 Minutes," when reporter Diane Sawyer questioned an Iranian politician about the restriction of women's rights in his country. He countered with the opinion that, in America, where women faced fewer restrictions in their dress and demeanor, women were miserable. Sawyer, looking at him in disbelief, asked "You mean, you think I'm miserable?" He demurred, looking at the smiling face of perhaps one of the few American women he had ever encountered, and said that while perhaps she in particular was not miserable, women in America in general were indeed miserable.

As noted in the discussion of meta-analysis, the frequency of extreme levels of behavior can make a strong impression on people. If the sexes are seen to differ in the frequency with which they engage in extreme levels of a particular behavior, this observation can contribute dramatically to gender stereotypes. Taking aggression as an example, it is likely that most of us have heard of many more instances of extreme violence perpetrated by men than by women, and thus it is easy for us to believe that men are much more aggressive than women. At most levels of aggression, however, the gender difference is probably much less dramatic; the behavior of a relatively small number of very violent individuals has a disproportionate impact on our beliefs about women and men in general.

In weighing the results of research against one's own observations, then, neither the research nor one's own observations should be taken entirely at face value. Apparent gender differences often reflect differences in situational role expectations and status. When researchers successfully control for these factors, they find smaller gender differences. Such findings say much about what the social world might be like if differential role and status expectations about women and men were abolished; they say less about the social world as it is. Moreover, the control and precise measurement required to carry out research often preclude the study of aspects of behavior that are less tangible or not as easily observed, in favor of the obvious and easily quantifiable. Many of the more complex and subtle aspects of behavioral gender differences may thus be overlooked by research, although they may be apprehended in a qualitative way by observers. It is dangerous to rely too heavily on one's casual observations, however, since they are heavily prone to bias.

Summary

Despite the fact that women and men are often referred to as opposites, psychological research finds gender differences to be relatively small in size or inconsistent in many areas of social behavior. Small differences favoring males have been found for aggressive and dominant behavior; small differences favoring females have been found for influenceability. In the areas of nurturance, empathy, and altruism, no across-the-board differences are found, but gender differences occur under particular circumstances.

For all of the social behaviors discussed here, status and role expectations seem to be important mediators of gender differences. The influence of role expectations is seen in the tendency for larger gender differences to appear when research participants are reporting their own feelings or are aware of being observed. The influence of status is seen in the tendency to find smaller gender differences under conditions in which an effort has been made to equalize the status of male and female participants. It is reasonable to expect, then, that the overall picture of gender differences in behavior will be different across cultural and historical situations in which role and status expectations for males and females vary. Currently, North America seems to be experiencing a period when gender roles are overlapping and merging more than they have in the past, a phenomenon that may be reflected in findings of smaller behavioral gender differences as the years go by.

The literature on gender differences in social behavior has many limitations. Behavior tends to be studied apart from its social context in order to achieve careful control of variables confounded with gender; thus, results are sometimes uninformative about the processes through which the social environment supports or discourages gender differences in behavior. Behaviors that are chosen for study tend to be the ones that are most easily measured; thus, many subtle, complex aspects of the relationship between gender and behavior may be lost. Despite its limitations, however, research on gender and social behavior provides an important corrective to the biases of the casual observer.

The newfound popularity of meta-analytic methods for examining patterns of gender differences has contributed a great deal to knowledge about the relationship between gender and particular behaviors. This approach has shown that even though a gender difference may be found reliably, its size may be quite small. More longitudinal and cross-sequential research is needed, however, in order to build understanding of the developmental and historical aspects of gender differences, and of within-gender variables that predict behavior.

For Additional Reading

Elshtain, Jean Bethke. (1987). *Women and war.* New York: Basic Books. Drawing on the historical records of wars and of peace movements, the author challenges the stereotypes of men as eager warriors and women as peacemakers, and helps the reader to think in new ways about gender and aggression.

Fausto-Sterling, Anne. (1985). *Myths of gender.* The author, a biologist, examines the myths that surround some of the gender-related differences discussed in this and other chapters.

5
Biology & Environment: The Relationship Between Sex & Gender

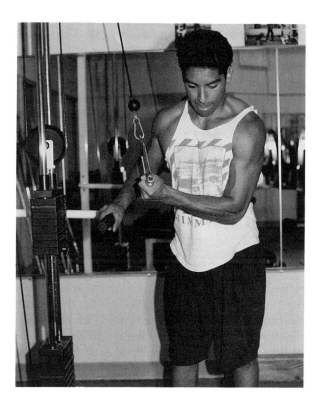

$\mathbf{A}$t the 1985 World University Games, in Kobe, Japan, a young Spanish track and field athlete was quietly summoned by officials and ordered to withdraw from a scheduled race. Heartsick and shaken, Maria Patino faked an injury during warmup and did not run because the officials had warned that the alternative was to make public a devastating discovery: She had "failed" the sex test. According to the results of the buccal smear, a test of the sex chromosome pattern in cells scraped from inside her cheek, Maria was not a normal female. Instead, her chromosome pattern was that of a male. The discovery made her an unwilling member of a small sorority: about a dozen women have been banned from Olympic competition for not being sufficiently female (Carlson, 1991).

Maria had never for an instant doubted her own femaleness. Months of subsequent medical examinations revealed that hers was a case of androgen insensitivity: a male chromosomal pattern that had not resulted in the development of a male body because of complete and permanent inability to respond to testosterone. She has no uterus, but she has female genitals, female body proportions, female secondary sex characteristics, and normal sexual response. Her insensitivity to testosterone means that she could not benefit from taking steroids.

Femininity testing was introduced by the International Amateur Athletic Federation (IAAF) in the late 1960s, after reports that men had been masquerading as women in female sport. Maria became the first woman to publicly challenge her disqualification. During her struggle for reinstatement, she lost her scholarship and her access to her coach. Her records and titles were stricken from the books. Her boyfriend and many of her friends left her. Finally, three years later, acknowledging that her body did not, in fact, give her any unfair advantage with respect to other female athletes, the International Olympic Committee officially requalified her. Furthermore, her case helped to convince the IAAF that the system of testing should be changed.

If Maria Patino's story sounds complicated, consider the following: Several years ago, a research team working in the Dominican Republic reported on the discovery of an unusual phenomenon. A small number of children who had been raised as girls developed male secondary sex characteristics at puberty. Their voices deepened, they grew beards, and developed adult-sized penises and scrotums. Almost all of these "girls" made successful transitions to being male, married, and fathered children (Imperato-McGinley, Guerrero, Gautier, & Peterson, 1974; Imperato-McGinley, Peterson, Gautier, & Sturla, 1979).

What is going on here? Surely, despite all the cautious talk about overlapping distributions of behavior for women and men, one can safely hold to the belief that, at least in biological terms, the categories "female" and "male" are discrete, nonoverlapping, and unambiguously separate? It turns out, in fact, that things are not so simple. The preceding examples are only two of a number of cases in which sex—biological maleness or femaleness—has turned out to be a more fuzzy category than it first appears. There are several biological indicators of sex: chromosomes, sex glands or gonads, hormones, internal reproductive organs, and genitalia. All of these indicators are usually congruent, all male or all female, but occasionally they are not. To make matters more complex, there are questions about the sexual differentiation of the brain, and about the relationship between all of these variables and behavior.

This chapter begins with an examination of the normal process of biological differentiation into female or male. This is followed by a discussion of what happens when something goes awry with this process, producing an individual with mixed indicators of biological sex. The relationship between biological sex and various aspects of gender has been the subject of a great deal of curiosity and controversy, so the study of the gender-related behavior of individuals whose indicators of biological sex are mixed has been regarded as a unique source of clues to this relationship. In this context, we will focus on studies of gender-role behavior and then on gender identity, asking what it is that governs a person's sense of maleness or femaleness. To further explore the question of gender identity, there follows a discussion of transsexualism, a rare and puzzling phenomenon in which an apparently biologically normal individual feels trapped in a body of the wrong sex. The impact of sexual differentiation on sexual orientation is discussed briefly, and the chapter concludes with an examination of attempts to link aggressive behavior with male hormone levels in normal individuals.

The Biological Process of Sexual Differentiation

The process of sexual differentiation is accomplished in several steps. First, the individual's sex is genetically determined at conception. Then, as the embryo develops, the "indifferent gonad" develops into male or female sex glands. In turn, these glands begin to secrete the appropriate male or female sex hormones, which circulate throughout the bloodstream and are responsible for the sexual differentiation of other bodily organs: the internal reproductive tract, the external genitalia, and, to a disputed extent, areas of the brain.

Genetic Determination of Sex

Every normal human cell contains 46 chromosomes, arranged in 23 pairs. One chromosome of each pair is contributed by the mother of the individual and one by the father. Twenty-two of the chromosome pairs carry genes that determine hereditary characteristics of the person. The twenty-third pair, called the *sex chromosomes,* differs for women and men. If the individual is female, the sex chromosomes are represented as XX; if male, the pair is designated as XY. The two types of sex chromosomes are illustrated in Figure 5.1. Only males carry a Y chromosome, which is very small and carries little genetic material. Thus, a person's genetic sex is determined by his or her father. If the sperm cell that happens to fertilize the egg at conception carries an X chromosome, the individual will be female; if it carries a Y chromosome, the individual will be male.

For the first five weeks, the anatomical development of XX and XY embryos seems to be identical. Each develops a "neutral" gonad or sex gland and begins to form two sets of internal reproductive structures: female (*Müllerian ducts*) *and* male (*Wolffian ducts*). Until the sixth week of development, then, all embryos have the potential to develop in either a male or female direction. Whatever genes are involved up until this point must be present in both sexes.

Sex-linked Characteristics. When the genes for a particular trait are carried partially or totally on one of the sex chromosomes, the trait is said to be *sex-linked*. Almost all of the relatively few traits currently identified as sex-linked are associated with genes carried on the X chromosome, and these traits are typically pathological. The presence of such X-linked genes accounts for the greater male than female susceptibility to certain genetic disorders. For instance, the gene for hemophilia is sex-linked and recessive. A father carrying this gene cannot transmit it to his son because he contributes only a Y chromosome to his son, and the gene is carried on the X chromosome. He can, however, transmit the gene to his daughter, to whom he contributes an X chromosome. His daughter, however, will not express any symptoms of hemophilia unless she has also inherited a hemophilia gene on the X chromosome contributed by her mother. If, as is normally the case, the genetic material on the X chromosome from at least one

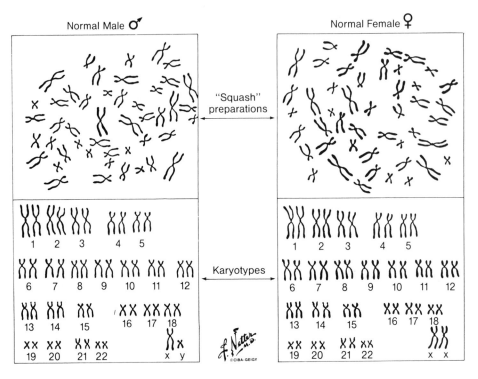

Figure 5.1
The 23 pairs of chromosomes in the normal male and the normal female person. The sex chromosomes are the 23rd pair.

of the parents is programmed for the development of a healthy blood-clotting mechanism, the daughter will not develop hemophilia. Because the trait of hemophilia is recessive, it will be masked by the presence of a normal blood-clotting gene on the other X chromosome. The daughter continues to carry the gene, of course, and may transmit it to her sons or daughters. If she does transmit to her son, the hemophilia will be expressed because the son has no other X chromosome (only a Y chromosome) carrying a normal dominant gene that would mask the recessive trait. Scientists have recently developed the technology for identifying the sex of 3-day-old embryos, with the objective of helping prospective parents who want to conceive a female in order to avoid passing on serious genetic diseases to males (Scientists identify sex, 1990).

Sex-limited Characteristics. Some traits are sex-limited rather than sex-linked. These traits are carried on genes that are not on either of the sex chromosomes but are, nonetheless, generally manifest in only one sex. In this case, the trait requires the presence of male or female sex hormones in order to appear. Baldness, for example, is a trait that is carried genetically but that requires the presence of a certain level of male sex hormones in order to be expressed.

Abnormalities.   Occasionally, through errors in cell division, an individual is conceived who has some chromosomal abnormality—extra or missing chromosomes. Such abnormalities are sometimes present in the sex chromosomes. For example, an individual may be born with a single X chromosome (XO), an extra X chromosome (XXX), an extra Y chromosome (XYY), or with patterns such as XXY (Klinefelter's syndrome) or even XXXY. In these rare instances, as long as there is at least one Y chromosome present, the body type will tend to develop as male unless some subsequent factor interferes. If no Y chromosomes are present, bodily development will be female. It is thought that an individual with only a single Y chromosome cannot survive since no person with this chromosome pattern has ever been found (Money & Ehrhardt, 1972). Various behavioral, personality, and intellectual difficulties have been ascribed to the presence of chromosomal anomalies, but the rarity of the conditions and the fact that in some cases they are noticed only when the individual gets into trouble or seeks help for a problem makes the evidence difficult to evaluate.

Some attempts have been made to demonstrate that particular abilities or behavioral tendencies are linked to the sex chromosomes. For example, there has been speculation that aggression might be partially linked to the Y chromosome since some studies showed that XYY males (men with an extra Y chromosome) were found in higher rates in prisons and institutions for the criminally insane. However, careful examination of the findings indicates that these men are no more likely, indeed less likely, to commit *violent* crimes than are normal males (Price & Whatmore, 1967a, 1967b), so there is no basis for the belief in a link between aggression and the extra Y chromosome. Investigators now attribute the overrepresentation of XYY males in institutions to their generally lower intelligence—a characteristic associated with excess genetic material provided by the presence of extra Y *or* extra X chromosomes (Witkin et al., 1976).

Gonadal Development

The influence of chromosomes on sexual differentiation appears to be most important during the sixth week of development, when the indifferent gonad begins the process of either male or female organization. At this point, if a Y chromosome is present, it promotes the synthesis of a protein called the H-Y antigen, which, among other things, helps the gonad to differentiate into an embryonic testis—the male sex gland. If no Y chromosome is present, the gonadal tissue begins, in later weeks, to differentiate into an ovary, the second step in female development.

Hormones

Once the gonads are formed, they begin to secrete the sex hormones. The rest of the process of sexual differentiation is directed by these hormones, chemical substances secreted into the bloodstream and carried to every cell of the body.

In the developing male embryo, the testis synthesizes testosterone, part of a group of chemically similar male hormones called androgens. Testosterone influences the male reproductive tract, the Wolffian duct system, to begin developing. At the same time, the testis secretes a hormone called the Müllerian Inhibiting Substance (MIS), which causes the female duct system to degenerate and disappear.

In the developing female embryo, the ovary begins to secrete the hormones estrogen and progesterone. The male duct system degenerates and the female system develops to form the internal organs of the female reproductive system. Exactly what controls this process in females is not known. Scientists have traditionally believed it is the absence of testosterone rather than the presence of estrogens that accounts for female differentiation at this stage, but recently more attention has been focused on the role of the ovarian hormones (Fausto-Sterling, 1985).

Although the androgens are often called male hormones and the estrogens and progesterone are called female hormones, individuals of either sex can synthesize these hormones. All three hormones can be produced in the ovaries, testes, or adrenal glands. Researchers who assayed the concentrations of two androgens, two estrogens, and progesterone from the umbilical cord blood of infants at birth found that the concentration of only one of these hormones, testosterone, differed for female and male infants. The level of the estrogens and progesterone actually varied more according to birth order than sex: firstborns of both sexes had higher levels of all three than did laterborns (Maccoby, Doering, Jacklin, & Kraemer, 1979).

At puberty, the sex hormones are responsible for the development of secondary sex characteristics such as breast development for females and beard growth and muscular development for males. It is the phenomenon of muscle growth in response to testosterone that motivates athletes—both male and female—to take steroids, despite their negative side effects. The extent to which hormonal influence extends beyond the anatomical differentiation of the sexes and into the realm of behavior is an issue that has generated much research and controversy. It will be addressed in detail later in the chapter.

Internal Reproductive Tract

In males, the androgens secreted by the embryonic testis organize the internal ducts into the male reproductive tract: vas deferens, epididymis, seminal vesicles, urethra, and prostate. Meanwhile, the MIS causes the still-present female ducts to atrophy. In females, the male ducts atrophy, while a female reproductive tract—Fallopian tubes, uterus, and vagina—develops from the female ducts.

External Genitalia

The external genitals of the male and female differentiate from the same basic structure, as shown in Figure 5.2. Until the eighth week of fetal life, the external genital appearance of both sexes is identical, and the genitals can differentiate in either direction. In males, under the influence of testosterone, the genital tubercle develops into a penis and the labioscrotal swelling becomes a scrotum. In females, by the twelfth week, the genital tubercle has turned into a clitoris, while the labioscrotal swelling has become the lips of the vagina. Female development at this stage has been attributed to

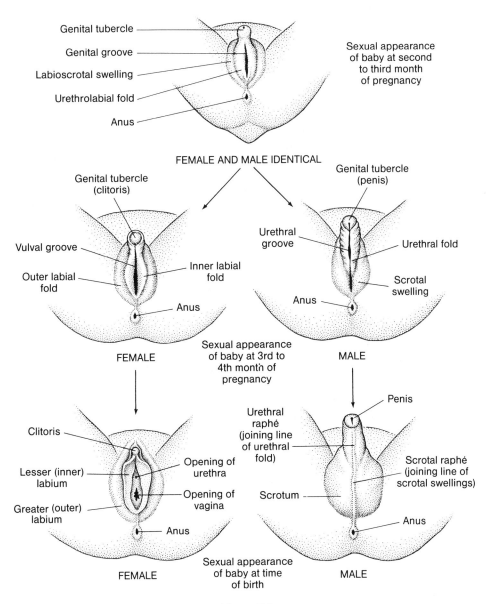

Genital tubercle
Genital groove
Labioscrotal swelling
Urethrolabial fold
Anus

Sexual appearance
of baby at second
to third month
of pregnancy

FEMALE AND MALE IDENTICAL

Genital tubercle
(clitoris)

Vulval groove

Outer labial
fold

Inner labial
fold

Anus

FEMALE

Genital tubercle
(penis)

Urethral
groove

Urethral fold

Scrotal
swelling

Anus

MALE

Sexual appearance
of baby at 3rd to
4th month of
pregnancy

Clitoris

Lesser (inner)
labium

Greater (outer)
labium

Opening of
urethra

Opening of
vagina

Anus

FEMALE

Penis

Urethral
raphé
(joining line
of urethral
fold)

Scrotal raphé
(joining line of
scrotal swellings)

Scrotum

Anus

MALE

Sexual appearance
of baby at time
of birth

Figure 5.2
Three stages of external genital differentiation in the human fetus. (From *Man and Woman,
Boy and Girl* by John Money and Anke A. Ehrhardt, Baltimore: The Johns Hopkins
University Press, 1972, p. 44. © 1972 by The Johns Hopkins University Press.
All rights reserved. Reprinted by permission of the publisher.)

the absence of testosterone, but the possible role of the estrogens or progesterone in the development of the genitals has not been explored.

Brain

"How Female Is Your Brain?" asks the headline of a recent *Washington Post* article (Moir & Jessel, 1991). The ten-item test includes queries about how well you can remember a song you recently heard, how likely it is that you would detect a clandestine affair between two of your friends, and how likely you would be to try to back your car into a tight parking space. Can the answers to such questions really tell us anything about the femaleness of our brains? According to the questionnaire authors, the answer is yes—female and male brains are better at different things because of the way they are organized, and that organization is the direct result of the early process of sexual differentiation: "What gives us a male or a female brain is the degree to which our embryonic brains are exposed to male hormone. The die is cast *in utero*; after that, the luggage of our bodies, and society's expectations of us, merely supplement this biological fact of life" (Moir & Jessel, 1991, p. K3).

Is it really true that hormone levels *in utero* somehow fix the brain in a male or female organization, in the same way as they determine the development of the genitals as male or female? Genital differences between females and males are obvious; brain differences are far less so. In light of the transactional perspective on the biology–environment relationship discussed in Chapter 3, the notion that everything that comes after a critical exposure to hormones before birth is merely "supplemental" to an essential biological fact is absurdly simplistic. However, that is not to say, necessarily, that prenatal hormone levels make no contribution to the brain organization of the developing fetus. Animal studies suggest that, in some species, sex hormone levels present at a critical prenatal or postnatal period *do* influence the development of the brain. In rats, exposure to testosterone at a critical period just after birth results in a subsequent sensitivity of the brain to male hormones and an insensitivity to female ones (Levine, 1966). This differential sensitivity is demonstrated in the response of the mature animal to hormone injections. For example, if testosterone is injected into a newborn female rat, the rat's normal female sexual receptivity behavior seems to be permanently lost. In adulthood, she fails to show the usual female response even when given large replacement injections of female hormones. Moreover, she tends to show extremes of *male* sexual behavior, including the motions associated with ejaculation, when injected with testosterone.

Research on rats also indicates that early hormonal exposure affects the part of the brain, the hypothalamus, that controls the pattern of release of gonadotrophins by the pituitary gland (Levine, 1966). The gonadotrophins, in turn, control the secretion of the sex hormones by the gonads. The presence of testosterone during a critical period causes a noncyclic pattern of hormone release to develop, while the absence of testosterone causes the development of the characteristically female pattern of cyclic release of hormones and the occurrence of ovulation at regular, fairly predictable intervals.

The findings for animals led to speculation that the human brain too may be affected by sex hormone levels at critical periods. However, the relevance of the animal literature to humans is limited in this area since human behavior is, in general, more subject to learning and the social environment and less governed by hormones than is that of animals lower on the phylogenetic scale. We can conclude little about human hormone–brain–behavior relationships from such relationships in animals. Thus far, the impact of prenatal and early postnatal hormone levels on the developing human brain remains an area of research and controversy. It has not been demonstrated that early exposure to androgens is the critical factor in establishing the pattern of hormone release in humans (Herbert, 1976). Nonetheless, it has been suggested that the presence of testosterone at critical periods of differentiation might "masculinize" the nervous system, organizing it so that the individual is predisposed or prepared to learn specifically masculine patterns of behavior. It is not clear *how* testosterone might act to differentiate the brains of human males and females, nor is there any certainty about the timing of the critical period, if there is one. Researchers have discovered that there is a sex difference in one part, now labeled the sexually dimorphic nucleus (SDN), of the preoptic area of the hypothalamus that becomes noticeable after the age of 2 to 4 years (Breathnach, 1990; Swaab & Hofman, 1988). However, the implications of this difference are not yet clear.

Do Physical Sex Differences Have Implications for Behavior?

Animal Studies

If there is any truth to the notion that the presence of testosterone at a critical differentiation period "masculinizes" the central nervous system so that the individual is predisposed to learn certain particularly masculine behaviors, then an animal who is injected with testosterone during the critical period should later show more "masculine" behaviors than one who was not. Some animal studies using this method have provided support for a link between critical period testosterone administration or removal and nonsexual behaviors such as rough-and-tumble play and threat.

A group of researchers (Goy, 1968, 1970; Phoenix, Goy, & Resko, 1968) found that young female rhesus monkeys whose mothers had been injected with testosterone during pregnancy showed more play initiation, rough-and-tumble play, threats, and chasing behavior than did normal females. These findings suggest that hormones may indeed, through action on the developing brain, influence behavior. However, the extent of the testosterone effect is difficult to assess, for two reasons. First, behavioral differences are ascertained through direct observation of the animals by investigators who cannot help but be aware of each animal's condition. Although this procedure probably has no serious effect on the measurement of gross and dramatic behavior differences, it may possibly have a biasing effect on the interpretation of more subtle ones. Second, animals castrated or treated with testosterone during early development may well differ in appearance, and even in smell, from their normal same-sex peers. Goy's androgenized female monkeys, for example, each had a scrotum and a penis. It is possible that their difference in appearance affected their treatment by their cohorts—accounting, perhaps, for at least some of their deviation from expected female behavior.

Human Studies

Humans depend greatly on the learning process in the development of behavior patterns. Our behavior is largely mediated by cognitive factors: our thoughts about the meanings of objects and actions. Also, human social organization is complex. These factors make physiological influences on human behavior difficult to isolate and interpret. The presence of strong social-environmental pressures toward behavioral gender differences is always a confounding factor in the assessment of physiological effects. Also, for ethical reasons, researchers cannot experiment with the hormone balance in human fetuses. Attempts to address the question of the behavioral implications of physical sexual differentiation in humans have thus been, of necessity, limited and not entirely conclusive.

Three major hypotheses, based on the early evidence, guided research on the behavioral impact of biological sex differences (Baker, 1980):

1. *Gender-role behavior* is influenced, in some respects, by the prenatal hormonal environment.
2. *Gender identity* is determined, not by chromosomes or hormonal influence, but by rearing. Furthermore, there is a critical period, between 18 and 24 months of age, after which it is very difficult or impossible to reassign a child successfully to the other gender.
3. *Sexual orientation* is determined more by rearing than by chromosomal, gonadal, or hormonal factors.

Most data on the effects of prenatal hormones on human development and behavior have come from the study of people whose sexual differentiation was disrupted *in utero* by hormonal imbalance. Such individuals, known as pseudohermaphrodites, form less than 1 percent of the population but have been extensively studied over the past three decades. The hormonal imbalance can be the result of drugs administered to the pregnant mother, stress experienced by her, or a glandular malfunction of genetic origin. As a result of the prenatal hormonal disruption, the individual is born with the sexual anatomy incompletely differentiated. For instance, a pseudohermaphroditic baby may be born with ambiguous external genitalia, or with genitalia incongruous with internal reproductive structures. By studying the behavioral and personality concomitants of the many varieties of human pseudohermaphroditism, investigators have hoped to discover the connection between specific aspects of physiological sex and behavior.

What happens to an infant whose sex at birth is ambiguous? In our society, an individual's sex is not allowed to remain ambiguous; it is thought crucial to assign the child as male or female as quickly as possible—even if that assignment is fairly arbitrary—and to provide treatment (drugs and/or surgery) that will help the child's body fit the assigned identity. To help make the assignment of identity as definite as possible, doctors routinely tell parents that an infant whose sex appears indeterminate is "really" male or female and simply needs corrective treatment to bring all bodily features in line with the "correct" sex (Kessler, 1990). However, the determination of sex assignment is not based on discovering the child's "true" sex (since the child possesses a mixture of sexual characteristics and is thus truly intersexual). Rather, it is based on an assessment of how well, given the physical characteristics present at birth and the possibilities for treatment, the child will be able to function as a female or male in later life. Such an assessment is necessarily based on sociocultural assumptions surrounding gender. For instance, in the late nineteenth century, women's ability to bear children was viewed as their essential characteristic. In that period, the presence or absence of ovaries was often the determining factor in assigning gender to hermaphroditic individuals. Current thinking, perhaps because of the emphasis on sexuality in our culture, appears to privilege the importance of external genital anatomy over internal reproductive organs. An infant with a normal-appearing penis would likely be reared as a male, even if normal female internal reproductive structures were present (Kessler, 1990)—because the alternative of surgically removing the penis is disturbing to physicians and parents.

We have little information, then, about what would happen to hermaphroditic children if they were left to grow up in our society with ambiguous sex assignment. Most of the research discussed in the following sections deals with individuals who did receive some form of treatment or intervention because of their ambiguous sex.

Gender-Role Behavior

Elevated Prenatal Androgens.   Studies of pseudohermaphroditic individuals have covered a wide range of disorders, and the interested reader is referred to reviews by Baker (1980), Hines (1982), Ehrhardt (1985), and to an important summary work by two pioneers in the field, John Money and Anke Ehrhardt (1972). Their most frequently cited set of studies deals with the effects of a specific hormonal problem: the adrenogenital syndrome (AGS). This syndrome, which is genetically transmitted, causes the adrenal glands of the fetus to malfunction. The malfunction results in a release of excess androgens from the prenatal period onward, thus setting the stage for a variety of masculinizing effects. Girls with AGS are born with masculinized genitalia, but the internal reproductive organs are female. If the syndrome is diagnosed at birth, these girls receive surgery to feminize their genitals and are placed on lifelong cortisone therapy to compensate for the continuing adrenal malfunction. These individuals, then, are in some respects comparable to the genetically female animals who were experimentally exposed to androgens during the early critical period of central nervous system differentiation. Boys with AGS are born with a normal masculine appearance. However, they too must be treated with cortisone, or the extra output of androgen will cause their puberty to occur years early.

If the presence of significant amounts of androgens during a prenatal critical period causes the brain and central nervous system to differentiate in a masculine direction, children with AGS might be expected to show evidence of this effect. Two early studies examined children born with this syndrome for signs of masculinization of behavior and personality. In both cases, the sample is small and covers an age range of young children to middle adolescence, so the reliability of the findings is difficult to assess. Nonetheless, the results of the two studies are quite consistent, and they provide us with some clues about possible effects of prenatal androgenization on humans.

The first study (Ehrhardt & Money, 1967, described in Money & Ehrhardt, 1972) compared 25 fetally androgenized girls (15 with AGS and 10 who had been androgenized by progestin taken by their mothers during pregnancy) with a control group of

25 normal girls, matched on the basis of age, IQ, socioeconomic background, and race. Data were collected by interviewing each girl and her mother, using a standard format. On the basis of the interviews, several significant differences were found between the two groups. The fetally androgenized girls were more likely to regard themselves as tomboys, tended to have a higher preference for athletic energy expenditure and for joining boys in energetic play, preferred practical rather than pretty clothes, showed less interest in dolls, and showed relatively more interest in a career and less in marriage than did the control girls. No differences were found in several other dimensions such as aggression, lesbianism, enjoyment of personal adornment such as jewelry and perfume, and observable amount of sexual play or interest. These interesting findings cannot be accepted uncritically, however. Data were collected by interview, and the interviewers apparently were not blind to the diagnostic category (androgenized vs. nonandrogenized) of the girls they were questioning. Thus, the possibility of unintentional researcher bias cannot be excluded. Furthermore, no observational data were collected, so that the conclusions rest heavily on self-report. Some critics have also noted that many variables are confounded with exposure to excess prenatal androgens in the AGS children. The social environments of the two groups may have been different. The families of the androgenized girls may have been affected by the birth of an "abnormal" child, and the girls may have received special treatment because of parental guilt over their condition or expectation of a tendency toward masculinity. Also, these children must take regular doses of cortisone to counteract the effects of the excess androgens. In adults, cortisone treatment can cause mood elevation and hyperactivity; thus, there may be reason to suspect that the differences between AGS children and controls were caused by the cortisone rather than the prenatal androgen exposure (Fausto-Sterling, 1985). Finally, the girls themselves, who were aware of their condition, may have felt they had more excuse than their counterparts to behave in a masculine way.

A second study (Ehrhardt & Baker, 1974) was designed to take account of some of the criticisms mentioned. In this investigation, 17 females and 10 males with AGS were compared with their unaffected same-sex siblings and parents. Thus, the possibility of general family differences between androgenized and control children was removed. Also, the inclusion of males in the study allowed for a broader examination of early androgen effects. Data were still collected through interviews, however, with interviewers aware of the diagnostic category of their subjects. This study found several differences between androgenized girls and their unaffected sisters and mothers: The androgenized girls were more often described by themselves and their families as having a high level of intense physical energy expenditure and showing a preference for boys over girls as playmates. Girls with AGS were less likely to show an interest in dolls or infants or to daydream or role-play about marriage or motherhood than were their sisters or their mothers during childhood. No differences between the groups were found on career interest. Significantly more of the AGS girls identified themselves as having been tomboys during all of their childhood, preferred functional clothing over clothing considered attractive for girls at that time, and showed low interest in jewelry, makeup, and hair styles. Despite these differences from their sisters and mothers, however, the androgenized girls were clearly identified in the female role and were not unhappy with being girls. Their behavior was not considered abnormal by themselves or their families, but followed a pattern of tomboyism that is quite acceptable for girls in this culture. Interestingly, a follow-up of this sample of girls when their mean age was 16 years showed that about half of them had become much more interested in their appearance, in self-grooming, and in dressing attractively (Ehrhardt & Baker, 1976).

For the males in this study, only one difference was found. Boys with AGS were more often reported as showing a long-term high energy expenditure level in sports and rough outdoor activities than were their brothers.

In this study, the investigators intensively interviewed parents to determine whether they had any ambivalence or anxiety about their AGS offspring's sexuality—anxiety that might be manifested in differential treatment. They were able to uncover none. Similarly, their interviews with the girls themselves revealed no significant, persistent concern with being "born different." The accuracy of these findings is difficult to ascertain because of the possibility of interviewer bias and evaluation apprehension on the part of the subjects.

On the whole, the two studies show results that are reasonably consistent: Girls in the AGS groups more often than control girls were described as showing behavior such as high energy expenditure, tomboyism, preference for functional over attractive clothing, and low interest in and rehearsal for marriage and motherhood roles. Since these are behaviors on which groups of normal boys and girls are thought to differ, on the average, the tentative conclusion has been drawn that prenatal androgenization, through action on the developing brain, masculinizes behavior. "Masculinizes" may not, however, be the most appropriate word. As Kaplan (1980) notes, the behavior of the AGS girls seems more androgynous—a combination of femininity and masculinity—than masculine. More problematic than the terminology used, though, is the confounding of the effects of prenatal androgenization with a number of other variables: cortisone treatment, knowledge of being different, parental attitudes, and behavior. The virtual impossibility of separating out the hormonal effects from these confounding variables means that conclusions about the impact of prenatal androgenization on behavior must be tentative at best.

What if the correlation between high levels of prenatal androgens and high levels of physically active play behavior in childhood does reflect a process whereby variations in hormone levels before birth predispose an individual to physically active play? Researchers who accept this explanation argue that it does not mean that behavior is mechanically predetermined by hormones:

> A predisposition possibly related to prenatal androgens simply means a greater likelihood of developing a certain behavior pattern. Whether and how the behavior will be expressed depends on the socialization process after birth. Girls who have a predisposition to physically active play behavior may frequently join boys rather than girls in active outdoor play. They are also more likely to be called tomboys. However, this will occur only if they grow up in a family and a large social context that permits and encourages this type of behavior for girls. If, on the other hand, the environment imposes a greater degree of sex stereotyping and explicitly discourages physically active play behavior in girls, the original predisposition may not be expressed at all or may lead to maladjustment and unhappiness. (Ehrhardt, 1985, pp. 45–46)

Androgen Insensitivity.   Some individuals who are genetically male have a genetically transmitted disorder that makes their cells partially or completely unable to respond to their high prenatal levels of androgens. They may be born with female or ambiguous external genitalia and are thus frequently reared as females. Studies of such individuals indicate that their gender-role behaviors are consistent with their sex of rearing (Masica, Money, & Ehrhardt, 1971; Money & Ogunro, 1974). When reared as females, these genetic males show no sign of the "masculinized" behavior patterns reported for the AGS girls. Once again, potential problems of observer bias and confounding variables make these findings difficult to interpret. The case of Maria Patino, described in the opening paragraph of this chapter, is that of an individual who is androgen-insensitive.

Elevated Prenatal Progesterone.   If prenatal exposure to androgens might possibly "masculinize" behavior, what about prenatal exposure to female hormones? Some research on individuals whose mothers were treated with progesterone during pregnancy hints that such exposure could have a "feminizing" effect on behavior. One double-blind study of 20 male teenagers who had been exposed prenatally to progesterone reported that these males were less assertive and aggressive, had decreased athletic coordination, fewer "masculine" interests, and less heterosexual experience than controls (Yalom, Green, & Fisk, 1973). A second study found that progesterone-exposed males had less interest in dating and marriage than did those in a matched control group, while progesterone-exposed females had less interest in tomboyish behavior and more interest in their appearance than did controls (Zussman, Zussman, & Dalton, 1975). In this research as well, there are possible confounds of hormonal exposure with other variables since mothers taking progesterone during pregnancy were usually doing so because of diabetes or some other risk factor; thus, the hormone-exposed boys were probably also products of more stressful pregnancies than the controls.

In all of the research cited here, the most basic difficulty in determining physiological influences on human gender-role behavior is that there are simply no clear, agreed-upon criteria concerning which behaviors are male and which are female; in most areas there is an enormous degree of overlap between the behavior of the two sexes. We cannot say for people, as we can for rats, for instance, that male sexual behavior always follows a certain pattern, beginning with mounting the female! Indeed, the range of male sexual behavior patterns that we would call both "masculine" and "normal" is wide enough that a change brought about by hormones would have to be very dramatic to capture our attention. Similarly, the tomboyish behavior of the AGS females in the foregoing studies would almost certainly have gone unnoticed had it not been specifically sought, since it falls well within the range of normal female behavior in this culture. In fact, the majority of girls and women report themselves to have been tomboys at some time during childhood (Hyde, Rosenberg, & Behrman, 1974).

If sex hormones, through their influence on the fetal brain, do produce the substrata for gender-role behavioral differences, these substrata merely provide basic predispositions that interact with environmental forces. Such interactions can produce a variety of behavioral outcomes. For instance, as noted by Ehrhardt (1985), though it is plausible that higher androgen levels affect the brain, predisposing boys to exhibit more physically active play, the socialization process widens this gap through a complex interaction of many factors. Being reinforced for physically active play, as boys more often are than girls, may encourage competition in active sports, which may in turn foster a competitive orientation, assertiveness, leadership skills, and dominance. The sex hormone difference may affect a specific, limited aspect of behavior, such as the threshold for expression of physically energetic play; however, this difference may be amplified and made more important by a variety of other factors.

Gender Identity

Gender identity is the individual's private experience of his or her gender: the concept of the self as male or female. This is such a powerful and important part of a person's self-concept that in most adults it is virtually impossible to change it. (If you don't believe this, try for a moment to think of yourself as still "you," but as the other sex.) Yet research indicates that physiological sexual differentiation notwithstanding, we are not born with a gender identity: It develops after birth.

Money and Ehrhardt (1972) describe a case in which a 7-month-old boy was the victim of a surgical accident that destroyed his penis. The boy had been normal in every respect, but the loss of the penis resulted in a decision by his parents to reassign his sex as female and to rear him as a girl. At the age of 17 months, the child's name, clothing, and hairstyle were changed to fit feminine norms, and surgery to feminize the genitals was undertaken shortly thereafter. Because the child had an identical twin brother, it became possible to compare the way in which two children with exactly the same genetic and prenatal background developed when one was assigned and reared as a boy and the other as a girl.

For this particular case, the records show that the child who was reassigned as a girl quickly developed typical feminine interests and behavior, whereas the other child maintained his masculine patterns. Moreover, the girl clearly thought of herself as a girl, whereas the boy's self-concept was unambiguously masculine. Thus, the gender identity of each child was apparently shaped by the sex of assignment and rearing more than by genetic or other physiological determinants.

A number of studies have compared the gender identities of pseudohermaphroditic individuals with the same physiological indicators of sex who were assigned and reared differently, either as females or as males. In most cases, gender identity develops consistent with the sex of assignment and rearing, as long as the assignment is made by between the child's eighteenth and twenty-fourth month of life and the parents communicate no ambiguity or doubt about the child's sex. The AGS girls discussed in the previous section all formed female gender identities. In cases of AGS where genetically female individuals have been reared as males, however, they form a male gender identity (Money & Daley, 1977). Similarly, among the subjects with a history of androgen insensitivity, almost all formed a gender identity concordant with their sex of rearing. In the same vein, the males with a history of prenatal exposure to progesterone had no difficulty with maintaining a male gender identity. On the whole, the evidence strongly suggests that people form their gender identities according to whether, from an early age, they are labeled and treated as males or females.

Once formed, how resistant to change is a person's gender identity? There is some controversy around this question. Early research showed fairly consistently that gender identity was "set" very early in life and thereafter could not usually be altered successfully. Some of the most dramatic findings in this respect were reported by Hampson and Hampson (1961), who studied 31 AGS females. In these patients, the syndrome had not been treated at birth, so that they continued to be exposed to excess androgens postnatally. Thus, they had grown from childhood with masculine-appearing genitalia, and had a tendency to develop male secondary sex characteristics at puberty. They had been raised as girls, however, by parents who had been told their daughters were genetically female. Despite the problems these girls must have had in coping with their paradoxical appearance, however, all but five of them established an unambivalently female gender identity. This identity did not change even when male secondary sex characteristics began to develop at puberty.

The study of a population of male pseudohermaphrodites in the Dominican Republic, cited at the beginning of this chapter, has challenged the conclusion that gender identity, once formed, is virtually irreversible in later life (Imperato-McGinley, Guerrero et al., 1974; Imperato-McGinley, Peterson et al., 1979). Imperato-McGinley and her coworkers identified a group of male pseudohermaphrodites whose condition was caused by a genetically transmitted enzyme defect that interfered with the body's ability to use testosterone for sexual differentiation. These genetic males were born with ambiguous genitalia—a clitoris-like phallus and an incompletely developed scrotum—and many of them had been reared as girls. Of 18 subjects who had been reared as females and for whom adequate interview data were collected, 17 had changed to a male gender identity at adolescence. These individuals recalled feeling different from other girls as they approached adolescence, usually because of physical differences. Their change in gender identity occurred gradually, paralleling to some extent the development of male secondary sex characteristics. Most of these subjects also successfully adopted the male gender role, and developed sexual relationships with women.

The findings of the Imperato-McGinley team were startling because they appeared to fly in the face of the notion that gender identity was "set" in the second to third year of life. A closer look at the research reveals, however, that the individuals studied by these researchers probably had not consolidated a female gender identity during childhood because they had not been unambiguously reared as females. In the first place, these children cannot have been regarded by their parents as proper girls since they did not possess a vagina and were thus incapable of intercourse and childbearing. In their village societies, where the feminine role was strongly focused around marriage and the bearing and rearing of children, these "girls" would have great difficulty finding a satisfactory niche. In the second place, the genetic disorder affecting these children was apparently common enough in this small society to have acquired a name. Affected children were labeled "guevote" (penis at twelve) or "machihembra" (first woman, then man). Such labels reflect an expectation that gender will change, and this expectation may have been incorporated into the developing child's sense of gender identity. It is unlikely, then, that the individuals met the criterion of unambiguous rearing as girls that would have been necessary for them to form a solid female gender identity in early childhood.

The controversy surrounding the Imperato-McGinley findings arose, not just because of the unusual reports of individuals changing gender identity at adolescence, but also because of the interpretation the authors gave for this change. They argued that the change to a male gender identity reflected biological predispositions based on prenatal androgen influences on the brain. In other words, these individuals had "masculinized" brains because of their exposure to male hormones *in utero* and, when their social environment allowed it, their brains were "activated" by the upsurge of testosterone at puberty into a readiness to adopt a male gender identity. Thus, these researchers used their findings to argue that gender identity is biologically determined.

While appearance and behavior are susceptible to hormonal influence, identity seems more likely to be socially constructed—though it might well be affected by appearance and behavior, and by the masculine or feminine labels applied to them. As discussed in earlier chapters, the very categories "female" and "male" are social constructions, agreed-upon classifications with characteristics assigned, to some extent, by social consensus. It is known, for example, that some groups, such as the Mandaya of the Philippines, have languages that do not use gender distinctions and use occupation or status rather than gender as ways of classifying people or activities (Yengoyan, 1982). It is difficult to believe, then, that brain organization directly predisposes an individual to adopt one or the other of these socially constructed gender identities. Yet, the findings of this study are challenging and provocative. They suggest that gender identity may be more fluid than once thought, evolving and becoming reintegrated as the individual develops. They raise more questions about the conceivable role of prenatal or postnatal hormones in affecting the brain's possible "predisposition" toward maleness or femaleness (Baker, 1980). However, the environmental and biological factors leading up to the observed shift in gender identity are so confounded with each other that there are no grounds for accepting the findings as proof that gender identity is biologically determined. Furthermore, studies of children in the United States who are affected by the same enzyme defect indicate that, in this cultural context, the children reared as females maintain their female gender identity, even after the development of male characteristics at puberty (Rubin, Reinisch, & Haskett, 1981). Clearly, there is much that is yet to be discovered about the process of gender identity formation, but the evidence is weighted heavily against the notion that gender identity is determined in any automatic way by hormones.

Transsexualism.   Over the last two decades, several individuals in the public eye have made headlines by going through surgical procedures to change their sex assignment. James Morris, a well-known writer and reporter, chose to become Jan Morris and told the story of the transition from male to female in a best-seller called *Conundrum* (1974). Renee Richards, playing on the female professional tennis circuit, created doubts and protests because she had previously been a man playing on the male circuit. What mysterious process would cause an adult with a settled, stable life to want to change his or her sex?

A transsexual is a person—male or female—who firmly believes that she or he was born with the body of the wrong sex. This conviction dates from early childhood, usually as far back as the person can remember. It is usually not amenable to change through life experiences, rewards for "normal" behavior, or therapy (Green, 1974). Transsexualism is an extreme form of "gender dysphoria" (Fisk, 1973), or discontent with one's biological sex. To all appearances, a transsexual has acquired the *wrong* gender identity, and, once acquired, this identity seems to be virtually unchangeable. Such individuals may lead lives that are outwardly congruent with their anatomical sex, but their conviction that their body is wrong for them is often strong enough to cause them to seek surgery in order to change it. Thus, a male-to-female transsexual may achieve a body congruent with a feminine self-image by taking regular doses of estrogen to acquire female secondary sex characteristics and having a vagina surgically constructed from the penile tissue. A female-to-male transsexual, on the other hand, may take male hormone treatments and have surgery to construct a makeshift penis. Of course, in neither case is chromosomal sex changed; the individual remains genetically male or female despite surgically and hormonally wrought changes in appearance.

A transsexual who is seeking surgery must convince doctors that she or he is reasonably emotionally stable. Then, before any surgery is performed, the transsexual is required to spend a significant period living the life of the other gender, adopting the appearance and mannerisms associated with that gender. The rationale for this requirement is to ensure that the individual will be comfortable in the new identity. Some critics have suggested, however, that by promising the surgery only to those people who can successfully live as members of the other gender, doctors are acting as agents of social control, promoting gender-stereotypic behavior by their clients (Raymond, 1979). During the one- to two-year trial period, transsexuals receive hormones to begin changing their bodies. A male is treated with estrogen to stimulate breast development, smoother skin, and reduced muscularity. A female takes testosterone to suppress menstruation and cause the growth of facial and body hair. After the trial period, if surgery is judged appropriate, a male-to-female transsexual has the penis and testicles removed and external female genitals constructed. The female-to-male transsexual has the breasts removed, and a penis is constructed from abdominal skin. Depending on the surgical method used, this penis may be semierect and may or may not be sexually sensitive.

There is much controversy over the benefits of sex-reassignment surgery. Some studies of postoperative transsexuals have found high levels of satisfaction with the surgery and the new life (Blanchard, Steiner, & Clemmensen, 1985; Pauly, 1968). Critics have charged, however, that such an outcome is comparable to the satisfaction neurotics feel when allowed to carry out their obsessive behavior, or that addicts feel when allowed access to their drug; it does not justify such drastic surgery. Defenders of the treatment argue that, within a medical framework, no other methods have been found effective for reducing the distress transsexuals experience (Blanchard et al., 1985). One interesting outcome of sex reassignment may be a change in economic status. Blanchard (1985) found evidence that taking on the male role was correlated with superior economic status for females, while reorientation in a female direction was associated with inferior economic status for males. Being male, no matter how it is achieved, is apparently associated with a higher income.

The origin of the transsexual's conviction of being born into the wrong sex remains a mystery. Suggestions that it may have a physiological basis have received no support since these individuals appear to be normally sexually differentiated and not pseudohermaphroditic in any sense. Bardwick (1971) proposed that the prenatal sexual differentiation of the brain in transsexuals may have proceeded in the wrong direction, causing their gender identity to differ from their anatomical sex. This explanation has never been supported, however, and it seems inadequate, given that transsexuals have generally been found not to differ physiologically from the rest of the population (Green, 1974) and that pseudohermaphrodites usually form a gender identity congruent with their sex of assignment and rearing.

Consistent patterns of socialization and rearing associated with transsexualism have also been hard to identify. Green (1974) reports that the parents of some of his transsexual patients appear to have wanted a child of the other sex and may have communicated this to the child at a young age, but this pattern is not *always* found. Although psychoanalytic theory might propose that the transsexual identified with the wrong parent at the Oedipal stage, there is little evidence with which to support or reject this notion. Social learning theory, which might suggest that the transsexual's difficulty had been caused by rewards for performing the behaviors of the other sex, does not easily explain why the transsexual often lives a successful life consistent with his or her anatomical sex while remaining firmly convinced that his or her gender identity is different. The cognitive developmental approach might interpret transsexualism as due to a child's initial faulty learning of the male–female concept or a mistaken gender categorization of the self at a critical period. It does not, however, suggest what forces might bring about such faulty learning.

Some writers have speculated that transsexualism is an outcome of the social definition and construction of gender roles. Raymond (1979), for example, notes that male-to-female transsexuals frequently adopt an exaggerated version of feminine role behavior, becoming more stereotypically feminine than most women. This tendency may be based on an extremely rigid view of masculine and feminine gender roles. Perhaps, Raymond suggests, if each sex were allowed greater latitude in terms of what behavior was considered appropriate for their gender role, individuals would not feel the need to change their bodies to match their behavioral preferences. There is, in fact, some evidence that in societies that allow for gender-role categories other than the usual male and female, individuals can sometimes live outside the limits of strict masculinity or femininity without feeling dissatisfied with their bodies. For example, Wikan (1977) describes a "third gender" in the Arab state of Oman, the *xanith*. The *xanith* are biologically men, but they do not adopt the traditional male role. They work as homosexual prostitutes and as skilled domestic servants. They have male names, adopt dress and hairstyles that are distinct from those of both men and women, and can, with impunity, violate the restrictions of *purdah,* the cultural system of female seclusion. Thus, they may speak with women on the street and see a woman's unveiled face. In addition, Wikan reports, the *xanith* are not irrevocably stuck in their role; they can adopt the male role simply by getting married and proving themselves able to perform heterosexual intercourse. Perhaps the existence of this third gender-role option undercuts the development in some men of an urgent sense that their bodies are wrong and must be changed.

The unanswered questions surrounding transsexualism illustrate the extent of our ignorance about how gender identity develops. Although on the one hand individuals with ambiguous sexual differentiation often hold firmly to the gender identity consonant with their assigned sex despite contradictory signals from their bodies, on the other, transsexuals refuse the gender to which they were assigned, even though it matches their bodies.

Sexual Orientation

Sexual orientation, the degree of erotic responsiveness to the other sex (heterosexuality) or to one's own sex (homosexuality) is a third aspect of behavior in which the sexes differ, on average. The available data on pseudohermaphroditic patients suggests that the sex of rearing is one decisive variable in the establishment of this orientation. Studies of AGS females in adolescence found that most of these prenatally androgenized girls developed a heterosexual orientation (Ehrhardt & Baker, 1976; Money & Schwartz, 1977) although a somewhat larger proportion of them than might be expected expressed a homosexual or bisexual preference (Money, Schwartz, & Lewis, 1984). Similarly, androgen-insensitive genetically male individuals reared as females generally were found to adopt a heterosexual orientation; many went on to marry men and adopt babies (Masica, Money, & Ehrhardt, 1971).

Some researchers have argued that there is a genetic component to male homosexuality, citing the finding that brothers of gay males are four to five times more likely than those of heterosexual males to be homosexual or bisexual and that identical twins usually show the same sexual orientation (Pillard & Weinrich, 1986). However, the rarer cases in which identical twins show different sexual orientations indicate that, if there is a genetic predisposition, it works in concert with other factors.

Although no conclusive evidence exists that prenatal hormones contribute to the determination of sexual orientation, some scattered evidence points to at least a possible link between the two. A "gestational neurohormonal" theory of human sexual orientation has been proposed, based on an overview of both animal and human research (Ellis & Ames, 1987). The theory suggests that, in all mammals, sexual orientation is primarily guided by the degree to which the nervous system is exposed to testosterone, estradiol, and other sex hormones while the organization of the brain and central nervous system is taking place (that is, prenatally, for humans). Based primarily on animal research, the theory is nonetheless consistent with certain observations about sexual orientation in humans—for example, the difficulty of altering a person's sexual orientation, the greater prevalence of homosexuality among males than females (based on the notion that sexual differentiation tends in a female direction at each stage unless some masculinizing process occurs), and the still insufficiently documented findings of differences between heterosexual and homosexual men in their bodies' responses to injections of estradiol (Gladue, Green, & Hellman, 1984). It is possible that prenatal hormones can have some effect on predispositions toward heterosexual or homosexual orientations, but the evidence is still far from conclusive, especially given the findings that so many individuals with known prenatal exposure to hormonal abnormalities establish a sexual orientation that follows their sex of rearing. However, hormones may play an indirect role through their effects on body build or gender-role behavior (Meyer-Bahlburg, 1980).

The findings of a recent study have been used to suggest that male homosexuality is correlated with specific aspects of brain organization. LeVay (1991), using brain tissue from autopsies of 41 individuals (19 men identified as homosexual, 16 men identified as heterosexual, and 6 women identified as heterosexual) found that one node of the hypothalamus was, on the average, significantly smaller (similar to the average size for the women) in the homosexual than in the heterosexual men. The sample is small and the correct interpretation of the correlational findings is impossible to determine with certainty. The brain difference, if found to be reliable, could be an effect rather than a cause of sexual orientation, or it could be an anatomical feature that happens to be correlated with homosexuality but does not contribute to it. Despite the headlines that greeted these findings: "Brain May Dictate Sexuality: Differences Found in Critical

Region" (Suplee, 1991), researchers are a long way from identifying the precise ways in which biological factors may contribute to male homosexuality.

As for female homosexuality, its determinants seem even more complex. Some women report that their lesbianism is an aspect of themselves that is beyond their control—something they were born with or that dates back to their early memories. Others describe lesbianism as a choice, often made later in life after considerable heterosexual experience (Golden, 1987). For the latter group, sexual orientation seems to be experienced as more fluid than popular notions of homosexuality–heterosexuality have described. These findings—so recent despite years of research on sexual orientation—remind us that researchers' assumptions often preclude the investigation of certain questions. It has taken psychologists a long time to examine the variations in lesbian experience instead of treating lesbianism as a unidimensional, single-cause phenomenon. The newer findings bring us face to face with the notion that people may not always be so easily classified as homosexual, heterosexual, or bisexual. Furthermore, they remind us of the gaps that remain in scientists' understanding of sexual orientation.

Variations in Normal Development

All males are not hormonally identical, and neither are all females. In fact, there is considerable variation within each sex as to the relative proportions of male and female hormones present in the body at any given developmental stage. This variation is most obvious at puberty, when the release of larger amounts of the appropriate sex hormones in the male or female body results in a more dramatic development of secondary sex characteristics. If hormones influence behavior in any way, then, they may contribute as much to individual differences as to sex differences. As Ehrhardt and Baker (1974) conclude in their report on AGS children:

> If prenatal hormone levels contribute to sex differences in behavior, the effects in human beings are subtle and can in no way be taken as a basis for prescribing social roles. In fact, we rather like to make an argument from the opposite point of view. If it can be documented that prenatal hormone levels are among the factors that account for the wide range of temperamental differences and role aspirations within the female, and possibly also within the male, sex, a great variety of adult roles should be available and can be adequately fulfilled by both women and men, and they should be equally acceptable and respectable for either sex. (p. 50)

Researchers have tried recently to uncover relationships between neonatal hormone levels and characteristics of normal children. They have found that within-sex differences in hormone levels are sometimes as important as sex differences in predicting what children will be like. Jacklin, Maccoby, & Doering (1983) assessed timidity in 6- to 18-month-old children for whom sex hormone levels in umbilical cord blood had been measured at birth. They found marginal male–female differences in timidity, with girls more timid than boys. However, among the boys, neonatal sex hormone levels were significantly related to across-age timidity scores. The higher their levels of progesterone and testosterone had been at birth, the lower was their timidity. On the other hand, boys' neonatal estrogen levels were positively related to later timidity. No relationship between hormone levels and timidity was observed for girls. Other work by these researchers showed that, among children in the first three years of life, simple sex differences in muscular strength were overshadowed by more complex hormonal effects (Jacklin et al., 1984). While there was a small tendency for boys to have higher average strength scores than girls, strength in both girls and boys was negatively related to levels of androstenedione (a male hormone) measured at birth. In addition, neonatal progesterone levels related differently to strength for boys and girls. Girls with high umbilical cord progesterone showed low strength, while boys with high progesterone showed high strength. Researchers do not yet know enough about the prenatal and postnatal action of hormones on the nervous system and the rest of the body to explain these findings, but they seem to bear out Ehrhardt and Baker's (1974) claim that hormones may contribute as much to individual differences as to group differences between females and males.

A note of caution is in order here. The results just cited are correlational; thus, it cannot be stated with any degree of certainty that neonatal hormone levels *caused* differences in timidity or muscular strength. Moreover, it is not even certain that neonatal hormone levels are related to later hormone levels, since hormones were measured only once, at birth. In general, a number of factors aside from sexual differentiation can affect the levels of sex hormones circulating in a person's body. Emotional stress can cause drops in both male and female hormone levels (Archer, 1979; Kreuz, Rose, & Jennings, 1972; Rose, 1969); sexual activity can increase testosterone secretion, as can winning in competition (Gladue, Boechler, & McCaul, 1989), while social isolation, defeat, and unavoidable punishment can decrease it (Ellis, 1982). If there is a causal relationship between hormones and behavior, then, there is no reason to suppose that it is a one-way street.

Aggression

One behavior that researchers have thought might be linked to variations in sex hormone levels is aggression. Controlled experiments with animals and research on humans who have been exposed prenatally to excess androgens suggest a link between prenatal androgen levels and rough-and-tumble play. For example, Goy (1970) found that female rhesus monkeys whose mothers had been injected with male hormones during pregnancy engaged in more rough-and-tumble play and chasing and threatening behaviors than did their female age-mates. Similarly, research on human females who were accidentally exposed to excess androgens *in utero* indicates that these girls may engage in more rough-and-tumble play than other girls (Money & Ehrhardt, 1972), although it is not clear that this difference can be attributed to prenatal hormones. However, even an unambiguous connection between male hormones and rough-and-tumble play would not suffice as proof that aggression is linked to prenatal androgen exposure. Most psychologists define aggression as behavior with intent to injure. Although the AGS children, both girls and boys, were described as more energetic and likely to engage in rough-and-tumble play than their normal counterparts, they were *not* reported to be more aggressive against other children or to initiate or engage in more fights. Across a number of studies of children prenatally exposed to excess androgens, the reporting of an effect on rough-and-tumble play is quite a bit more consistent than the finding of an effect on aggression (Hines, 1982). Indeed, recent research indicates a clear distinction between rough-and-tumble play and aggression (DiPietro, 1981). Children have little trouble distinguishing between playful, mock fighting, which requires a great deal of cooperation, and real aggression, although rough-and-tumble play can lead to aggression through accidental injury or through increased sensitivity to threatening stimuli. If there is a connection between prenatal hormones and aggression, then, it cannot simply be assumed on the basis of a correlation between hormones and rough-and-tumble play.

One study examined the relationship between prenatal hormone exposure and a measure of aggressive orientation (Reinisch, 1981). Boys and girls whose mothers had been treated with various forms of progesterone during pregnancy were compared with their siblings on a test that asked them to choose one of four solutions to each of six common conflict situations. The choices involved physical aggression, verbal aggression, withdrawal, and nonaggressive coping. Boys whose mothers took progesterone during pregnancy were twice as likely as their brothers to choose the physical aggression response; girls whose mothers had taken the hormones chose physical aggression 1.5 times more often than their sisters. These findings are difficult to interpret, but such difficulties are themselves instructive: They show why hasty conclusions can be perilous in this area of research. In the first place, aggressive orientation was linked with exposure to progesterone—a female hormone—while the supposition has always been that it is male hormones that are related to aggression. As it turns out, the type of synthetic progesterone taken by the mothers of some of these children was a chemical that the body apparently converts into testosterone. However, the progesterone taken by some of the other mothers in the sample seems to behave as a female hormone and has been studied by other researchers for its potential feminizing influence (Fausto-Sterling, 1985). Thus, it is not clear that all of the children in this study had been exposed prenatally to masculinizing hormones. In the second place, the average daily dose of progesterone taken by the mothers during pregnancy was a small one, between one-third and one-tenth of the amount being naturally produced by the mother. The mothers' blood hormone levels were not measured, so it is not certain that the treatment significantly raised the already high level of progesterone in the mothers' bloodstream. Given these difficulties, it is far from certain that the differences in aggression-related responding between the two groups of children can be attributed to the fact that one group was exposed to extra progesterone prenatally while the other was not. Fausto-Sterling (1985) suggests an equally plausible explanation: that the mothers who were treated with progesterone during pregnancy were having more difficult than average pregnancies. Women who receive hormone treatments are usually suffering from specific complications or risks during pregnancy, and thus may be experiencing more than the usual stress of pregnancy. Perhaps it is the stress itself, rather than the hormone treatments, that causes the children of such pregnancies to differ from the children of more problem-free pregnancies. The data do not allow us to choose between the two explanations. The evidence for an organizational effect of prenatal exposure to masculinizing hormones on predisposition to later aggression is equivocal.

Taking a different approach to the androgen-aggression connection, some researchers have examined the possible activational effect of testosterone: the relationship between testosterone levels in the blood of adult men and their aggression levels. The assumption that testosterone levels and aggression were related has been so strong until recently that violent male criminals were sometimes castrated as a way to reduce their aggressive tendency. Currently, treatment with synthetic female hormones has replaced surgery for this purpose, but follow-up studies indicate that neither method is particularly effective at reducing violent aggressive behavior (Kling, 1975; Whitehead, 1981).

Studies of normal men, in which both aggression and testosterone levels in the blood have been measured, show mixed results. Some studies show little evidence of a correlation between circulating testosterone levels and aggression (Doering, Brodie, Kramer, Becker, & Hamburg, 1974; Meyer-Bahlburg, Boon, Shavma, & Edwards, 1974; Moyer, 1974), although some studies of male prisoners indicate a positive relationship between testosterone levels and history of arrests or aggressive behavior in prison (Kling, 1975; Kreuz & Rose, 1972) and history of violent crimes (Dabbs, Frady, Carr, & Besch, 1987). One study showed hockey players' testosterone levels were strongly correlated with response to threat when faced with an aggressive situation in a game or practice (Scamarella & Brown, 1978). Positive correlations between testosterone levels and dispositional aggressive tendencies have been found for college-age men (Christiansen & Knussman, 1987) and younger adolescents (Susman et al., 1987).

A recent study of nearly 4500 U.S. male military veterans found that testosterone levels were correlated with a variety of antisocial behaviors: delinquency, drug use, alcohol abuse, military AWOL (Dabbs & Morris, 1990). The relationship between testosterone and these behaviors was considerably weaker in high socioeconomic status than in low socioeconomic status groups, however, indicating that social class moderates the relationship between hormones and behavior. Furthermore, the size of the effect is small; it becomes noticeable mainly at extreme levels of testosterone. Another series of studies, using small samples of men in different occupations, found that actors tended to have higher testosterone levels than ministers (Dabbs, de La Rue, & Williams, 1990). The latter finding proves nothing about aggression per se, but the authors suggest that the two types of occupations are differentiated by the amount of dominance and antisocial tendencies they require. However, the small sample sizes and such inconsistencies as the fact that football players did not differ significantly from physicians or professors in their testosterone levels, cast some doubt on this interpretation.

Three studies suggest that men's levels of testosterone can change in response to victory or defeat in male-male competition. Testosterone levels were found to stay elevated longer among winners than losers of a tennis match, but no such pattern differentiated winners and losers of a lottery (Mazur & Lamb, 1980). Among wrestlers, testosterone levels declined more quickly among losers than among winners (Elias, 1981). And winners of a competition involving computer-driven reaction-time tasks showed higher postcompetition testosterone levels and a slower decline of those levels than did losers (Gladue et al., 1989). These findings are not directly relevant to aggression; however, they suggest the possibility of a link between testosterone and the experience of dominance. Here, though, there is no implication that high testosterone levels cause dominant behavior; rather, it is the experience of prevailing in competition that appears to cause changes in hormone levels.

On the whole, then, the demonstration of a causal connection between circulating levels of male hormones and aggressive behavior is tenuous. The issue begins to seem even more complex when consideration is given to the sheer number of hormones in the human body, many of which vary simultaneously and interact with one another. When the levels of so many different hormones are changing at once, measuring only one of them and focusing on the connection between that particular one and a social behavior such as aggression may well be an overly simplistic approach.

Summary

The biological categories "female" and "male," often thought of as completely discrete, have been shown to have some potential for overlap. Physiological differentiation of the sexes begins at conception with the genetic determination of sex and continues through several stages of fetal development: the differentiation of the gonads, their secretion of sex hormones, and the resulting differentiation of the internal reproductive organs and the external genitalia. In addition, some researchers believe that the sex hormones also have an impact on the developing brain, differentiating it in some respects for males and females. The existence, extent, mechanism, timing, and implications of sexual differentiation of the human brain remain controversial.

Under normal circumstances, the differentiation proceeds in the same direction at every stage, producing an individual who is unambiguously either female or male at birth. However, on rare occasions the process is disrupted, and the individual differentiates as male at some stages and as female at others. Such individuals, called pseudohermaphrodites, are a source of valuable information about the relationship between the physiological and psychological aspects of sex and gender.

Many questions have been raised about the biological bases of sex dimorphic behavior—behavior on which groups of females and males tend to differ. Research using pseudohermaphroditic individuals has focused on three types of behavior: gender-role behavior, gender identity, and sexual orientation. At present, the evidence linking sexual orientation to irregularities in the sexual differentiation process is inconclusive. For gender identity, most of the research suggests that children adopt an identity that is congruent with their sex of assignment and rearing, regardless of biological abnormalities that may tend to contradict it. Researchers believe that, for the latter pattern to hold, sex assignment must be done before the third year of life, and the individual must be reared unambiguously according to the gender to which she or he was assigned. There is more for scientists to learn about gender identity, though, as illustrated by the Imperato-McGinley findings of gender identity shifts in adolescence among one group of male pseudohermaphrodites, and by the puzzling phenomenon of transsexualism. For gender-role behavior, some evidence suggests a connection between prenatal exposure to androgens and such "masculine" behaviors as rough-and-tumble play. However, since early hormonal exposure is usually confounded with other variables, such as continuing cortisone treatments, the awareness of having been born different, and perhaps parental anxiety, the evidence remains equivocal.

Even among normal individuals, both male and female hormones are synthesized by both sexes, and there are wide individual variations in the levels of circulating sex hormones. These variations affect the development of secondary sex characteristics at puberty, and so may affect gender-related behavior indirectly by helping to create a more or less stereotypically masculine or feminine body build and appearance. Studies on muscle strength and timidity in young children suggest that within-sex individual differences in hormone levels at birth may be as important as sex in predicting these qualities. Attempts have been made to relate within-sex differences in male hormone levels to aggression; however, the evidence on this point remains weak. Scientists still have much to learn about biological influences on human behavior in general, and on human sex and gender in particular. Nothing that has been uncovered so far, however, points to chromosomes, hormones, or anatomy as direct unilateral determining factors in gender-role behavior, gender identity, or sexual orientation.

For Additional Reading

Garber, Marjorie. (1991). *Vested interests: Cross-dressing and cultural anxiety.* New York: Routledge. This is a wide-ranging study of transvestism that questions why men sometimes dress as women and vice versa.

Morris, Jan. (1974). *Conundrum.* Scarborough, Ontario: New American Library of Canada. A transsexual journalist who lived a successful life as a man until middle adulthood tells the story of her early life and her transition to a feminine body and gender role.

6
Perceptual & Cognitive Abilities: Gender Similarities & Differences

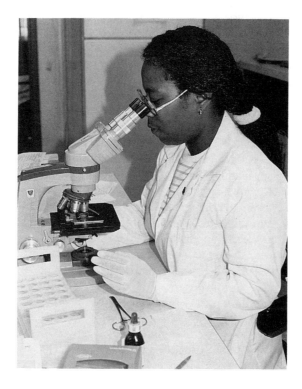

In 1903, James McKeen Cattell, an influential professor of psychology at Columbia University published a study of one thousand eminent persons. In title and content it was, in fact, a study of eminent *men*; only 32 women were included in Cattell's list. Cattell himself made no apologies for the dearth of female representation in his catalogue of eminence, noting that it was well known that women were much less likely than men to depart from average levels of ability (Cattell, 1903).

Cattell's argument was completely in step with his times. Only a few years earlier, the famous Francis Galton, after testing 9337 persons in his Anthropometric Laboratory in England, had declared that women were inferior to men in all their capacities (Boring, 1929). And one of the founders of social psychology noted that "all psychologists who have studied the intelligence of women . . . recognize today that they represent the most inferior forms of human evolution and that they are closer to children and savages than to an adult, civilized male" (LeBon, 1879, quoted in Gould, 1981,

p. 104). Indeed, many of the research efforts of the new discipline of psychology in the early part of the twentieth century were devoted to demonstrating the assumed biological inferiority of women (Shields, 1975) and non-Caucasian racial groups (Guthrie, 1976).

Many psychologists and educators of Cattell's generation held firmly to the belief that men, as a group, were more variable than women—that men were more likely than women to be found at the high and low extremes of intelligence. Men were more likely than women to be geniuses; they were also more likely than women to be mentally subnormal. Women, on the other hand, were most likely to be of average intelligence.

The belief in greater male variability was congenial to those who were interested in maintaining the status quo between the sexes. In the first place, the greater variability claimed for the male sex was considered a positive quality—a progressive force in the evolution of the human species. Greater variability was one more plank in the platform of male superiority, as was the idea that the greater male variability meant that most geniuses would be male. It was an idea that provided ammunition to those who wished to exclude women from graduate and professional schools and to channel educated women into low-paying, low-status jobs.

The idea that males varied more in intelligence than females was probably accepted as a truism by many early twentieth-century observers. Most areas where eminence could be achieved were clearly dominated by men; males also tended to outnumber females in institutions for the mentally retarded. The notion that these male–female differences might be explained by causes other than sex differences in the distribution of intelligence received little consideration. In the end it was a female psychologist, Leta Hollingworth, who most successfully cast doubt on the greater male variability hypothesis (Silverman, 1989).

Hollingworth knew from bitter personal experience that the road to eminence for a woman had as much to do with social custom and prejudice as with her degree of intelligence. Her graduate education in psychology occurred in a climate in which graduate scholarships were not open to women, most faculty members had never worked professionally with women or taught female students, the chairperson of her department was an active campaigner against higher education for women, and the dean of her faculty stated publicly that few women were capable of truly advanced, original work (Rosenberg, 1982). Her own major advisor, E. L. Thorndike, a believer in the variability hypothesis, argued that "in particular, if men differ in intelligence and energy by wider degrees than do women, eminence in and leadership of the world's affairs of whatever sort will inevitably belong oftener to men. They will oftener deserve it" (Thorndike, 1910, p. 35). It was while working at her first job, as a tester at New York City's Clearing House for Mental Defectives, that Hollingworth began to focus her attention on the variability hypothesis. Although most of the retarded children referred to her for testing were boys, a situation predicted by the variability hypothesis, she noted that the disproportionate number of males was due largely to the large number of boys under the age of 16. Her observations led her to believe that boys of below average intelligence were likely to come to the attention of the law at a much earlier age than were their female counterparts. Boys were less restricted, and so were more likely to get into trouble; moreover, the undemanding social expectations for girls—that they be passive and dependent—made it less likely that low intelligence would be noticed. In adulthood, a low-intelligence female sometimes found a niche as a housewife, domestic worker, or prostitute, and came to a mental institution only when illness or the death of the man on whom she was depending intervened; a low-intelligence male had fewer options and was likely to end up in a mental institution much sooner (Hollingworth, 1922). Social factors rather than differences in the variability of intelligence, then, could explain the preponderance of males in institutions for the mentally retarded.

Hollingworth believed that the apparent underrepresentation of women at the top end of the distribution of intelligence could also be explained by social factors. After reviewing measurements made on 20,000 infants at birth, she concluded that there was no difference in variability between females and males. She went on to chastise psychologists for failing to consider the impact of domestic and childrearing tasks—"a field where eminence is impossible"— on women's capacity to achieve the distinction associated with genius (Hollingworth & Montague, 1914). Only when the latter explanation had been ruled out, she argued, should psychologists consider differences in intelligence or variability as an explanation for sex differences in the attainment of eminence.

After Hollingworth's articles on sex differences in mental traits appeared in the prestigious *Psychological Bulletin* (Hollingworth, 1916, 1918), the greater male variability hypothesis was discredited. Arguments have continued to rage, however, about whether the sexes differ in intellectual abilities or in cognitive style—the way they think and approach problems. Even the discredited variability hypothesis has not been allowed to die entirely, despite a lack of supporting data (e.g., see Lehrke, 1972). This chapter reviews the recent findings on gender and intellectual abilities. Because intellectual abilities can be measured only through performance on various tests, the discussion will also encompass some of the many nonintellectual affective factors that can influence performance on such tests.

Gender Differences in Intellectual Performance

Many of the popular stereotypes of women and men are based on the assumption that the two sexes approach the task of thinking in very different ways. It is widely held, for instance, that men are logical and women are intuitive, that it is a rare woman who has a "head for figures" and that men are more quickly frustrated and bored when performing simple repetitive tasks. Is there any basis to the idea that males are better suited to the task of calculating formulas or that females are better at spelling and typing? Researchers in this area have found a few gender differences in performance, but they tend to be smaller than the stereotypes would lead us to expect.

General Intelligence

There are no differences between male and female performance on tests of general intelligence (Maccoby & Jacklin, 1974). This finding is not surprising: IQ tests were constructed by balancing subscales on which females tended to score better with those on which males tended to score better, thus effectively eliminating gender differences in overall scores. In addition, there is little evidence linking intelligence to specific biological indicators of sex, such as the X or Y chromosomes (Wittig, 1979) or prenatal hormones (Hines, 1982). One interesting finding is that gender-role nonconformity is positively related to IQ for both sexes (Maccoby, 1966).

Sensation, Perception, and Motor Skills

From the age of 4 onward, females tend to outscore males on tests of perceptual speed and accuracy (Antill & Cunningham, 1982; Fairweather, 1976; Feingold, 1988). Boys over the age of about 9 show faster reaction times than their female counterparts; however, in situations where semantic or symbolic information must be processed in order to choose a response, females react faster than males, and the female advantage increases as the amount of information to be processed increases (Fairweather & Hutt, 1972).

In childhood and adulthood, females show more sensitivity to touch in the fingers and hands than males do (Weinstein & Sersen, 1961), as well as more sensitivity to pressure on various parts of the body (Gandelman, 1983). In the realm of manual dexterity, findings are mixed (Thomas & French, 1985). On a pegboard task, females usually outperform males; however, this finding appears to be due to females' smaller finger size rather than dexterity (Peters, Servos, & Day, 1990). The only other fine motor task on which female–male differences are consistently found is finger tapping, on which men perform better (Dodril, 1979). Motor tests of gross strength and speed favor males, who are larger and stronger (Thomas & French, 1985).

Studies on auditory threshold indicate that females have better high frequency hearing than men do (Hull, Mielke, Timmons, & Willeford, 1971; McGuinness, 1972; Gandelman, 1983). Evidence also suggests that females react more strongly than males to sound intensity. Females are more intolerant than males of loud sounds; by about the level of 85 decibels, females may hear a sound as twice as loud as males do (McGuinness, 1972). Females also seem to be more sensitive than males to changes in sound intensity (Zaner, Levee, & Gunta, 1968). In the visual mode, men seem to be more sensitive than women to intensity changes; in dark conditions, however, women adapt more rapidly than men to lower light levels and show more sensitivity at these levels (McGuinness, 1976).

In auditory search tasks, when males and females are asked to tell, by listening to a list of words, where a particular sound or letter occurs in each word, males perform much more poorly than females (McGuinness & Courtney, 1983). These researchers conclude that males have more trouble than females in forming a visual image of a word while operating in an auditory, or listening, mode. They suggest that this difficulty may be a factor underlying some gender differences in linguistic performance.

There is some evidence that male and female infants differ in the kinds of visual stimuli to which they pay most attention. Girls show greater interest in and greater ability to discriminate among faces than boys do (Fagan, 1972; Lewis, 1969). Boys, on the other hand, have been found to show stronger attentional responses to blinking lights, geometric patterns, and novel objects (Cornell & Strauss, 1973; Kagan & Lewis, 1965; McCall & Kagan, 1970). In an interesting experiment with adults, McGuinness and Symonds (1977) presented pairs of photographs to subjects stereoscopically (that is, one photograph is presented to one eye, while the other photograph is simultaneously presented to the other eye). In this situation, the two stimuli compete to be "seen," and the person sees either one of them at a time or an image that combines them in some way. Each pair of photographs contained one picture of an object and one picture of a person. Male subjects reported seeing objects more than people, while females reported the reverse. This phenomenon was tested again, this time using a simple measure of time spent looking at each of two pictures (Jobson & Watson, 1984). These researchers too found a gender difference in the attention paid to objects versus persons, but only for younger subjects. For subjects older than 35, there was no gender difference: Both females and males spent more time looking at pictures of persons.

The implications of male–female differences in perception and attention are uncertain. Some of them, such as females' greater perceptual speed and accuracy and their greater tactile sensitivity in the fingers and hands, have been used to argue for women's "suitability" for clerical work, such as typing. They could just as logically be used to argue that women would make better neurosurgeons than men. The fact that such an argument is seldom seen is a reminder of how easily the "neutral" findings of science can be used to justify the status quo. It has been suggested that male–female differences in sensory processing may underlie gender differences in cognitive performance; however, in most cases, no connection has yet been established.

Learning and Memory

A review of the literature by Maccoby and Jacklin (1974) indicated no gender differences in learning and memory. The stereotype that females are better at rote learning and males are better at learning complex tasks receives no support. Some research suggests that women may process information more rapidly than men (McGuinness & Pribram, 1978). Most studies show no female–male differences on tests of memory (e.g., Joseph, McKay, & Joseph, 1982; Villardita, Smirni, LePira, & Zappala, 1981). However, others have found a female advantage on tests of verbal memory (Trahan & Quintana, 1990). Some apparent gender differences in the recall of visual material have been attributed to gender differences in verbal fluency: Females may simply be better than males at describing what they remember, rather than at remembering itself (McGuinness & McLaughlin, 1982). Where gender differences in learning or memory are found, they can usually be traced to gender differences in familiarity with or interest in the topic at hand. For example, in one study, words that had been previously classified as "masculine" were better recalled by males, while "feminine" words were better recalled by females (Brown, Larsen, Rankin, & Ballard, 1980).

The tendency to learn and remember gender-related information better than non–gender-related information seems to be strongest among individuals who are highly sex-typed (Cann & Garnett, 1984; Hepburn, 1985). This finding is perhaps best explained by gender schema theory—the notion that individuals who are sex-typed have learned to perceive and process information in terms of gender categories (Bem, 1985).

Verbal Performance

For years, it was consistently reported in the psychological literature that females outperform males on verbal tasks (Anastasi, 1937/1958; Hyde, 1981; Maccoby & Jacklin, 1974; McGuinness & Pribram, 1978; Tyler, 1947/1965). While the gender difference in verbal performance appeared consistent, its size was very small. A meta-analysis by Hyde (1981) showed that gender accounted for an average of only 1 percent of the variance in verbal performance scores. Most reviewers concluded that knowing a person's gender allows us to predict very little about that person's verbal ability (Plomin & Foch, 1981).

Research comparing test performances of samples of children between 1947 and 1983 shows that gender differences in verbal performance, as well as in other cognitive skill areas, has declined drastically over the years (Feingold, 1988). A more recent meta-analysis, using 165 studies, found no gender differences in verbal performance, either across all types of verbal tests or within such specific tests as vocabulary, reading comprehension, and essay writing (Hyde & Linn, 1988). However, some researchers continue to report gender differences in verbal performance. For instance, a study of high school students in Japan and the United States indicated that in both countries girls averaged significantly higher scores than boys on a word fluency test (Mann, Sasanuma, Sakuma, & Masaki, 1990).

Quantitative Performance

Meta-analyses done more than a decade ago showed a tendency for males to outperform females on mathematical tests; however, only between 1 percent and 5 percent of the variance in mathematics performance could be explained by gender (Hyde, 1981; Rossi, 1983). Meta-analyses that include more recent studies indicate that the gender gap in mathematics performance is decreasing (Friedman, 1989; Hyde, Fennema, & Lamon, 1990a) and is often negligible. Figure 6.1 shows two overlapping distributions that approximate the size of the gender difference in mathematics performance, averaging over the more than 100 samples (representing almost 4 million subjects) used in the latter meta-analysis.

In this meta-analysis, gender differences in mathematics performance were found to be greater for white Americans than for black, Hispanic, or Asian Americans, or for Canadian or Australian samples. A similar pattern of larger gender differences in samples of white American students than in samples of minority students emerged in the Friedman (1989) meta-analysis.

Until early adolescence, the majority of studies show no gender differences in performance on general mathematics achievement tests—a finding that holds across a variety of cultures (Lummis & Stevenson, 1990). Girls show a slight advantage in computation in elementary and middle school. Some studies find that boys do better than girls on one type of quantitative performance, mathematical problem solving, as early as the first grade (Lummis & Stevenson, 1990). In the latter study, first-grade males outperformed females in problem solving by equivalent amounts across samples in three countries: the United States, Japan, and Taiwan. Although Japanese girls achieved higher average scores on problem solving than did American boys, the gap in problem-solving performance between Japanese boys and Japanese girls was as great as that between American boys and American girls. This difference occurred despite girls' and boys' apparently equivalent adeptness at computation and understanding of the mathematical operations needed to solve the problems.

Gender differences favoring males in mathematical problem solving appear most reliably in high school and are maintained or increased in college. The estimated size of the gender difference is such that about 43 percent of high school females and

Figure 6.1
Two normal distributions that are 0.15 standard deviations apart (i.e., $d = 0.15$. This is the approximate magnitude of the gender difference in mathematics performance, averaging over all samples.)

57 percent of high school males will score above the average score for the whole high school sample (Hyde et al., 1990a). Problem solving, then, appears to be the only area of mathematics achievement in which the gender difference may be a cause for concern. As Hyde and her colleagues note, problem-solving skill is critical for success in such fields as engineering and physics.

On the whole, gender differences seem to be smallest, and may favor females, when the samples studied are from the general population. The differences are larger with more selective samples, and appear largest for samples of highly precocious persons (Hyde et al., 1990a). There are some indications that gender and social class interact with respect to mathematics achievement test results. Smaller gender differences in performance are found in samples from lower than from higher socioeconomic groups (Fischbein, 1990).

Despite the finding that by high school males tend to outperform females on standardized tests of mathematical problem solving, girls often obtain higher grades in mathematics than boys do (Kimball, 1989). This anomalous finding is shrugged off by researchers convinced of male quantitative superiority as being due to girls' better behavior in school (Benbow & Stanley, 1982). It may, however, reflect differences between the two types of testing situations such that boys are advantaged in the standardized testing situation and girls are advantaged in classroom testing situations. Such differences could involve issues such as test anxiety (Crocker, Schmitt, & Tang, 1988) or content of items included on the tests.

Some researchers have linked performance in mathematics and science to visual-spatial ability, since correlational studies show a strong relationship between spatial abilities and mathematical reasoning (Linn & Petersen, 1985). However, as discussed in the next section, the kinds of spatial tasks that show the strongest gender differences do not correspond to the processes required for good mathematical performance. The correlations that do exist may reflect the shared degree of general or analytic ability required for the two types of tasks. Research with children in the sixth through eighth grades indicates that children who differ in visual-spatial skill do not differ in their ability to solve mathematical problems (Fennema & Tartre, 1985). However, poor spatial performance seems to be linked more strongly to poor mathematical performance for girls than for boys (Ethington & Wolfle, 1984; Fennema & Tartre, 1985). There are no obvious explanations for this correlational finding, and more research is needed before any conclusions are drawn about the impact of spatial ability on gender differences in mathematical performance.

Considerable interest in the possibility of gender differences in mathematical ability has been aroused by the work of Benbow and Stanley (1980, 1982, 1983; Benbow, 1988). These researchers examined scores on the SAT-M (a standardized test of mathematical reasoning) for about 50,000 seventh- and eighth-grade children identified by the Johns Hopkins National Talent Search. To be included in the sample, a child had to score in the top 3 percent nationally on a standardized achievement test. Among these high-ability children, Benbow and Stanley found a mean difference in performance favoring boys of 30 points. Although this difference is statistically significant, it represents only about three-eighths of the size of the combined standard deviations for males and females in the sample. Benbow and Stanley's most striking finding, however, was the ratio of boys to girls among the highest scorers. In the upper reaches of the distribution, the higher the score, the greater the ratio of males to females who attained it. Among children who scored above 500, the ratio of boys to girls was 2.1 to 1; among those scoring above 600, the ratio of boys to girls was 4.1 to 1; among those scoring over 700, boys outnumbered girls 13 to 1 (Benbow & Stanley, 1983).

Although the research carried out by Benbow and Stanley has provided a wealth of useful information about gifted children, it is easy to make too much of these dramatic-sounding results. In the first place, they are based on a sample of girls and boys who are much more mathematically talented than average. Furthermore, these children, as voluntary participants in the Talent Search, were to some extent self-selected for motivation and interest. As noted earlier, gender differences in mathematics performance are found to be greatest in the most select samples. Benbow and Stanley's research provides no information about gender differences in mathematical performance among average males and females. In the second place, their focus on male–female ratios among extremely high scorers makes gender differences in mathematics performance appear more important than they are (Rossi, 1983). For example, in their sample, which already represents only the top 3 percent of intellectually talented children, only about 7 of every 1000 boys and 5 of every 10,000 girls score over 700. At this rarified level, so few individuals are actually affected that even a large difference in the proportions of males and females has little practical significance. Benbow (1988) reports that follow-up data on the mathematically gifted children in her sample show that, of the 47 percent who went to graduate school, 42 percent of the men and 22 percent of the women chose scientific or mathematical fields—statistics that show, by implication, that the majority of even this highly gifted sample did *not* take up science or mathematics as a career. In the third place, the gender differences occur specifically on the SAT-M, a test that seems, perhaps because of its content or administration, to produce larger gender differences in performance than other tests (Hyde et al., 1990a) although in the general student population the gender difference in SAT-M scores has decreased steadily since 1981 (Friedman, 1989). Finally, some critics have noted that there was a great deal of variability in males' performance at the top levels; in fact, variability among the males was consistently greater than among the females (Becker & Hedges, 1988). For example, in one year, 19 percent of the boys out-performed the highest scoring girl in the sample, while in another year the highest scoring girl did better than all but 0.1 percent of the boys (Tobias, 1982). Thus, the significance of gender differences in mathematical performance remains a matter of debate.

Visual-Spatial Performance

Visual-spatial abilities are those that enable us to visually perceive and locate objects and their interrelationships. This broad class of abilities includes, among other things, the capacity to mentally rearrange and rotate objects or figures, and to pick out or "disembed" a simple figure or shape from its background.

Gender differences in visual-spatial performance favoring males have been reported more consistently than any other cognitive differences (Cohen & Wilkie, 1979; Connor & Serbin, 1985; Maccoby & Jacklin, 1974; Willis & Schaie, 1988). The actual size of the difference is small, however, with gender accounting for less than 5 percent of the variability on visual-spatial tests (Hyde, 1981). There are some indications that this difference is decreasing (Feingold, 1988; Rosenthal & Rubin, 1982) and that, like the gender differences in mathematical performance, it appears largest in the most highly select samples (Becker & Hedges, 1984). Gender differences often involve speed of responding rather than accuracy (Blough & Slavin, 1987).

Critics of the research in this area argue that visual-spatial ability has not been defined precisely or separated from spatial abilities in general, and that different measures of visual-spatial ability actually tap different abilities (Caplan, MacPherson, & Tobin, 1985; Linn & Petersen, 1985). Linn and Petersen concluded that at least three different types of spatial ability are represented in the literature on gender differences: spatial visualization, spatial perception, and mental rotation. Spatial visualization, most often measured using the Embedded Figures Test (see Figure 6.2 for an example) involves complicated, multistep mental manipulations of spatial information. Subjects may be asked to "disembed" a simple figure from a complex background or to imagine how a piece of paper would look when folded a certain way. This type of task, which seems to require analytic ability, shows no reliable gender differences at any point in the life span, according to Linn and Petersen's meta-analysis. The second type of ability, spatial perception, involves determining spatial relationships with respect to one's own body orientation, in spite of distracting information. It is often measured by the Rod and Frame Test, in which a subject must adjust a tilted rod inside a tilted frame to true vertical, in the absence of visual context clues. This ability is a spatial, but not necessarily visual, one. Good performance requires the use of kinesthetic cues (cues relating to body motion, position, and gravity). Linn and Petersen found that beginning at age 8 males show a small advantage over females on this type of task, and the size of the gender difference is larger (two-thirds of a standard deviation) for samples in which subjects were older than 18. The third type of spatial ability, mental rotation of figures, is the only one for which Linn and Petersen concluded that strong gender differences exist. Performance in the latter category is measured by showing the person a picture or object, and asking questions about it that require the visualization of that picture or object from another angle. Scores are based on speed rather than

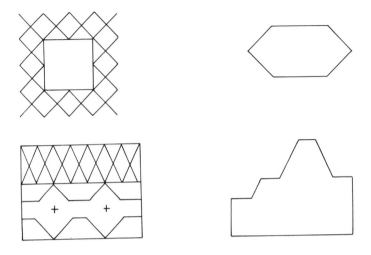

Figure 6.1
Examples of drawings used in the embedded-figures test.

accuracy of rotation (accuracy tends to be very high). Gender differences favoring males were detected across all ages on this type of task, although the size of the effect varied from one-quarter of a standard deviation to an entire standard deviation, according to the specific test used. The reason for better male performance on this type of task is not yet clear. It may reflect the acquisition and/or use of different cognitive strategies for finding a solution that could, in turn, be related to differences in males' and females' experiences with this type of task.

The consistent reporting of gender differences in certain visual-spatial abilities may tend, by focusing attention on them, to exaggerate their implications. For example, Caplan and her colleagues (1985) note the frequency with which anecdotal examples of female inferiority in spatial ability are cited (e.g., the shortage of female chess masters), in contrast to equally valid examples of female spatial competence:

> The buying of furniture with a view toward how it can be rotated and fitted within a particular space; learning to type without watching the keyboard . . . and the designing and using of clothing patterns that must be turned, flipped, and inverted, and then worked on while the user visualizes how they will look when re-turned, reinverted and reflipped." (p. 789)

An implication of the erroneous stereotype that there are large and important differences between the sexes in visual-spatial ability is that such differences account for the shortage of women in professions that require this ability, such as architecture and engineering. However, this is demonstrably not the case. Hyde (1981), making the initial assumption that a person would have to be in the top 5 percent of the range of spatial abilities to be qualified for a profession such as engineering, calculated that if spatial ability were the only determining factor, the ratio of males to females in such professions would be 2 to 1. Since, in actual fact, the proportion of women in the engineering fields has been less than 5 percent for many years, gender differences in spatial ability could potentially explain only a small part of the male dominance in the engineering profession.

Creativity

Creativity, the ability to produce unique and novel ideas, is measured by tests in which people attempt to generate new uses for common objects and new associations for words. Maccoby and Jacklin's (1974) review of studies in this area found that females tended to score better than males on creativity tests requiring verbal fluency, while few reliable gender differences were found on nonverbal tests of creativity. Research since that time has tended to support Maccoby and Jacklin's conclusions, although findings are mixed. For example, researchers in the United States (Chusmir & Koberg, 1986) and in India (Kelgeri, Khadi, & Phadnis, 1989) report no gender differences in creative thinking; researchers in Canada (Kershner & Ledger, 1985) report higher verbal creativity scores for girls; and researchers studying the mathematical creativity of Indian high school students report higher scores for males (Tuli, 1982).

The correlates of creativity have also been investigated. A positive relationship between self-esteem and creativity seems to be greater for females than for males (Goldsmith & Matherly, 1988). A study of managers suggests that creativity is predicted by need for achievement in men and by need for affiliation in women (Chusmir & Koberg, 1986). Some research indicates that androgyny is positively related to creativity for both sexes (Harrington & Anderson, 1981). For creativity, as for other abilities discussed in this chapter, there is little in the way of gender differences that would explain or justify the differences in eminence achieved by women and men outside the psychology laboratory. The relative shortage of female, as compared to male, well-known artists, for instance, cannot be attributed to gender differences in creativity.

Explaining the Differences

Despite the relatively small size and limited nature of the observed gender differences in performance on some cognitive tasks, psychologists have invested a great deal of energy in trying to explain these differences. The result is an often bewildering array of possible explanations for the existence of differences that may or may not be important. Most of the differences are too small to worry about, but some, such as the difference in mathematical problem solving, may have practical implications for education. Understanding the cause of gender differences in performance could provide clues to educational strategies that would minimize those differences.

Biological Explanations

Many researchers have searched for biological explanations for female–male performance differences. A demonstration that performance differences are partially based in biology is often mistakenly interpreted as a sign that they are inevitable and immutable. As we have seen in earlier chapters, however, biology and environment interact so closely that a biologically based predisposition in the direction of a particular behavior or ability is usually only one of many determining factors in the development of gender differences.

Genetics.   Most attempts to link genes with cognitive gender differences have focused on visual-spatial performance. The suggestion has been made that some aspect of visual-spatial ability may be X-linked (Bock & Kolakowski, 1973; Stafford, 1961). However, the research evidence does not consistently support that hypothesis (Linn & Petersen, 1985). Because it is so difficult to separate the effects of an individual's environment from those of his or her genetic endowment, attempts to link a specific ability to genetic factors face many difficulties (Wittig, 1979). For example, greater similarity between mother–son than father–son performance levels, sometimes taken as a clue that an ability is carried genetically on the X chromosome, could be due to an environmental factor: fathers' lesser contact than mothers' with their sons. Because sex is a stimulus variable—serving as a cue to other people in the environment about how the individual should be treated—conclusions about the impact of genetic, as well as other biological aspects of sex, must always acknowledge the impact of the social psychological context.

Hormones.   There are two ways in which hormones can potentially influence ability and/or performance: The actual level of hormones circulating in the bloodstream might somehow have a direct effect, or there might be an indirect effect of prenatal hormones through their action on the developing brain. In this section, we examine research that deals with the first possibility: an impact of circulating hormones. The following section, on brain lateralization, includes a discussion of the second possibility.

One of the problems with trying to relate hormone levels to cognitive task performance has been the difficulty in measuring hormone levels. Some researchers have tried to get around the problem by inferring hormone status from hormonally influenced physical characteristics such as muscle versus fat distribution, body shape, penis or breast size, and pubic hair distribution. Presumably, more masculine physical characteristics indicate high levels of androgens, while more feminine ones indicate higher levels of female hormones. Petersen (1976) measured spatial visualization, which requires perceptual restructuring, and fluent production, a rapid accurate production of names, for male and female adolescents. At ages 16 and 18, males who were less sex stereotypic in physical appearance (and thus, presumably, had lower levels of male hormones) were better at spatial visualization than at fluent production, while males who had more extremely masculine physical characteristics (and thus higher levels of male hormones) were better at fluent production than spatial visualization. For the females, good performance on the spatial visualization task was also related to less sex stereotypic physical characteristics, but fluent production was completely unrelated to physical appearance.

How do Petersen's findings relate to gender differences? The finding of within-sex correlations between inferred hormone levels and spatial visualization performance is not indicative of a simple relationship between circulating hormone levels and sex-related differences in cognitive performance. In the first place, it is not the case that high levels of male hormones relate to good performance on spatial tasks while high levels of female hormones relate to good performance on verbal tasks, as the pattern of observed gender differences in cognitive performance might lead us to expect. In the second place, we have already seen that the sexes do not differ reliably in spatial visualization performance. Thus, this line of research has so far produced no conclusive evidence that gender differences in cognitive performance can be explained by a simple, linear relationship between sex hormones and cognitive abilities. In fact, men with lower levels of testosterone actually perform better on spatial tasks than do their counterparts with higher levels of testosterone; for women, the relationship between testosterone levels and spatial performance is the reverse—a pattern of findings that may suggest that, for spatial ability at least, there is an optimal androgen/estrogen balance that is slightly below that of the average man and above that of the average woman (Kimura, 1987).

Some researchers interested in the relationship between circulating hormone levels and cognitive performance have studied women's performance at various phases of the menstrual cycle, when levels of circulating estrogen are high or low. Findings are that women perform somewhat better on verbal articulation tasks (e.g., saying "A box of mixed biscuits in a biscuit mixer" five times in a row as quickly as possible) and fine motor skill tasks at times in their cycle when estrogen levels are high rather than when they are low, and somewhat better on certain spatial tasks, such as the rod-and-frame task, at times when estrogen levels are low rather than when they are high (Hampson, 1990a, 1990b). However, the differences related to menstrual cycle phase were small in comparison to individual differences among the women. Fluctuating hormone levels in men, such as the drop in testosterone between morning and evening, might also show some small relationship to cognitive performance, but so far these relationships have not been examined. Researchers studying men have, however, found a negative relationship between levels of FSH (follicle-stimulating hormone) and tests of some forms of visual-spatial functioning (Gordon & Lee, 1986). This line of research, then, provides some suggestive evidence for a link between circulating hormone levels and cognitive-perceptual performance, but the effects are small and may be of little practical significance. Menstrual and other hormonal cycles will be discussed in more detail in Chapter 8.

Brain Organization.   The notion that sex-related cognitive differences are caused by sex differences in brain organization has received a good deal of press in the last few years. "Women's Intuition Linked to Thicker Nerves in Brain," proclaimed a newspaper headline (Women's intuition, 1986); "Male Brain, Female Brain: The Hidden Difference," proclaimed *Psychology Today* (Kimura, 1985).

The idea that male and female brains are different has a long history. At one time, the explanation for women's "obvious" intellectual inferiority was their smaller brains —an idea that was quickly dropped when it was demonstrated that, relative to body weight, women's brains were proportionally larger than those of men (Shields, 1975). The current focus, however, is not on brain size, but on the organization of functions within the brain.

Although the human body appears relatively symmetrical—the left side looking more or less like a mirror image of the right—we are not symmetrical in terms of our competence at different activities. A person is better at writing with one hand than with the other, kicks a football better with one foot than the other, prefers one ear over the other when listening closely. The majority of people are right-handed; handedness may or may not be consistent with foot or ear preferences. The tendency for individuals to be better at certain activities using one side of their body than the other has been taken as evidence for the way functions are organized in the brain.

The human brain is divided into left and right halves, or hemispheres, connected by a mass of nerve fibers called the *corpus callosum*. (See Figure 6.3.) Each hemisphere of the brain governs the activities of the opposite side of the body (that is, the left side of the brain controls the right hand, the right ear, the right leg, and the right visual field). Scientists also believe that, to some extent, the two hemispheres of the brain are the locations for different abilities. In normal right-handed people, the capacities for language and for analytical, mathematical, and sequential information processing tend to be located in the left hemisphere. The right hemisphere is the site for more holistic and nonverbal information processing skills, musical ability, and certain types of spatial skills. These generalizations do not hold for left-handed individuals; nor is it the case that the locations of various abilities are simply reversed for left-handers.

Since verbal and certain spatial skills seem to be located on different sides of the brain, researchers have found it tempting to speculate that female superiority on verbal tasks and male superiority on some spatial tasks might be related to sex differences in the development of the left and right hemispheres. Could it be that females have a better-developed left hemisphere (to explain the rapidly disappearing female advantage in verbal skills) and males have a more well-developed right hemisphere (to explain the male advantage in some spatial skills)? At first blush, the explanation sounds seductively simple. But wait: In addition to verbal skills, the left hemisphere also seems to be the location for analytic and sequential skills, in which the sexes do not differ. If earlier or stronger left-hemisphere development explains female superiority on verbal tasks, might it not also be reasonable to expect that the same process would guarantee female superiority in mathematical performance? If brain organization does relate to gender differences in cognitive performance, the relationship must be more complex than each sex simply being better developed on different sides of the brain.

The focus of research has been on possible sex differences in the degree to which particular functions are localized in one side of the brain (that is, the degree of hemispheric lateralization or specialization). Levy (1972) proposed that greater hemispheric lateralization for spatial ability enhances performance for that ability, and that male superiority on spatial tasks was due to greater lateralization of spatial skills among men than among women. Her proposal laid the groundwork for a dizzying flurry of research in which males and females were compared for their lateralization of verbal and spatial abilities.

Three sorts of evidence have been used to gauge lateralization in women and men: clinical studies of brain-damaged patients, behavioral tests of normal individuals, and studies of brain activity and anatomy. These studies have been reviewed by McGlone (1980) and Springer and Deutsch (1981), and the whole field has been critiqued by Alper (1985). In general, clinical studies have found that, for men, damage to the left hemisphere is associated with more impairment of verbal than nonverbal performance, while damage to the right side of the brain is associated with greater impairment of nonverbal than verbal performance. For women, however, verbal and nonverbal performance do not seem to be differentially affected by the side of the damage, suggesting that verbal and nonverbal abilities are distributed across both hemispheres. Several

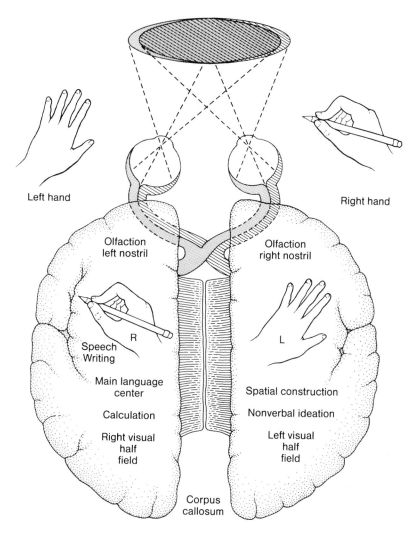

Figure 6.2

Sensory inputs to and functions of the two brain hemispheres for the normal right-handed person.

studies have failed to confirm this pattern, however, finding no differences between males and females in the effects of damage to the left or right hemispheres (Bornstein, 1984; Herring & Reitan, 1984; Snow & Sheese, 1985). Moreover, the earlier work has been criticized on a number of grounds, including the lack of similarity to the general population of the samples used and the confounding of sex with other variables. Recent research with brain-damaged patients by Kimura and her colleagues indicates that no single rule about sex differences in brain organization holds across all aspects of thinking (Kimura, 1985, 1987). They are finding that, for producing speech and making hand movements that contribute to motor skill, women's brains seem to be more focally organized than those of men (that is, these abilities seem to be localized in a more restricted area of the brain for women than for men). Basic speech function appears to be more dependent on the anterior (front) than the posterior (back) region of the brain for women, and more equally distributed between the two regions for men. However, for tasks such as defining words the sex difference appears to go in the opposite direction: Women's brains are organized more diffusely than men's. Finally, for a variety of other verbal tests, there is no obvious sex difference in brain organization. Clinical research, then, does not support the simple view that men's brains are more lateralized, in general, than women's brains. According to Kimura (1987), her research with brain-damaged persons demonstrates differences in brain organization between human females and males. She notes, however, that there are wide individual variations within each sex, that sex is only one of several individual-difference variables that are correlated with brain organization, and that "the population differences in abilities that we see between men and women do not have a high predictive value for individuals. As a means of screening for admission to occupations or life activities, genital sex is a very poor instrument" (p. 146).

Behavioral tests with normal subjects use tasks in which two different stimuli are presented simultaneously to the different sides of the brain, with subjects later tested to determine which inputs are best recalled. Perhaps the most common of such tests is the dichotic listening test, in which different lists of numbers or spoken syllables are simultaneously presented through earphones to the subject's left and right ears. If the subject later shows a tendency to remember the stimuli presented to one ear better than those presented to the other, the result is taken as evidence that the person's verbal abilities are more strongly lateralized in the brain hemisphere corresponding to that ear. If males are more strongly lateralized than females for verbal abilities, we would expect men to show a greater right-ear (left-hemisphere) advantage than women on this test. Of 14 such studies cited by McGlone (1980), 9 showed no relationship between sex of subjects and right-ear advantage, 4 found a stronger right-ear advantage in men, and 1 found a right-ear advantage in women. Studies in which information is presented to the right and left visual fields and studies in which the response required is nonverbal rather than verbal also show a mixed pattern of results, although when male–female differences *are* found they are more likely to be in the direction of greater lateralization for men than for women. The sexes do seem to differ reliably in manual asymmetry— the degree to which one hand is dominant—but in this case it is the women who show more "handedness," and thus, presumably, greater lateralization. On the whole, then, the results of behavioral studies, like those of the clinical studies discussed earlier, do not provide overwhelming support for the idea that men's brains are more lateralized than women's.

Studies of brain anatomy have reported some evidence of small differences between male and female brains, which have been interpreted as implying more laterali-zation for males than females (de Lacoste-Utamsing & Holloway, 1982; Wada, Clark & Hamm, 1975). In particular, researchers have focused on the corpus callosum, the "bridge" between the left and right hemispheres. If that "bridge" is more developed in one sex than the other, would that mean that transmission between the two hemispheres is more efficient for that sex? Some research on brains examined at autopsy suggests that the corpus callosum is larger, at least in the posterior of the brain, in women than in men (Kimura, 1987). Two recent studies of the brains of living human beings, using magnetic resonance imaging, contribute to the controversy by providing contradictory results. In one of these studies, no male–female difference in the size or surface area of the corpus callosum was found. However, a striking difference in the *shape* was observed: the posterior region of the corpus callosum (the splenium) was more bulbous-shaped in females and more tubular-shaped in males (Allen, Richey, Chai, & Gorski, 1991). This difference was not evident in children younger than 16 years. Another study did not find sex differences in the posterior region (Byne, Bleier, & Houston, 1988). According to the latter group of researchers, the most striking finding was the large variation in the size and shape of the corpus callosum, irrespective of gender or age. Clearly, research in this area is not yet at the stage when it can be cited with confidence to prove or disprove the hypothesis of greater male than female later-alization. To further complicate the issue, researchers are increasingly convinced that sex differences in brain anatomy may vary across the life span, indicating that what-ever sex differences in brain organization exist may be dynamic rather than static, pres-ent at some periods of life but not at others (Kimura, 1985).

On the whole, then, there is no overwhelming evidence that males are more later-alized in general than females. However, the possibility exists that, at least for some particular abilities, the brains of the two sexes may differ in their organization. Sus-pending all doubts for a moment and accepting the hypothesis as true, we would still be left with two basic questions: Does brain organization really make a difference to cognitive performance, and, if so, how?

Most of the theories about the relationship between brain organization and per-formance focus specifically on lateralization. We have already seen, however, that what-ever sex differences in lateralization may exist are more likely to be specific to particular types of abilities, such as speech production or vocabulary than to encompass broad categories such as "verbal abilities" or "spatial abilities." Yet most of the research designed to explore the relationship between brain organization and performance in women and men has been aimed at showing a relationship between gross measures of lateralization (that is, is one sex more lateralized than the other?) and broad categories of abilities. The studies are ingenious, but they cannot provide completely useful answers because they are focusing on the wrong questions.

For example, Hines and Shipley (1984) tested the hypothesis that prenatal hor-mone levels affect the degree of brain lateralization, which, in turn, affects cognitive abilities. The idea that prenatal hormone levels may indirectly affect cognitive abilities by influencing the developing brain is a popular one that has received support from ani-mal research and forms the basis for some theories about male–female differences in cognitive abilities among humans (e.g., Kimura, 1987; Nyborg, 1983). The research by Hines and Shipley (1984) provides one of the few direct tests with humans of these proposed prenatal hormone/brain organization–cognitive performance links. They compared women who had been exposed prenatally to DES, a synthetic estrogen, to their nonexposed sisters, hypothesizing that the DES-exposed women would show greater hemispheric lateralization and a more masculine pattern of cognitive performance (that is, better visual spatial performance and poorer verbal performance) than their sisters. (Although DES is an estrogen, it is now thought by researchers to have a masculinizing effect since it is now known that testosterone converts to estrogen.) They found, in fact, that the DES-exposed women did seem to be more lateralized, at least as measured by their performance on a dichotic listening task. Thus, it is possible that prenatal hormone levels affect brain lateralization, although more research is needed to confirm this. However, they found *no* relationship between lateralization and cognitive performance. The DES women did not differ from their sisters on verbal or visual-spatial measures. Although this one study does not rule out the possibility that lateralization is related to cognitive abilities, it certainly indicates that the relationship is too weak to be measured in a small sample of women and may be of minor significance. Thus, even if sex differences in lateralization were unequivocally demonstrated, there is as yet no clear evidence of how these differences are linked to specific cognitive abilities.

It is worthy of note at this point that sex differences in brain asymmetry, if they exist, could be the result of environmental as well as genetic or hormonal factors. For example, some studies suggest that children's lateralization of verbal skills is affected by the quality and quantity of their exposure to language (Borowy & Goebel, 1976; Geffner & Hochberg, 1971). Thus, if the sexes do differ in brain lateralization, the difference is as likely to be a function of such environmental factors as the amount of talking parents do to their male and female infants as it is to be a product of different hormone levels.

One further line of research attempting to tie brain lateralization to cognitive functioning involves the rate of physical maturation. Waber (1977) attempted to show a relationship among verbal and spatial performance, degree of hemispheric specialization, and rate of physical growth at adolescence. Girls and boys aged 10 to 16 years were classified by a medical examination as early or late physical maturers and were tested for verbal performance, spatial performance, and lateralization of speech perception. The results were striking because they indicated that the relationship between sex and spatial performance was overshadowed by the relationship between maturation rate and spatial performance. Late-maturing adolescents, male or female, performed better on tests of spatial ability than did early-maturing adolescents. No significant relationship between verbal performance and rate of maturation was found. However, the older an individual subject was at the onset of puberty, the better was his or her performance on spatial relative to verbal tests. These data fit with the general observation that boys, on the average, mature physically later than girls and also tend to do better than girls on some spatial tasks. Some subsequent research supports the link between late maturation and spatial performance (e.g., Sanders & Soares, 1986), but such a link is not always found (e.g., Waber, Mann, Merola, & Moylan, 1985).

How does hemispheric specialization fit into these results? Waber found, among the older children only, that the late maturers showed greater hemispheric specialization for speech perception than did early maturers of the same age and sex. She postulated that maturation rate had physiological correlates, probably having to do with hormone levels, that were present from an early age and that influenced the development of the organization of brain functions. She suggested that late maturers show more hemispheric specialization of abilities than do early maturers and that this difference in specialization mediates the effect of maturation rate on spatial ability. Her data do provide partial support for this suggestion, as does some later research (Vrbancic & Mosley, 1988; Waber, Bauermeister, Cohen, Ferber, & Wolff, 1981), but some other researchers have failed to find support for it (Bryden & Vrbancic, 1988; Petersen, 1976). At this point it is not certain that maturation rate relates to spatial ability or that, if it does, the relationship occurs through the impact of maturation rate on hemispheric specialization. In fact, an interesting alternative explanation for a relationship between maturation rate and spatial performance was suggested and tested by Newcombe and Bandura (1983). They noted that timing of puberty is known to be associated with personality differences. For one thing, there appears to be more cross-sex typing or androgyny among late maturers of both sexes than among early maturers. Early-maturing girls date earlier and develop more conventional feminine interests than their late-maturing counterparts; similarly, late-maturing boys are found by some researchers to be lower in masculine orientation and aggression than their early-maturing peers. Newcombe and Bandura suggest that these differences in gender-role–related interests and orientation between early and late maturers may help to shape the relationship between maturation rate and spatial performance, perhaps by affecting participation in particular activities. In their study of sixth-grade girls, they found that later maturation was positively related to good spatial performance *and* to stereotypically masculine personality traits and interests. However, they found *no* relationship between maturation rate and lateralization, between lateralization and spatial performance, or between gender-role orientation and spatial performance. Thus, the study provides no definitive answer to the question of what mechanism might be responsible for the observed link between spatial performance and the timing of puberty, but it tends to undercut the notion that maturation rate affects spatial ability through differences in hemispheric lateralization. A subsequent longitudinal study showed that personality characteristics at age 11 were predictive of spatial ability at age 16 (Newcombe, 1987).

Before leaving the topic of brain organization, a final comment is in order. Understanding of the organization and functioning of the human brain is still far from complete. Furthermore, the emphasis on lateralization as the most crucial feature of brain organization is rapidly diminishing (Efron, 1990). The network of connections in individual human brains may be so unique as to make the individuality "of fingerprints or facial features gross and simple by comparison" (Sperry, 1982, p. 1223). Divisions of the brain other than left/right (e.g., up/down, front/back) might yet prove to be important; moreover, scientists are still trying to understand the way the brain functions as a coherent whole (Sperry, 1982). One commentator compares our current understanding of the brain with that which might be achieved by someone totally unfamiliar with cars if he experimented by removing parts of the car:

> He removes different parts of the car, observing that the
> removal of a wheel makes the ride bumpy, draining the brake
> fluid makes it difficult to stop, and removal of the battery or

> engine prevents forward motion altogether . . . he thus localizes
> some functions . . . [but] . . . uncovers little information about
> their mechanisms. (Fausto-Sterling, 1985, p. 48)

Fausto-Sterling may be too harsh in her evaluation of the current state of neuropsychology. Nevertheless, given the contradictory evidence and the large gaps in our knowledge about the brain, we should be extremely cautious about jumping to conclusions about a simple relationship between hemispheric lateralization and gender differences in cognitive performance.

We probably should also be cautious about the practical significance of some of the findings relating hormones or brain organization to performance. Scientists have, for example, found some evidence for relationships among handedness, testosterone, allergies, myopia (short-sightedness), and mathematical performance (Benbow, 1986; 1988; Geschwind & Behan, 1982). But how useful is it to confirm such interrelationships? If we could say for certain that left-handed myopic males with a lot of allergies make the best mathematicians, would we give up on everyone else? And, as McGuinness (1988) asks, how would such a finding help us to understand the majority of mathematically talented people, who simply do not fit such a category?

Social/Affective Explanations

Anyone who has ever taken a test knows there is more to success or failure than intellectual competence. There are matters of long-term training and immediate preparation, mood, fatigue, confidence, and motivation—all of which may be, in turn, influenced by the expectations of others, the cultural or institutional climate, and immediate situational factors.

When the cognitive performance of females and males is compared, it is necessary to examine the ways in which the kinds of emotional and social factors just listed might systematically differ for the two sexes and thus help to explain differences in their performance on certain kinds of tasks. We will look briefly at the possible roles of direct training, gender-role socialization with respect to the development of particular skills, and gender-related differences in self-confidence and motivation as causes of some of the observed gender differences in cognitive performance.

Training and Experience.   Even in cases where the level of a particular ability is partially determined by physiological factors, the ability is usually susceptible to training. For example, while some of us may have more potential than others to become great athletes, all of us can improve our athletic skills to some extent through instruction and practice. It is quite clear, likewise, that spatial, verbal, and mathematical skills can all be increased through training.

Evidence now shows that both sexes show a positive relationship between experience and practice on visual-spatial tasks; the more a person has participated in visual-spatial activities, the better she or he is likely to score on tests of visual-spatial ability (Baenninger & Newcombe, 1989; Connor & Serbin, 1985; Newcombe, Bandura, & Taylor, 1983). Since traditionally masculine toys and activities involve more visual-spatial skills than feminine ones do, it may be that the male–female differences in performance on visual-spatial tasks mainly reflect differences in their spatial experience.

However, these correlational findings may imply only that people who are good at spatial activities seek them out. A stronger argument for the effect of experience on performance comes from experimental studies of training in spatial skills. A meta-analysis of such studies shows that both females and males benefit, apparently equally, from direct training (Baenninger & Newcombe, 1989).

It appears that the gender difference in mathematics performance can also be partially explained by the fact that females simply take fewer math courses than males (Benbow & Stanley, 1982; Fox, 1981). When the number of courses taken is held constant, gender differences in mathematics achievement are greatly reduced, although not always eliminated (De Wolf, 1981; Ethington & Wolfle, 1984; Fennema & Sherman, 1977). Since gender differences in the number of mathematics courses taken is apparently decreasing (Chipman, Brush, & Wilson, 1985), the already small difference in performance may shrink.

Researchers have noted, however, that even when males and females take the same courses in mathematics, they do not necessarily receive the same training. In the first place, mathematically gifted males are more likely than gifted females to engage in extracurricular study and activities related to mathematics (Fox & Cohn, 1980; Kimball, 1989) and are more likely to receive parental encouragement for mathematics achievement (Fox, 1981). In fact, a study of the parents of the mathematically gifted children in the Johns Hopkins National Talent Search found that parents of the boys were considerably more likely than those of the girls even to be aware that their child was mathematically talented (Tobias, 1982), and parents of boys were more likely than parents of girls to have given their children science-related gifts such as science kits, telescopes, and microscopes (Astin, 1974). In the second place, even within the same mathematics class, boys and girls may not be getting the same education. When one team of researchers observed 33 second-grade teachers in the classroom, they found that these teachers spent more classroom time teaching reading than mathematics to individual girls, and more time teaching mathematics than reading to individual boys (Leinhardt, Seewald, & Engel, 1979). In high school mathematics classes, boys are consistently spoken to and called on more and receive more social interaction, individual instruction, feedback, and encouragement (Becker, 1981; Koehler, 1986; Stallings, 1985). Researchers have also shown that, when working in small groups in mathematics classes, girls receive less information from their peers than boys do (Webb & Kenderski, 1985; Wilkinson, Lindow, & Chiang, 1985).

Further evidence for the importance of training and practice on mathematics achievement comes from recent findings showing that the international gap in math achievement between the United States and China and Japan is far greater than the average male–female gap observed within countries. Researchers who tested kindergarten, first-, and fifth-grade children in these three countries found no differences in reading or general intelligence, but they did find increasing international differences in mathematics performance with increasing age. (No significant male–female differences in mathematics performance were found for any of the grade levels.) American first-graders were surpassed by those in China and Japan by an average of 10 percent on a standard math test. By the fifth grade, the top American class scored, on average, below the lowest Japanese class and the second-lowest Chinese class. Of the 100 highest scoring fifth-graders, only one was American (Stevenson, Lee, & Stigler, 1986). Rather than looking for biological explanations, as they might have done had they been reporting gender differences, these researchers searched for social explanations for these vast international differences. What they discovered is that, in the first place, Chinese and Japanese students receive more formal school training in mathematics than their American counterparts: They spend 240 days a year in school compared to the Americans' 180. In the second place, Japanese and Chinese parents gave their children more help with math homework than U.S. parents. The basis for the difference in parental actions can be found in their beliefs about the reasons for academic success: American parents attributed success more often to ability, Chinese and Japanese parents attributed it to effort.

For verbal skills as well, evidence points to the impact of specific training. Starting in infancy, females are vocalized to more often than males, which may, in turn, lead to increased vocalization by female infants (Bee, Mitchell, Barnard, Eyres, & Hammond, 1984; Maccoby & Jacklin, 1974). Regardless of the reason for the original difference, the two processes probably act in an ever-strengthening feedback loop to increase females' experience and practice with speech production skills at an early age. This pattern does not seem to hold across cultures, however. In Greece, where there is strong cultural preference for male over female infants, mothers speak more affectionately to male than female infants, and home-reared male infants seem to be more vocally responsive and interactive with their mothers than do females—a finding that researchers have speculatively linked to other studies showing that Greek males tend to outperform females in cognitive tasks, even verbal ones (Roe, Drivas, Karagellis, & Roe, 1985). Even in North America, some research shows that by the time children are toddlers mothers' speech to boys and girls differs significantly on dimensions thought to stimulate cognitive development. Mothers' communication to their sons included more questions, more numbers, more verbal teaching, and more action verbs than did their communication to their daughters (Weitzman, Birns, & Friend, 1985). It is becoming increasingly clear that early parent–child interactions have an impact on the child's cognitive development and that these interactions may differ in many subtle ways for girls and boys. Much more research is needed to understand just how this process works.

Gender-Role Socialization.   In North America, female and male gender roles fit neatly into the observed pattern of performance differences between women and men. Even among children and adolescents, mathematics and technical and mechanical pursuits based on spatial ability are thought to be masculine domains, while verbal and artistic skills are considered feminine (Hill, Hobbs, & Verble, 1974; Nash, 1979; Stein, 1971). A study of elementary school students in Taiwan, Japan, and the United States found that, as early as first grade, children and their mothers in all three countries believed that boys were better at mathematics and girls were better at reading (Lummis & Stevenson, 1990).

From preschool onward, children set very gender-stereotypic occupational goals (Archer, 1984; Franken, 1983). These findings are not surprising, given that the activities and toys encouraged for boys and girls are so different. For example, boys are given more mechanical toys such as models and tools; not only do such toys encourage the development of spatial ability, but their definition as "boys' toys" encourages the attitude that this type of ability is a masculine one. It has also been found that fathers tend to engage in gender stereotypic play with their sons and daughters, while mothers are likely to use feminine toys and activities with both boys and girls (Maccoby & Jacklin, 1974)—a pattern that is bound to result in girls' having fewer opportunities than boys to engage in play that involves mechanical and spatial skills.

The fact that children learn to label various tasks as masculine or feminine is clearly relevant to their performance on these tasks. Many studies support the contention that children perform better, work longer and harder, and evaluate the appeal of the same task as greater when it is labeled as appropriate to their own gender than when it is labeled as appropriate to the other gender (Hargreaves, Bates, & Foot, 1985; Montemayor, 1974; Stein, Pohly, & Mueller, 1971), although some researchers have found the effect of gender-typed labeling to be stronger for boys than girls. For both sexes, mathematics achievement in elementary and junior high school is positively correlated with the belief that mathematics is gender-role appropriate (Paulsen & Johnson, 1983). The impact of gender-labeling of tasks can be seen even more clearly when cultures are compared. In cultures that label reading as a masculine-appropriate skill, for example, males' performance on reading and vocabulary tests equals or exceeds that of females (Finn, 1980).

Some authors have suggested that the gender-appropriateness of particular academic subjects may be conveyed through the gender of the teacher. Because, beginning in junior high school, more mathematics teachers are male and more English teachers are female the notion that math is for boys and English is for girls may be reinforced (Nash, 1979). Moreover, gender-of-examiner effects have been found for children's performance: Males do better when tested by male examiners and females do better when tested by female examiners (Pedersen, Shinedling, & Johnson, 1975).

The impact of gender labeling of academic subjects has potentially serious implications beyond immediate academic performance, since it can affect children's course choices and thus, eventually, their career paths. For example, a belief that mathematics is a male domain has been found to relate to females' lower self-confidence in learning math (Sherman, 1982) and avoidance of mathematics courses in high school (Sherman & Fennema, 1977). The avoidance of mathematics courses in high school closes a number of college study options for women, thus helping to perpetuate male–female segregation into different careers. Actually, males are more likely than females to stereotype mathematics as a male domain (Hyde, Fennema, Ryan, Frost, & Hopp, 1990b). It is likely that, especially during adolescence, females are sensitive to these male stereotypes and may avoid mathematics and technical subjects in response to them (Lips & Temple, 1990).

Not only the labeling of specific tasks and skills as masculine or feminine, but also the overall flexibility of gender-role socialization may affect cognitive performance. For example, research has uncovered larger gender differences in spatial visualization among the Temne tribe in Sierra Leone than among the Canadian Inuit, for whom no gender differences are found (Berry, 1966). Among the Temne, females are more strictly controlled than males, while the Inuit encourage independence and autonomy for both sexes.

Self-Confidence. Some of the effects of gender-role socialization on cognitive performance may have their impact through gender differences in self-confidence. Simply labeling a task "for girls" or "for boys" raises the expectations of the "appropriate" group for success on that task (Montemayor, 1974; Stein et al., 1971). Males are more likely to expect to do well on masculine tasks and intellectual areas (Crandall, 1969; Deaux & Emswiller, 1974). Females are more confident of success on feminine-typed tests, such as verbal ones, and less confident on masculine-typed tests, such as spatial ones (Lenney, 1977). In high school and university, males have more self-confidence than females do in their mathematical, scientific and technical abilities (Erlick & Lebold, 1975; Fennema & Sherman, 1977; Hyde, et al., 1990b). Mathematics self-efficacy expectations (beliefs about one's ability to perform a given task) are consistently and significantly stronger for college males than for college females (Betz & Hackett, 1983). Even when girls are doing well in mathematics, they do not feel competent (Levine, 1976).

Parents seem to expect more from their children in gender-stereotypic areas. Thus, for instance, parents expect higher achievement from sons than from daughters in mathematics (Levine, 1976) and credit sons with more talent than daughters for successful mathematics performance (Yee & Eccles, 1988). Research suggests that, particularly in the realm of mathematics achievement, parents' differential expectations for their sons and daughters are communicated to their children at a young age (Entwisle & Baker, 1983). After tracking 1100 children semester by semester over the first three grades, these researchers noted that, despite the fact that the boys' arithmetic marks or general aptitude did not exceed girls' in first grade, boys developed higher expectations for their performance in mathematics than did girls. These higher expectations do not seem to be based on past performance or teachers' evaluations, but rather on parents' expectations for their children's performance. Other research also shows that parents' beliefs about their children's math aptitude are better predictors of the children's attitudes toward math than are measures of past performance (Parsons, Adler, & Kaczala, 1982).

There are many indications that gender-role socialization predisposes females and males to different levels of general self-confidence. Girls receive strong messages that they are *incapable* of doing certain things, such as mathematics, while boys' gender-related prohibitions are based on the notion that they *should* not do certain things, such as playing with dolls, rather than on the notion that they cannot do them. Jeanne Block (1984) has argued that the end result of the differing patterns of socialization for females and males in our culture is that males tend to develop "'wings'—which permit leaving the nest, exploring far reaches, and flying alone" (p. 137), while females tend to develop "'roots'—roots that anchor, stabilize, and support growth" (p. 138). Boys, she concludes, are encouraged to explore, to be independent, to try difficult things. Girls, on the other hand, are "oversocialized"—closely supervised close to home and given fewer chances to master the environment or to figure out how things work, to make decisions, or to take risks. Small wonder, then, if girls and boys differ in their confidence at tackling the new, abstract, and sometimes difficult material that is presented in mathematics courses.

Motivation. A potentially useful framework for understanding gender differences in achievement choices is the expectancy/value model developed by Eccles and her colleagues [Eccles, 1985; Eccles (Parsons) et al., 1983]. The model proposes that the decision to pursue achievement in a particular area is most directly linked to expectancy for success and to the importance or value an individual attaches to achievement in that area. We have already seen that male and female expectancies for success may differ for mathematical, verbal, and spatial tasks. Do the sexes also differ in the value they attach to success in these areas?

There is some evidence from studies of achievement in mathematics and science that males and females do differ in the way that they attach values to various achievement activities. As early as the seventh grade, boys see mathematics as more useful than girls do (Fennema & Sherman, 1977; Hilton & Berglund, 1974; Sherman & Fennema, 1977). One study of fifth- and sixth-graders found that girls were relatively unaware of the relevance of mathematics to careers other than strictly scientific ones. A program that emphasized the applications of mathematics to art and social problems had a positive impact on these girls: they felt better about school, reported liking mathematics more, and even showed some increased interest in scientific careers (Fox, 1976).

Among high school students, the value that males attach to mathematics achievement is strongly related to their performance history: The better they have done in the past, the more highly they value mathematics achievement (Eccles, 1985). For females, on the other hand, the value placed on mathematics achievement is much more independent of their past performance. Behr (1973) found that girls' mathematics grades could be predicted more accurately from their attitudes to mathematics than could boys' grades. The reason for this gender difference is not yet clear, but Eccles (1987) suggests that gender roles influence achievement patterns mainly through their effect on the value that females and males attach to different achievement options.

Other research supports the idea that task value is an important determinant of achievement behavior and that males and females differ in the factors that influence these values. One study of mathematics and science participation among female university students found that the reason given most often for avoidance of math and science was a lack of interest in and enjoyment of these academic subjects (that is, low intrinsic value)—a reason that was cited far more often than perceived difficulty or lack of career relevance (Lips, 1984). In a study of computer-related attitudes among university students, women's intentions to major in computer science were related more strongly to interest and enjoyment of computers than to a more pragmatic desire to find a high-paying, advancement-oriented job, while the reverse pattern was true for men (Lips & Temple, 1990). Research suggests, as well, that one reason for college males' greater tendency to choose courses and career goals in mathematics and science is their concern with status and success. College men and women see science careers as equally difficult and demanding, but men seem to see that demandingness as a more positive feature than women do (Lips, 1992). Thus, females and males, at least in high school and college, may be motivated by different factors in their pursuit of achievement in mathematical, scientific, and technical fields. The precise origin of these differences, how they affect performance, whether they extend to other areas, and how early they begin to appear, are all matters that await further investigation.

In general, it appears that all four of the social/affective factors discussed in this section—training, gender-role socialization, self-confidence, and motivation—work in interlocking ways to help produce small performance differences between males and females in certain verbal, mathematical, and visual-spatial tasks. Girls and boys are taught, implicitly and explicitly, that mathematical and visual-spatial tasks are masculine while verbal tasks are feminine. In concert with this differential labeling goes differential training, starting with parental vocalization to infants and toddlers, and continuing with sex-typed toys and activities and different amounts of teaching in school. The labeling also produces gender differences, both in self-confidence on these tasks and in the value attached to achievement in these areas, which, in turn, relate to decisions about trying to achieve and to performance itself.

Summary

Despite psychology's long history of searching for intellectual differences between the sexes, such differences have, for the most part, proven small and elusive. There is some evidence for male–female differences in sensation and perception: Females outscore males on tests of perceptual speed and accuracy, show more sensitivity to touch in their fingers and hands, and are more sensitive than males to changes in sound intensity. Under lighted conditions, males seem to be more sensitive than females to changes in the intensity of visual stimuli. Male and female infants have been found to differ in the kinds of stimuli to which they pay the most attention, with females showing stronger responsiveness to faces and males responding more to blinking lights and other novel objects.

Most of the recent research attention has, however, concentrated on cognitive rather than perceptual performance differences. Traditionally, males and females have been thought to differ in their performance on verbal, quantitative, and visual-spatial tasks. Generally speaking, research now shows only a negligible tendency for females to outscore males on tasks that require verbal skills, and small differences favoring males on mathematical problem-solving tasks and tasks requiring spatial perception. A somewhat larger difference favoring males is found for visual-spatial tasks that require rapid mental rotation of pictures or objects. For these broad areas of cognitive performance —verbal, quantitative, and visual-spatial—the presence and magnitude of a gender difference depends on the specific aspect of performance being tested and the specific population being studied. Given the current state of the research, it is no longer appropriate to make general statements about one gender outperforming the other in one of the three broad areas. And of the specific differences that have been observed, none are nearly large enough to explain the disproportionate number of males, as compared to females, in the scientific and technical professions.

Psychologists have spent a great deal of energy trying to explain the observed small gender differences in certain aspects of verbal, mathematical, and visual-spatial performance. A number of biological mechanisms have been postulated as causal factors: genetic linkage of particular abilities to the X-chromosome, direct action of circulating sex hormones, sensitizing effects of prenatal hormones on the developing brain, and the degree of lateralization of specific functions in the left and right hemispheres of the brain. At present, evidence for the X-linkage explanation is very weak, new evidence is emerging in support of some aspects of the circulating hormones hypothesis, and, under the glare of a great deal of research attention, the hypothesis linking cognitive performance differences to greater lateralization of functions in the male than female brain has begun to look overly simplistic. Some evidence suggests, however, that some particular abilities may be organized differently—some more diffusely and some more focally—in female and in male brains.

Several social/affective factors appear to play interlocking roles in helping to produce gender differences in cognitive performance. Some verbal tasks are gender-typed as feminine while mathematical and certain visual-spatial tasks are labeled masculine. As a consequence of this labeling, boys and girls receive different amounts of direct training and parental encouragement for achievement in these areas. The labeling, training, and parental support all influence children's self-confidence and the value they attach to success on particular tasks, which, in turn, influence performance. These social/affective factors, in interaction with whatever small biological predispositions toward gender differences exist, help to increase gender differences in performance. Yet despite all these pressures in the direction of differences, the result is only a small gender gap on a few cognitive tests. For tasks in all three cognitive areas, the gap is most noticeable at the top extreme of the performance distribution, and appears to be decreasing. Sizeable gender differences continue to be observed in curricular and career choices; however, it appears that these differences have little to do with cognitive abilities and a lot to do with gender-related expectations and cultural barriers to participation.

None of the research discussed in this chapter provides any justification whatsoever for sex discrimination in education, employment, the law, or any of our social institutions, or for the segregation of jobs according to gender. The finding that gender differences in abilities are so few in number and so small in size indicates clearly that individual differences rather than gender differences are the ones to be kept in mind when deciding what educational programs are best suited to various people, what roles each spouse should play in a marital relationship, or who is the best person for a particular type of job. As a favorite women's movement slogan puts it: "The best man for the job is often a woman," and we might add, "The best woman for the job is often a man."

For Additional Reading

Hollingworth, Harry L. (1990). *Leta Stetter Hollingworth: A biography*. Bolton, MA: Anker. The woman whose research first challenged the variability hypothesis was considered a "scientific pillar" of the women's movement. Here, her life and work are described in respectful detail by her husband.

Keller, Evelyn Fox. (1983). *A feeling for the organism: The life and work of Barbara McClintock*. San Francisco: W. H. Freeman. The author describes the work of one of the few women scientists to have won a Nobel Prize, and raises questions about whether women and men approach science differently.

7

Sexual Lives & Orientations

"**W**omen need a reason to have sex," muses Billy Crystal's character, Mitch, in the movie *City Slickers,* "men just need a place." The comment reflects something of the popular opinion about gender differences in a realm where such differences may seem especially relevant: sexuality.

Two of the most well-known sexual gender stereotypes involve the reluctant, disinterested female and the male who is always ready. Such beliefs in fundamental male–female differences in sexual response, drive, and desires have served as a justification for practices and institutions as diverse as prostitution, stag parties, "men's entertainment magazines," romance novels, men-only clubs, and the custom of veiling women from head to toe in certain cultures. Basic to the gender stereotypes about sexuality has been the notion that men have a much stronger sex drive than women do. Conveniently paired with this belief has been the idea that there are, however, "two kinds of women": the promiscuous, seductive ones who tempt men away from their more important pursuits and who fill the roles of prostitutes and performers in pornographic films, and the virtuous ones who are restrained and selective in their sexual behavior. While such stereotypes have begun to fade in some quarters, there are many indications that people expect women and men to differ in their approach to sexuality.

How do these expectations relate to the facts about male and female sexuality? This chapter presents some answers by reviewing the findings on the physiology of sexual response for women and men, the types and frequency of sexual behavior by the two sexes, sexual attitudes, and sexual orientation. Also discussed will be theories about the underpinnings of sexual behavior and research on some important issues that involve both sexuality and power and aggression: erotica and pornography, rape, and incest. The first step, however, is an examination of a constellation of beliefs that for centuries has promoted differing sexual values for women and men: the double standard.

The Double Standard

The double standard means just that: two different standards of sexual behavior, one for women and one for men. It is based on the assumption that males have a greater desire and need for sexual activity than females do. This supposed difference in males' and females' need for sex makes it appropriate for men to be the sexual aggressors and pursuers and for women to be the sexual gatekeepers, making sure that things don't get out of hand. Believers in the double standard do not hold a man responsible for pushing an unwilling woman to engage in sexual activity; rather they hold that it is the woman's responsibility to set limits. *He* supposedly cannot help himself; *she,* with her supposedly weaker sex drive, can.

This set of assumptions carries enormous implications for the sexual behavior and experience of women and men and for the power relationship between them. First of all, it trivializes women's sexual feelings, refusing to allow for the possibility that female sexual desire is important in its own right. Secondly, it trivializes men's capacity for self-control, making it appear that men are helpless before their sexual impulses. It means that women more than men risk ruined reputations by becoming known as sexually active, that men more than women risk ruined reputations by becoming known as sexually inactive, and that women who have been sexually assaulted, harassed, or raped are often blamed for their own victimization. Fallout from the double standard may include men's failure to learn that there are ways of controlling their sexual responses, women's failure to learn about their own capacity for sexual pleasure, and a reluctance of sexual partners to communicate with each other about their feelings.

Despite its long history, the double standard is not rooted in fact. Women and men are very similar in the physiology of sexual response, and women have an enormous capacity for sexual pleasure. It may be, in fact, that the gender differences we observe in sexual behavior are a result of the different ways in which social disapproval is dished out to women and men because of the double standard, and of women's awareness that, if sexual activity results in pregnancy, it is their own lives that will be most dramatically affected (Rubenstein, 1983).

The Physiology of Sexual Response

Until the 1960s most people's knowledge about the body's response to sexual arousal was limited to their own (and what they could tell about their partners') experience. Because sexuality was considered an extremely private matter, the idea that researchers could actually observe and measure in the laboratory the bodily reactions of people engaged in sexual activity was unthinkable. However, in 1966, the pioneers of this type of research, Masters and Johnson, published data on 382 women and 312 men whom they had observed in thousands of cycles of sexual arousal and orgasm (Masters & Johnson, 1966).

Sexual Response: Four Phases

One thing that Masters and Johnson did not find was a fundamental difference between women and men in their patterns of sexual arousal and orgasm. For both sexes, the physical response to sexual stimulation can be described as four phases: *excitement, plateau, orgasm,* and *resolution.* The two basic physiological processes involved in these phases are *vasocongestion* (the accumulation of blood in the blood vessels of a particular region) and *myotonia* (muscle contraction). The four phases, described in the following sections, are diagrammed for females and males in Figures 7.1 and 7.2.

Excitement.   This initial stage can be triggered by any of a variety of sexually arousing stimuli. Vasocongestion of the genital organs begins to occur. In males, this increased blood flow to the genitals causes the penis to erect, a reaction that tends to occur within a few seconds of the stimulation. In females, the increased blood flow causes fluids to seep through the membranes of the vaginal walls, producing lubrication. This lubrication, which signals the beginning of arousal, begins within 30 seconds after the arousing stimuli. The glans of the clitoris also swells as a result of vasocongestion. In both sexes the nipples may harden and erect as a result of contraction in muscle fibers.

During the excitement phase, the lips of the vagina swell and the upper two-thirds of the vagina expands. In males, the scrotum is pulled closer to the body and the testes begin to be elevated. In both males and females, there is an increase in heart rate and blood pressure. Although this phase is governed by the same physiological processes—vasocongestion and myotonia—for males and females, the different anatomies of the two sexes dictate different physical and social consequences. The erect penis cannot be ignored as easily as the moist vagina.

Plateau.   If sexual stimulation continues with sufficient intensity, a peak level of vasocongestion is reached in the plateau phase. Rate of breathing, pulse rate, and blood pressure increase further. The male's penis becomes fully erect and the testes swell and are further elevated. In females, the clitoris retracts, the vaginal lips deepen in color, and the tissues surrounding the outer third of the vagina swell to form the "orgasmic platform"—a change that has the effect of narrowing the opening to the vagina. As stimulation continues, both vasocongestion and myotonia continue to build toward the tension required for orgasm. If stimulation is withdrawn before orgasm, the person enters directly into the resolution phase. However, without the discharge of tension that occurs in orgasm, the resolution phase progresses slowly and can be quite uncomfortable. Men call this condition "blue balls"; women do not

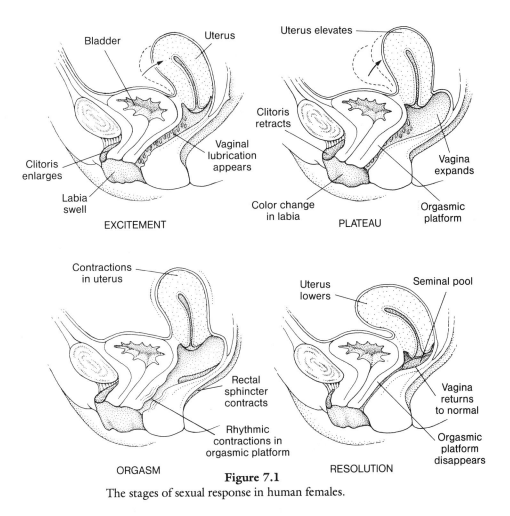

Figure 7.1

The stages of sexual response in human females.

seem to have an equivalent phrase, despite the fact that, as will be discussed later in the chapter, not reaching orgasm is a more common experience for them than for men.

Orgasm. In both sexes, when arousal reaches a critical point, it triggers orgasm, a series of involuntary rhythmic contractions of the pelvic organs. For males, the first part of orgasm involves the contraction of the vas, seminal vesicles and prostate to force the ejaculate into position in a bulb at the base of the urethra. Once this has happened, ejaculation is inevitable. Next, the bulb and the penis begin rhythmic contractions, causing the ejaculation of the semen.

For females, orgasm is a series of contractions of the orgasmic platform and the uterus. Surrounding muscles may also contract. In both sexes the pulse rate, blood pressure, and breathing increase sharply, and muscles throughout the body, such as

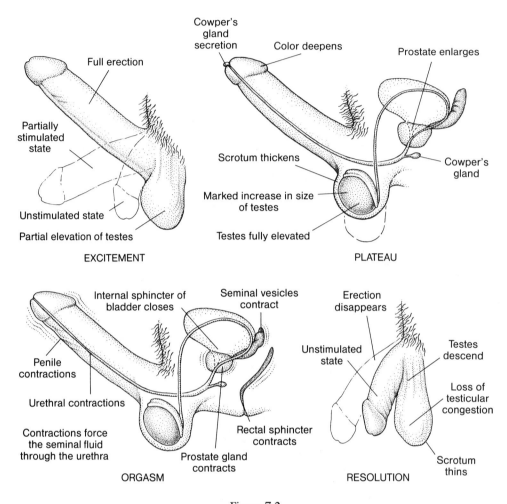

Figure 7.2
The stages of sexual response in human males

legs, thighs, and back, may contract. The whole process lasts only a few seconds. Some research has raised the possibility that some women also ejaculate during orgasm (Perry & Whipple, 1981). These researchers discovered a fluid that is chemically similar to seminal fluid spurting from the urethra during orgasm in a few women. Female ejaculation has been speculatively linked to an organ called the *Grafenberg spot* (or *G-spot*), located on the top side of the vagina. The whole notion of female ejaculation is still very controversial, however. The G-spot cannot be located for all women and, even among those for whom it can be, there is not always evidence of ejaculation. In one study, chemical analysis of the fluid ejaculated by women found it to be similar to urine rather than to male semen (Goldberg et al., 1983).

Whether or not the sexual partners experience simultaneous orgasm, or whether there is even a partner, orgasm is the same physiological process. For females, however, there is greater individual variation in duration and intensity of orgasm than there is for males. Also, for women, orgasm achieved through masturbation appears to be more intense than orgasm from intercourse, probably because a woman has better control over the type and intensity of stimulation during masturbation. Women seem to attach much importance to the interpersonal aspect of sexuality, however, as masturbation has not threatened to replace intercourse.

People would not go to so much trouble to have orgasms if they were simply a set of muscular contractions. The sensations of orgasm are very intense and pleasurable, and the release of sexual tension leaves the individual feeling satisfied and relaxed. These feelings are much the same for women and men. In one study, male and female college students gave written descriptions of what an orgasm felt like. A panel of experts (doctors and psychologists) who read the descriptions could not reliably distinguish between those that had been written by women and those that had been written by men (Vance & Wagner, 1976).

Resolution. Following orgasm, the body enters a fourth phase, resolution. The processes that led up to orgasm—vasocongestion and myotonia—are reversed. Muscular tension is relaxed and blood is released from the engorged blood vessels. In women, the clitoris shrinks to its normal size, the orgasmic platform relaxes, and the vagina and uterus return to normal. In men, the erection of the penis is lost and the scrotum and testes return to normal. In both sexes the pulse rate, breathing, and blood pressure gradually return to unaroused levels.

Resolution usually takes 15 to 30 minutes after orgasm. However, when orgasm has not occurred, it can take up to an hour. Among women who frequently experience sexual arousal without orgasm, the buildup of vasocongestion without discharge by orgasm can produce a great deal of discomfort.

One notable sex difference in response occurs in the resolution phase: Men experience a refractory period, lasting from a few minutes to 24 hours, during which they typically cannot be restimulated to erection and orgasm. No such refractory period occurs for women, making it possible for them to experience multiple orgasms.

Sexual Response: Issues

The Myth of the Vaginal Orgasm. One of the most popular misconceptions about orgasm, arising from Freudian theory, is that females can experience two distinct kinds of orgasm: one kind due to clitoral stimulation and a different (better) kind due to stimulation of the vagina by the penis during intercourse. As mentioned in Chapter 2, Freud believed that part of the psychological maturation process for women involved abandoning the attainment of orgasm through clitoral stimulation and shifting to a preference for orgasm attained through heterosexual intercourse. Indeed, his theory characterized the clitoral orgasm as "infantile," and many women seeking to avoid this label spent hours (and fortunes!) in psychiatrists' offices trying to figure out what unconscious fixation was blocking them from reaching orgasm with their partners without clitoral stimulation.

Masters and Johnson's research undercut the distinction between the clitoral and vaginal orgasms by showing that there is no physiological difference between orgasms that occur during intercourse and those that occur as a result of manual or oral stimulation of the clitoris. In fact, almost all orgasms involve stimulation of the clitoris. The vagina is a relatively insensitive organ—a useful feature given that one of its main functions is to serve as a route through which childbirth occurs. It is, however, sensitive to pressure, and it is this sensitivity that makes insertion of the penis pleasurable (Barbach, 1976). The clitoris, which (as discussed in Chapter 5), grows from the same fetal structure as the penis, is an exquisitely sensitive organ—so sensitive, in fact, that direct contact can be painful. (This is probably why the clitoris retracts during the plateau phase of sexual arousal.) Vaginal intercourse can indirectly stimulate the clitoris by pulling on the inner lips of the vagina, which in turn causes the clitoral hood to move back and forth against the clitoris. Thus, clitoral stimulation is usually what triggers orgasm, and the distinction between the clitoral and vaginal orgasm does not make sense.

Multiple Orgasm. Masters and Johnson found that women did not enter a refractory period after orgasm and that many women were capable of having a series of orgasms within a short period of time. During the resolution phase, if a woman is stimulated again, she can often be aroused, return to the excitement or plateau phase, and have another orgasm. Much less stimulation is required for these subsequent orgasms although they can be just as intense as the first, and the cycle can be repeated several times. Masters and Johnson found that, using masturbation, a woman could sometimes have 5 to 20 orgasms—up to 50 if she was using a vibrator!

Not all women experience multiple orgasms, and even those who do can often feel satisfied with just one. It should also be noted that some men may be capable of multiple orgasms, although data supporting this are scant (Robbins & Jensen, 1977; Zilbergeld, 1978).

Sexual Dysfunction. Impairments of sexual functioning, such as the inability to get an erection in men and the inability to have an orgasm in women or men, are common problems that cause a great deal of anxiety to the individuals experiencing them. Besides the obvious fact that they interfere with sexual pleasure, there are other reasons why these problems are sources of so much distress: People feel they cannot discuss them with others, and the cultural labels attached to the problems (e.g., "impotence" and "frigidity") are very negative ones. Masters and Johnson's research dispelled a lot of the secrecy surrounding sexual dysfunction and fostered a commonsense approach to treatment (Masters and Johnson, 1970).

The sexes are not so different with respect to sexual dysfunction. Both males and females can experience difficulty with arousal and orgasm, painful intercourse, and low sexual desire. However, there are differences in the frequencies with which these problems occur for women and men. Women are considerably more likely than men to report difficulty achieving orgasm. Men, on the other hand, are much more likely than women to have a problem with their orgasm happening too quickly (premature ejaculation).

It is estimated that about 50 percent of men experience occasional difficulty in getting an erection (Kaplan, 1974). Such difficulties can affect men at any age. Some popular attention has been given to the alleged "new impotence": a supposed rise in the numbers of men experiencing erectile difficulties due to the threatening emergence of the sexually liberated, sexually demanding woman (Ginsberg, Frosch, & Shapiro, 1972). However, no good data exist to support this notion. It is quite likely that, if sex therapists are seeing an increase in the numbers of men seeking treatment for erectile dysfunction, it reflects the publicity given to sex therapy and the increased social acceptability of admitting the problem (Hyde, 1986).

Early sex surveys found that about 30 percent of women reported never or only occasionally having orgasms during intercourse (Kinsey, Pomeroy, Martin, & Gebhard, 1953; Terman, 1951), while more recent ones show only about 10 to 15 percent of women saying they seldom or never have orgasm (Hunt, 1974). The latter study also uncovered some evidence for orgasm inconsistency in men, particularly under the age of 25. Perhaps, then, the gender difference in orgasm consistency is diminishing. On the other hand, the discrepancy between the early and later surveys may partly reflect a difference in the populations sampled. One of the difficulties with sex surveys is that the people who choose to respond to them may not be representative of the "average" population. Kinsey's research took place at a time when sexuality was a taboo topic. Thus, not only may he have had trouble obtaining honest responses, but his respondents, by agreeing to discuss their sexual habits with him, showed themselves to be a rather daring segment of North American society in the late 1940s. Hunt tried hard to obtain an unbiased sample of the U.S. population, but did not succeed completely. We do know that the Kinsey and Hunt samples are not completely comparable in terms of the age, race, marital status, and socioeconomic status of the respondents. Another possible problem with the comparability of the two surveys is that it may have been more acceptable in the 1940s for women to admit to difficulties with orgasm. Now, in the age of the multiple orgasm for women, it may simply be harder for women to admit orgasm inconsistency, even on an anonymous questionnaire.

The finding that women report more difficulty with orgasm than men do may be largely a function of ineffective stimulation of the woman. Women can masturbate to orgasm about as quickly as men can; it is during intercourse that they tend to experience difficulty or slowness in responding.

Sexual Desire. In 1978, and again in 1982, researchers conducted studies in which college students were approached by attractive females or males and asked one of the following questions: "Would you go out tonight?" "Will you come over to my apartment?" or "Would you go to bed with me?" (Clark & Hatfield, 1989). Not surprisingly for those of us familiar with sexual norms for women and men, men were more willing than women to accede to sexual invitations from potential partners. The great majority of men were willing to have a sexual encounter with the woman who approached them; however, not one woman agreed to such an encounter.

Do these findings mean that women are less interested in sex than men are? Not necessarily. The double standard of expectations for females and males affects the way that female-to-male and male-to-female propositions are interpreted. The women might have been worried about what the attractive man would think of them if they agreed to have sex with him so casually. The men who were propositioned would have few such worries. Moreover, their opinion of the woman issuing the invitation was no doubt lowered by the very fact that she would invite a stranger to have a sexual encounter with her. Beyond the double standard, another consideration might well have inhibited women from accepting the man's invitation: fear. As discussed in a later section, women have good reason to fear sexual violence, and women may well be cautious about making themselves vulnerable.

Despite the possible competing explanations of the double standard and the fear of sexual violence, a traditional stereotype has held that women desire intercourse less frequently than men. Kinsey and his colleagues noted that wives wanted intercourse less often than their husbands did; however, according to the Hunt survey, fewer than 5 percent of the wives wanted intercourse less often than their husbands did, and in a survey conducted by *Redbook,* one-third of the wives reported a wish for more frequent intercourse (Levin & Levin, 1975). It is difficult to infer a trend here because the samples may be very different. The more recent findings do indicate, however, that many women are interested in intercourse. That interest is not limited to married adults. A *Seventeen* magazine survey of a national sample of single females and males between the ages of 14 and 21 found that, of those who were sexually active, 99 percent of the males and 91 percent of the females reported that they enjoyed intercourse (Pesmen, 1991).

Perhaps, in the attempt to study sexual desire, it is inappropriate to focus on the desire for intercourse. We have already seen that intercourse may not be the most satisfying form of sexual activity for women. If middle-class wives prefer, as one study found, to read a book rather than engage in sexual activity with their husbands (Mancini & Orthner, 1978), that preference may reflect not a lack of sexual desire but a lack of sexual satisfaction through intercourse.

When it comes to sexual activity, women and men may differ, not so much in the frequency with which they desire the activity, but in the kinds of activities they desire. Research with college students and newly married couples shows that women desire more activities in sex that demonstrate love and intimacy, while men want more activities that are sexually arousing (Hatfield, Sprecher, Pillemer, & Greenberger, 1988). Another study focused on sexual urges and fantasies outside of heterosexual activity (Jones & Barlow, 1990). Male and female undergraduate students self-monitored their sexual fantasies (internally generated sexual thoughts), urges (externally provoked sexual thoughts), and masturbatory fantasies for seven consecutive days. Women and men did not differ in the frequency of their sexual fantasies. However, men reported more urges and masturbatory fantasies than women did.

Some writers have suggested that women's sexual desire may fluctuate with the menstrual cycle. A peak in desire may occur at the ovulation phase for some women and at the menstrual or postmenstrual phase for others (Adams, Gold & Burt, 1978; Gold & Adams, 1981; Kinsey et al., 1953). While such correspondence between the menstrual cycle and sexual desire may be experienced by individual women, there is, as yet, no evidence that women as a group show any regular pattern of cyclic fluctuation in sex drive.

Sexual Activity

Information about the type and extent of people's sexual activity generally comes from self-reports elicited through surveys (e.g., Bell, Weinberg, & Hammersmith, 1981; Hite, 1976, 1981; Kinsey, Pomeroy, & Martin, 1948; Kinsey et al., 1953; Pesmen, 1991). Although such surveys have proven invaluable in providing knowledge about sexual activity, there are reasons to be skeptical about the degree to which the survey results reflect the sexual behavior of the general population. Volunteer participants in sex research tend to be more experienced and less inhibited in their sex lives than most people (Kaats & Davis, 1971; Maslow & Sakoda, 1952), so they are not an unbiased sample of the population. Making the sample still more biased may be the deliberate exclusion of particular groups. For example, the Kinsey report did not include black respondents, and Hunt, in an effort to make his sample comparable with Kinsey's, dropped black respondents when comparing his results with the Kinsey report. In addition, the reliance on self-reports of sexual practices has some potential pitfalls. Respondents may distort reality by tending to exaggerate or minimize their sexual activity, they may be unable to remember accurately events that are long past, and they may have difficulty estimating frequencies and time spent in certain activities. Given these drawbacks, it might be more appropriate to take the data provided by these surveys as rough approximations of the experience of the general population than as completely accurate representations of it.

Heterosexual Intercourse

Kinsey's data, collected in the 1940s, indicated that, by the age of 25, 33 percent of women and 71 percent of men had had premarital sexual intercourse. The Hunt report indicated that, by the 1970s, the comparable percentages were 97 percent for men and 67 percent for women. Other surveys show a similar increase in premarital sexual activity among adolescents and young adults, with a larger increase evident for women than for men and a trend toward first intercourse occurring at earlier ages (Hopkins, 1977). A survey by Zelnick and Kantner (1980) showed that 69 percent of females and 77 percent of males reported having premarital intercourse by the age of 19. The *Seventeen* magazine survey (Pesmen, 1991) indicated that 51 percent of both single males and single females in the 14 to 21 age range had had sexual intercourse and 71 percent of young women aged 18 to 19 were sexually active. There is little evidence, however, that the average young adult has a great deal of variety in sexual partners before marriage. Surveys taken in the early seventies suggested, for example, that more than half of the women who engaged in premarital intercourse had only one partner, often their fiancé (Hunt, 1974; Kantner & Zelnick, 1972) and that married men had typically had about six premarital partners. The average number of premarital partners may have increased for women (Zelnick & Kantner, 1977); however, the majority of young single women report that they prefer to date one person exclusively (Pesmen, 1991).

Sexual activity is affected by a variety of factors. Currently, the AIDS epidemic, as well as the prevalence of other sexually transmitted diseases, may be a factor in people's decisions with respect to whether or not, and with whom, to be sexually active. These issues are discussed in later sections.

First intercourse is often greeted with different reactions by females and males, at least among the adolescents studied by Sorenson (1973). Males were more likely to report feeling positive: excited, joyful, and mature. Females, on the other hand, were more likely to say they felt negative emotions: guilt, sorrow, disappointment. Disappointment may be a common reaction for women. One sample of college women, rating their experience of first intercourse on a 1 to 7 scale (1 = didn't experience pleasure at all, 7 = strongly experienced pleasure) gave it an average rating of only 3.9 (Weis, 1983).

Among married couples, there is a great deal of variability in the frequency of coitus. According to the surveys, the average couple in their mid-twenties has intercourse between two and three times per week, with the frequency declining gradually over the years (Hunt, 1974; Westoff, 1974). Women report slightly less satisfaction with marital sex than men do, but both women and men express relatively high levels of satisfaction (Hunt, 1974). On surveys, men are more likely than women to say that they have engaged in extramarital sex, with about half of the men and one-quarter of the women engaging in it at least once. The incidence of extramarital sex for women seems to have increased since the 1960s (Thompson, 1983), but, in general, the affairs do not seem to be casual ones. Many of the women who have had extramarital sex have done so with only one partner (Blumstein & Schwartz, 1983).

Most surveys report a higher incidence of heterosexual activity for men than for women. A greater proportion of men than women say they are sexually active, and men report having more partners than women do. This finding is a difficult one to explain. Since each act of heterosexual intercourse involves one man and one woman, where are the women with whom the male respondents in these surveys claim to be having intercourse? Phillis and Gromko (1985) list three possible explanations for the men's reported higher number of partners: (1) overreporting by men and/or under-reporting by women of sexual activity; (2) the existence of a minority of women who have many partners; and (3) males and females in the surveys, or their partners, are drawn from different populations. Phillis and Gromko's own study of students at a midwestern university revealed no evidence for the existence of a small group of women having intercourse with a large number of men: 6 percent of sexually active women and 9 percent of sexually active men reported having 12 or more partners. Furthermore, there was no evidence that the men were finding a disproportionately larger number of partners away from the campus than the women were. Phillis and Gromko finally concluded that the differences in the proportions of males and females reporting sexual activity could be explained by the unequal sex ratio at the university (57 percent women and 43 percent men). Their reasoning went like this: Suppose that, on an island populated by 300 women and 100 men, 80 percent of the men are heterosexually active. If each sexually active male has one female partner, then 80 men are paired with 80 women. In terms of proportions, though, a researcher could report that 80 percent of the men but only 27 percent of the women report heterosexual activity! When Phillis and Gromko corrected for the unequal proportions of males and females in their own sample, the gender difference in reported heterosexual activity disappeared. They tried to test the generalizability of this finding to the Kinsey, Hunt, and other sex surveys, but were unable to find the information on sex ratios needed to do so. Nonetheless, their findings suggest that the commonly accepted finding of greater male than female heterosexual activity may be more illusory than real, at least in some populations.

Homosexual Activity

The Kinsey surveys indicated that 37 percent of men and 13 percent of women had at least one homosexual experience leading to orgasm during adulthood (Kinsey et al., 1948, 1953). However, only 4 percent of males and 2 percent of females reported that they were exclusively homosexual. Hunt's (1974) data reveal a somewhat similar frequency of homosexual experience: 20 to 25 percent for men, 10 percent for married women and 20 percent for unmarried women.

Some of the reported gender differences in homosexual behavior seem to parallel those reported for heterosexual activity. Males report more sexual activity with more partners than do females, and females are more likely to want and to be involved in long-term, emotionally close relationships (Bell & Weinberg, 1978; Hunt, 1974; Meredith, 1984; Peplau, 1981). Since women in our culture are socialized more strongly than men are to value close relationships, this finding is not surprising.

Within homosexual relationships, the amount of sexual activity varies widely, just as it does in heterosexual relationships. This variation can be seen in the conflicting results obtained by researchers studying lesbian sexuality. One review of the literature led to the conclusion that lesbian women and heterosexual women are similar in the frequency with which they have sex (Peplau & Amaro, 1982); by contrast, however, a large-scale survey indicates that lesbian couples have sex much less frequently than any other type of couple (Blumstein & Schwartz, 1983).

Like heterosexual activity, homosexual activity is responsive to the norms of the surrounding culture. For example, studies of the history of lesbian relationships show that, under some conditions, lesbian couples of the 1940s and 1950s adopted the sexual roles of "stone butch" and "fem" (Davis & Kennedy, 1990; Newton, 1984). The butch was the sexual initiator or doer, while the fem was the more passive partner, receiving sexual pleasure. The ideal of the "stone butch" was to be untouchable: to gain sexual pleasure from giving pleasure, and not to allow her partner to reciprocate. Although, at first glance, these roles may seem to echo traditional male–female heterosexual roles, they were actually quite different. The active, butch, partner's main goal was to give, not take, sexual pleasure. Her fulfillment came from satisfying her partner. The fem, while more passive, was able to acknowledge and focus on her own sexual responses, to demand and receive sexual pleasure. These roles were socially constructed as ways of expressing lesbian cultural identity and female–female sexual love, and they were enforced by the norms of the lesbian community of the times (Davis & Kennedy, 1990). Currently, the emphasis on these roles has greatly diminished, as lesbian communities have found other ways to express their distinct identity:

> In the late sixties in Buffalo, with the development of the political activities of gay liberation, explicitly political organizations and tactics replaced butch-fem roles in leading the resistance to gay oppression. Because butch-fem roles were no longer the primary means for organizing the community's stance toward the straight world, the community no longer needed to enforce role-appropriate behavior. (Davis & Kennedy, 1990, p. 397)

Masturbation

Both the Kinsey and Hunt surveys indicated a large gender difference in the proportion of respondents who had masturbated to orgasm. Almost all males but only about two-thirds of females had masturbated. Furthermore, males began masturbating at an earlier age than females. Current data support these findings (Clement, Schmidt, & Kruse, 1984). Although part of the gender difference may be attributable to males' greater willingness than females' to report masturbation, it is interesting to note that females *do* report more of some kinds of sexual activity in recent surveys than they did in earlier ones, suggesting that they now feel freer to admit sexual activity than they did in Kinsey's day. However, the percentage of women reporting that they masturbate has remained relatively constant.

Some experts feel that there is a connection between the finding that a large proportion of women do not masturbate and the finding that many women have difficulty reaching orgasm. Women who have not masturbated may be unaware of the kind of stimulation that gives them the most pleasure and may not learn to be comfortable with their own body and sexual responses. Kinsey's data did, in fact, suggest that women who masturbate to orgasm before marriage are more likely to experience orgasm during sex with their husbands (Kinsey et al., 1953). At least one writer has argued that sex, like any other skill, must be learned and practiced; learning about one's own body through masturbation can build a sense of independence and can make the experience of two-person sex more positive (Dodson, 1974).

Contraception

Despite the emphasis on sexuality in our culture, there is a curious reluctance to connect sexuality with pregnancy. Media depictions of sexual encounters have increased in number and explicitness in the last decade (Brown, Childers, & Waszak, 1990). However, these depictions virtually ignore the reproductive potential of sexual intercourse: Never does the heroine of a romance novel stop to put in her diaphragm before she allows herself to be seduced by the hero, and even the most sensitive of movie heroes never seem to use contraception themselves or inquire of their sex partners whether they are using birth control before jumping into bed. Yet, in reality, the possibility of pregnancy cannot help but affect heterosexual relationships, and, given that women are the ones who get pregnant, the effect is bound to be different for women and men. Women are more likely than men to report that fear of pregnancy interferes with the free expression of their sexuality (Pesmen, 1991; Rubenstein, 1983).

One of the sources of the fear of pregnancy has traditionally been the disgrace associated with unwed motherhood. That stigma has lessened somewhat. In the United States, more than one million babies (26 percent of all newborns) were born to unmarried mothers in 1988—the majority to women in the 20 to 24 age range (Births to unmarried, 1991). Similarly, in England and Wales, the proportion of babies born to unmarried mothers has reached an all-time high: 29.6 percent in the first quarter of 1991, up from 6 percent in 1961 (Stigma of unmarried mother fading fast, 1991).

The fear of pregnancy, while still real enough, is less salient to present-day North American women than it was to women in the first half of this century. The provision of birth control information to women was technically illegal in the United States until 1918, when the law was changed as a result of the energetic efforts of Margaret Sanger and her colleagues in the National Birth Control League. Sanger, who started her career as a nurse, was moved to tears and anger by her repeated exposure to the plight of poor women worn out from a continuous series of pregnancies that they could not prevent, and dying in childbirth or from self-induced abortions. These women begged her for the facts about how to prevent pregnancy; however, even her nurse's training had not included that information. A turning point came for Sanger after a woman whom she had helped to save from death in the aftermath of an abortion pleaded with the doctor to tell her how she could avoid becoming pregnant again. The doctor laughed and told the woman to get her husband to sleep on the roof. Three months later, the woman died of another abortion, and Sanger left her nursing career behind to devote herself full-time to making birth control available to women. During the struggle, she was publicly reviled, jailed, and frequently subjected to frustration and humiliation. In the end, however, she and the organization she founded prevailed; it became legal for doctors to give contraceptive information to women, and a network of birth control clinics was eventually established (Sanger, 1938). In Canada, too, the birth control movement, under the guidance of women such as Mary Elizabeth Hawkins and Dr. Elizabeth Bagshaw, had a positive impact on the availability of contraception for women—although as late as the mid-1930s, an Ottawa social worker was charged with criminal activity for distributing family planning information (Van Preagh, 1982).

Despite the current availability of effective methods of birth control, many sexually active adolescents apparently do not use them consistently. One American survey shows that only about 75 percent of sexually active single males and females aged 14 to 21 say they use contraception "absolutely all of the time" or "nearly all of the time" (Pesmen, 1991). In some developing countries, the rates of contraceptive use are far lower. For example, one study of Guatemalan teenagers found that only 10 percent of sexually active teens were using contraception (Berganza, Peyre, & Aguilar, 1989).

Recent years have seen an alarming rise in the rate of teenage pregnancies. In the United States, there are approximately 1¼ million adolescent pregnancies each year (Kisker, 1985), 1 in every 9 girls between the ages of 15 and 19 gets pregnant (Ventura, Taffel, & Mosher, 1985), and 30,000 pregnancies per year occur among girls younger than 15 years of age (Byrne, 1983). Seventeen thousand women below the age of 15 and 399,000 women aged 15 to 19 had legal abortions in the United States in 1985 (U.S. Department of Commerce, 1990). In the United States in 1987, births to teenage mothers made up 10.4 percent of those to white women, 22.6 percent of those to black women, and 16.3 percent of those to women of Hispanic origin (U.S. Department of Commerce, 1990). Teen pregnancy takes a greater toll on the black American population than on white Americans. By their eighteenth birthday, 22 percent of black females and 8 percent of white females have become mothers (Ladner, 1987). Among whites, adolescent pregnancies are most likely to be ended by abortion; for blacks, they are most likely to result in single parenthood (Buchanan & Robbins, 1990).

The United States has the highest teen pregnancy rate in the Western world. The causes may lie partly in a lack of information about or easy access to birth control techniques; other Western countries make contraceptives and birth control information more easily accessible to adolescents (Ladner, 1987). Studies of black and Hispanic inner-city teenagers show that these young people are often aware of contraceptive methods but do not know how to go about getting them and know little about how effective they are (Herz & Reis, 1987; Smith, Chacko, & Bermudez, 1989). However, attitudes toward sexual activity, some of them based on our old friend the double standard, also seem to contribute to the problem (Adler, 1984; Byrne, 1983). The gender-role norms that say women do not take the initiative in sex may make it especially difficult for a young woman to prepare actively for the possibility of intercourse. However, the attitude that women should be the gatekeepers of sexuality means that the responsibility for preventing pregnancy is usually placed squarely on their shoulders, making men less likely to take responsibility for contraception.

The consequences of adolescent pregnancy can be serious for both the female and male involved. Women who become mothers, and men who become fathers, before their eighteenth birthday are, respectively, 50 and 40 percent less likely to graduate from high school than are their counterparts who put off parenthood until the age of 20 (Ladner, 1987). Adolescent males involved in a pregnancy show more psychological distress as young adults than do their counterparts who did not have a girlfriend become pregnant. This is true whether the pregnancy ends in abortion, in the assumption of fathering responsibility, or in the abdication of parenting responsibilities to the girlfriend (Buchanan & Robbins, 1990).

Throughout the adult years of fertility, women are far more likely than men to take the responsibility for preventing pregnancy. When college students submit anonymous written questions about sexuality, the women ask twice as many questions about contraception and pregnancy as men do (Valois & Waring, 1991). The most frequently used methods of birth control among American women have been those that do not require male cooperation: sterilization and the birth control pill. Less common, but also widely used, are the diaphragm, vaginal spermicides, and the intrauterine device (IUD). The use of methods that depend on male cooperation—vasectomy (male sterilization), condom, withdrawal, and rhythm—was reported by a combined total of only 20 percent of women surveyed by Forrest and Henshaw in 1983.

Recently, however, experts have begun to urge sexually active persons to use condoms, not just for the prevention of pregnancy, but for protection from sexually transmitted diseases such as herpes or AIDS. This new emphasis on the importance of condoms, in combination with the greater visibility of condom advertising, has apparently led to an upsurge in their use in some populations. One survey indicates that 72 percent of teenage girls and 79 percent of teenage boys who have had sexual intercourse have used condoms, compared to 48 percent and 61 percent in a comparable 1986 survey (Pesmen, 1991). This survey suggests that, among teenagers at least, condoms are the most popular method of contraception, used by 82 percent of those who regularly use contraception. This method is followed in popularity by the birth control pill (61 percent), while other methods, such as contraceptive foams and jellies, contraceptive sponge, and diaphragm, are used by 5 percent or less of this group.

Sexually Transmitted Diseases

Americans were stunned in November 1991, when basketball superstar Magic Johnson called a news conference to announce that he was retiring from the game because he had become infected with the virus that causes AIDS (Basketball star, 1991). In that news conference, Johnson urged young people to heed his message that "safe sex is the way to go." Johnson's high profile and popularity brought new attention to bear on the issues of safe sex and AIDS—attention that may cause at least some people to take more seriously the risks associated with sexually transmitted diseases.

A host of potentially serious diseases is transmitted through sexual contact: AIDS, herpes, chlamydia, syphilis, gonorrhea. Two and one-half million American adolescents contract a sexually transmitted disease every year (Pesmen, 1991). Yet fear of such diseases apparently plays little part in many adolescents' decision to become sexually active (Jedlicka & Robinson, 1987). In addition, knowing that the risk of contracting AIDS and other diseases can be reduced significantly by using condoms does not necessarily mean that condoms will be used. One study found that while 90 percent of teenage girls knew that unprotected sex put them at risk for contracting AIDS, fewer than 40 percent had used condoms the last time they had intercourse (Fishbein, 1988).

The source of the most serious concern about sexually transmitted disease has been the discovery of and publicity given to AIDS (acquired immune deficiency syndrome). AIDS is caused by the HIV (human immunodeficiency) virus, a slow-acting retrovirus. An individual who tests positive for the presence in the blood of antibodies to this virus (that is, an individual who is HIV-positive) does not necessarily have AIDS. However, current thinking in the scientific community is that 40 percent of persons with HIV will develop AIDS within five years. The virus attacks the immune system, the body's natural system for fighting off disease, allowing other diseases, such as rare cancers and infections, to go unchecked. Although there are some long-term survivors of the disease, most victims have a short life expectancy. In industrialized countries, the average survival rate after AIDS diagnosis is one to two years; in the developing world, death usually occurs within a year. Women have a shorter survival span than men (Gillespie, 1991).

As far as researchers can tell, the disease is transmitted through blood or semen, sometimes by carriers who have no symptoms themselves (Ho et al., 1984). The virus is known to be passed from person to person through sexual contact, blood transfusions, the use of contaminated hypodermic needles (e.g., among intravenous drug users), and from an infected mother to the fetus in her womb. During heterosexual contact, the disease is 17 times more likely to be passed from a man to a woman than vice versa (Padian, Shiboski, & Jewell, 1991). In North America, the disease was at first thought to be specific to gay men. However, this misconception has been shown to be false. In some sub-Saharan African countries it is more common among heterosexuals; worldwide, heterosexual intercourse is responsible for 60 percent of all transmission of HIV (Gillespie, 1991) and the incidence of heterosexually transmitted AIDS is increasing in North America. However, because the disease is sexually transmitted, and because it made its first appearance in North America in the gay male population, it has tended to be transmitted within that population and to have its biggest impact within those boundaries. Despite this, massive testing in the U. S. military for the presence of the AIDS virus has revealed that one-third of those who test positive are heterosexuals, and as many as 15 to 18 percent are women who deny using intravenous drugs (Fisher, 1986). This and other evidence has made it clear that the risk factor for AIDS is not sexual orientation but frequency of sexual contact.

The World Health Organization estimates that at the end of the 1980s, 8 to 10 million people were HIV-infected (Gillespie, 1991). In North America, the incidence of HIV disease has increased rapidly since the first cases were reported in 1981. More than 125,000 Americans have died of AIDS since then. Women are the fastest growing category of people with AIDS in the United States (Stuntzner, 1991), and AIDS is the leading cause of death for women ages 20 to 40 in major cities in North and South America, Western Europe, and sub-Saharan Africa (Gillespie, 1991). For women, the disease is complicated by its relationship to reproduction: An HIV-infected pregnant woman has a 25 to 40 percent chance of having an infected baby.

The fear of catching AIDS through sexual activity has had a large impact on the gay sexual lifestyle. Gay men are now cautioned to practice "safe sex": to use condoms when having sex, to avoid anal intercourse, and to limit their number of sex partners. This advice is apparently being heeded; there has reportedly been a shift away from casual sex in many gay communities (Lyons, 1983). The advice about condoms and caution with respect to casual sex is equally and urgently applicable to persons who practice heterosexuality, but change in practices has been slower in this population. Meanwhile, researchers are racing against time to develop an effective treatment for and a vaccination against the disease.

Life-Span Issues

Sexuality changes across the life span, and the patterns of change seem to be different for females and males. For one thing, women often find themselves much more able to enjoy sexual activity in middle age than they did when they were younger. Women are more likely than men to report increases from young adulthood to old age in measures such as frequency of orgasm, subjective pleasure in sexual activity, and satisfaction with sex life (Adams & Turner, 1985). Kinsey's survey indicated that women had orgasms more consistently at age 40 than they did as young adults. Men, on the other hand, are more likely to enjoy sexual activity from adolescence onward. One analysis (Kaplan & Sager, 1971) suggests that teenage males in our culture have an intense genitally focused sexuality. With the passing years, male sexual desire becomes somewhat less urgent, so that by age 30 a man is satisfied with less frequent orgasms. The adult man expands his sexuality from a narrow focus on genital pleasure to include the broader sensual and emotional aspects of sexuality. In women, on the other hand, there is an early appreciation of the sensual and emotional aspects of sexuality, but the genital response is often limited and inconsistent in adolescence and young adulthood. Often it is only in later adulthood that women develop a capacity for intense genital pleasure.

It is important to note that the pattern just described is not necessarily "natural." In different cultures, the male and female patterns of sexuality can vary widely from this one; thus, our socialization and expectations in the area of sexuality are highly likely to affect our experience of it. For example, researchers have described the sexual practices in two contrasting societies: a small Irish community on the island of Inis Beag (Messenger, 1971) and a South Pacific island called Mangaia (Marshall, 1971). On Inis Beag, where there is an attitude of secrecy and fear about sex, premarital sex is all but unknown, intercourse is something that happens infrequently and quickly, and many people cannot imagine that female orgasm exists. On Mangaia, by contrast, both boys and girls receive sexual instruction from adults and are encouraged to have sexual experience with several partners before marriage, and all the women apparently learn at a young age to have orgasms. These two cases are not isolated instances of variation in human sexual customs and expectations. Anthropologists have uncovered a wide variety of rules for handling sexuality in different cultures. For example, among the Truk of the Caroline Islands in the western Pacific Ocean, a man may sleep with the wives of any of his brothers-in-law and a woman may sleep with her sisters' husbands; also, men, but not women, can demand a divorce on grounds of adultery. In many foraging societies, there is little or no sexual double standard, and virginity is not an important issue. Among the Hagen of New Guinea, conversely, virginity is highly prized in brides, and wives are supposed to be chaste. However, sex is thought to be unclean and dangerous for both men and women, and hence the value placed on abstinence is almost as great for males as it is for females (O'Kelly & Carney, 1986). Clearly, sexuality can vary dramatically with cultural context.

The influence of culture on sexuality is particularly striking in the way our society regards sexuality and aging. Elderly people are often considered asexual (Kay & Neelley, 1982), so that, as people age, they commonly fear the loss of sexual interest and ability. Also, sexuality among the aged is sometimes thought of with disgust in our youth-oriented culture—the same behavior that might be taken as evidence of "virility" at 25 is called "lechery" at 65 (Rubin, 1965). North America is not the only part of the world where such myths flourish. Japanese researchers, for instance, have found that a decline in sexual activity among the elderly is partly attributable to cultural expectations (Mamiya, 1984).

The myths about aging and sex affect women and men somewhat differently, both because of gender roles and because of the difference in male and female life spans. The performance-oriented male sexual role is threatened when erections start to occur more slowly, and the female sexual role as an attractive object is threatened when her appearance no longer conforms to the youthful stereotype that is synonymous with beauty in our culture. Physiological changes that occur with age can slow down sexual response: Men may have slower erections with more need for direct genital stimulation, women may lose fatty tissue around the vagina, making intercourse uncomfortable without added lubrication. However, good health and regular sexual activity can promote men's and women's sexual functioning into their seventies and eighties, if they do not fall victim to the myth that "old" means "sexless." A particular difficulty for women in heterosexual relationships, however, is that they are extremely likely to outlive their mates. Because there is a shortage of men in the over-65 age group, and because men in our culture tend to seek out younger rather than older women as sexual partners, widowhood often implies forced celibacy for women whose orientation is exclusively heterosexual.

Sexual Motives, Values, and Attitudes

Motives

Females and males, at least during the college years, respond differently to the question "What are your motives for having sexual intercourse?" Women tend to stress love and commitment to their partner (e.g., "emotional feelings that were shared"), whereas men emphasize physical needs and pleasure (e.g., "need it," "to gratify myself") (Carroll, Volk, & Hyde, 1985). Twice as many male as female teenagers say they would have sex with a date simply because they were sexually attracted (Pesmen, 1991). Given the changes that are hypothesized to occur over the life cycle in female and male sexuality, we would not necessarily expect to find the same pattern of differences for adults in their thirties or older.

One researcher examined the correlates of sexual experience for women and men, in an attempt to test the hypothesis that sexual experience serves a compensatory function by bolstering self-esteem and self-confidence (Newcomb, 1984). His research found that, for men but not for women, sexual experience was correlated with assertiveness, education, self-esteem, and self-perceptions as highly masculine and invulnerable. This finding could be interpreted to mean that sexual experience enhances self-esteem and self-confidence for men—or it could simply mean that highly self-confident men are better at attracting sexual partners. In any case, the fact that no relationship was found between self-esteem variables and sexual experience for women does suggest a difference in the reasons women and men have for engaging in sexual activity.

Values

There is a stereotype that women and men value different things in heterosexual relationships. For instance, the accepted wisdom says that women place a higher value on love, intimacy, and togetherness, while men tend to emphasize the importance of the physical relationship and sexual variety. Evidence on these points is mixed. Clark and Hatfield (1981, cited in Hatfield, 1983), for example, found some support for the notion that men are more interested than women in sexual variety. They interviewed casual dating and newlywed couples about their desire for variety in sexual experience and found that men tended to wish their sex lives were more exciting, while women were more likely to be satisfied with the way things were. On the other hand, the idea that love is more important to women than to men in sexual relationships is supported by some findings and not by others. One study found that 45 percent of college females but only 8 percent of college males answered "Always" to the question "For you, is emotional involvement a prerequisite for participating in sexual intercourse?" (Carroll, et al., 1985). The latter researchers estimated that 29 percent of the variability in attitudes toward casual premarital sex could be explained by gender, suggesting that gender differences are quite a bit larger on this dimension than they are on measures of aggression or cognitive performance, as discussed in earlier chapters. Research also suggests that women in heterosexual couples feel more passionate and companionate love for their partners than men do, at least until old age (Hatfield, 1983). However, researchers have also found that men tend to be more romantic than women: more likely to fall in love quickly, view the relationship in romantic terms, and suffer terribly when the relationship ends (Hatkoff & Laswell, 1979; Hill, Rubin, & Peplau, 1976; Rubin, Peplau, & Hill, 1981).

One study (Cochran & Peplau, 1985) examined the importance that university students placed on three kinds of values in heterosexual relationships: attachment (having a close and secure love relationship), autonomy (the freedom to have separate interests apart from a primary relationship), and equality (both partners having equal say in decisions within the relationship). Despite the stereotype that women are more oriented toward intimacy and men toward independence, these researchers found that women and men did not differ in the value they placed on attachment. Women and men were equally concerned with having a secure, committed, sexually exclusive relationship. Also in violation of the stereotype, women placed significantly more value on autonomy and independence than men did. Finally, women gave more importance to equality than did men.

On the whole, there is evidence for both differences and similarities in the value orientations of women and men in sexual relationships. Because most of the research has been conducted with middle-class college students, however, it is impossible to draw general conclusions from these data about the impact of gender on values in sexual relationships.

Attitudes

Attitudes toward sexual activity have changed quite dramatically over the last several decades. In general, Americans, particularly those under the age of 30, have become more permissive of sexual activity, especially premarital sex. A Harris poll taken in the early 1980s showed that 79 percent of men and 70 percent of women aged 18 to 29 approved of sexual intercourse for regularly dating couples (Fink, 1983). A survey of Americans aged 14 to 21 recently showed that 28 percent of the females and 16 percent of the males said they did not intend to have sex before marriage (Pesmen, 1991). These percentages are in sharp contrast to surveys taken in 1937 and 1959, in which 56 percent and 54 percent of respondents, respectively, disapproved of premarital intercourse (Hunt, 1974).

Until the mid-seventies, it was taken for granted that women had more conservative sexual attitudes than men did. However, in the context of the recent general shift toward more sexual permissiveness, women's attitudes seem to have changed more than men's—perhaps because they had more latitude for change (King, Balswick, & Robinson, 1977; Perlman, 1974; Walsh, Ferrell, & Tolone, 1976). Surveys among university students, however, indicate that women are still somewhat more conservative than men. Astin's (1985) nationwide representative survey of college freshmen revealed that nearly two-thirds of the men but less than one-third of the women approved of sexual intercourse between "people who like each other." In a more recent survey of American adolescents, there was more permissiveness. However, females continued to appear somewhat more conservative than males: Only 6 percent of the females and 21 percent of the males agreed that it was okay to have sex with someone simply because it's fun (Pesmen, 1991). Among university students in another study, males scored higher than females on every item of a scale measuring sexual permissiveness (Hendrick, Hendrick, Slapion-Foote, & Foote, 1985). The differences were not extreme, however, and the researchers characterized the males as "moderately permissive" and the females as "moderately conservative."

Sexual attitudes involve more than permissiveness, and the latter study, which compared males and females on a spectrum of sexual attitudes, found gender differences on several dimensions. Females tended to score higher than males on sexual responsibility, an orientation that included concern with pregnancy and other consequences of sexual activity for a relationship. Women also scored higher than men on sexual conventionality, a scale concerned with the acceptability of such sexual practices as masturbation, using "sex toys," and using "dirty" words. There was also some tendency for women to give stronger endorsement than men to items measuring sexual communion, an attitude that sex involves close communication and can be "the ultimate in human interaction"; and for men to give stronger endorsement than women to items assessing sexual instrumentality—a self-centered, physical orientation to sex. However, the latter two differences did not appear when the individual item scores were summed to form scales.

In summary, although there is evidence that the sexual attitudes of women and men are becoming more similar, differences still exist. Researchers are not sure whether the trend toward convergence of male and female sexual attitudes will continue or whether there will be a shift toward more conservatism, reflecting political trends. A major determining factor in the trend will be the media portrayal of sexuality. There is little doubt that our sexual attitudes are shaped by the way sexual relationships are depicted in movies, television, music videos, magazines, and books. If these media continue to emphasize a double standard of sexual behavior, an absence of sexual responsibility for males, and a greater concern among females than males for the relationship context of sexuality, then these attitudinal gender differences are likely to persist.

Sexuality and Power: Erotica, Pornography, and Coercive Sexuality

Part of the stereotype that men have a stronger sex drive than women is a belief that men are more frequently and more easily sexually aroused by erotic material. The consequences of this belief for women's and men's feelings about their own sexuality and for the sexual power relationship between the sexes are enormous. Most material that is meant to be sexually arousing is produced for a male audience. Perhaps because it is explicitly geared to men rather than to both sexes, this material tends to present a view of women that is simultaneously idealized (in terms of physical beauty) and belittling (women are portrayed as passive objects of sexual desire, as bodies rather than people). Not surprisingly, women have never been encouraged to view this type of material; its very presence sometimes renders a store, a pub, or an entire section of a city virtually off-limits for women. One impact of the presence of large amounts of male-oriented erotic material, then, is to make real live women feel unwelcome and out of place in the areas where images and fantasies of sexuality are sold. Such a situation is highly unlikely to foster in women a sense of empowerment and joy in their own sexuality! To make matters even more difficult, there is an increasing trend toward the portrayal of brutalization and degradation of women in sexually oriented materials, a development that makes such materials even less palatable to women and that reinforces the myths of male sexual dominance and female sexual powerlessness and passivity. The development of an entire industry dedicated to producing and marketing sexually arousing materials specifically for a male audience obviously makes at least good economic sense: The pornography industry makes millions of dollars per year in sales to men. But does it make sense on any other dimension? Are women really not interested in erotic materials? What impact does the consumption of existing erotica and pornography have on men? And how does pornography fit into the larger problem of coercive sexuality?

Responses to Erotica

The women in the early Kinsey surveys reported less responsiveness than the men to most types of erotic materials. However, more recent studies suggest that women and men are not very different in their arousal to erotic stories, pictures, and films. For example, Schmidt and Sigusch (1970) showed erotic slides and movies to 128 male and 128 female university students. Gender differences in self-reported responsiveness were small, with 40 percent of the women reporting stronger sexual arousal than the average man.

There is an obvious problem with relying on self-reports to assess sexual responsiveness to erotic material: People may not want to admit they are sexually aroused. Thus, researchers in this area often try to obtain physiological measures of sexual arousal as well as self-reports. For men, such a physiological measure can be obtained using a device called a penile strain gauge—a flexible loop that fits around the base of the penis and measures vasocongestion. For women, arousal is also measured through vasocongestion, using a photoplethysmograph—a tampon-like acrylic cylinder that fits inside the entrance to the vagina. A groundbreaking study by Julia Heiman (1977) used these devices to show that what subjects report about sexual arousal in response to erotica does not always reflect what their bodies are experiencing. Heiman had male and female subjects listen to one of four kinds of tapes: erotic (explicit descriptions of heterosexual sex), romantic (a couple expressing affection and tenderness but not engaging in sex), erotic-romantic (containing both explicitly sexual and romantic elements), and control (neutral conversation). Each set of tapes also contained variations in the stories according to who initiated the activity (female-initiated vs. male-initiated) and whose physical responses were the focus of the description (male-centered vs. female-centered). In general, she found few differences between males and females in their physiological and self-reported arousal to the tapes: Both men and women showed the most responsiveness, both physiologically and in their self-reports, to the tapes containing explicit sex, both the erotic and erotic-romantic tapes. Neither sex tended to respond to the romantic or control tapes. Also, for both males and females, the female-initiated, female-centered tape was the most arousing. One difference did emerge, however. Although both women and men showed a high correlation between physiological and self-reported measures of arousal, women were significantly more likely than men to "miss" their physiological arousal. When men were physically aroused, they never failed to notice and report it. About half of the women, conversely, did not rate themselves as aroused when physiological measures indicated that they were. As noted earlier in the chapter, it is harder to ignore an erect penis than a moist vagina; it appears that women can sometimes be unaware of the early stages of their own physical arousal.

The gender difference in awareness of arousal may have as much to do with differences in sexual attitudes as with anatomy. Perhaps the prevalence of the double standard causes some women to internalize their "gatekeeper" role so strongly that they inhibit acknowledgment of sexual arousal. Support for the latter notion comes from a study by Morokoff (1985), who found that women who were high in the tendency to feel guilty about sex reported less arousal but showed higher physiological arousal while watching erotic videotapes than did women who were low in sex guilt. The tendency to regard sex as "forbidden," then, may be associated with both a refusal to acknowledge sexual arousal and a tendency to respond with strong physiological arousal to the erotic stimuli.

Impact of Erotica and Pornography on Behavior

There are several areas in which it might be reasonable to expect an impact as a result of viewing or listening to sexually arousing material. There might be an effect on the level of sexual interest, on the performance of particular sexual acts, on the perception of one's sexual partner, or satisfaction with one's sexual relationships. There is little evidence that exposure to erotica has any long-term effects on sexual interest or behavior, but there are indications that it can affect the sexual interest and behavior of both sexes in the short term. For instance, one study of male exposure to sexually explicit slides found that, in the week following, there was no increase in sexual activity although there was a significant increase in masturbation on the day of exposure (Brown, Amoroso, & Ware, 1976). Schmidt and Sigusch (1970) found that women but not men showed an increase in petting and sexual intercourse in the first 24 hours after seeing erotic slides and movies.

Exposure to erotic material may affect a man's evaluation of his mate. Men, but not women, who saw a series of nude photographs from *Playboy, Penthouse,* and *Playgirl* magazines later rated their mates as less sexually attractive than did their counterparts, who were exposed instead to pictures of abstract art (Gutierres, Kenrick, & Goldberg, 1983). Research does not appear to have addressed the question of how exposure to erotica and pornography affects women's and men's own self-perceptions and body image. One might, for example, predict that exposure to the photographs of apparently flawlessly beautiful women in magazines such as *Playboy* could shake a normal-looking woman's self-confidence in her own attractiveness.

Because so much of the sexually arousing material that is produced for men tends to portray women more as objects than as human beings, it is not surprising that there has been a trend toward increasing portrayals of violence against women in such material. When explicit violence is added to sexually arousing material, the issues of impact become even more complex. There is concern that a viewer who learns to associate sexual arousal with depictions of rape scenes, for example, may be tempted to try rape in real life. Moreover, in pornography, a woman who is raped, humiliated, or brutalized is usually shown to resist initially, but eventually to become sexually aroused by the way she is treated. Exposure to this type of fantasy may encourage men to behave in sexually coercive ways, in the mistaken belief that the experience will not ultimately be a bad one for the woman. Research now indicates that exposure to sexually violent pornography can increase men's acceptance of interpersonal violence against women and of rape myths such as "every woman secretly wants to be raped" (Demaré, Briere, & Lips, 1988; Malamuth & Check, 1981). Repeated exposure to violent pornography also results in decreased sensitivity to female victims of violence in nonsexual contexts (Linz, Donnerstein, & Penrod, 1984). Furthermore, laboratory studies in which males are exposed to aggressive or nonaggressive pornography and then given the opportunity to behave aggressively against another person by delivering electric shocks show that exposure to aggressive, but not nonaggressive, pornography increases the aggressive behavior of male subjects against females but not against males (Donner-stein, 1980, 1983; Malamuth, 1984). Exposure to aggressive pornography is strongly related to arousability to rape scenes, acceptance of rape myths, and self-reported likelihood of committing rape (Briere, Corne, Runta, & Malamuth, 1984). Finally, a survey of college males indicates that self-reported use of sexually violent, but not nonviolent, pornography plays a significant role in predicting self-reported likelihood of using sexual force or rape against women, and of self-reported use of actual sexual coercion or force (Demaré et al., 1988; Demaré, Lips, & Briere, 1991).

In summary, although exposure to pornography does not seem to have a major, lasting impact on sexual behavior, there is evidence that violent pornography can have an impact on men's aggressive behavior against women, as well as on their attitudes toward violence against women and toward female victims. Little research has addressed the impact of exposure to violent pornography on women, probably because men are the main consumers of pornography. However, since violent pornography is now a fairly visible feature of the media environment (e.g., in 1981, 17 percent of the covers of pornographic magazines depicted bondage or domination images—Dietz & Evans, 1982), it may well be having an impact even on those who are not its intended audience. Individual women often report that they feel humiliated and angry when forced to stand next to a rack of pornographic magazines at the checkout counter of their local store; such feelings are compounded when women have their children with them. Women speak of feeling violated and hurt when confronted with the violent anti-woman images in pornography, particularly when they discover that their male partners are consumers of such images. There seems little doubt that exposure to pornography affects women's feelings about themselves and their attitudes toward men, although these relationships have not been formally researched.

Coercive Sexuality

Relating sexually to another person implies exposing oneself to that person, at least physically and often emotionally. That exposure gives the partners some power over each other. In addition, knowing that one is desirable and desired sexually can confer a sense of power and secure self-esteem. Thus, sexuality almost always involves issues of vulnerability and power. Perhaps it should not be surprising, then, to find that power and dominance can sometimes overwhelm the relationship aspects, even the physical pleasure aspects, of sexuality—that sex can become an expression of dominance rather than of love or lust. There is a very noticeable gender difference here: Sexual coercion or violence is much more likely to be used by men than women. In a social context that tends to accept and encourage male dominance in so many situations, such a gender difference is almost inevitable.

Rape. Rape—forcing sexual relations on someone without that person's consent—is a common crime of sexual violence. Interviews with a random sample of San Francisco women led researchers to conclude that a woman faces a 26 percent chance of being raped during her lifetime (Russell & Howell, 1983). Although this figure is much higher than police reports of rape, it is widely acknowledged that rape is one of the most underreported crimes (Amir, 1971; Clark & Lewis, 1977). According to the recently released results of the federally funded National Women's Study, 683,000 American women were raped in 1990 and 12.1 million American women have been raped at least once (Estimate of rape victims is quintupled, 1992). Moreover, there is an entire category of rape that is not counted as a crime in some jurisdictions: marital rape, the rape of a woman by her husband. One study found that 14 percent of a sample of women who had ever been married had been raped by a husband or ex-husband (Russell, 1983b); another study found marital rape to be a common correlate of wife-battering (Frieze, 1983).

Men have less reason to fear rape than women, unless they are in prison, where homosexual rape is common (Lockwood, 1980). However, there are rare instances in which men are raped by women (Sarrel & Masters, 1982). Although the latter occurrence might seem physically impossible, it is not; penile erection is not under strict conscious control and may occur in response to such emotions as anger or fear.

College students have been found to estimate that 45 percent of men would commit rape if they could be sure they would not be caught and that 32 percent of women would enjoy being raped if no one would know about it. When these same students were asked to project their own reactions, 51 percent of the men reported at least some likelihood that they would commit rape if they would not be caught, but only 2 percent of the women reported any likelihood at all that they would enjoy being raped (Malamuth, Haber, & Feshbach, 1980). The average number of college males indicating some possibility that they would rape a woman under certain conditions appears to be about 35 percent (Malamuth, 1981), although in different samples it can be as high as close to 60 percent (Briere & Malamuth, 1983) or as low as 17 percent (Demaré et al., 1988). The self-reported likelihood of rape is correlated with acceptance of rape myths, fantasies about forced sex, and sexual arousal to rape depictions.

Attitudes about the acceptability of force in sexual interactions have an early start. When Zellman and Goodchilds (1983) questioned a broad spectrum of Los Angeles teenagers, they found that only 21 percent of them replied that, under each of nine specific conditions, it was definitely not all right for "a guy to hold a girl down and force her to have sexual intercourse." Force was viewed as most acceptable in cases where the girl had led the boy on or gotten him sexually excited, or when the couple had been dating for a long time. Both male and female teenagers were reluctant to define forced sex as rape, particularly when the couple involved was portrayed as dating steadily, and they tended to assign some of the blame for forced sex to the female. These findings reflect the presence of the traditional double standard in modern teenagers' attitudes, particularly in the stereotype that it is the girl's responsibility to control sexual behavior. Against such a background, it is perhaps not surprising that a significant number of college males say there is some possibility that they would commit rape.

College students' self-reported attitudes about rape may stem in part from the prevalence of rape on college campuses. As many as 25 percent of college women have experienced rape or attempted rape (On the legislative front, 1990). Few women report their experience, however, perhaps because campus administrations have traditionally treated rape as a prank that got out of hand rather than as a crime. However, the consequences of academic institutions' silence in the face of rape are very negative for female students: Victims may drop out of classes or even leave school, and a ripple effect through the female student population may diminish confidence levels and assertiveness (Hirsch, 1990). The words of one young college graduate, several years after being gang-raped at a fraternity party during her junior year, provide some sense of the pervasive, lasting effects of such an experience: "I'm a lot more hesitant about things, more cautious. I'm much more comfortable with things I'm used to. I think I'm probably more scared. Like, I'm much more comfortable just being home" (quoted in Hirsch, 1990, p. 56).

Why Is Sexual Assault So Common?　The finding that many ordinary men say there is some likelihood that they would commit rape lends support to the argument, often made by feminists (e.g., Brownmiller, 1975; Russell, 1984), that a tendency toward sexual aggression against women is part of the traditional masculine gender role. Males are socialized to be dominant and aggressive, and there are many messages, including those contained in violent pornography, that it is appropriate to express these tendencies in a sexual context. Clearly, rape is not simply an outcome of a sexually frustrated male's need for an outlet: Self-reported adequacy and importance of his sex life are not related to a man's self-reported likelihood of rape (Briere & Malamuth, 1983). The high incidence of gang rape (rapes committed by more than one assailant) also points to the conclusion that rape is a way of proving masculinity and dominance, rather than achieving sexual release. The feminine gender role may also contribute to rape, in that females are socialized to be passive, weak, and fearful—prime qualities for the construction of vulnerable victims (Russell, 1975). In fact, research on the avoidance of rape suggests that women whose socialization does not reflect the traditional feminine image are more successful at avoiding attempted rape (Bart, 1980). Bart found that background differences involving women's autonomy, competence, and self-reliance were related to the ability to avoid rape—for example, size and weight, never being married, regular sports involvement, knowledge of first aid and self-defense, and assertiveness training. Moreover, in the actual attempted rape situation, women who used the most strategies to avoid rape were the most successful; the likelihood of being raped increased when the woman relied on only one strategy to avoid it. These data suggest that women should be prepared to use many methods of avoiding rape, and that overreliance on such "feminine" modes of influence as pleading and reasoning with the rapist is ineffective.

A set of social norms, based on the double standard, that suggest that only "virtuous" women deserve full protection from sexual assault also contributes to the prevalence of rape. The rape of a prostitute is thought by some to be a contradiction in terms. One Australian judge, for instance, noted during sentencing of a man who had raped a prostitute at knifepoint that rape was less traumatizing for prostitutes than for other women because prostitutes were involved in sex as a business (Magazanik, 1991).

Interestingly, a man's rape of his wife has also been thought, until recently, to be a contradiction in terms. The thinking was that marriage gave a man full sexual access to his wife, so there could be no such thing as rape in the marriage relationship. The wife's willingness to engage in sex on any particular occasion was not relevant. Many countries have now changed their laws to make it possible for a woman to charge her spouse with rape. In 1990, France became one of the latest countries to rule that rape could exist within marriage (Rapist husband, 1990).

Incest.　Incest, defined as sexual relations between relatives, is often coercive and exploitative, since in many cases it involves an older powerful relative forcing sex on a younger, inexperienced one. Studies show that female children tend to be sexually victimized by adult males more often than male children are victimized by males or females. Between 4 and 12 percent of all women surveyed report a childhood sexual encounter with an adult male relative, and, for 1 woman in 100, that adult male relative is her father (Herman, 1981). Fewer men report being sexually victimized by an adult during childhood; among those who do, the adult is far more likely to be male than female. It appears that men are far more likely than women to try to take sexual liberties with children. This may be because men tend to hold more power in the family situation than women do, giving them a sense that they have a right to impose their will on other family members, and making it unlikely that others will interfere. It may also be due partly to our culture's sexual socialization of men and women: Men are conditioned to be attracted to sexual partners who are young, delicate and naive—the qualities of children—whereas women do not learn to associate these characteristics with sexual desirability.

Sexual Orientation

In May 1991, Heidi Leiter, a 17-year-old high school senior, broke new ground at her high school prom: The date she brought was a woman. The pair became the first openly lesbian couple to attend a high school prom in their region (Masters, 1991). Reaction of Heidi's classmates was generally unenthusiastic, and her choices have apparently isolated her from other students. However, the fact that she was able to be open about her sexual orientation at all bespeaks the changes that are beginning to occur in public attitudes about homosexuality.

In recent years, the gay liberation movement has had a dramatic influence on public awareness of differences in sexual orientation. Individuals whose sexual preference is homosexual, long a virtually invisible minority, are shedding their negative labels, refusing to accept stigmatization as either "sick" or "corrupt," and fighting for an end to discrimination against them. Despite the new openness, however, many people hold mistaken beliefs about sexual orientation: what it means, how many people fall into the various categories, how the different orientations come about.

Heterosexuality, Homosexuality, and Bisexuality

Sexual orientation refers to a person's preference for sexual partners of the same or other sex. A heterosexually oriented person prefers partners of the other sex, a homosexually oriented person prefers partners of the same sex, and a bisexually oriented person can be attracted to partners of either sex. The terms *gay* and *straight* are often used to refer to homosexuals and heterosexuals, respectively, and female homosexuals are called *lesbians*, after the island of Lesbos. In ancient Greece, Lesbos was the home of the poet Sappho, famous for her love poetry to women.

It is difficult to say how many people practice heterosexuality, homosexuality, or bisexuality because these orientations seem to be points on a continuum rather than completely discrete categories. The data do seem to indicate, however, that more males than females have homosexual experiences and that males are more likely than females to practice exclusively homosexual lifestyles (Hunt, 1974; Kinsey et al., 1948, 1953).

A study that investigated sexual orientation in one sample of adults, based on reported percentage of sexual fantasies and sexual experiences with women and men, found that one-third of both females and males reported at least occasionally fantasizing about sexual encounters with same-sex partners. In addition, one-third of the males also reported having at least one intimate sexual experience with another man; only 10 percent of females reported an intimate homosexual experience (Ellis, Burke, & Ames, 1987).

As discussed earlier in the chapter, people can have homosexual experiences without labeling themselves as homosexual, and many people who think of themselves as gay still relate sexually to other-sex partners. Kinsey's conceptualization of heterosexuality–homosexuality as a continuum with many points in between was an important breakthrough in understanding sexual orientation. More recently, Storms (1980) offered a new model of sexual orientation based on two independent dimensions—homoeroticism and heteroeroticism—instead of a single continuum. In this model, a person who is high only in heteroeroticism (sexual attraction and arousal to members of the other gender) tends to be involved only in heterosexual sexual relationships; a person high only in homoeroticism (sexual attraction and arousal to members of his or her own gender) tends to be involved only in homosexual sexual relationships; and a person high in both tends to be involved in both. This scheme allows us to think of homoeroticism and heteroeroticism as different dimensions rather than opposites: being high on one does not automatically mean being low on the other.

A major difficulty with research into the frequency of different sexual orientations, the reasons for the differences, and the characteristics of different sexual orientation groups is the lack of agreed-upon conceptual and operational definitions of sexual orientation. One survey of 228 research articles found that only 28 of them provided a conceptual definition of sexual orientation. These definitions varied from study to study, including or excluding such elements as physical sexual activity; affectional attachment; erotic fantasies; arousal; self-identification as bisexual, heterosexual, or homosexual; and awareness of attraction to one sex (Shively, Jones, & De Cecco, 1983/1984). There is confusion even among researchers, then, about the exact meaning of sexual orientation. Indeed, some researchers have called for an abandonment of such categorical labels as heterosexual, bisexual, and homosexual, arguing that vast individual differences within each category make the distinctions artificial (Paul, 1985). Others have called upon researchers to stop imposing identities and labels on people and to focus instead on articulating a descriptive language of relationships (De Cecco & Shively, 1983/1984). It is possible that researchers' struggle to come to grips with the meaning of sexual orientation will eventually lead to a major reevaluation of our understanding of sexual desire and sexual relationships.

Scientists really do not know what causes people to develop different sexual orientations. There is a fair amount of negative evidence—studies failing to find relationships between various factors and particular sexual orientations. As discussed in Chapter 5, for example, there is suggestive, but still insufficient, evidence for a biological basis for homosexuality. Evidence for various environmental causes is just as weak. One very comprehensive study of homosexuality found no evidence that homosexuality could be traced to disturbed parental relationships, being labeled by others as a homosexual, unpleasant early heterosexual experiences, or being seduced at a young age by an older person of one's own sex (Bell, Weinberg, & Hammersmith, 1981). A study that set out to investigate the idea that traumatic sexual experiences with men might be a significant factor in the development of lesbianism found no support for this notion (Brannock & Chapman, 1990). The only significant difference found between lesbians and heterosexual women was that heterosexual women reported more categories of traumatic heterosexual experiences than did lesbians!

Why has it been so difficult to uncover the antecedents of sexual orientation? Perhaps because researchers have allowed their assumptions about sexuality to narrow their approach to the question. First, despite increasing evidence that there are many kinds of homosexual and bisexual preferences, just as there are many kinds of heterosexual preferences, researchers have tended to look for a single cause to explain each sexual orientation. Probably there are many different causes and combinations of causes that lead to many different shades of sexual orientation. Second, researchers have often been guided by theories that suggest that sexual orientation is always "set" very early in life. In fact, many individual case histories suggest that sexual identity and orientation can evolve and change across the life span; for example, many bisexual women do not have their first homosexual experience until middle age (Blumstein & Schwartz, 1976). Finally, researchers have operated under the assumption that heterosexuality is the natural state, and they have spent their energy trying to explain the occurrence of the "deviant" orientations of homosexuality and bisexuality. An alternative approach might be more fruitful. For example, what if bisexuality were considered as the natural state (Hyde, 1986)? Then the important questions would concern, not what errors in development and upbringing lead to homosexuality, but rather what leads people to reject half of the population as potential sex partners in order to become exclusively heterosexual or exclusively homosexual. Or what if no particular object choice, but only the existence of sexual desire, were considered natural? Then research would focus on the combinations of factors leading to different possible foci of that sexual desire.

Attitudes Toward Homosexuality

Homosexuality is still considered a stigma in our culture, so much so that Lehne (1976) coined the term *homophobia* to describe the widespread irrational fear and intolerance of homosexuality. Gay individuals risk discrimination in employment and housing, and "coming out" as gay can involve the loss of support of friends and family.

Discrimination on the basis of sexual orientation, not prohibited by the Civil Rights Act of 1964, is still sometimes legally sanctioned. In Virginia, a law banning gay bars was overturned only in 1991 (Harris, 1991). More than 13,300 service persons have been dismissed from the U.S. military over the past decade because of their homosexuality. Often these have been people whose military records were outstanding, as in the case of Col. Margarethe Cammermeyer, a 30-year veteran with meritorious service in Vietnam and a Bronze Star, who admitted her lesbianism during an interview in which she was being considered for the position of chief nurse of the National Guard. The epitaph of one discharged Air Force veteran, Leonard Matlovich, points to the irony in the way he was treated: "When I was in the military, they gave me a medal for killing two men and a discharge for loving one" (Duke, 1991).

One apologist for the military's position on homosexuality, Col. Michael McAleer, is quoted as saying that it is the military's sworn duty to defend the beliefs of

Americans—and part of what Americans believe is that homosexuality is against Christian ideals (Duke, 1991). Many people do indeed hold negative attitudes about homosexuality. A 1984 national survey in the United States revealed that 73 percent of the respondents thought that sexual relations between two adults of the same sex were always wrong, and 40 percent felt that an admitted homosexual man should not be allowed to teach in a university (Davis & Smith, 1984). Only 17 percent of females and 14 percent of males in a survey of American adolescents said they had "no problem" with the idea of homosexuality (Pesmen, 1991).

Homosexuality is more negatively sanctioned in males than in females (Morin & Garfinkle, 1978), perhaps because, as members of the higher-status sex, males can be less easily forgiven for deviating from their assigned role than females can. Homosexuality also receives more disapproval from males than females (Astin, 1985). The bias against homosexuality is apparent in the evaluation of lesbian and gay love relationships. In one study, heterosexual undergraduates presented with identical information about a hypothetical couple described that couple as "less in love" and "less satisfied with their relationship" when the couple was portrayed as gay or lesbian than when it was portrayed as heterosexual (Testa, Kinder, & Ironson, 1987).

These negative attitudes have made it difficult to study homosexual lifestyles. They make the gay population difficult for researchers to identify, a situation that may result in the use of biased samples to draw conclusions about gays. In addition, these attitudes have a direct impact on the lifestyles and feelings of people who are homosexually oriented, making it difficult, for instance, for researchers to unravel the correlates of identifying oneself as homosexual or of living a lifestyle that incorporates homosexuality from those of being labeled a deviant or of being a victim or potential victim of discrimination.

The words of Joseph Beam, an African American gay writer who died of AIDS at the age of 33, capture some of the feeling of isolation that can accompany the self-recognition of homosexuality:

> In the winter of '79, in grad school, in the hinterlands of Iowa, I thought I was the first black gay man to have ever lived. . . . I lived a guarded existence: I watched how I crossed my legs, held my cigarettes, the brightness of the colors I wore. I was sure that some effeminate action would alert the world to my homosexuality. . . . Several years passed before I realized that my burden of shame could be a source of strength." (quoted in Trescott, 1991, p. C5)

A contributor to negative attitudes toward homosexuals, particularly gay men, has been the discovery of and publicity given to the AIDS disease. In North America, AIDS is found most often in gay or bisexual men; some evangelists have pointed to it as a "plague" or a judgment on homosexuals for their immoral behavior. The atmosphere of fear surrounding the disease has intensified homophobic attitudes, leading, in some cases, to the treatment of all gays as if the slightest contact with them were potentially deadly.

As noted in the previous section, there is no justification for such treatment; the HIV virus that causes AIDS is not transmitted through casual contact but through the exchange of blood and/or semen.

Explaining the Gender Differences in Sexuality

Where differences between males and females in sexual behavior exist, they seem to be in the direction of more sexual activity for males although there seem to be no gender differences in the intensity of sexual response. Men are also more likely than women to be sexually coercive. Several theories have been applied in an effort to explain these differences.

Physiology and Anatomy

Since some animal research links testosterone to sexual behavior, there has been some speculation that, in humans, men's higher levels of sexual activity are due to their having higher levels of testosterone than women do. The logic of this argument is not overwhelming. It is quite possible, for instance, that women's bodies are more sensitive to testosterone than men's are (Sherfey, 1966; Sherwin, 1988). Some research does link androgen secretion to sexual arousability in humans (Knussman, Christiansen, & Couwenbergs, 1986; Sherwin, 1988), but social factors and past experience apparently outweigh the hormonal effects (Barfield, 1976).

The male–female difference in sexual anatomy has also been postulated as a source of gender differences in sexual behavior. As noted earlier in the chapter, males can easily see their sexual organs and their arousal has obvious, visible signs. Females, on the other hand, can visually examine their own genitals only by squatting over a mirror, and their arousal response is not as obvious and unmistakeable as the male's erection. This difference may lead males to discover masturbation earlier and to feel more comfortable with their sexual anatomy and responses than females do. This explanation may provide part of the reason for the gender differences in masturbation and other sexual activity.

Sociobiology

As discussed in Chapter 2, the sociobiological approach to behavior postulates that much of our social behavior has evolved as strategies to ensure reproductive success —to produce as many healthy offspring as possible. For sociobiologists, reproduction is the main function of sex, and the differences in male and female sexual behavior stem from the different conditions that favor reproductive success for the two sexes (e.g., Symons, 1979). According to sociobiology, since males can produce millions of sperm, the best way for them to ensure that their genes will be reproduced is to impregnate as many women as possible; hence, the tendency to greater promiscuity among males. Since females can produce only one egg per month, on the other hand, their best reproductive strategy is to be very selective about whom they mate with, choosing someone who is healthy and likely to sire healthy children, and perhaps who will provide safety and security for those children. The sociobiologists even extend their theory to coercive sexuality, arguing that rape is simply a way for men to maximize their reproductive fitness by mating with as many partners as possible (Barash, 1979).

The limited approach taken by sociobiology ignores all the nonreproductive aspects and functions of sexuality. The logic becomes particularly strained when attempting to explain homosexuality and other sexual behaviors that are irrelevant to the production of offspring (see Futuyma & Risch, 1984, for a review and critique of the sociobiological approach to homosexuality). The theory also ignores recent data on female sexuality that shows women to be sexually responsive to erotica and to be capable of intense, prolonged sexual pleasure. Although evolution may be one of several influences that has shaped gender differences in sexuality, the evidence for this possibility is still weak. Convincing evidence would involve demonstrating both that the behavior in question had a genetic basis and that it was adaptive for reproductive fitness.

Sociocultural Influences

The double standard has long dictated that women restrict and are restricted in their sexuality more than men. This difference in what males and females are implicitly given permission to do may well influence the sexual expression and experiences of both. Women, more often watched and warned about sexuality than men, and encouraged to play a "gatekeeper" role, may learn to inhibit their sexual responses. Later, when they have no reason for inhibition, they may find they have learned the lesson too well: They find it difficult to let go. Men, on the other hand, who are allowed more leeway in terms of masturbation, exposure to erotica, and heterosexual activity, and who may even learn to view sex as a way to "prove" their masculinity, may learn early on to treat sex as a goal-oriented activity—the goal being to produce an orgasm and/or to "score." This narrow focus may cause them to miss out on some of the pleasure of sexual experience. The "sexual scripts" that lead women to associate being "good" with avoiding sex and lead men to associate sex, not with intimacy, but with achievement and conquest, tend to limit the sexuality of both women and men. They are also the source of a good deal of grief, especially in adolescence and young adulthood, as the two genders find themselves working at cross purposes in their attempts to develop satisfying sexual relationships. As noted in our discussion of sexual attitudes, there has been some relaxation of the double standard in recent years—a change that may explain why males and females have become more similar in their sexual behavior.

The double standard itself is based on the notion that male sexual needs are stronger, and therefore more important, than female sexual needs. This notion is one more reflection of the greater power and status accorded to men than women in our culture. Perhaps we have not come so far from the time when Freudian theory could describe the whole process of psychosexual development as revolving around male anatomy. Despite the vast increase in technical knowledge about sex since Freud's day, some of the assumptions remain unchanged. Sex is still often defined in terms of the penis; it is, as Rotkin (1972) argues, phallocentric. "Real" sex involves male ejaculation into the female vagina. The terms *foreplay* or *afterplay* underline this point. Anything that occurs before or after intercourse is somewhat beside the point, even if it includes female orgasm. Children are still sometimes taught that the female sexual organ is the vagina, when in fact the clitoris is the center for female sexual gratification. Men are still made to feel inadequate if they cannot bring a woman to orgasm during intercourse, despite the research showing that the thrusting of the penis in the vagina is not a particularly effective way to stimulate a woman to orgasm. When the aim of sexual activity is reproduction, intercourse is, of course, necessary. However, when the aim is sexual pleasure and intimacy, intercourse is not necessary, as many gay and lesbian couples will attest. It is quite likely that both women and men would be happier in their sexual relationships if sexual intercourse were defined as just one of the possible expressions of sexuality rather than as the most important one. A redefined sexuality that places as much emphasis on the clitoris as the penis, and that removes the performance-in-intercourse orientation for males, may help to make sex, not one more expression of the status difference between women and men, but rather a source of pleasure, self-esteem, and empowerment for both.

Summary

Research on gender and sexuality has occurred in the context of a double standard of behavior for women and men. Men have been thought to have the stronger sex drive, and thus have been implicitly given more permission to engage in sexual activity. However, research on human sexual response indicates that, physiologically, there are strong similarities between males and females in their response to sexual stimulation. The main difference is that females are capable of multiple orgasms while most males are not. On the other hand, women are more likely than men to report difficulty in achieving orgasm, at least during intercourse. Both sexes can masturbate to orgasm quickly and easily; however, women are considerably less likely than men to masturbate. Women who do masturbate are less likely to have trouble reaching orgasm during sexual activity with a partner.

There is an increasing frequency of premarital intercourse, especially among women, leading to a reduction in the gap between men and women in the extent of such activity. Men still tend to have more sexual partners before marriage than women do, and are more likely than women to feel positive about their first experience of intercourse. Men are more likely than women to report engaging in extramarital sex. Among heterosexuals, the possibility of pregnancy impacts more strongly on female than on male sexuality: Women are more likely than men to report that fear of pregnancy interferes with the free expression of their sexuality, and are more likely than men to take reponsibility for birth control.

The AIDS epidemic appears to be having some impact on sexual attitudes and behavior. Sexually active teenagers of both sexes worry about contracting the disease although they often do not take steps to reduce the risk by using condoms. Gay males have become significantly more cautious in their sexual behavior.

Men are more likely than women to report engaging in homosexual activity and to define themselves as exclusively homosexual. Homosexuality is more negatively sanctioned in men than women in our culture, and men also express more disapproval of homosexuality than women do. The AIDS epidemic has stimulated increased levels of discrimination against gay men, worsening an already difficult situation. On the positive side, individuals in gay and lesbian relationships do not have to accommodate the gender-role expectations that have such a powerful impact on heterosexual relationships.

Some gender differences exist in the motives, attitudes, and values surrounding sexuality. In general, sex seems to be more closely linked to emotional and affectional ties for women than for men in our culture. However, *within* sexual relationships defined as love relationships, men are as concerned as women are (some research suggests even more concerned) with attachment. In general, women hold less sexually permissive attitudes than men do, and show some tendency to be more conventional and responsible in their approach to sexual activity.

Both men and women can be easily aroused by erotic material or fantasies. However, most commercially produced erotic material is aimed at heterosexual males. Much of that material depicts sexual violence against women as sexually arousing. Research suggests a link between men's consumption of such sexually violent material and tendencies to accept violence against women, to actually behave aggressively against women in laboratory situations, to report some likelihood of raping a woman if given a clear opportunity, and to report having achieved intercourse with a woman through coercion or physical force. The availability of violent pornography is only one source of the message to males in our culture that the use of aggression and power in a sexual context is often permitted and approved. The high incidence of rape and incest seems to flow, not from uncontrollable male sexual desire, but from masculine socialization toward sexual dominance and an ideology that allows males to feel they have a right to impose their will on females. Females' frequent lack of success in combatting these assaults stems partly from the feminine gender-role socialization toward passivity and powerlessness.

No single explanation seems to account for gender differences in sexual behavior. Differences in anatomy may provide some of the basis for the differences in the way males and females explore their feelings and are socialized, by both parents and peers, with respect to sexuality. Different cultural standards of sexual behavior for women and men contribute to the development of different value orientations, attitudes, and behavior. The cultural tendency to define sexuality in terms of male anatomy and needs leads to coercive sexual behavior by males and often to frustration and dissatisfaction for both females and males in heterosexual relationships. Yet, despite all this, a reasonable number of people achieve happy, satisfying heterosexual relationships. Apparently males and females are not so different that their shared humanity and concern for relationships cannot transcend the difficulties wrought by anatomy, gender-role socialization, and the cultural ideology of male dominance—at least some of the time!

For Additional Reading

Laqueur, Thomas. (1990). *Making sex: Body and gender from the Greeks to Freud.* Cambridge, MA: Harvard University Press. A social historian looks at the ways in which scientific thinking about sex has mirrored social attitudes and morality.

Sang, Barbara, Warshow, Joyce, & Smith, Adrienne. (Eds.). (1991). *Lesbians at midlife: The creative transition.* San Francisco: Spinsters Book Company. This anthology by and about lesbians from 40 to 60 includes personal perspectives on topics such as mother–daughter relationships, menopause, body image, couple relationships in transition, and being single at midlife.

Scully, Diana. (1990). *Understanding sexual violence: A study of convicted rapists.* Boston: Unwin Hyman. A sociologist interviews men convicted of and incarcerated for rape.

8
Hormonal & Reproductive Connections

In England, during the past decade, several women have been given reduced or probated sentences for murder because they committed the crimes during the week before the onset of their menstrual cycle—and each used the defense that she suffered from severe premenstrual syndrome (PMS) (Sommer, 1984). PMS was cited as a source of diminished responsibility, making the women prone to uncontrollable acts of violence during the premenstrual period. More recently, a Virginia physician, arrested for driving under the influence of alcohol, successfully used PMS as her defense (PMS defense successful, 1991).

There are numerous other anecdotes of women's hormonal or reproductive physiology being labeled a source of instability. Several years ago, a Canadian judge disallowed the evidence given by a woman in her fifties because, he said, women at that stage of life (presumably referring to menopause) were known to imagine things. And recently, during an interview about my research on the psychology of pregnancy, a reporter greeted my finding that most pregnant women did not report unusual emotional difficulties with open astonishment and disbelief: "Everyone knows," she sputtered, "that women go a little crazy for nine months when they're pregnant"! "Everyone knows," indeed, that the hormonal changes involved in female reproductive processes—menstruation, pregnancy, childbirth, postpartum adjustment, breastfeeding, menopause—render women less emotionally stable than men. But is "everyone" correct? Are the physiological processes involved in reproduction really debilitating to women? Are *men* affected by these processes: Are their moods affected by hormonal cycles? Is there such a thing as the "male menopause"? Are there cycles besides the menstrual cycle that might be linked to emotions or behavior in both women and men? To answer these questions, it is necessary to move beyond the stereotypes to the research.

As explained in Chapter 5, one consequence of physiological sexual differentiation is the development of an approximately month-long cycle of sex hormone release in women and not in men. The most obvious consequences of this difference are female menstruation and the fact that, whereas a woman can become pregnant only during a particular part of her monthly cycle, a man's potential to impregnate a woman is apparently not limited by any cyclic variations. The implications of this difference between the sexes, however, have been carried far beyond the area of fertility. For centuries, the existence of the menstrual cycle has been used to characterize women as unstable and therefore unfit for certain responsible social and economic positions. This is, of course, in contrast to men, whose physiological state has been thought to be relatively constant (although, as will be noted later in the chapter, male hormone levels are *not* particularly constant). In fact, women's reproductive anatomy and physiology have long been considered a source of danger to both physical and emotional health. At the turn of the century, some educators took strong stands against coeducation in adolescence on the basis that daily association with boys would interfere with the "normalization" of a girl's menstrual period; the suggestion was also made that if girls were forced to exercise their brains at puberty, they would use up the blood needed later for menstruation (see Shields, 1975). In fact, for well into the twentieth century, doctors viewed women as more or less always potentially sick by virtue of the mere possession of a uterus and ovaries; menstruation, pregnancy, and menopause were seen as physical diseases and intellectual handicaps (Ehrenreich & English, 1979). In addition, even dry scientific texts tend to wax lyrical when discussing menstruation, sometimes describing it as a sign that a woman's body *wants* to have children! For example, Ganong's (1977) *Review of Medical Physiology* unabashedly notes that "Menstruation is the uterus crying for the lack of a baby" (quoted in Laqueur, 1990). The echoes of these beliefs still haunt our culture's approach to women and to reproduction.

The Menstrual Cycle

In women, the cyclic pattern of sex hormone levels is maintained through a negative feedback system involving the hypothalamus, the pituitary gland, and the ovaries. The ovaries, which produce the sex hormones, estrogen and progesterone, are regulated by the pituitary gland, which in turn is regulated by the hypothalamus, which responds to the levels of estrogen and progesterone produced by the ovaries. The cycle, which lasts approximately 28 days on the average, but which may vary a great deal among individuals and even within the same individual, happens in four phases: (1) in the first, or *follicular* phase, the pituitary secretes follicle-stimulating hormone (FSH), stimulating a follicle in one of the ovaries to secrete estrogen and to bring an egg to maturity; (2) in the second phase, *ovulation,* the follicle ruptures to release the mature egg. At this point, the estrogen level is high—a condition that stimulates the hypothalamus to produce LH-releaser, which in turn causes the pituitary to produce LH (luteinizing hormone). The high estrogen level also inhibits production of FSH. In the uterus, the high levels of estrogen stimulate the lining of the uterus to thicken and form glands that will secrete substances to nourish the embryo if conception occurs; (3) in the third, or *luteal* phase, the LH stimulates the follicle to turn into a glandular mass of cells called the *corpus luteum,* which in turn manufactures progesterone. As the progesterone levels rise, they stimulate the glands of the endometrium, or uterine lining, to secrete nourishing substances. They also inhibit the pituitary's production of LH, eventually causing the corpus luteum to degenerate and the levels of both progesterone and estrogen to drop sharply after 10 to 12 days. However, if the egg has been fertilized and implanted in the womb, the hormone levels will not drop and the next phase will not occur; (4) the final phase, *menstruation,* involves the shedding of the inner uterine lining, the endometrium, which flows out through the cervix and the vagina. Levels of progesterone and estrogen are low, and FSH levels are beginning to rise again in preparation for the beginning of another cycle. Although menstruation is technically the end of the cycle, the first day of menstruation is counted as day 1 of the cycle because it is the easiest to identify. The changes in the levels of ovarian and pituitary hormone levels across the cycle are shown in Figure 8.1.

Given the dramatic shifts in the levels of estrogen and progesterone over the 28-day cycle, we should not be surprised by the suggestion that the cycle variation affects moods, feelings, performance, and behavior. In fact, many women do report symptoms such as periodic shifts in mood that seem to correlate with their menstrual cycle. Some women report that they become depressed and irritable just before or during their menstrual period. Others report physical symptoms such as cramps or headaches at this time of the month. There is a lack of universal agreement on what symptoms occur when, but because a reasonable number of women report *some* symptoms that seem to vary with the phase of their menstrual cycle, it seems worthwhile to pursue the issue of what might cause such symptoms. It must be remembered that the fact that certain symptoms may correlate (that is, occur together) with certain phases of the menstrual cycle does not necessarily imply that they are *caused* by the hormonal changes that characterize that part of the cycle. It is very difficult, in fact, to ascertain whether these reported symptoms are due to physiological changes in the woman's body or to her learned expectations of menstrual effects, since research (e.g., Schacter & Singer, 1962; Walster, 1974) indicates that people actually tend to label their moods according to their expectations about how they should feel in certain situations.

Expectations about the menstrual cycle vary widely across times and places. Great powers, danger, and impurity have been attributed to menstruating women. According to the Roman historian Pliny, the touch of a menstruating woman would cause new wine to turn sour, razors to become blunt, and boiled linen to turn black. In some societies a menstruating woman is viewed as polluting anything she contacts, and sometimes, as among the Arapesh of New Guinea, women are secluded in menstrual huts during their periods to protect others from their dangerous powers. In other

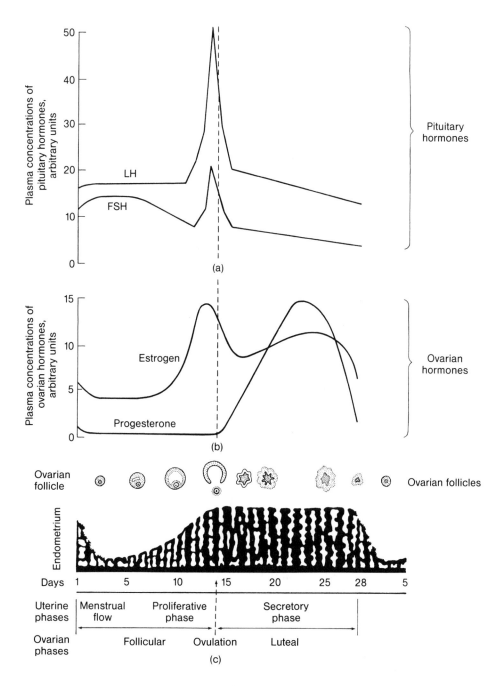

Figure 8.1
Changes in hormone levels across the menstrual cycle.
(a) Levels of hormones produced by the pituitary. (b)
Hormones produced by the ovaries. (c) Changes in
follicles in the ovary and the endometrium of the uterus.

cultures, there are positive—albeit less powerful—images for menstruation. According to Japanese tradition, a girl's first menstruation is "the year of the cleavage of the melon." One Indian phrase for menstruation is the "flower growing in the house of the god of love" (Delaney, Lupton, & Toth, 1976).

Emotional, Behavioral, Sensory, and Cognitive Correlates of the Menstrual Cycle

Mood.   For decades, psychologists have referred to a "premenstrual syndrome" of high tension, depression, and irritability that is said to occur during the days immediately preceding the onset of menstruation (Dalton, 1964; Frank, 1931). Some research has found that women report more anxiety, hostility, or depression during the premenstrual and menstrual phases than at other times (e.g., Golub, 1976; Hamilton, Gallant, & Lloyd, 1989; Paige, 1971). However, some other studies have found no relationship between mood and the menstrual cycle (e.g., Golub & Harrington, 1981; Laessle, Tuschl, Schweiger, & Pirke, 1990; Mansfield, Hood, & Henderson, 1989) and others have reported findings contradictory to those expected (e.g., McFarlane, Martin, & Williams, 1988; Parlee, 1982). Some support for a hormonal cause for mood fluctuations comes from the finding that women taking oral contraceptives (and thus not experiencing normal cyclic variations in hormone levels) tend not to report cyclic mood changes (Paige, 1971; Rossi & Rossi, 1977). However, there is another possible explanation for the absence of mood fluctuations in women taking oral contraceptives: Oral contraceptives reduce the monthly menstrual flow and make it more predictable—and negative moods may be due to anticipated flow and the bother that goes with it rather than to hormone levels (Paige, 1971; Parlee, 1982).

When women are asked to keep daily records of their moods and symptoms over several months, the results generally indicate a great deal of variability in individual women's patterns, with individual records showing very little evidence of rhythm. However, when the records of many individual women are combined, some studies show regular cyclic changes in such things as fatigue, abdominal pain, breast tenderness, appetite, headaches, and irritability (Laessle et al., 1990; Parlee, 1973). However, different studies tend to show cyclic changes in different patterns, and these inconsistencies remain unexplained. Accurate estimates of the proportion of women who experience mood fluctuations across the menstrual cycle are unavailable; different studies provide substantially different numbers. One reviewer estimates that 50 to 75 percent of women show some mood fluctuation, while at least 25 percent show none at all (Hyde, 1986). Moreover, despite the menstrual cycle, the variability in women's moods does not seem to differ appreciably from the variability of men's moods, as shown by a study in which husbands and wives charted their daily moods for two months (Dan, 1976). Finally, the influence of the menstrual cycle on mood seems to pale in comparison to that of other variables. Studies show, for instance, that environmental and social variables account for more variability in mood than does cycle phase (Good & Smith, 1980; Landers, 1977; Mansfield et al., 1989).

Even in cases where a relationship between the menstrual cycle and mood has been demonstrated, interpretation is difficult. Most people assume that hormonal changes associated with the cycle cause the mood change. However, the direction of causality in some cases may be precisely the reverse, as it has long been known that psychological stress can delay menstruation or cause it to begin ahead of schedule (Parlee, 1973). Another problem is that the focus of investigation has often been on negative symptoms, the assumption being that women experience more negative moods than "normal" during the premenstrual and menstrual phases. However, when researchers look for positive changes in the premenstrual phase, they can find those as well. In one study, 66 women out of a sample of 100 reported at least one positive change associated with premenstruation. In all, seven different positive changes were reported: increased sexual interest, tendency to clean or tidy, increased sexual enjoyment, tendency to get things done, more attractive breasts, more energy, and more creative ideas (Stewart, 1989).

Others have looked for positive symptoms at midcycle. Perhaps women feel "normal" most of the time, except for feeling especially positive at midcycle, a pattern that would be impossible to detect using only negative symptom measures. Sommer (1975) had subjects complete daily checklists of positive and negative moods for 4½ weeks. When the results were analyzed, the only statistically significant finding was an increase in positive affect at midcycle. It is interesting to speculate on the changes in attitudes toward the menstrual cycle that might take place if women began to think of the midcycle as a high point rather than focusing on the premenstrual and menstrual phases as times of extraordinarily low moods.

Behavior and Performance.   Some investigators have looked for correlations between phases of the menstrual cycle and the occurrence of specific behaviors. Cyclic changes have been reported in behaviors such as volunteering to be a subject in a study (Doty & Silverthorne, 1975), consumption of sweet food (Bowen & Grunberg, 1990), deciding to seek psychological services (Surrey, Scott, & Phillips, 1975), alcohol consumption (Dumas, Calliet, Tumblin, & King, 1984), and maternal response to a child's illness (Tuck, 1975). Parlee (1973) notes that investigators have tended to report that abnormal behaviors are most likely to occur in women during the premenstrual or menstrual phase of their cycle. The alleged link between these behaviors, which include commission of violent crimes, loss of control of an aircraft, suicide, and admission to hospital with acute psychiatric illness, might seem at first glance to imply that women are a menace to themselves and others for a few days every month! However, as Parlee's careful critique shows, such a general conclusion is unwarranted. Some of the reports are based on extremely small samples of women, and many have used methods such as retrospective reports of cycle phase, the accuracy of which is highly suspect. Moreover, she cautions, correlational data from special groups of women (e.g., female criminals) should not be used to make general statements about all women or about other special groups of women (e.g., female artists). Even supposing that women disposed to commit violent crime are more likely to commit it premenstrually, we cannot assume that women with strong inhibitions about violent behavior will be significantly more likely to commit violent acts at a particular point in the menstrual cycle. One group of reviewers concludes that, among women who are potential committers of pathological acts, the period surrounding the beginning of menstruation is a likely time for such acts to occur (Friedman, Hurt, Arnoff, & Clarkin, 1980). However, others have concluded that there is no acceptable evidence linking the menstrual cycle to criminal behavior and that the lack of scientific knowledge is so glaring that evidence about menstruation and crime should not be admissible in criminal trials (Harry & Balcer, 1987).

Popular opinion holds that women perform tasks more poorly during the premenstrual phase of the cycle. Most objective measures do not show any general impairment in cognitive tasks, work and academic performance, or perceptual-motor performance associated with the menstrual cycle (Sommer, 1973, 1983). Studies using standard cognitive tests, academic examinations, reaction time measures, quantity and quality of factory production, typing, and keypunching all fail to show menstrual cycle–related changes in performance. However, studies do show that women *believe* that their performance is lower during the premenstrual and menstrual phases.

Female college students say they believe their academic performance is impaired by premenstrual symptoms. However, their performance, when measured objectively by tests and examination scores, does not show cyclic variation (Richardson, 1989). Another study examined the performance of female professional typists throughout the menstrual cycle (Black & Koulis-Chitwood, 1990). This study found no evidence for any variation in typing performance (errors or speed) as a function of the cycle. A study of hand steadiness, conducted by military researchers to assess individual differences in the skills necessary to perform such tasks as holding and firing a handgun, did show that women with normal menstrual cycles showed a drop in hand steadiness during the premenstrual phase. On the whole, however, normally cycling women showed more steadiness than did a comparison group of men (Hudgens, Fatkin, Billingsley, & Mazurczak, 1988).

Cognition and Sensation.   A number of studies have examined sensory responsiveness across the menstrual cycle. Visual, auditory, olfactory, taste, and touch sensitivity have all been studied in relation to the cycle, along with skin conductance (GSR) and brain wave activity (EEG). Some studies have found changes in sensitivity to such stimuli as tactile vibrations and auditory thresholds. Others have examined heart rate and blood pressure reactivity to stressors, some finding a correlation between reactivity and cycle phase (Tersman, Collins, & Eneroth, 1991) and others finding no such correlation (Weidner & Helmig, 1990).

Much of the research is reviewed by Parlee (1983) and Sommer (1983). There is a great deal of variation in the findings: Some studies report cyclic fluctuations in sensitivity, while others do not. The studies that do report variation, particularly for visual and olfactory thresholds, tend to find increased sensitivity or responsiveness in the middle of the cycle, and reduced sensitivity around menstruation. Pain thresholds seem to be lower in the premenstrual phase. However, conclusions are hampered by a number of problems: (1) much of the research was designed to uncover the reasons for cognitive impairment associated with the menstrual cycle—impairment for which there seems to be little evidence; (2) many of the findings have never been replicated; (3) in many studies, measures are not taken often enough during the cycle to provide an accurate and complete picture of the pattern of fluctuations in sensitivity; and, (4) there is a wide variation in the way cycle phases are defined. Menstrual cycle effects on sensory processes are probably very small; it may be too early to try to explain them, given the large discrepancies that exist in the findings. However, it is important for researchers to be aware of the possibility that changes in the action of the central nervous system may accompany the cyclic changes of the menstrual (or, indeed, any other) cycle.

Special Difficulties: PMS and Dysmenorrhea

PMS.   In recent years, most women's magazines have devoted considerable space to the topic of the Premenstrual Syndrome (PMS). The articles tend to be negative in tone, emphasize negative aspects of the menstrual cycle, and support the stereotype of women as maladjusted by virtue of their normal reproductive processes (Chrisler & Levy, 1990).

Treatment groups for PMS have sprung up at women's health clinics around the continent, and the shelves of health food stores display a variety of products supposedly geared to the relief of this syndrome. The advertisements for such products are calculated to heighten women's anxiety about the possible debilitating side-effects of menstruation, and their widespread visibility encourages the assumption that the majority of women suffer from severe menstrual problems. Clearly, popular interest in PMS is high.

The publicity and interest surrounding PMS is fascinating, given that it is a poorly defined cluster of severe premenstrual symptoms that appears in a very small proportion of the female population. The number and type of symptoms said to characterize PMS varies from study to study. However, there seems to be agreement that the syndrome can include emotional problems (e.g., tension, anxiety, depression, irritability, and hostility), physical problems (e.g., abdominal bloating, swelling, breast tenderness, headache, backache), and behavioral problems (e.g., avoidance of social contact, change in work habits, increased tendency to pick fights, and crying spells) (Abplanalp, 1983). As all of these are common symptoms that may be experienced in varying degrees of severity by almost anyone at any time of the month, some caution is indicated in labeling women as sufferers of PMS. In general, PMS should involve, on a regular basis, a significant increase in moderate to severe physical *and* psychological symptoms during the premenstrual phase, with marked relief associated with onset of menstruation. When stringent criteria are used to define PMS, it is difficult to find enough women from a large unselected sample to study it; severe, disabling premenstrual symptoms are reported by relatively few women (Abplanalp, 1983).

Despite the difficulties in diagnosing PMS, a formal psychiatric diagnosis, "Late Luteal Phase Dysphoric Disorder" (LLPD), is being considered for inclusion in the upcoming revision of the American Psychiatric Association's catalog of psychiatric disorders, the DSM-IV. Much more research is needed before such a diagnostic category could be used with confidence (Hamilton & Gallant, 1990).

Various treatments for PMS have been heralded by the press. So far, there is no good evidence that any of them work. Most of the studies allow for the contamination of treatment effects with the effects of expectations since women who are given the treatment are told that they are getting something that will cure their problem. A high proportion of women with PMS report benefiting from treatment, no matter what is used; in other words, they show a "placebo effect"—an effect apparently caused by the *expectation* that the treatment will help rather than by the treatment itself (Elsner, Buster, Schindler, Nessim, & Abraham, 1980). When double-blind, controlled studies are conducted (that is, studies in which neither the researcher nor the subject knows until the study is over which women have been given the treatment drug and which have been given an ineffective placebo), none of the treatments turn out to be any more effective than the placebo (Sampson, 1981; Steiner & Carroll, 1977). This conclusion holds even for progesterone therapy, the most widely acclaimed treatment for PMS, now shown to be ineffective (Robinson & Garfinkel, 1990; Sampson, 1979). Current research suggests that the most effective management of PMS involves simply stress control and sensible levels of diet and exercise (Robinson & Garfinkel, 1990).

Various interests have been quick to cash in on the popularity of PMS: A good way to sell a lot of vitamins, for example, is to help convince a lot of women that their problems are due to PMS, and that PMS can be relieved by a certain new vitamin formula. This strategy has been widely used, despite the lack of evidence either that there is a high incidence of PMS or that any particular treatment is effective. Perhaps one of the reasons why so many women have been quick to accept the media-backed notion that PMS is a widespread disease is that the syndrome provides a "valid" label for menstrual-related discomfort and represents one of the first times that menstrual complaints have been taken seriously by doctors. However, the level of discomfort experienced by most women is not severe or disabling enough to qualify as PMS, and it is dangerous to women to foster the idea that large numbers of them experience the normal fluctuations of the menstrual cycle as a disease. There is no reason to return to the era when women's "raging hormonal influences" were thought to disqualify them from important jobs, for example. This is not to say that the severe premenstrual problems experienced by a few women are not real or important, but that PMS should be acknowledged for what the evidence shows it to be: a rare disorder, and one that is as yet poorly understood.

Dysmenorrhea. *Dysmenorrhea,* or painful menstruation, is the most common menstrual problem, reported by from 31 to 92 percent of women (Friederich, 1983). The frequency and severity of discomfort vary widely among women, and even in the same woman over time. Under normal conditions, the cause of the problem is now thought to be the release of *prostaglandins*—hormonelike substances—from the lining of the uterus (Budoff, 1980). These chemicals cause excessive contractions in the uterine muscles, decreased blood flow, and increased sensitivity to pain, all of which contribute to menstrual cramps. Women reporting severe menstrual pain have been found to have unusually high levels of prostaglandins. Various prescription antiprostaglandin drugs are used to treat menstrual pain, and studies show that about 80 percent of women are helped by these drugs (Friederich, 1983). Aspirin, which is a mild antiprostaglandin, is also effective for some women. In addition, strategies to increase blood flow and release congestion are helpful. Thus, physical exercise may be a good idea, and many women report that orgasm, whether achieved through masturbation or sex with a partner, works very well to relieve menstrual cramps.

Social and Cultural Influences on the Menstrual Experience

According to historical and anthropological evidence, menstruation has never been merely a physiological event. The menstruating woman has often been regarded as a participant in a strange and dangerous process, as someone who is unclean or who is especially powerful. In many cultures she was secluded during her period, forbidden to prepare food or to have any contact with men. She could be punished with death if found concealing the fact that she was menstruating (see Weideger, 1977, for an account of the rituals surrounding menstruation). Even today in our culture, menstruation is sometimes referred to as "the curse," some religions regard menstruating women as unclean, and some people hold a taboo against sexual relations during the menstrual period. Some have argued that cultural reactions to menstruation reflect attitudes toward women. Gloria Steinem (1983), for instance, fantasizes that if men could menstruate, cyclic fluctuations would be viewed as an advantage rather than a liability. At any rate, as many observers have noted, societal concerns about the possible debilitating effects of menstruation seem to have resurfaced with every new push for gender equality.

It would be surprising if the cultural meanings attached to menstruation did not have an influence on how women experience it. Indeed, it is probable that the biological influences of the menstrual cycle on women's experience are magnified many times by the cultural influences. Research on cultural attitudes toward menstruation, and the impact of these attitudes on women's experience, are examined in the following sections.

Menarche. *Menarche,* the first onset of menstruation, represents an important developmental milestone in women's lives; one study of 137 women aged 18 to 45 found that every one of them remembered their first menstruation and most could describe the surrounding events in detail (Golub & Catalano, 1983). Yet such is the air of embarrassment surrounding menstruation in our culture that menarche usually occurs, not only without fanfare, but often in relative secrecy. In addition, research on menarche has, until recently, been in short supply (Golub, 1983). Studies of premenarcheal girls and their male classmates indicate that a substantial proportion of them have negative beliefs about menstruation—for example, that it is accompanied by physical discomfort, increased emotionality, and disruption of activities (Brooks-Gunn & Ruble, 1980). One study of 9- to 12-year-old girls found that, while most of them equated menstruation with growing up and being normal, almost a third of them believed menstruation to be embarrassing, a nuisance, or disgusting, and many of them believed that menstruating women should not swim or be active in sports (Williams, 1983). Eighty-five percent of these girls thought that a girl should not talk about menstruation to boys; 40 percent thought she should not discuss it even with her father. It appears, then, that negative attitudes toward and expectations about menstruation are part of the anticipation of menarche for many girls. The advertisements for tampons and sanitary napkins may well contribute to these negative attitudes. Such advertisements tend to suggest that their product will help get the menstruating woman through a difficult and embarrassing time, that its use will make the woman able to carry on "almost as if she were her normal self." Not surprisingly, at the time of menarche, mixed feelings, such as fear and excitement, are commonly reported (Petersen, 1983), and a substantial number of women recall it as a negative event (Golub & Catalano, 1983). There is some evidence that early-maturing girls have special difficulties adjusting to menstruation, perhaps because it thrusts them into a new stage not yet encountered by their peers (Petersen, 1983).

Some researchers have wondered whether the social events and emotional experiences surrounding menarche may set the stage for how a woman will experience menstruation in subsequent years. One group has suggested that, in order to overcome some of the negative meanings associated with menarche, a positive new tradition or ritual should be developed (Logan, Calder, & Cohen 1980, cited in Golub, 1983). These researchers wrote five brief stories describing possible responses to a girl's first period. They gave the stories to girls between the ages of 8 and 17, mothers of girls in this age range, and female psychologists. The mothers and daughters chose "Congratulations, our little girl is growing up" as the best response to being told about the beginning of menstruation, while the psychologists preferred "Something special has happened." What symbolic gesture might be appropriate? Mothers favored a special toast to the girl from both parents, or a meal in her honor. However, the girls themselves, shying away from a situation in which they would be the center of attention, thought that the best gesture would be a hug or kiss and a gift to mark the occasion. It is difficult to be sure what effect such a positive celebration of menarche would have on women's later menstrual experience, but it should certainly help to counteract the negative expectations and attitudes with which many girls approach menstruation.

Attitudes, Expectations, and Their Impact on Menstrual Symptoms.   A survey of 1034 Americans, a representative sample over the age of 14, indicates that a significant minority of people associate menstruation with some degree of impairment: 35 percent believe menstruation affects a woman's ability to think, 26 percent believe women cannot function as well at work when menstruating, and 30 percent believe that women need to restrict their physical activities during menstruation (The Tampax Report, 1981). Eighty-seven percent of the respondents agreed that women are more emotional when menstruating although, when asked about their (or their partner's) most recent menstrual period, 42 percent and 58 percent, respectively, reported no mood or personality changes either menstrually or premenstrually. Even among well-educated women, knowledge of the menstrual cycle is often incorrect and negatively biased (Koff, Rierdan, & Stubbs, 1990).

Widespread cultural stereotypes exist about menstruation. Parlee (1974) asked women and men to complete a symptom questionnaire according to their beliefs about what women in general experience at various cycle phases. Both men and women gave responses that showed fluctuations of symptoms across the menstrual cycle—fluctuations similar to the self-reports of menstrual symptoms found in other samples. Koeske and Koeske (1975) used a questionnaire to measure subjects' reactions to a written excerpt from a hypothetical student's interview with a college counselor. They examined the effect of information about the student's menstrual cycle phase, mood, and environment on subjects' formation of attributions about the student. Results showed that subjects displayed a clear-cut attributional pattern in which they linked the negative moods of depression and irritability to the occurrence of the premenstrual phase of the student's cycle. It appears that our culture provides an emotional label of "premenstrual tension" to any negative moods that may occur at this point in a woman's cycle. The researchers note that this attribution pattern presents a number of dangers. It obscures the very wide individual variation among women in menstrual and premenstrual symptoms. It uses women's biology to explain negative, but not positive, moods, and it may result in the exaggeration of the likelihood or recall of negative moods. If a woman accepts this attribution for her own emotions, it might even reduce the likelihood of her taking action to alter an upsetting external situation since she would believe that premenstrual tension, not the external situation, was the source of the upset.

Do women accept the stereotypic beliefs about menstruation with respect to their own experience, or only for "women in general"? In one study (Brooks, Ruble, & Clarke, 1977), college women were asked to respond to a symptom questionnaire *as if* they were premenstrual or intermenstrual. Their responses indicated that they expected to experience more severe symptoms in the premenstrual than in the intermenstrual phase, a result that parallels the stereotypic expectations for women in general found in previous studies.

If cultural expectations about menstrual symptoms are so prevalent, might they not influence the self-reports or even the actual experience of menstrual symptoms? Probably. When they are told that the menstrual cycle is the focus of a daily symptom-reporting study, women report significantly more negative psychological and physical symptoms at premenstrual and menstrual cycle phases than do women who are given a different rationale for the study (Aubuchon & Calhoun, 1985).

In one study, women completed daily questionnaires in which they reported their physical and emotional symptoms. Later, some of these women were asked to recall the ratings they had made on a day when they were menstruating; others recalled a day when they were not menstruating. Finally, the women completed a questionnaire about how they thought they were "typically" affected by menstruation. The women who thought that menstruation was typically associated with distress tended to remember their menstrual days as distressing—more distressing, in fact, than they had reported at the time. The more a woman believed in the phenomenon of menstrual distress, the more exaggerated were her recollections of her negative menstrual symptoms (McFarland, Ross, & DeCourville, 1989).

When obtaining symptom reports from women, how do researchers know how much of the symptomatology is caused by the biological changes associated with the menstrual cycle and how much is caused by expectations and stereotypic beliefs? One researcher (Ruble, 1977) used a creative approach to separate the effects of expectations from the effects of biology. She told her 44 undergraduate subjects that new scientific techniques made it possible to predict the expected date of menstruation. Then, after using this bogus technique on each woman (hooking her up to an EEG machine), she informed her, according to the group to which the subject had been randomly assigned, that (1) her period was due in 1 or 2 days (premenstrual group); or (2) her period was not expected for 7 to 10 days (intermenstrual group); or (3) no information was given about cycle phase (control group). Thus, these women were given supposedly accurate information about their cycle phase, but the information each was given was, in reality, randomly determined and independent of her actual cycle phase. After being given this information, each woman went to a second room, where another experimenter, unaware of the group to which the woman had been assigned, asked her to rate her experience of a set of supposedly menstruation-related symptoms. All of the women were really in the 21st or 22nd day of their cycles, since their testing had been scheduled on the basis of a menstrual history taken earlier. However, regardless of their actual cycle phase, women who believed they were premenstrual reported more premenstrual symptoms than did those who believed they were intermenstrual! These findings suggest that expectations can and do influence women's self-reports of menstruation-related symptoms, and indicate caution in the interpretation of such studies.

How are expectations about menstrual symptoms formed and maintained? By administering a questionnaire to a large sample of Protestant, Catholic, and Jewish women, Paige (1973) explored two issues: (1) the possibility that women use menstruation to explain bodily discomfort and psychological distress that actually have origins in other events, and (2) the possibility that different religious-cultural groups may promote attitudes conducive to different levels of menstrual symptoms. Her findings demonstrate that learned social attitudes play a significant role in determining women's reactions to the menstrual cycle. They indicate first that women *learn* to attribute various forms of physical discomfort to menstruation and second that groups of women with similar menstrual cycles but different subcultural religious backgrounds differ in the way that social factors relate to their reports of menstrual distress.

Paige found, first of all, that women who reported many menstrual distress symptoms were also significantly more likely than other women to report higher psychological stress, greater use of drugs, and more illnesses in general. It appears that, for some women, menstruation merely represents a specific, socially acceptable explanation for symptoms that actually occur all month long and that, at midcycle, would be attributed to external causes such as overwork, family disputes, or other stressors. Secondly, she found that, although there were no overall differences among religious groups in quantity of menstrual symptoms reported, the three groups differed in the ways that various social factors were related to symptom reporting.

For Paige's Jewish subjects, the only dimension that seemed to relate strongly to complaints of menstrual distress was menstrual social behavior. Those women who found sex during menstruation unenjoyable or embarrassing and/or tended to follow certain prescribed social rituals connected with menstruation were the women most likely to report menstrual problems. Among Catholics, on the other hand, the factors that related most strongly to reported menstrual distress were sexual experience and family/motherhood orientation. Catholic women with more sexual experience were less likely to report menstrual symptoms. Also, among Catholics, the women who indicated most strongly that a woman's place was in the home and who listed no personal career ambitions were those most likely to report menstrual problems. For the Protestant group, no especially strong relationship between reported menstrual distress and any of the social factors was demonstrated.

The relationships that Paige found cannot be used to prove that certain social factors *cause* menstrual distress or vice versa, but, since there is no reason to believe that the women in different religious groups differed in their menstrual cycle patterns, her demonstration of intergroup differences in the correlates of menstrual discomfort provides considerable support for the idea that social and cultural factors have an impact on women's reactions to menstruation. As Paige notes in her article, this should not be particularly surprising, since we are quite aware that cultures label and control other basic biological functions. For example, eating is obviously a response to a basic biological need controlled by physiological processes. Yet, as Paige reminds us, our culture has a tremendous influence on what, when, where, how, and with whom we eat!

Although there is reason to believe that hormonal changes during the menstrual cycle may affect mood and behavior, the research indicates that sociocultural factors play a major role, perhaps the most significant role, in determining these effects. There are still many unanswered questions, however. For instance, we know little about the specific reasons for the wide individual variations among women (or even in the same woman over time) in the level of menstrual and premenstrual symptoms. Issues such as diet, stress, and fatigue may well be important, but they remain to be investigated. Also, it is clear that most women must continue to perform their jobs in the workplace or home despite any menstrual symptoms they may experience. It would be interesting and practical to study the strategies used by the women who cope most successfully with recurring menstrual symptoms.

Hormones and the Male Experience

Male Puberty

The onset of puberty occurs about two years later for boys than for girls. In both sexes, the physical changes of adolescence are triggered when the hypothalamus increases secretions that cause the pituitary gland to release gonadotrophins in large amounts. *Gonadotrophins,* hormones that stimulate the gonads to activity, are chemically the same in males as in females, but their presence produces different results in the two sexes because the gonads they act upon are different. In males, they stimulate the testes to increase testosterone production; in females, they cause the ovaries to produce estrogen.

Under the influence of increased hormone levels, both sexes experience a growth spurt and the development of secondary sex characteristics. Internal reproductive organs also undergo further development. In girls, this development has a dramatic manifestation in menarche. In boys, the penis and testes increase in size, as do the prostate gland and seminal vesicles. When the prostate and seminal vesicles begin functioning under the influence of increasing testosterone levels, ejaculation becomes possible. The first ejaculation (spermarche) usually occurs about a year after the growth spurt has begun, often at age 13 or 14, but the timing can vary widely among individuals. Early ejaculations may or may not contain viable sperm, as the timing of sperm production also varies.

Just as girls may be shocked and upset by menstruation when they are unprepared, boys may be frightened by their first experience of ejaculation. While boys are typically used to masturbating before puberty, and have experienced orgasms, they are often taken by surprise the first time that masturbation leads to ejaculation. As one man, looking back on his first ejaculation during masturbation, commented to a researcher, he "couldn't believe it when something shot out of my penis" (Crooks & Bauer, 1987, p. 460). A major worry, he went on to say, was that God was punishing him for his sinful behavior.

One study suggests that boys are often unprepared for their first experience of ejaculation but that the lack of preparation is not necessarily associated with a negative reaction to the event (Gaddis & Brooks-Gunn, 1985). Only 3 of 13 adolescent boys interviewed had had ejaculation explained to them, in all cases by an adult male; most had obtained their information from reading. Furthermore, only four had discussed their first ejaculation after the experience. The majority of the boys reported that they had experienced strong positive feelings at spermarche. No one was upset or strongly ashamed; however, one was very embarrassed, and two were very frightened. It appears that first ejaculation is less likely to be discussed than is first menstruation, and that, for a minority of boys, this lack of discussion can contribute to negative reactions to the event.

Male Cycles

If the menstrual cycle is associated with some changes in mood and behavior for a certain proportion of women, one possible implication is that women are, on the average, more variable in mood and behavior than men are. This suggestion is based, of course, on the assumption that men are not subject to any cycles of their own. Investigation of this assumption dates back to Leta Hollingworth (1914), who painstakingly followed six women and two men with daily tests of cognitive performance over four months. She found no female–male differences in performance variability or patterns of performance change. More recently, Dan (1976) followed 24 married couples for two months, using tests of mood and problem-solving performance. She also found no differences in variability between women and men.

If the menstrual cycle contributes to variability in women, and women on the whole are not more variable than men, men must have their own sources of variability. It is of interest, then, to look briefly at the issue of *male* cycles, an issue that has been virtually ignored by researchers. Is it possible that men experience physiological cycles that create as much variability and vulnerability as does the female menstrual cycle, but that have been ignored by the culture and hence not magnified in their effects by social expectations? Indeed, it is. Researchers studying biological rhythms in males have identified monthly cycles of efficiency and irritability (Hoffman, 1982).

Cycles are a universal aspect of life. Both men and women experience daily rhythms on physiological dimensions such as body temperature, blood sugar levels, and sleeping/waking. Such cycles can affect alertness, mood, or performance (Monk, Moline, Fookson, & Peetz, 1989). There may also be seasonal cycles. One Italian study of suicide records over 12 years identified different seasonal variation cycles in suicide for women and men (Micciolo, Zimmerman-Tansella, Williams, & Tansella, 1989). Ramey (1972) reviewed limited evidence that men show cyclic mood variations ranging in periodicity from four to nine weeks. The studies suggest that there may be a great deal of variability among individual men in the cyclic patterns of their moods and physical symptoms, just as there are large individual differences among women. Thus, the female menstrual cycle may be only one of a number of human biological cycles that have a potential impact on mood or behavior.

Ramey (1972) cites one study, carried out in Denmark, in which fluctuations of testosterone levels in male urine were followed for 16 years. Reportedly, a 30-day rhythmic cycle of hormone levels was found. Another study cited by Ramey involved male managers and workers in a factory. The investigator in this case measured not hormones, but mood, and found an emotional cycle of four to six weeks in which low periods were characterized by apathy, indifference, and overreactions to minor problems and high periods by feelings of well-being, energy, lower body weight, and a decreased need for sleep. A study by Doering, Brodie, Kraemer, Becker, and Hamburg (1974) measured both hormonal fluctuations *and* moods in 20 men for two months and found evidence supporting a link between the two. They reported a significant positive correlation between levels of self-reported depression and concentration of plasma testosterone in the blood. Their data, however, showed only weak evidence for rhythmic changes in testosterone levels.

We have seen that women's responses to the biological changes of the menstrual cycle are subject to sociocultural influences. It is logical to suppose, as well, that men's mood fluctuations are sensitive to social forces. One demonstration of this phenomenon is reported by Rossi and Rossi (1977), who found that the "social time" of the seven-day week may be as important as "body time" of the menstrual cycle. These researchers had 67 female and 15 male college students complete daily mood adjective checklists for 40 days. While many of the women showed menstrual-cycle–related variations in mood, the day of the week effect was more pronounced for males, making overall mood variability the same for both sexes. A similar study of couples aged 25 to 45 years found that, even for women, day of the week accounted for more mood variability than did menstrual cycle phase: For females and males, negative moods and arousal levels decreased on weekends (Mansfield, Hood, & Henderson, 1989). Yet a third study also shows more fluctuation in women's moods over the days of the week than over the menstrual cycle (McFarlane, Martin, & Williams, 1988). It appears that "social time" creates important cycles for both women and men.

Another possible source of variability in males is the influence of their female partners' menstrual cycles (Dan, 1979). Such an effect could have both social and biological components. In one study, after 90 days of daily mood reporting, the only significant effect associated with the menstrual cycle was that *men's* arousal scores were higher during their wives' menstrual phase than during their follicular phase (Mansfield et al., 1989).

Much more research remains to be done before male hormonal cycles are understood. Other cycles do not have the clear marker of menstruation to help researchers determine cycle phase, making the discovery of fluctuations more difficult. The lack of an obvious marker also makes it difficult for the individual man to be aware of any regular fluctuations he may be experiencing in mood or performance. It is interesting, however, to speculate on the possible impact on men of knowing or not knowing about their own cycles. It may be that men, lacking a knowledge of their own cycles, are more disadvantaged by them than women are by the menstrual cycle. When they experience a "low" time, they may be unaware of any cycle-based reason for it and so may wrongly attribute difficulties to their own incompetence, dislike of their work, or unreasonable coworkers. On the other hand, knowledge of an upcoming "low point" in his emotional cycle might, through a self-fulfilling negative expectation, cause a man to be more depressed or to perform more poorly during this time than he would have had he not been given this information about his cycle (as suggested for women in Ruble's 1977 research). As researchers begin to attend to the issue of male cycles, we begin to see that the menstrual cycle in women is not unique among human cycles in the magnitude of its effects. We are also beginning to understand how effects on female and male mood and performance are produced by awareness of and learned expectations about cyclic physiological changes.

Pregnancy and Childbirth

Physical and Emotional Aspects of Pregnancy

When a woman becomes pregnant, her normal monthly hormonal cycle is interrupted, and she experiences a state in which both estrogen and progesterone levels are more or less constantly high. Hormonally, pregnancy is most similar to the phase of the menstrual cycle that occurs just after ovulation and that has been characterized by some researchers as one of generally positive moods. In our culture, it is not unusual to hear pregnant women described as happy, content, fulfilled, and glowing. Could it be that a sense of well-being associated with pregnancy is produced by high hormone levels?

Conversely, there is much to suggest that pregnancy, far from being viewed as a time of particularly positive feelings, is seen by many as a disability. Medical research on pregnancy often seems based on the notion that the pregnant woman is to some extent disabled, and tends to focus on negative symptoms. So pervasive is this focus that it is difficult to find a pregnant woman described as healthy or normal in the medical literature. As Rothman (1982) notes, healthy pregnant women are classified simply as "low risk." Social scientists too have been influenced by the notion of pregnancy as a time of special difficulty and vulnerability for women. Psychological research on pregnancy has until recently been dominated by the psychoanalytic idea that pregnancy brings up a host of unconscious conflicts about femininity, sexuality, and the woman's relationship to her own mother (see, for example, Bibring, 1959; Deutsch, 1945). Thus, there has been a tendency, in both medical and psychological research, to focus on the problems of pregnancy, and only recently have researchers begun to examine the normative aspects of the experience.

Physical Symptoms of Pregnancy.   Research on the pregnancy experience of normal women indicates that a group of physical symptoms is commonly reported during pregnancy, but that the variation among women is tremendous (Lips, 1982a, 1985b). Perhaps the symptom most commonly linked to pregnancy in the popular consciousness is morning sickness—a tendency toward nausea and vomiting shortly after rising. It has been difficult to get an accurate estimate of the proportion of women who suffer from morning sickness during their pregnancies. To complicate the issue, women who have been pregnant several times often report that each one was different with respect to this symptom. The lack of frequency data has not, however, inhibited physicians and researchers from theorizing that the symptom has a psychological basis! It has been suggested that women who experience nausea or related difficulties during pregnancy are denying their femininity (Deutsch, 1945), are unconsciously rejecting or expressing their ambivalence toward their unborn child (Chertok, 1969), or are just generally neurotic (Pajntar, 1972). Since these explanations accompany a stereotype that *most* pregnant women suffer from morning sickness, they seem to reflect a view of women that is uncomplimentary, to say the least. It is a view that sees women teetering precariously on the brink of neuroticism, requiring only the normal changes of pregnancy to push them over. A review of the research on pregnancy nausea provides little support for any of these explanations; researchers still do not know why some women experience these symptoms and some do not (Macy, 1986).

My own research on a sample of 108 normal, healthy middle-class women revealed that 24 percent of them reported moderate to high levels of nausea and vomiting when questioned between the third and fifth months of pregnancy. That this rate of nausea is linked to pregnancy can be seen by the rate at which it was reported by three comparison groups: 3 percent for expectant fathers, 5 percent for nonpregnant women, and 3 percent for husbands of nonpregnant women. Thus, a substantial minority of pregnant women do report this particular symptom, but it appears, nevertheless, that the majority do not.

Responses to a 55-item list of symptoms showed that pregnant women could be distinguished from comparison groups by a small cluster of physical symptoms (Lips, 1982a, 1985a). In the first half of pregnancy, this cluster included nausea and vomiting, a desire to take naps and stay in bed, dizziness or fainting, and a definite lack of bursts of energy and activity. In the sixth to eighth month of pregnancy, it included feelings of heaviness and excessive weight gain. In the ninth month, it included feelings of awkwardness, discomfort, heaviness, swelling, general aches and pains, and backache. However, while more pregnant women than other people reported these symptoms on the average, many pregnant women did not.

Emotional Symptoms of Pregnancy.   Our cultural "script" for pregnancy includes a variety of emotional dimensions. We allow pregnant women to act a little unreasonable and are tolerant of emotional outbursts and strange requests. Conversely, as noted earlier, there is an expectation that the pregnant woman will "glow." The self-reports of pregnant women provide little support for these generalizations. Pregnant women do not differ from other women in the tendency to describe themselves as beautiful, attractive, and radiant—the "glow" factor—and a group of adjectives describing negative emotionality (irritability, mood swings, tension, depression, anxiety, and upset) failed to distinguish pregnant women from comparison groups at any stage of pregnancy (Lips, 1985b). Some studies have, however, found higher rates of depression among pregnant than nonpregnant women (Lips, 1985b; Tobin, 1957) and increased rates of depression as pregnancy progresses (Gjerdingen, Froberg, & Kochevar, 1991). In addition, pregnancy does not seem to be associated with increased psychological well-being for most people. According to one study, fewer than 15 percent of women and 10 percent of men report increased psychological well-being during pregnancy (Condon, 1987).

It is theoretically possible that hormone levels may tend to predispose the pregnant woman toward positive moods, at least during some stages of pregnancy. However, if this tendency exists, the mixed evidence about the types of emotions actually experienced by pregnant women suggests that it can be overwhelmed by other factors. These factors might include the fatigue and other physical discomforts sometimes associated with pregnancy, changes in body image, anxiety about new responsibilities, or resentment of an unwanted pregnancy (Lips, 1982c). Even the positive moods associated with pregnancy are undoubtedly not totally explainable by hormone levels. Pleasure and excitement about having a child could certainly produce a positive mood shift during pregnancy. Furthermore, in a culture that still emphasizes childbearing as the route to fulfillment for women, women are actually socialized to "glow" when pregnant, and pregnant women sometimes comment that they feel guilty or inadequate if they display negative emotions.

Social and Cultural Influences on the Pregnancy Experience

Besides being a biological state, pregnancy is also part of a social role. Pregnancy apparently is a social stimulus, eliciting particular responses from people with whom the pregnant woman interacts. Two researchers did an experiment in which a woman made up to look pregnant rode a busy elevator in a high-rise building (Taylor & Langer, 1977). She stood in one back corner of the elevator and another woman, carrying a parcel so that she would take up as much space as the "pregnant" woman, stood in the other back corner. The reactions of people, particularly men, boarding the elevator were striking: They studiously avoided crowding the "pregnant" woman, sometimes almost trampling on the other woman in the process. Moreover, they did a lot of staring at the "pregnant" woman—a reaction people often display to someone with an obvious physical handicap or stigma. It is no wonder that pregnant women sometimes feel self-conscious about their appearance or notice that people seem to be treating them differently. They are reacting to a real change in their social environment.

Other research indicates that people think of pregnant women as emotional, irritable, and suffering from various physical symptoms. In one study, university students were given a description of a day in the life of a young woman and were asked to give ratings of her mood as well as to rate various factors on their importance in determining the woman's mood (Lips, 1980). In half of the descriptions, the woman was said to be five months pregnant while in the other half no mention of pregnancy was made. The students generally rated the woman's mood as more positive when she was described as pregnant. However, when trying to give reasons for the woman's mood, they used pregnancy more often as an explanation for negative than for positive moods. Moreover, pregnancy was, almost without exception, described as a source of stress by students who mentioned it spontaneously. Clearly, these students, most of whom had never been pregnant, had learned the social stereotypes about pregnancy. They are not alone. Recently, I asked another group of university students to complete a symptom checklist "as if they were a woman who was five months pregnant." In general, their answers indicated that they thought pregnancy was characterized by a variety of physical symptoms, notably nausea, feeling overweight, and fatigue. For pregnancy, as for menstruation, there is apparently a well-known set of cultural expectations.

In trying to determine the links among physiological changes, expectations, and emotions, it cannot always be assumed that causality works in a particular direction, from physiological to emotional change. A case in which emotional changes apparently have physiological consequences is pseudocyesis or pseudopregnancy. The physical symptoms that characterize pseudocyesis are similar to those associated with pregnancy: menstrual disturbance, abdominal enlargement, swelling and tenderness of the breasts, softening of the cervix, enlargement of the uterus, nausea and vomiting, and weight gain. Pseudocyesis patients have even reported that they can feel fetal movements. According to a review of the literature (Barglow & Brown, 1972), the symptoms of pseudocyesis, although not common, are not extremely rare, appear most frequently in women who are sterile, and can appear occasionally even in men. Key causal factors are thought to be a fear of, or wish for, pregnancy.

Another instance in which emotions appear to lead to the physiological reactions of pregnancy rather than vice versa is the *couvade syndrome* (Trethowan, 1972), in which expectant fathers suffer from physical symptoms during their wives' pregnancy or labor. These symptoms are sometimes, but not always, similar to those experienced by the pregnant woman: nausea and vomiting, alterations of appetite, abdominal pain, swelling, and spurious labor pains. In one study, expectant fathers were found to have significantly more backaches, colds, and headaches than a comparison group of men. In addition, the expectant fathers showed unintentional weight gain, particularly during the third trimester (Clinton, 1987). There is speculation that the symptoms are caused by the man's high anxiety about his wife's pregnancy. Trethowan, who suggests that the expectant father is not usually aware of the connection between his symptoms and his wife's pregnancy, estimates that 1 out of every 4 or 5 expectant fathers experience this syndrome. However, other research suggests that the syndrome is much less common than this (Lips, 1982b).

The couvade syndrome takes its name from a set of customs in various cultures that anthropologists have named "couvade" (from the French verb *couver*—to brood or hatch). Couvade rituals are expressions of father involvement in the birth process. One form that such rituals may take is that of the father-to-be, simultaneously with his wife's confinement, taking to his bed, simulating labor and delivery, and receiving attention comparable to that received by the laboring mother. The practice may be carried out to protect the mother and infant by decoying evil spirits away from them during the vulnerable time of childbirth, to help the woman in her efforts, or to announce in a powerful nonverbal way that a particular man is the father of the child. The couvade syndrome, when observed in our industrialized society, is not part of such a ritual, yet it may, in a sense, reflect some of these same motives.

The existence of pseudocyesis and the couvade syndrome, despite their relative rarity, underlines the complexity of the interaction that can occur between hormones and social-emotional factors in the production of physical symptoms. The finding that nonpregnant women, and even men, sometimes experience symptoms that simulate those of pregnancy lends weight to the notion that our culture teaches us how a pregnant woman is supposed to feel and act. If most members of the culture acquire this information through a process of social learning, then those who eventually find themselves pregnant may develop the symptoms they (and others) have learned to expect, and it is difficult to determine the extent to which expectations and/or hormones are responsible for this development.

Pregnancy and the New Reproductive Technologies. New technologies such as artificial insemination, in vitro fertilization, fetal monitoring, ultrasound, embryo transplants, and surrogate motherhood have expanded some people's choices in the area of childbearing, and have implications for the psychology of childbearing. The psychological, not to mention political, implications of some of these technologies have not been adequately explored. For instance, little is known about what a surrogate mother —a woman who agrees, or contracts, to carry a pregnancy to term and then to turn the baby over to someone else—can expect to experience and what factors might shape that experience.

One issue that has been studied to some extent is the effect on expectant parents of knowing the sex of the fetus. Yet the findings here are mixed. For instance, one study found that parents' reactions to their infants were unaffected by knowledge of fetal sex before birth (Sweeney & Bradbard, 1989), while another found that parents who knew the sex of the fetus scored lower on attachment to the fetus than did parents who did not know the sex (Wu & Eichmann, 1988).

Knowledge of fetal sex can and has been used by some parents to select the sex of their children (by aborting fetuses not of the desired sex). There is a long tradition in many cultures of preference for male children, especially for male firstborns, and this preference may be reflected in the way so-called "sex selection technology" is used. One recent study of American undergraduate students found the preference for a male firstborn still in place. In this sample, of those who indicated a willingness to use sex selection, 73 percent preferred sons—a finding that held across race, religion, age, and income levels (Steinbacher & Gilroy, 1990).

Expectant Fatherhood

While the expectant father does not experience the dramatic physiological changes of pregnancy, he is not altogether exempt from its effects. It has now become common for the father-to-be to take an active role in pregnancy: attending childbirth preparation classes with his spouse, working with her on prenatal exercises, and being present during childbirth to provide support. The change has been relatively recent. In 1972, one survey showed that fathers were permitted in the delivery room in only 27 percent of American hospitals; by 1980, this number had increased to 80 percent (Parke, 1981).

Some expectant fathers say that they feel caught in a double bind: encouraged to participate in pregnancy and birth, but simultaneously excluded from the childbearing experience, with few good models to point the way to active, involved fatherhood (Jordan, 1990). They may have a number of concerns, such as queasiness, increased responsibility, uncertain paternity, and worry about losing the spouse; however, men often keep these concerns to themselves (Shapiro, 1987). Despite the adjustment they are making and the possibility of couvade symptomatology, however, expectant fathers show a lower rate of health-care seeking during their wife's pregnancy than before conception or after delivery (Quill, Lipkin, & Lamb, 1984).

Psychological theories about expectant fatherhood, like those concerning expectant motherhood, have until recently emphasized a psychoanalytic approach. His partner's pregnancy has been thought to stir up the man's underlying conflicts about his own masculinity and femininity, his relationship to his father, and his needs to be dependent and nurtured (Coleman & Coleman, 1971; Lacoursiere, 1972). If such feelings are experienced, some of them may be directly attributable to the social norms regarding the father's role in pregnancy and childbirth. It is not surprising to find that a man may feel anxious and dependent at a time when his partner is involved in a life-changing experience from which he is excluded. More recent studies, carried out in the new social climate of father participation in pregnancy and childbirth, suggest that, although it involves a certain amount of anxiety, expectant fatherhood is experienced positively by many men (Fein, 1974; Grossman, Eichler, & Winickoff, 1980; Lips, 1982c). In one study of middle-class couples expecting a child, the themes mentioned most frequently by the men in response to an open-ended question about how their lives had changed since the beginning of the pregnancy were a new emphasis on planning for the future, concern with finances, and an increased necessity to help with the housework (Lips, 1982c). Contrary to what many pregnant women think, men do not necessarily count the woman's pregnant body as a disadvantage of pregnancy. Men frequently report finding their pregnant wives attractive, and they complain about a diminished frequency of sexual activity (Miller & Friedman, 1988). What expectant fathers said they liked most about the pregnancy was the anticipation of the baby and their wives' happiness; what they liked least was their wives' discomfort and fatigue. A positive aspect of pregnancy, especially first pregnancy, for many modern fathers, is that the shared experience draws them closer to their spouse (Lips & Morrison, 1986).

For years, research on expectant fatherhood lagged behind that on pregnancy, probably because the father's inclusion in the preparation for and experience of childbirth has been relatively recent and because the father experiences no physiological changes comparable to those of pregnancy. Research is still particularly lacking on certain issues that are unique to fathers and prospective fathers. Little is known, for example, about the psychological aspects of fatherhood achieved by proxy—through the woman's artificial insemination with another man's sperm. Still less is known about men's reactions to the loss of a potential child through women's decisions to abort a pregnancy, to give up a baby for adoption, or to refuse to acknowledge a man's paternity.

Childbirth and the Postpartum Experience

Childbirth, which used to be a female domain from which men were largely excluded, has changed dramatically in our culture during the past century. Two changes in particular stand out: (1) The process of childbirth is now largely governed by medical procedures, and (2) fathers are frequently present at the birth of their children. During the transition, women have lost considerable control over childbirth. Midwives and female relatives have been replaced by doctors and husbands, and while such changes may have positive aspects, they also have negative ones. The management of birth is now considered a medical specialty; birth is treated as a physical-mechanical process, rather than a spiritual or social one. In our society, the doctor, not the woman, is said to deliver the baby. The husband may be present to support and "coach" his spouse, but the real control is in the hands of the physician. In this context, it is easy for a woman to feel powerless and vulnerable during labor and delivery—feelings that no doubt color her experience of childbirth and its aftermath. On the other hand, the woman experiencing childbirth in a modern medical context need worry considerably less than her nineteenth-century counterpart that she will die in childbirth, a factor that must also impact on the way she approaches and experiences the birth.

The experience of labor and delivery in our North American context is a dramatic, emotional, and physically draining experience for the mother, and often for the father as well. Both women and men often report that it was a "peak" experience (Lips & Morrison, 1986) although, if difficulties or complications arise, it can be frightening and very painful. But, while both partners can share the experience up to a point, only the mother's body goes through the physical trauma of childbirth. During labor, the woman experiences increasingly strong and frequent contractions of the uterus as the baby moves into and down the birth canal. These contractions, although painful, can often be made tolerable by the woman's use of special breathing techniques and by the partner's use of massage and focusing exercises. After the delivery, the woman is likely to be exhausted, but this fatigue is not the only physical change she experiences. Some researchers estimate that during labor a woman's progesterone level drops so rapidly as to represent the greatest change in concentration of this hormone she experiences in her lifetime, compressed into a few hours (Hamburg, Moos, & Yalom, 1968).

One researcher has argued that both childbirth and breastfeeding have a sexual pleasure component for women that has been ignored (Newton, 1971). Childbirth in particular, she notes, shares some physical and psychological similarities with orgasm. Breathing patterns, facial expression, uterine and abdominal contractions, clitoral engorgement, lowered inhibitions, increased physical strength, greater flexibility, and decreased sensitivity to external stimuli are similar in childbirth and orgasm; in fact, some women experience orgasm during childbirth. (This does not mean that the pain of childbirth is pleasurable for women. It is the combination of pressure and vasocongestion that may trigger orgasm.) Immediately after childbirth, as after orgasm, there is typically a sudden return of sensory acuity and feelings of joy and well-being. The possibility of a woman's experiencing sexual pleasure in childbirth is rarely mentioned, probably because our culture views any sexual connotations of this event as inappropriate.

For women, physiological and social factors conspire to make the period following the birth of a child (the postpartum period) a stressful one. Many new mothers experience some negative emotions in the days, weeks, or months after childbirth. Clinicians and researchers have labeled these negative feelings *postpartum depression*, a label that may be misleading since it is used to refer to several different types of experience. Experts now acknowledge three kinds of postpartum depression: (1) the "blues," characterized by emotionality and readiness to cry, which lasts for the first few days after delivery; (2) "neurotic" postpartum depression, characterized by depressed feelings and symptoms such as loss of appetite and insomnia, which lasts at least two weeks and occurs within the first few postpartum months; and (3) postpartum psychosis, a serious breakdown in the ability to cope, often including delusions and suicidal thoughts, and requiring psychiatric care. Indications from the research literature are that the blues occur in between 50 to 80 percent of women (Harris, 1980; Hopkins, Marcues, & Campbell, 1984; Oakley, 1980), while postpartum psychosis occurs in less than 1 percent (Herzog & Detre, 1976; Kaij & Nilsson, 1972). For the intermediate category of neurotic depression, frequency estimates range from 10 to 30 percent (Cutrona, 1982; Hopkins et al., 1984; Oakley, 1980).

Some researchers have theorized that the large drop in the woman's progesterone level at delivery and the dramatic drop in estrogen levels during the first postpartum week are responsible for postpartum depression. However, a causal link between the hormonal change and the emotional change has not been demonstrated. Studies in which hormone levels were measured during pregnancy and the postpartum period have found no consistent differences in these levels between those women who developed postpartum depression and those who did not (Cutrona, 1982). However, since some studies find that women who experience severe menstrual problems are more likely to experience postpartum depression, Cutrona speculates that there may be a small group of women whose depression is due to an unusual sensitivity to hormonal changes.

Researchers have investigated a number of psychological and cultural-environmental correlates of postpartum depression. Their findings suggest that stressful life events, delivery-related stress, lack of social support from others, and prior history of psychiatric symptoms are all factors that may be important in predisposing a woman to postpartum depression (Cutrona, 1982). In addition, there are reports of postpartum depression in new fathers (Liebenberg, 1969; McEwan, 1985; O'Hara, 1985; Richman, Raskin, & Gaines, 1991) and in adoptive mothers (Melges, 1968), suggesting that the hormonal changes occurring during labor are not necessary to precipitate these feelings. In the postpartum period, as with pregnancy and the menstrual cycle, the relationships that may exist between hormone levels on the one hand and feelings and behavior on the other are complicated by the presence of many social and environmental factors.

Of course, there is more to the postpartum period than depression. Attachment to the baby develops gradually in both parents over the first several months (Leifer, 1980). This process of attachment can be influenced by a number of variables. Fathers present at the birth of their infants show more intense attachment to the baby (Peterson, Mehl, & Leideman, 1979). Mothers who have experienced marital problems and ambivalence about the pregnancy are more likely to be depressed and to have difficulties interacting with the baby (Field et al., 1985). Conversely, despite popular concern about the psychological impact of birth technology, interventions such as caesarean section have not been shown to have an adverse effect on the mother–infant relationship (Bradley, 1983). On the whole, it is clear that both parents have the capacity to develop an intense attachment to the new baby, given the close contact necessary to do so.

Abortion

Every year, hundreds of thousands of women in North America end their pregnancies through abortion. The decision to terminate a pregnancy is a difficult one for many women, often made more problematic by the raging political controversy that surrounds the issue. However, despite the difficulties, most women seem to cope with the experience of legal abortion reasonably well. Studies of abortion on request have found that most women do not suffer severe psychological trauma, and that, on average, women tend to feel relief and happiness after the termination of an unwanted pregnancy (Adler, 1975; Shusterman, 1976; Turell, Armsworth, & Gaa, 1990). However, these emotions may be combined with mild to moderate feelings of guilt and regret. It is important that the woman reach the decision herself: Women who are pressured into abortion when they are uncertain about it are more likely to experience negative psychological consequences (Greenglass, 1976). Other factors that may predispose a woman toward distress after abortion are lack of support from significant others, younger age, having no other children, abortion during the second trimester of pregnancy, and strong religiosity (Turell, Armsworth, & Gaa, 1990).

Regardless of the ultimate decision, confronting the choice to have or not to have an abortion can force a woman to grapple with the balance between her own needs and those of others (Gilligan, 1982). Thus, counseling during the decision period can be very important. Yet, sometimes abortion counseling is inadequate to help women explore their feelings surrounding the issue, instead taking the narrow emphasis of handing out contraceptive information and warning women not to become pregnant again (McDonnell, 1984). While this emphasis is prompted by social concern over the large number of repeat abortions, it is possible that the problem would be better addressed by helping women to work through feelings about their pregnancy and abortion.

In men, one reaction to abortion may be a sense of helplessness and loss of control. Anecdotal reports suggest that men may also feel isolated, angry at themselves and their partners, and worried about emotional and physical damage to the woman. Among men who are supportive of their partner, many focus on concern for her and hide or deny their own feelings (Wade, 1978). They may keep silent about the decision in an attempt to allow the woman to make her own choice, but some women may experience this silence as an abdication of responsibility. On the other hand, many men truly do abdicate their responsibility in this situation, leaving the woman to cope on her own with whatever decision she makes.

Many aspects of the psychology of abortion are still poorly understood, perhaps because it has been difficult to separate the reasons for and impact of abortion itself from the legal and ethical controversies that surround it. However, it is an experience that affects enormous numbers of people, and a better understanding of it should be an important item on psychologists' research agenda.

Some research has examined the values, belief systems, and characteristics of the people who take active stands either against abortion or in favor of choice with respect to abortion. Sociologist Lorna Erwin studied members of Canadian groups who identify themselves as "pro-life" and "pro-family" (Rauhala, 1987). She found that religion was the single most important factor distinguishing these people from the general public in Canada. They were far more likely than the average Canadian to say that religion was important to them and to attend church more than once a week. More than 85 percent of them were concerned about feminism and about homosexuality as threats to the family, and a majority disapprove of the mothers of preschoolers working outside the home. Luker (1984), who studied American pro-choice and anti-abortion activists, found that more than 80 percent of the highly involved persons on both sides of the issue were women, and that these two groups of women differed in many ways besides their views on abortion. The typical pro-choice activist has one or two children, is married to a professional man, has some professional training herself, is employed, and has a relatively high family income. Religion is not an important part of her life and she rarely attends church. By contrast, the typical anti-abortion activist has three or more children, is a high school graduate, is married to a man who runs a small business, and enjoys a family income that is about $20,000 per year less than that of her pro-choice counterpart. Religion is very important to her, and she attends church at least weekly.

The pro-choice activists tend to believe that men and women have equal rights and responsibilities, that parenthood is not a "natural" role for women, but rather one that should be chosen freely, and that sex is for pleasure and enhancing intimacy rather than only for procreation. By contrast, the anti-abortion women tend to believe that women are naturally more suited than are men for filling nurturing family roles, that men are more suited for work in the public sphere outside the home, and that the main purpose of sex is procreation. Thus, the two groups of women differ sharply in their values and life choices, and Luker argues that their stances on abortion act to rationalize and justify these personal commitments. Women who have made traditional motherhood and family roles central to their lives may well feel threatened and devalued by a movement that would give women the power to restrict their involvement in such roles. Women who have defined themselves not just as mothers but also as workers outside of the family circle, are profoundly uncomfortable with an ideology that enshrines motherhood as the primary role for most women. Abortion is the issue over which these two groups of women have come into obvious conflict, but Luker argues that the conflict actually encompasses a struggle between two very different ways of life.

Menopause

At about age 40, a woman's ovaries begin to stop responding to stimulation by pituitary hormones to produce estrogen and progesterone. Over the next 10 to 15 years, the menstrual periods become irregular and eventually stop. When a woman has had no menstrual periods for one year, she is said to have reached *menopause* (Voda & Eliasson, 1983). As estrogen levels fall, the woman may experience a number of physical changes. It is not known whether the drop in estrogen *causes* these changes, and there is some debate about the proportion of women who experience them. For example, in one study of 40- to 60-year-old women, those going through menopause reported no greater frequency of physical symptoms than pre- or postmenopausal women (Frey, 1981). The most common symptoms attributed to menopause are hot flashes, vaginal dryness, urinary problems, and bone thinning (osteoporosis). Hot flashes are perhaps the most well known of menopausal symptoms although their cause is not well understood. During a hot flash, the blood vessels in the woman's skin dilate and her skin conductance increases—and she feels extremely hot (Freedman, 1989; Swartzman, Edelberg, & Kemmann, 1990).

All of the physical symptoms of menopause can be ameliorated by taking replacement estrogen. However, there is some uncertainty about whether estrogen use may increase a woman's risk of developing uterine or breast cancer, blood clots, liver tumors, and other problems. On the positive side, some researchers feel that estrogen therapy may significantly reduce the risk of cardiovascular disease (Stuenkel, 1989; Voda & Eliasson, 1983). To complicate the issue, there is evidence that estrogen therapy merely postpones the symptoms: Hot flashes return when estrogen is stopped. There are also nonestrogen treatments for dealing with some menopausal symptoms. Nonestrogen creams and jellies are effective against vaginal dryness, and osteoporosis can be prevented or slowed by a high calcium diet, regular exercise, and the avoidance of cigarette smoking and heavy drinking. Women who are physically active and aerobically fit experience fewer symptoms (Wilbur, Dan, Hedricks, & Holm, 1990).

Some women report increased depression and irritability around the time of menopause. To put these reports in perspective, consider the findings of Neugarten and Kraines (1965), who studied "menopausal" symptoms among women of different ages. They found the highest levels of symptoms in menopausal women and adolescents, and the lowest level among postmenopausal women. Adolescents reported more psychological symptoms; menopausal women noted more physical ones. Thus, psychologically, adolescence may be a more difficult time for women than menopause. At any rate, there is no evidence for a general increase in depression at menopause (Lennon, 1987; Weissman & Klerman, 1977).

The emotional changes that some women experience around menopause may well be linked to social-environmental variables. A woman at this stage is losing her ability to bear children—an ability that our culture tends to emphasize as crucial to the feminine role. If she has children, they are growing up and moving away and are no longer dependent on her, a change that may be experienced by her as either positive or negative. She may also be conscious of "losing her looks" as she ages, and may feel that this change in appearance jeopardizes her relationship with her husband or partner. There are reasons here for a woman to reappraise her life and her priorities, and possibly to become depressed if she decides that she is losing everything that is worthwhile. One study of middle-aged women indicated that depression at menopause was strongly related to the degree of role loss a woman was experiencing, and linked menopausal depression to the "empty nest" (Bart, 1971). This researcher also found that in cultures where a woman is still gaining rather than losing status as she ages, negative emotional reactions at menopause are rare. Other research has found that many women are, in fact, overjoyed to have an empty nest again—to be free of the responsibilities of parenthood so that they can reorganize their lives and try something new (Rubin, 1979). Yet another study has shown that the most marked increases in depression among postmenopausal women were associated with multiple causes of worry and stress, including adolescent children, ailing husbands, and aging parents (McKinlay, McKinlay, & Brambilla, 1987). These findings indicate once more that cultural-environmental factors can strongly modify a person's reaction to physiological changes.

"Male Menopause"

In men, there is no sudden change in hormonal level at a particular age. Rather, a man's level of testosterone and sperm production decreases very gradually from the age of about 30 onward. One physical change that is fairly common for men over the age of 40 is enlargement of the prostate gland. This enlargement, which is thought to be related to changes in hormone levels, causes urinary problems; it can be remedied by surgery. Another change is a gradual drop in libido (Davidson, 1989).

Although the physical changes are very gradual, some men seem to experience a psychological crisis at middle age—a crisis that has sometimes been dubbed "male menopause." Research shows that men in their forties show higher depression scores and more alcohol and drug use than other adult men; however, they do not differ from other men in anxiety, life satisfaction, or happiness (Tamir, 1982). The problems that men in this age range experience have been attributed not to their changing hormone levels, but to psychosocial factors. For example, Gutmann (1972) refers to the male mid-life crisis as a "loss of the future." He claims that by about the age of 50, many achievement-oriented men begin to feel that they are not going to become any more successful or move any closer to their goals. Gutmann's interviews with men in this age group in several different cultures offer some support for this concept. His research suggests that a man may greet the realization that he cannot improve his future either with a relieved sense of "letting go" and a moving out of the "rat race," or with an inner crisis in which he struggles with the fact that he has not achieved his goals to his own satisfaction. This theme of an aspiration-achievement gap for middle-aged men is echoed by Levinson (1978).

Another explanation that is offered for a male mid-life crisis is the change in family relationships that occurs at this time. Children are moving away from home, leaving their parents alone together for the first time in many years. Women, freed from their parental roles, may return to work or school, developing new interests and responsibilities and forcing a renegotiation of the couple's relationship. These changes may be experienced as threatening by the man; conversely, they may be viewed as opportunities to explore new directions.

It is clear that both women and men can experience negative emotional reactions to the important changes in role that occur at mid-life. Women, however, have been taught to expect these changes and to label them as menopausal. These expectations probably contribute to the strength of the symptoms they experience and to their coping strategies. Although some mid-life symptoms are related to the physical aspects of aging, it seems reasonable to suggest that both women and men may react negatively when they find themselves no longer able to fulfill the roles that society has defined as central for them: childrearing for women and successful career achievement for men. As feminine and masculine gender roles become more flexible, perhaps mid-life will be regarded increasingly by both women and men as a welcome opportunity to shift gears and try something different.

Summary

Women's menstrual cycle makes it obvious that they are experiencing cyclic fluctuations of hormone levels, whereas men display no easily discernible signs that their physiology is not completely stable. However, research shows that both women and men are subject to a variety of biologically and socially induced cycles that relate to mood and behavior, and women are no more variable than men in mood and performance. There is also strong evidence that relationships between biological cycles and such correlates as symptoms, moods, or performance can be modified dramatically by factors in the person's environment. Furthermore, although women are subject to the special processes of pregnancy, childbirth, and menopause that involve both large hormonal changes and culturally recognized sets of physical and emotional symptoms, men are not unaffected by the drastic life changes that go along with having a child or losing an important role. Thus, even with regard to the particular experiences of pregnancy and menopause, causality of symptoms cannot be attributed simply to hormonal changes, but must be considered a blend of biological and social factors.

In general, research on hormonal and reproductive issues seems to have been guided by the assumption that they are "women's problems," and has focused on trying to understand them by reference to hormone levels. Accordingly, research on male reactions to these events has been scanty. Much more research on both women and men is needed before the myths about "raging hormones," pregnancy, postpartum depression, and menopause can be replaced with facts.

For Additional Reading

Rothman, Barbara K. (1982). *In labor: Women and power in the birthplace.* New York: Norton. A sociologist describes the ways that the medical approach to pregnancy and childbirth affects women's experience of these processes.

Taylor, Dena, & Sumerall, Amber Coverdale. (Eds.). (1991). *Women of the 14th moon: Writings on menopause.* Freedom, CA: The Crossing Press. Nearly one hundred women write about their experience of the physical, sexual, and emotional aspects of menopause.

9
Mental & Physical Health: Stress, Change, & Adaptations

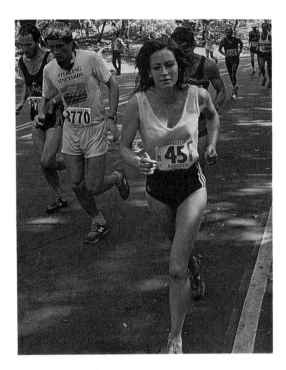

Our culturally accepted gender roles associate femininity with weakness, delicacy, and vulnerability, and masculinity, in contrast, with images of strength, toughness, and invulnerability. It is perhaps not surprising then that women's physical and mental health has been considered fragile in comparison to men's, and that the history of professionalized health care has, at least until recently, been largely one of male doctors giving advice to female patients (Ehrenreich & English, 1979). Women's vulnerability to both physical and mental ill health was once believed to be traceable in large measure to their reproductive physiology and anatomy: The mere possession of a womb rendered a woman susceptible to a variety of disorders. During the nineteenth century, doctors argued that normal feminine functions put all women at risk. As one physician put it, those women who were not "crippled on the breakers of puberty" might be "dashed to pieces on the rock of childbirth" or "ground on the ever-recurring shallows of menstruation, and . . . the final bar of menopause" (Engelmann, 1900, quoted in Ehrenreich & English, 1979, p. 110). Furthermore, doctors asserted that in women diseases of the stomach, liver, heart, lungs, and other organs were usually no more than sympathetic reactions to disorders of the womb. Even tuberculosis, which was attributed to environmental causes when contracted by males, was believed to be a result of menstrual malfunction when it occurred in females (Ehrenreich & English, 1979). Most famous of all female disorders, however, was *hysteria*—named for the Greek word meaning uterus—a mysterious disease marked by fainting or fits and a variety of symptoms such as loss of voice or partial paralysis, with no apparent physical cause. It was considered a disease of the uterus, despite the lack of evidence that the symptoms had any organic basis whatsoever. Sigmund Freud eventually redefined hysteria as a mental rather than physical disorder; nevertheless, it was still considered a feminine disease. In retrospect, modern commentators have explained it as a result of the stifling restrictions attached to the role of the upper-class woman during the nineteenth and early twentieth centuries.

Vulnerability and Strength

The idea that women are the weaker, more vulnerable sex while men are stronger and more able to withstand the rigors of life and work both stems from and provides a convenient justification for the social arrangements of the cultures in which it prevails. In fact, however, the evidence pertinent to the issue provides a rather mixed picture of male–female differences in vulnerability and strength. In brief, although some studies show that women report more minor physical symptoms and seek medical help more often than men do, men are more vulnerable than women to serious illnesses at every stage of life, and the male's life span is shorter than that of the female. Women and men each report higher rates of certain mental illness symptoms. In terms of muscular strength, men generally outperform women, but the gap is not necessarily as large as the "tough man–fragile woman" stereotype would suggest.

Physical Vulnerability and Mortality

Males are more likely than females to suffer injury or death prenatally or during the birth process and to be victims of childhood diseases. Although 108 to 140 males are conceived for every 100 females, by the time of birth, the ratio of males to females has dropped to between 103 and 106 to 100 in the United States. Miscarriage, stillbirth, and death from birth-related injuries are more likely to affect males than females. Male infants are more likely than females to suffer from congenital malformations and from a wide variety of genetically linked diseases, and to die during the first year of life. During the teenage years, males are more likely than females to die in accidents. The survival rate of women from such conditions as starvation, exposure, fatigue, and shock is better than that of men. In the United States, females outnumber males by the early twenties; by the age of 65 there are about 3 women for every 2 men, and among those who live to be 100, the ratio of women to men is 4 to 1. The sex differential in longevity has traditionally been smaller among African- and Hispanic-Americans, whose life expectancy is as much as six years shorter than that of European-Americans. This effect is likely due to low income, which tends to be correlated with race. As the life expectancy of these minority groups increases, so does the gender difference in that expectancy, thus leading to increased rates of widowhood in these groups (Markides, 1989).

In developing countries, where poverty and malnutrition are more prevalent, sex differences in life expectancy are narrower: closer to two years than to the seven years found in developed countries. In three south Asian countries (India, Nepal, and Pakistan), men's life expectancy actually exceeds that of women by one year (Sivard, 1985). This higher female mortality has been linked to the low cultural value placed on females relative to males. Boys are given better care, including better nutrition and access to medical treatment, than girls, who are more likely to be neglected.

Although the possession of a uterus does not endanger a woman's health in the way that nineteenth-century doctors claimed, it does present one potentially serious risk to women's health and survival: childbearing. The World Health Organization estimates that in Third World countries deaths from maternal causes (pregnancy and childbirth) are among the five major causes of death for women aged 15 to 44; in one-third of the countries, these causes rank first or second in overall death rates. In the United States, complications of pregnancy and delivery account for less than 1 percent of the deaths of women between 15 and 49, but in developing countries, these causes may account for up to one-quarter of such deaths. Even when it does not directly lead to the mother's death, pregnancy is a serious drain on women's health in countries where women do not have access to enough food to meet their increased caloric and nutrition requirements. Countries with the lowest life expectancy for females also tend to have the highest fertility rates (Sivard, 1985).

Illness Rates

Men are more likely than women to die from heart disease, cancer, lung disease, pneumonia and flu, and liver disease. Women are more likely than men to die from strokes or diabetes, and they account for almost all of the deaths from breast cancer. In addition, the rates of death due to suicide and homicide are strikingly higher for men than for women (Harrison, 1978; U.S. Department of Commerce, 1984). Men use and abuse alcohol and illegal narcotics more than women do; however, women are more likely than men to be treated with drugs for their mental and emotional problems (Fidell, 1982).

These statistics can be somewhat misleading. An emphasis on the differences between women and men obscures the fact that, depending on a variety of conditions, both sexes can be threatened by such serious illness as heart disease and cancer. For example, although more young men than young women die of heart disease, heart disease is the leading killer of American women older than 55, and a woman's first heart attack is more likely than a man's to be fatal. Women who both smoke and take oral contraceptives are at substantially increased risk for heart attacks. African-American women between the ages of 35 and 74 die from heart disease one and a half times as often as their European-American counterparts, partly because they are more likely to have high blood pressure (Long, P., 1991).

Across all ages, women report more physical illness symptoms than men do, take more prescribed and nonprescribed medication, and visit the doctor more often (Pennebaker, 1982). The *types* of symptoms reported by women and men also differ:

Women report more headaches, sore throats, urinary problems, constipation, and weight problems, whereas men report more ulcers, asthma, stomach symptoms, and eye problems. Also, when the definition of mental illness is restricted to diagnoses involving mental disorganization (e.g., confusion, disorientation) or personal discomfort (e.g., anxiety, depression) women are considerably more likely than men to be diagnosed and treated for mental illness (Gove, 1979; Russo & Sobel, 1981). This finding holds across all ethnic groups but not across all types of marital status. In fact, it is only among the married population that women are more likely than men to receive psychiatric treatment. When particular categories of mental disorders and treatments are examined, the pattern of observed gender differences is mixed. Men have higher rates of treatment for alcohol and drug disorders, while women far outnumber men in depression, and the sexes are diagnosed and treated for schizophrenia with about equal frequency (Belle & Goldman, 1980). Women are far more likely than men to suffer from the eating disorders anorexia and bulimia.

Fitness and Strength

As a group, women are shorter, lighter, and less muscular than men and are regarded in our society as generally unable to perform heavy manual work. Research has demonstrated, however, that young women (college students without special training) are able to do strenuous work, expending 2369 kilocalories for 8½ hours (Wardle, 1976). This expenditure of energy is approximately equal to that required in un-mechanized coal mining—usually considered one of the most demanding occupations. Thus, although women have, on average, less muscular strength than men, it would be a mistake to characterize them as weak. This conclusion is strengthened by a look at women in other cultures. For example, researchers working in a University of Nairobi laboratory have found that an African woman who is accustomed to the task can easily carry on her head a load that is equal to two-thirds of her body weight, and do it by expending far less energy than a male U.S. army trooper hauling an equivalent load (Maloiy, Heglund, Prager, Cavagna, & Taylor, 1986).

Men's advantage in muscular strength has been amply demonstrated by their performance in athletic competition. In Olympic events in which both sexes participate, men consistently obtain better performance records. However, the differences between men's and women's records in track, field, and swimming events are decreasing rapidly as female athletes receive proper training. For instance, during the 12 years between 1972 and 1984, the women's record for the marathon dropped more than 23 minutes, while the men's dropped only 22 seconds. The world swimming record set by Janet Evans in the 400-meter freestyle in the 1988 Olympics was two seconds *faster* than Mark Spitz's 1968 world record in the same event (Swardson, 1991). In events that require endurance as well as speed, such as the ultramarathon, women can win out over men. Women hold the speed record for swimming the English Channel in both directions. In 1988, Paula Newby-Fraser won the women's division of the famous Ironman Triathlon—with a time that placed her ahead of all but 10 of the hundreds of male contestants. In 1988, Susan Butcher became the first person to win a third consecutive Iditarod, a grueling long-distance sled dog race. And in 1989, Ann Trason won the mixed-sex TAC/USA 24-Hour Race in New York City.

Among nonathletes, men generally are stronger than women and participate in more physical activity than women do. On the average, women have lower levels of cardiovascular fitness than men do at all age levels, although in North America neither men nor women meet the standards for cardiovascular fitness set by health organizations (Bailey, Shephard, Mirwald, & McBride, 1974). Women are not as accurate as men are at judging their own fitness levels; in the previous study, the 20 percent of women who thought they were of above-average fitness had the lowest group average aerobic power. For both sexes, fitness levels improve markedly with regular physical exercise.

According to these three lines of evidence—vulnerability and survival rates, illness rates, and measures of fitness and strength—the reliability of the strong man–weak woman stereotype is far from clear-cut. Let us turn next to an examination of gender-related patterns in specific areas of physical and mental health, and their underlying causes. Physical and mental health are discussed under separate headings, but it will soon become clear that they are strongly interrelated, each one unavoidably affecting the other.

Gender and Physical Health

General Health and Fitness

We have seen that men have a shorter life expectancy than women and that males are more likely than females to succumb to a variety of serious diseases. Part of the explanation for these differences is genetic: Males, as seen in Chapter 5, are more likely than females to inherit a variety of sex-linked disorders. Other biological explanations have been offered for some of the gender differences. Women's relatively high estrogen levels may offer them at least temporary protection against heart disease (Hazzard, 1986); heart attacks increase for women as their estrogen decreases (Barfield, 1976). Another suggestion is that women's lower metabolic rate and relatively greater percentage of body fat than men's contributes to their survival in difficult conditions. Support for the biological vulnerability explanations of gender differences in health comes from studies in which populations of males and females living very similar lifestyles are still found to differ in life expectancy. For example, a study of 40,000 American monks and nuns, all of whom were, of course, unmarried, did not smoke or drink alcohol, had similar diets, and were teachers, found that, despite the similarity in lifestyle, the women had a life expectancy advantage of more than five years by the age of 45 (cited in Nicholson, 1984). Other research, however, has shown that there is a tendency for males and females to die at equal rates from specific diseases when their environment and lifestyle are similar. For example, among male and female long-term psychiatric patients the death rate from heart disease is similar for the two sexes, whereas in the general population men are four times more likely than women to die of heart attacks (Craig & Lin, 1984).

Several writers have argued that gender roles make an important contribution to gender differences in health. One way in which this might happen is that the masculine role prompts men to behave in ways that are dangerous to health (Harrison, 1978; Waldron, 1983). Brannon (1976), for example, has argued that the stereotyped masculine role contains four elements: the avoidance of femininity, the need to be superior to others, the need to be self-reliant and independent, and the need to be more powerful than others. The attempt to live up to such a role may cause a great deal of anxiety. The stress of not meeting his achievement aspirations, for instance, may be difficult for a man to handle, and a man trying to live up to the "self-reliant" part of the masculine role has another potential handicap: He cannot allow himself to relieve his anxiety by talking about his problems. The physical effects of stress generated by a competitive orientation may be worsened by the man's attempts to relieve that stress through drinking, smoking, or other drug use. Furthermore, the desire to appear powerful may lead a man to engage in risky behaviors, such as driving dangerously or fighting. All of these factors, each one stemming in some way from the masculine role, contribute to the likelihood of an earlier death for men than for women (Ortmeyer, 1979). As women take on more and more of the stresses traditionally associated with the masculine role, the male–female difference in mortality may begin to decline. For example, recent statistics show that from 1975 to 1990, the number of women drivers killed in traffic accidents rose by about 60 percent, while the number of men drivers killed dropped about 10 percent. In concert with this finding, note researchers, the arrest rate for driving under the influence of alcohol is up for women and down slightly for men (Fehr, 1992).

The feminine gender role may also contribute to gender differences in health patterns. The feminine ideals of expressiveness and intimacy may help women to avoid the stress-generating patterns of competitiveness and suffering in stoical silence that are encouraged by the masculine role. The lack of necessity to show off strength or power may keep women out of risky situations. There is a potential trade-off here, of course: While men die during their risky undertakings, women may die of boredom! In fact, boredom, the lack of a sense of purpose, and the absence of intellectually challenging work *has* been cited as a source of ill health for women caught in restrictive roles—from the affluent "hysterical" women of the early part of this century to the middle-class housewives experiencing the numbing malaise that Betty Friedan in *The Feminine Mystique* (1963) characterized as "the problem that has no name."

A direct and obvious contribution of the feminine role to women's lower levels of fitness has been the notion that strength is unfeminine and that athletic activity is primarily for men. In recent years, there has been an explosion of female athletic activity in the United States, due largely to the equality of access to athletic training and facilities in schools and colleges legislated by Title IX and to corporate sponsorship of "big-time" sports events for women. However, the attitude that muscles and sweat are not ladylike still holds for many people. Not until the 1984 Olympics in Los Angeles was a woman's marathon considered an appropriate event; little girls are still sometimes taught to do special "girls' push-ups," to throw a softball underhand, to play certain sports less intensively than boys, and to rule out participation in other sports altogether. Females participate less regularly in physical exercise than males do, and studies show that a variety of sports activities continue to be perceived as essentially masculine (Nicholson, 1984). Attitudes are changing, however: Female athletes are becoming "stars" that girls are happy to emulate. The names of tennis stars such as Monica Seles and Jennifer Caprioti, track and field athletes such as triathlete Paula Newby-Fraser and heptathlete Jackie Joyner-Kersee, and others such as speed skater Bonnie Blair, have become household words—at least in some households. Girls and women with disabilities are also presented with athletic role models, such as Jean

Driscoll, world record holder in the wheelchair division of the Boston Marathon, or Laura Schwanger, gold medalist in the pentathlon at the 1991 World Wheelchair Games. The visibility accorded such women may gradually erode the stereotype that women are, or should be, weak and fragile.

A particular source of concern about physical exercise for women has been the relationship between exercise and reproduction. Some women who follow a very demanding exercise schedule experience a temporary disruption or cessation of their menstrual cycle. This is most likely to occur in women with a history of irregular menstruation (Butler, 1985) although menstrual periods tend to return when the athlete reduces the intensity of her training regimen. Research also indicates that, on the average, menstruation does not interfere with the performance of female athletes (Sherif, 1980). Thus, there seems little reason to use menstruation as a justification for restricting women's exercise levels. Similarly, research shows that there is no reason for the average woman to avoid moderate exercise during pregnancy; such exercise helps to keep the mother healthy and seems to have no adverse effect on the fetus (Lutter, Lee, & Cushman, 1984). Until very recently, however, expectant mothers have been cautioned to "take it easy"—advice that may actually contribute to the fatigue that many women report during the second half of pregnancy.

More evidence that women's and men's health may be related to gender roles and stereotypes comes from statistics comparing the health status of married and unmarried individuals. Unmarried men who live alone have a mortality rate almost double that of married men; unmarried women living alone also have a higher mortality rate than their married counterparts, but the difference is much smaller (Kobrin & Hendershot, 1977). The authors of this study propose that two social variables, social ties and social status, promote long lives, with social ties being the more important of the two. According to gender stereotypes, status is associated more with masculinity, while affiliation is a feminine behavior. A married couple in a society that adheres to these stereotypes may gain much of their social status through the man and maintain many of their social ties through the woman. On the other hand, a man alone may have status because of his role, but lack social ties without a family; a woman is likely to have social ties even if she lives alone, but is less likely to have high social status.

Occupational Health and Safety

Since women and men often do different kinds of work, they are vulnerable to different kinds of job-related injuries and illnesses. Exposure to toxic chemicals is common for women in such female-dominated occupations as lab technology, computer chip manufacturing, laundry and textile work, and cosmetology. Exposure to radiation may be a problem for dental hygienists, X-ray technicians, and some nurses. The necessity to sit or stand for long periods of time places workers such as secretaries, telephone operators, waitresses, and sales clerks at risk for circulatory diseases and back problems (Stellman, 1978). The female-dominated jobs of school teaching, child care, social work, and health care all carry a high risk of infection. The male-dominated jobs in trades and construction make their occupants vulnerable to accidental injury, as do certain factory jobs. Police and military work, also male-dominated, carry risks of death and injury through accidents and violence.

Some occupational hazards, such as radiation and toxic chemicals, may be especially problematic for women of childbearing age, as they may affect a developing fetus. Thus, some companies have tried to exclude fertile women from jobs that involve this kind of dangerous exposure (Randall, 1985). The economic implications for women of such restrictions can be enormous; some women may choose sterilization in preference to losing a high-paying job. However, some analysts have argued that the focus on pregnancy risks obscures the issue that exposure to toxic chemicals or radiation is not good for anyone, and that, rather than excluding fertile women from certain jobs, companies should find ways to reduce dangerous exposure for *all* workers (Stellman, 1977; Win-O'Brien, 1980). This argument gleans support from findings that not only the female reproductive system is at risk from toxins: Occupational exposure of male workers to certain chemicals can damage their reproductive abilities as well. For example, exposure to lead can lead to reduced sexual drive, decreased ability to produce normal sperm, and sterility in males (Gold, 1981).

Both women and men who are employed outside the home report more Type A coronary-prone behavior (a behavior pattern characterized by competitiveness, impatience, and aggression) and more marital disagreement than do women at home (Haynes & Feinleib, 1980). For both employed women and men over the age of 45, the psychosocial risk factors associated with coronary heart disease are Type A behavior and suppressed hostility. For both men and women, these behaviors may be encouraged by high-pressure jobs; however, in women they may also stem from such job-related frustrations as discrimination and juggling work and family obligations. Employment in general, though, does not make women more vulnerable to health problems. In fact, employed women report fewer illnesses and fewer days in bed than housewives do (Verbrugge & Madans, 1985; Waldron & Herold, 1984).

Socioeconomic Risk Factors

In general, the poor are more vulnerable to illness and disabilities than are upper- and middle-income groups (Coe, 1978; Gladwell, 1990). Blue-collar workers are about 2.3 times more likely to die of heart disease than are managers and professionals; people making less than $10,000 annually report getting sick more than 4½ times as often as do those making at least $35,000. Since poverty is becoming increasingly "feminized" all over the world (in the United States, about 2 out of 3 adults living below the poverty line are women), women, particularly black women, are at higher risk than men for health problems associated with low socioeconomic status. In the United States, a black woman is almost three times more likely to be poor than is a white woman; an Hispanic woman is 2½ times more likely than a white woman to be poor (Shortridge, 1989). The risk of sudden death by heart attack is greater for black women than for any other group, and, in a reversal of the pattern for the white population, hypertension is a greater problem for black women than for black men (Albino & Tedesco, 1984). Low-income women of color are more likely than other women to die from complications of pregnancies and abortions. Stress levels associated with being poor and belonging to a marginalized group are potential contributors to health problems. Ratings of stress have been found to be higher among female immigrants from Central America than among Mexican- or Anglo-Americans (Selgado de Snyder, Cervantes, & Padilla, 1990).

Among men, blacks are more likely than whites to die from injuries suffered at work, and they have higher death rates from heart disease, hypertension, cancer, strokes, cirrhosis of the liver, tuberculosis, diabetes, and lung diseases (Gary, 1981).

Health and Illness Behaviors

There is evidence that women and men differ in some of the behaviors that are related to maintaining health, responding to symptoms of illness, and treating health problems. These differences, which frequently seem to reflect gender-role expectations, may well explain some of the differences in illness rates and life span between the sexes.

Maintaining health involves proper nutrition, rest, exercise, and cleanliness; the avoidance of self-destructive activities such as smoking, overindulgence in alcohol and other dangerous drugs, and overexposure to the sun; and preventive health care such as medical and dental checkups and self-examination for signs of cancer and other problems. Women seem to engage in such health-oriented behavior more than men do. Women are more knowledgeable about and interested in health than men (Feldman, 1966), place a higher value on health (Kristiansen, 1984), have more eye examinations and dental and medical checkups (Woods, 1981), and engage in fewer behaviors that are a direct risk to health (Langlie, 1979). Women's greater use of preventive health-care services may help to account for both their higher illness rates and lower mortality rates than men, since they will tend to be diagnosed and treated earlier for certain diseases that cause death in men. However, despite their tendency to use health services more than men do, American women still make less than optimum use of preventive health care. Less than a third of American women obtain regular screenings for breast cancer, and less than 60 percent of 40- to 70-year-old women have regular pap smears (Campaign for Women's Health, 1991). This may be because so many women are not adequately covered by health insurance, which is almost exclusively tied to full-time employment.

One difference in men's and women's behavior that can be linked to their different mortality rates is smoking. Years ago, in a rare and dramatic example of gender-role stereotypes exerting a protective effect on women, it was considered unladylike to smoke. Tobacco companies have done all they can to reverse this stereotype. Advertising campaigns reminding women that they've "come a long way" are designed to link smoking with women's liberation, and smoking has increased among teenage girls and older women during the past two decades; only recently has smoking among this group begun to decrease (Burger & Gochfeld, 1989). At the same time, deaths from lung cancer showed a fivefold increase among women over 30 years, as compared to a twofold increase for men (U.S. Bureau of the Census, 1982). Women now account for almost one-third of new cases of lung cancer and 31.5 percent of lung cancer deaths (U.S. Department of Health and Human Services 1987). Recent research shows that, in contrast to rates for American men, which are relatively steady, tobacco-related deaths among American women under 70 have been rising dramatically since 1965 (Brown, 1992). Taking a more global perspective, for middle-aged men in industrialized countries, 415 of every 100,000 deaths were attributable to smoking—a number that is projected to rise to 452 by 1995. For middle-aged women, however, the projected increase is more striking: more than doubling from 28 of every 100,000 deaths in 1965 to 86 in 1995.

When illness symptoms do arise, women are more likely than men to try to do something about them, by treating them or by seeking medical help. Part of the explanation for this gender difference may be that women are more attentive than men are to their internal state (Pennebaker, 1982). In addition, admitting weakness and seeking help is an acceptable part of the feminine, but not the masculine, role making it easier for women than men to report illness (Verbrugge, 1979). Finally, women are more likely than men to be socialized to pay attention to and deal directly with symptoms of illness, since mothers have traditionally taken primary responsibility for health care in families. Once medical advice has been sought, however, women and men are equally likely to comply with their doctor's recommendations (Albino & Tedesco, 1984).

Health Care

Although women use the health-care system more than men do, it frequently does not meet their needs. Medicine is still dominated by men, despite the influx of women into medical schools and the fact that women fill most of the support roles in health care. Gender stereotypes abound in what medical students are taught. Disorders specific to women are often trivialized or described as psychological in origin, while men's symptoms are more likely to be seen as physically than emotionally based; small wonder that physicians and nurses tend to attribute women's symptoms to psychological rather than organic causes (Fidell, 1980; Long, P., 1991; Wallston, DeVellis, & Wallston, 1983). A clear illustration of the tendency was found by two researchers who examined standard medical texts for discussions of dysmenorrhea, nausea of pregnancy, pain in labor, and infant behavior disorder (Lennane & Lennane, 1973). They found that each of these problems was routinely attributed to the women's mental or emotional state, despite the lack of any evidence that these problems are psychological in origin and a great deal of evidence in the other direction.

There is some evidence that doctor–patient interactions may differ for male and female patients, although the data are based on male physicians only. Researchers analyzed more than 300 taped interactions between doctors and patients, looking for patterns of seeking and offering information (Wallen, Waitzkin, & Stoeckle, 1979). Doctors spontaneously offered information equally often to men and women, but women asked more questions than men and so received more informative statements. However, when total time spent explaining rather than number of explanations was measured, there were no differences between male and female patients—a finding that suggests that men received fuller explanations without asking as many questions. There was also a tendency for the doctors to "talk down" to the female patients. It appears that women may have to work harder to extract information from doctors, at least male doctors. If so, the outcome may be to reinforce women's dependence on the medical care system. Some women may give up trying to get information and simply go along with whatever their doctor advises, thus becoming trapped in a situation where they must seek medical advice and/or reassurance every time they experience symptoms.

Further insights into the ways doctors treat women and men come from a study showing that male and female patients with similar symptoms were treated differently by physicians (Armitage, Schneiderman, & Bass, 1979). Male patients were given more extensive lab tests and other forms of attention—a finding that led the researchers to conclude that women were given less medical attention than were men for the same problem.

A women's health movement has emerged as women try to reduce their dependence on the medical system and assume an active role in their own health care. The focus has been on education and empowerment in the area of health, encouraging women to obtain full information, be aware of treatment consequences, exercise the option to refuse treatment when appropriate, and seek complete access to their medical records. The approach is one that puts as much knowledge and power as possible in the hands of the patient, rather than treating the patient as a passive responder to physician recommendations. Although the movement has arisen among women because they were dissatisfied with the male-dominated medical system, such an approach could also be empowering for male patients.

The Politics of Health Research

A 1984 report by the American National Institutes of Health entitled *Normal Human Aging* was based entirely on data obtained from men (Horwitz, 1990). A prestigious large-scale study of the relationship between coffee consumption and heart attacks used 45,589 subjects—all of them men. Similarly, a study testing the efficacy of low daily doses of aspirin against migraine headaches included 22,071 male subjects—and no females (Adler, 1990). These examples are illustrative of a general pattern in the way health research dollars have been spent in the United States: Until very recently most of those dollars have been spent studying the health of men.

Why the omission of women from health research? Until 1985, studies funded by NIH and other agencies routinely excluded females (even female mice or rats)—because their menstrual cycles complicated the findings. The idea that such "complications" should be studied because of their very relevance to women's health appears to have been overlooked. Official NIH policy is now to include females in clinical research, but the guidelines have yet to be stringently enforced. Federal Food and Drug Administration policy continues to exclude women of childbearing potential from many drug trials.

Because research on women's health has been neglected for so long, the extent to which many health issues are gender-related has not been well explored. Attempts to remedy the situation include the Women's Health Equity Act proposed in 1991. This Act included bills to establish an NIH Office of Research on Women's Health and a women's research office in the Alcohol, Drug Abuse, and Mental Health Administration, as well as provisions to include more women as subjects in publicly funded research (Freiberg, 1991b).

Women, Men, and Mental Illness

Patterns of diagnosis and treatment for mental illness are very different for women and men. Because surveys of communities to determine the incidence of mental health problems have not included all the different kinds of disorders, no firm conclusions can be reached about whether men or women experience higher rates of mental illness in general (Goldman & Ravid, 1980). However, it *is* clear that gender differences exist in the prevalence of specific forms of mental illness. Women are more than twice as likely as men to suffer from clinical depression (Weissman & Klerman, 1977). Ninety-five percent of the cases of anorexia nervosa, an eating disorder characterized by self-starvation, are female (Oakes, 1984). Women are more likely than men to develop phobias and anxiety neuroses; men are more likely to suffer from personality disorders, alcohol and drug addiction, and pathological gambling. It is quite possible that feminine and masculine roles predispose women and men to express their distress in different ways, and to seek help with different frequencies, thus laying the groundwork for these gender-differentiated patterns of symptoms. It is also possible that gender stereotypes affect the way that symptoms are responded to by others and how they are diagnosed.

Two sets of findings are often used to illustrate the impact of gender roles on patterns of mental illness. The first is that women are more likely than men to talk about and seek treatment for their symptoms (Klerman & Weissman, 1980; Phillips & Segal, 1969). The feminine role makes it acceptable for women to acknowledge weakness and to seek help; the masculine role encourages men to "tough it out" when they experience problems. The extremes of both styles are problematic. The drawbacks of the masculine role can be seen in the findings that, while women are more likely than men to seek treatment for depression, men are more likely to deal with depression by turning to drugs or alcohol (Williams & Spitzer, 1983), or by committing suicide. Conversely, the disadvantage of the feminine, help-seeking, approach is that it can encourage dependence and low self-esteem. Women learn to feel that they cannot solve their own problems and must rely on the authority of a doctor or therapist. Such dependency may reinforce the very feelings of overwhelming helplessness that produced the symptoms in the first place, and contribute to a prolongation of the illness. A frequently serious outcome of depending solely on medical treatment to solve certain emotional problems is an addiction to mood-altering prescription drugs. The majority of the prescriptions for mood-altering drugs, such as tranquilizers, are written for women, and women are the major abusers of these drugs (Verbrugge, 1982a).

The second set of findings pointing to a major impact of gender roles on mental illness is that the relationship between marital status and mental illness rates differs dramatically for women and men. Among married people, the rate of mental illness is considerably higher for women than for men. However, among single people, the pattern is reversed: Men show higher rates of mental illness than women do (Gove, 1972; Walker, Bettes, Kain, & Harvey, 1985). Some researchers have blamed the traditional gender-role expectations associated with marriage for this difference. The married woman tends to suffer a loss of autonomy since the husband is still often considered the "head" of the family (Maracek, 1978). Moreover, if she stays at home and is not employed, or if she works part-time and thus earns a low income with few benefits, she becomes dependent on her husband for money and for status. Her work as a homemaker tends to be unstructured and invisible, with few objective standards of performance and few rewards for doing well (Gove, 1972). For a man, however, marriage has traditionally meant no loss of status, but a gain in social support and in having someone to "look after him" in many small domestic ways. Also, since the masculine role discourages men from talking about their anxieties with other men, a wife is sometimes the only person who can serve as a confidant in certain areas. The reverse is not true for women; the feminine role makes it quite acceptable for them to share their anxieties with other women, making them less dependent on marriage for this type of emotional relief. In certain ways, then, marriage may be protective for men and emotionally dangerous for women. These conclusions are complicated, however, by studies of positive well-being that suggest that marriage is positively associated with reports of happiness and life satisfaction for both women and men—but more so for women (Wood, Rhodes, & Whelan, 1989). These authors note that women, long encouraged to pay attention to the emotional aspects of intimate relationships, may be more sensitive than men to both the emotional lows *and* highs associated with marriage.

Both the masculine and feminine role differences in the acceptability of seeking medical help and the gender differences in the relationship between marriage and mental health point to the impact of gender roles on the patterns of mental illness in women and men. Their influence is most obvious in certain specific diagnostic categories. We turn briefly now to an examination of four particular types of mental illness for which gender differences have been found: depression, alcoholism, eating disorders, and agoraphobia.

Depression

Serious, clinical depression is signaled by feelings of extreme sadness and hopelessness and by a loss of interest in most activities. Women are more likely than men to experience serious depressions (Chino & Funabiki, 1984; Nolen-Hoeksema, 1987) and to be diagnosed and treated for depression (Weissman & Klerman, 1977). Married, divorced, and separated women are more likely to be depressed than their male counterparts, while single men and widowers are more likely than comparable women to experience depression (Radloff, 1980). According to the National Task Force on Women and Depression, American women are twice as likely as men to be depressed (Freiberg, 1991b).

The relationship between depression and gender may vary according to ethnicity. Greater female than male rates of depression have been found among European-Americans (Radloff, 1980) and among Cuban-Americans (Narrow, Rae, Moscicki, Locke, & Regier, 1990) and other Hispanic-American groups (Russo, Amaro, & Winter, 1987), but some studies show no gender difference in depression for African-Americans (Markush & Favero, 1974).

The female–male difference in depression rates may sometimes be explainable by the presence of a few women who score very high on measures of depression (Golding, 1988). In addition, the gender effect may be an indirect reflection of other factors such as employment, low socioeconomic status, and stress. For example, one study of depression in an employment setting showed that, after the effects of salary, age, education, and job classification had been taken into account, no gender differences in depression remained (Maffeo, Ford, & Lavin, 1990).

The theories that have been proposed to account for the gender differences in depression include (1) the notion that the feminine role predisposes women to depression by encouraging them to feel and act helpless, (2) the idea that women face more stress than men and so are more likely really to *be* helpless or powerless, (3) the possibility that women are particularly sensitive to stressors that are related to the disruption of interpersonal relationships, and (4) the hypothesis that the differences in depression are biologically based. No general agreement among researchers has been reached about which explanation is best; it is quite likely that each of the following theories captures a portion of the truth.

It has been argued that the feminine role makes women susceptible to depression by encouraging them to feel helpless and by literally teaching them to respond to stress in powerless, helpless ways (Cox & Radloff, 1984; Radloff, 1980). When a person discovers that the rewards or punishments in a given situation are independent of her or his actions, that person learns that she or he is helpless in that situation. The sense of helplessness, that one's actions make no difference, can generalize to new situations if experienced strongly or regularly. A generalized "learned helplessness" is related to depression; in particular, the expectation that one's responses will be ineffective may produce failure to cope and a susceptibility to depression. A great deal of evidence suggests that female socialization is more likely than male socialization to lead to the belief that one's responses are ineffectual, and thus to a susceptibility to depression. Radloff (1980) notes, for example, that females are stereotypically expected to be weaker, less competent, and more in need of help than males, that the actions of boys are more likely than those of girls to have consequences of reward or punishment, that female competence is more likely than male competence to be ignored or greeted with ambivalence, and that work produced by females is less rewarded with pay, promotions, or status than similar work produced by males. One possible source of gender differences in depression, then, is that males are socialized more strongly than females to believe that their responses make a difference, that they can affect their rewards or punishments by the way they act.

A second possible explanation for the preponderance of women in the depressive diagnostic category is that women lead more stressful lives than men do. If this is true, it would mean that women have more problems and changes to cope with, and so objectively have more difficulty than men do being in control of their lives. Thus, an actual rather than a perceived difference in controllability of rewards and punishments would explain gender differences in depression. As seen in the section on stress later in this chapter, the evidence pertaining to gender differences in exposure to stressors is mixed. Research on whether women or men experience more stressful life events is inconclusive; however, women are more likely than men to have low status and to live under a variety of chronically stressful life conditions. Thus, it is possible that some of the gender difference in depression can be explained by gender differences in exposure to or reactions to stress. In particular, women tend to face threats of rape and other forms of sexual abuse, domestic violence, and sexual harassment at considerably higher rates than men. As one depression researcher has commented, "Simply reducing the number of women who are victimized should reduce the number of women who are depressed" (Nolen-Hoeksema, quoted in Freiberg, 1991a, p. 39).

Weissman and Klerman (1977) have proposed a third explanation for the higher rates of female depression: Women may be more sensitive than men are to disruptions in close personal relationships. It is difficult to evaluate this hypothesis. On the one hand, researchers have found that women are more concerned than men about rejection and abandonment (Pidano & Tennen, 1985), and that the loss of an important relationship is a more common trigger of depression for women than for men (Scarf, 1979). On the other hand, there is quite a bit of evidence, as discussed in Chapter 7, that men are more devastated than women by breakups of intimate relationships. Researchers and clinicians have long acknowledged that relationship loss is an important precursor of depression for both women and men. It remains to be seen whether women are more affected by it than men.

One proposed explanation for the female preponderance in depression is a biological one: Depression may be linked to the hormonal changes associated with women's reproductive processes. This idea stems from the long-held belief that menstruation, the postpartum period, and menopause are times when women are at significantly higher risk for depression. As seen in earlier chapters, however, menopause is not linked to an increase in depression, and the research linking depressed mood to the menstrual cycle and to the postpartum period has not demonstrated that the link has a hormonal basis. Thus, some researchers suggest, although some part of the female–male difference in depression can perhaps be explained by hormone levels or changes, this factor alone can account for only a portion of the large difference in depression that has been observed (Klerman & Weissman, 1980).

Finally, a fifth theory to explain female–male differences in depression focuses on the ways that women and men respond to depressive episodes (Nolen-Hoeksema, 1987). The theory is based on findings that men and women show different patterns of responding to their own feelings of depression. In general, there is evidence that men, when depressed, tend to engage in activities to distract them from their feelings. Women, on the other hand, tend to react to depression by reflecting on it, thinking about its possible causes and implications. These differing response styles are in tune with gender roles: Men are taught to be active and to ignore feelings of weakness, while women are taught to be concerned with their feelings.

Nolen-Hoeksema (1987) argues that a ruminative, inactive response set for depression might amplify and prolong a depressive episode in several ways, while an active response set might dampen and shorten it. Reflecting on the depression might interfere with concentration on other tasks, leading to failures and an increased sense of helplessness. Conversely, becoming active in response to depression leads to more chances for controlling one's environment and obtaining positive rewards. Focusing on the depression might activate a storehouse of negative memories, which strengthen the depressed mood and reinforce negative interpretations of events. Becoming active, however, might distract an individual from the mood and negative thoughts, breaking the cycle and dampening the depression. Finally, ruminating on a depression increases the likelihood that an individual will generate depressing explanations for things that are happening, thus increasing the depression further. This theory suggests that constant attention to one's own mood may be counterproductive, and that mildly depressed women might be best helped by advice that stresses an active response to depression and discourages thinking about it too much. The author also notes, however, that the other extreme—denying the signs of a severe depression—can be equally counterproductive. Although expectations associated with masculinity might prevent a seriously depressed man from seeking help, expectations associated with femininity might encourage a mildly depressed woman to pay too much attention to her mood and thus to become moderately or severely depressed. This theory illustrates one more way in which cultural gender roles may be influencing the incidence of mental illness in women and men.

Alcoholism

It is well documented that men are more likely than women to drink and to abuse alcohol (Leland, 1982; U.S. Department of Health and Human Services, 1988). This finding holds even though women, because they have less body mass and less of the stomach enzyme that breaks down alcohol than men do, become impaired more easily than men do when they drink. Data from both the United States and Canada indicates that, among problem drinkers, the ratio of men to women is about 3 to 1. The groundwork for this gender difference may be laid very early; research shows that, even among adolescents, males report more use of all drugs except cigarettes (Kandel, 1980). These findings fit the gender stereotypes about drinking; when people think of a skid row alcoholic they usually think of a man. The image of a temperance advocate is inevitably female.

Two gender-role theories have been proposed to explain the large ratio of male to female alcohol abusers: the *power theory* (McClelland, Davis, Kalin, & Wanner, 1972) and the *dependency theory* (Bacon, 1974). The power theory suggests that men drink as a way of enhancing their feelings of power—feelings that are much more important for the masculine than for the feminine role. In this framework, the increased energy and adrenalin levels that accompany alcohol intake are thought to produce a sensation of increased strength. Women, who are not expected to be strong and powerful, supposedly have less need than men do for alcohol as a source of power feelings. The dependency theory proposes, conversely, that alcohol creates feelings of security, warmth, and acceptance and allows the drinker to feel dependent. Men, who are pressured by society's stereotype of masculinity to hide their dependency needs, are thus more inclined than women are toward the relief from this pressure provided by alcohol.

The two theories propose opposing motives for and effects of drinking; hence, more research is needed to know which, if either, is correct. A more straightforward explanation for the gender difference in alcohol abuse may be simply that women receive more negative societal responses than men do for heavy drinking. A common tradition exists that when a drug is regulated by a society, the rules of access, both formal and informal, are different for men and women, and alcohol is no exception (Gomberg, 1982). Female drunkenness is viewed with less tolerance than is male drunkenness, and alcoholism is judged more negatively in women than in men. Part of the gender difference in alcohol abuse may well stem from social rules that encourage women to find expressions other than drinking for their distress. Thus, for instance, the finding that male relatives of alcoholics often become alcoholics, while female relatives of alcoholics show a greater tendency toward depression (Cotton, 1979) might be interpreted to mean that alcoholism and depression are gender-specific expressions of similar underlying problems.

Eating Disorders

Two eating disorders, anorexia nervosa and bulimia, have been the objects of a surge of professional and public interest over the past 15 years. Anorexia involves self-starvation in an effort to maintain an unrealistically low body weight. It is characterized by an intense fear of becoming obese and by a disturbed body image—a tendency to "feel fat" even when grossly underweight (American Psychiatric Association, 1980). Bulimia, which involves a pattern of "binge" overeating followed by self-induced "purging" through a variety of means, including dieting, vomiting, or laxatives, is also characterized by an obsession with food and with body weight. Both syndromes are far more common among women than men, with most studies indicating that females comprise 85 to 97 percent of cases (Bruch, 1973; Garfinkel & Garner, 1982; Hall, Delahunt, & Ellis, 1985). The "typical" sufferer from one of these disorders is a white, middle-class woman under the age of 25. Subgroups of young women for whom thinness is especially important, such as modeling students, athletes, and professional dancers, show a higher than average incidence of eating disorders (Brooks-Gunn, Burrow, & Warren, 1988; Szymanski & Chrisler, 1990/91).

A number of writers have suggested that sociocultural factors, particularly the current emphasis on thinness, play a part in the development of eating disorders (e.g., Boskind-White, 1985; Chernin, 1981; Wooley & Wooley, 1985). An increase in the incidence of eating disorders over the past 20 years has occurred simultaneously with a shift toward thinness in the ideal of feminine beauty and a rise in interest in diets and weight reduction. Fat people, especially fat women, are disparaged as unattractive in our culture. The more dependent a person is on physical attractiveness for self-esteem, the more vulnerable she or he is to such cultural messages. Since women tend to be more identified in terms of their appearance than men are, it is perhaps not surprising that more women than men fall victim to eating disorders. Moreover, research shows that, in contrast to males, females tend to see their bodies as heavier than the ideal figure or than the figure that would appeal to the other sex (Fallon & Rozin, 1985). Among college students, women are more likely than men to see themselves as overweight and to diet. One survey found that nearly one-third of a sample of college females reported either self-induced vomiting or laxative use as a weight-loss strategy (Connor-Greene, 1988).

The cultural premium on thinness, then, particularly for women, may stimulate the obsession with food and weight that helps to generate the distortions of body image and appetite characteristic of eating disorders.

Agoraphobia

Phobias, defined as persistent, irrational fears of and desire to avoid specific objects, activities, or situations, are more common among females than males (Brehony, 1982). *Agoraphobia,* the most common, involves a fear of being in public places from which escape might be difficult or help unavailable in case of sudden incapacitation (American Psychiatric Association, 1980). Sufferers from this disorder may fear such situations as busy streets, crowded stores, elevators, or public transportation; thus, they may literally be trapped in their own homes by the fear of venturing out. The symptoms may represent a passive way of avoiding stressful situations. Among individuals diagnosed as agoraphobics, women outnumber men 3 to 1 (Fodor, 1982).

Researchers are still unsure of the reasons for the female preponderance among agoraphobics, but the most popular theories center on the different expectations for coping with fear that are built into the masculine and feminine roles. Research has shown that, until adolescence, girls and boys are fairly similar in fearfulness, but that, from adolescence onward, males admit to many fewer fears than females do (Macfarlane, Allen, & Honzik, 1974). Masculine socialization encourages boys to confront and master their fears while girls are reinforced, not for mastery, but for expressing their fears and remaining helpless and dependent (Hoffman, 1972). Agoraphobia, which most often begins in the mid-twenties, within a few years of marriage, may be triggered when an individual who has been socialized to be dependent and apprehensive becomes pressured instead to be competent and independent. For a woman in a traditional marriage, this pressure may occur in the context of fulfilling the homemaker role, or in the context of discontent with that role and a desire to pursue alternatives (Fodor, 1982). The stress may cause these women, conditioned by a lifetime pattern of avoidance, to become increasingly helpless and dependent—a reaction that may be reinforced by the attention and sympathetic responses of those around her. Although men may have similar reactions of fear and helplessness, they are far less likely than women are to be reinforced for them. Moreover, since the men are more likely than the women in this group to be employed and to be the major economic provider for the family, they simply cannot afford to avoid leaving the house (Jassin, 1980). Thus, men who have a tendency toward agoraphobia may instead display symptoms of alcoholism or anxiety neuroses.

For agoraphobia, then, as for the other disorders discussed in this section, at least part of the explanation for the gender difference in incidence may well be found in gender-role expectations. Psychological distress is manifested in different symptoms and diagnosed differently for women and men. The differences seem to derive, not from a differential vulnerability to mental illness, but from the different patterns of behaviors that are reinforced for the two sexes and the different kinds of pressures built into the masculine and feminine roles.

The Politics of Diagnosis

We have already seen one of the implications of deciding how to diagnose and "count" mental illness: When certain categories of mental illness are excluded from the tally, women appear to suffer more from mental illness than do men. However, when these categories are included, the overall gender difference in mental illness rates tends to disappear. It is important to remember that sexist biases built into the diagnostic categories may well influence perceptions of whether women and men are psychologically healthy. If the categories are based on an idea that male behavior represents the norm or standard for health—an idea that is certainly not inconceivable in view of the historic male domination of the psychiatric profession—then women who are behaving in ways that are normal, given their socialization and the situation of women in society, may be diagnosed as mentally ill. For instance, since women learn to deal with their emotions differently than men do, they may become very enmeshed in their feelings without losing their sense of self. Thus, "many women diagnosed as borderline may actually be functioning in a normal way for a woman, even though their behavior may make male-identified therapists anxious" (Walker, L. E., 1984b, p. 15).

There is a danger that the mental health system will apply diagnostic categories in gender stereotypic ways (Kaplan, 1983). Indeed, the diagnoses that are most commonly applied to members of specific subgroups of the population tend to embody the roles and stereotypes attributed to those groups (Landrine, 1987, 1989). Landrine (1987) gave stereotyped descriptions of lower-class men, single middle-class women, married middle-class women, and married upper-class men to a sample of clinical psychologists and psychiatrists. The clinicians were asked to provide diagnoses for these "cases," and were explicitly reminded that the cases might be normal. Landrine found that the stereotype of the lower-class man was labeled antisocial, the stereotype of the married middle-class woman was labeled dependent, that of the single middle-class woman was labeled histrionic/hysterical, and the stereotype of the married upper-class man was labeled prototypically normal. There were no differences in the ways male and female clinicians, or psychoanalytic and feminist therapists, labeled the cases—suggesting that all were influenced by prevailing social stereotypes.

An example of the politics of diagnosis has occurred recently in the controversy over the inclusion of several new diagnostic categories in the DSM-III-R, the diagnostic manual of the American Psychiatric Association. Two of these categories, "premenstrual dysphoric disorder" (now called Late Luteal Phase Dysphoric Disorder) and "self-defeating personality," have the effect of labeling female experiences and stereotypically feminine traits as signs of mental illness. Controversy over the inclusion of these diagnostic categories in the manual was intense; more than six million North Americans signed petitions and wrote letters opposing their inclusion. However, both categories have now been assigned official numbers and included in an Appendix to the manual.

What if stereotypically male traits were grouped together and labeled "sick"? In an article that satirizes the labeling of gender-related behavior patterns as "disorders," Kaye-Lee Pantony and Paula Caplan (1991) highlight the bias implicit in diagnostic politics. They propose, with feigned seriousness, the inclusion of a new diagnostic category—Delusional Dominating Personality Disorder—in the diagnostic manual. The "symptoms" of this disorder (first detailed by Caplan & Eichler, 1989) include, among others, the "tendency to use power, silence, withdrawal, and/or avoidance rather than negotiation in the face of interpersonal conflict or difficulty," and a "tendency to feel inordinately threatened by women who fail to disguise their intelligence" (Pantony & Caplan, 1991, p. 121). The incidence of this disorder is, according to the authors, highest among males but occasionally present in females, and tends to be pronounced among "leaders of traditional mental health professions, military personnel, executives of large corporations, and powerful political leaders of many nations" (Pantony & Caplan, 1991, p. 121). The "disorder" proposed by Pantony and Caplan seems absurd precisely because it characterizes as "sick" the attitudes and behaviors of powerful and successful people. Their approach underlines the point that mental health policy as it relates to gender and other social categories is not value neutral, but tends to define the behavior of powerful groups as normative and that of other groups as sick.

Gender and Mental Health

Good mental health is more than the absence of serious mental illness; it is often viewed as satisfaction, or as adjustment to, acceptance of, and ability to cope with one's life situation. Women, on average, report greater life satisfaction and happiness than do men—a seemingly paradoxical finding in view of women's higher rates of depression

(Wood, Rhodes, & Whelan, 1989). It is not clear whether this gender difference represents a difference in experience, a difference in the willingness to report extreme emotional responses, or a difference in sensitivity to internal emotions. A recent study indicates that women respond with greater emotional intensity to stimuli than men do, suggesting that women's more intense positive emotions may help to balance their higher levels of negative feelings (Fujita, Diener, & Sandvik, 1991).

There is a catch-22 in the "adjustment" definition of mental health: The more difficult and stressful one's situation, the more problematic it is to adjust to it. Although most of us would consider it mentally healthy for a person to accept and adjust to the necessity of working for a living rather than clinging to the improbable hope of winning a lottery, we would not counsel a woman who is being beaten regularly by her husband that it is mentally healthy to "adjust" to the situation. Thus, the conception of mental health as adjustment must be tempered by a keen awareness of both the situation to which a person is being expected to adjust and whether an acceptance of that situation will ultimately be beneficial or harmful to him or her.

In the past, gender roles have figured strongly in psychology's notions of what represented proper adjustment—and thus good mental health—for women and men. People who conformed to gender expectations, masculine men and feminine women, were considered healthier than those who did not. Indeed, "rejecting" one's femininity or masculinity was considered cause for psychotherapy. Over the years, however, three major problems with this approach have been recognized. The first is that the gender role to which women are expected to adjust is inherently less healthy, in terms of coping abilities and a sense of self-worth, than is that to which men are expected to conform. The second is that rigid adherence to one's gender role, like too much rigidity in any area, interferes with a person's capacity to cope with a variety of situations, and thus can be counterproductive for mental health. The third is that society's gender roles channel women and men into situations that differ in the kinds of stress they exert and the requirements for coping they demand. An acceptance of one's gender role often means, not just acceptance of a certain style of interpersonal behavior, but of a certain position in the family, in the workplace, and so on.

The Double Standard of Mental Health

The influence of gender stereotypes on standards of mental health for women and men was demonstrated in a landmark study of the ideals of mental health professionals (psychologists, psychiatrists, and social workers) for healthy adult men and women (Broverman, Broverman, Clarkson, Rosenkrantz, & Vogel, 1970). These researchers found that clinicians actually held different ideals for a healthy, fully functioning adult male than for a healthy, fully functioning adult female. The ideal healthy woman was described as being more submissive, less independent and adventurous, more easily influenced, less aggressive and competitive, more easily excitable in minor crises, more easily hurt, more emotional, more vain about her appearance, less objective, and less interested in math and science than the ideal healthy man. Also, the clinicians' ideal of the healthy man was similar to that of a healthy, mature adult (gender unspecified), but their ideal of a healthy woman was quite different from both. It appeared, then, that women were caught in a double bind. If they met the mental health standards for their own gender, they automatically fell short of those for the general adult population. If they met the standards for a healthy adult, they were automatically defined as unfeminine—and thus poorly adjusted.

The double standard of mental health seems to have gone underground in recent years. Therapists no longer list very different characteristics as desirable for mentally healthy women and men (Davidson & Abramowitz, 1980; Phillips & Gilroy, 1985), but some studies find that, in practice, clinicians' judgments about their clients are influenced by gender roles (Abramowitz & Herrera, 1981; Teri, 1982). Therapists may have become sensitive to the issue of gender bias and so are unlikely to respond in a biased way to a questionnaire or a hypothetical situation presented to them on paper. A meta-analysis of 30 studies of gender bias in counseling and therapy (Smith, 1980) found little overall evidence for the existence of bias, and the greatest bias that was shown was found in the earlier studies. However, naturalistic studies, in which the therapist is confronted with a real live client instead of a hypothetical one, suggest that gender bias is alive and well (Hare-Mustin, 1983).

Cultural pressures on women to adjust to the feminine role is antithetical to the development of the healthy behaviors of independence and competence, just as pressure on men to adjust to the male role interferes with the healthy behaviors of expressiveness and warmth. Moreover, the association of good adjustment with gender-role conformity may mask problems for both women and men. It has been argued, for instance, that when women in our culture exhibit signs of hysteria or masochism, these signs often go unnoticed because of their similarity to the prescribed stereotype of feminine behavior (Belote, 1976). Similarly, when men in our culture exhibit the aggressiveness and disregard for others characteristic of the antisocial personality, they may be perceived as acting within the boundaries of the normal masculine role (Doyle, 1983).

Gender-Role Flexibility and Mental Health

Research over the past 15 years has increasingly challenged the notion that conformity to gender stereotypes is associated with good mental health. Indeed, for both women and men, the rigidity associated with strong adherence to gender roles may interfere with coping and adaptability in a variety of situations. For example, Pleck (1981) has argued that many men overconform to the masculine role out of anxiety about possible violations. Such overconformity prevents the exploration of potentially satisfying behaviors and interests. Women too may suffer adverse consequences from conforming too closely to traditional feminine roles. One study that followed a group of women from the 1950s to the early 1980s found that, although traditionality of role was related to positive well-being and effective functioning at age 21, such traditionality was related to negative changes in psychological and physical health by age 43 (Helson & Picano, 1990).

A series of studies by Sandra Bem and her colleagues using the BSRI (discussed in Chapter 1) indicated that strong gender-typing in the direction of either masculinity or femininity was associated with restricted behavior in certain settings. For example, they demonstrated that in a situation that required the "feminine" behavior of nurturing a small baby, subjects of both sexes who were classified as either feminine or androgynous performed significantly better than masculine men and women (Bem, Martyna, & Watson, 1976). In another study, Bem (1975) demonstrated that masculine and androgynous subjects of both sexes performed better than feminine subjects at a task that required the stereotypically "masculine" behavior of independence in the face of social pressure. A third study (Bem & Lenney, 1976) demonstrated that masculine men and feminine women were more likely than androgynous women or men to choose activities that were "appropriate" for their own gender and to reject out-of-role activities. After performing cross-gender activities, masculine men and feminine women also reported experiencing more discomfort and feeling worse about themselves than did androgynous subjects of either sex. These findings were taken as evidence that "appropriate" gender-typing, as measured by the BSRI, is related to behavioral inflexibility and a tendency not to adapt one's role to the requirements of unfamiliar situations—hardly a hallmark of good mental health.

More recent research indicates, however, that the relationship between gender stereotypes and mental health cannot be summarized adequately by the motto that "androgyny is good; sex-typing is bad." For one thing, androgyny may be more of an advantage for women than for men in this culture (Heilbrun, 1984; Wiggins & Holzmuller, 1981). Some studies have found that people with masculine qualities—those who score either androgynous or masculine on the BSRI or other scales—show the most adaptive behavior and social effectiveness, have higher subjective well-being and self-esteem, and report lower stress (Jones, Chernovetz, & Hansson, 1978; Long, 1989; Long, V., 1991; Lubinski, Tellegen, & Butcher, 1981; O'Heron & Orlofsky, 1990). The instrumental qualities tapped by contemporary measures of masculinity, then, are apparently very important for successful social functioning in our culture. Thus, although the research is inconclusive about whether androgyny is preferable to masculinity (at least as assessed by current tests) in terms of behavioral flexibility or other aspects of mental health, it seems safe to conclude that there is no mental health advantage to women to being "properly" sex-typed as feminine. In fact, feminine sex-typed individuals, especially women, show more depression, anxiety, and low self-esteem than do those scoring as masculine or androgynous (Burchardt & Serbin, 1982; Heiser & Gannon, 1984; Tinsley, Sullivan-Guest, & McGuire, 1984). Although rigid adherence to gender roles may interfere with behavioral flexibility for both women and men, the consequences for women, at least in a culture that is structured so that most rewards are obtainable only through the instrumental behaviors we associate with masculinity, may be more serious.

Gender Roles and Environmental Stress

It is sometimes argued that the environments in which women and men are expected to function differ in terms of stress, a difference that would help to explain women's higher rate of mental health problems. *Stressors* are external events or conditions that are appraised as threatening by an individual, and thus are the source of upset, worry, discomfort, and general distress. Researchers examining this issue have looked at both life events and life conditions. In general, they have found little evidence to suggest that women and men differ in the quantity or quality of stressful life events they experience, but there is strong evidence that women are more likely than men to experience stressful long-term life conditions.

Stressful Life Events.   A great deal of research suggests that life events that involve change or disruption are experienced as stressful and that the onset of both physical and mental illness is often preceded by a cluster of such events: accidents, job loss, promotion, pregnancy, divorce, wage increase, family arguments, and so on. Since women and men differ in both their daily lives and their patterns of mental illness, it seems reasonable to ask whether they experience different numbers of stressful life events. As it turns out, there is little evidence that they do; most research shows no gender differences in the number of stressful life events reported (Makosky, 1980; Mulvey & Dohrenwend, 1984). How, then, to explain women's apparently higher rate of mental illness? Perhaps the contents of the life-events lists are biased so as to include more of the stressful events that men rather than women face. Perhaps the life changes faced by men are more likely to be positive ones, and thus less distressing, than are those faced by women. Or perhaps women may experience more stress than men do in response to the same life events. Each of these possibilities has received some attention from researchers.

There are good arguments for the notion that the item content of the life-change lists used in stress research may produce misleading life-change scores for women (Makosky, 1980). For example, most lists do not include items about events happening to significant others that may be stressful to oneself (e.g., spouse fired or promoted, child changed schools)—yet some research has shown that women are far more likely than men to report the occurrence of such events (Dohrenwend, 1976, cited in Makosky, 1980). Also missing from most lists are some items of particular concern to women: rape, changes in child-care arrangements, incidents of sexual harassment, physical abuse by spouse. It is difficult to define a list of life changes that is equally appropriate to everyone; yet if group comparisons are to be made, the list must reflect fairly the changes likely to be important for each group.

Researchers have found no gender differences either in the desirability of stressful life events or in the degree to which individuals say they are able to anticipate such events. However, in one study, when subjects were asked about the extent to which they could control the occurrence of stressful events, an unexpected and counterstereotypic gender difference was found: middle-aged and late middle-aged men reported less control over their life events than did women (Mulvey & Dohrenwend, 1984). In the same study, young men reported *more* control over life-change events than any other group. The researchers speculate that men may feel an exaggerated sense of control when young, so that the obstacles and unrealized goals they face later in the life span seem more problematic in contrast to their earlier expectations. Women, they suggest, are accustomed to obstacles and low status from an early age and do not experience the same sense of relative deprivation as they age.

There is some evidence that the same stressor may result in different amounts of stress for women and men. For example, when subjects were asked to imagine how much stress they would be experiencing at the present time if specific events (e.g., deaths, separations, arguments, threats to self-image, financial threats, general changes) had occurred one week ago, one month ago, and so on up to three years ago, women rated all the sets of events as more stressful than men did (Horowitz, Schaefer, & Cooney, 1974). Also, it has been argued that such events as separation, divorce, widowhood, and childbearing are more stressful for women than for men because women tend to experience greater financial loss, are less likely to remarry, and are more likely to have the major burden of child care (Makosky, 1980).

On the whole, then, although there is no direct evidence for gender differences in the *number* of stressful life events, there are many unanswered questions about how such events are experienced by women and men, and even about whether the same list of such events is appropriate for use with both genders. More research is needed before the relationship between stressful life events and gender differences in patterns of mental illness can be delineated with certainty.

Stressful Life Conditions.   In contrast to stressful life events, stressful life conditions are chronic environmental factors that have a long-term impact on individuals. In terms of such conditions, we have already noted that women are more likely than men to be poor; they are also more likely than men to be employed in low-status, low-paying jobs and to be heading single-parent families. They are also more likely than men to be victims of unpredictable, uncontrollable family violence. Finally, they are more likely than men to be trying to perform two concurrent full-time jobs: homemaker/mother within the home and paid employee outside the home. It is fairly easy to argue that, on the average, life conditions are more stressful for women than for men.

Particular groups of women and men may be exposed to different kinds of chronic stressors. One newly developed measure of stress for African-American women (Watts-Jones, 1990) includes items that reflect the following chronic stressors: inadequate resources (e.g., unable to afford your own place, living in a neighborhood with high crime), work-related stress (e.g., working at a boring job), relationship conflict/dissatisfaction (e.g., man is possessive/jealous), role functioning (e.g., being a single parent), racism (e.g., working with prejudiced coworkers), and personal health (e.g., being overweight).

Poverty is associated with mental health problems, and the combination of poverty with responsibility for young children is devastating for women. One study of married women living in central London showed that the rate of mood disorders was 5 percent for middle-class women, 25 percent for working-class women, and 42 percent for working-class women with preschool children (Brown, Bhrolchain, & Harris, 1975). Other research indicates that women who are single parents are at even greater risk for emotional problems (Pearlin & Johnson, 1977). It is unlikely that there is anything specifically "feminine" about this pattern of reactions; men living in poverty with sole responsibility for preschool children would probably get depressed, too.

One reason for the link between chronic conditions such as poverty, discrimination, and fear of violence on the one hand and emotional problems such as depression on the other is the lack of control over one's life that these conditions engender. It is difficult to maintain a sense of well-being and self-esteem when it is impossible, despite one's best efforts, to feed and clothe one's children properly, or to keep the household running smoothly. However, for some women, one potentially stressful life condition can add to their sense of control and self-esteem instead of detracting from it—that is, combining having a family with outside employment.

Employment is certainly a potential source of stressors for both women and men. However, it is also a potential source of satisfaction, accomplishment, and mastery, as well as a reason for leaving the isolation of one's own home. Some analysts have argued that one reason for high mental illness rates among housewives is that they have only one role from which to derive a sense of satisfaction, whereas the typical employed man has two (Gove & Tudor, 1973). Some evidence seems to suggest that people with few roles are vulnerable to mental and physical health problems; for example, Verbrugge (1983) found that the women with the poorest health profile were those without employment, husband, or children, while Baruch, Barnett, and Rivers (1983) found the highest overall indications of mental health among women with the most roles. Among employed black and white women and men, job satisfaction is positively related to life satisfaction, and occupational status is positively linked to perceived control for women of both racial groups (Crohan, Antonucci, Adelmann, & Coleman, 1989).

However, lack of outside employment is not necessarily linked to discontent for women. Some researchers have found that married, full-time homemakers with young children express more pleasure and satisfaction with their lives, and have fewer worries than other women (Baruch et al., 1983; Veroff, Douvan, & Kulka, 1981). The ability to *choose* roles, not just the *number* of roles, seems to be crucial to mental health (Sales & Frieze, 1984). Homemakers who are dissatisfied with their role have high rates of depression, physical and mental problems, and drug use (Pearlin, 1975; Verbrugge, 1982b).

For women who have good marriages and who have adequate resources to handle child care, employment during the early childrearing period may be less stressful than staying home. The additional demands imposed by juggling two roles can be balanced by the fact that the satisfactions of one role can act as a buffer for the problems and frustrations encountered in the other (Brown et al., 1975; Stewart & Salt, 1981). Thus, just as men have traditionally been able to forget temporarily about failures and anxieties at work by coming home to families where the relationships and tasks are different, so employed mothers may be able to avoid becoming trapped in feelings of frustration and anxiety about childrearing by having the additional set of goals, rewards, and concerns that the workplace provides. In addition, outside employment reduces the isolation often experienced by new mothers.

In general, researchers have found that employed women, both middle-class and working-class, are in better mental health than those who stay at home, at least on some dimensions. Women who work outside the home report fewer symptoms and use mental health services less than do women who stay home (Wheeler, Lee, & Loe, 1983). They also report greater feelings of mastery, but not more positive feelings about life (Baruch et al., 1983). Thus, employment may be linked to only certain aspects of mental health. For example, employed women may have stronger feelings of competence and self-esteem, but be no happier on the whole than other women (Sales & Frieze, 1984). Furthermore, researchers cannot yet say unequivocally that employment *causes* women to be more mentally healthy; it may be simply that healthier women choose to seek employment. Yet employed women no longer represent an elite or unusual minority; more and more women enter the work force out of economic necessity. The fact that, with increasing numbers of women entering the labor force, the positive relationship between employment and mental health has remained stable suggests that employment does make a contribution to women's well-being (Sales & Frieze, 1984).

For women with unsatisfying marriages, inadequate resources to guarantee good child care in their absence, or jobs that are stultifying or unpleasant, the mental health costs of combining employment and motherhood may sometimes outweigh the benefits. Moreover, there may be an "overload" point at which the positive relationship between role involvement and mental health reverses; beyond a certain limit, it may be unhealthy to juggle too many roles at once (Verbrugge, 1983). Single working mothers, for example, are often overstressed and vulnerable to illness.

In summary, women tend to have to cope with more stressful life conditions than men do, a difference that may help to explain why women are more likely than men to become depressed. Paradoxically, however, women who add to their potential stressors by combining employment with motherhood often report fewer symptoms of stress than do women who stay at home, perhaps because employment confers an additional source of self-worth and control. Heavily overloaded women, however, may be very distressed by the demands of multiple roles.

Treatment of Emotional Problems

Psychotherapy.   A common response to mental or emotional distress is to seek psychotherapy. An individual who enters therapy has often failed to find solutions to problems using other strategies and hopes that the therapist will be able to provide help, support, and guidance in dealing with painful, difficult situations. Often, these hopes are realized. Therapy has helped many people to solve serious problems. However, as we shall see, therapy as an institution can reflect some of the same sexist biases that are found in the diagnostic arm of the mental health system. The potential consumer of therapy services is well advised to evaluate therapists with care before choosing one.

Women are much more likely than men to consult a therapist, and some writers have argued that psychotherapy as an institution, like marriage as an institution, poses some inherent dangers for women (Chesler, 1972; Tennov, 1975). The danger stems partly from the reinforcement of the dependency and helplessness that are built into the feminine role. Therapy, like marriage, can put a woman into a dependency relationship with an authority figure. If the therapist is male, the process may further reinforce the notion that a woman needs a man to solve her problems.

A therapist may hold strongly to particular values that work against the growth and problem-solving capacity of the client. If a client is trying to transcend gender-role stereotypes, a therapist who believes implicitly in the appropriateness of these stereotypes is unlikely to provide much support. For example, a woman struggling to find the courage to leave or renegotiate a stifling marital relationship is unlikely to be helped much by a therapist who adheres strongly to the belief that the man is the natural head of the family. Likewise, a man whose relationships are failing because he is unable to express any warmth and tenderness may receive little useful advice from a therapist who believes that the most important qualities for male adjustment are autonomy and independence.

Sexism may well affect the psychotherapeutic process. There are many reported instances of therapists fostering traditional gender roles, telling sexist jokes, refusing to take violence against women seriously, and seducing their female clients (American Psychological Association, 1975). Furthermore, therapists are often simply uninformed about the psychology of women and about sexual and reproductive issues (Sherman, Koufacos, & Kenworthy, 1978). Ignorance about women's experience may be particularly serious when the client is a minority or low-income woman. Many clinicians limit their attention to intrapsychic issues, ignoring such potential contributors to emotional distress as inadequate income, poor health, substandard housing, unsafe neighborhoods, and racial discrimination. One researcher found that only 7.7 percent of the white psychologists in his sample said that socioeconomic problems were among the most common ones experienced by the black families who were their clients, while white social workers and black psychologists and social workers saw such problems as widespread (Boyd, 1979). The ignorance or denial of the importance of environmental factors can lead therapists to negative stereotyping of low-income and minority women, women who are victims of violence, and other individuals exhibiting stress-related emotional problems.

One area in which therapist knowledge and understanding is often crucial to the success of treatment is sexual assault. According to some surveys, anywhere from 13 percent to 48 percent of female psychiatric patients have histories of sexual assault (Dye & Roth, 1990). Women who have been sexually victimized may suffer psychological distress for years. They may develop depression, phobias, sexual dysfunction, social withdrawal, and other symptoms. Yet victims of sexual assault are often the targets of negative social attitudes: blame for the assault and social derogation. If therapists hold such negative attitudes, their reactions to female clients who have experienced sexual assault will not be helpful.

Some research shows that therapists are not very likely to endorse rape myths (such as "every woman secretly wants to be raped"). Younger age and being female are associated with less acceptance of such myths; psychiatrists are more likely than other mental health professionals to accept rape myths. Therapists who hold more negative stereotypes about sexual assault victims are more likely to endorse and to employ treatment approaches that blame the victim for the assault (Dye & Roth, 1990).

Some efforts have been made to reduce bias in psychotherapy through education. Both the American and Canadian psychological associations have published guidelines for therapy with women (American Psychological Association, 1978; Canadian Psychological Association, 1980). The Canadian Psychological Association has prepared a handbook of educational materials geared to help therapists confront and deal with their own gender biases and to practice nonsexist therapy or "sex-fair" counseling (Canadian Psychological Association, 1982). Nonsexist therapy is based on the idea that women and men should be treated in similar ways and should be viewed as individuals rather than as women or men. Some excellent examples of such nonsexist therapy and counseling approaches have appeared in the psychological literature (Pyke, 1979; Rawlings & Carter, 1977). Because of the availability of such materials it may become easier, in the long run, for people seeking therapy to find a therapist who has struggled to overcome sexist (and racist) biases.

Feminist Therapy.   Awareness of the potential problems in the therapeutic relationship, particularly with respect to gender roles, has given impetus to the development of feminist therapy (Brodsky, 1980; Rosewater & Walker, 1985). There are many versions of feminist therapy, but they tend to share the following features. Feminist therapy explicitly discards traditional gender stereotypic assumptions about behavior, and the stereotypes themselves are openly discussed rather than ignored or assumed. Therapy incorporates instead the assumption that the differential roles and statuses prescribed for women and men are potentially harmful to both sexes, particularly women. The approach rejects the notion of the therapist as an authority figure, emphasizing instead the empowerment of the client. Moreover, instead of focusing only on individual difficulties and failings, this approach encourages the client to see her or his problem in its social/political context. Most importantly of all, the client, not the therapist, defines the changes that are desirable.

Both female and male therapists can adopt the principles of feminist therapy. However, in the current context of lower status for women, some debate has surrounded the issue of whether women should be treated by male therapists at all. Beginning with Chesler (1971), many feminists have argued that a female therapist provides a better role model for female clients, and also that women seeing female therapists are spared the opportunity to reinforce feelings of dependency on men— feelings that may be the source of problems. Also, as Rosewater (1984) notes, "Women therapists share with their women clients the experiences of being second-class citizens" (p. 271), making it easier to develop mutual understanding and respect. Thus, it may be advantageous to women to have a female therapist, given the current intergroup relations between women and men. For some of the same reasons, there may be advantages for a man in having a male therapist—someone who can empathize with the difficulty of shedding some aspects of the male gender role, and who can provide a good model of the possibilities for male nurturance and self-disclosure. This is not to say, however, that a woman cannot be helped by seeing a feminist male therapist, or that a female feminist therapist cannot do useful work with a male client. Personal as well as social contextual variables influence the success of any client–therapist relationship; individuals must seek a therapist whose style meshes successfully with their own.

Heterosexism in Psychotherapy.   The problem of finding a suitable therapist may be especially difficult for gay and lesbian individuals. Research shows that therapists, particularly males, tend to rate homosexual clients as less healthy than heterosexual clients and to set different therapeutic goals for them (Garfinkle & Morin, 1978). A therapist may show such biases by devaluing same-sex relationships, by emphasizing a search for the cause of the homosexuality rather than dealing with current problems, or even by expecting the client to be able to be impervious to the widely publicized negative images of homosexuality (Riddle & Sang, 1978). It is difficult for a gay or lesbian client to be helped by interactions with a therapist who defines homosexuality as the problem, or who does not help the client to see her or his difficulties in a social context. Because of the negative attitudes toward homosexuality in our culture, lesbians and gay men lead more stressful, and often more isolated, lives than many heterosexual individuals—a difference that must be acknowledged in the therapeutic process. In addition, since much of the stress on individuals is created by negative social responses to behavior that is considered strange or unhealthy simply because of the sex of the person who is engaging in it, the promotion of mental health for all groups of women and men involves changing homophobic and sexist attitudes in society.

Drug Prescriptions

Psychotherapy is not the only treatment for emotional or mental distress. A common clinical response to such problems is to prescribe psychoactive (mood-altering) drugs such as antidepressants or tranquilizers. Women are far more likely than men to receive drug prescriptions for psychological problems (Cafferata & Meyers, 1990; Fidell, 1982). Apparently, physicians are less reluctant to medicate women than men. One study showed that psychiatrists were more likely to recommend drug treatment for a hypothetical female client than for a male client described as having the same symptoms (Schwartz & Abramowitz, 1975). Physicians' biases in this direction are reinforced by drug advertisements in psychiatric journals; most of the clients depicted in such advertisements are women, and the messages are extremely gender stereotypic (Prather & Fidell, 1978).

In the realms of both psychotherapy and drug treatment, the presence of gender bias is being highlighted by concerned researchers and therapists. Yet breaking down these biases is likely to be a long process. For the present, mental health, mental illness, and the treatment of mental illness continue to be gender-defined.

Summary

The "strong man–fragile woman" stereotype is far too simplistic to describe gender differences in physical and mental health. Males are more vulnerable than females to death and serious physical illness across the life span, and they have a shorter life expectancy. Females, however, report more physical and emotional symptoms and seek treatment for physical and mental illnesses more often than men. Men are muscularly stronger than women and have higher fitness levels (at least in North America), but women can outperform men in some endurance situations.

An examination of the patterns of gender differences in health and illness suggests strongly that gender roles and stereotypes make a significant contribution to these differences. Part of men's higher death rate from disease and accidents, for example, is attributed to the dangers of trying to live up to the competitive, achievement-oriented, risk-taking masculine role. Women's higher rates of depression and agoraphobia are linked to the lack of independence and control built into the feminine role.

Not only role expectations but the whole social and physical environment may well provide different stresses and be the source of different problems for women and men. Women are more likely than men to be poor and to be single parents. Marriage, which often involves a loss of status and autonomy for women but not for men and a larger gain in social support for men than for women, tends to be physically and emotionally protective for men but may be dangerous in some ways for women. Employment, which often means the addition of one full-time job to another for a woman with children, may have different health implications for women and men. Even the health-care system, strongly influenced by gender stereotypes, responds differently to women and men and sometimes labels people as unhealthy when they violate norms of femininity, masculinity, or heterosexuality. The promotion of good physical and mental health for women and men requires, in many instances, that such stereotypic thinking be confronted, questioned, and changed.

For Additional Reading

Butler, S., & Rosenblum, B. (1991). *Cancer in two voices*. San Francisco: Spinsters. The statistics about the epidemic of breast cancer among women become terribly personal in this book. The story of three years in the lives of two women who, as partners, must confront the diagnosis of breast cancer in one of them and her eventual death is told through the journals of both women.

Nelson, M. B. (1991). *Are we winning yet? How women are changing sports and sports are changing women*. New York: Random House. The author, an athlete herself, explores the issues surrounding gender equality in sports through interviews with a wide variety of female athletes.

10

Sex & Gender & Childhood

A researcher tells the following story about her own experience of discovering the seriousness with which young children take gender stereotypes. While interviewing 3- to 6-year-olds about their career aspirations, she asked each of them what they would want to be when they grew up if they were members of the other sex. Their responses showed that not only did most of the children choose careers that fit the stereotypes for the other gender, but also that their perceptions of the limitations imposed by gender were sometimes quite extreme. One little girl confided with a sigh that her true ambition was to fly like a bird, but that she could never do it because she was not a boy! One little boy put his hands on his head, sighed deeply, and said helplessly that if he were a girl he'd have to grow up to be nothing (Beuf, 1974).

A study of the way 3- to 5-year-old children made up stories in response to such story beginnings as "Two children are playing outside one day. They discover a secret door," showed that, given the same starts, girls and boys developed very different fantasies (Libby & Aries, 1989). The girls' stories tended to involve caretaking and responding to others' needs. Their stories often contained friendly figures who offered assistance to female characters. The stories told by the boys centered more often on aggression and on attempts to master challenging situations. At this early age, these children were already reflecting gender-stereotypic expectations.

Research on a wider age range of children shows that they feel that a change in their gender would cause a dramatic change in the behavior that was possible and acceptable for them (Baumgartner, 1983). The general notion one gets from reading the responses of these third- to twelfth-grade students is that a change from male to female would involve a restriction of activities and horizons, while a change in the opposite direction would involve a widening of possibilities. For instance, girls noted that as boys they would be more outspoken, noisier, rowdier, have to adhere to fewer rules, worry less about their appearance, and be closer to their fathers. Boys thought that, as girls, they would have to be quieter and more reserved, less active, more restricted in what they were allowed to do, worry more about their appearance, worry about safety, and do fewer things with their fathers. The boys, especially the younger ones, tended to view the possibility of becoming a girl with revulsion; girls, on the other hand, were likely to see advantages to being male.

Clearly, the impact of gender roles and rules on a child's social world begins very early, and one big part of that impact is that males learn to expect more choices and more power and control over their lives than do females. In Chapters 1 and 2, we discussed some of the mechanisms through which this impact occurs. Children, we noted, learn quickly that gender categories are important and pervasive and develop "gender schemas" for processing information according to those categories. Certain activities, certain clothes, certain toys, are found to be appropriate only for girls or only for boys and are duly assigned to "masculine" or "feminine" categories. The child's efforts to categorize things correctly are helped along by modeling, reinforcement, and explicit instruction. In short order, children become quite confident that "boys don't play with dolls" or "girls can't be pilots," and their social relationships reflect and strengthen these expectations.

This chapter examines some of the social forces that push children in the direction of traditional gender stereotypes: parental socialization, the media, and language. It also explores the ways that two of the processes involved in growing up—friendship formation and the search for achievement—affect and are affected by gender stereotypes and roles.

"Getting the Word": Sources of Early Gender Learning

Parents and Children

Parents are the first source of children's gender learning, and indications are that parents both hold and communicate different expectations for males and females. Researchers who interviewed 30 first-time parents within 24 hours after childbirth found that parents of boys and girls had already begun to view their infants differently (Rubin, Provenzano, & Luria, 1974). Those with daughters saw their babies as softer, finer featured, and more delicate than did those with sons; those with sons saw them as firmer, stronger, better coordinated, hardier, and more alert. These differences in describing male and female infants were most marked among fathers. Since objective measures of the size and health of the infants showed no differences between females and males, it appears that parental perceptions were influenced by gender-stereotyped expectations.

Once parents get to know their infants, do the stereotyped perceptions and expectations give way to ones that more accurately reflect the children's individual differences? The answer to this question seems to be mixed. Strong differences in the way parents treat their daughters and sons have not been found in all studies (e.g., Bee et al., 1984; Bellinger & Gleason, 1982). Researcher Carol Jacklin has commented on the surprising lack of evidence in the Stanford Longitudinal Study for the existence of parental pressure on preschoolers to conform to gender stereotypes, providing examples such as the burly father who looked sheepish but made no protest as his hair was rolled into curlers by his young son (Jacklin, 1985). A recent meta-analysis on studies of parents' different socialization of girls and boys found that, on most dimensions (such as amount of interaction, discipline, warmth), differences in the ways parents treat their sons and daughters appear small and nonsignificant (Lytton & Romney, 1991). Some tendency was found for parents to inflict more physical punishment on boys than on girls and to stimulate motor behavior in sons more than in daughters.

Conversely, many studies do indicate that parents treat daughters and sons differently in areas specifically related to gender expectations: giving them different toys, dressing them differently, and assigning them different tasks. One study of middle-class preschoolers' bedrooms showed that boys' rooms were filled with sports equipment, toy vehicles, military toys, and toy and live animals; girls' rooms were more likely to contain dolls and dollhouses, and to be decorated with floral wallpaper and lace (Rheingold & Cook, 1975). Another study of the household tasks performed by boys and girls between the ages of 2 and 17 years found that the boys were mowing the lawn, shoveling snow, taking out the garbage, and doing other yard work; girls were cleaning the house, washing dishes, cooking, and babysitting for younger children (White & Brinkerhoff, 1981). Lytton and Romney's (1991) review showed that the dimension on which parents were most likely to treat girls and boys differently was encouragement of gender-typed activities.

There is evidence that parents play and interact with boys and girls differently. They are more likely to talk with their daughters and to roughhouse and play actively with their sons (Tauber, 1979). Parents asked to work on a jigsaw puzzle with their 6-year-olds and to teach them to remember a series of picture cards were found to use different strategies for sons and daughters. They were more performance and task-oriented with sons, tried to teach them more general problem-solving strategies, and were both more directive and more approving and more disapproving of sons than daughters. With daughters, parents interacted in a more cooperative, concrete way, and daughters were given more feedback about their performance (Frankel & Rollins, 1983).

It is quite possible that parents have no idea of the extent to which they are treating boys and girls differently. For example, in one study of the way that 11 mothers interacted with a six-month-old infant, 5 of the mothers played with an infant who was dressed in blue pants and called "Adam," and 6 later played with the *same* infant wearing a pink dress and called "Beth" (Will, Self, & Datan, 1976). These mothers were more likely to offer a doll to "Beth" and a toy train to "Adam," and to smile at and hold the baby more closely when they thought they were dealing with Beth than when they thought they had Adam. Actually, the infant was male, yet two of the mothers later commented that Beth was a "real girl," since she was sweeter and cried so softly. Moreover, in later interviews every one of the 11 mothers said that boys and girls were alike at this age and should not be treated differently, and that they would not treat their own sons and daughters differently.

It is not only in middle-class North America that parents socialize their sons and daughters differently. Cross-cultural studies indicate that it is not uncommon for parents to pay more attention to boys than girls, to interact more sociably with girls, and to emphasize more achievement and autonomy with boys. For example, in a study of Mexican families, fathers, but not mothers, were found to differ in their behavior toward daughters and sons:

> Boys were listened to and shown how to do things, which would seem to convey the message that what they have to say is important and that they are capable of mastering new skills. Girls, on the other hand, were treated especially gently, and at the same time, with a lack of full attention and an imposing of opinions and values. The gentle treatment would seem to convey the message that they are fragile and docile. . . . The inattention and imposing of opinion would seem to communicate the view that what females have to say is less valuable than what males have to say, so that females need to be told what to think and do, and can more readily be interrupted or ignored. (Bronstein, 1984, p. 1001)

Further evidence for differential socialization of boys and girls comes from an examination of childrearing data from more than 100 societies (Zern, 1984). This research confirmed that boys are more strongly pressured in the direction of self-reliance, achievement and general independence than girls are, although both sexes receive some pressure in this direction.

Within North America, there is some evidence that parents in different social class and racial groups do not follow identical patterns of gender-role socialization. Gender stereotyping tends to be stronger and restrictions on females greater in working-class than in middle-class families (McBroom, 1981). Research on African-American families suggests that parents in this group may socialize their daughters more toward economic responsibility and a commitment to employment than white parents do (Smith, 1982). Black women report androgynous patterns of gender-related traits, suggesting that they were socialized to have a mixture of instrumental and expressive qualities (Binion, 1990). It is probably inappropriate, therefore, to assume that the patterns of differing parental treatment for girls and boys that have been found in white, middle-class families hold in all respects for other class and racial groups. More careful research of the patterns followed in a variety of groups is needed. However, it does appear that children's gender is a relevant dimension to parents in every group—a dimension that helps to shape parent–child interaction.

Media

The average North American child spends more time in the first 15 years of life watching television than doing any other waking activity (Clark, 1972). Add to this the time spent listening to the radio, watching movies and music videos, and reading, and it becomes very clear that, for most children beyond infancy, the media is the most potent and pervasive source of information about their social world. Gender stereotypes form a significant component of the media message.

Television.   By the age of 17, the typical American adolescent has viewed some 350,000 television commercials. What messages about gender are touted along with the products in these commercials? That males are the authorities, for one thing. Approximately 90 percent of the narrators in commercials are male. Although differences in the portrayal of women and men have decreased over the past 15 years, women are still more likely than men to be seen in domestic settings and less likely than men to be shown as employed (Bretl & Cantor, 1988).

Studies of the content of children's television have shown that males are over-represented among the characters and that males and females are usually portrayed in gender-stereotypic ways. In one early study, Sternglanz and Serbin (1974) analyzed ten commercially produced children's programs and found striking differences in the depictions of male and female characters. Males were shown as more aggressive and constructive, and were more likely than females to be portrayed as rescuing others from dangerous and distressing situations; females were depicted as submissive and inactive. In addition, males both showed more behaviors and received more rewards for their behavior, while the behavior of female characters often seemed devoid of consequences.

Other studies have found similar results. Long and Simon (1974), in a study of the portrayal of women in children's and family programs, concluded that, not only were women numerically underrepresented in these shows, but they were presented in a distorted way. Women were almost always portrayed in comic roles or as wives and mothers; none were shown as simultaneously married and working outside the home. The female characters were subservient and dependent on men, behaved less rationally than their male counterparts, held no positions of authority, and tended to be silly and overemotional. Moreover, most of the women in these programs fell into a single narrow image: well-groomed, under 40 years of age, attractive, and extremely concerned with their appearance. Barcus (1978), in an analysis of children's programs broadcast on weekends and weekday afternoons, found that male characters outnumbered female characters by a 3 to 1 margin. Lott (1989) found that, in a sample of the television programs most popular with eighth-graders, female characters appeared less often than male characters and when they did appear they were more likely to be shown interacting with men than with other women. Comparable findings were reported by Nolan, Galst, and White (1977) and Feldman and Brown (1984), whose examination of Saturday morning cartoons led them to conclude that children were receiving greater exposure to male than female models, and that the male models were more likely than females to be shown as having an impact on their environment and as holding positions of power. Even the commercials directed at children uphold gender stereotypes: Males are over-represented in advertisements for all kinds of toys except dolls, and girls are more likely than boys to be portrayed as passive (Feldstein & Feldstein, 1982; Streicher, 1974).

An interesting aspect of the gender stereotyping presented in children's cartoons involves physique. One study (Busby, 1974) found that married men tended to be portrayed as overweight with poor physiques; heroes and other single men were sleek and agile. (Married men were never portrayed as heroes!) Ironically, both married and single women were also shown as trim and agile despite their apparent avoidance of all physical activities; husbands' participation in sports activities such as baseball and bowling did not seem to ameliorate their tendency to be overweight. The message conveyed, according to Busby, is that once trapped into marriage by a woman a man loses his physical prowess!

The kinds of occupations filled by women and men have also tended to be portrayed stereotypically on children's television. Male characters dominate professional occupations such as lawyer, doctor, police officer, while female characters dominate the lower-status service occupations such as nurse, secretary, and waitress (Miller & Reeves, 1976). In a study of cartoons, Busby (1974) found male characters in 42 different jobs and female characters in only 9.

There is little doubt that children notice the different ways that female and male characters and feminine and masculine content are portrayed on television. When children aged 8 to 13 were asked, in one study, to rate the behavior of the characters in Saturday morning cartoons, they evaluated the characters in ways consistent with extreme gender stereotypes. Male characters were described as brave, dominant, intelligent, making decisions easily, not having to be rescued, independent, keeping out of trouble, acting as leaders, harsh, aggressive, and unconcerned about appearance. Female characters, conversely, were rated as needing to be rescued, easily excited in a crisis, having a strong need for security, and crying easily (Mayes & Valentine, 1979). But children's comprehension of gender-related messages on television is not limited to the content of those messages: It also encompasses form—the different ways in which feminine and masculine content is presented. Form of presentation includes visual techniques such as cuts, fades, and dissolves; auditory features such as music, sound effects, and types of speech; and variables such as action level and pacing of the presentation. Research has shown that masculine and feminine content on children's television tends to be presented with different formal features. For example, commercials designed for boys have rapid action, frequent cuts, loud music, sound effects, and many scene changes, while those designed for girls have background music, fades and dissolves, and female narration (Welch, Huston-Stein, Wright, & Plehal, 1979). As early as first grade, children seem to be aware of the connotations of these different forms. When presented with pseudocommercials in which the content was identical but the formal features were either "masculine" or "feminine," 6- to 12-year-old children were able to identify correctly each form as appropriate for advertising either a toy truck or a baby buggy and for advertising directed to girls or to boys (Huston, Greer, Wright, Welch, & Ross, 1984). It is possible, then, that the form of presentation of various objects and activities on television influences children's attention and interest in subtle ways, cueing them as to the gender-appropriateness of particular content. If this is indeed the case, then television can act as a powerful agent of gender-role socialization even in the absence of content that explicitly defines certain activities as appropriate only for girls or only for boys.

Research has made it quite clear that television viewing is related to gender-stereotypic attitudes among children and teenagers. Children who watch more than

25 hours of television per week have been found to hold more traditional gender stereotypes than those who watch less than 10 hours per week (Frueh & McGhee, 1975). A similar positive relationship between heavy viewing and adherence to traditional gender stereotypes has been found in several studies with children from preschool age to adolescence (Gross & Jeffries-Fox, 1978; Eisenstock, 1984; McGhee & Frueh, 1980; Zuckerman, Singer, & Singer, 1980). Does watching television actually contribute to children's gender stereotypes, or is it just that those who already hold strong stereotypes spend more time than their counterparts do in front of the television set? At least one study suggests that heavy TV viewing may help to produce an increase in gender stereotyping. Teenagers responded twice (two years apart) to a questionnaire measuring sexism so that researcher Michael Morgan (1982) could assess whether heavy viewing was associated with an increase in sexism. What the research revealed was that those subjects who were the least sexist to begin with, high-IQ girls, seemed to be most affected by watching television. After two years, girls in this group who had watched a lot of television showed more sexist attitudes than they had earlier; those who were light viewers, on the other hand, showed no increase in sexism.

Some studies have shown that television messages have a direct effect on children's attitudes. A mere five minutes of viewing commercials about either traditional (housewives and mothers) or nontraditional (professional businesspeople) women has been shown to affect the attitudes toward women of third- and eighth-grade children (Pingree, 1978). Similarly, five minutes of exposure to two television Muppets labeling a toy as appropriate only for the other sex was enough to make 4- to 6-year-olds refuse to play with the toy (Cobb, Stevens-Long, & Goldstein, 1982).

In adolescence, much of the TV viewing is focused on rock music videos. These videos frequently enshrine gender stereotypes, portraying women as emotional, frivolous, and passive, and men as aggressive, "cool," and adventuresome (Hansen & Hansen, 1988). The videos sometimes portray rape and other forms of sexual aggression against women. Is there a cumulative effect of exposure to such material? Apparently yes. Frequent viewing of rock videos increases the probability that the viewers will later judge women's and men's behavior in gender-stereotypic ways (Hansen & Hansen, 1988). Even listening to heavy-metal music, without the video, has been found to increase young men's gender stereotyping and negative attitudes toward women (St. Lawrence & Joyner, 1991).

The Printed Word.   Stereotyped portrayals of females and males in children's books parallel those found on television. Male characters outnumber females; far more stories are boy-centered than girl-centered; and males are portrayed as adventurous, brave, competent, and clever while females are depicted as incompetent, fearful, and dependent on others (usually males) to solve their problems (Davis, 1984; Weitzman et al., 1972; Women on Words and Images, 1975). Despite some improvement in recent years in the ratio of males to females portrayed, and some avoidance of obvious sexism, children's books continue, for the most part, to reflect traditional gender roles (Davis, 1984; Kolbe & LaVoie, 1981). However, these "traditional" gender roles are now more fictional than real. For instance, while books written for children continue to show mothers working only in the home, the majority of North American mothers in fact hold outside jobs.

Like television, books appear to influence children's behavior. For instance, nursery-school boys have been shown to work longer and harder on a task after hearing a story about achievement behavior by a male character than after hearing about the same behavior by a female character, while the reverse trend is found for nursery school girls (McArthur & Eisen, 1976). It has also been shown that preschoolers are more likely to choose a gender-stereotypic toy after exposure to a stereotypic picture book, and a nonstereotypic toy after exposure to a nonstereotypic book (Ashton, 1983).

The stereotyped picture of males and females presented to children in books and other media may well have a strong influence on the children's capacity or willingness to imagine a world that is free of such stereotypes. A recent, disturbing finding is that children's own writing reflects the very same stereotypic thinking that is evident in the books that are written *for* them. When the creative writing of children from grades 1 to 6 attending a "young authors conference" in Michigan was examined, it was found to reflect social perceptions of gender roles (Trepanier & Romatowski, 1985). Male characters outnumbered female ones in the stories written by both girls and boys, although females did include more girls in their stories than the boys did. Not only did male characters outnumber females, but more attributes—both positive ones, such as courageous and determined, and negative ones, such as mean and nasty—were ascribed to male than to female characters. Moreover, when occupational roles were considered, there were dramatic differences in the number of such roles assigned to male and female characters. Of 127 occupational roles assigned to their characters by these young authors, 111 (87 percent) were assigned to male characters and only 16 (13 percent) to female characters. The roles themselves were stereotypic. For example, a female could be a princess, cook, teacher, babysitter, or nurse; a male could be a doctor, astronaut, dentist, clown, professor, or police officer. Even at this young age, then, children seem to have "gotten the message" that females are less interesting, less important, and have narrower horizons than males.

Language

Most of an individual's relations with the social world are mediated by language, and the learning of language is one of the first and most important tasks facing a developing child. Furthermore, as discussed in Chapter 2, at least one theorist (Constantinople, 1979) has suggested that children's development of gender identity and gender role is inextricably bound up with the acquisition of language. The labels that children learn—*boy, girl, man, woman, daddy, mommy*—help them to form the categories around which they build a fundamental understanding of gender and help them to guide their thinking about this concept.

A problem with the role language plays in children's learning about gender is that the language contains built-in biases about gender—biases that reflect the sexism and gender stereotypes of the culture. In English at least, these biases are reflected in the way language ignores females or labels them as special cases. The masculine gender is used to refer to people in general (e.g., *mankind, the nature of man, sons of God, everyone must do his part*). Females are labeled in ways that indicate they are exceptions, often with the additional implication of inferiority. A male, for instance, is a "real" poet, while his female counterpart is a *poetess*. And a female colleague and myself were once referred to as *professorettes*!

Does the sexism built into language affect children's learning and thinking about gender? The evidence is clear that it does. Children in kindergarten, first, third, and fifth grades give male-biased responses to story cues that contain the pronoun *he,* as do college students (Hyde, 1984a; Fisk, 1985). In Hyde's study, when the pronoun in the sentence cue "When a kid goes to school, _____ often feels excited on the first day" was *he,* only 12 percent of the stories were about females, as compared to 18 percent when the pronoun was *they* and 42 percent when the pronoun was *he* or *she.* Clearly, the masculine pronoun makes children think of males. Moreover, fewer than one-half of the children, even by fifth grade, indicated an awareness that *he* could be used as a generic term referring to people in general. Perhaps even more telling is the impact of masculine, feminine, or neutral pronouns on children's evaluation of how well women or men could perform the fictional job of *wudgemaker.* When the pronoun used in the job description was *he,* children's ratings of how well a woman could perform the job were lowest. The ratings were intermediate when neutral pronouns were used and highest when *she* was used. It appears that the choice of pronoun influenced children's perception and gender categorization of the neutral, fictional *wudgemaker* job. The implications for children's gender stereotyping of occupations labeled policeman, draftsman, or chairman of the board are obvious.

Hyde concludes that most elementary school children have learned to think of males when they hear *he* in a gender-neutral context, and do not know that *he* can refer to both males and females. Since they are exposed to a constant stream of information using the masculine gender as normative, they learn to think of the typical person as male—an important step toward the cultural assumption that the male is normative and the female atypical or deviant.

Some steps have been taken toward a more gender-egalitarian language. Publishers of textbooks now frequently use guidelines to eliminate sexist writing, advising their authors to avoid the use of *he* when they really mean *he* or *she* and to use gender-neutral terms to refer to occupations. Teachers attend workshops on the use of nonsexist language. A few writers, such as Marge Piercy in her science fiction novel *Woman at the Edge of Time,* have experimented with the use of a neutral singular pronoun (Piercy used *per*). Yet, it may be many years before our language reflects these changes in a general way. In the meantime, children are using gender-biased language as the cornerstone of their initial concepts of sex and gender.

Language joins parental socialization and the media as a potent source of information and social pressure with respect to gender roles. As described in Chapter 2, children use the information and reinforcement provided by these and other sources to build an understanding of gender and a set of behaviors congruent with that understanding. These cognitive and behavioral aspects of gender affect virtually all areas of the child's life. The remainder of this chapter looks at how gender-role socialization in childhood and adolescence affects two major aspects of the developing individual's life: the formation of friendships and the emergence of achievement goals.

Constructing an Identity: The Relational and Individual Self

A developmental task faced by every person is the construction of an identity or sense of self. This sense of self includes the sense of belonging to particular social groups, such as the individual's gender, ethnic, racial, social class, sexual orientation, or religious groups. It encompasses the qualities the person sees as part of the self, as well as the acceptance for the self of labels, such as "feminist" (Freedman & Lips, 1992; Lips & Freedman, in press).

Identities are not static, but tend to alter in response to changes in the individual's social environment and life stage. For example, the formation of the ethnic aspect of identity takes place over time, as young people explore and make decisions about the role of ethnicity in their lives. This process may occur in several stages, beginning with a phase in which ethnicity is largely unexamined and is taken for granted, moving through a period of questioning and exploring the meaning of one's ethnicity, leading finally to a committed ethnic identity (Phinney, 1989, 1990). The exploration stage may be triggered by a significant event that "awakens" the person to an awareness of the implications of her or his ethnicity (Kim, 1981).

Gender-related expectations may play a part in the way a person responds to ethnic identity issues. For example, in some cultures there is an assumption that women are the carriers of ethnic traditions.

Traditional theories about how a person forms an identity or sense of self have tended to emphasize separation-individuation as the basic task of human development (e.g., Erikson, 1950). In order to develop a clearly defined, separate sense of self, this approach stresses, the person must disconnect to some extent from relationships. Thus, for example, the child must weaken ties with the mother, must gradually become less dependent and more self-reliant, and must develop an individual set of goals and sense of purpose. Contemporary theorists argue, however, that this traditional conception of development is based largely on masculine role expectations and ignores a different and equally important aspect of identity: the development of a sense of *self-in-relation* (Surrey, 1983, cited in Kaplan & Surrey, 1984). The sense of oneself as a relational being, someone who is developing and growing in the ability to connect with and relate to others, is arguably as much a core aspect of identity as is the sense of oneself as a separate, independent being striving for one's own particular goals. Although theorists have noted that the self-in-relation aspect of identity may be an especially important factor in women's psychological development, it must be important to men as well. It is likely that both males and females must construct identities that include both individuated and relational aspects, although gender-related expectations may lead them to place differential emphasis on the two components. The following discussion of development therefore focuses on both relational and individual achievement issues.

Friendship

Childhood

From the beginning, girls and boys learn different expectations about friendship. Girls receive many messages that personal relationships are an important, perhaps *the* most important, life priority. They are encouraged to develop the qualities on which relationship skills are built: empathy, nurturance, expressiveness, sensitivity to others. They are urged to consider the needs of others when making their own decisions and plans. Boys, although not taught that relationships are unimportant, are often more strongly encouraged to be independent, self-reliant, assertive, and achievement-oriented than to give high priority to friendships. This difference in emphasis for girls and boys is probably related to the traditional expectations for females and males: that, for females, security and success ultimately reside in their ability to form and maintain relationships with others, while for males, they reside in individual achievements.

Beginning in early childhood, boys and girls tend to separate into same-sex play groups, and best friends are almost always of the same sex (Katz & Boswell, 1984; Maccoby, 1990). This separation is no doubt influenced by cultural norms that encourage girls and boys to play different games and to engage in different kinds of activities; however, segregation prevails even during gender-neutral activities. The reason for children's strong preference for same-sex play appears to be twofold. First, the rough-and-tumble play and orientation toward competition and dominance that characterize boys' interaction seem to make girls nervous. Second, girls find boys unresponsive to their influence attempts—and so do not enjoy interacting with them (Maccoby, 1990).

The same-sex peer groups that develop during childhood reinforce cultural norms and play a powerful role in maintaining gender differences. Children make harsh judgments about peers who do not conform to gender-role standards (Fagot, 1984; Hartup, 1983); two of the most deprecating epithets that can be flung at one child by another are "sissy" and "tomboy." For boys in particular, the same-sex peer group seems to play an important role in reinforcing masculine gender identity and male dominance, a process that occurs largely through the derogation of girls and all things feminine.

The kinds of relationships that characterize girls' and boys' friendship groups differ in some respects, perhaps in response to gender roles that stress intimacy for females and adventurousness for males (Berndt & Hoyle, 1985; Humphreys & Smith, 1987; Sharabany, Gershoni, & Hofman, 1981). Boys' groups tend to be larger, providing them with more friends but less intimacy, and giving them a "gang" with which to embark on explorations of their world. Certainly, this is the image of male childhood friendships that has been celebrated in movies and television. Girls, however, limit the size of their friendship groups and tend to have fewer, more intense friendships—relationships that provide the arena for exploring interpersonal concerns. Even in childhood, girls seem to be more comfortable than boys are with intimacy. In one study of 7- and 8-year-olds, same-sex pairs of children either sat close together and drew pictures of each other (high-intimacy condition) or sat with a screen separating them (low-intimacy condition). The girls smiled more and laughed less than boys did in the high-intimacy condition—an indication, according to the researchers, that they were more comfortable than the boys were in this situation (Foot, Chapman, & Smith, 1977). The same study found similarities for boys and girls in the effects of being with a friend. Children who watched a cartoon when paired with a friend showed more social responsiveness—laughing, smiling, talking, looking at their partner, and touching—than did those who were paired with a stranger. Clearly, there are gender similarities as well as differences in children's friendships.

The different kinds of activities encouraged for school-age boys and girls may help to maintain the pattern of small intimate friendship groups for girls and larger "gangs" for boys. Team sports such as softball, hockey, and football form a large part of boys' recreational activities. The boys who play these sports may well learn to associate having fun with being in the company of a fairly large, diverse group of peers. Until fairly recently, only a minority of girls has been given the opportunity to engage in team sports. Researchers have yet to examine the interesting question of whether there is a relationship between friendship patterns and participation in team sports. Another male–female difference in recreational activities is in the use of computerized "video games," a pastime much more common among boys than girls. This activity, far from fostering the development of a large friendship group, promotes a one-on-one relationship of boy to machine! It is difficult to say what impact the widespread use of this form of recreation may have on boys' friendship patterns in the future. However, casual observation suggests that, although boys play these games as individuals, they often come and go from the game situation in groups, and that their individual success with the games is a matter of status in the group.

One of the most interesting aspects of children's preference for all-girl and all-boy groups is that different styles of interaction develop in groups of girls and groups of boys. Boys' groups show more concern with dominance. Boys are more likely than girls are to interrupt one another, command and threaten, boast, refuse to comply, give information, and call other boys names. Girls, conversely, seem more interested in sustaining social relationships. They are more likely than boys to say they agree with another speaker, acknowledge points made by other speakers, and pause to allow another girl to speak (Maltz & Borker, 1983). The interaction styles characterizing boys' and girls' groups have been labeled, respectively, *constricting* and *enabling* (Hauser, Powers, Weiss-Perry, Follansbee, Rajapark & Greene, cited in Maccoby, 1990). Since groups of girls and boys differ in their habitual interaction styles, and since children spend so much time interacting in same-sex groups, girls and boys are socialized by their peers into different ways of relating. These different styles of interaction apparently carry over into adolescence and adulthood.

As Maccoby (1990) notes, the different ways in which males and females have learned to interact with others from childhood onward have implications for later, cross-sex, relationships:

> What happens . . . when individuals from these two distinctive "cultures" attempt to interact with one another? People of both sexes are faced with a relatively unfamiliar situation to which they must adapt. Young women are less likely to receive the reciprocal agreement, opportunities to talk, and so on that they have learned to expect when interacting with female partners. Men have been accustomed to counterdominance and competitive reactions to their own power assertions, and they now find themselves with partners who agree with them and otherwise offer enabling responses. It seems evident that this new partnership should be easier to adapt to for men than for women. (Maccoby, 1990, p. 517)

Adolescence

Adolescence is a time when friendships often become very intense, perhaps because it is a time of personal transition and uncertainty. The pattern of fewer, more intimate friendships for girls and larger, less intimate friendship groups for boys persists.

Moreover, there is some evidence that relationships are more important to girls than to boys during this period. When teenagers were asked to rank-order a number of concerns in order of their importance, both sexes ranked identity and sexuality at the top of the list, but girls placed interpersonal relationships third, while boys chose autonomy as their third most important concern (Strommen, 1977). Researchers have also found that high school girls express greater concerns about their friendships than do high school boys (Schneider & Coutts, 1985). Adolescent girls are more likely than their male counterparts to share information about their emotional state with their parents and friends (Papini, Farmer, Clark, Micka, & Barnett, 1990).

Boys may be less concerned with friendship *or* boys may simply be inhibited about admitting an interest in same-sex friendships. College males are significantly more reluctant than females to volunteer for studies listed as investigations of same-sex friendship, and are even unwilling to sign up for studies of issues unrelated to friendship that require them to bring along a same-sex friend (Lewis, Winstead, & Derlega, 1989). Furthermore, teenage boys who are highly affiliative (that is, very interested in being with other people) report more negative emotional states, both when they are alone and when they are with friends, than do teenage girls who are highly affiliative (Wong & Csikszentmihalyi, 1991). This finding may reflect boys' expectations that they should be independent, coupled with the suspicion of homosexuality that our culture imposes on male–male friendships.

An extensive study of adolescent friendships points to gender differences in the focus and quality of these relationships (Douvan & Adelson, 1966). For girls in their midteens, sensitivity to others and mutual trust are cited as important qualities in a friend. Girls in this age range describe a friend as someone who will provide emotional support during personal crises and who will not gossip behind one's back. By contrast, boys in the same age range list relatively impersonal qualities (e.g., easy to get along with, does favors) as the important ones for a friend to have. In addition, boys are more likely than girls to view the friendship group as a source of support against adult authority and to mention that a friend is someone who stands by you when you are in trouble with that authority. A popular film about male adolescent friendship, aptly titled *Stand By Me,* is built largely on this aspect of peer relationships. Four boys, feeling unloved by parents, scorned by teachers, and persecuted by older teenagers, find in their relationship not only solace but a source of humor about adult authority and the courage to challenge it. Movies about female adolescent friendship are in short supply, perhaps because most filmmakers are still men.

It appears that friendships during childhood and adolescence tend to follow patterns that support girls and boys as they follow the paths laid down by traditional gender roles. Girls' friendships are geared to helping them explore and deal with personal relationships. Boys' friendships provide support for defiance of authority and assertion of independence. Of course, the differences in emphasis are not always so pronounced, particularly in later adolescence. Some studies of college student friendships have found more gender similarities than differences (Caldwell & Peplau, 1982; Rose, 1985).

One factor that may influence social relationships in different ways for girls and boys during adolescence is the timing of physical maturity. In general, girls reach puberty sooner than boys. However, maturing earlier or later than one's peers has different implications for the two sexes. For a girl, early development of breasts and a more sexually mature appearance is likely to be associated with early pressures in the direction of the traditional feminine role. Parents may place new restrictions on her, while older boys may begin to pressure her for sexual behavior (Golub, 1983; Katz, 1986). The early maturing girl may be dating at an age when her cohorts are still relying heavily on same-sex friendships to explore interpersonal issues. In fact, dating may actively interfere with a girl's same-sex friendships. To the extent that males keep the role of initiator in the heterosexual dating situation, females simply react to male invitations. Thus, a girl may often find herself unable to pick the times when she can get together with a boy. Rather, her only control in the situation lies in saying yes or no to a specific invitation. Under these circumstances, girls often find themselves forced to choose between previously established plans with their girlfriends and the chance to go out with a boy they like. It is perhaps not surprising, then, that girls sometimes break plans with same-sex friends in order to accept a "date." Some evidence shows that such early dating is disadvantageous to girls' self-esteem (Golub, 1983; Simmons, Blyth, Van Cleave, & Bush, 1979), perhaps because girls are not yet equipped emotionally to handle the sexual and affective pressures of the dating situation, or perhaps because of the loss of control over her life that "waiting to be asked out" can involve for a girl. Moreover, some have speculated that a girl who is physically well developed at an early age receives more reinforcement for following a traditional feminine script, making it less likely that she will explore alternatives such as a career (Katz, 1986). Early-maturing girls also tend to be dissatisfied with their weight and their appearance, causing them to focus more concern on these issues. Overall, early physical maturation appears to be linked to changes in the pattern of girls' social relationships—changes that involve increased pressure to be "feminine."

For a boy, on the other hand, early maturation is not likely to be associated with increased parental restrictiveness although it may be associated with an increase in responsibilities. Also, since our culture has traditionally placed males "in charge" of the dating situation, there is less likelihood that early dating will cause problems for them. The boy who is quicker than his peers to develop the muscularity, strength, and physique of the adult is likely to be regarded with envy. If he begins to develop relationships with girls, it is still unlikely that he will significantly loosen his ties with his male friendship group. He may gain increased status in that group, however, and be expected to provide leadership. These pressures are in line with masculine role expectations.

In comparing the experience of the early-maturing girl and the early-maturing boy, it is clear that both involve earlier than usual stress on gender-role conformity. However, this early pressure has quite different implications for girls and boys. For girls, it means more curtailment of their activities, significant loss of control over their social relationships, and being placed in the role of sexual object before having a chance to explore their own sexual feelings. For boys, it often means less rather than more curtailment of their activities, increases in responsibility and status, and the frequently unnerving challenge of initiating (or, at least, appearing to initiate) heterosexual relationships.

Given the gender segregation of activities that occurs through childhood and adolescence, it is not surprising to find that cross-sex friendships are relatively rare. Some such relationships do appear in adolescence (Sharabany et al., 1981); however, the cultural inclination to define any female–male relationship in sexual terms makes it difficult for them to thrive.

In middle and late adolescence, there is an increased focus on sexuality, and dating becomes a prominent concern. Girls, who must attract boys, become very concerned with physical appearance and social skills. Although boys display a parallel concern with their attractiveness to girls, the development of heterosexual relationships is far from their only priority since they receive a great deal of reinforcement for such other activities as athletic pursuits and scholarly achievement. Nonetheless, for both females and males at this stage, peers of the other sex become quite important as sources of social approval and status. This pattern seems to hold even for those individuals who will eventually identify themselves as gay or lesbian. In fact, there is some evidence that lesbians and gay males tend to begin dating earlier than their heterosexual counterparts (Saghir and Robins, 1973). These researchers also found that about half of both the gay and the heterosexual adults they studied remembered having a romantic attachment to a member of the other sex before the age of 14. By the same age, 80 percent of the gays, but only 6 percent of the heterosexual men and 25 percent of the heterosexual women had also formed same-sex romantic attachments. Most of these same-sex romantic attachments were to peers and did not involve sexual contact. In fact, the relationship between adolescent sexuality and adult sexual preference is not particularly clear-cut. As the early Kinsey surveys show, although up to 10 percent of adolescents who engage in homosexual behavior go on to identify themselves as gay in adulthood, most do not; moreover, many gay adults report having no same-sex sexual activity until after high school (Schofield, 1965). Regardless of their ultimate sexual orientation, then, it appears that male and female adolescents tend to form some cross-sex attachments and to experience the gender-role pressures involved in dating.

For young women and men who are moving toward affirmation of an identity as lesbian or gay, dealing with gender-role pressures in relationships is only part of the task they must face. If they embrace a homosexual identity, they are embracing a self-definition that is stigmatized by the dominant culture. One model of homosexual identity formation (Cass, 1979) proposes a series of six steps, beginning with the initial realization that particular thoughts, feelings, or behavior can be identified as homosexual. This realization feels incongruous, given that the person and the environment have assumed that the person is heterosexual. Gradually, the individual begins to come to terms with the social alienation that the new identity represents, and then to establish contacts with other homosexuals in order to obtain a sense of community and a validation of homosexuality as an identity. The individual develops a sense of pride in the new identity, but must still confront the incongruity between strong self-acceptance and society's negative labeling of homosexuality. The incongruity produces anger; the person may become interested in confronting the dominant heterosexual culture. At this stage, she or he may become increasingly open about homosexuality. Finally, the model suggests, the person reaches a stage in which public and personal sexual identities can be synthesized. Homosexuality then becomes, not an all-encompassing identity, but only one aspect of the self. The whole process embodies a gradual movement from denial of a self-view that is seen as negative to the embracing of an identity that is ultimately seen as positive. It may be complicated by the intersection of sexual identity with ethnic, religious, or other aspects of identity. For instance, Espín (1987) reports that Latina lesbians sometimes feel they must make a choice to emphasize either their ethnic or their lesbian identities, since lesbianism is labeled even more negatively in Latin cultures than in mainstream North American society.

It is clear that on the interpersonal dimensions of affiliation, friendship, and sexuality the developing child and adolescent is strongly influenced by gender roles and expectations. Does gender play a role of comparable importance in the more individualistic dimension of achievement? As the following section will indicate, the answer is a resounding yes.

Achievement

From an early age, children are expected to respond to the query: "What do you want to be when you grow up?" They soon learn that their gender is relevant to the answer; indeed, the influence of gender exists at every stage in the development of achievement goals and orientation. The different ways in which girls and boys are treated in task-oriented situations results in different levels of self-confidence, expectations for success, and feelings of self-efficacy and control for the two sexes. The kinds of expectations for their future that are portrayed for them by parents, teachers, school counselors, peers, and the media, and the kinds of interests in which they are encouraged or discouraged, help to shape the specific achievement pathways that girls and boys choose to follow and the tasks they try to accomplish.

Socialization for Achievement

When psychologists discuss achievement motivation, they usually mean a person's disposition to seek success: a stable, general personality disposition to strive for success in any situation where standards of excellence are applied (McClelland et al., 1953). Many researchers have stressed the importance of the parent–child relationship in the development of the child's motivation to achieve. Interestingly enough, the conclusions about the best way to socialize a child to be achievement-oriented differ for boys and girls. For example, parental warmth (accepting, affectionate, child-centered behaviors) has more often been found to be positively related to the achievement orientation of males than to that of females (Manley, 1977). Whereas high levels of maternal warmth and affection were associated with strong achievement orientation in boys, moderate warmth and slight hostility related most strongly to girls' achievement orientation. Similarly, maternal warmth appears to relate to boys' but not girls' ego development (Richards, Gitelson, Petersen, & Hurtig, 1991). A number of explanations for the apparently paradoxical situation have been offered. Crandall, Katkovsky, and Preston (1960) suggested that girls who do not receive as much maternal affection turn to achievement as an alternate source of satisfaction. These authors also suggested that the less nurturant mother may be more involved with her own achievement and thus be providing her daughter with a female achieving role model. However, some of the research results themselves may be suspect on the grounds that behavior labeled "hostility" when directed toward girls might not be so labeled when directed toward boys (Hoffman, 1972). Finally, it must be noted that if parental warmth does relate differently to girls' and boys' achievement orientation, the existence of the relationship does not specify cause and effect. It is just possible that whereas parents who see a daughter becoming independent and achievement-oriented may withdraw a small portion of their warmth from her, a son exhibiting similar behavior may be the recipient of extra praise and approval. In other words, nurturant parents may be reinforcing accepted cultural definitions of appropriate behavior for girls and boys. There are, in fact, indications that such a pattern is sometimes present in the interactions of children with their teachers. One study of fifth- and sixth-grade children (Sears, 1963, cited in Crandall, 1963) showed that teachers switched from positive ratings in the fall of high-IQ task-oriented girls to negative ratings in the spring on dimensions such as their liking for the student. However, bright girls who were "socially" work-oriented (that is, who worked well in a social context) rather than simply task-oriented, received consistently positive ratings. It appears that the teachers were reinforcing female achievement orientation only when it was manifested in a social context. This pattern was not found for boys.

An important factor in the socialization of achievement is the presence of models. We have already noted the scarcity of achieving female role models in the media; the presence of real live role models is also important. Where girls are provided with achieving female models, their attitudes toward success and career attainment seem to be favorably affected. The literature on the effects of maternal employment indicates that, in middle-class families, daughters of employed women have higher educational and occupational aspirations than do daughters of women who are full-time homemakers (Etaugh, 1974; Stein & Bailey, 1973). Daughters of employed women also regard the professional competence of women more highly than do those whose mothers work in the home (Baruch, 1972), and there is a correspondence between mothers' and daughters' career interests and aspirations (Zuckerman, 1981). Among black female university students, those pursuing nontraditional careers were more likely than their more traditional counterparts to have mothers who were well educated and working in nontraditional fields themselves (Burlew, 1982). One study found that, as early as kindergarten and first grade, girls whose mothers were working in nontraditional fields also tended to aspire to less gender-stereotypic careers (Selkow, 1984). In fact, in the same study, both girls *and* boys whose mothers were currently employed chose a greater number of future occupations and showed less gender-stereotypic vocational aspirations than did children of nonemployed mothers. Because more than half of the mothers of young children in North America are now employed outside the home, a gradual reduction in the strength and pervasiveness of occupational stereotyping by gender may be occurring. Most college women now believe that they will have careers in addition to family responsibilities (Baber & Monaghan, 1988; Bridges, 1987). However, many social forces still support the stereotype that men are more achievement oriented, intelligent, competent, and independent than women.

Self-Confidence, Self-Esteem, and Expectations for Success

In adolescence and early adulthood, males show higher self-esteem than females do (Keltikangas-Jarvinen, 1990; Richards et al., 1991). One survey of 2400 girls and 600 boys in the fourth through tenth grades suggests that the gender gap in self-esteem widens during adolescence (Freiberg, 1991a). At the ages of 8 and 9, 60 percent of the girls and 67 percent of the boys reported feeling confident and positive about themselves. Among high schoolers, however, the percentage who reported feeling positive about themselves had dropped to 29 percent for girls and 46 percent for boys, leaving a considerably larger gap between the two groups. When the findings were broken down by race, it became clear that many more African-American girls maintained high self-esteem in high school than did their European-American or Hispanic counterparts. However, with age, the African-American girls showed large drops in positive feelings about their teachers and school work. Hispanic girls expressed less confidence in themselves than did African-American girls, and between elementary school and high school, their confidence dropped farther than either of the other two groups.

What is responsible for girls' drop in self-esteem and self-confidence during the transition to adolescence, and how do African-American girls manage to resist the trend? One researcher who has interviewed many girls making this transition argues that, as girls move from childhood to adolescence, they become aware that there is a conflict between the way they see themselves and the way others (teachers, authorities) view them. They suddenly confront a message of female inferiority, exclusion, and subordination (Gilligan, 1990). They can respond to this conflict by submerging their own feelings and accepting the view of reality conveyed by adult authorities—or by insisting on their own feelings and knowledge. Many girls follow the first strategy. However, a substantial number of African-American girls, buoyed perhaps by the support of their families, choose the second. In so choosing, they may become alienated from the educational system, but their self-esteem apparently remains intact.

Socialization and the presence of gender stereotypes have an impact on the way that females and males react to their own achievements. As early as the third grade, boys begin to predict more successful task outcomes for themselves than girls do, a difference that seems to last into adulthood (Crandall, 1969; Erkut, 1983; Vollmer, 1984). The gender difference reflects both an overestimation of their performance by males and an underestimation of their performance by females. Some factors limit this effect. For example, there is evidence that expectancies are affected by the gender-role appropriateness of the task. Stein, Pohly, and Mueller (1971) found that when presented with the same tasks, girls predicted better performance for themselves when the task was labeled "girls generally do better" and boys expected more success when the task was labeled "boys do better." Among a sample of college students, women reported lower occupational performance expectations than men did for male-dominated occupations but higher expectations for female-dominated occupations (Bridges, 1988). However, perhaps due to the stereotyping of achievement itself as masculine, even "feminine" tasks are sometimes greeted with more male than female self-confidence (Lippa & Beauvais, 1983). The timing of the assessment may also affect the findings; girls expect less success than boys do early in the school year, but these differences sometimes disappear as the year progresses (Dweck, Goetz, & Strauss, 1980).

The tendency for boys to have higher achievement expectations than girls may be mainly a white, middle-class phenomenon. Much of the literature suggests that black females have higher career aspirations and expectations than both black males and white females (Kirkpatrick, 1973; Smith, 1982). One study of black adolescents found that higher male than female expectations for success were chiefly evident in middle-class schools (Teahan, 1974). Moreover, when samples include a high proportion of black and low socioeconomic status children, gender differences in expectations for success on specific tasks are not found (Fulkerson, Furr, & Brown, 1983).

The different pattern of gender differences for white and black children may relate to teachers' expectations. Studies show that both black and white elementary school teachers hold lower expectations for black males than for black females (Grant, 1984; Washington, 1982). Even when teachers are presented with hypothetical case histories in which all qualities are held constant except gender, the teachers consistently hold lower expectations for black males than for black females (Ross & Jackson, 1991).

The study of how gender-differentiated patterns of self-confidence in achievement situations are transmitted to children has occupied researchers for many years. One of their chief findings has been that girls and boys are treated differently in the classroom, and the differences are such as to produce relatively more feelings of control among boys and relatively more feelings of helplessness among girls (Dweck, 1975; Dweck, Davidson, Nelson, & Enna, 1978; Dweck, Goetz, & Strauss, 1980). In elementary school classrooms, teachers allow boys more than girls to talk and interrupt them—a practice that ensures not only that more time will be spent on boys' than girls' problems, but that both groups will learn that male concerns take first priority. African-American girls escape this pattern in the earliest grades, often receiving more attention and feedback than European-American girls. However, by the middle of elementary school, black girls have apparently been socialized into the same pattern of inconspicuousness to the teacher as their white counterparts (Irvine, 1986).

Teachers tend to punish boys and girls for different kinds of behavior—boys for being unruly and girls for academic mistakes. However, when praise is handed out to girls, it is likely to be for good appearance or conduct, while for boys it is more likely to be for good academic performance. The lessons are obvious: Girls learn that the route to appreciation is by being "good," while boys learn that they are appreciated for their academic efforts. Most damaging of all, perhaps, is the way that teachers encourage girls and boys to react to their own mistakes. A boy giving the wrong answer is encouraged to keep trying until he gets it right. A girl is frequently told not to worry about a mistake, and the teacher spends less time suggesting new approaches and encouraging her to keep working on a problem until it is solved. In fact, girls are more likely than boys to be simply left in the dark about the quality of their answers. Teachers often do not tell them if their answers are excellent, need improvement, or are completely wrong (Sadker & Sadker, 1985). The differences in teacher interactions with boys and girls may communicate that teachers expect more and better thinking from boys. Thus, boys are more likely to learn to respond to an unsolved problem as a challenge, while girls are given the message that failure is beyond their control.

Even in preschool, teachers pay more attention to boys and respond more to boys who act aggressively and to girls who act dependently (Serbin & O'Leary, 1975). Yet teachers are apparently unaware that they are treating boys and girls differently. The pattern of greater teacher attention to males carries through to university, where women experience the classroom atmosphere as less encouraging for themselves than for men because of an aggregation of small, nonconscious discriminatory actions on the part of professors. Students report that instructors know the names of more male than female students, and that female students are more likely than males to be "squeezed out" of lab projects and demonstrations and are more hesitant to intrude on an instructor's time by asking for help (Schnellmann & Gibbons, 1984). Even more serious, it is becoming clear that sexual harassment is a common problem faced by female students. In one recent survey of more than 1100 university students, 17 percent of the females and 2 percent of the males reported having been sexually harassed by teachers. More than one-third of the incidents reported by these students had occurred in high school (McCormack, 1985). Many schools do not have an adequate system for dealing with student reports of sexual harassment, and the absence of such a system communicates to students that the problem is not considered common or serious.

The cumulative effect of the differential experiences of females and males in the educational system is a decrease in the self-confidence of female students—this despite the fact that females generally obtain higher grades than males at every academic level. It is difficult for education to have an empowering effect on girls and women as long as the subtle messages behind teacher–student interactions remain that females are valued less than males, that females are valued more for their appearance and good behavior than for their competence and intellectual skill, and that sexuality can be used as a weapon against female students.

Attributions for Success

If different treatment in school helps to create different expectancies of success for females and males, just how do these differing expectations relate to actual achievement? First, research shows that people who expect to do better on an achievement task actually do perform at a higher level (Battle, 1965; Feather, 1966). Second, a person's performance expectations probably influence the way she or he assigns causality in trying to explain success and failure. For example, an unexpected outcome is more likely to be attributed to luck or chance. Such attributions, in turn, influence the individual's response to success or failure: Will she or he try doubly hard next time or give up?

Four frequent explanations for achievement outcomes (success or failure) are ability, effort, luck, and task ease or difficulty (Weiner et al., 1971). Ability and effort are internal factors, considered to originate within the individual, whereas luck and task ease are environmental factors, external to the individual. Also, ability and task ease are thought of as relatively stable and unchanging, but both effort and luck are unstable factors that can conceivably fluctuate widely.

Within the foregoing framework the causal attributions that a person makes for success or failure have implications for both self-esteem and future achievement striving (Frieze, 1975). For example, a person views success with maximum pride and security when he or she perceives it as being due to the internal, stable factor of ability; success attributed to external factors produces less pride. Attributions for failure are also important; if lack of ability is seen as the main cause of a failure, there is little tendency to "try again" because the person does not believe that the failure can be changed to success at a future time.

Maximum self-esteem would theoretically be associated with internal, stable attributions for success and external or unstable attributions for failure. The motivation to keep working on something should be strongest when a person believes that successes are linked to ability or effort and that failures are a result of bad luck or of not working quite hard enough. Researchers have found that, by adolescence, middle-class white males and females show somewhat different patterns of attribution for success and failure, with males more than females following the pattern that leads to higher self-esteem and greater future effort. Some studies show that males rely more heavily on ability and females on luck or effort to explain success. In contrast, females tend to attribute failure to lack of ability or to another stable cause, while males are more likely to attribute failure to external and/or unstable causes such as an unfair test or lack of preparation (Bar-Tal & Frieze, 1977; Brown, Fulkerson, Furr, Ware, & Voight, 1984; Erkut, 1983). When respondents are asked to recall real failure experiences, however, the gender differences in attributions for failure are not very consistent across achievement domains (Farmer & Vispoel, 1990). Also, some research indicates that African-American females and males do not differ from each other in their patterns of causal attributions for success and failure (Murray & Mednick, 1977). It appears that achievement is seen as more gender-appropriate for black females than for their white counterparts.

There are disadvantages to the attribution patterns favored by each gender. The girls' pattern of taking little personal credit for success and blaming themselves for failure leads to discouragement and decreased self-confidence. Researchers have found that girls are more discouraged than boys after failure in both classroom and laboratory situations and that such discouragement translates into a generalized low expectancy for success (Dweck et al., 1980). The boys' pattern of taking credit for success and blaming failure on external or unstable factors, although enhancing self-confidence, may make them defensive and unable to learn from their mistakes or admit failure. The self-protective masculine attribution pattern has one big advantage, however: It supports continued achievement striving by emphasizing the individual's capacity to control achievement outcomes.

Gender differences in patterns of achievement attribution are certainly not inevitable. First, different patterns can be learned (Dweck, 1975). Second, the gender differences are not apparent in all cultural and ethnic groups. Third, the differences are apparently affected by a variety of factors, are often small in magnitude, and are not always found (Frieze, Whiteley, Hanusa, & McHugh, 1982; Sohn, 1982). Yet even small differences can translate into major consequences if they mean, for instance, that girls are more likely than boys to withdraw from achievement situations. A series of apparently minor decisions to avoid challenging tasks (e.g., taking no more mathematics courses, avoiding "advanced" classes) can snowball by the end of adolescence into a situation in which the individual's life choices have been considerably narrowed.

Competition and Cooperation

Much of what is labeled "achievement" in our society is linked to competition, to winning. Gender stereotypes suggest that boys are more competitive than girls, and some research supports the stereotypes. For example, females behave less competitively than males in some experimental game situations (e.g., Miller & Pyke, 1973), and a large-scale survey of elementary and high school students found cooperative attitudes higher among girls and competitive attitudes higher among boys, with the greatest differences appearing in grades 8, 9, and 10 (Ahlgren & Johnson, 1979). However, there are some indications that cooperation and competition may mean different things to boys and girls, so the gender difference may not be as straightforward as it appears. One study examined the possibility that cooperation and competition in school might be linked with somewhat different attitudes for girls and boys (Ahlgren, 1983). The results showed that, during the early school years, competition is a more positive construct for boys than for girls. For elementary school boys, competitive attitudes are positively related to sense of personal worth as a student and to internal motivation, but no such relationships are observed for elementary school girls. In the same age range, however, both sexes show a positive relationship between cooperative attitudes and personal worth. By senior high school, the sexes have become similar in some respects: Both show a positive link between competition and sense of personal worth and internal motivation, and neither females nor males show any links between cooperation and negative school attitudes. Nevertheless, some differences still exist: Although boys lose all negative correlates of competition, for girls competition retains some negative associations. Also by senior high school, boys show no correlation between cooperative attitudes and sense of personal worth, while girls still show a link between these two attitudes. In summary, then, by senior high school, cooperation has become completely positive for both sexes, but girls link it more strongly than boys do to their sense of personal worth. Competition, on the other hand, has become positive for both sexes, but girls retain some negative associations with it. Thus, changes in the affective connotations of cooperation and competition follow a somewhat different pattern for girls and boys during the school years, and girls seem to end up feeling less comfortable with competition and more conscious of the importance of cooperation than boys do. In view of the strength of gender stereotypes that characterize boys as task-oriented and competitive and girls as relationship-oriented and cooperative, these findings are not surprising. Thus, girls may find themselves more uneasy than boys are in the many achievement situations in our society that stress competition at the expense of cooperation. Where cooperation is the requisite orientation for success, however, girls may have the advantage.

Person Orientation versus Task Orientation

The common wisdom born of gender stereotypes suggests that males are task-oriented and females are person-oriented: that males tend to be intrinsically interested in the task at hand whereas females, who are more interested in relationships than in tasks, tend to focus on the social consequences of performing well or poorly. In other words, for females affiliation needs predominate over achievement needs, often interfering with females' performance. To date, the evidence in support of such a hypothesis is weak at best. Females do score higher than boys do on paper and pencil measures of need for affiliation (Maccoby & Jacklin, 1974; Schneider & Coutts, 1985). However, Maccoby and Jacklin's (1974) extensive review of the literature uncovered no evidence to indicate that boys were more intrinsically interested in task performance than were girls, with the exception that preschool-aged boys showed more exploratory behavior than did their female counterparts. In terms of person orientation, the same review suggests that task performance of males is more likely to be affected by the presence of peers than is task performance of females, a finding that argues for more person orientation in males than in females.

Some research suggests that, at least during high school, person orientation may interfere more with male than female academic achievement. Starting from evidence that schoolwork and academic achievement may be viewed by high school students as more female-appropriate than male-appropriate (Stockard et al., 1980) and that boys may be more susceptible than girls to peer pressure against conforming to adult standards (Andersson, 1979), Schneider and Coutts (1985) formulated the hypothesis that boys would be more likely than girls to report a negative influence of peers on their achievement behavior. Their survey of students in grades 10 and 12 supported that hypothesis: Boys reported less positive pressure from peers to get good grades and more negative peer pressure against achievement striving than did girls. Neither boys nor girls viewed high grades as very important for attaining popularity with either their own or the other sex. However, boys ranked scholastic excellence significantly lower in importance to popularity than girls did. Moreover, boys were more likely than girls to report that they wished they could work harder in school but didn't because of what their friends would think, and that it was harder to study if their peers were going out. Also, among twelfth-grade students, boys were more likely than girls to report that they thought they would study harder and improve their grades if members of the other sex were not present in their classes. The researchers concluded that high school boys were more susceptible than girls to peer influences that interfered with their achievement strivings.

It has often been suggested that affiliation needs are more likely to interfere with achievement for girls than for boys; however, the findings of the preceding study indicate that affiliation–achievement conflicts may be very relevant to understanding the academic achievement behavior of *males*.

Choosing Career Paths

Even in elementary school, children are quizzed about "what they are going to *be*"; by high school, there is considerable pressure on boys and girls to choose a career path. It is a truism in vocational psychology that the choice of an occupation is the choice of a means to implement one's self-concept (Super, 1951); thus, it is not surprising that such choices reflect gender-role socialization.

One aspect of current gender roles that has implications for career paths is experience with computers. Since computers are technical, there seems to be a general assumption that boys will take to them more naturally than will girls. This assumption is reflected in both the opportunities provided for boys and girls to use computers and the behavior of the children themselves. Studies show that boys using computers in school outnumber girls by as much as 2 to 1, that 40 percent of boys but only 7 percent of girls use computers outside the classroom, and that 25 percent more boys than girls live in homes with computers (Boy still meets girl, 1987). Some observers have noticed that boys are more assertive than girls about getting access to scarce computer time and getting help with computer problems (Linn, 1985; Rosser, 1982), and a number of researchers have found that boys like computers more than girls do at every grade level (Collis, 1985; Wilder, Mackie, & Cooper, 1985). However, girls respond positively to educational strategies aimed at equalizing computer use (Fish, Gross, & Sanders, 1986).

In an occupational climate that is increasingly dominated by computer technology, females are destined to be relegated once again to low-level jobs if they do not obtain some basic understanding of computers and learn to master some of the skills associated with computer technology. Yet the strong social message still exists that expertise in computer technology is for males—and girls and young women are quick to pick up this message.

Social pressure against choosing occupations that are seen as gender-inappropriate are strong. Children and adolescents continue to express gender-traditional career choices (Hammond & Dingley, 1989; Houston, 1991). Nontraditional occupational choices are seen as less appropriate than traditional choices for both women and men (Fitzgerald, 1980); in fact, there is some evidence that men have even less support than women for choosing nontraditional occupations (Yanico, 1978). The greater pressure on males to follow a traditional path may stem from homophobia; the fear of being thought homosexual apparently plays a role in the restriction of male career choices. Male nurses, for example, report that their sexual identity is often called into question (Etzkowitz, 1971).

What factors are related to the choice of *non*traditional career aspirations? For both black and white American college women, choosing a nontraditional career is related to holding nontraditional gender-role attitudes and having high educational aspirations. Black women display less conflict over combining professional and family roles in such careers than do their white counterparts (Murrell, Frieze, & Frost, 1991).

Vocational counselors play a part in the guiding of males and females into traditional careers. One study, for example, found that practicing counselors reacted more negatively to and were less willing to work with a hypothetical male client who aspired to a "feminine" (nurse) than to a "masculine" (physician) occupation (Fitzgerald & Cherpas, 1985). However, a number of other factors also serve to orient males and females toward traditional career paths, not the least of which may be an awareness of the very real difficulties associated with breaking from the traditional route.

One interview study of 150 Canadian teenagers found a tendency for girls to make traditionally feminine occupational choices and to express less confidence than boys that they would reach their occupational goals (Baker, 1985). About three-quarters of the girls planned to hold paying jobs as adults; however, they tended to see the responsibility for housework and child care as primarily theirs and to assume that paid work must fit in with these other duties. These girls showed little awareness of skilled or technical positions, of the economic penalties for part-time work, of the potential problems in finding suitable child care, or of the probability that, by age 30, they would be working for pay as a matter of economic necessity rather than choice. In another interview study (Gaskell, 1985), girls from working-class families also assumed they would have primary responsibility for domestic work and that paid work outside the home would have to take second priority. These assumptions seemed to be based on their own experience that men were unwilling to share domestic responsibilities and that women earn less money than men. Gaskell argues that these girls are probably being quite realistic, and that planning in a gender-unequal labor market leads to traditional choices.

Clearly, for adolescents planning their future, there is a potential conflict between career and family life. The conflict is more intense for females, who are more likely than males to anticipate having to juggle two sets of responsibilities. Perhaps for this reason, there has long been an assumption in vocational psychology that, for females, commitment to career goals and commitment to home and family goals were opposite ends of a single continuum: the stronger the commitment to one, the weaker the commitment to the other. However, that particular piece of conventional wisdom has now been challenged. Using girls in grades 8, 10, and 12, Holms (1985) found no negative relationship between the two types of commitment; the two dimensions were independent.

There are many signs that females are aspiring in greater (though still small) numbers to traditionally masculine careers (e.g., Geller, 1984; Women and minorities continue to grow in workplace, 1984); however, the reverse trend is much weaker for males. If gender-role socialization becomes less restrictive, perhaps both boys and girls will learn to base their occupational aspirations more heavily on their individual talents and the needs of the marketplace, and less on the arbitrary limitations of masculine and feminine roles.

Summary

Beginning in early childhood, girls and boys learn that a different set of expectations holds for each sex. Parents are the first to communicate these expectations, but their influence is quickly built upon by the media. Even the patterns of everyday language reinforce the notion that different tasks and occupations are more suitable for one gender than the other, and that males represent the norm while females are the exceptions.

In developing a sense of identity, the growing child must develop both a sense of self-in-relation to others and a sense of separateness and individual purpose. Traditionally, the relationship aspect of development has been stressed for girls, while the individualistic, achievement-oriented aspect has been emphasized for boys. Although some research does support the idea that, probably as a result of gender-role socialization, relationships are more important to girls and achievement to boys, other research indicates that, for both sexes, concern with either of these two domains can interfere with the other. Boys sometimes allow interpersonal concerns to inhibit their achievement strivings, while girls may permit concern over achievements in the social arena (e.g., getting a date for Saturday night) to interfere with ongoing important relationships.

Girls and boys differ in their friendship patterns, with girls having fewer, more intense friendships than boys, and boys more than girls depending on their friends to back them up in conflicts with authority. They also differ in their achievement patterns. Despite a tendency to get better grades at every scholastic level, girls display less confidence than boys in their ability and seem more easily discouraged by failure. These differences may be a result of differential treatment of male and female students by teachers, who tend to pay more attention to boys than girls and to reward boys more for good performance and girls more for good behavior.

Finally, as girls and boys begin to develop their occupational goals, they are influenced by gender-role expectations. Boys assume they will someday work to support a family; girls assume that their paid work will take second priority to domestic responsibilities. Perhaps with these assumptions in mind, girls report less confidence than boys do that they will achieve their career goals. By adolescence, then, the impact of gender-role expectations has had its effect—through parental admonishments, cartoons and children's books that show males in a wide variety of occupational roles and females in very few, teacher expectations, and counselor bias—on the life goals of girls and boys. Girls and boys have been taught to expect different amounts of control over their lives, and they have been channeled in different directions; as adults, their lives will consequently differ in many respects.

For Additional Reading

Elgin, S. H. (1984). *Native tongue*. This feminist science fiction novel imagines a world in which women develop their own secret language. The narrative provides a good feel for the power of language and its importance in maintaining power relations between women and men.

Fine, M. (1992). *Disruptive voices: The possibilities of feminist research*. Ann Arbor, MI: University of Michigan Press. The author introduces some of the possibilities that can be opened up when feminist scholarship is applied to such issues as adolescent sexuality, the education process in public schools, and reactions to rape.

Gilligan, C., Lyons, N. P., & Hanmer, T. J. (Eds.). (1990). *Making connections: The relational worlds of adolescent girls at Emma Willard School*. Cambridge, MA: Harvard University Press. This is a collection of the accounts of researchers who have listened to adolescent girls as they talked about connection and separation, their relationships, and their conflicts.

11

Family & Friends: Attachment, Intimacy, & Power

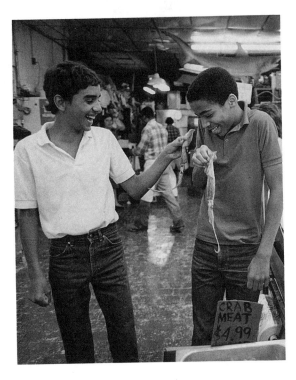

In a village in the remote Himalayas, it is common practice for a woman to have several husbands—all brothers. The system ensures that most men will find wives in this land where men outnumber women 4 to 3. It also holds advantages for the women, who need not endure being left alone for long periods of time while one husband is away from home and whose children have several fathers to care for them. Since women are in short supply, they need not put up with an intolerable family situation. Divorce is easy, and every time a woman changes husbands she commands a larger bride-price, usually in recognition of her increased experience and proven fertility (Zorza, 1986).

This example is often surprising to North American observers, yet it is only one of a variety of reasonably satisfactory ways that human beings have devised to structure their family and other intimate relationships. Depending on the culture, various versions of polygyny (one husband having several wives at the same time), polyandry (one wife having several husbands at the same time), or serial monogamy (an individual having a series of mates, one at a time) may be taken for granted as accepted practice. People may have most of their needs for intimacy met by their mates, other kin, or same-sex friends. Fathers may be expected to become deeply involved with their children or to have only distant, formal relationships with them. Apparently no single arrangement of important relationships is uniformly preferred across human societies.

Relationships with family and friends both reflect and reinforce the gender stereotypes and roles of a society. They help to define the amount and kinds of influence and power available to men and women, and to shape the quality of their social lives and their sense of personal well-being. This chapter focuses on the ways that close relationships are experienced by women and men, how those experiences are influenced by cultural understandings about gender, and how they are related to the actual and felt control that women and men have in their social environments. We turn first to an examination of close relationships in adulthood: close friendships, couple relationships, and loneliness (the experience of being unable to meet one's relationship needs). Next, we examine the formalization of close relationships in marriage. Finally, we conclude with a discussion of parenthood.

Close Relationships in Adulthood

Relationships serve important needs for women and men alike. Close relationships fill emotional needs for intimacy and sharing; both close and more casual relationships can fill social needs for companionship, social stimulation, and status. A variety of types of relationships can provide the individual with many forms of social support—everything from comfort in times of deep emotional distress to investment advice to the confidence that someone else will be around to restock the refrigerator when she or he has the flu and cannot venture out. Clearly, such forms of support are important to both women and men, yet the two gender groups have been found to differ somewhat in their expectations of relationships and, to some extent, in who they count on for what.

Same-Sex Friendships

A pervasive stereotype has held that friendships between males are stronger and deeper than those between females. The notion was eloquently expressed by Montaigne: "The ordinary capacity of women is inadequate for the communion and fellowship which is the muse of the sacred bond of friendship, nor does their soul feel firm enough to endure the strain of so tight and durable a knot." In more recent times, anthropologist Lionel Tiger (1969) proposed the hypothesis that men have a genetically based tendency, reinforced by society, to form nonerotic bonds with other males, and that these male bonds are stronger and more stable than those formed between females. However, despite the credence often given such notions of the superiority of male–male ties, research generally has failed to support them. Men tend to be lower in affiliation motivation and affiliation values than women (Mazur, 1989). Studies indicate that, although men may report more same-sex friendships than women, male friendships tend to be less close and less intimate than female friendships. College males are more likely to consult with and make intimate self-disclosures to close female friends than to close male friends (Komarovsky, 1974, 1976; Lewis, 1978; Olstad, 1975). Aged males are less likely than their female counterparts to have intimate same-sex friends and to replace lost friends (Powers & Bultena, 1976); however, the friendships that they do have are more likely to be seen as equitable (Roberto & Scott, 1986). Married men depend less on same-sex friends than women do for emotional support and guidance (Nye, 1976).

When women and men are questioned about their friendships, strong similarities appear in their responses (Caldwell & Peplau, 1982; Gibbs, Auerbach, & Fox, 1980). However, there are some differences: Women place more emphasis on talking and sharing emotions, while men focus on shared activities (Caldwell & Peplau, 1982). In conversations with their best friends, men are more likely to discuss what is going on in the external world—current events, sports, business—while women are more likely to include discussions of feelings and personal concerns (Davidson & Duberman, 1982). However, although the kinds of things women and men do with their friends are different, their reports of subjective satisfaction with such friendship activities are about the same (Mazur, 1989). Some research suggests that women's friendships include less hostility and greater emotional involvement than men's do (Bell, 1981; Gibbs et al., 1980).

An in-depth interview study of friendship attitudes among young, middle-aged, and older adults provides some insights into the differences in female and male friendships in adulthood and the ways in which these differences may change with age (Fox, Gibbs, & Auerbach, 1985). The researchers found that males consistently tended to be more instrumental, or goal-oriented, in their friendships while females tended to be more expressive, or emotion-centered. This difference was particularly noticeable among the young (aged 18 to 22) adults. Young men described their friendships as dating back to childhood, often formed through playing on sports teams together, and as durable in the face of disagreements over dissimilarities or disagreements in attitudes or behavior. They avoided confronting friends who did or said things they didn't like, preferring to preserve the friendship rather than to change the friend's behavior. Young women, conversely, described their friendships as less durable and more fragile. They were more willing than males to confront their friends over things that disturbed them, and felt it was important to express their feelings even if it meant sacrificing the friendship. Thus, it appears, young men were more able to enjoy friendships with people with whom they disagreed, perhaps because, as suggested in earlier research, their major emphasis was on shared activities rather than shared talk. Young women were much more sensitive to disagreement with their friends, feeling perhaps that their definition of true friendship—emotion sharing—could not be achieved with someone whose beliefs or values differed strongly from their own.

Young men appeared to be less aware than young women of the emotional needs that friendship could fill. They spoke far less than the women did about the role of empathy and altruism in friendship; women, however, stressed the importance of being able to reveal themselves and of accepting their friends' innermost feelings. The authors of the study speculate that the greater intimacy of female friendships may be related to girls' early closeness with their mothers and the absence of a comparable closeness between boys and their fathers. Most of the young women named their mothers as close friends; none of the young men mentioned their fathers.

Among mid-life (aged 35 to 55) subjects, the instrumental–expressive differences in men's and women's friendship attitudes was still evident. However, men in this age group were more concerned and thoughtful about friendship than were younger men, while the women were more tolerant and less confrontational than younger women. Both sexes expressed a desire to hold on to their friends. Men were negative about too much dependency in friendships, and their concept of need—an instrumental one that included various kinds of concrete help—differed from women's more expressive emphasis on the need to talk, to be comforted, to share.

Among the older (56 and older) sample, both women and men held long-term friendships and were less likely than the mid-life sample to be confrontational with their friends. In this age group, men's attitudes toward friendship appeared more idealistic than those of their mid-life counterparts. However, men's friendships still differed from those of women in the sense that they tended to originate at work and to focus on shared activities and discussions of such externals as taxes and politics. Women continued to emphasize expressiveness in their friendships.

The authors of this study conclude that major differences exist between women and men in their experience and expression of empathy and altruism in friendship. Women are more likely than men to consider the sharing of feelings a central aspect of friendship. As the authors themselves comment, "Men as well as women defined a friend as someone you could talk to about anything, but when questioned further, the 'anything' for men was sports, politics, and business, and for women was feelings and problems" (p. 499). Clearly, women and men both have strong needs for friendship, but their friendships differ in the extent to which they provide emotional intimacy.

Various explanations have been suggested for the gender differences in friendship orientation just described. Perhaps men do not need as much emotional intimacy as women do, or perhaps they focus more of these needs on their female friends or partners. A number of authors have discussed the potential barriers to emotional intimacy between men, citing in particular the competitiveness that is socialized into the masculine role (Komarovsky, 1974; Lewis, 1978). The aura of competition among males makes it difficult for men to be open with other men, to "let down their guard," lest it provide these other men with a competitive advantage. It is seen as safer, perhaps, for a man to disclose his feelings to a female friend or partner—someone who is not perceived as a competitor.

Another barrier to intimacy in male friendships is homophobia, negative attitudes toward and fear of homosexuality (Lewis, 1978; Morin & Garfinkle, 1978). Although data that demonstrate a causal connection are not available, many writers on the subject of male friendship speculate that the fear of being labeled homosexual inhibits the development of emotional intimacy in men's relationships.

Cross-Sex Friendships

In North America, a strong emphasis is placed on the importance of having an intimate, loving, sexually exclusive relationship with another person: being part of a couple. In fact, the pairing of women and men into such intimate relationships is taken so much for granted that people seem to find it difficult to conceive of female–male relationships that do not fit this pattern. Often there is an assumption that any friendly overture from a woman to a man or vice versa is an expression of sexual interest, or that any strong bond between a man and woman must have a sexual component. One case in point: When Canadian mountain climber Sharon Wood, the first North American woman to reach the summit of Mount Everest, was interviewed on television recently, the male interviewer began the session by focusing eagerly on how sleeping arrangements had been managed during the ascent! Had she shared a tent with the men or had she had one to herself? When Ms. Wood responded patiently (no doubt she had faced this question before) that she had slept in her sleeping bag, in the same tent as her male co-climbers, who were all her good friends, the interviewer produced a knowing leer. Clearly, he had no conception of the possibility that a woman could live and work closely with a group of men as partners in a challenging expedition without sexuality becoming a big issue—even in the cold, exhausting, oxygen-poor environment of high-altitude climbing!

This tendency to assume a sexual aspect to male–female relationships seems to be stronger in men than women, and was illustrated experimentally by Abbey (1982). Inspired by her own experience and by the anecdotes of other women about having their gestures of friendliness misinterpreted by men as indications of sexual interest, Abbey devised an experiment to see whether the phenomenon was a prevalent one. In the experiment, a series of male–female pairs of subjects participated in five-minute, unstructured conversations in the laboratory, while a hidden female and male observed the interaction. After the interaction, both actors and observers were asked to rate the actors on a number of trait adjectives and to respond to questions about their sexual attraction to and interest in dating the opposite-sex actor. She found that the college males in her study did indeed show a tendency to misperceive female friendliness as an indication of sexual interest. Male actors and observers rated the female actor as being more promiscuous and seductive than did female actors and observers. Males were also more sexually attracted to the opposite-sex actor than females were. Surprisingly, males also rated the *male* actor in a more sexualized way than females did, suggesting that men may be more likely than women to view the world in sexual terms. The tendency for men to perceive less friendliness but more "sexiness" in women's behavior than women do has also been demonstrated in a series of three studies that included not only peer interactions but also videotaped exchanges between a male store manager and a female cashier and between a male professor and a female student (Saal, Johnson, & Weber, 1989).

Cross-sex friendships are more likely to be reported by young adults than by middle-aged and older adults, perhaps because marriage makes it practically difficult for individuals to pursue cross-sex relationships except in the context of couple relationships (Fox et al., 1985). Among mid-life adults, employed women have more cross-sex friendships than nonemployed women, whereas employment is not related to men's cross-sex friendships (Dickens & Perlman, 1981). Some research suggests that cross-sex friendships are experienced as less satisfactory than same-sex friendships, especially by women. Among a sample of young adults, cross-sex friendships were reported by both men and women as providing less help and loyalty than same-sex friendships, and the women said that the cross-sex relationships were less accepting and intimate, but provided more companionship, than did same-sex ones (Rose, 1985).

Couple Relationships

For many adults, the most important close relationship is a romantic-sexual one in which two individuals develop strong bonds and think of themselves as a couple. Whether the couple is dating, cohabiting, or married, and whether the relationship is heterosexual or homosexual, gender is one of the most important influences on the structure and functioning of the couple relationship.

Choosing a Partner and Falling in Love. Among heterosexuals, both women and men are drawn to partners who are physically attractive. Men tend to place greater value on physical attractiveness than women do (Feingold, 1990). Physically attractive men initiate more contact with women and rate these contacts as more meaningful and disclosing than do less attractive men; however, women's physical attractiveness is unrelated to their involvement with men (Reis et al., 1982). This apparent discrepancy may be due to the still accepted pattern that men take more direct initiatives in making contact with women than vice versa and that they seek out women who, they think, will accept them. A man's chances may indeed be better with a moderately attractive than with a highly attractive woman because, as Reis and his colleagues demonstrated, physically attractive women tend to be less trusting of men.

Social factors seem to affect the way people perceive attractiveness in potentially eligible romantic partners. A study of bar patrons found that men rated the attractiveness of female patrons higher as the evening wore on, while women showed a similar pattern in their ratings of male patrons (Gladue & Delaney, 1990). This effect was unrelated to the amount of alcohol consumed and suggests that people's perceptions of attractiveness are influenced by the availability of a potential partner. The "availability" effect may work in reverse as well: Individuals who are already involved in romantic relationships see other potential partners as less attractive than do individuals who are unattached (Simpson, Gangestead, & Lerma, 1990).

Heterosexual women and men give different responses when asked what characteristics are desirable in a mate. In one study of adult married couples, the women rated the following characteristics as significantly more desirable than the men did: considerate, honest, dependable, kind, understanding, fond of children, well liked by others, good earning capacity, ambitious and career-oriented, good family background, and tall. The men, on the other hand, rated these qualities as significantly more desirable for a spouse than the women did: physically attractive, good looking, good cook, and frugal (Buss & Barnes, 1986). Interestingly, the sexes differ in the way that their expressed preference for particular spousal qualities relates to the type of mate with whom they end up. In the preceding study, the wives of husbands who preferred kind-considerate spouses tended to be agreeable, extroverted, and gregarious, while husbands of wives who preferred kind-considerate spouses tended to be submissive, unassertive, and socially passive. In a similar vein, wives of men who preferred spouses to be domestic tended to be warm, agreeable, submissive, and feminine, while husbands of wives who preferred domestic spouses were low on dominance and ambition but showed no special evidence of warmth and agreeableness. It appears that a trait such as kindness/considerateness can mean different things in women than in men, or that the pool of available people seen to possess a particular characteristic is different or more restricted within one gender group than within the other.

Once a relationship has begun, the individuals explore the possibilities for increased commitment. The influence of gender on this process can be considerable. For one thing, young men seem more ready to fall in love than their female counterparts—perhaps because the men are focusing on the partners' physical attractiveness while the women are looking more pragmatically at the man's education and earning potential (Adams, 1982; Huston & Ashmore, 1986). If men do fall in love more quickly, it may mean that early in the relationship, men are more motivated than women to try to make a good impression and to work at maintaining the relationship (Huston & Ashmore, 1986). At any rate, for both women and men, creating a good impression may often involve fulfilling gender-role expectations (Zanna & Pack, 1975).

Communicating.   Although there is a great deal of evidence that women prefer more self-disclosure in intimate relationships than men do, reciprocity may dictate similar levels of disclosure between partners. Thus, the amount of self-disclosure in a relationship may reflect a compromise between the preferences of both partners (Peplau, 1983). When differences do exist, it is usually the woman who discloses more. Gender differences in the content of self-disclosure have been observed by some researchers, with men being more likely than women to reveal strengths and hide weaknesses.

Gender differences have also been found in the communication patterns of intimate couples. In heterosexual couples, women provide more support to male speakers than men provide for women. Women ask more questions and use "mm's" and "oh's" more to indicate attention and interest than men do (Fishman, 1978). After analyzing more than 50 hours of spontaneous conversations between the members of three couples, Fishman found that 96 percent of the topics introduced by males "succeeded" (resulted in a conversation in which they were discussed), while only 36 percent of those introduced by the females did so. Men frequently did not respond or responded minimally to topics raised by women, while women almost always responded to those raised by men. Perhaps because talking does not always get the results they want, women often turn to nonverbal communication to get their point across. Wives have also been found to be better at sending nonverbal messages to their husbands than vice versa (Noller, 1980).

Permanence/Stability and Exclusivity.   There is little direct evidence as to whether women and men differ in their concern with stability or permanence in intimate relationships. Some research suggests that men are more devastated by breakups of intimate relationships than are women (Bloom, White, & Asher, 1979; Rubin, Peplau, & Hill, 1981).

Comparisons of heterosexual and lesbian cohabiting couples have found that heterosexuals express greater confidence than do lesbians that their relationship will continue in the future (Schneider, 1986). A factor that may be either a cause or an effect of this difference in confidence is the difference in degree of financial interdependence described by the two sets of couples. Heterosexual couples were more likely than lesbian couples to have joint bank accounts and to have life insurance and wills naming the partner as beneficiary. Among both lesbian and gay male couples, high values placed on dyadic attachment (desire for intimacy in close relationships) are associated with expectations of permanence in the relationship and with willingness to move if necessary to maintain the relationship (Peplau & Cochran, 1981; Peplau, Cochran, Rook, & Padesky, 1978).

It is in the area of exclusivity that a striking difference among the relationships of gay men, lesbians, and heterosexual couples emerges. When samples of these three groups were asked if they had had sex with someone other than their primary partner during the past two months, 54 percent of the gay men said yes, compared to only 13 percent of the lesbians and 14 percent of college-aged dating men and women (Peplau & Cochran, 1981). This difference may reflect to some extent gender differences in attitudes toward sexuality, specifically the tendency for men to learn that sexual behavior can be separate from love and intimacy (Gagnon & Simon, 1973).

Relationship Quality and Satisfaction. One of the qualities related to the success of a close relationship is trust—a multifaceted construct that includes faith that one's partner will act in loving ways whatever the future holds and belief in the partner's behavioral predictability and personal dependability (Remple, Holmes, & Zanna, 1985). Although trust is seen by both women and men as crucial in close heterosexual relationships, it is viewed somewhat differently by them. For women, the three components of trust are integrally related. For them, trust includes not only faith in the partner's future caring, but also belief that the partner is a dependable person, as consistently confirmed by predictable behavioral evidence. For men, conversely, the three components of trust appear to be less integrated; they can, for instance, focus on faith in a partner's future caring without putting too much emphasis on the more pragmatic concerns of dependability and predictability. Remple and his colleagues (1985) offer two possible explanations for the gender difference. First, women may be more concerned with the practical aspects of interpersonal behavior because they are often in positions of greater dependency in close relationships. Men, being less dependent, can perhaps afford to take a more romantic viewpoint. Second, and equally plausible, is the possibility that women are more sensitive to relationship issues than men are, and so are more likely to evaluate the future of a relationship with reference to its past and present.

Another aspect of relationship quality that apparently has different implications for women and men in close heterosexual relationships is intimacy maturity—the levels of relationship maturity in terms of other-orientation, caring/concern, sexuality, commitment, and communication that may be found within an intimate relationship (White, Speisman, Jackson, Bartis, & Costos, 1986). For husbands in the sample studied by White and her colleagues (1986), intimacy maturity was significantly and positively related to perceived marital adjustment; for wives there was no relationship between the two scores. Wives' marital adjustment score *was* predicted by husbands' intimacy maturity, however: The more mature the husbands, the better adjusted the wives! However, wives' intimacy maturity was unrelated to husbands' marital adjustment. Clearly, the connections between intimacy and marital adjustment are not the same for the two sexes. These findings may reveal a similar dynamic to those on trust, just discussed. Wives, more oriented to husbands' actual behavior, may be more sensitive to manifestations of their husbands' intimacy maturity, while husbands, maintaining a more abstract, idealistic view of their relationships, may be relatively uninfluenced by wives' behavior in their perceptions of marriage.

Some research has compared the relationship quality of couples in heterosexual, gay, and lesbian relationships (Blumstein & Schwartz, 1983; Kurdek & Schmitt, 1986a, 1986b). Many similarities exist among these different types of couples in the factors that relate to relationship quality. For example, poor relationship quality has been linked in all three groups of couples to arguing about money management, intrusion of work into the relationship, spending much time apart, and nonmonogamy (Blumstein & Schwartz, 1983); also, love for partner has been linked to the perception of many barriers to leaving the relationship and to high dyadic attachment (Kurdek & Schmitt, 1986b). However, some differences are evident among the different kinds of couples. Reciprocal dependency and equality of power have been found to be particularly important for the relationship quality of lesbian couples, while financial equality and similarity of educational level have emerged as especially important for the relationship quality of gay male couples (Blumstein & Schwartz, 1983). In a comparison of heterosexual married, heterosexual cohabiting, gay, and lesbian relationships, Kurdek and Schmitt (1986b) found that the four partner types differed both in relationship quality and in the variables that predicted relationship quality. Cohabiting heterosexual partners had the lowest love for partner and relationship satisfaction scores relative to the other three groups, who were indistinguishable from one another on these scores. Married partners reported the most barriers to leaving the relationship, while cohabiting heterosexual partners reported the fewest. Gay male partners were more likely than the other groups to believe in "mindreading"—a belief that partners should know each other's thoughts without having to say them out loud. Lesbian couples exceeded all other groups in shared decision making. Gay and lesbian couples perceived less social support from friends and family for the relationship than did either the married or unmarried heterosexual couples. Despite these differences, however, the major correlates of relationship quality were similar across the different groups of couples. Dyadic attachment was an important predictor of love for each partner type and an important predictor of liking for married, gay, and lesbian partners. For each partner type, relationship satisfaction was predicted by seeing few good alternatives to the relationship, high shared decision making, and few beliefs that disagreement is destructive to the relationship. The authors of this study argue that the results support the existence of a general model of relationship quality, applicable to the various types of intimate couple relationships, that includes dyadic attachment, alternatives to remaining in the relationship, shared decision making, and beliefs regarding the value of disagreement (cf. Sternberg, 1986).

Another factor whose influence seems to be similar across all couple groups is gender-role self-concept (Kurdek & Schmitt, 1986a). In gay, lesbian, and heterosexual couples, androgynous and feminine subjects reported higher relationship quality than did masculine and undifferentiated subjects. Relative to other couples, couples in which one or both partners were androgynous or feminine reported the highest relationship quality, whereas those in which one or both partners were masculine or undifferentiated reported the lowest relationship quality. The reason for these differences may perhaps be found in the characteristics displayed by individuals falling into the four gender-role self-concept categories (Cook, 1985). Both androgynous and feminine individuals appear to have qualities that are conducive to interpersonal relations. Androgynous people are poised, outgoing, concerned about others, likeable, assertive, and self-disclosing. Feminine individuals are submissive and sensitive to expressive cues. Masculine persons, however, have been found to be task-minded, hostile, dominant, egotistical, demanding, and low in nurturance; undifferentiated people tend to be self-centered, withdrawn, poorly socialized, depressed, and lacking in intimacy—hardly the qualities that would enhance a close relationship.

The research on relationship satisfaction within marriage suggests that wives and husbands have a tendency to emphasize different things when determining satisfaction. For example, as a knowledge of traditional gender roles might lead one to expect, husbands' satisfaction is related more strongly to their wives' performance of household activities than it is to how affectionate their wives are; the reverse pattern is found for wives' satisfaction (Huston & Ashmore, 1986). In a similar vein, wives' satisfaction is related to husbands' employment stability and income, while the reverse is not consistently found for husbands' satisfaction. Although such findings are likely a direct consequence of gender-role expectations that the husband should be the main provider and the wife the main caretaker of the home, researchers do not seem to have directly tested this question.

Another difference found between husbands and wives is that conflict is more strongly related (negatively) to wives' than to husbands' feelings of love for their partners (Huston, McHale, & Crouter, 1985; Kelly, Huston, & Cate, 1985). Some authors have suggested that this difference is a consequence of the greater power held by men than women in marriage. Conflict may interfere less with love for the person who generally wins than for the person who generally loses. Research has shown that the perceived use of bullying tactics by one's partner is negatively related to satisfaction with the relationship, and to estimates of how long the relationship will last (Howard, Blumstein, & Schwartz, 1986). The issue of power in intimate relationships, and in marriage in particular, is discussed at length later in this chapter.

How do individuals decide how satisfactory their relationship is? Some social psychologists have argued that one of the most powerful standards applied by both women and men in evaluating a relationship is that of fairness or justice. According to this model, the partners ask themselves if they are getting benefits out of the relationship that are fair with respect to their contributions and to their partner's benefits and contributions. The contributions and benefits that partners put into their implicit equations may include such intangibles as love, understanding, and sympathy, as well as more concrete factors such as money, status, and the performance of needed tasks. The difficulty with studying fairness, however, is that what seems perfectly fair to one person may appear profoundly unjust to someone else! Indeed, many of us have observed close relationships in which the participants seem quite satisfied despite what appears to be a most inequitable arrangement. Nonetheless, researchers have shown that perceived equity—the extent to which the ratio of each partner's contributions to rewards is seen to be equal—predicts marital satisfaction for both women and men (Utne, Hatfield, Traupmann, & Greenberger, 1984), and equity theorists argue that it is the participants' weighting of the contributions and benefits that determines perceived equity, not some outside observer's assessment of the situation. Thus, for example, one couple may think it a perfectly fair exchange for the wife to do all the housework and child care while the husband earns all the income and looks after the car, while such an arrangement might appear grossly unjust to another couple. Attitudes about how particular contributions and benefits should be weighted are influenced to some extent by self-interest (e.g., each individual may see the tasks she or he performs as being more important and/or more difficult than those that the other performs) and by cultural and peer attitudes and expectations (e.g., in a social environment that takes traditional gender roles for granted, the arrangement described in the preceding example would seem more fair than it would in a less traditional environment). Equity may not be the last word on satisfaction, however. One study of premarital couples showed that, while perceived equity did predict marital satisfaction, it was a less reliable predictor than perceived equality (the view that both partners are giving and getting equal amounts in the relationship) and perceived rewardingness of the relationship (Cate, Lloyd, Henton, & Larson, 1982).

Power and Influence in Intimate Relationships.   Even in the most intimate of relationships, both partners do not always want the same thing. Thus, each partner must face the problem of asserting his or her own wishes and of getting the other partner to comply or at least not interfere with them. There are two questions of interest here for students of the psychology of gender: whether gender is related to the relative amount of success that one partner has in influencing the other, and whether gender is related to the *way* in which one partner goes about trying to influence the other. These are questions of interpersonal power: the ability of one person to get another person to do what the first person wants, in the face of resistance from the second person.

As noted in several earlier chapters, men are often seen to hold more status and power, as a group, than women. It might be reasonable to expect that this power asymmetry would be reflected in the intimate relationships between individual women and men and, perhaps, that same-sex intimate relationships would be characterized by greater equality of influence between the partners than would heterosexual relationships. Furthermore, it might be expected that, given female–male differences in status, access to resources, and learned gender roles, the influence tactics used in intimate relationships might differ for women and men. Are such expectations confirmed by the research? The answer is yes, to some extent—but, as usual, the pattern of gender differences is not as simple as the theory predicts.

Before examining the research findings on power in intimate relationships, we need to look briefly at theories of power in general. One of the basic ideas in this area is that power is based on control of resources (French & Raven, 1959; Raven, 1965), and thus on one person's ability to affect the outcomes that occur to the other person (Thibaut & Kelley, 1959). The more resources relevant to another person's life that you control, the more you are able to affect what happens to that person, and thus the more power you have relative to that person. It is important to remember, though, that the translation of power into the ability to influence another is based on both individuals' perceptions of the situation. If the other person does not realize, for instance, how much power you have to affect his or her life, your attempt to influence that person may not work. However, if the other person imagines that you have control over resources or outcomes that you really do not have, that person may give way to your influence despite your objective lack of power. The kinds of resources on which power can be based include various types of rewards and punishments, expertise, legitimacy of position, the ability to inspire identification and liking (referent power), and information (French & Raven, 1959; Raven, 1965). In any intimate relationship, each partner has some resources on which to base power, but one partner may have more than the other. The situation is made even more complex by what social exchange theorists call the *principle of least interest*: the person who is least dependent on the other for rewards—who needs the relationship least—has the most power (Homans, 1974).

In intimate relationships, we might expect that access to bases of power and the amount of interpersonal dependence would affect both the amount of influence and the influence tactics employed by the partners. We might also expect that such issues of power and dependence would be related to the gender of the partners involved—that, for instance, in heterosexual couples, men would be likely to control more resources such as money, expertise, and status by virtue of their privileged position in society. In most heterosexual couples, the man is also bigger and stronger than the woman—a not insignificant power advantage. Finally, in a patriarchal society, the man is seen, normatively, as the dominant partner or the "head of the house," and this perception endows him with power based on legitimacy. Power based on liking or attraction, on the other hand, may well be equally distributed between the partners, or may favor the woman. In homosexual couples, there is less reason to expect particular power asymmetries although particular imbalances may well exist in individual couples.

Falbo and Peplau (1980) examined the influence strategies that members of heterosexual, gay, and lesbian couples reported they used in their intimate relationships. They were able to categorize the strategies along two dimensions: directiveness (direct-indirect) and interactiveness (unilateral-bilateral). The directness dimension refers to the openness or obliqueness that characterizes an influence attempt. A straightforward request or order would be a direct influence tactic, for instance, whereas a behind-the-scenes manipulation of the situation to favor one's own preferred outcome would be an indirect tactic. The interactiveness dimension refers to the degree of mutual engagement with the partner required in the influence attempt. An extremely unilateral strategy, such as giving an order or walking out on the other person, involves no mutual engagement at all; a bilateral strategy, such as arguing or bargaining, requires considerable engagement and interchange. Using these dimensions, Falbo and Peplau found that influence strategies varied according to the partners' perceptions of power in the relationship. In heterosexual, gay, and lesbian couples, individuals who preferred and perceived themselves as having more power than their partner reported the use of more direct and bilateral influence strategies. Conversely, those who saw themselves as having less power than their partners reported using more unilateral and indirect tactics to get their way. Finally, as suggested by the intergroup gender differences in power and status, gay and lesbian partners were less likely than were heterosexual partners to want more power than their partners or to view themselves as having such a power advantage, and women in heterosexual relationships were more likely than were men to feel at a power disadvantage. Across the groups, women showed a greater preference than men did for equal power in their relationships.

Perceptions of power are situational, and may vary from interaction to interaction for the same couple. One study showed that both wives and husbands were more likely to be demanding (exerting pressure through emotional requests, criticisms, complaints) when discussing a change that *they* wanted and to be withdrawing (retreating into defensiveness and passive inaction) when discussing a change that the *partner* wanted. On the whole, however, men were more likely than women to withdraw from their spouses during marital conflict (Christensen & Heavey, 1990).

Another study of the relationship between gender and power in intimate relationships examined the relative importance of the following on the influence tactics used in same-sex and cross-sex intimate relationships: gender, gender-role orientation, control over structural resources (money, education, age), physical attractiveness, and dependence on the relationship (Howard et al., 1986). Unlike Falbo and Peplau, whose respondents were university undergraduates in relationships that were relatively new, these researchers studied a cross-section of adults in long-term relationships. They identified six categories of influence strategies: (1) manipulation (e.g., dropping hints, flattering, behaving seductively), (2) supplication (e.g., pleading, crying, acting ill or helpless), (3) bullying (e.g., threatening, insulting, becoming violent), (4) autocracy (e.g., insisting, claiming greater knowledge, asserting authority), (5) disengagement (e.g., sulking, leaving the scene), and (6) bargaining (e.g., reasoning, offering to compromise). Stereotypically, manipulation and supplication are weak strategies, while bullying and autocracy are strong ones. The researchers expected that the use of the "weak" strategies of manipulation and supplication would be linked to being female, being relatively less masculine and more feminine, having relatively less structural power, and being more dependent on the relationship than one's partner. What they did find was that, although the actor's gender did not relate to influence tactics, the partner's gender did. Both females and males with male partners were more likely to use the weak influence strategies than were females and males with female partners. As the authors suggest, "The power associated with being male thus appears to be expressed in behavior that elicits weak strategies from one's partner" (p. 107). Other aspects of the hypothesis were supported. Having control of fewer resources, such as having less income or seeing oneself as less attractive than one's partner, is linked to greater reported use of supplication and manipulation, as is greater dependence on the relationship. However, these differences in structural power did not themselves account for the effects of gender on influence tactics. In other words, gender was related to power in these intimate relationships above and beyond other forms of power and dependence. Men's capacity to elicit deferent behavior cannot be completely explained by their access to money and expertise; rather, being male in our culture is correlated with so *many* sources of power (e.g., status, legitimate authority, size, strength) that it would be difficult to measure them all in one study. Moreover, it is likely that, growing up with all these indicators of power, males, perhaps not even realizing it, develop behavior patterns that tend to elicit deference and "weak" influence strategies from others. There is much yet to learn about the dynamics of interpersonal power and influence, but it is certainly clear that gender and power are linked in intimate relationships—a link that is probably both caused by and supportive of the intergroup gender differences in power and status.

Loneliness

We have seen that gender has implications for both friendship and intimate "couple" relationships. It seems also to have implications for the way that perceived scarcity or deficiency in such relationships—loneliness—is experienced. Given the differences that have been noted in males' and females' orientation to close relationships, it might be expected that females would be more likely than males to notice and to be bothered by deficiencies in their relationships, and thus to feel lonely. Some researchers have indeed found that women report more loneliness than men do (e.g., Weiss, 1973). However, given the difficulties with intimacy that some researchers have noted among male subjects, it might be expected that males would report more loneliness than do females—and some researchers have found this pattern as well (e.g., Schultz & Moore, 1986). In an effort to make sense of the evidence on this issue, Borys and Perlman (1985) classified the existing studies into those that had used a standard questionnaire measure of loneliness, the UCLA Loneliness Scale (Russell, Peplau, & Cutrona, 1980), and those that had used a self-labeling measure of loneliness (responses to questions such as "How often do you feel lonely?"). They found that, although most studies using the UCLA scale showed no gender differences in loneliness, those that did find a difference almost always found males scoring as lonelier than females. However, among the 11 self-labeling studies, 9 showed that women were more apt than men to label themselves as lonely. Borys and Perlman suggest that the incongruent results for the two types of studies derive from the way that questions are asked. The UCLA scale asks respondents about the quality of their relationships but does not ask them if they would label themselves as lonely. Perhaps men, because of social influence pressures, are simply more reluctant than women to admit to being lonely. In support of this explanation, Borys and Perlman offer the results of their own study (1985) indicating that college students are more rejecting of a lonely male than of a lonely female. Their findings suggest that the negative consequences of admitting loneliness are less for women than for men, at least among young adults.

One study (Schultz & Moore, 1986) has shown that there may be qualitative as well as quantitative gender differences in loneliness. These researchers examined the factors that were associated with loneliness for female and male college students. They found that lonely males were more likely than were lonely females to suffer from negative mood and negative self-evaluations—a finding that may mean that males tend to blame loneliness on their own failures, whereas females are more likely to blame it on external circumstances. This study also showed that loneliness was more strongly linked to a reported lack of social risk taking for males than it was for females. This finding is not surprising, the authors suggest, given that gender roles place more of the onus for initiating social contact, especially cross-sex contact, on males than on females. Taken together, the two findings suggest that, at least for college students, the relatively greater degree of control over heterosocial relationships that is assigned to the masculine role can backfire on men. Charged with the responsibility for making contacts, men who are hesitant to take social risks may not only feel lonely but also blame their own inadequacies for their loneliness. Women, whose feminine role gives them more support for waiting to be approached, can at least blame some of their loneliness on the social ineptitude of their male acquaintances! In the realm of close relationships, then, it appears that even reactions to the *absence* of such relationships is influenced by gender-related expectations.

Marriage: The Intimate Economic Partnership

When an intimate heterosexual relationship is legally formalized through marriage, or acknowledged by the partners to be a permanent living-together arrangement, new issues must be faced. Besides such emotional concerns as love, trust, and satisfaction, the spouses must now confront problems of dividing up the household work, sharing income, and making joint decisions regarding employment, housing, children, and so on. The partnership is more than a close personal relationship: It is an economic and legal one as well. If a couple is formally married or, in some jurisdictions, become common-law spouses simply by living together for a specified length of time, they have agreed, albeit often without realizing it, to abide by the terms of a marriage contract. The terms of the marriage contract are not negotiable by the two partners; they are legal rights and responsibilities spelled out by the government. The terms cover such things as how property is shared during the marriage and divided upon divorce, sexual exclusivity, financial support, inheritance, responsibilities for children, even the woman's right to keep her own name. As Sapiro (1986) notes, the marriage contract is virtually the only one that most people enter without knowing the terms, and that can be changed by a third party (the government) while it is in force and without notification of the involved parties. Moreover, private agreements between a wife and husband that contravene the terms of the marriage contract are not enforceable by law.

Although the marriage contract used to be based on the notion that a woman, upon marriage, came under the more or less complete authority and ownership of her husband, legal changes, such as the introduction of community property laws, have removed some of the inequality built into the marriage contract. However, the idea that women are subordinate to their husbands is still built into the marriage contract in many jurisdictions. For example, in many jurisdictions, the husband has the right to choose where the couple will live. If a wife refuses to move with her husband, she is legally considered as abandoning him—grounds for divorce.

The economic laws and customs surrounding marriage are still largely based on assumptions about family structure and stability that do not fit current social patterns. The core of these assumptions is that women and children will have a man to provide for them. However, instead of a relatively permanent arrangement that includes one employed spouse, one homemaker, and children, families in the 1990s must often respond to divorce, remarriage, out-of-wedlock births, and the necessity for two incomes. When family-disruptive events such as divorce, job loss, or disability occur, women are more likely than men to experience significant drops in their access to resources and well-being (Burkhauser & Duncan, 1989).

The Division of Labor

Traditionally, the basic assumptions of the marital economic arrangement in middle-class urban families were that the husband was responsible for the economic support of the wife and children, while the wife was responsible for most of the domestic labor. It has even been suggested that our society measures a man's masculinity by the size of his paycheck (Gould, 1973). The husband's breadwinner role is often considered his most important function by men and women alike (Slocum & Nye, 1976), and a survey by Yankelovich (1974) suggests that, for about 80 percent of employed married men, the provider role gives purpose and meaning to life and to jobs that are otherwise not very satisfying. The assumption that the man should be the chief breadwinner and the woman his helpmate and homemaker has not disappeared, but it is widely questioned or rejected outright as women move into the paid work force in large numbers. In fact, what appears to be happening in many cases is that the woman is keeping most of the domestic role while taking on an increasingly larger share of the breadwinner role. For instance, between 1950 and 1980, both black and white women's poverty rates increased relative to men's in all age groups. Much of the increase was due to changes in parental obligations among nonelderly women: Women are increasingly likely to head single-parent families. This change accounted for 70 percent of the increase in poverty rates among black women aged 18 to 64 and 86 percent of the increase among white women aged 25 to 64 (McLanahan, Sorensen, & Watson, 1989).

Women do not have to be single heads of households to find themselves filling more than one role. Studies show that the movement of wives into the paid labor force has not been accompanied by a complementary shift of husbands into greater participation in housework (Atkinson & Huston, 1984; Fasting & Sisjord, 1985; Golding, 1990; Pleck & Rustad, 1980; Robinson, Yerby, Fieweger, & Somerick, 1977). Employed married women spend fewer hours doing household tasks, but their husbands put in little, if any, time on household chores to compensate for their wives' busier schedule. Most of the housework is done by wives, regardless of their employment situation. In fact, one examination of national sample data on time use found that husbands of employed women actually had more free time than husbands of women not in the labor force, while employed married women had significantly less free time than their husbands or their nonemployed female counterparts (Robinson et al., 1977). Cultural and ethnic attitudes and traditions may make the dismantling of gender-typed division of household labor even more difficult. For example, among Mexican-American couples, women have been found to do a larger share of the housework than among non-Hispanic white American couples (Golding, 1990). Even when a woman is at home full-time, the assignment of *all* domestic tasks to her results in a division of labor that burdens her unfairly. One writer (Kaye, cited in Kome, 1986) has calculated that a full-time homemaker with two preschool children works 206 hours a week— more hours than a week actually has!

An obvious explanation for the continuation of a fairly traditional spousal division of household labor in the face of changing ideologies about gender roles is that women and men each feel more skilled at the tasks that fall within their traditional spheres. Beginning in childhood, females and males are assigned tasks on the basis of their gender appropriateness (White & Brinkerhoff, 1981), so it is not surprising if men and women each have more confidence in their skill at gender-traditional chores. Indeed, one study shows that men's and women's perceived skill can be a good predictor of the extent to which they perform household tasks traditionally done by members of the other sex (Atkinson & Huston, 1984). However, life repeatedly confronts us with the necessity of learning new activities, and most household tasks are far from impossible for an intelligent adult to master. Why, then, does the traditional division of labor persist? Part of the answer lies in an examination of power inside and outside the marital relationship.

Issues of economics and exchange cannot be separated from issues of power and control, and one factor that slows down the change away from the traditional division of economic responsibilities in marriage is that the change threatens men's "legitimate" power as head of the household. Social norms are such that a man can still feel that his masculinity is impugned if he does too much housework or if he appears too responsive to his wife's demands for sharing in the area of domestic chores. In fact, a comprehensive review of the literature on power in marriage indicates that the lowest marital satisfaction and happiness is reported in couples where the wife is dominant in decision making—perhaps because both partners are acutely conscious of the extent to which their arrangement violates social norms (Gray-Little & Burks, 1983). Moreover, most people will agree that housework is generally not "fun," and that if a person can get away with letting someone else do it, she or he will. In many marriages, men *can* get away with letting their wives do the housework by using power based on the legitimacy of gender roles ("It's not my job—it's the wife's job") or helplessness ("I can't do it as well as you can"). The assignment of the bulk of household tasks to women is further supported by the imbalance of financial contributions brought to the marriage by each spouse. Even when both spouses are employed, the husband usually earns more than the wife, making her more economically dependent on the relationship and hence more influenceable (Blood & Wolfe, 1960) and more likely to try to maintain equity in the relationship by contributing in nonfinancial ways (Scanzoni, 1972). Increased sharing of domestic chores within a marriage is intricately bound up with changes in gender-related ideology and actual gender equality in the larger society.

If the division of household labor is partially influenced by the degree of financial contribution brought by each spouse to the marriage, it might be expected that a shift in the balance of such contributions would cause a corresponding shift in the division of household labor. Research on couples' reactions to the husbands' job loss has shown such a pattern. Couples in which the husband was unemployed reported lower contributions by the wives to household work than did couples in which the husband was employed full-time (Aubry, 1986). However, there was no indication that the unemployed husbands took on more household work.

There are other issues of power and control that may help to explain women's lack of insistence that men share the housework. For a woman, the domestic sphere may sometimes represent an area of control within her marriage that she is reluctant to give up, even if that reluctance translates into more work for herself. That explanation is the one given by Robinson and his colleagues (Robinson et al., 1977) for their finding that only 19 percent of the women in their national sample answered yes to the question "Do you wish your husband would give you more help with the household chores?"

Women do the larger share of the *social* work in families as well. Not only do they take more of the responsibility for childrearing (Hoffnung, 1989), but they also do the bulk of the work of caring for aged parents (Brody, 1981). This large share of family relationship work may be even greater for African-American women, who are frequently the central figures and primary sources of socialization in their family units (Wilkinson, 1984).

Nontraditional Families.   Some families have broken dramatically with tradition in their division of labor. According to some estimates, for instance, there are between 1 and 2 million men in the United States who have taken on the role of "househusband" (Doyle, 1985). These men stay at home and take the major responsibility for housework and child care, while their wives are employed full-time. The few studies that exist of these men suggest that their role is experienced as a positive one (Beer, 1982). However, for the majority of these men, the househusband role is not taken on by choice but conferred on them by circumstances; not surprisingly, those who have freely chosen the role are most happy with it (Lutwin & Siperstein, 1985). Studies in both the United States (Radin, 1982) and Australia (Russell, 1982) indicate that fathers who become the primary caregivers experience an improved relationship with their children.

Consistent with the availability of the "househusband" option is the finding that a significant minority of married women now earn more than their spouses do. In 1981 the figure was 12 percent, one-third of which were couples in which the wife was the sole breadwinner and two-thirds of which were couples in which wives earned more than their working husbands (Bianchi & Spain, 1983). Interestingly, the majority of wives who earn more than their husbands are not college educated and are not in professional or managerial jobs. It remains to be seen whether this group will grow in size and what kinds of problems they will encounter.

Not all families are based on the unions of heterosexual couples. Although the legal aspects of marriage are not applicable to them, homosexual couples often form permanent relationships and rear children together. One such family is described in a recent article by Lindsy Van Gelder (1991). Two women in a committed lesbian relationship wanted to have a child. They searched for and found a man who was willing to be the biological father of that child. That man, also gay, ended up making a commitment to maintaining a relationship, both emotional and financial, with the child he had fathered. The child, Sarah—now a little girl of 6—consequently has a family of three adults: Nancy, her mother; Amy, her mother's lover; and Doug, her father. The three adults are good friends, and all share the parenting of Sarah. The arrangement produces some difficulties in terms of explaining the family to the rest of the world, but it has many advantages as well: Three adults rather than two share the responsibilities, and barriers exist that prevent the family from falling into the stereotypical divisions of labor and power often found in more traditional families.

Marital Violence

More frequently than we care to admit, coercive power within the marriage relationship is exercised through physical violence. In Canada, a conservative estimate suggests that 1 out of every 10 women living with a husband or lover is battered by that man (MacLeod, 1980). American estimates of the percentages of marriages in which battering takes place range from 25 to 60 percent (Pagelow, 1984), although these figures include marriages with relatively low levels of violence. Physical violence in intimate relationships can begin even before marriage: Studies have found that about 22 percent of courting couples report that physical violence has occurred in their relationships (Cate, Henton, Koval, Christopher, & Lloyd, 1982; Makepeace, 1981).

Violence within marriage is linked historically to a legal definition of the family that made it acceptable for a man to exercise his authority over his wife by beating her (MacLeod, 1980). From ancient Greece and Rome through to Europe in the Middle Ages, men could beat or kill their wives with impunity. As late as the nineteenth century, British law books stated that the husband could exercise his power and dominion over his wife by beating her, although the beating must not be cruel and violent! Even in the present day, there is some tendency for judges to avoid "interfering" in wife abuse cases because family matters are supposed to be private. One judge in Nova Scotia was recently suspended after years of complaints from women's groups because he persisted in ordering battered women to "go home and submit to your husband."

Marital violence is usually initiated by the husband, but, as the pattern continues, the wife will often fight back (Saunders, 1986). The violence usually increases in severity over time (Frieze, 1986), becoming so dangerous that in about one-third of the cases the victim must seek medical treatment for her injuries (MacLeod, 1980). The female victim often becomes isolated from other people and faces a growing sense of powerlessness and helplessness as she tries and fails to change the situation in some way that will stop the violence (Walker, 1979). Eventually, the woman may try to leave the relationship but often returns because she has nowhere to go or feels too frightened and inadequate to make it on her own (Frieze, 1986). As the violence becomes even more extreme, she may finally leave because she fears for her life or the lives of her children (Frieze, 1979), or she may actually try to kill her husband. One study of marital homicides in Ontario found that all of the female offenders had been seriously assaulted by their victims (Chimbas, cited in MacLeod, 1980).

The likelihood that a woman who is being assaulted by her partner will be rescued by the justice system is small. According to one researcher, the probability that wife assault will be detected by the criminal justice system is only 6.5 percent, and, if detected, the probability of an arrest is about 21.2 percent. Taking all stages of the justice process into account results in the estimate that, given that a man assaults his wife, he has only a 0.38 percent chance of being punished by the courts (Dutton, 1987a).

People who do not know the facts about wife abuse often believe that women stay in abusive relationships because they are masochistic. In fact, the reasons for staying in a violent marriage have much more to do with situationally determined issues of power and control in the family than with personality dispositions. The woman who wants to leave an abusive marriage often faces a lack of external resources for doing so: no monetary resources to draw on, no way to protect herself against violent retaliation from her husband if he comes after her, no friends or family who can help her, and no accessible shelter for battered women (Frieze, 1986). Moreover, her sense of self-confidence has been drained by the relationship. Physically abusive husbands are usually verbally abusive as well, and wives often endure long strings of insults about their competence, their appearance, and their sexuality along with the beatings (Walker, 1979). All of these factors conspire to place the abused woman at a huge power disadvantage with respect to her husband. Add to this some common beliefs, such as that all men are violent anyway or that her violent husband needs her, and it becomes easy to see how strong are the pressures on an abused woman to remain in the relationship (Frieze, 1986).

Although both men and women may behave violently toward their partners, it is men who inflict the most serious abuse (Straus, Gelles, & Steinmetz, 1980). Moreover, the factors associated with violent behavior toward a spouse or intimate partner are quite different for men and women. Men who have a high need for power are more likely to abuse their partners, but women's need for power is unrelated to abusive behavior (Mason & Blankenship, 1987). Assaultive men are found to be not only high in the need for power but low on verbal assertiveness toward their spouses, suggesting that violence may sometimes stem from the frustration of not having the verbal skills to exert influence (Dutton & Strachan, 1987).

Women who report behaving violently toward their spouses are usually being treated violently by these same spouses; however, men who report being physically or psychologically abusive toward their partners are frequently not receiving the same kind of abuse (Mason & Blankenship, 1987). Also, young women's expression of and receipt of violence in adult love relationships appears to be more strongly correlated with having been abused as children than does young men's violent behavior in such relationships (Marshall & Rose, 1990).

Studies of men who repeatedly assault their wives suggest that the men tend to blame their wives or external circumstances for their aggressive behavior. One analysis of wives' reports of their husbands' behavior after a "typical" battering incident showed that only 8 percent of the men apologized and 80 percent acted as though nothing had happened (Dobash & Dobash, 1984). A comparison of wives' and husbands' causal attributions for an assault by the husband indicated that the husbands tended to externalize the cause for their behavior by blaming it on their wife's behavior or on alcohol, while wives tended to see the assault as due to their husband's emotional state, personality, or other causes internal to the husband (Shields & Hanneke, 1983). One study of 75 men with histories of repeated wife assault found that about one-fifth of them excused their assault as not their responsibility, but accepted that the act was wrong. The other four-fifths of the men accepted personal responsibility but found ways to justify their actions—by blaming the victim, saying that they had been too angry to control themselves, or claiming that their behavior was in line with the norms of their particular subcultural or ethnic group (Dutton, 1986). In this study, men who blamed their wives for the assault were more likely than other men to minimize the frequency, severity, and consequences of their violence.

Some men who assault their wives may, without realizing it, be trying to face down the specter of abandonment. Research shows that assaultive men become more angry and aroused than other men do when they watch videotaped scenes of male–female arguments in which there is a strong perceived threat of the female abandoning the male (Dutton, 1987b). In addition, researchers who have studied *desperate love*, a type of emotional attachment in which the lover feels desperate for contact with the loved one and fearful of being left, have found that in men, but not in women, desperate love is strongly related to an attachment style involving aggressive or destructive impulses (Sperling & Berman, 1991).

The majority of men (about 75 percent) do not approve of the use of physical violence by a man against his wife (Stark & McEvoy, 1970). However, as seen in Dutton's (1986) research, even men who see such violence as wrong sometimes engage in it. It appears that men who batter their wives are rewarded in certain ways for this behavior. Dutton and Browning (1983) describe the feelings that are connected with wife assault for some men: power, agency (a sense of taking action), and increased sense of control over aversive stimuli. Among other strategies, then, the clinical treatment of male batterers must include teaching these men not to depend on violence as a source of feelings of power and control (Sonkin, Martin, & Walker, 1986).

It is clear that intimate relationships involve issues of power as much as issues of attachment and caring. Marital relationships exist, not in a social vacuum, but against a background of social norms and legal rules that encourage or tolerate certain kinds of behavior. As long as those norms continue to encourage inequality between husbands and wives and to tolerate the use of violence as a way of exercising power in these relationships, marital violence, particularly wife abuse, will continue to be a problem.

Women and Men as Parents

In the popular imagination, one of the largest assumed gender differences is in parent–child relationships. People often think of women as naturally nurturant, with a built-in instinct for mothering, and of men as second-class parents, more clumsy and less involved with their children. In fact, the notion that women have an inborn maternal instinct played a large role in shaping the history of psychology's study of human caretaking behavior (Shields, 1984). Many early psychologists saw motherhood as women's most important function, and, until recently, psychologists concerned with the study of parenting examined only mother–child relationships.

Our culture abounds with images of mother nurturance. Anthropologist Ashley Montagu's (1952) comments are representative: "The sensitive relationships which exist between mother and child belong to a unique order of humanity, an order in which the male may participate as a child, but from which he increasingly departs as he leaves childhood behind" (p. 142). Hoffnung (1989) describes what she calls the "motherhood mystique"—a constellation of romanticized attitudes about motherhood that has influenced women to feel guilty or inadequate if they do not have children or if they do not devote themselves full-time to their children. The mystique says that only by having a child can a woman actualize her full potential and achieve the ultimate meaning of her life. Motherhood, according to this myth, is complementary with and does not interfere with the other traditional feminine roles of wife and homemaker. Furthermore, a "good" mother is always patient and content, never resentful, and is available to her child 24 hours a day. This mystique surrounding motherhood, which dates only from the eighteenth century (Harris, 1979), has formed the basis for what Adrienne Rich (1976) calls the institution of motherhood: the set of social prescriptions and norms that limit women's choices in and shape their experience of motherhood. Our society has institutionalized motherhood in such a way that mothers are assumed to have primary responsibility for children, are given little recognition and almost no support in this task, are isolated with their children much of the time, and are expected to experience nothing but fulfillment and a self-sacrificial glow as they live out this role. Rich (1976) attempts to convey some of the ambivalence experienced by a woman caught in this institution of motherhood:

> The physical and psychic weight of responsibility on the woman with children is by far the heaviest of social burdens. It cannot be compared with slavery or sweated labor because the emotional bonds between a woman and her children make her vulnerable in ways which the forced laborer does not know; he

can hate and fear his boss or master; loathe the toil; dream of revolt or of becoming a boss; the woman with children is a prey to far more complicated, subversive feelings. Love and anger *can* exist concurrently; anger at the conditions of motherhood can become translated into anger at the child, along with the fear that we are not "loving"; grief at all we cannot do for our children in a society so inadequate to meet human needs becomes translated into guilt and self-laceration. This "powerless responsibility" as one group of women has termed it, is a heavier burden even than providing a living—which so many mothers have done, and do, simultaneously with mothering—because it is recognized in some quarters, at least, that economic forces, political oppression, lie behind poverty and unemployment; but the mother's very character, her status as a woman, are in question if she has "failed" her children. (pp.35–36)

The motherhood role may be institutionalized differently in different cultures. In Japan, for example, traditionally the role of mother has been associated with independence and power. Mothers have had almost complete control over childrearing, have directed their children's education, and have been able to influence government and community leaders when speaking as guardians of the new generation. Japanese women have perhaps been able to gain status, respect, and a personal sense of self-worth from their role as mothers (Bankart, 1989). As the options open to women in Japan increase, however, young women appear to be very realistic about the amount of work involved in motherhood and reluctant to accept motherhood as their sole route to fulfillment.

One of the goals of the feminist movement has been to gain for women the right to choose or refuse motherhood. Although the advent of effective contraception and safe access to abortion has made it much easier than it used to be for women to put off or avoid motherhood, the social expectations that continue to surround motherhood still make it difficult for women to combine motherhood with other goals. Whereas men rarely face a choice between career and parenthood, that choice is still a painful reality for many women. As Betty Friedan (1981), who has argued persuasively that feminism must not deny or devalue the human importance of love, parenthood, and family, notes:

The price of motherhood is still too high for most women; the stunting of abilities and earning power is a real fear, because professions and careers are still structured in terms of the lives of men whose wives took care of the parenting and other details of life. The point is that *equality*—the rights for which women have been fighting for over a century—was, is, necessary, for women to be able to affirm their own personhood, and in the fullest sense of choice, motherhood. The point is, the movement to equality and the personhood of women isn't finished until motherhood is a fully free choice. (p. 87)

As women approach motherhood, they are not oblivious to the problems associated with it. Among first-time expectant parents, age and duration of marriage are positively linked to good feelings about the pregnancy for men, but not for women (Lips, 1983). Apparently, the older and more established in her life a woman is, the more she knows she will have to give up in becoming a mother. The older the woman in this sample, the more likely she was to agree that she could have a fulfilling life without children. Despite this awareness, however, women were more likely than men to link having children with fulfillment of their gender roles and with having a satisfying life.

All of the preceding is not to say that parenthood is not a potential source of joy and transformation for both mothers and fathers. Expectant and new parents—female and male—often report strong feelings of happiness, hope for the future, and a change in their concept of relationship from "couple" to "family" (Lips, 1982c; Lips & Morrison, 1986). Yet, in general, the behavioral correlates of these attitudes are quite different for mothers and fathers. Estimates of the amount of time fathers spend in direct contact with their infants include a low of less than a minute per day (Rebelsky & Hanks, 1971), 15 to 20 minutes a day (Lewis & Weinraub, 1974), and a high of just over 3 hours per day (Golinkoff & Ames, 1979).

Fathers are more likely to play with and to engage in caregiving behaviors with their infants if they view fatherhood as a self-enriching experience (Levy-Shiff & Israelashvili, 1988) and if they are not overwhelmed with other life concerns (De Luccie & Davis, 1991). From the beginning of the baby's life, fathers are more likely to be found playing with the baby, while mothers are more likely to be found feeding, changing, dressing, or cleaning it. Studies have shown that up to 75 percent of fathers have no regular responsibility for taking care of their infants (Kotelchuk, 1976) and that, in general, fathers spend considerably less time than mothers do in infant feeding and other caretaking activities (Rendina & Dickerscheid, 1976; Richards, Dunn, & Antonis, 1977). In fact, regardless of the espousal of egalitarian ideals by couples, or of social class or dual- or single-earner status, the birth of a baby is the occasion for a shift toward a gender-traditional division of roles (Arbeit, 1975; Cowan, Cowan, Coie, & Coie, 1978; Lewis & Cooper, 1988; Moss, Bolland, Foxman, & Owen, 1987). This shift is associated with more stress and dissatisfaction among mothers than fathers.

There is some evidence that the amount of time fathers spend with their children increases as the children grow older (Lewis & Weinraub, 1976). This increase has been noted especially in the case of male children, with whom fathers often become involved in particularly "masculine" aspects of socialization such as sporting activities. Like mothers, fathers may feel inadequate in their parental role because they give their children less attention and care than they think they should (Heath, 1976). There are also indications that fathers' involvement with children is increasing. For example, Meg Luxton (1980), studying the changes in women's work in the home across three generations of women in a northern Canadian town, noted a distinct change across generations in the amount of father participation in childcare reported by these women. Women in the youngest generation, those with small children at the time of the study, were the envy of the older women because of the amount of help their husbands gave them. The older women claimed that during their childbearing years their husbands had refused all involvement with pregnancy, childbirth, or child care; the younger women felt they had a right to expect help from their husbands in this sphere. However, the husband's participation was still viewed as "helping out," and there was little thought that he should or could be an equal participant in the job of raising the children.

Despite the "motherhood mystique" and the lack of adequate child-care participation by fathers, mothers of young children have entered the paid labor force in large numbers. These "working mothers" often experience a great deal of conflict and guilt about the possible harm they may be doing to their children by not being more available to them. However, research on the effects of maternal employment on children indicates that school-aged children suffer no emotional or intellectual deprivation as a result of maternal employment (Hoffman, 1974), that preschoolers often benefit socially and intellectually from childcare outside the home (Clarke-Stewart, 1991), and that some women are better mothers when they are employed (Schubert, Bradley-Johnson, & Nuttal, 1980). Even infants do not seem to be adversely affected by being cared for extensively by caretakers other than the mother (Mott, 1991). Of course, the impact of maternal employment must vary with the kind of child-care arrangements that mothers are able to make (Zaslow, 1991), as well as with such variables as the mother's attitude toward employment and the support she gets from her partner. When women are given the same supports that men are for working—the knowledge that their children are being well cared for in their absence and that their paid work is valued by other family members—maternal employment is apparently a positive, rewarding choice for women and their families. However, only a lucky minority of women have access to such support.

The gender differences in parental behavior, like so many other gender differences, can be at least partially understood with reference to learned social roles, ongoing social expectations, and access to power. First, the socialization process tends to strengthen the female's and minimize the male's attachment to children; the feminine and masculine roles have a strong influence on responsiveness to the young (Berman, 1980). Second, the social arrangements that support these feminine and masculine roles—the unavailability of paternity leave, the demand that "work" take place from 9 to 5 each day—make it difficult for people to be flexible, even if they are so inclined. In a study of new parents, McHale and Huston (1984) found that the extent of involvement in child-oriented activities was predicted by involvement in the paid labor force for women but not for men, and by perceived skill at child-care tasks for men but not for women. Also, fathers' involvement with their children was more related to their own and their spouses' attitudes than was mothers' involvement. In concrete terms, the more the mother worked outside the home, the less central was the child to her activities when she was at home, and the more competent and interested a man was in child care before becoming a father, the more he actually did with his child later on. As the authors of the study note, these findings can be explained as stemming from social norms that give mothers little leeway with respect to child care and fathers little freedom of choice with respect to employment. In other words, individual differences in attitude are more likely to influence behavior when the person is free to decide whether or not to engage in the behavior.

The McHale and Huston (1984) study has some practical implications for increasing fathers' involvement in child care. They found strong correlations between fathers' perceived skill at child-care tasks before their babies' birth and these fathers' later involvement in child care. This finding, which is in line with other studies, suggests that giving fathers practice or training in child-care activities may increase their participation in the care of their infants. The researchers also found that the extent to which the mothers were nontraditional in their gender-role attitudes and role preferences was positively related to their spouses' involvement in child care—suggesting, perhaps, that "women must be willing to step back from the role of primary caregiver if fathers are to become more involved in caring for their sons and daughters" (p. 1360). Women may be unwilling to step back, however, if they feel that child care is their major sphere of influence and expertise in the family. Moreover, the "motherhood mystique" ensures that a woman will feel guilty at first for giving up any aspect of the traditional mothering role, no matter how competent and willing her partner is.

Although most of the research on parenting has focused on women and men in two-parent, heterosexual families, parenting obviously takes place in a variety of family contexts (e.g., see Hanson, 1985; Nieva, 1985). Besides dual-earner and wife as sole earner families—the more commonly acknowledged variations on the traditional family—parenting takes place in stepfamilies and single-parent families, by parents who do not live with their children and see them only on weekends, and by gay fathers and lesbian mothers. All of these groups encounter special difficulties, but perhaps their greatest shared problem is their invisibility. We continue to think of families in traditional terms and to assume that families that differ from the "normal," two-biological-parent model generate problems for their members. Such an assumption has, for example, been behind the notion that the 40 percent of black American families that are headed by women have problems that stem from the way the family is structured rather than, as seems more likely, from the fact that female-headed families are much more likely than are two-parent families to be living below the poverty line (Blackwell, 1985). Similarly, the assumption that families should conform to the "man as provider, woman as nurturer" model has been responsible over past decades for the insistence that Native American groups abandon their own family traditions and conform to those of the dominant white culture (Almquist, 1989). Even in the white middle-class population, however, there is much more diversity among families than existed a decade ago. For example, the number of single-parent families has risen dramatically in recent years. Our vision of the family and our research have not kept pace with these changes.

Summary

The influence of gender on peer and family relationships is rooted in our socialization into feminine and masculine patterns of behavior and maintained by social arrangements that favor these patterns. Girls learn at an early age that intimate, self-disclosing friendships are rewarding and socially approved. Boys learn equally early that too much intimacy with another male is often regarded with suspicion in a society influenced by competitive and homophobic attitudes. The narrow emphasis on sexuality in female–male relationships makes it unlikely that cross-sex friendships will develop, and the separation of males and females into different kinds of jobs and even different domestic roles contributes further to this situation.

Intimate sexual relationships between women and men share many features with intimate sexual relationships between men or between women. However, a major difference between heterosexual and homosexual intimate relationships is that there tends to be more emphasis on equality between the partners in lesbian and gay relationships than in heterosexual relationships. This difference probably derives from the difficulty heterosexual couples have in separating their relationship from a social context in which men are accorded more status and have access to more bases of power than do women. The influence of this context is particularly apparent in the institution of marriage, where the authority of husband over wife is legally entrenched in some respects. The impact of assumptions about gender differences and the man's right to have authority over the woman can be seen in the problems that beset many male–female couples: inequitable division of household labor and the use of violence by men against their partners.

Relationships between parents and their children are also conditioned by gender-role ideology and the power differences between women and men. Women are supposed to be naturally interested in and good at parenting, by virtue of their sex. The motherhood mystique encourages them to feel guilty if they find motherhood uninteresting or problematic, or if they try to combine it with other goals. Men, by contrast, are not expected to be particularly interested or involved in child care, although there is some evidence that these expectations are slowly changing.

Changes in families over the past 15 years—the increase in employment among mothers, the rise in single-parent families—have led to fears that the family is disintegrating. Some have even accused the feminist movement of destroying the family. Perhaps what is being destroyed is the monolithic conception of the family as a patriarchal structure in which the husband is the breadwinner and head, the wife is the caregiver and supporter, and the children grow up lacking all but the most superficial contact with adults other than their parents. According to Betty Friedan (1981), the family is now a "feminist frontier"—an institution that must be, not destroyed, but changed to accommodate the full personhood of both women and men. Such an accommodation would no doubt mean, in part, that many different kinds of families would be considered "normal" and that, within such families, women and men would not be locked into expectations of submission and dominance, caregiver and breadwinner, as they have in the past. Although some movement in this direction has certainly happened, it remains to be seen how readily this particular "feminist frontier" can be crossed.

For Additional Reading

Ehrenreich, B. (1983). *The hearts of men*. New York: Anchor Books. The author examines the ways that ideas about masculinity have changed and how those changes relate to changes in the marriage relationship.

Nardi, P. M. (Ed.). (1992). *Men's friendships*. Newbury Park, CA: Sage Publications. The contributors to this volume present a variety of different perspectives on how gender and social forces shape friendships.

Tannen, D. (1990). *You just don't understand*. New York: Ballantine Books. A linguist writes about the complexities of female–male communication. She argues that women and men have different underlying goals in much of their communication: connection for women and status seeking for men.

12

Economic & Political Life: Power, Status, & Achievement

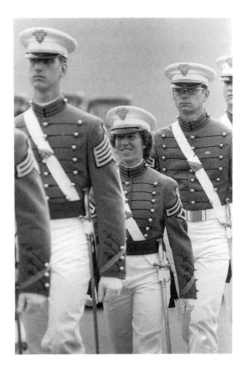

A common retort to advocates of equality between the sexes is, "If women are as capable as men, why are there so few great women artists? Where are the eminent women novelists, composers, philosophers, economists, chemists, politicians?" Writer Virginia Woolf would have provided a swift and decisive answer to such questions. In her haunting essay, *A Room of One's Own* (1929/1957), she describes the obstacles of prejudice and economic hardship that beset women would-be writers until the present century. What, she muses, would have become of a sister to William Shakespeare, a sister whose talent rivaled that of the famous bard?

> It seemed to me that any woman born with a great gift in the sixteenth century would certainly have gone crazed, shot herself, or ended her days in some lonely cottage outside the village, half witch, half wizard, feared and mocked at. For it needs little skill in psychology to be sure that a highly gifted girl who

> had tried to use her gift for poetry would have been so thwarted
> and hindered by other people, so tortured and pulled asunder
> by her own contrary instincts, that she must have lost her health
> and sanity to a certainty. (p. 51)

Woolf is only one of many individuals who have argued persuasively that women's invisibility relative to men in terms of recognized achievements is due, not to a lack of talent, but to barriers imposed by discrimination and other external factors.

It is clear that in most fields few women relative to men have managed to achieve positions of eminence and power. Although they make up half of the world's enfranchised population, women hold 10 percent of the seats in national legislatures; in one-third of all governments there are no women members of the highest decision-making body of the country, the executive council (Sivard, 1985). Women make up an extremely low percentage of the conductors of major orchestras, the directors of major motion pictures, the members of the National Academy of Sciences, the recipients of the Nobel Prize. When Nadine Gordimer was awarded the Nobel Prize for literature in 1991, she became the first woman novelist in a quarter of a century to receive this honor. The awarding of the 1991 Nobel Peace Prize to a woman, Burma's imprisoned opposition leader Aung San Suu Kyi, was also highly unusual. Women of color, often the targets of double discrimination, have even less representation in the ranks of the eminent. For instance, the first Ph.D. in mathematics awarded to a black woman, Evelyn Boyd Collins, was granted in 1946; the first American black woman to gain a Ph.D. in physics, Shirley Jackson, graduated in 1976; and only in 1987 did the NASA astronaut training program select its first black female astronaut, Dr. Mae Jemison (Thomas, V. L., 1989).

Although women have made considerable progress in gaining access to the labor force in recent years, they have been relegated mainly to traditionally feminine occupations or to the lower ranks of male-dominated occupations. As organizational sociologist Carolyn Dexter (1985) puts it, "Regardless of the type of work or the type of organization involved, women's employment is characterized by limited power over their own and others' activities, few economic or symbolic rewards, and low prestige" (p. 240).

An understanding of the large gender gap in positions of eminence, prestige, and influence requires that we examine the psychological and social issues surrounding power and achievement. In earlier chapters we noted that females and males are socialized differently with respect to achievement, that males are often automatically accorded more status than females, and that women and men frequently differ in their access to the resources on which power is based. This chapter will focus on the ways in which such differences are translated into a social structure in which men occupy a disproportionate number of the positions of prestige and eminence and dominate most aspects of economic and political activity. It begins with an examination of a typical, personality-based explanation for the gender differences in economic and political power: "Women aren't as motivated as men are to get to the top." This section will show that, in fact, there is no evidence that women and men differ in the strength of their motivation to achieve success or power. The next section delves into the question of what power and achievement mean to women and men. Do the two genders satisfy their needs for power and achievement in different ways? Gender roles and a society structured to maintain those roles often make it easier for women to seek achievement and power vicariously or indirectly and for men to seek them directly. The very definitions of "success" and "power" may thus differ for men and women. The third section looks at social influences on the access that men and women have to bases of power and at the impact of this differential access on the influence strategies that women and men use. This is followed by an examination of the ways in which power is gained and maintained in politics and in organizational settings, and the reasons why women so often find themselves at a disadvantage in those arenas. The chapter concludes with a discussion of the self-perpetuating nature of power: the ways in which power transforms its users and the ways in which people in a hierarchical power relationship maintain the power difference through their behavior.

Motivation: The Driving Force?

Many psychological theories are based on the assumption that individuals differ in the strength of their motives—their tendencies to need and to seek particular outcomes. Both the achievement motive and the power motive have been studied energetically by psychologists looking for clues to explain individual differences in behavior. The achievement motive is defined as a general personality disposition to strive for success in any situation where standards of excellence are applied (McClelland, Atkinson, Clark, & Lowell, 1953), while the power motive is defined as the tendency to strive to feel that one is having an impact on others (Winter, 1973). Both motives are measured using the Thematic Apperception Test (TAT; Murray, 1937), a projective test in which the respondent is asked to tell stories about a series of pictures. The stories are then scored for the presence of themes indicating an orientation toward or concern with achievement or power.

The Achievement Motive

Almost all of the original research on the achievement motive was done with male subjects. McClelland and his colleagues (1953) found that for men, achievement motivation could be shown to relate to performance in competitive situations in the lab as well as to later career performance. They also found that men's achievement motivation scores tended to rise, often dramatically, when subjects were given "achievement-involving" task instructions—that is, instructions that stressed that subjects' task performance would reflect their intelligence, organizational ability, or leadership capacity. These relationships did not hold for female subjects, however. McClelland and his colleagues summarized their findings on gender differences in achievement motivation as follows: (1) Women get higher achievement motive scores than men do under neutral conditions; (2) women do not show an increase in achievement motive scores when given achievement-involving instructions; and (3) women's achievement motive scores relate to their performance in the same way that men's do (p. 178).

The finding that women's achievement motivation did not seem to be easily aroused by the instructions that researchers had found to be achievement involving for men was interpreted by many people to mean that women simply had less need for achievement than did men. This interpretation fit nicely with the observation that women did indeed appear to be achieving less than men in many fields of endeavor and reinforced the assumption that women did not have great achievements because they weren't particularly interested. Since achievement appeared to be mainly a male preserve, researchers focused on males. Atkinson's (1958) classic work on achievement motivation mentions women in only a single footnote, and McClelland's (1961) book, *The Achieving Society,* omits any mention of women. It was only in the context of interest generated by the feminist movement that researchers again turned their attention to achievement orientation in females.

When researchers finally tackled the problem of why women, who seemed to have the same basic amount of achievement motivation as men, did not pursue achievement in many situations, they zeroed in on the differing rewards attached to success for women and men. They began to realize, for example, that women and men might each attach higher value to performing well in gender-appropriate than in gender-inappropriate areas of achievement. Thus, for instance, two psychologists who reviewed the literature on achievement socialization in females noted that, in contrast to intellectual, artistic, mechanical, and athletic skills, social skills are somewhat unique in being viewed as "feminine" in our culture—and women tend to respond with increased achievement arousal when given achievement-involving instructions emphasizing social skills (Stein & Bailey, 1973). The research that brought the most attention to how people's motivation to achieve might be affected by their awareness of the gender-linked consequences of success focused on a motive that was labeled *fear of success.*

Fear of Success.   According to a widely accepted analysis of achievement motivation (Atkinson & Feather, 1966), the motivation to achieve that is aroused in a given situation depends on three things: the strength of the person's underlying achievement motivation, the probability of success, and the incentive or reward value of success in that situation. Using this approach, it can be seen that even if a person has a very strong motive to achieve, this motive might not be aroused in a particular situation if, for example, the person perceives that the consequences of such success would be negative (that is, if the incentive value of success is low).

Matina Horner (1968) hypothesized that since achievement in many areas is considered inappropriate, or at least unusual, for women, a woman achieving in one of these areas might feel she was losing some aspect of her femininity. Thus, success for a woman would be an ambivalent experience, having both the positive consequences of self-respect and external recognition and the negative consequences of smarting under the real or imagined disapproval of others for being unfeminine. If the negative consequences appeared to outweigh the positive ones, motivation to achieve in a given situation would be low.

Horner's theory arose from her own observations that successful career women often seemed to feel a need to demonstrate that besides being successful in their vocational sphere, they were also successful as "real" women—that they were loving mothers, devoted wives, marvelous cooks, and impeccable housekeepers. These women perceived that society found it unacceptable for a woman to be outstandingly successful at her career if that success led her to give short shrift to her "proper" feminine role. Such observations led Horner to postulate that for women, the negative consequences in terms of loss of femininity would often outweigh the positive consequences of success, leading to a situation where the woman developed a motive to *avoid* success. Since success for a man rarely implies any loss of masculinity, Horner predicted, a motive to avoid success would appear much less frequently in men than in women.

Horner (1968) began testing her predictions on a group of University of Michigan students by giving them a projective test that she hoped would measure "fear of success" (the anticipation of negative consequences for success). In the test, female students were asked to complete a story beginning with the following sentence: "After first-term finals, Anne finds herself at the top of her medical school class" (Horner, 1970, p. 59). Males completed a similar story about a medical student named John. As Horner had predicted, many of the women (65 percent) told stories that incorporated either negative consequences of Anne's success (social rejection, anxiety over her normality or femininity) or denied the possibility of that success by attributing it to an error in marking, cheating, and so on. A common theme in many of the stories was that Anne's success threatened her relationship with the man in her life or with men in general. In contrast, fewer than 10 percent of the men told stories in which any negative consequences came to John because of his success.

Horner's findings at first appeared to support her theory that, because of their gender-role socialization, women and men had acquired different amounts of the motivation to avoid success. The theory struck a chord with the popular media, and magazine articles explained glibly that the reason women so seldom achieved eminence was because they had a basic flaw: They were afraid of success. The ready acceptance of the theory was not surprising in an era when discrimination against women in many areas was just beginning to be seriously questioned. After all, it blamed women in large part for their failure to make an impact. However, the acceptance turned out to be premature, as researchers who followed up on Horner's work were quick to discover (Condry & Dyer, 1976; Tresmer, 1976).

Some critics argued that, first, there was no certainty that Horner's projective test actually tapped a stable internal motive. Perhaps the negative consequences described in the stories represent not a personal fear of success but simply an awareness that negative consequences can result from success, particularly for women. This argument gains support from the finding that male subjects, given the opportunity to tell a story about Anne instead of John, also tend to include many negative consequences for her success. Similarly, women as well as men tend more often to complete the story about John without negative consequences (Monahan, Kuhn, & Shaver, 1974). Thus, the results of this type of test may be reflecting a cultural stereotype that success is often aversive for women, instead of (or as well as) an actual motive to avoid success. Research does show that successful individuals, male or female, are described as more masculine than unsuccessful individuals (Gerber, 1984). In addition, women are apparently more sensitive than men to others' evaluations of their performance (Roberts, 1991), making it likely that they will be bothered by any negative reactions others might have.

Second, it can be argued that the gender difference in fear of success is more apparent than real. In a summary of 64 studies, Paludi (1984) found that the proportion of females showing fear of success ranged from 6 percent to 93 percent, with a median of 49 percent, while for males the proportions ranged from 7 percent to 95 percent, with a median of 45 percent. The reason for the wide variation may lie partly in the story cues used. Cherry and Deaux (1978) found that men indicated more fear of success when writing about John in nursing school than in medical school, whereas the reverse was true for women writing about Anne. They concluded that although both women and men have an awareness and perhaps a fear of the negative consequences of succeeding in a "gender-inappropriate" situation, there is little reason to believe that women fear success in general more than men do. Research using black female and male graduate students also supports the interpretation that fear of success represents a flight from inappropriate situations (Fleming, 1982). Both the men and the women in Fleming's sample showed fear of success that could be interpreted as motivation to avoid subjectively role-inappropriate behaviors. Women who showed fear of success were trying to develop career interests compatible with a strong commitment to home and husband, while the men who showed fear of success "seemed to be reacting to negative racial stereotypes and attempting to live up to a new image of the black male" (p. 339). Fear of success, then, may be a situational rather than a motivational variable, with women or men showing more fear depending on the particular situation described. In fact, when no situation is described, and subjects are merely told that "Anne (or John) succeeded," no difference in fear of success is seen between male and female stories (Gravenkemper & Paludi, 1983).

If the fear of success stories are really reflections of a realistic appraisal of the negative consequences that might arise from success in gender-inappropriate situations, it might be reasonable to predict that the more traditional an individual is, the more that person's achievement-related feelings and behavior might be affected by situational variables. Some researchers have found fear of success scores to be associated with low "masculinity" scores and feminine gender-typing (Cano, Solomon, & Holmes, 1984; Mulig, Haggerty, Carballosa, Cinnick, & Madden, 1985; Wong, Kettlewell, & Sproule, 1985). However, this relationship seems to hold for men as well as women, so it seems to be a low level of instrumentality, the quality most clearly measured by the masculinity scales on gender-typing questionnaires, rather than adherence to traditional roles, that is related to fear of success scores.

In summary, there is no reason to believe that women and men differ in the strength of their basic motivations toward success. However, the research stimulated by the fear of success concept has shown clearly that individuals are sensitive to the social consequences of their achievement behavior, and that such consequences are perceived to be different for women and men in particular situations. Perceived institutional and social barriers rather than motivational ones are responsible for the different achievement behaviors of women and men.

The Power Motive

Research on the power motive has followed much the same pattern as that for achievement. Early research was conducted on male subjects, but when female subjects were eventually studied, it was found that the two gender groups did not differ in their power motive scores under neutral conditions. Also, both women and men responded with increased power motivation scores to power-arousing procedures

(Stewart & Winter, 1976; Winter & Stewart, 1978). For both women and men, a high need for power is associated with acquiring formal institutionalized power through leadership roles or offices, and with choosing careers that involve having direct, legitimate interpersonal power over others (Winter & Stewart, 1978). Once again, then, it appears that the difference in men's and women's ascendance to positions of prestige and influence cannot be attributed to gender differences in motivational variables.

Defining Achievement and Power

Some research suggests that women and men may differ in the way they define *achievement* and *power,* and thus in the ways they find to satisfy these needs. For example, for women more than for men, success at social relationships may be experienced as an achievement, since the area of social relations is one in which it is acceptable for females to excel (Stein & Bailey, 1973). Congruent with this idea, women who are oriented toward the traditional feminine role show high achievement motivation only under conditions designed to arouse affiliation, whereas women who accept achievement behavior as part of the feminine role respond to the same kinds of achievement-arousing conditions that men do (Gralewski & Rodgon, 1980).

The definition of achievement used in most psychological measures of motivation is likely too narrow, tapping only the traditional, male-oriented factors of direct, competitive achievement. People view not only public mastery situations but also personal and interpersonal events in achievement terms (Travis, Phillippi, & Henley, 1991). In fact, when separate components of the achievement motive are studied, males are generally found to score higher than females on the drive to compete with and be better than others, while females are found to outscore males on orientation to work for its own sake (Spence & Helmreich, 1978). Another difference between the two gender groups may be that, following the dictates of their gender role, more women than men may try to satisfy their achievement needs vicariously through the successes of their spouses, children, or bosses, rather than directly through their own achievements (Lipman-Blumen & Leavitt, 1976). The latter pattern may be true for the satisfaction of power needs as well.

Where differences do exist between women and men in the outlets they find for their achievement needs, such differences may be due not so much to definition as to opportunity and self-confidence. We have seen that people are quite sensitive to the social approval or disapproval that their achievement behavior elicits. Women trying to achieve in a masculine-oriented arena hold overly negative self-evaluations (Beyer, 1990). No doubt many women have found that they face fewer negative and more positive consequences for achievement when they avoid competition with males and when they support the achievement efforts of their families rather than themselves. Similarly, men have discovered that competition and winning is a core aspect of the masculine role (Cicone & Ruble, 1978) and that such an approach to achievement gains them more points than does a strictly task-oriented approach. Thus, differing styles of achievement for women and men reflect, to some extent, a reaction to social expectations imposed by gender roles. However, constraints are forged by more than simple approval or disapproval. A woman who is at home caring for children may find few opportunities for achievement other than through her husband; a secretary may find it more practical to bask in the satisfaction of her boss's successes than to find any source of public recognition for herself.

The stereotypically masculine and feminine patterns of meeting achievement needs can both be problematic. The literature of the feminist movement is filled with examples of women's dissatisfaction with the expectation that they limit their achievement drives to achieving social success or to achieving through the lives of those whom they nurture (e.g., Bernard, 1974; Friedan, 1963). For men, on the other hand, the emphasis on competition and the material rewards of achieving can be the source of considerable stress and can interfere with personal relationships and the exploration of less prestigious, but potentially more satisfying lifestyles. An interesting perspective on the male side of the problem can be gleaned from an examination of the "fear of success" stories told by males. Although the stories told by females tend to stress fear of social rejection as a result of success, those told by males often involve discovering the emptiness of success (Basow, 1986).

Women and men may also differ in the way they define and experience power. For one thing, men and boys consistently describe themselves as more powerful and stronger than do women and girls (Maccoby & Jacklin, 1974). This perception is not always accurate in terms of behavior. For example, in one study, high school women were more assertive than their male counterparts in response to simulated social situations, but these same women were more likely than the men to deny their own impact on others (Smye, Wine, & Moses, 1980).

Some theorists have suggested that women and men may conceive of and seek power differently: men by dominating others and women by developing a sense of their own abilities and strengths (Miller, 1977; Rich, 1976). Research has shown, though, that, when asked explicitly about what power means to them, college women and men do not differ in the proportions of each group that include themes of influence over others and achievement/self-worth in their definitions (Lips, 1985a). However, certain types of experiences were more linked to feelings of power for men than for women: having material possessions, being physically strong, and participation in sports. Other researchers have noted that men and women may satisfy their power motives differently, according to how the two gender groups are expected to behave (McClelland, 1975), and that the expression of a need for power is somewhat more likely to be tempered by socialization toward responsibility in females than in males (Winter & Barenbaum, 1985).

In considering gender differences in the way needs for achievement and power are expressed, it is important to remember that the value and prestige assigned to particular positions and accomplishments are not decreed by some absolute authority but are decided by social consensus. That consensus, in an androcentric or male-centered culture, reflects a tendency to value traditionally masculine accomplishments more than feminine ones. Thus, in our society, becoming a corporation president, writing a best-selling novel, hitting the million mark in record sales, hitting a record number of home runs, or getting a large research grant are considered achievements; raising three children is not. The popular definition of achievement has emerged in such a way that success in the traditionally feminine domain of home and family is simply taken for granted rather than treated as an accomplishment. When asked what she does, the woman who is a full-time homemaker has learned to answer diffidently that she is "just a housewife," although her job may well involve more work and higher levels of skill than many others that are more prestigious.

Perhaps nowhere can the disregarding of traditional feminine achievements be seen more clearly than in the difficult quest for the history of women (e.g., Miles, 1988; Rasmussen, Rasmussen, Savage, & Wheeler, 1976). A reading of traditional history books might well give one the impression that women had not even been present during most major historical events or at least that they had made no noticeable impact on the way things turned out. In North American history, one reads references to "the pioneer and his wife" (is the wife not also a pioneer?) with the realization that even when working against terrible odds and under the most difficult and dangerous conditions, a woman devoting herself to her home and family is considered merely to be doing her duty rather than accomplishing anything special. Thus, although men and women are encouraged to pursue achievement and power in different ways, these ways are neither equally visible nor equally valued.

Access to Resources

Power and achievement merge to some extent into a single concept when power is conceptualized as the ability to get things done (Goodchilds, 1979). As noted in Chapter 11, the exercise of power depends on access to certain types of resources: the capacity to reward or punish others, credentials of expertise, legitimacy of authority or position, being identified with or liked by others, and information (French & Raven, 1959). Within these categories fall such specific resources as money, education, employment, physical health and strength, status, legal rights, and time. Individuals differ widely in their access to resources, but the group differences between women and men are consistent: In almost every category of resource, men have more access and control than do women. In addition, when women try to increase their access to these resources, their efforts are often regarded as illegitimate because they are violating established norms. In North America, employed women earn less than two-thirds of what men earn (Abella, 1984; Sapiro, 1986). Although the majority of women are in the labor force, they are clustered in low-status jobs with little chance for advancement. Women also do considerably more unpaid household labor than men do, a situation that puts women at a disadvantage with respect to the precious personal resources of time and energy to accomplish other things (Lips, 1986b). Women are much more likely than men are to live below the poverty line; this is especially true for women of color. In the United States, among blacks, about 18 percent of all men and 30 percent of all women fall below the poverty line, as compared to 7.3 percent of white men and 11 percent of white women (Shortridge, 1989). In Canada, native women and Central and South American women have the lowest incomes of all groups, earning only 77 percent of the already low national female average (Abella, 1984). Women have less access to political power than men do. Of the 11 oldest democracies in the world, 10 waited until the twentieth century to give women the right to vote, ending with Switzerland in 1971. Women are underrepresented in political decision-making positions. In the United States, men outnumber women 98 to 2 in the Senate and women make up only about 6.2 percent of the House of Representatives. In Canada, women had only achieved a representation of 13.6 percent in the federal Parliament by 1988. Females' and males' access to schools is about equal in North America; however, from a world perspective, the situation with respect to education is less egalitarian. Around the world, 80 million more boys than girls are receiving a primary and secondary education, and 130 million more adult women than men have not learned to read and write (Sivard, 1985). These statistics could go on for pages, but the ones already listed make the point: Men as a group have more access than women do to the resources on which power is based. Yet women who complain about these inequities are still frequently treated as if they are being unreasonable, and those who have pioneered women's entry into the many arenas that have been closed to them have been, at every stage, the subject of disapproval and ridicule. Sometimes this disapproval has come, and continues to come, from other women. While the British suffragettes were struggling to gain the vote for women, they were being opposed by Queen Victoria herself, who was, she said, "most anxious to enlist everyone to join in checking this mad wicked folly of Women's Rights, with all its attendant horrors" (quoted in Nunes & White, 1973, p. 10). While North American feminists have been struggling to improve women's access to resources, they have been vigorously opposed by an anti-feminist women's movement in the United States (Ehrenreich, 1981) and by the R.E.A.L. (Realistic, Equal, Active for Life) women in Canada (Dubinsky, 1985; Eichler, 1986).

A conflict theory perspective on the opposition to the feminist movement suggests that such opposition stems from the fact that certain groups benefit while others are systematically deprived under the traditional pattern of gender relations. Those who benefit are more likely to be men than women, but many women may be convinced that a system in which males hold most of the authority is ultimately beneficial for all concerned. In fact, it has been argued that, in order for a group to exert effective control over a society, that group must not merely secure power but also establish, in the eyes of subordinate groups, its *right* to wield such power (Weber, 1965). In Weber's words, the group needs to *legitimate* its power, thus achieving authority over—or the right to dominate—subordinate groups. It appears that men have been, and remain, quite successful at convincing women that male dominance of society is legitimate. Weber's analysis, which lists three basic sources for legitimizing power, offers some clues as to how male authority became so entrenched. Authority can stem from tradition (ruling groups may rule because they have always done so), from charisma (leaders of ruling groups have personal magnetism or charm that induces others to follow them), or from rational means (the use of legal and judicial mechanisms). Male authority certainly has tradition on its side, and, once in authority, it is easier to have access to the legal and judicial mechanisms to reinforce that authority. Even charisma, which might reasonably be expected to be evenly distributed between women and men, may lie more strongly with men because men more than women are taught to be assertive and to expect others to follow them. Thus, all three sources of authority can be seen to work to make male dominance of society appear legitimate. Furthermore, as Weber also notes, once a group is in power, it can maintain its legitimacy in the eyes of subordinate groups partly through the control and dissemination of ideas—and we have already noted the difficulties that have traditionally greeted women writers, politicians, and other activists. Once in place, the dominance of one group by another is reinforced by so many factors that it is extremely difficult to dismantle, and the pattern of differential access to resources is not easily changed.

Women's and men's differential access to resources has implications on both the group and individual levels. It affects the capacity that each group has to make an impact, and it affects the chances that female and male individuals have to achieve particular goals. For example, a female politician, even if she does not want to be identified with so-called "women's issues," must deal with the fact that she is in a minority position and that this position will color her acceptance by others and affect her ability to be effective in her job. As Agnes Macphail, the first woman elected to the Canadian House of Commons, recalled about her 14 years as the lone woman in that institution,

> I found that I couldn't quietly do my job without being ballyhooed like the bearded lady. . . . I couldn't open my mouth to say the simplest thing without it appearing in the papers. I was a curiosity, a freak. And you know the way the world treats freaks. (Cochrane, 1977, p. 42)

Men, too, cannot evade the implications of their gender group membership when it comes to achievement and power. In mixed-sex situations, men are more likely than women are to be assigned leadership roles, whether they seek them or not (Lockheed & Hall, 1976; Nyquist & Spence, 1986), and unsuccessful men are subject to more negative evaluations than are unsuccessful women (Fogel & Paludi, 1984). Perhaps because more resources are assigned to men, more is expected of them. Thus, both genders carry the weight of their intergroup differences in access to resources when they are in situations involving power and achievement. These differences influence not only what women and men can accomplish, but how they try to accomplish it and how their accomplishments are evaluated by themselves and others. As described in the following section, the strategies that women and men employ to gain influence and make an impact are shaped by the fact that women, more often than men, are operating from a position of weakness in terms of resources, and that people tend to see efforts to change the accepted distribution of resources as illegitimate and threatening.

Strategies of Influence

People use a bewildering array of strategies in their attempts to use the resources they have to exert influence and to acquire more resources. Psychologists have made various attempts to categorize these strategies (e.g., Cody, McLaughlin, & Jordan, 1980; Falbo, 1977; Kipnis, Castell, Gergen, & Mauch, 1976) and to examine the relationship between the resources a person controls and the particular interpersonal influence strategies she or he favors. Persons who operate from positions of relative strength (that is, who control more resources) tend to use "strong" authoritative influence techniques, while those in weak positions rely on "weaker" tactics based on accommodation and dependency (Kipnis, 1984; Howard, Blumstein, & Schwartz, 1986). Furthermore, those who control more resources or who are in initially dominant positions tend to use a greater variety of influence strategies than do those with less power (Kipnis, Schmidt, & Wilkinson, 1980).

The extent to which such findings on interpersonal influence would generalize to intergroup influence is not certain. However, when groups are in a hierarchical power relationship, as men and women are, group membership itself becomes a resource for interpersonal influence. Not surprisingly, then, researchers have examined the relationship between gender and influence tactics.

Paula Johnson (1976), a pioneer in research on gender and power, suggests that there are three major dimensions on which the use of power to exert influence is affected by gender stereotypes: directness, concreteness, and competence. According to her analysis, gender norms dictate that men's influence styles can be direct, concrete, and competent, while women's should be indirect, personal, and based on helplessness or dependence.

Indirect vs. Direct Influence.   Whereas direct influence is demonstrated when a person uses power openly, by giving an order or making a request, indirect influence is exercised when the individual obtains the desired outcome while trying to keep the other person unaware of the influence. Indirect influence is often called "manipulation." Johnson (1976) suggests that in our society there are many constraints against directness by women and that, consequently, women more than men tend to rely on indirect influence. Many feminist writers have noted that a woman who uses direct power is quickly labeled unfeminine, castrating, and bitchy. Furthermore, even a casual perusal of the popular magazines devoted to advising women about interpersonal relationships indicates that women are actually instructed to use manipulative rather than direct strategies to get what they want ("Let him think it was his idea").

The use of indirect influence, although potentially effective in the short run, may have long-term negative consequences for the user. When the source of influence is concealed, the person wielding it may not be regarded as powerful, may be kept in a subordinate position, and is not likely to see herself or himself as a strong person. A person who is actually wielding a good deal of influence indirectly may get little credit for it. Being the "power behind the throne" or the woman behind the successful man may have its gratifications, but probably not as many as being *on* the throne, or claiming the success for oneself.

Personal vs. Concrete Resources.   An individual's attempt to exercise influence is given weight by the amount and nature of resources that person controls. The implied threat in any influence attempt is that a refusal will be met by invoking the resources at the power holder's command in order to induce compliance. Johnson (1976) suggests that resources can be divided into two categories: those that depend on personal relationships, such as liking and approval, and those that are concrete and independent of relationships, such as money, knowledge, and physical strength. She argues that in our society men have considerably more control over concrete resources than do women (an argument borne out by the statistics given at the beginning of this section) and that women therefore rely on personal resources more than men do.

Personal resources are certainly not unimportant. The threat of a denial of love, affection, or sex can be a very powerful way to induce cooperation from a person to whom that denial matters deeply. Nonetheless, as Johnson (1976) points out, this type of influence is effective only in the context of a personal relationship. Also, it has the disadvantage of leaving the influencer highly dependent on others. Although a woman may hold great personal power in an individual relationship, it is often not the sort that generalizes beyond the relationship or holds up in a court of law. For example, a woman may hold a great deal of power based on personal resources such as affection and sexuality with respect to her husband, easily gaining his compliance to her wishes. This same woman could, in some parts of North America, be threatened with divorce on the grounds of desertion if she refused to move with her husband to a new home; no legal threat for comparable behavior could be applied to the husband.

Helplessness vs. Competence.   It is sometimes possible to get others to do things for us either by acting competent, taking charge, and giving orders, or by acting incompetent and helpless, and throwing ourselves on their mercy. A major theme in our gender roles is that men are strong and competent, women weak and helpless—a theme that is reinforced in everything from children's stories about the handsome prince rescuing the damsel in distress to television serials in which, week after week, heroes such as "McGyver" and "Jake" (of "Jake and the Fat Man") save hapless women from pursuit by crazed killers or KGB agents. Johnson (1976) suggests that because women are often in situations where they are not regarded as or do not feel competent, they tend to rely on helplessness as a mode of influence more than men do. By acting helpless, women can get men to take on responsibilities and do tasks for them, particularly those tasks that fit society's expectations for the masculine role. It should be mentioned, though, that men are not above using helplessness themselves as an influence tactic, as many women have discovered when they first asked their spouse to do laundry, cook supper, or change the baby's diaper.

Johnson suggests that helplessness, though effective in the short run, does not establish its users as strong influencers and may contribute to both low status and low self-esteem.

Do Women and Men Really Use Power Differently?

Johnson's (1976) research on people's reactions to power use in a hypothetical situation (one student trying to get another to change his or her opinion on a legal case) suggests that men and women are *expected* to use power in different ways. Given a list of 15 different methods of influence in the hypothetical situation, respondents were asked to indicate whether the influencer was male or female. Results showed that coercion based on concrete resources, competence based on legitimacy or expertise, and the direct use of informational power were expected more of male influencers, while the use of reward based on personal resources and sexuality was seen as significantly more characteristic of females. Johnson suggests that men are allowed to use many different forms of influence, depending on the situation, while women are more severely restricted to the less aggressive types. This finding is reminiscent of the finding by Kipnis and his colleagues (1980), cited earlier in this chapter, that persons operating from strong positions use a greater variety of influence tactics than do those whose positions are weaker. If men really are allowed to use more kinds of influence strategies than women are, perhaps it is no wonder that some women resist the changes in gender roles advocated by feminists. These women may fear that if they are "liberated," their traditional feminine modes of influence may no longer be effective (e.g., if women are recognized as being as competent as men are, they can't get their way by acting help-less), and yet they do not anticipate being comfortable with or good at the more direct, competent tactics. Consequently, they may foresee a "liberation" that results in a net loss, rather than a net gain, of power for women.

Although Johnson's (1976) research addresses the question of what influence styles are stereotypically associated with women and men, it does not answer the question of whether women and men actually do use power differently. Earlier research by Johnson herself and more recent studies by other researchers do indicate, however, that different influence strategies tend to be favored by the two gender groups, and that the target of the influence makes a difference as to the choice of strategy (Cowan, Drinkard, & McGavin, 1984; White, 1988). Johnson, P. (1974) gave male and female group leaders a choice of six influence messages to persuade their group to work faster at a task. The male leaders often chose the persuasive message that stressed their own exper-tise, while female leaders avoided it. The female leaders were more likely to use the per-suasive message that emphasized their own helplessness and dependency on the workers—a strategy that male leaders, without exception, rejected. In a study using a simulated organizational setting, another group of researchers placed women and men in positions of equal power and investigated whether they would use different strategies to influence their subordinates (Instone, Major, & Bunker, 1983). They found that, relative to males, females made fewer influence attempts, used fewer types of influence strategies, and relied more on coercion and less on reward. These differences seemed to be mediated by lower self-confidence among the women than the men. Other or-ganizational research also suggests that males are more likely to use direct, assertive strategies, while females are more likely to use indirect, submissive ones (Fairhurst, 1985). However, one study of employees in a business environment found that men were more likely than women to report that they relied on charm, manipulation, and appearance to achieve personal and organizational objectives (DuBrin, 1989).

Although the frequency with which women and men report using various strate-gies differs, women and men do not seem to differ overall in their *order* of preference for particular strategies. For both men and women, the influence strategy ranked highest in order of preference is "use reason and logic," followed by "simply state my desires," "offer to compromise," and "convince, persuade, and coax" (White & Roufail, 1989). Yet, in terms of absolute frequency of reported use, men are more likely than women to use high-pressure tactics such as arguing and yelling, threatening force, and forceful assertion as first-choice strategies; women are more likely than men to report using negative emotion (pleading, crying, acting cold, getting angry and demanding) as their first choice.

One reason for a gender difference in influence strategies may well be the impact of social expectations for women and men. For example, direct, assertive influence attempts by women often engender social disapproval in a way that similar strategies by men do not (Gervasio & Crawford, 1989). Gender differences in the use of influence strategies probably stem not just from role expectations, however, but from initial power differences. It has already been noted that people operating from a position of strength can use stronger, more assertive influence strategies, and a wider range of such strategies. Women frequently control fewer resources than men do, and are thus operating from a position of relative weakness in their influence attempts. An interesting case in point revolves around the resource of legitimacy. In many cultures, including our own, men hold more of the positions of authority than women do—positions that give them a legitimate right to make decisions and command obedience. In fact, in a culture that tends to ascribe higher status to males than to females and to consider that the man is the head of the family, even men who are not in formal positions of authority are still viewed as having some rights to exert authority over women. Obviously, a position of authority lends considerable force to any attempt to exercise influence directly. As Rosaldo (1974) notes, however, a person who tries to exercise a significant amount of influence independent of authority is regarded as manipulative, disruptive, and troublesome, and is generally not taken seriously as a powerful person. Thus, women must be cautious about open attempts to exercise influence from subordinate positions in organizations, and the woman who allows her power in the marriage relationship to show in public may risk an unflattering label (Bernard, 1972).

Legitimacy may vary according to the situation, of course, and with it the acceptability of certain kinds of influence tactics for females and males. Johnson and Goodchilds (1976) found that in a dating situation where the issue of sexual intimacy occurs, men are seen as using direct methods to influence a woman to have sexual intercourse and women are perceived as being capable of equal directness in turning a man down. In a reversal of this situation, however, subjects suggested that a woman would be quite indirect in her efforts to seduce a man and the man would be correspondingly indirect in refusing her. The researchers use these results to suggest that a person engaging in an out-of-role influence attempt is likely to be less direct than someone operating within his or her role expectations. A more general explanation might be, however, that the more legitimate a person perceives his or her demands to be, the more direct will be the mode of influence used.

Pat Mainardi's (1970) essay on the politics of housework provides a good example of the way that the perceived legitimacy of a person's argument can affect the influence tactics that are used. In it, she outlines the helpless and indirect tactics her husband used in his attempts to avoid doing his share of the housework. Of course, as a man, he was well within the rights of the traditional masculine role in refusing to do many household chores. However, in the course of the marriage, he had acknowledged the legitimacy of his wife's argument that housework should be shared, and this acknowledgment disallowed him the use of direct means of influence such as flat refusal. The arguments that he did use were as indirect ("Housework is too trivial to even talk about"), irrelevant ("Women's liberation isn't really a political movement"), and helpless ("I don't mind doing the housework, but I don't do it very well") as one might ever hope to find.

If it is indeed the case that the legitimacy of one's position increases one's capacity to use direct modes of influence, it would seem that the feminist attempts to legitimize the demands of women for equal rights will eventually make it easier for women to exercise direct power in a wide range of situations. There is, however, a fly in the ointment. "Rocking the boat" is almost always seen as illegitimate. Since, in challenging men's authority, feminists are trying to change a system that is considered by many to be not only normative but normal and natural, they may have trouble commanding the resource of legitimacy, and their influence attempts are bound to be regarded by some as merely disruptive, troublesome, and annoying.

Some Implications of the Differences.   The definition of power implicitly includes some freedom to decide how to act, while powerlessness implies a situation in which one is not free to decide or to act. When a person feels free to behave in a certain way, and then senses a threat to that freedom, the reaction is predictable: what psychologists label "reactance" (Brehm, 1966). *Reactance* is basically an effort to protect or regain the behavioral freedom that is threatened. It can manifest itself as anger and hostility toward the individual or institution that is doing the threatening. Because a threat to a person's freedom to behave in a particular way often comes from an influence attempt that is directed at that person, reactance is an important concept for understanding the effects of different influence tactics.

When a person is the target of influence based on coercion or expertise, he or she may feel a threat to behavioral freedom and be motivated to regain control by resisting the influence attempt (Rodin & Janis, 1979). However, when persons do comply with expert, coercive, or reward-based influence, they tend to attribute their compliance to external reasons and to suffer some loss of their sense of control. Both of these patterns are helpful in understanding the impact of stereotypically masculine and feminine influence styles on their users and targets. Women, operating from a weaker power base, often cannot afford to provoke reactance in their influence targets; they use more subtle, indirect influence strategies that are less likely to make the target feel threatened. Men, on the other hand, frequently having access to more resources with which to back their influence attempts, can be direct enough to arouse anger, hostility, and resistance. In a male–female relationship, if the woman uses an indirect and personal style of influence while the man tends to be more direct and concrete, it is likely that the two people will attribute their compliance to very different causes. When the woman complies with the man's wishes, she will attribute her behavior to pressure from him and she may thus feel little sense of control over or responsibility for her behavior. When the man complies with the woman, however, he may not even view his behavior as compliance. Instead, he may be responding to a manipulation that allows him to see his behavior as stemming from his own decision. He is thus able to maintain a sense of control and responsibility, and the couple's initial difference in the sense of power is reinforced. It is possible, then, that under certain conditions gender differences in influence styles can become a self-perpetuating cycle.

Resources, Strategies, and Political Power

For some people, the word *power* is synonymous with politics. Can the psychological analysis of power differences between women and men be applied to their behavior in the political arena? The answer to this question must begin with an examination of gender differences in political behavior.

In a democracy, one of the most basic political behaviors is voting in elections. In most countries, women have had to fight for the right to vote; among half the countries responding to a survey of embassies by the World Priorities organization, the average delay between men's and women's suffrage was 47 years. In the United States and Canada, women have had the right to vote since 1920. When suffrage for women was new, some women still felt that voting was inappropriate, and women's participation in elections lagged behind men's. In addition, women tended to be less educated than men, and studies show that education is related to political participation. However, the gender differences in voter turnout have now disappeared in both countries (Brodie & Vickers, 1982; Klein, 1984). Women are also now almost as active as men in grass roots–level politics; both groups do a lot of campaigning and behind-the-scenes work for political parties. Women's most common areas of political activity involve issues related to the social position of women and children (Deckard, 1983). At the citizen level, then, there is little difference between the political participation levels of women and men. Politics is still seen as a "masculine" endeavor by many people (Rosenwasser & Dean, 1989), however, and female (but not male) high school political activists see future family life as limiting the possibility for involvement in politics in adulthood (Romer, 1990).

At levels of politics above the grass roots level, gender differences are quite dramatic. Women make up only a small percentage of the holders of public office and are less likely than men to be in leadership or elected governmental positions (Center for the American Woman and Politics, 1984). Within political parties, there has been a tendency for women to be assigned the supportive and "housekeeping" tasks (Brodie & Vickers, 1982). Some changes are evident, however. In Canada in 1991, the New Democratic Party became the first major party in North America to decide that women would comprise half of its nominations for federal elected office.

A power analysis of the situation described here suggests many reasons why women's and men's relatively equal participation in citizen level politics does not translate into more equal participation at the higher levels. First, gender ideology and custom still give men more legitimacy than women as leaders, political or otherwise (Brown 1979; Butler & Geis, 1990; Porter & Geis, 1981). Specifically in the realm of politics, surveys show that about 30 percent of Americans think that women do not belong in politics (Welch & Sigelman, 1982), about 10 percent say they would not vote for a woman under any circumstances (Sloane, 1983), and many voters tend to shy away from female candidates unless they are clearly better qualified than their male opposition (Basler, 1984; Sigelman, Thomas, Sigelman, & Ribich, 1986). Women also tend to have less access than men to the power base of expertise. They rate their understanding of politics lower than men do, although research does not support this perceived difference (Sapiro, 1983). Within political parties, women are much less likely than men to be chosen to perform strategic leadership tasks—tasks that are often the first step toward building the expertise and the loyal support that are crucial for seeking public office (Brodie & Vickers, 1982). When women do run for office, they are often hampered by a lack of access to funds, a concrete resource that is now the sine qua non of an effective campaign. Moreover, the campaigns that they wage are, much more often than for men, for "lost cause" seats. For years, female candidates have been the "sacrificial lambs" in elections, gaining their parties' nominations most easily in constituencies where there was little realistic expectation that they would be elected (Brodie & Vickers, 1982).

Despite the disadvantages under which women have labored in the political arena, there are signs that female candidates and female holders of high political office are gaining more legitimacy. In both the United States and Canada, more women are running as candidates in elections than ever before. During the 1980s, Americans had their first opportunity to vote for a female vice-presidential candidate—Geraldine Ferraro—on the ticket of a major party. The 1980s and 1990s have also seen the election of female governors in several states, including Texas—stereotypically a bastion of male power. Canadians have seen the roles of Speaker of the House of Commons, governor general, and provincial premier filled by women for the first time. In both countries, women have gained some power during election campaigns as a special interest group. In Canada, the 1985 federal election saw, for the first time, the leaders of the three major parties stage a televised debate specifically on "women's issues," and subsequent years have seen the selection of a woman to lead one of the three major political parties. Beyond North America, too, changes can be seen. For instance, in France, where women did not get the vote until 1944 and where, until 1964, a woman had to have her husband's permission to open a bank account or get a passport, an outspoken feminist woman, Edith Cresson, was appointed prime minister in 1991. In Ireland, a strong feminist woman, Mary Robinson, was elected president in 1990.

It is no accident that political parties have started to put somewhat more emphasis on women as an interest group. Over the past decade, women have organized to increase their power as a pressure group—by increasing their political skills and expertise, setting up funds to support women candidates or to lobby for specific issues, and by organizing mutually supportive coalitions among groups of women. Women's caucuses within the political parties push for the adoption of issues important to women as platform planks. Nonpartisan organizations such as the League of Women Voters in the United States and the National Action Committee on the Status of Women in Canada keep these issues visible both during and after the elections. The political system is still largely dominated by men, but women are building the power to make an increasing impact.

Power in Organizations and Institutions

As we indicated in the preceding discussion of political power, even when women's and men's access to particular institutions is nominally equal, or almost so, women are more likely than men to be relegated to marginal positions within the institution and to wield relatively less power. Sometimes it is suggested that men have more of "what it takes" to hold leadership positions than women do. However, the reasons for the gender differences in organizational power are more complex than that. They are built into the structure of the organizations themselves, and into the social context in which these organizations exist.

Research within organizations indicates that particular constraints and requirements in the way organizations run affect the power available to individuals within them. For instance, Rosabeth Moss Kanter's (1975) research, which began as an attempt to isolate the variables that separate women from career success in organizations, showed that the leadership behavior of individuals was more strongly related to the position they held than to their gender. Poor leadership and success skills were found among people in token positions, people in dead-end jobs, and people in positions of nominal leadership that carried no real power. People in these positions were characterized by rigidity and hostility toward outsiders and powerful superiors, and they appeared to have more concern for socializing than for advancement. Unfortunately for women, they tended to hold more of these problematic positions than did men. Kanter concluded that the stereotypes about women being poor managers were based on women's relegation to powerless organizational positions.

One thing that researchers have found to be an important determinant of an individual's power and success in an organization is that person's access to informal networks of communication and exchange. Managers must coordinate the activities of many people within a work group, as well as negotiate with members of other groups or organizations. In performing these functions, managers cannot rely solely on the formal power that goes with their positions, but must use informal power based on reciprocation of favors and sharing of information. Doing this successfully requires maintaining a large number of good relationships. However, for a number of reasons, the maintenance of such networks may be more difficult for women than for men. First, the woman is often in a minority or token status and so does not easily fit in to the informal networks of her male colleagues. In fact, in what Bernard (1976) has called the "stag effect," women may find that the most important informal meeting places for their male colleagues are off limits, or at least unwelcoming, to women. Second, women are more likely than men to be doing double duty as homemakers and businesspersons, and so simply have less time for informal discussions after work or other "optional" activities. Third, informal organizational networks are often based on male modes of communication and shared experiences, making it more difficult for women, with less background in common, to fit in (Hennig & Jardim, 1977).

Women's relative lack of access to informal networks within and outside of an organization limits their influence. They may have more trouble obtaining rewards for their subordinates, for instance. Such a situation can become a vicious circle, as subordinates may lose respect for a manager who appears powerless, thus further diminishing her power (Kanter, 1979; Ragins & Sundstrom, 1989). In addition, a lack of access to informal networks can hinder a woman's chances of being hired or promoted. For example, Dexter (1985) notes that women have difficulty achieving partnerships in major accounting firms, largely because of their lack, relative to men, of third-party relationships. Partners are expected to bring business into the firm, and they fulfill this function by maintaining large networks of relationships with community and business leaders through formal and informal organizations. Since many businesses are headed by men, and the organizations in which the socializing takes place are restricted to men or at least are extremely male-dominated, women have many fewer opportunities than men do to contact other business leaders. Making a woman a partner in the firm is thus viewed as a risk to the profitability of the firm.

In looking at the larger culture that provides the setting for organizations, it is not difficult to see how the ideology surrounding gender contributes to the maintenance of male dominance of them. As Barbara Polk (1974) notes in an article on the sources of male power, since men have shaped society's institutions, they tend to fit the value structure of such institutions. Thus, for example, the masculine gender role matches certain professional and business roles (lawyer, business executive, university president) better than does the feminine gender role. In a pattern that would be comic if it were not so aggravating, women trying to fit their behavior to the requirements of such roles are sometimes accused of acting masculine.

Certain institutions are imbued so strongly with the notion of male dominance that women are barred from even trying to fit into leadership roles. Many religions, for example, are built on the idea of a male god ruling the universe from outside. Such an image serves to legitimize male control of worldly institutions and acts very specifically as a barrier to women's participation in such formal and ceremonial leadership positions as priest, minister, rabbi, or ayatollah. Many feminists have argued that the pervasive image of "God the Father" runs deeply in our culture, affecting even people who have consciously rejected religious dogmas, and that such imagery must be replaced if the culture is to develop a new vision of women and men (e.g., Daly, 1973; Ruether, 1983; Starhawk, 1979). Certainly, since religion has a large impact on people's values and their conceptions of what is right and wrong, the pervasive acceptance of male dominance within major institutional religions is not a trivial matter for women and men.

Maintaining the Status Quo: How Hierarchies Perpetuate Themselves

Although many people, female and male, say that they believe in equality between the sexes, male dominance is not easily banished from most situations. The problem is that many of women's and men's habits of thought and behavior act to perpetuate the power difference between them: Learned patterns of verbal and nonverbal behavior perpetuate status distinctions; implicit stereotypes bias perceptions before they even register in awareness; and the metamorphic effects of holding power have sometimes caused men to justify their dominance by inflating their sense of their own worth and devaluing that of women.

Verbal and Nonverbal Behavior

In an earlier chapter, the role played by language in maintaining the status difference between females and males was noted. The habitual use of *he* to mean any person, of *man* to mean people, makes people feel as if females are exceptions. Women who have changed their linguistic habits to avoid the generic *he* actually think more easily of females in response to sex-indefinite cues than do those who use traditional linguistic forms (Khosroshahi, 1989). The terms of address used for males and females also help to reinforce the status difference. Men are men, but women are girls or gals, chicks or broads. It is not uncommon to hear 50-year-old women referred to as *the girls*, or to hear a male manager refer to his middle-aged secretary as *my girl*. Even a woman's name often incorporates her marital status (Miss or Mrs.), and when a woman marries she is still generally expected to take her husband's name rather than vice versa. Finally, the use of the term *ladies*, with its implied delicacy, for adult females is incompatible with the idea of those adult females holding jobs as construction workers, police officers, perhaps even politicians.

Dominance is also conveyed by the degree to which one can control a conversation: how successfully one can interrupt another speaker and how much attention and response one is able to draw from others. Researchers have found that men talk more than women and that they maintain this difference partly by interrupting women and by not listening or responding to them (Eakins & Eakins, 1978). Such tactics, commonly used by males in cross-gender conversations, tend to discourage females and subdue their efforts at participation, allowing the males conversational control. These patterns of verbal participation tend to reinforce status differences between females and males.

Communication involves more than words, however, and psychologist Nancy Henley (1977; see also Henley & Freeman, 1989) was one of the first to suggest that nonverbal communication is even more influential than language in maintaining the power differential between women and men. Henley noted that much of the nonverbal communication that characterized male–female relationships followed a pattern parallel to that characterizing superior–subordinate relationships. Subordinates and women, for example, tend to show controlled, circumspect nonverbal behavior, to contract into a small amount of space, and to be touched by other people. Men and powerful people, on the other hand, tend to be more relaxed and expansive in their nonverbal behavior and to "touch downward" in the status hierarchy. Henley further suggested that when women break these rules by staring, touching men, or loosening their demeanor, their actions are interpreted not as power plays, which are unexpected in females, but as sexual invitations.

For several reasons, nonverbal behavior may pose a particularly resistant barrier to change in gender power relations (Mayo & Henley, 1981). First, a great deal of nonverbal behavior lies outside of awareness, so people often do not realize they are communicating power-related cues. Even if they do realize it, the habits are so strong and so routinized that they are very difficult to break. Second, much nonverbal behavior is learned through socialization by family, friends, and media and based on norms that are extremely slow to change. Third, women tend to be nonverbally adaptive—more partner-oriented than men in their nonverbal behavior. Studies of movement show that when men communicate dominance, their female partners tend to respond with low-power gestures; men, however, tend not to show similar nonverbal accommodation to high-power moves by women (Davis & Weitz, 1981). This tendency for women to adapt to men's behavior may slow down behavioral change for both genders. Finally, nonverbal behavior is particularly effective at communicating covert power messages. All types of nonverbal behaviors—gesture, touch, use of space, movement, gaze, facial expression—can be used to communicate power differentials. Moreover, they can be used even in situations where a power differential is verbally unacknowledged, or even denied. Thus, even in a male–female dyad in which both persons say that their status is equal, nonverbal behavior may reveal male dominance.

If nonverbal behavior is so potentially important to gender power relations, perhaps women and men should work hard at trying to change their nonverbal behavior. In fact, there is mixed evidence about how effective such a strategy would be. Some research suggests that, because of gender stereotypes, the same nonverbal cues that communicate power for men may not work for women. Porter and Geis (1981) found that, whereas for men, sitting at the head of the table is associated with being viewed as the leader of the group, this same cue had no impact on the perception of women as leaders in mixed-sex groups. They suggest that nonconscious gender stereotypes bias people's perceptions, making it difficult to "see" women as leaders, even when they engage in the very same nonverbal behavior that has helped men to establish leadership.

On the positive side, some research indicates that conscious manipulation of non-verbal cues can sometimes affect power-related aspects of the way a person is viewed and treated. Both female and male observers can accurately interpret different levels of visual dominance displayed by a woman who is interacting with either a man or another woman, rating her as more powerful in the conditions where her use of visual dominance cues is high (Ellyson, Dovidio, & Fehr, 1981). Thus, with some nonverbal behaviors at least, it may be possible to change the perception of one's status by changing one's nonverbal behavior. Nonverbal communication, then, can act either as a barrier to or facilitator of change in the power relationship between females and males (Mayo & Henley, 1981).

The Metamorphic Effects of Power

One more factor that tends to perpetuate status hierarchies is the effect of power on the power holder. According to a model developed by Kipnis (1972; Kipnis et al., 1976), if power holders use strong, controlling means of influence to gain compliance, they tend to believe that they have caused the other person's compliance. This belief leads them to devalue the other person, take credit for that person's performance, and try to increase social and psychological distance from that person. A powerful person, gaining a lot of compliance and a lot of (perhaps false) feedback that his or her ideas are good, easily develops an inflated sense of self-worth. Kipnis's model can readily be applied to the male–female situation. In many situations, men hold power over women, and women are taught to build up men's egos in order to keep them happy. In such a situation, it is quite likely that men develop an exaggerated sense of superiority with respect to women—a feeling that has the potential to become addictive. One of the reasons why the cycle of power differences between women and men is difficult to break, then, is that the very existence of a power difference probably has a tendency to make men feel they are superior to women. The converse of this pattern is that women, having so frequently been given second-class status, may learn to accept it as a true reflection of their worth. It appears that the power difference between men and women will not be easily wiped out, even when many people consciously see it as anachronistic. The narrowing of the gender gap in power requires a reshaping of many habits of thought and behavior.

Summary

There is a large difference in the visibility of women and men in positions of eminence and power. Research has established that no gender differences in basic achievement or power motivation account for these differences in visibility. It has indicated, however, that social barriers against achievement and power are often different for women and men, and that both sexes are sensitive to these barriers and tend to adjust their behavior accordingly. Consequently, attempts to change patterns of gender-related achievement without altering the social structure in which these patterns are embedded will probably not be overwhelmingly effective at getting more women into positions of visible eminence or power.

Power comes in many forms, and women and men may tend to use it differently. Men hold more of the concrete resources, such as wealth, than do women. Thus, men have more opportunities than women to wield power that involves threats or rewards based on these resources and to wield that power openly and directly. Women, on the other hand, may often find themselves in positions where the only way they can exert influence is through subtle manipulation or an appeal to personal, relationship-based resources. However, there is not necessarily any built-in gender difference in styles of influence. Rather, the difference is a result of a social structure that awards men higher status and stereotypes them as more competent than women. When women are in positions of authority or are making a demand that is perceived as legitimate, they can more easily use strong, direct influence styles.

As we have seen in this chapter, however, it is no small task to make a dramatic increase in the proportion of women holding positions of authority or eminence. The male–female status differences tend to be self-perpetuating, not only because of stereotyping but also because of women's relative exclusion from the "old boy" networks of influence in business, politics, and the professions, and because of habits of thought and behavior that frequently place women and men in complementary submissive–dominant roles. It has been noted, for instance, that such subtleties as who touches whom, who controls the conversation, and which pronoun is used to refer to humans in general all help to create a climate where power differences between women and men go unquestioned.

In closing this chapter, we might do well to remember that status hierarchies, power differentials, and dominance–submission are not necessarily "natural" aspects of the human condition. As Fromm (1973) noted in his classic work on human destructiveness, many so-called primitive hunting-gathering societies have been characterized by an absence of dominance or even permanent leadership associated with high-status qualities or skills. He suggested that the social structure adopted by a group of people determines, in large measure, their need for power differences and status hierarchies among themselves, and that the psychology of dominance–submission is an adaptation to a social order rather than a natural human condition that generates a particular social structure. Fromm's point is a good one to keep in mind while contemplating the kind of future society that might emerge in the course of women's struggle for a society in which *female* is not automatically associated with lower status than *male*. Men themselves now sometimes complain that the traditional masculine role, with its built-in authority, can be restrictive and burdensome. Perhaps, in the process of making changes in the power relationship between the sexes, the social structure will be altered in ways that make the dominance aspect of power less important.

For Additional Reading

Higonnet, A. (1990). *Berthe Morisot*. New York: Random House/Burlingame. This book tells the story of one woman's achievements: how she became a "great woman artist" though deprived of the encouragement, training, and rewards that were available to her male counterparts.

Lips, H. M. (1991). *Women, men, and power.* Mountain View, CA: Mayfield. A wide-ranging examination of the relationship between gender and power, including chapters on images of power, interpersonal power, and power in family, work, and politics.

Miles, R. (1988). *The women's history of the world.* New York: Harper & Row. The author unveils a wealth of economic and political achievement by women who have been overlooked or omitted from the history books.

Russell, D. E. H. (1989). *Lives of courage: Women for a new South Africa.* A sociologist provides firsthand portraits of the achievements of 24 women activists who have been part of the struggle to end apartheid.

13

Issues in the Workplace

HILARY LIPS AND NINA COLWILL

In 1990, Houston's chief of police, Elizabeth Watson, only three months into her new job, discovered that she was pregnant. As she prepared to leave her position, she braced herself for what she felt would be the inevitable flood of comments along the line of, "That's what you get when you put a woman in the job." Instead, to her surprise, her announcement was greeted with arguments that she should *not* quit— strong promises of support from the mayor, her five-member board of assistant chiefs, community members, and her husband. She stayed in the job, becoming probably the first American big-city police chief to have a baby during her tenure (Ryan, 1992).

Chief Watson's case is noteworthy because it is still unusual, not only for a woman to be so visibly successful in a male-dominated line of work, but also for that woman to receive so much encouragement and support for combining career and family responsibilities. Women have always worked—even in male-dominated fields—but rarely has their work achieved the same status and recognition as men's, and they have frequently been penalized for trying to "have it all."

To work, to be judged as competent in one's line of endeavor, to be recognized as a contributing member of society—these are important ingredients of the self-concept. One's employment forms such a critical part of one's identity that it is common practice to ask new acquaintances to disclose their occupation within seconds of being introduced to them. This question often takes the form "What do you do?" indicating that it is a basic question, the answer to which will classify the speaker. This very question provides a clue to the impact of gender stereotypes on social attitudes about work, for it is more likely to be addressed to a man than to a woman. Women are sometimes asked "Do you work?" or "What does your husband do?"—questions that reveal an expectation that women are unlikely to be in the work force. Such an expectation is based on ignorance of the facts: About 57 percent of Canadian and American women over the age of 16 are employed outside the home or actively looking for a job, and women make up about 47 percent of the paid labor force in the United States and Canada. Among women aged 25 to 34, the percentage of employed women rises to 72 percent for white women and 74 percent for black women. The frequency with which women are asked "Do you work?" also reveals a pervasive bias in the way that work is defined: No activity can be counted as work unless one gets paid for it. Unpaid work in the home, an activity to which many women devote a significant portion of their time and energy, is not granted the status of "real" work.

Because work defines an individual's place in society—social standing, lifestyle, prestige, and respect—it is not surprising that many of the battles for gender-role liberation have been fought in the workplace. And the reasons for the battles are many. Historically, women have been kept out of many areas of employment. In the 1990s, the average full-time employed woman continues to earn only 68 percent of what the average full-time employed man earns. Women earn less than men in nearly every occupation: The earnings ratio of female to male physicians is 82 percent, that of female to male bus drivers is 76 percent, that of female to male high school teachers is 94 percent, that of female to male billing clerks is 74 percent. De facto vertical and horizontal occupational segregation of the work force keeps most women in a few low-paid occupations, while men have access to a wider variety of jobs. Occupations with a high percentage of women and minority workers are likely to have a high percentage of low-wage workers (people whose hourly wages are not sufficient to maintain them above the poverty line). Minority women are 4 times more likely, white women 3 times more likely, and minority men 1.5 times more likely than white men to be low-wage earners (Hartmann & Spalter-Roth, 1991). Even in the face of unemployment, women fare worse than men. It takes men an average of five to seven months to find a new job, but it takes women about two months longer (Kleiman, 1991).

This chapter examines some of the issues facing men and women in the workplace. It begins with an examination of the division of labor by sex—what has come to be the "men's work" and the "women's work" of our society—and the changes that are being wrought in this familiar system. It then addresses the sex discrimination faced by women and men as they try to disassemble the division of labor by sex. From there we move to the inevitable conflict facing every person who has a life outside of the workplace—the stress of combining work and family—and we look at how those stresses differ for women and men. And finally we examine sexuality in the workplace in its romantic as well as its coercive forms.

Division of Labor by Sex

Women's Entry into Male-Dominated Professions

How quickly are changes in the gender composition of the professional and managerial labor force taking place? Most of the research that addresses this question has been directed at women. In 1975, for instance, Bennett and Loewe (1975) argued that it would be fully a century at the rate of change that was taking place in the 1970s before women would be represented in management in the same proportion that they were represented in the work force. There is some possibility that women may gain equal representation in management more quickly than predicted, however, because more women are now entering professional schools than even the most optimistic forecaster would have predicted in the early 1970s.

Let us look at some recent American figures. In 1982, women hit the majority point in the college population at 52 percent, and that year they earned 49 percent of all bachelor degrees and 51 percent of all master's degrees. Between 1972 and 1982, women more than doubled, and in some cases, tripled or quadrupled, their representation in architecture, medicine, economics, law, accounting, and pharmacy. Women's participation in business programs has quadrupled since 1970, when their representation was 10 percent, and by the 1980s women were earning 30 percent of four-year computer degrees—up from 0 percent in the early 1970s (The feminization of the professional workforce, 1986). However, women still account for only 1 in 3 scientists and only 1 in 25 engineers (National Science Foundation, 1990). The representation is lower among minority women; for example, only 2 of the 77 American women who received doctorates in mathematics in 1987 were black (Bozeman, 1989).

If women continue to enroll in programs that train them for the male-dominated professions, the sex composition of accounting, law, medicine, and architecture will soon change, but that of engineering, mathematics, and the physical sciences have farther to go. However, although the male-dominated professions control much of the power in society and thus have a strong impact that extends beyond a narrow occupational sphere, they employ a minority of North American men and women. Perhaps more telling to those who study the division of labor by sex is the fact that women are not entering male-dominated blue-collar occupations and that men are not entering any of the female-dominated occupations fast enough to warrant our notice.

The Forgotten People

Although there have been millions, probably billions, of words written about gender-role issues in the workplace over the past 20 years, most of these words have been addressed to two visible but small groups of people: women in management and male-dominated professions, and the people who study them. Hundreds of articles have reported research on female professionals and female managers; dozens of books have advised them on their clothing, their family lives, and their sex lives; and have dissected their ambition, their past, and their probable future. Yet very little attention has been paid to the women who enter male-dominated blue-collar jobs or to the men who enter female-dominated occupations. Even more surprising, researchers' and the media's seemingly insatiable interest in employed women has rarely extended itself to the majority of employed women who work in female-dominated occupations.

Women in Female-Dominated Occupations.   Nurses, home economists, nursery-school teachers, secretaries, typists, and switchboard operators: Most of these people share a common characteristic—their femaleness. These are the women who work in female-dominated occupations—the women who are doing "women's work." They do not enjoy the prestige that their formal education, on-the-job training, and responsibility would suggest; their pay is lower and their opportunities for advancement fewer than those in male-dominated occupations. Yet, every year young women enter the female-dominated occupations in large numbers. There has been surprisingly little public relations aimed at increasing the public image of these occupations and surprisingly little effort aimed at lowering their female domination by recruiting men.

Women in female-dominated occupations cluster into two groups: those who are in such female-dominated professions as nursing, social work, elementary school teaching, home economics, and librarianship, and those who are in clerical and "pink collar" jobs such as secretarial positions, bookkeeping, sales, or food service. As we shall see, research suggests that the reasons for selecting and remaining in the female-dominated occupations vary between these two groups of women workers.

The female-dominated professions are sometimes called "semi-professions" because, although to some extent they share with professions the requirement for advanced education and specific credentials, they tend to lack the authority, autonomy, and monopoly over a knowledge base that characterizes such professions as law or medicine (Fox & Hesse-Biber, 1984). What are the characteristics of women in female-dominated professions? In one study in which female nurses and businesswomen were matched for age, education, and managerial level, nurses tended to be less achievement-oriented, less production-oriented, and less likely to see themselves as having characteristics ascribed to managers or to men (Moore & Rickel, 1980). Nurses had more children and considered the domestic role to be more important, although the two groups did not differ in the importance they placed on their career or in their perceptions of their husbands' attitudes. Because this study focused specifically on nurses, it is difficult to know if these are characteristics that one might expect to find among women in other female-dominated fields, or if these are characteristics particular to nurses. Furthermore, it is difficult to know if women with particular characteristics seek out female-dominated professions or if there are different effects of working in female-dominated and male-dominated fields that cause the differences reported in the study. Perhaps the women who choose these professions are balancing their desire for a professional career against the perceived obstacles to a family life associated with the more prestigious, male-dominated professions. Educational data do indicate that women who enter the female-dominated professions have planned their choice; they tend to follow gender-typed patterns of preparation and entry. The educational choices that many women make at the university level (for example, their disproportionate representation among degree recipients in education, health, and library science) suggest that they anticipate entry into one of the female-dominated professions (Grimm, 1978). Furthermore, many women entering female-dominated professions say that they expect their careers to be interrupted by childrearing.

It has been noted that high school girls who plan to enter male-dominated fields tend to attribute their successes to ability and their failures to lack of ability, as men are usually found to do, and that females who plan to enter female-dominated fields are more likely to attribute their failures to lack of effort and interest and their successes somewhat to effort, but more strongly to luck (Wergers & Frieze, 1977). In addition, qualities of assertiveness and self-efficacy are positively related to college women's willingness to engage in nontraditional, but not traditional, career activities (Nevill & Schlecker, 1988). Although these findings suggest that there is a self-selection factor that propels some women into male-dominated and others into female-dominated occupations, the extent to which these young women actually followed nontraditional or traditional career paths is not known.

Not just individual, but also structural factors act to guide women into the female-dominated professions. Gender stereotyping of academic areas such as mathematics and science may channel female students away from courses needed to pursue the male-dominated professions. The perceived lack of availability of parental leaves and child-care alternatives may discourage women from pursuing careers that require a 60-hour workweek, as some of the male-dominated professions do. The very male domination of some professions means that a woman needs an extra dose of courage just to claim her place in that world. Sex discrimination, both blatant and subtle, still blocks women's entry into some professions. All of these structural factors are discussed in more detail later in this chapter.

The vast majority of women who do not enter the female-dominated professions enter the labor force as clerical workers. These women tend to work for reasons of income and to maintain an identity separate from their family roles, just as do their counterparts in the professions. They also find work important as a way of forming and maintaining social connections and as a way of structuring their time and feeling useful (Glenn & Feldberg, 1989). They tend to be committed to working, although not necessarily to their specific jobs. Some research indicates that women may choose clerical jobs even though they find them boring because they see few options for themselves and because they do not expect to be in the work force for an extended period of time (Gaskell, 1981).

More than one-third of the female work force in both Canada and the United States is employed in the clerical sector (Canadian Advisory Council on the Status of Women, 1985; Glenn & Feldberg, 1989). A full 99 percent of today's secretaries, 94 percent of typists, 97 percent of receptionists, and 91 percent of data entry clerks are female (Spalter-Roth & Hartmann, 1990), and although several authors have predicted that we are due for a secretarial crisis (Colwill, 1985; Kiechel, 1983; Stead, 1983), secretaries seem to labor invisibly in a world in which all eyes are on their sisters in management. North American organizations are still reaping the secretarial benefits from the day when women seldom extended their occupational choices beyond nurse, teacher, and secretary; and managers have come to expect highly talented people to fill top-level secretarial positions. However, the stereotype of a secretary as a bright young woman temporarily marking time in a job while she waits to get married is no longer (if it ever was) accurate (Colwill, 1985). The average secretary is 35 years old, married, and economically responsible for children (Spalter-Roth & Hartmann, 1990). Although often highly skilled, she is undercompensated for those skills, particularly over a long tenure in the work force. This future is not an attractive one for young women currently making occupational choices. As more and more highly intelligent, highly motivated women enter male-dominated fields where they can expect to be better paid for their efforts, recognized for their talents, and given opportunities for advancement, however, a critical shortage of good secretaries is beginning to hit the job market (Stead, 1983) at the same time that a variety of new stressors in the form of advanced technology are changing the face of secretarial work. It is difficult to predict the changes that this crisis will engender, but one optimistic possibility is that, in order to attract top-notch secretarial help, top management of large organizations will begin to envision the secretarial position as a training ground for management, and offer secretaries with some management training or secretaries who are prepared to gain management training, the opportunities for advancement that have always been offered to entry-level men. The secretarial position requires many skills required of middle managers—skills such as independence, organization, the ability to take orders, and the ability to gain satisfaction from the accomplishments of others. It also offers an ideal location to learn the workings of the organization, and a case could be made for establishing the secretarial position as a common route into management for women and men (Colwill, 1985). In a day in which every forward-looking university student knows how to type and use a word processor, and typing is no longer considered to be a female ability, such a move might help solve the secretarial crisis while helping to disassemble the division of labor by sex.

Women in Blue-Collar Jobs. For decades women have been edging their way into hospitals as nurses, into educational systems as primary school teachers, and into offices as clerical workers and secretaries. Men in those fields have accommodated themselves to the presence of women in nurturant and helpmate roles in the workplace, and women's steps to equality in those industries, although slow, have been easier than they have been for blue-collar women. There is no need for nurturance in carpentry and plumbing, however, and the helpmate role in the trades has been filled by male apprentices, male college students, and young men who are "finding themselves" (Colwill & Colwill, 1985).

It is no accident that more women are entering male-dominated professions than are entering male-dominated blue-collar jobs. Women have long benefited from a gender-role stereotype that labels them as good students, and women who enter occupations based largely on "book learning," even though they may be considered "uppity," can take advantage of this stereotype. On the other hand, technical, spatial, and mechanical abilities and physical strength—the characteristics deemed necessary for male-dominated blue-collar work, particularly the trades—are characteristics that women are seen to be lacking (Colwill & Colwill, 1985). Furthermore, as Walshok (1981) has argued, professional women come to their jobs equipped with degrees that serve as recognized proof of their competence—degrees that they earned in an atmosphere in which everyone else was equally naive. Because a blue-collar woman learns most of her visible skills on the job rather than in the classroom, however, she must undergo her training in an extremely vulnerable situation, often as the only neophyte in the group. Thus, there are few visible skills by which the entry-level female blue-collar worker can be assessed. In situations such as this, where there are few cues available to evaluate ability, evaluators tend to rely more heavily on external characteristics, such as gender, as a means for judging a worker's competence (Hodgins & Kalin, 1985).

Given these problems, it's not surprising that blue-collar women have remained in lower-paying female-dominated industries. Women are the textile workers, making just over minimum wage, rather than the steelworkers, making more than $13 per hour (U.S. Department of Commerce, 1991), and when they do enter the higher-paying industries, it is into different and lower-paying jobs than men have traditionally occupied: Women are the small electronic component assemblers, while men build jet engines (O'Farrell, 1982). As late as 1981, O'Farrell (1982) reported, American women in occupations designated as the trades and crafts ranged from a low of 0.1 percent of brickmasons to a high of 3.4 percent of machinists. The situation has changed little since then; in 1989, women made up only 2.1 percent of persons employed in the construction trades and 3.4 percent of those employed in occupations labeled mechanics and repairers (U.S. Department of Commerce, 1991). Statistics compiled by the International Labour Office (1991), which aggregate a broader range of construction-related occupations, show that in 1990, women made up 8.6 percent of employees in construction in the United States. In many other Western countries, the percentages of women in construction in 1990 were comparable: The percentage was 10.9 in Canada, 9.1 in the United Kingdom, 10.4 in Germany, 12.8 in Australia. However, even fewer women are working in these jobs in many other countries, such as Spain (3.2 percent), Brazil (2.6 percent), Hong Kong (4.4 percent), and the Philippines (1.8 percent).

When a woman does venture into a male-dominated trade, her sense of isolation resembles that of the top-level female executive. She is unlikely to have a female peer and even less likely to have a female boss (Colwill & Colwill, 1985). As a recent job entrant, her advancement, which is probably based solely on seniority, will be slow, her potential for layoff high (Deaux & Ullman, 1983). In addition, virtually every study of women in trades shows some evidence of resentment among coworkers and first-line supervisors; these women were subjected to practical jokes, threats of violence, sexual harassment, and actual violence—although few men actually participated in these activities (Colwill & Colwill, 1985). The woman who enters a male-dominated blue-collar job when a woman before her has failed at that job is particularly likely to experience the resentment of this small minority of male coworkers (O'Farrell, 1982).

Deaux (1984a), who has researched extensively in this area, is not optimistic about the future of women in high-paying, male-dominated, blue-collar jobs. She argues that the recession (and, one might add, robotics) has resulted in seniority-based layoffs that have adversely affected many of the few women who have entered the trades. Women, she believes, may have arrived on the scene too late to enjoy the high wages and lucrative benefits that have characterized the trades, and she suggests that women should look to new industries with no history of male dominance—industries that have yet to establish gender-role stereotypes.

Men in Female-Dominated Occupations.   There is no doubt that women in male-dominated occupations suffer discrimination from people who feel that their reach exceeds their grasp, and women in female-dominated occupations suffer from association with that which is female, and therefore low in prestige. But the few men who enter the female-dominated occupations—nurses, infant care workers, home economists, and secretaries—can sometimes have an even tougher row to hoe. To emulate one's status superiors, as women do when they enter male-dominated occupations, is a forgivable deviation from the norm in an achieving society, but to emulate one's status inferiors, as men do when they enter female-dominated occupations, gives cause for alarm. There is evidence that people tend to attribute homosexuality to males, but not to females, who do not conform to gender-role stereotypes (Deaux & Lewis, 1984). More specifically, Levinson's (1975) research indicates that men are less likely than women to be considered for an occupation nontraditional for their sex, and that their sexual orientation may be called into question. These findings probably come as no surprise to the male telephone operators who told an interviewer on a recent CBC radio show that several customers had asked them if they were gay.

The situation is far from bleak for men in most female-dominated occupations, however. Regardless of the occupation, from clerical work to such professions as nursing and librarianship, men are represented disproportionately for their numbers in senior and administrative positions (Spalter-Roth & Hartmann, 1990). In nursing, a field that is 97 percent female, nearly half of the small number of men hold administrative positions (Grimm & Stern, 1974). Although women make up the vast majority of elementary school teachers, 95 percent of school superintendents and 72 percent of school principals are men (Jordan, 1992). Similar patterns are found in social work and librarianship. Moreover, the tendency for men to make more money than women do carries over into female-dominated occupations. Even among clerical workers, males get paid more than their female counterparts with similar education and job qualifications (Spalter-Roth & Hartmann, 1990). It appears that even when men do enter female-dominated occupations, the division of labor along gender lines is maintained through the clustering of men in the higher-status, higher-paid segments of these occupations.

The division of labor by sex will not subside until men enter female-dominated occupations in large numbers. Currently, men *are* entering female-dominated jobs at a faster rate than women are entering male-dominated jobs (Ott, 1989), with the unfortunate result that some women will be denied jobs in their traditional strongholds, even as some men are now denied jobs in their traditional strongholds because of increased female competition. If history repeats itself, men's entry into female-dominated occupations will raise the status of the jobs and the salaries of the incumbents, but not without pain for the men who are treated as gender-role deviants and for the women whose jobs are lost. Only when this transition is complete—only when jobs cease to be identified as "men's work" and "women's work"—will it be possible to objectively evaluate the contribution to the labor market made by any particular occupation.

Sex Discrimination

Pay Equity

In the not too distant past, it was considered perfectly acceptable to pay females less than males for the same work. Anyone arguing against the unfairness of such a system was told that supporting a family was the primary responsibility of the man of the house, and that even single men must prepare financially for that responsibility. There were, of course, single women with children; there were women who supported their husbands and their children; and there were single men and women who never married or had children. The social conscience of North America was not easily activated by gender-role issues in those days, however, and social policy was rarely affected by deviations from the norm.

In more recent times, society's collective conscience *has* been activated by sex inequalities, and two new concepts have been introduced into the workplace. The first was the notion that women and men should be paid the same wage for the same work. Although this concept, known as *equal pay for equal work,* is supported by legislation, it has yet to become reality for all women and men throughout the labor force. Another idea, the widespread acceptance of which was begun only in the 1980s and 1990s, has also been considered: the notion that the work traditionally done by women and that traditionally done by men can be considered equal in value and should be remunerated accordingly. Implementation of this idea requires that the value—the composite of skill, effort, responsibility, and working conditions—of jobs normally filled by women and jobs normally filled by men within the same organization be established and compared. For example, how does the value of the work of a mail clerk (usually male) compare with that of a secretary (usually female)? How does the work of a grocery store shelving clerk (usually male) compare in value to the work of a cashier (usually female) in the same store? If the values of the jobs are determined to be similar, the salaries should be similar, according to the principle of *comparable worth* or *equal pay for work of equal value.*

There is an increasing amount of legislation and increasing social pressure to support the second as well as the first of these principles, but these two facets of the same problem of pay equity—that men and women should be paid the same for the same work and that men and women should be paid the same for jobs of comparable worth—are far from being resolved. It has been argued, for instance, that employers will react to the pressures to pay women for the real worth of their work by refusing to hire women at all (Block, W., 1984). This argument is based on the unspoken assumption that any employer would, given the choice, prefer a male to a female employee, and points to the need for a broader approach to this issue. Although the concept of equal pay for work of equal value is considered to be an economic issue, it has been argued that it is merely a symptom of a much broader social psychological phenomenon that manifests itself in the devaluation of women and that which women do (Colwill, 1984). Because women and men are valued differently, work that is gender-labeled "masculine" has a different connotation attached to it than has work that has been gender-labeled "feminine," and it is extremely difficult, if not virtually impossible, for anyone who has been conventionally socialized in North American society to evaluate the worth of an occupation independent of the gender labeling of that occupation (Baron & Newman, 1990; Steel & Lovrich, 1987). Thus, Canadian and American employers, union leaders, legislators, and policymakers face a monumental task as they attempt to come to grips with the concept of "equal pay for work of equal value." To tackle that issue is to tackle the most basic tenets of our gender-role socialization, the most basic assumptions behind sex discrimination.

Discrimination in Hiring and Evaluation

Although sex discrimination in the workplace has been illegal for over 20 years, researchers continue to find evidence of its existence, and most of this discrimination is directed at women, who are more likely than men to be seen as stepping out of their "place." One particularly telling area of study is discrimination within the working of unions; the primary function of unions is to protect their worker-members, yet women are underrepresented in the top levels of virtually all unions (White, 1980) and rarely find their way into union executive positions unless they belong to a union in which women form a clear majority (Chaison & Andrappan, 1982).

One basis for sex discrimination in evaluation is a general tendency to devalue the things that women typically do. In a series of studies, men and women were given an advantage when they employed the power strategies that are typically used by men (Colwill, Perlman, & Spinner, 1982; 1983) or when they were identified as being in a male-dominated (engineering) rather than a female-dominated (home economics) profession (Colwill, Pollock, & Sztaba, 1986). Furthermore, Colwill and Sztaba's (1986) research indicates that both women and men are seen as less effective when they speak in the traditionally feminine manner: using superlatives ("the most wonderful"), qualifiers ("This product is, perhaps, the best on the market"), tag questions ("You will, won't you?"), and highly descriptive and explicit words such as *mauve, ecru,* and *lovely*—what has come to be known as female "genderlect" (Dickerson, cited in Kramer, 1974).

In any case, sex discrimination against women and sex discrimination against men seem to take different forms. Women tend to be the recipients of prejudice and discrimination in situations in which their competence and credibility, particularly to do malelike things, are at stake. Men, conversely, tend to have discriminatory attitudes and behaviors directed at them when they incur the hostility of others by doing femalelike things that are considered to be beneath them. Thus, as suggested earlier, women are punished as incompetents for trying to emulate their social superiors and men are punished as deviants for trying to emulate their social inferiors. This difference was probably best demonstrated in Levinson's (1975) field study, in which men who applied for traditionally female jobs were often told that the job was too simple, too dull, or too low-paying. Women applying for "men's jobs," on the other hand, were more likely to be told that the job was too difficult or that it required too much strength or time commitment for a woman.

But haven't prejudice and discrimination been reduced dramatically in the years since 1975, when Levinson's research was published? Few longitudinal data examine this question directly, but in one study of MBA students' attitudes toward female executives done in 1975 and again in 1983, males' attitudes toward women as managers remained consistently negative, and females' attitudes remained significantly more positive than did those of their male counterparts (Dubnos, 1985). Surveys show that negative attitudes toward female managers persist, especially among men (Frank, 1988; Wiley & Eskilson, 1990). Data concerning the career paths of managers continue to show that women in high-status male-dominated occupations are the targets of prejudice and discrimination. One study of 1000 top female and male managers at the top 20 American companies showed that, even when women had the same qualifications as men—the same education, similar levels of job tenure, equivalent work experience in the same industries and job areas, similar willingness and ability to relocate—they received lower salary increases and fewer opportunities to relocate over a five-year period. Over that five-year period, women received pay increases and bonuses averaging 54 percent of their salaries, compared to 65 percent for men (Stroh, Brett, & Reilly, 1991, cited in Kleiman, 1992).

It appears that the strongest prejudice against women in a traditionally male occupation is likely to occur when people are considering hypothetical situations, among men who have had little exposure to women in that particular job, or in situations in which people are lacking data that would help them make an informed decision about the worth of a woman's work. It is known, for example, that women and men who have been managed by women have fewer negative stereotypes about female managers (Ezell, Odewahn, & Sherman, 1981; Wheeless & Berryman-Fink, 1985) and that discrimination against women is more likely to occur if managers are given insufficient information to make a personnel decision based on competence, as Gerdes and Garber's (1983) study of engineers has demonstrated.

There has been a tendency in the past for both men and women to show prejudice against women, leading many people to believe that everyone prefers to work with and for men. However, numerous studies now show that women are more accepting of female managers than are men (Die, Debbs, & Walker, 1990; Stevens & DeNisi, 1980; Wheeless & Berryman-Fink, 1985). In one such study, female employees expressed a preference for female coworkers (Haefner, 1977), and in another, female managers evaluated managerial women more positively than they evaluated comparably qualified men. Female managers in the latter study were judged as being more intelligent, more likeable, more successful, and more able than their male counterparts, and the future of female managers was seen as more satisfying (Jabes, 1980). Similarly, the MBA women in Mikalachki and Mikalachki's (1984) study gave more favorable ratings to female than to male managers. Finally, in a study that suggests that pro-female biases may sometimes benefit women, Dalton and Todor (1985) found that union grievances were 50 percent more likely to be settled in favor of female grievers, and that this effect was maintained even when the researchers controlled for severity of grievance or the level at which the case was settled. (There were five possible levels, from meeting with first-level supervisor to arbitration.)

Whether gender-role stereotypes favor women or men, the consequence is an inequitable workplace, because stereotypes almost invariably lead to discrimination. There is increasing evidence that stereotypes may have other deleterious effects: They may actually motivate the stereotyped person to behave in a manner consistent with the stereotype. This process, known as the *self-fulfilling prophecy,* was demonstrated in a study by von Baeyer, Sherk, and Zanna (1981), in which women were interviewed by men whom they were led to believe held either traditional or nonstereotypical views about women. Women who were interviewed by the "traditional" men dressed for the interview in a more "feminine" manner, and were more likely to wear jewelry, scarf, and makeup than were women who were interviewed by the "nontraditional" men. In addition, women who thought they were being interviewed by men with traditional attitudes were more likely to adopt subservient nonverbal gestures: to stare at the interviewer when he was talking and to look away when they answered his questions.

Stereotypes may create a vicious circle. We have certain attitudes about a person—she or he becomes aware of these attitudes and behaves in a manner consistent with our stereotypes, and our stereotypes are reinforced. The von Baeyer, Sherk, and Zanna (1981) study demonstrated the link between perceived stereotypes and the stereotyped person's behavior. A second study by Towson, MacDonald, and Zanna (1981) demonstrated the reinforcement of the stereotyper's original attitudes. In this study, the researchers had male actors conduct interviews with female actors playing one of two roles: the role of a "feminine" woman (jewelry, scarf, makeup, and subservient nonverbal communication) or the role of a "nonfeminine" woman (same clothing, but no jewelry, scarf, or makeup; and she looked at the interviewer when he *and* she were speaking). In addition, the feminine woman said that she would quit work to raise her family; the nonfeminine woman said that if she were to get married and have children, she would organize her life so that family commitments and career advancement would not conflict. Videotapes of these interviews were shown to men who had been pretested as having either traditional or nontraditional gender-role attitudes. Men with traditional attitudes were less likely to predict job success for any of the female applicants. Furthermore, feminine women were seen as being better fitted for jobs in female-dominated occupations and nonfeminine women were judged as being more appropriate candidates for traditionally male jobs.

Sex discrimination is apparently still with us and will not be easily banished. Women and men are readily classified into two groups, and the myriad stereotypes about these two groups, which are inextricably intertwined with sexual mores, religious teachings, and family roles, cannot help but affect workplace attitudes. Sex discrimination helps us to preserve the status quo, and the status quo, whatever its shortcomings and whatever its unfairness, has the advantage of familiarity. Perhaps because of this familiarity, or perhaps because they cannot bear to face the reality of its unfairness, women tend to underrate the amount of sex discrimination that is visited upon them personally, even when they are quite aware that women in general experience sex discrimination. This phenomenon is known as *denial of personal discrimination* (Crosby, 1984). Women, and probably all people who are the objects of discrimination, apparently adopt cognitive strategies that protect them from feeling deprived—by using reference groups similar to themselves (other women in similar situations) rather than by facing the incongruity associated with comparisons to more privileged groups (Abbondanza, 1982, 1983).

Clearly, people prefer to protect themselves from feelings that they are being treated unfairly. Despite their lower salaries, women are less likely than men to report dissatisfaction with their pay (Jackson, 1989; Steel & Lovrich, 1987; Summers, 1988). When given the opportunity to compare their pay with that of other workers, participants in one study chose to see the pay of the same-sex and same-job group first (Major & Forcey, 1985). The same study also showed that both men and women assigned to a "feminine" job expected less pay and rated their obtained pay as fairer than did those in "masculine" jobs, and that women thought they deserved less pay for their work than did men, regardless of their job assignment. People are apparently so used to evaluating their own and others' pay expectations by making implicit same-sex comparisons that they do not question the fairness or appropriateness of restricting their comparisons in this way. Interestingly, for women at least, looking beyond one's own sex for comparison purposes may be linked to discontent. One study of professional women indicated that women with male reference groups perceived a greater gap between what they had and wished to have, were more pessimistic about their futures, and were more dissatisfied than were their counterparts who compared themselves to other women (Zanna, Crosby, & Loewenstein, 1987).

We can do little to eliminate the fact that women and men belong to two identifiable groups, and are thus susceptible to sex discrimination. We can do even less to overcome sex discrimination based on the fact that gender-role change disturbs the status quo. We can, however, through education, particularly education directed at the women and men who believe that they are not personally the targets of sex discrimination, help to break down one of the barriers to social change—the denial of personal discrimination. This process is particularly important in the lives of men and women who find themselves in token positions, for they are particularly vulnerable to discrimination.

Minorities and Tokenism

Women and men in occupations nontraditional for their sex often find themselves holding token positions—positions in which they are treated as symbols or representatives of their sex. Kanter (1977) makes a clear distinction between tokens and minority members. She argues that in skewed groups, where there is a large preponderance of one sex over the other (a ratio of 85:15, for example), the minority members are truly tokens or symbols of their group. It is only when their proportions rise to a ratio of, say, 65:35, that we can speak of *minorities* and *majorities* rather than of *tokens* and *dominants,* for only then do the minority members have the opportunity to be seen as individuals, differentiated from one another. At this point they can form coalitions and have the opportunity to affect the group culture.

Kanter's sociological study of "Indsco," an anonymous company in which she conducted research in the 1970s, has provided a great deal of information about people in token positions. From her research it has become clear that tokens tend to be perceived as members of the outgroup rather than as individuals, and that their every action tends to be seen either as typical outgroup behavior or as behavior that is unusual for a member of the outgroup, rather than as the action of one unique person.

The token status places one in a particularly visible, and thus vulnerable, position, and both male and female tokens may find it difficult to relax and do their jobs as competently as they would be capable of doing under less adverse circumstances. In a study that attempted to duplicate the situation in which tokens find themselves (Lord & Saenz, 1985), subjects believed that they were interacting, via television screen, with three other people, discussing opinions on several noncontroversial topics. In reality, they were being videotaped giving their opinions, but were watching prerecorded videotapes of three confederates. In the nontoken condition of this experiment, the confederates were the same sex as the subject; in the token condition, the three confederates were the other sex. The results indicated that tokens, even in this relatively nonthreatening situation of expressing opinions on everyday topics, and even though they were treated no differently than nontokens, seemed to exhibit a memory deficit: They could not remember as well as nontokens what they had said or what the three others had said. In a second part of the experiment, subjects serving as observers watched the four videotapes—the three videotapes watched by the subject, plus a videotape of the subject himself or herself. These observers were more likely to remember the opinions of the token than they were to remember the opinions of the nontokens or confederates. The authors argue that the tokens' memory difficulties resulted from the feeling of being scrutinized by an audience of other-sex peers. If this phenomenon generalizes to the work situation, and there is no reason to believe that it does not, the token is in a particularly vulnerable position: she or he is unable to remember the details of interactions that take place in a situation in which she or he is obviously the center of attention, and a memorable one at that. Moreover, if tokenism alone is enough to cause cognitive difficulties, the added pressure of differential treatment in the workplace may well compound the problem.

Because most of the tokens at Indsco were women, Kanter's (1977) research has focused mainly on the roles that token women find themselves playing in organizational settings in which they are seen primarily as "women" rather than "workers":

- the *mother* to men in the group—the comforter, the button-sewer, the emotional specialist
- the *seductress* or sex object—the object of sexual competition or male "protection" from the sexual advances of other men
- the *pet* or mascot of the organization—the good-humored cheerleader whose competencies are fussed over as being exemplary performance for a woman
- the *iron maiden* who expects full rights of group membership—the "women's libber" for whom no passages are smoothed

These four roles share two commonalities: They are blatant caricatures of the female gender role and they rob the role players of the chance to be seen in their worker role. Thus, Kanter argues, every effort should be made not to introduce lone employees into a work situation in which they are surrounded solely by members of the other sex. Although that is undoubtedly the ideal, it is equally important that managers not postpone the integration of their organization until the day when they can introduce two or more employees into nontraditional work situations, for there is evidence that mere exposure to a token can create more positive attitudes toward the group to which the minority member belongs. In one particularly dramatic study, Shomer and Centers (1970) found more positive attitudes toward feminism among men in a group with one woman than among men in an all-male group, *even though group members did not have the opportunity to talk to one another.*

The workplace stresses of the token are numerous because the token position contains several dilemmas and contradictions: Tokens are treated as representatives of their group, yet as exceptions to their group; they are visible, yet backstage; they stand apart, yet are stereotyped; they can relax least in "relaxing" situations in which formal organizational roles are dropped (Kanter, 1977).

Either women or men can be tokens in a workplace setting dominated by the other group. Is the *token* experience the same for men as it is for women? Two studies suggest it is not—that, in fact, for men gender stereotypes act to ameliorate the negative aspects of being a token. In the first, a study of young concession stand workers, findings revealed that the token man did not experience the negative consequences—high visibility, contrast, and assimilation—that the token woman did. Rather, token men identified with (male) supervisors and advanced more quickly than did nontoken men and women (Yoder & Sinnett, 1985). In the second study, a comparison of the experiences of female police officers and male nurses, the female, but not the male, tokens reported that they did not feel accepted by their peers, that they felt extremely visible, and they had been sexually harassed (Ott, 1989).

One thing that tokens, minority members, or new members of a group may do to reduce stress is to search for solidarity among themselves. They may isolate themselves from majority group members, interacting more frequently and positively with one another than with more established members of the group (Schein, 1968). Although such solidarity can be helpful, it also has a major drawback: It can slow down the process by which newcomers are assimilated into the group (Moreland, 1985). This finding underlines the dilemma inherent in the position of a woman or man entering an occupation or workplace in which their sex is underrepresented. Not only must they cope with the many problems associated with token or minority status, but even their attempts to seek support from others in the same position may present a danger to their ultimate acceptance. The brave souls who persevere in such situations surely deserve the label *pioneers*. These pioneers are not the only people who experience workplace stress, however. Let us turn now to an examination of the stresses inherent in the interface between work and family.

Two Spheres in Contact: The Interaction of Family and Employment Issues

How simple (and how dull) life would be for the average working person if the only responsibilities he or she faced were those connected with the job! For most of us, however, a job represents only one of the sets of tasks and sources of worry, pride, frustration, and fulfillment that fill our lives. No serious examination of gender-related issues in the workplace can ignore the fact that, when women and men leave the workplace and head for home, they are faced with different amounts and kinds of responsibilities.

Combining Job and Family: Stresses and Rewards

It used to be expected that women would set aside their own work and achievement needs in order to provide support for those of their husbands. Consider the comments, made in 1972, of one of the gifted women from Terman's longitudinal study of high-IQ individuals:

> A person of Henry's talent and drive desperately needs a partner to take care of family, home and all of the social needs and other involvement. . . . My husband's multifaceted career has been the central factor in my life. Ours has been a partnership in many ways, as I have carried most of the home, family, and social responsibilities. This has enabled him to devote full time to his creative work, his teaching, etc. I wish I could have achieved creatively myself, but what small talent I might have had was absorbed in his great gifts. (Quoted in Tomlinson-Keasey, 1990, p. 217)

Traditional gender roles, by assigning women to the home and men to the working world, have allowed a certain amount of separation between the employment and family spheres. The entry of women in large numbers into the labor force now means that the tidy separation is crumbling. For women, especially, this new situation is likely to result in increased stress. Women who work outside the home usually find themselves faced with another full-time job in their "off" hours: cooking, cleaning, and caring for children. Even in dual-career families, mothers continue to assume the major responsibility for the care and socialization of young children and for housework (Bielby & Bielby, 1988; Cunningham, 1983; Pleck, 1983). Employed women report that a major source of stress is the conflicting set of demands generated by work and family roles (Canadian Mental Health Association, 1984; Duxbury & Higgins, 1991; Koberg & Chusmir, 1989). Women garment workers interviewed in one study reported that worry over finding adequate day care for their children was more stressful than the unhealthy working conditions at their plant (de Koninck, 1984). Studies of some populations show that women are more likely than men to report work–family role conflict (Mashal & Kalin, 1985; Wiersma, 1990); others show that, although both women and men complain of the conflict between work and family roles, women complain more of exhaustion and the difficulty of trying to schedule everything while men complain of overwork (Crosby, 1982).

In recent years, a new load has been added to the domestic side of women's double burden by an emerging demographic phenomenon: increasing longevity, and the concomitant demand that middle-aged people spend years caring for their aged parents. The people called on to be the caregivers in this situation are usually women, as are most of the dependent elderly, since women live longer than men. These female caregivers have been characterized as "women in the middle" by gerontologist Elaine Brody (1981), not only because their age places them in the position of being expected to care for both their parents and their children, but also because they are juggling so many competing demands on their time and energy—job, husband, health problems, college-age children. According to Brody's research, three-fifths of these heavily burdened women felt guilty about not doing enough for their mothers.

Stress among employed women comes not only from the burden of unpaid, unrecognized domestic work added to their outside employment, but also from conditions on the job. Women are more likely than men to face pay inequities (Abella, 1984), underutilization of skills (Belanger, 1984; de Koninck, 1984), sex discrimination in performance evaluation and promotion (Larwood & Wood, 1977), and tokenism (Kanter, 1977)—all of which, along with work–family role conflict, have been related to negative physical and psychological stress symptoms (Greenglass, 1985a, 1985b, 1991).

If the strain of combining work and family responsibilities is so great for women, what is there to be said in favor of doing it, other than the obvious financial payoff? It is clear that women can reap psychological and physical, as well as economic, benefits from the effort of juggling two roles, particularly if they have support from family and friends (Amatea & Fong, 1991; Epstein, 1983). In fact, employed women appear to be happier and healthier than homemakers, except when they have infants to care for (Walker & Best, 1991). One study of women in the 40- to 59-year age range found that work outside the home may play an important role in the psychological well-being of middle-aged women. Employed women at mid-life had higher self-esteem and less psychological anxiety than did homemakers, and also reported being in better physical health (Coleman & Antonucci, 1983). Taken alone, these correlational data do not prove that holding jobs caused women to feel happier, healthier, more self-confident, and less anxious; perhaps happy, healthy, self-confident, calm women are simply more likely to seek and find jobs. However, in the Coleman and Antonucci study (1983), employment was the only significant predictor of self-esteem in mid-life women, in contrast to income, education, marital status, and family life-cycle stage—none of which predicted self-esteem. This finding led the researchers to speculate that employment in and of itself may affect women's well-being. They suggest that the stabilizing impact of employment enables women to avoid some of the possible negative effects of family role loss that occur at mid-life: empty-nest syndrome, feelings of inadequacy, loss of purpose. They further suggest that working outside the home may have a similar stabilizing influence at other crucial transition periods of the life cycle, such as early parenthood, divorce, or death of a spouse. Perhaps it simply helps to keep life in perspective when one can look at it from the viewpoints of two very different roles. This suggestion receives support from Crosby's (1990) study of divorce and work life among women managers. She noted that work was explicitly recognized by the women managers as a source of pride and repair to damaged self-esteem.

For men, stress in the workplace has long been recognized as a problem. The early research on Type A behavior—a hard-driving, job-devoted behavioral style characterized by excessive competitive striving, time urgency, and aggressiveness that has been linked to coronary heart disease (Friedman & Rosenman, 1959)—was concerned only with men. The Jenkins Activity Survey, which measures Type A behavior, was developed for men (Jenkins, Rosenman, & Friedman, 1967) and was only later adapted for use with women (Davis & Cowles, 1985). Although Type A behavior is more common among men than among women (Waldron, 1976), it seems to be related more to gender role than to sex. When employment or college status is controlled for, the Type A personality shows up equally often in women and men (DeGregorio & Carver, 1980; Waldron, 1978), and Type A behavior correlates significantly with masculinity but not femininity scale scores (DeGregorio & Carver, 1980; Grimm & Yarnold, 1985). Many of the correlates of Type A behavior are similar for the two sexes, as seen in Chapter 9.

Some research indicates that a major source of stress for men may be that, because of expectations linked to the masculine role, they rely too heavily on their job and their breadwinner role for their sense of identity. When this role is threatened through unemployment, men may show increased symptoms of stress, such as ulcers, heart attacks, elevated blood pressure, and strokes (Kasl & Cobb, 1979; Liem & Rayman, 1982). Moreover, these negative effects of unemployment are not limited to the out-of-work men themselves; stress and ill health are common among the wives of men who have lost their jobs (Grayson, 1983). Perhaps, then, the benefits of combining two roles are not limited to women who add employment to their traditional domestic tasks. Perhaps men can also gain from dividing their commitment more evenly between the spheres of work and family. Certainly there is a good deal of evidence that men who increase their involvement with parenting find the experience to be a positive and rewarding one, as discussed in Chapter 11. It is quite likely that, given mutual support, both men and women can benefit by not putting all their eggs in one basket—by finding sources of identity and satisfaction in both job and family.

Dual-Career Couples: Finding a New Job–Family Balance

For the growing number of families in which the two adult partners are pursuing careers, many of the traditional expectations about the division of household tasks, the supportive role played by the wife for the husband, and family mobility to accommodate the career moves of the male partner become unworkable. Even in the absence of any ideology about female–male equality, the pressures on a two-career cou-ple force them in the direction of a more equitable division of family tasks. As this type of family structure becomes more common, the male members of these couples are dis-covering firsthand two of the major difficulties that have traditionally plagued career women: (1) the limitations imposed on career accomplishment by the necessity to per-form such survival activities as shopping, cooking, cleaning, and laundry; and (2) the frequent assumption by employers that anyone who takes family responsibilities seri-ously lacks career commitment.

A well-worn assumption in the corporate world has been that men bring two peo-ple to their jobs, while women bring less than one (Kanter, 1977). Men, according to this assumption, come equipped with wives, whose unpaid work enhances men's productivity on the job. Furthermore, the assumption goes, wives not only free their husbands from the necessity of spending energy on daily concerns such as clean shirts and school lunches, they also help host business associates and maintain smooth social relations among the husbands' colleagues and coworkers. Although expectations are changing somewhat, the average female employee rarely has anyone doing these things for her and, indeed, is often trying to do them for someone else. Clearly, a single man, or one whose partner spends her energy on her own career rather than on supporting his, is at a disadvantage similar to that faced by most women. Although he is not likely to be in the desperate situation faced by many married career *women* who juggle employment and the lioness's share of domestic responsibilities, he is still denied the opportunity to focus all of his energy on his career and leave the details of daily living to someone else.

When men do try to take on a serious share of family duties, they may run into trouble at work. Although an employer may show some understanding and flexibility in making adjustments to accommodate a female employee whose work and family responsibilities conflict, a man experiencing similar conflicts can expect a less sym-pathetic response (Rosen & Jerdee, 1973). Traditionally, people who have allowed fam-ily considerations to "distract" them from their jobs have been judged to be less than serious about their work, and have been passed over for promotions and raises.

It is interesting to speculate on the changes in job and family expectations that may evolve in response to the issues confronted by two-career couples. As male as well as female employees must increasingly give priority to domestic and interpersonal responsibilities, job expectations may change to accommodate these responsibilities. Issues such as parental leave, flexible work schedules, and on-site child care, already finding their way into employment contracts, may eventually be taken for granted. Women or men who show strong commitment to family roles will not be suspected automatically of low career dedication. A sign of the increasing acceptance of two-career families is that the official employment guide for new Master of Business Ad-ministration graduates provides a rating on "dual-careers potential" for major U.S. urban centers (Association of MBA Executives, Inc., 1981). Some organizations, at least, are recognizing that fewer and fewer of their employees can make career decisions independent of family considerations or can blithely leave all family responsibilities in the hands of a spouse.

Not only job conditions but also family expectations must change as couples adapt to a two-career lifestyle. Such couples must wrestle with questions of whether and when to have children; they face enormous challenges each time one spouse is asked to relocate; and they sometimes spend years in long-distance "commuter" relationships. Because some of the differences in wage levels between men and women with the same educational background seem to be explained by geographical relocations based on the husband's career (Frank, 1978; Gallaway, 1969), the option of living apart is seen as preferable to relocation by some couples. This solution is still considered a drastic departure from society's expectations about marriage, and couples who adopt it may have to face the disapproval of family and friends along with the inevitable difficulties of the separation. However, studies of these couples reveal some advantages to this difficult lifestyle: The suspension of spousal role demands allows individuals to devote long hours to their work; the absence of a more well-established spouse allows the other to begin a career without relying on or being overshadowed by him or her; and individuals find opportunities for personal growth and development independent of the spouse (Douvan & Pleck, 1978; Farris, 1978; Gross, 1980). The disadvantages, though, are equally compelling: loneliness, the expense of maintaining two residences, long distance phone calls, commuting, and the lack of a partner with whom to share domestic responsibilities (Green & Zenisek, 1983).

As both individuals and employers gain experience with dual-career relationships, perhaps the lifestyle will become less difficult. In the meantime, dual-career couples are serving not only as pioneers but as role models for the 94 percent of male and female adolescents who expect to end up married to spouses who work outside the home (Tittle, 1981, cited in Green & Zenisek, 1983).

Career Paths of Women and Men

In recent decades, the pattern of labor force participation for North American women has been quite different from that of men. Although men have tended to enter the workplace and continue employment until they retire, women's participation has shown a sharp dip during childbearing years, followed by a rise as women whose children are grown return to work. Because of its shape on the graph and its significance, this pattern has sometimes been labeled the M curve—M for mother (Farley, 1980). With each passing year, however, the M curve is disappearing; fewer women are leaving the labor force during their childrearing years, and the so-called women's pattern of employment participation is becoming increasingly like men's (Treiman, 1985). In the 1980s, more than half the mothers of preschool children and two-thirds of mothers of school-aged children were employed. Over 70 percent of employed women having babies now return to work within two years. If current trends continue, it is projected that by 1995 2 out of 3 preschool children and 3 out of 4 children aged 6 to 13 will have mothers in the labor force (Hofferth & Phillips, 1987).

For women who do leave the work force, the break is a costly one. Labor force discontinuity is one of the factors responsible for the salary and status differentials between employed women and men. According to one estimate, earnings foregone in the year of birth (or adoption) and in the two subsequent years amount to $14,400 (in 1986 dollars) per woman (Institute for Women's Policy Research, 1990). Not only does the discontinuity limit a woman's opportunity to build experience and seniority, but it places her in a poor bargaining position when she wishes to reenter the job market. She is likely to find, despite her experience, that her opportunities are limited to entry-level jobs (Treiman, 1985). Research supports a link between labor force discontinuity and job advancement: Women without children tend to be in the labor force continuously and experience slight upward mobility in occupational status by age 32, while those with children experience slight downward mobility (Sewell, Hauser, & Wolf, 1980). Even women with continuous labor force participation do not achieve upward mobility levels comparable to those of men, however, so this variable alone cannot account for the female–male differences.

Life-span developmental researchers have noted that work force participation is related not merely to such concrete factors as income and occupational status, but also to psychological variables. One recent study showed that the employment status of the female member of a couple was a key factor in predicting women's and men's changes in masculinity and femininity across the family life cycle. Employed women had lower femininity scores and their male partners slightly lower masculinity scores than nonemployed women and their partners, respectively (Cunningham & Antill, 1984). This finding is especially interesting in view of a previous research emphasis on demonstrating a link between parenthood and gender-typing. Although some research had suggested that the anticipation and presence of children was largely responsible for changes in couples' masculinity and femininity scores over the course of their relationship (Feldman, Biringen, & Nash, 1981), it now appears that employment may be a more important predictor of these changes.

In recent years, despite a minor flurry of cautionary tales in the popular press about the dangers for women of trying to "have it all," the trend of women combining family and employment shows no sign of slowing down (Schoonmaker, 1986). Indeed, for many families, losing the wife's income, even for a few years, would mean the impossibility of adequate housing, occasional family vacations, and college education for the children. Moreover, should marriage breakdown occur, as it does in one-third to one-half of cases in Canada and the United States, the woman who has been out of the labor force is at an extreme economic disadvantage. Under California's no-fault divorce law, for example, a woman's standard of living drops an average of 73 percent in the first year after her divorce, while her former husband's increases by 42 percent (Weitzman, cited in Schoonmaker, 1986). Finally, the choice of staying home with children rarely means being in a completely ideal setting, with adequate resources and an available, supportive male partner. For most people, the home comes no closer to perfection than does the workplace; if both were restructured to accommodate the needs of people who are seriously committed to both family and employment responsibilities, women and men would have less stress and more time with their children and each other.

What if solutions could be found to all the dilemmas faced by women and men in trying to fulfill both work and family roles? Would sex and gender no longer be important issues in the workplace? The answer is no, for there is at least one other major arena in which gender expectations can interact with work roles: sexuality.

Work, Sexuality, and Power

One of the traditional concerns about integrating women and men in the workplace has been that sexuality will interfere with job performance. A few years ago, the proposal to assign women to work alongside men on U.S. naval ships at sea caused a public outcry, fueled by the specter of sailors having romantic liaisons when they should be swabbing the decks. Husbands and wives of male and female managers may feel stabs of jealousy when business meetings last late into the evening or when their mates take business trips with a member of the other sex. Because changes in the gender composition of the workplace have most frequently involved the addition of women to a previously all-male preserve, these worries about sexuality are most commonly used as arguments for keeping women out. It appears, however, that the issue of sexuality in the workplace is not a simple matter of women's presence turning men's fancy to thoughts of romance. Men and women have learned ritualized ways of relating to one another, often adopting reciprocal gender roles based partially on sexuality, and these roles are not easily shed at the entrance to the workplace. Who, for example, has not encountered the man or woman who cannot seem to relate to members of the other sex without flirting? And who has not observed a change come over a group of men or women at coffee when they are joined by a single member of the other sex? It would be extremely naive to ignore the impact that sexuality can have on our perceptions of and responses to the people with whom we work.

Sexuality has implications for both women's and men's power and achievement in the workplace, and also for the smooth functioning of the workplace itself. An individual can use sexuality as a power resource for influence or advancement at work or, coercively, as a weapon to keep others in line. The intimate bonds that can form in noncoercive sexual relationships at work, although sometimes good for morale and motivation, can promote the formation of coalitions that interfere with group decision making in the workplace. Moreover, public awareness of the existence of such a relationship has a variety of implications for the participants. Let us look briefly at the implications of both coercive and noncoercive sexuality in the workplace.

Coercive Sexuality: Sexual Harassment on the Job

In 1991, one of the first female neurosurgeons, Dr. Frances Conley, a professor at Stanford University School of Medicine, shocked students and colleagues when she announced her resignation. The 51-year-old physician had established an outstanding reputation over the 17 years of her career. Why was she leaving? She said that she had endured a career-long pattern of sexual harassment from her medical colleagues and superiors. She was tired of being asked, for effect, in jest, to go to bed with her colleagues. She was tired of being called "honey" by male doctors in front of her patients. She was tired of the constant sexual innuendos and putdowns to remind her that she was not a real member of the "club" (A surgeon cuts to the heart, 1991).

Sexual harassment—the unwanted imposition of sexual demands or pressures, usually in the context of unequal power relationships—is now recognized as a major problem in the workplace. Although both female and male workers can be sexually harassed, females are the most frequent victims. The U.S. Merit Systems Protection Board (1981) found that 42 percent of women workers, as compared to 15 percent of men workers, reported experiencing sexual harassment. According to a 1983 survey by the Canadian Human Rights Commission, 1.2 million women and 300,000 men say they have been sexually harassed at work. This harassment is not limited to any particular employment sector. A study by the American Medical Association found that

55 percent of the women in a sample of third-year medical students reported being sexually harassed by residents, interns, and faculty (Friend, 1990). A survey of United Methodist clergywomen revealed that 77 percent of them had experienced incidents of sexual harassment—41 percent of them by colleagues or other pastors (Women clerics, 1990). And, in the aftermath of law professor Anita Hill's testimony charging Supreme Court nominee Clarence Thomas with sexual harassment, a flood of anecdotes by women working on Capitol Hill has illustrated that working for an elected representative of the people is no guarantee of safety from unwanted, often humiliating, sexual attention (Sharpe, 1992).

Although gender is by far the best predictor of sexual harassment, other factors also seem to play a part. White women in their thirties who are living with a man to whom they are not married report the most instances of harassment (Gutek & Nakamura, 1983). However, women from virtually every age, racial, and marital status group report sexual harassment to some extent. The people doing the harassing are preponderantly male: 95 percent of the female victims and 22 percent of the male victims in a large survey of federal employees in the United States reported harassment by males only (Tangri, Burt, & Johnson, 1982). In both the United States and Canada, sexual harassment is now recognized as a form of sex discrimination.

Reports by women who are pioneers in male-dominated jobs suggest that they may be at special risk for sexual harassment. Studies of blue-collar women, mentioned earlier, indicate that they face resentment from coworkers and supervisors—resentment that is manifested in practical jokes, threats, violence, and sexual harassment (Colwill & Colwill, 1985). And six female members of the Royal Canadian Mounted Police (RCMP) caused a sensation with complaints to the press about years of being propositioned and victimized by crude sex jokes. As one woman who quit the force after five years commented, "I got tired of being propositioned by senior officers who thought you were a lesbian if you didn't or a slut if you did" (RCMP accused, 1986). Not surprisingly, RCMP records show that the resignation rate for women is five times higher than that of their male counterparts.

The consequences of sexual harassment can be serious, both in terms of the victim's personal well-being and her or his job performance and advancement. Gutek and Nakamura (1983) report that 17.3 percent of the women and 4.8 percent of the men in their samples had quit a job because of sexual harassment; 7.1 percent of the women and 2.4 percent of the men had missed work for the same reason. In another study, 96 percent of the victims of sexual harassment reported emotional stress manifested in nervousness, fear, anger, or sleeplessness; 63 percent developed physical reactions such as headaches, nausea, and weight losses and gains (Crull, 1980). Sexual harassment, with its implicit message that noncompliance will lead to reprisals, creates an intimidating and unhealthy work environment for the victim. In a precedent-setting decision a few years ago, the Workers Compensation Board in Quebec ruled that extreme stress, depression, and physical symptoms caused by sexual harassment from a coworker during working hours is a work-related injury for which compensation should be paid (Lipovenko, 1985).

For victims of sexual harassment, the economic consequences may be as severe as the emotional ones. Noncompliance with the harasser or the lodging of a complaint may lead to retaliation: workloads increased, raises and promotions withheld, jobs lost, and references jeopardized. Victims who are fired or leave their jobs report that prospective employers tend to be skeptical when they cite sexual harassment as their reason for leaving previous jobs, and some have even been refused unemployment benefits (Crull, 1980).

Despite acknowledgment by governments, unions, and researchers that sexual harassment is a serious problem for workers, there is still disagreement about the kinds of behaviors that should be included as sexual harassment. Behaviors reported as harassment include actual or attempted rape or sexual assault; unwanted letters, phone calls, or materials of a sexual nature; unwanted pressure for sexual favors or for dates; unwanted deliberate touching, leaning over, cornering, or pinching; unwanted sexually suggestive looks or gestures; and unwanted sexual teasing, jokes, remarks, or questions (Tangri, Burt, & Johnson, 1982). The U.S. Equal Employment Opportunity Commission (1980) defined sexual harassment as follows:

> Unwelcome sexual advances, requests for sexual favors, and other verbal or physical conduct of a sexual nature constitutes sexual harassment when (1) submission to such conduct is made either explicitly or implicitly a term or condition of an individual's employment, (2) submission to or rejection of such conduct by an individual is used as the basis for employment decisions affecting such individual, or (3) such conduct has the purpose or effect of unreasonably interfering with an individual's work performance or creating an intimidating, hostile, or offensive work environment. (p. 746)

Despite the presence of this and other "official" definitions of sexual harassment, however, individuals may disagree about whether a specific incident constitutes harassment, and victims, even when they do experience harassment, are reluctant to report it. Research findings suggest some reasons why sexual harassment is often unrecognized by anyone but the victim, and why the whole problem has been ignored for so long. In one study (Cohen & Gutek, 1985), college students who were interpreting a possible case of sexual harassment placed little emphasis on variables directly related to the sexual and harassing nature of the incident (relative power of the individuals, appropriateness of the behavior), and paid more attention to the personal aspects of the incident (the degree to which the behavior in question was friendly, complimentary, and/or insulting) and the interpersonal relationship (amount of liking and respect) between the two parties. Furthermore, they focused on the positive aspects of the incident and tended to ignore the problematic aspects. It seems also that behavior is most likely to be labeled as sexual harassment when it violates the ordinary expectations of the actor's social role—expectations that often include the perceived power of the actor over the target. Thus, subjects in a study by Pryor (1985) rated the same comment as more harassing when made by a professor than when made by a fellow student. In addition, Pryor's research showed that if the actor behaved consistently toward the target over time and similarly toward other women, subjects showed a greater tendency to label the behavior as sexual harassment. Finally, one study shows that the frequency of the behavior is related to its perceived offensiveness, which is, in turn, related to the likelihood of reporting the harasser (Brooks & Perot, 1991). Taken together, these studies suggest that observers (and victims) are reluctant to conclude that sexual harassment is taking place, but that they are most likely to notice and label it when the behavior seems out of role or surprising, when it is performed consistently by a particular individual, and when it occurs with more than one target person.

Some people have argued that sexual harassment is simply a normal result of biology: Put women and men together in the workplace, and what can you expect? Tangri, Burt, and Johnson (1982) examined the responses of a stratified random sample of more than 20,000 federal employees to questions about their experience of sexual harassment, in an effort to assess the adequacy of three explanations for its widespread existence:

- natural social–sexual attraction
- the hierarchical way that organizations are structured
- the way society stratifies power and status between women and men

They concluded that sexual harassment was not a single, unitary phenomenon, and that each of the explanations was probably applicable, alone or in combination, to certain cases. The fact that women who sexually harass men are likely to be young, single, and subordinate suggests that the first explanation, social–sexual attraction, is operating in many of these cases. The fact that for both sexes being a "pioneer" in the job, being young, and needing the job badly are related to being sexually harassed supports the second explanation. Finally, the fact that women are, so much more often than men, the victims of sexual harassment lends support to the third explanation. The authors conclude that sexual harassment of women conforms more to an intimidation explanation, while that of men conforms more to an attraction explanation.

There is a popular myth that coercive and exploitative sexuality is not limited to sexual harassment but is widespread in another area: women deliberately exploiting and "selling" their sexuality for gain. Women are said to be able to reap huge professional and financial rewards by "sleeping their way to the top." One cannot help but suspect that this idea owes its popularity to a reluctance to attribute competence to women. Certainly there are some women *and* men who depend on their sexuality as a source of power and advancement at work. As Backhouse and Cohen (1978) point out, however, the penalties for this behavior make it a dangerous one. Not only do people who obtain their promotions, raises, and so on, through sexual payoffs experience self-doubts about their own abilities, but they are frequently the objects of vicious office gossip and sabotage. Moreover, for a person in this position, the end of the affair may also mean the end of the job. It appears that sexuality is only a temporary passport to power in the workplace.

Noncoercive Sexuality: Romance at Work

Fewer than 2 percent of top male executives in one American study reported having an affair with a woman in the office (Johnson, H. J., 1974). We have seen no comparable data on women or on nonoffice work environments. Although the actual number of "office romances" is difficult to determine, the amount of concern generated by the possibility of such liaisons is great (Mainiero, 1986). Some authors, in fact, have argued that the fear of sexual entanglements can lead to such extreme interpersonal vigilance that normal friendly relationships between female and male coworkers cannot develop (Bradford, Sargent, & Sprague, 1975).

Not surprisingly, proximity is a major factor in the development of romantic relationships at work (Quinn, 1977). People whose work throws them together have more opportunities to develop intimate relationships with each other. Motivation also plays a role. Quinn's research shows that observers attribute office romances to three types of motives: ego (excitement, adventure, conquest), job security or advancement, or love. Three kinds of relationships were described most frequently: (1) the "fling," characterized by ego motives on the part of both participants; (2) the "utilitarian relationship," in which the female was pursuing job-related goals while the male was seeking ego satisfaction; and (3) true love, in which both participants had sincere feelings for each other.

The impact of romance in the workplace is not limited to the participants. Observers are quick with stories of how the participants in workplace romances changed for better or for worse—becoming, for example, more efficient and competent, or less available than previously (Quinn, 1977). Such changes have a ripple effect on other relationships in the workplace, sometimes with disastrous results. Quinn argues that the disasters typically result from a distortion of the power and reward system created by the new relationship. He reports several cases of romances involving a male superior and a female subordinate in which the male informally increased the female's power, ignored complaints about her, and became inaccessible except through her. Coworkers who found such situations frustrating and unfair felt powerless and demoralized, and resorted to tactics ranging from complaining and ostracizing to blackmailing and quitting. Some of the hostility in such cases stems from the perception that a lower-ranking person has unfairly been given authority to interfere with people who are technically her superiors. Resentment may also flare when coworkers perceive that their confidences have been broken by one of the romantic partners—that, because of the special relationship, one partner is privy to information that other employees do not or should not have. The situation is fraught with potential not only for ruining employee morale, but also for torpedoing the career of the (usually female) subordinate in question. Apparently viewed as more dispensable, the female, who is usually subordinate, is twice as likely to be fired as is the male.

Even when the office romance is between two equals, it may generate problems. It may cause traditional superior–subordinate gender roles to interfere with the equality that has been established in the workplace between, say, two vice-presidents—a female and male. The sexual double standard may cause the woman to lose status and respect in the eyes of coworkers, and the man may feel angry and out of control because of his inability to protect her from slurs and vicious gossip (Collins, 1983).

It is with a view to dangers such as these that Margaret Mead (1980) proposed a new taboo on sex at work: "You don't make passes at or sleep with the people you work with" (p. 55). Arguing that the ruling out of coworkers as potential sexual partners would enable women and men to develop honest, respectful working relationships, Mead suggested that giving up sex in the workplace was an important step toward the development of true equality between women and men. Whether or not her solution is correct, Mead's article clearly summarized the problem: As long as women and men relate to each other mainly in sexual terms, their attempts to work together will be filled with tension.

Summary

Although both women and men have always worked, the traditional division of labor in industrialized societies has mandated that they work in different spheres: women in the private sphere of the home, men in the public (and paid) sphere of employment outside the home. Until very recently, when women ventured into the world of paid employment, they were automatically relegated to low-status, low-paid jobs. Although vertical and horizontal segregation of the work force by gender still keeps most women in a few clerical and service occupations, a significant minority of women are now entering male-dominated professions. By contrast, there is a much less noticeable influx of men into female-dominated occupations.

A strong factor in the maintenance of the division of labor along gender lines has been discrimination. Sex discrimination has been manifested in a tendency to pay women less than men for the same or comparable work, to evaluate women's work performance less highly than men's, and to give preference to men over women when hiring. Some research suggests that men also can sometimes be the victims of sex discrimination in evaluation and hiring when the job is defined specifically as female-appropriate. In recent years, legislation has been introduced to counteract sex discrimination in hiring and to promote pay equity between women and men. Although these legislative approaches have solved some problems (for instance, by making it more difficult for employers to practice obvious sex discrimination), they have opened the door to others. Controversies now rage about the extent to which male-dominated and female-dominated jobs are comparable in worth, and women who have been hired into male-dominated occupations find themselves dealing with all the pressures that go with token or minority status.

A second factor that helps to maintain gender-based occupational segregation is the assignment of most homemaking and child-care tasks to women, even in dual-career families. Many employed women carry a double burden of responsibility; the consequent stress, fatigue, and time pressure may well limit their capacity to take the steps necessary to move out of female-dominated occupations. However, research indicates that both women and men benefit when they take on a balance of occupational and family responsibilities. A small but growing minority of two-career couples are dividing family tasks more equitably and trying to place equal priority on the careers of both partners. Under pressure from such people, some employers are beginning to make structural changes that acknowledge and allow for the family responsibilities of their employees.

A third barrier to gender equality in the workplace has been the emphasis on sexuality in male–female relationships. Concern over the development of sexual liaisons at work has been the reason sometimes voiced for resistance to the integration of women into male-dominated occupations. Some people have little practice relating to members of the other gender on an equal footing, in ways that are task-oriented and businesslike, and they fear the necessity of doing so. When sexual liaisons *do* develop between people at work, problems sometimes result—and those problems can result in job loss for the member of the couple (usually the woman) who has the least seniority. Moreover, sexual harassment is a common problem in the workplace, especially for women, and even more especially for women in token or "pioneer" positions. Such harassment can serve to keep the gender-based division of labor in place by forcing the victims from their jobs or interfering with their job performance.

Despite the barriers to gender equality in the workplace, significant steps in the direction of that equality have been and continue to be achieved. Perhaps the most important change has been the recognition and questioning of the barriers—a process that may eventually transform the work situation for women and men.

For Additional Reading

Barkalow, Cpt. C., & Raab, A. (1990). *In the men's house.* Captain Barkalow's story of her career in the army offers insights into the difficulties faced by women who try to make a place for themselves in institutions that are profoundly sexist.

Cantor, D. W., & Bernay, T., with J. Stoess (1992). *Women in power: The secrets of leadership.* This study of 25 American women who hold high elective office provides interesting glimpses into the barriers women must overcome to enter politics and the ways in which such challenges can be met.

Clayton, D., & Crosby, F. J. (1992). *Justice, gender, and affirmative action.* Ann Arbor, MI: University of Michigan Press. Research on relative deprivation led these authors to the conclusion that affirmative action, which operates without the necessity for victims of discrimination to come forward on their own behalf, is a necessary policy.

Cohen, S. S. (1989). *Tender power: A revolutionary approach to work and intimacy.* Reading, MA: Addison-Wesley. The author discusses the ways in which the entry of women into management positions may influence how power is wielded by both women and men at high corporate levels.

England, P. (1992). *Comparable worth: Theories and evidence.* Hawthorne, NY: Aldine de Gruyter. Here is an overview of research on such controversial questions as how comparable worth can be decided, the economic and legal aspects of its implementation, and whether such strategies are justified.

14

Justice, Equity, & Social Change

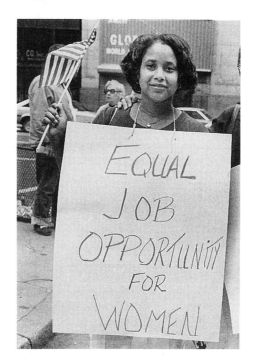

J ustice is often depicted in the form of a woman—a blindfolded woman holding the scales on which human deeds are balanced by their outcomes. The image says a lot about society's dominant conception of justice: the equity-based notion that people deserve outcomes (rewards or punishments) in proportion to their actions. However, the depiction of justice as a woman is more than a little ironic, since there exists a long history of pronouncements by male "experts" that women are morally inferior to men and less able to develop a strong, clear sense of justice unclouded by personal emotional biases. Within psychology, this tradition began with Sigmund Freud (1925/1974), who argued that women's weaker superego made them less capable than men of impersonal justice. Echoes of this attitude have appeared in some of the most widely accepted psychological theories of moral development.

There is another sense in which the depiction of justice as a woman is ironic: Society's formal institutions of justice—the laws and the judicial system—have been developed and dominated by men. Most lawyers and judges are still men. Women have had to struggle to be considered equal with men under the law, and many of those struggles are still underway. In Canada, women were not legally considered "persons" until 1929. In the United States, it has proven so far impossible to amend the Constitution with the words "Equality of rights under the law shall not be denied or abridged by the United States or any state on account of sex." Although nearly 100 countries have ratified the United Nations Convention on the Elimination of All Forms of Discrimination Against Women, some nations have not yet agreed to it. It appears that, as Florynce Kennedy (1970) once noted, justice really is blind—blind to the existence of sexism.

This chapter examines various issues of justice as they pertain to gender. It begins with an overview of research on gender differences and similarities in the perception and actualization of justice. Included here is a discussion of the ways in which the desire to see the world as fair and just shapes people's perceptions of social arrangements, helping them to rationalize the treatment of women and men as fair even when it is clearly unequal. A section on gender and the law then examines some concrete results of the formal application of the justice system to women and men. Finally, the chapter closes with a discussion of the social change that might result from the challenges posed by the feminist movement to society's traditional notions of justice.

Gender and Conceptions of Justice

Two streams of research within psychology have examined the relationship between gender and conceptions of justice: studies of reward allocation and studies of moral development. Both areas reveal evidence for both differences and similarities between women and men.

Reward Allocation and Personal Entitlement: Equity or Equality?

Differences between women and men in the way they allocate rewards to themselves and to others have been found consistently. In general, women tend to pay themselves less than men do when dividing rewards between themselves and others (Kahn, O'Leary, Krulewitz, & Lamm, 1980; Major & Deaux, 1982; Major, 1987). Women report as much satisfaction with their jobs as men do, despite the fact that they tend to hold jobs that are lower status and more poorly paid than men's (Hodson, 1989). In addition, there is a tendency for women to favor an equality norm in the distribution of rewards for task performance, allocating the same degree of reward to each participant, while men tend to favor an equity norm, allocating rewards differentially according to task performance (Major & Adams, 1983). Also, men report more satisfaction than women do with an exchange relationship that is equitable (Brockner & Adsit, 1986). It has sometimes been argued that these differences in reward allocation stem from the socialization of women to be more interpersonally oriented than men are, so that women place more emphasis on maintaining good relationships with their coworkers than on getting a fair share of the reward (Kahn et al., 1980). A second possible explanation is that women and men differ in their own personal feelings of entitlement—of what *is* a fair reward for their efforts (Major, McFarlin, & Gagnon, 1984; Major, 1987).

Studies have shown that women's standards of what is fair pay for themselves are lower than those of men (Callahan-Levy & Messe, 1979; Major et al., 1984). When women and men are asked to work on a task for a period of time and then to assign themselves fair pay for their performance, women pay themselves significantly less money than do men, and they also report that less money is fair pay for their work. This happens even when men and women do not differ in their evaluations of their own performance. Moreover, when asked to do as much work as they think is fair for a given amount of money, women work longer, do more work, and perform more correctly and efficiently than men do (Major et al., 1984). Many plausible explanations have been offered for these findings. Perhaps women have lower expectations for pay because of the history of wage discrimination against them. Or perhaps women tend to compare themselves to other women—a lower reference group standard than men because women typically are paid less than men. A third possibility is that women and men may place different values on rewards. Women may value money less and interpersonal relationships more than men do. Yet another perspective is that women are more likely than men to devalue their own work and hence to underreward it, or, conversely, that men overvalue and overreward their own work. Finally, it has been suggested that gender-role socialization leads women to see a weaker connection than men do between their work and pay.

All of these explanations may have some merit in particular situations, and several have received some experimental support. Major and her colleagues (1984) found that gender differences in personal entitlement did not occur when information was available about the pay of other people—a finding that suggests that women are no more likely than men to pay themselves less than others whom they see as comparable. These researchers did find evidence, however, that when no obviously appropriate comparison group was available, people tended to use generalized same-sex comparisons. People seemed to match their behavior to what they thought others of their own sex would do—and both women and men thought that women would pay themselves less than men for the same work, and that women would work longer than men given the same pay.

This study also provides evidence that women tend to undervalue and/or men to overvalue their own work. Although women did more and better work than men for the specified amount of pay, men and women did not differ in the value they assigned to their own work or in their satisfaction with their pay. However, no evidence was found to support the notion that men value money more than women do; there were no gender differences in the importance placed on the money earned.

Finally, this research also suggests that gender differences, not only in personal entitlement but also in interpersonal orientation, may have something to do with women's and men's allocation of rewards to themselves. Women, but not men, worked longer when they knew they were being observed by the experimenter—a finding that suggests that women's balancing of work inputs with pay outputs was more influenced by concerns about making a good impression or pleasing the experimenter than was men's. However, the fact that women overworked or underpaid themselves relative to men in all conditions, even when not being observed, indicates that gender differences in interpersonal orientation are not enough to explain the tendency for men to allocate more rewards to themselves than women do.

The tendency for women and men, when not provided with any comparison information, to think that they deserve differing amounts of pay for the same work apparently does not have a single cause, but many. Most of these causes, however, are probably traceable to a social structure that has traditionally provided fewer tangible rewards to women than to men for their work. If there is a norm, accepted by both sexes, that women expect less pay than men do for the same amount of work, that norm did not emerge in a vacuum, but from many generations of social consensus.

Gender differences in reward allocation extend beyond individuals' allocations to themselves. Researchers have found that, at least under some conditions, men and women differ in the way they distribute rewards to other people, such as coworkers or subordinates. Gender differences in this behavior are not always found, but when they do appear they show men favoring a distribution system in which people are rewarded in proportion to their work inputs (equity) and women favoring a system in which people are rewarded equally, regardless of differences in work inputs (equality). The most popular explanation for this difference has been that women have been socialized to be more concerned with interpersonal relations than men have, and so they distribute rewards in ways that will maintain interpersonal harmony rather than emphasize differences in performance. This explanation has received some support. However, situational factors are also apparently very important in determining the way that women and men distribute rewards. For example, Major and Adams (1983) found that even when men and women were equivalent in their scores on a questionnaire measure of interpersonal orientation, women still tended to allocate rewards more equally than did men. On the other hand, Zanna and Bowden (1977) showed that both women and men allocated rewards equally when relating to others as persons, but equitably when relating to others as positions or roles. Nevertheless, when the situation was ambiguous, traditional males allocated equitably and traditional females allocated equally. Another study showed that when pressured to improve their group's productivity, males, but not females, allocated rewards more equitably; when pressured to improve worker relationships, females, but not males, tended to allocate rewards more equally (Stake, 1985). Finally, Major and Adams (1984) showed that, under certain conditions, women relied more heavily on equity, distributing rewards more in proportion to merit, than men did! The crucial factor was whether people were dividing a shared reward between themselves and their partner, or whether they were allocating independent rewards to themselves and their partner (that is, when the allocation they made to themselves did not affect the allocation to their partner, and vice versa). Both women and men divided the reward more equally when asked to divide a joint reward than when asked to allocate independent rewards to themselves and their partner. Surprisingly, however, when subjects were allocating rewards separately to themselves and their partners, women allocated the rewards more in proportion to merit than did men. The researchers speculate that women do not ignore merit or different levels of performance when giving out rewards; rather, they are uncomfortable when rewarding themselves for better performance means that their partner will receive less. When some of the stigma of taking more for the self is removed by making the two allocations independent, women are more comfortable differentiating between their performance and that of their partner by giving themselves a larger reward. The study does not explain *why* women should be more sensitive than men to the negative connotations of taking more for oneself at the expense of someone else, even in the case where this can be justified by better performance. It does point, however, to the importance of such situational factors as the privacy of allocation decisions, the expectation of future interactions with the partner, and the nature of the reward on the justice decisions of both men and women. It may well be that situational factors in reward allocation settings provide cues about what behavior is appropriate for both genders. When researchers have identified all of these cues, we may be in a better position to explain the gender differences in reward allocation.

Regardless of the reasons for gender differences in justice decisions, the existence of such differences in certain situations has some interesting possible implications. In the workplace, for example, what might the implications be if male and female managers favored equity and equality, respectively, in dealing with the performance of their subordinates? Perhaps the subordinates of the female manager would be more cooperative with one another and less inclined to compete than would the subordinates of the male manager. Or perhaps the subordinates of the female manager would be demoralized and resentful, knowing that their less competent coworkers were being rewarded equally with themselves. Without knowing more about the specific organizational context and the people involved, it is impossible to predict the outcome. As yet, however, there is very little evidence from such field situations about whether, in fact, male and female managers do differ in their preference for equity or equality when dealing with subordinates. Most of the research on reward allocation has been done in laboratory situations using university students as subjects, and one study that has focused specifically on justice in manager–subordinate relations is no exception. In this study, Dobbins (1986) asked students to play the role of a manager who must choose what corrective action should be taken toward an employee who demonstrated poor performance by making two serious shipping errors. He found that the males relied solely on equity to decide what corrective action should be taken, responding most harshly when poor performance appeared to be caused by the employee's disposition rather than by situational factors. Females, however, used a mixture of equity and equality in their corrective action decisions. Although they too were harshest with the employee when the error appeared to be that individual's fault, they were also, in contrast to the men, more influenced in their decisions by the likableness and gender of the employee. Female "managers" were less harsh when the employee was female and/or likable; male "managers" were not influenced by these factors. This study has many limitations. The subjects had no real management experience, the situation was hypothetical, and there was no actual contact with a subordinate but only a written description of the subordinate's behavior. It cannot be used to draw conclusions about the behavior of real male and female managers, then, but it raises some issues worthy of further investigation.

On the whole, research on the way females and males allocate rewards to themselves and others suggests that men and women have learned to take different perspectives toward distributive justice in particular situations. The differences in behavior may reflect differences in the sense of personal entitlement or deserving, differences in interpersonal orientation, and/or differential sensitivity to particular social cues—but what these latter differences reflect is not yet clear. Major and her colleagues' (1984) argument that the gender differences stem from individuals' attempts to match their behavior with their awareness of norms for their own sex is a persuasive one—and as long as it is normative to reward women at lower rates than men, it signals real, not theoretical, problems for women. Research shows that initial expectations for pay tend to be self-confirming; that is, expecting and requesting a high salary tends to be associated with *receiving* a higher salary (Major, Vanderslice, & McFarlin, 1984). Women, expecting lower salaries, may keep on getting exactly what they expect.

Gender Inequality and the Perception of Justice.   The finding that both women and men tend to subscribe to norms that women will be rewarded less for their work or will do more work for less pay is congruent with many of the other findings discussed in this book. There appears to be a great deal of acceptance and rationalization of situations that amount to sex discrimination. How are people able to square their acceptance of such situations with their notions of justice?

If there is one general principle that cognitive social psychology has demonstrated, it is that human beings are capable of Olympic feats of rationalization. When people see a situation that they either cannot or do not wish to change, they are extremely good at thinking up reasons why that situation is fair. For example, research has shown that people have a need to believe that the world is a just place, and that people generally get what they deserve (Lerner, 1970, 1974). Individuals often seem to satisfy this need by seeing victims as, by definition, deserving of the harm inflicted on them. Such a general tendency may provide a partial explanation for accepting discrimination against women. Men and women may justify discrimination by believing that women's work is less valuable than men's, that women are less competent, need money less, or are less interested in their work than men are. As long as people can think of reasons why women *deserve* less than men, their belief in a just world can coexist comfortably with their awareness of sex discrimination.

A parallel explanation for the acceptance of female subordination stems from the study of the relationship between power and justice. As noted in Chapter 11, the group with the most power in a hierarchy not only gains control of more resources than other groups but also evolves a social philosophy that supports its right to monopolize these resources (Walster & Walster, 1975). According to equity theory, this philosophy will tend to become accepted by the entire community as justification for the status quo; if the entire group accepts the status quo, everyone avoids the discomfort of a relationship viewed as inequitable or unfair. Research has shown that both exploiters and victims can and frequently do convince themselves that even the most unbalanced of exchanges is perfectly fair (Walster, Berscheid, & Walster, 1973). The ideology of dominance, then, tends to be self-perpetuating: The more power a group obtains, the more its members convince themselves and others that such power is deserved and stems from superiority. For many people, recognizing that a system that discriminates against women is unfair is tantamount to admitting that their own decisions and actions have been unfair or that they have been victims of unfair treatment—possibilities that, according to equity theory, can result in considerable discomfort for individuals on either side of the equation.

Moral Development and Moral Reasoning

Several psychological theories have postulated that males and females differ in the way they develop moral reasoning, the ability to make judgments about right and wrong. Freud's (1925/1974) psychoanalytic theory suggested that, because of differences in the resolution of the Oedipal complex (see Chapter 2), males develop a superego that is more internalized, rigid, and demanding than that of females, with the consequence that the moral character of men is more strongly defined than is that of women. Piaget's (1965) cognitive-developmental theory of morality posited a similar belief in male moral superiority. He argued that equity, which involves taking into account the personal circumstances of each individual, was a more useful and advanced form of justice than equality, and noted that boys prefer equity while girls prefer equality.

Perhaps the most well-known theory of moral development was elaborated by Kohlberg (1964, 1984). This theory proposes that moral development progresses through three levels in six stages, the highest of which is not reached until adulthood, or may never be reached. Individuals progress from basing moral judgments on fear of consequences to themselves, to basing them on concern for social approval, harmony, and law and order, to basing them on abstract principles of universal rights for all persons. Kohlberg indicates that most women and men develop at least to the middle, conventional level of moral reasoning, but that, within this level, women prefer Stage 3 reasoning based on good intentions and social approval while men prefer the more advanced Stage 4 reasoning based on maintaining the social order. Furthermore, men are more likely than women to reach the highest level of moral reasoning; women supposedly do not reach these top two stages unless they take on occupational positions similar to men's. Otherwise, "while girls are moving from high school or college to motherhood, sizeable proportions of them are remaining at Stage 3, while their male agemates are dropping Stage 3 in favor of the stages above it. Stage 3 morality is a functional morality for housewives and mothers; it is not for businessmen and professionals" (Kohlberg & Kramer, 1969, p. 108).

Kohlberg's theory reflects some strong biases, not only about males and females and the moral requirements of their respective roles, but also about the superiority of certain kinds of moral reasoning to other kinds. The possibility that different forms of moral reasoning might be equally useful and valid is not acknowledged in his theory. Furthermore, the theory was developed using data only from males; thus, males provide the standard for what is humanly normal. Psychologist Carol Gilligan (1982) proposed a new cognitive-developmental theory of morality in an effort to correct the masculine bias of this and other theories.

Gilligan's Theory: Two Moral Principles.   When Gilligan analyzed the responses made by girls and women to questions about morality, she did not limit herself to looking for the kinds of themes that would indicate stage of moral development according to Kohlberg's theory. Rather, she tried to find out whether there were themes in women's moral reasoning that had been missed by Kohlberg's scoring system. Her research led her to suggest that, besides the principle of rights that had emerged as the basis of moral reasoning in Kohlberg's work, another principle was frequently invoked as her respondents struggled to explain why a particular decision was right or wrong— the principle of caring and responsibility. Moral judgments based on the principle of caring stressed the necessity to be responsible in one's relationships, to be sensitive to the needs of others, and to avoid giving hurt. Gilligan's research led her to conclude that there were stages in the development of the care orientation to morality, just as there were stages in the development of the rights orientation. Individuals moved from an initial stage of caring only for the self, to a middle stage of trying to be "good" by caring for others (sometimes called *maternal morality* by Gilligan because it is the type of morality that is urged on women in their maternal role), to a mature stage of caring for truth, which involves achieving a balance of care for the self and others.

Gilligan argues that, although both the rights orientation and the care orientation can be found in the moral reasoning of women and men, men tend to place more emphasis on rights, while women place more emphasis on care. The difference in emphasis, she suggests, is due to the different goals of development for women and men: attachment and relationship for women, separation and achievement for men. The goals are different because the problems and challenges faced by females are different from those faced by men, partly because society expects different things from them and partly because their biological differences make them vulnerable to different experiences in the area of reproduction. Gilligan argues, however, that neither the rights orientation nor the care orientation represents a superior type of moral reasoning. Rather, they are different, in some sense complementary, orientations: "two disparate modes of experience that are in the end connected. . . . In the representation of maturity, both perspectives converge in the realization that just as inequality adversely affects both parties in an unequal relationship, so too violence is destructive for everyone involved" (p. 174).

Many people have found Gilligan's theory appealing, while others have criticized it for reifying the stereotype that women are emotional and nurturant and men are logical and clearheaded. Although agreeing that her contribution has been immense in drawing attention to the dimension of care and responsibility in moral judgments, many investigators have been more cautious in accepting her claim that women and men differ in their reliance on this orientation. Of course, the traditional way of checking the value of a theory is to test it with research, and in recent years careful investigations have been made of both Kohlberg's and Gilligan's theories with respect to gender differences.

L. J. Walker (1984) performed a meta-analysis of studies on moral reasoning as measured by Kohlberg's interview method in 106 samples of children, adolescents, and adults. Of all these samples, only 8 clearly indicated significant differences favoring males. Moreover, several of these 8 were inconclusive because gender was confounded with occupational-educational differences. Walker suggests that, rather than arguing over the extent to which sex bias is inherent in Kohlberg's theory, it would be more appropriate to ask why, in the face of so little evidence, the myth persists that males are more advanced in Kohlberg's levels of moral reasoning than females are. He concludes that, in fact, the moral reasoning of men and women is remarkably similar, especially given publication and reporting biases that make differences more likely to be reported.

The failure to find empirical confirmation for the notion that males operate at higher levels of moral reasoning than females do is echoed in a meta-analysis of 56 samples including over 6000 subjects (Thoma, 1986). The findings showed that at every age and educational level, small but reliable gender differences appeared—with females scoring significantly higher than males on moral reasoning.

Another review of the literature on moral development, this one including not only studies using Kohlberg's measure but also those using a variety of other measures, found that 60 percent of the studies found no differences between males and females with respect to moral development (Lifton, 1985). Among the studies that did report a significant male–female difference in moral development, most used Kohlberg's measure, and the differences sometimes favored females, particularly for children. In his own research, Lifton (1985) found no evidence of male–female differences in moral development among adolescents or adults, using either Kohlberg's measure of moral judgment or his own measure of moral character. He did, however, find significant differences in stage of moral judgment between masculine and feminine persons of both sexes, suggesting that Kohlberg's measure may favor masculine over feminine persons.

Some researchers have tried specifically to evaluate Gilligan's theory that an ethic of care is more prevalent among women and an ethic of rights is more prevalent among men. Gilligan and Attanucci (1988), using real-life dilemmas, found that women and men used both care and justice orientations, but that care-focus dilemmas were more likely to be presented by women and justice-focus dilemmas were more likely to be presented by men. Stiller and Forrest (1990) also found that men emphasized justice and women emphasized care in their moral reasoning. Other studies that have examined individuals' moral reasoning about competitive athletic encounters (Crown & Heatherington, 1989) and interpersonal relationships (Pratt, Pancer, & Hunsberger, 1990) have found no gender differences in such reasoning.

Ford and Lowery (1986) conducted a study specifically designed to compare women and men on their use of the principles of rights and care in their moral judgments. They asked male and female undergraduates to describe three important moral conflicts in their lives, and to rate the importance of those conflicts and the degree of difficulty they experienced in deciding what to do. Next, the students read summary descriptions of the rights and care orientations to moral judgment and rated, on 7-point scales, the degree to which each orientation was a part of their own approach to the conflicts they had described. They also completed a measure of gender-role orientation and a scale evaluating the two moral orientations along good-bad, powerful-weak, and active-passive dimensions. The results of the study offered some, but not overwhelming, support for Gilligan's theory. Men and women did not differ significantly in the degree to which they used the rights and care orientations. However, women were more consistent from one conflict to the next in their use of the care orientation than in their use of the rights orientation, while men were more consistent in their use of the rights than of the care orientation. Interestingly, for both female and male subjects, the importance and difficulty ratings for the conflict situations were significantly associated with care ratings but not with rights ratings. For this college student sample, the most important and difficult moral decisions encountered so far had been related more to issues of care than to issues of rights. A later study (Friedman, Robinson, & Friedman, 1987), which also found a lack of support for Gilligan's hypothesis that gender is related to differences in moral judgments, similarly suggests that Gilligan is correct in her proposal that care is a distinct and important dimension of moral reasoning.

The only longitudinal study that has examined the possibility of gender differences in care and responsibility orientations suggests that, for most individuals, there is little consistency in these orientations over time (Walker, 1989). This study, in which persons aged 5 to 63 years were interviewed twice, two years apart, revealed no gender differences in justice and care orientations for children and adolescents, and none at any age using standard moral dilemmas. The only gender difference found was among adults using real-life dilemmas—for whom there was a tendency for women to use the care orientation more frequently. This gender difference in orientation appeared to be confounded with a gender difference in the content of the real-life dilemmas recalled by the respondents. Women were more likely to recall personal, as opposed to impersonal, real-life moral dilemmas—and, for both women and men, personal dilemmas were strongly associated with the use of the care orientation.

In the Ford and Lowery (1986) study, although females and males did not differ significantly in their use of the care and rights orientations, both groups rated the care orientation as a feminine response and the rights orientation as a masculine response. It appears that the belief in different styles of moral judgment for women and men existed even in this sample where only minimal evidence for such female–male differences could be found. This finding brings us back to the question posed by L. J. Walker (1984): Why does the belief in gender differences in moral reasoning persist so strongly in the face of such weak or contradictory evidence? Brabeck (1983) addresses the question of why so many people find an intuitive appeal to Gilligan's theory, despite its lack of clear empirical support. She notes that stereotypes about gender differences in morality abound; for instance, studies have found that girls and boys develop different reputations for altruism, even when their actual behavior is very similar (Shigetomi, Hartmann, & Gilford, 1981). In some way, she suggests, a belief that males and females are morally different meets our cultural and emotional needs—but it does so by distorting our vision of human beings:

> There is an essential tension between autonomy and interdependence, between the requirements of justice and the demands of mercy, between absolute moral principles and situation specific moral action, between reason and affect. To resolve this tension by assigning half to males and half to females when evidence does not support that division is to reduce the complexity of morality, to cloud truth with myth, to do an injustice to the capacities of both sexes and to lose an opportunity to revise and modify our theories of morality. (p. 287)

Although the last word is certainly not in on the possibility of gender differences in moral orientation (for example, it may be that the situations men experience as moral conflicts are more likely to involve rights while those women experience as conflicts are more likely to involve care), the evidence to date suggests that women and men are unlikely to bring very different principles of moral judgment to any particular moral dilemma. The controversy continues to stimulate research, and thus far it has had the effect of broadening our understanding of moral reasoning and of conferring new respect on a dimension of morality that, whether it actually differentiates the sexes or not, has always been trivialized because it was stereotyped as feminine.

Gender and the Law

Social notions of justice are formalized into a legal system of laws and courts that, in the tradition of justice as "blind," are supposed to treat everyone with equal favor, regardless of economic, social, or political status. Not surprisingly, however, this formal justice system reflects and even perpetuates the prevalent stereotypes and prejudices about gender. Such biases are evident in the induction of lawyers and judges into the system, in laws concerning the rights of women and men, and in the treatment of male and female criminals and victims who come into contact with the legal system.

Participation in the Legal System: Lawyers and Judges

Early in this century, when women in Canada were petitioning for the opportunity to become lawyers, one judge ruled that their exclusion was perfectly reasonable. His rationale: a "lady lawyer" would have to subject her delicate ears to courtroom testimony concerning rape—a subject about which no woman should have to hear (Smith, 1987). In 1873, a woman named Myra Bradwell was barred from practicing law in Illinois because, the judge said, woman's natural place was in the home (Agate & Meacham, 1977), and also because the state restricted the right of married women to make legally binding contracts. No client would want to deal with an attorney who could not be held accountable for the agreements that she signed. The law in this case placed women in a frustrating double bind: first, by limiting their accountability for their actions, and then by acting to protect others from the consequences of this lack of accountability.

Although women have now been admitted to the practice of law, they are still hampered by the stereotype that women are more emotional and less rational than men in their orientation toward justice. Furthermore, although their numbers are increasing, women are still a definite minority among lawyers and judges. In 1982, 16 percent of all American lawyers were women (Change over a decade, 1985); comparable figures for Canada show that fewer than 10 percent of lawyers were women in 1980 (Abella, 1984). Women held only 17 percent of American judgeships in 1980, most of these in lower courts (Schmid, 1984); Canadian figures for the same year indicate that there were fewer than 250 female judges and magistrates. In 1987, 19.7 percent of American lawyers and judges combined were women (Kaufman, 1989); that figure had risen to only 22.3 percent by 1989 (U.S. Department of Commerce, 1991).

The gender distribution of positions in the legal profession is changing; between one-third and one-half of entrants to many law schools in the United States and Canada are women. By 1988, women were earning 40 percent of law degrees (Institute for Women's Policy Research, 1991). However, reports suggest that all is not yet clear sailing for women in law school, and that the legal profession may be unwilling to grant full acceptance to women, particularly if they persist in pointing out inequities in the legal treatment of the sexes. McIntyre (1987), in a searching and painful description of her first year on the faculty of a prestigious Canadian law school, describes experiences of hostility and harassment from male students and colleagues in response to her feminist views. Particularly instructive, in view of the issues of power already discussed in this book, is her description of how female law students were silenced and intimidated when they tried to articulate feminist arguments or when they challenged traditional legal approaches to particular problems. For example, two women in her seminar on labor law expressed discomfort with the assumptions of adversarial relations and conflict built into the working model of labor law and labor relations that the class was using. They were interrupted, contradicted, and shouted down by male students:

> I . . . asked the class to reflect on what had just happened. Two usually silent women had spoken and explained why they had trouble participating. One was interrupted and called "wrong"; then the subject was changed; then their contribution was characterized as non-law. I suggested their contributions

introduced an alternative model of law and labor relations which we might try to explore. Again there was an uproar. I was shouted down by the left-wing male and denounced as a "bourgeois feminist". . . . I proposed we draw up two models for a first contract: one under the working model premised on conflict, power, inequality and private property; the other premised on codetermination, communal interests and equality. . . . About five male students put down their pens, pulled back their chairs and glared at me, refusing to participate. No one invited the two women who had advanced an alternative model to articulate what their vision might include. They went silent. A few men ventured some possibilities, but were met with open anger from other men who interrupted, laughed or talked over them. (p. 8)

This example illustrates just how difficult it can be for female students, even with the support of a female professor, to challenge the structure or built-in assumptions of a legal system that has always been articulated and dominated by men. Such difficulties are not unique to law schools, of course, but they may be aggravated in the law school atmosphere of adversarial justice. A reading of McIntyre's article makes it painfully clear that women who survive law school may have had much of their interest in questioning established legal assumptions and priorities ground out of them in the process.

Sex, Gender, and Legal Rights

In 1986, the Ontario Court of Appeal in Canada ruled that Justine Blainey, a 12-year-old girl who had been chosen to play on a first-class hockey team in Toronto but had been barred from play by the Ontario Hockey Association, could legally play on the team. This was the first sex equality case to be decided by an appeal court under Canada's then new *Charter of Rights and Freedoms*, and is one highly publicized example of the way in which sex discrimination can be fought by legal means (Brodsky, 1986).

More recently, in a decision with far-reaching implications, the United States Supreme Court ruled that companies may not use "fetal protection" as a reason to bar women of childbearing age from jobs that pose reproductive hazards (Marcus, 1991). The case involved a Milwaukee-based battery manufacturer that barred female employees from jobs that exposed them to high levels of lead. Lead can damage a developing fetus. The legal action was brought on behalf of a 50-year-old divorced woman who was transferred from her position and another who chose to be sterilized in order to keep her job. The Court held that it was illegal for a company to force a woman to decide between having a child and having a job, and noted that discrimination on the basis of a person's ability to become pregnant amounted simply to a form of sex discrimination.

In recent years, we have seen an escalation of efforts, international in scope, to achieve equal rights under the law for women and men. A major push has been made toward the adoption by all countries of the United Nations Convention on the Elimination of All Forms of Discrimination Against Women. This convention includes, among other things, the assurance that women and men will be equal before the law, including laws governing property and contracts, have equal rights to family benefits and bank credit, have the same rights and responsibilities during marriage and its disso-lution, and have equal pay for work of equal value. At this writing, nearly 100 coun-tries, including Canada but not including the United States, have ratified this convention.

Within North America, attempts to promote equality under the law for men and women have frequently foundered on arguments about what definition of *equality* is most appropriate. This argument turns on the perception of justice: Although a group of individuals may agree that women and men should be treated the same way under the law in many circumstances, they may disagree about which legal distinctions between the sexes, if any, should be preserved. The problem is a difficult one, because, as discussed earlier in this chapter, perceptions of fairness are so often conditioned by what we are used to and by "the way things have always been." As an illustration of this point, consider the following list of situations in which the law, in certain jurisdictions, discriminates on the basis of sex:

- Certain social service benefits are available to mothers who stay home with their children but not to fathers who do the same thing.
- The child of a married couple can be given the father's surname but not the mother's.
- The father of a child born "out of wedlock" can be sued by the mother for the support of the child; however, a father who has custody of a child born "out of wedlock" cannot initiate similar proceedings against the mother.
- "Protective" labor laws in some jurisdictions establish a maximum number of hours a woman may work.
- Proposed legislation in several states would deny custodial single parents, 95 per-cent of whom are women, increases in welfare benefits if they have additional children and would allow married couples to retain more of their earnings than single-parent families.

For years such laws have seemed so "natural" that few people considered them unfair, despite their discrimination on the basis of sex. It is only in consciously stepping back from traditional assumptions about sex differences and gender roles that people become aware of the arbitrariness of laws such as these.

Within the legal system, a debate is still going on about how gender equality should be defined under the law. There are at least three perspectives (Lahey, 1984). (1) The first is *absolute equality*, which would require legislation to be *sex-blind* and *gender-neutral* and to deny the existence of any meaningful differences between women and men, with the exception of reproductive differences. A feminist-inspired variation on this perspective is the *sex-specific/gender-neutral* approach (Lahey, 1984), which would try to achieve equality by drafting legislation specifically geared to the needs of women as a disadvantaged group, but written using such neutral terms as *parent* and *spouse* so that protections and benefits would be available to both women and men. (2) A second alternative is the *gender-specific* approach, which acknowledges biological, social, and economic differences between the sexes and recognizes women as a disad-vantaged group. This approach would strike down legislation that was detrimental to women but retain provisions that were beneficial to women in order to redress the ine-qualities between women and men. (3) Another possibility is *equality with recognition of real differences*. This would involve a standard in which equal treatment is the norm, but strong statistical evidence that women and men are in unequal positions can be used to uphold unequal treatment. This third standard reflects the current reasoning applied by the U.S. Supreme Court.

All of these approaches to gender equality have potential pitfalls. The problem with a gender-specific approach to equality is that gender-specific legislation can be used in the service of inequality as well as equality. For example, the recognition that women as a group are physically weaker than men has in the past been used to construct gender-specific legislation that "protected" women from being hired for jobs that required the lifting of heavy loads. The sex-specific/gender-neutral approach, despite its neutral language, could possibly reinforce existing gender stereotypes. For instance, laws designed to meet the needs of employed mothers may reinforce the stereotype that child care is "naturally" women's work, even though the actual wording of the legislation is in terms of *parental* rather than *maternal* leave. Even the absolute equality approach has its share of potential problems. Absolute equality denies male–female differences, but does so in the context of a legal system that was designed with males in mind, so that females and female experiences end up being judged according to a male standard. An example of how ludicrous this "gender-neutral" approach to justice can become in the hands of an unsympathetic judge can be found in the ruling on a sexual assault case in Canada. A young woman had been approached by a man who, against her will, grabbed and fondled her breasts. The man was charged with sexual assault. The court, however, ruled that, since breasts were female secondary sex characteristics, just as beards were male secondary sex characteristics, for a man to fondle a woman's breasts was no more a case of sexual assault than it would be for a woman to stroke a man's beard (Smith, 1987). This ruling was eventually overturned by the Supreme Court of Canada. However, it is clear that attempts to make the laws treat both sexes fairly can backfire against either women or men and that, since laws are interpreted in courts by judges, gender bias can be a factor in the justice system even when the laws themselves are unbiased.

Gender and Crime

An important aspect of society's concern with justice has to do with preventing and punishing criminal behavior. In this area as well, gender has an impact on justice. Women and men differ in their criminal behavior, in which of their behaviors are considered criminal, and in the way their crimes are punished. Women and men also differ in their experiences as victims of crime.

Women and Men as Criminals.   Men commit more crimes than women, and men's crimes tend to be more serious and violent than women's crimes (Gove, 1985). The reported incidence of crimes by women, particularly property crimes, have increased at a faster rate than those of men in recent years (Mann, 1984), but all over the world most crimes, especially violent ones, are still committed by men.

It is difficult to evaluate how well the statistics on crime reflect gender differences in criminal behavior because there are gender biases in the criminal justice system's treatment of offenders. Among adolescents, females, but not males, tend to be charged with so-called *status offenses*, such as promiscuity or running away from home (Mann, 1984; Figueira-McDonough, 1987). These behaviors are violations of social norms for young women; it is hard to imagine a male being detained on the grounds of "promiscuity." Also, a female juvenile can apparently sometimes be detained because her behavior is "unladylike." Among adults, on the other hand, women have traditionally been less likely to be arrested and have tended to be given more lenient treatment than their male counterparts (Parisi, 1982; Weisberg, 1982), perhaps because gender stereotypes support the notion that women can't really be as "bad" as men. The stereotypes can backfire for women accused of particularly unfeminine crimes, however; these women sometimes receive particularly punitive sentences (Parisi, 1982). There appears to be a trend now away from automatic leniency for female criminals (Heilbrun & Heilbrun, 1986).

Certain criminal laws discriminate directly on the grounds of sex. For example, in some jurisdictions, both statutory rape and homosexual acts are legally considered crimes only when performed by males, whereas, in others, prostitution is an exclusively female crime. Other laws, for the most part now changed, were based on the double standard with respect to sexuality in marriage. For example, in some jurisdictions, murder was considered a justifiable reaction for a man who found his wife in bed with another man, but not for a wife who found her husband in bed with another woman. Clearly, criminal law as well as civil law contains built-in inequalities with respect to gender, and these inequalities are related to social stereotypes about women and men.

An aspect of the criminal law that has been the target of much criticism for its inequitable treatment of women and men is that surrounding prostitution: the selling of sex for money. Most prostitutes are women although there are gay male prostitutes and there are also men who sell sex and companionship to women—but not usually on the street. Although the law in most jurisdictions defines soliciting or prostitution as a crime, not all the participants in the crime are usually charged, or even liable to be charged. Generally, the woman who sells sex is charged with breaking the law if she is caught; the man purchasing her services is not. For example, in Toronto, a jurisdiction where both prostitutes and their customers are liable for prosecution, over a four-year period, from 1979 to 1982, 71 percent of the charges for soliciting as prostitutes or customers were laid against women, while 29 percent were laid against men (Canadian Advisory Council on the Status of Women, 1984). A study of prostitution-related arrests in Buffalo, New York, between 1977 and 1979 showed a similar pattern: Only 12.9 percent of the female prostitutes, but 73.0 percent of the men arrested for patronizing them, were released after the arrest to await trial (Bernat, 1984).

The sex discrimination shown in applying the law on prostitution has always been very blatant, perhaps because it fits so well with the double standard of sexual behavior (discussed in Chapter 7) and with the established power differences between women and men. The following comment, made in a 1914 report on prostitution in Europe, reflects a sentiment that has changed little in the intervening years:

> The professional prostitute being a social outcast may be periodically punished without disturbing the usual course of society. . . . The man, however, is something more than a partner in an immoral act: he discharges important social and business relations, is as father and brother responsible for the maintenance of others, has commercial or industrial duties to meet. He cannot be imprisoned without deranging society. (Flexner, 1914, p. 108)

The existence of prostitution, and its lopsided gender distribution and punishment, is to some extent a symptom of the inequality between the sexes. In one version of a gender-equal society, women and men would be equally likely to be prostitutes and customers, to sell and purchase sex. In another version, prostitution would not exist at all because there would be no market or social support for impersonal, commercialized sexual relations. However, prostitution will continue to be the path of least resistance for a large number of women until the economic and social pressures that disadvantage women are changed. Women's poverty and low socioeconomic status with respect to men, and the gender-role socialization of both sexes, make prostitution one of the very few alternatives for some women. The impact of these pressures is highlighted by the difficulties that women encounter when they try to get out of prostitution and get a "respectable" job:

> The prostitute who can generally set her own hours of work and who lives in a world of cash exchanges, whose money may come as easily and quickly as it goes, and who is not linked firmly to the "disciplines" of work in a bureaucratic setting, is likely to find it very difficult to make the transition to that new world. A woman who has spent a significant portion of her early adult life in a marginal or even "outlaw" occupation is unlikely to have the skills and knowledge required for most standard jobs. Nor is she likely to have contacts to help her find a job in the regular working world. Aside from these difficulties, there is the distinct possibility that jobs in the "straight" world will be unappealing and low paying. An ex-prostitute is faced with the fact that the jobs which she can get, like the jobs most women hold, are neither as interesting nor as well-paid as the jobs any man, even if equally marginal, is able to get. (Canadian Advisory Council on the Status of Women, 1984, p. 94)

Traditional gender-role socialization with respect to work does not help the situation. Many young women still expect that their employment, whatever it is, will be an unimportant and temporary stage in their lives before they take on their "real" job as mothers. The young women who go into prostitution are no exceptions. As one 15-year-old Winnipeg prostitute said wistfully when asked in a television interview what she would ideally like to do with her life, "I want to have children, and a husband to look after me." This is a fantasy that is supported by myths and fairy tales and movies such as *Pretty Woman*.

Clearly, prostitution is one area of the law where justice is not meted out equally to women and men. However, the inequality in the law has roots that stretch deeply into other, even more basic inequalities between women and men.

Victims of Crime. On December 6, 1989, in a tragedy that has since become known as the "Montreal Massacre," Marc Lepine rampaged through the school of engineering at the University of Montreal with an assault rifle, killing 14 women and wounding 9 other women and 4 men. The preponderance of females among Lepine's victims was no coincidence. He ordered men out of the way and rounded up women to be shot, screaming at his victims that they were "all fucking feminists." Found among his belongings after he turned his gun on himself were a suicide note blaming all his failures on women, as well as a "hit list" of prominent Canadian women (Caputi & Russell, 1990). This terrible incident reflects the disastrous intersection of three destructive forces: a bitter, angry, troubled individual; the availability of an automatic weapon to such an individual; and a cultural context that often legitimizes attitudes of male superiority and the notion that women who challenge traditional roles or male authority deserve to be victimized.

Despite the horror of the Montreal Massacre, and despite what some experts argue are increasing levels of viciousness in crimes against women (Caputi & Russell, 1990), homicide statistics show no increase in the murder rate for women (Bergman, 1991). Across countries, time, and age groups, studies show that men are more often victimized by crime than are women, but women express greater fear of being victimized than men do (Bergman, 1991; Female victims of crime, 1985). A recent Gallup Poll showed that 56 percent of adult Canadian women and 18 percent of men were afraid to walk in their own neighborhood after dark (Bergman, 1991). Women's greater fear may stem from their socialization that they are incapable of protecting themselves, but it probably also relates to the *type* of crimes to which women are most vulnerable. Women are considerably more likely than men to live in fear of physical violence from a person in their own household. Women are most likely to be killed by people whom they know intimately, and are more likely to be murdered in their own homes than anywhere else (Bergman, 1991). Victimization surveys also show that women are 7 times as likely as men to experience a sexual assault. Not only are such victimization experiences especially traumatic in themselves, but reporting them tends to expose the victim to stigmatization. Women who have been raped or who have been beaten by their husbands are often assumed to have done something to encourage or provoke their attacker. The possibility of encountering such attitudes often causes a female victim to not report the crime. Estimates are that only 1 of every 4 rapes and 1 of every 10 incidents of wife assault are reported; one large Canadian survey indicated that fully 62 percent of female sexual assault victims did not report the crime to the police (Female victims of crime, 1985).

Gender prejudice has played an important role in the legal treatment of victims of rape and wife assault. For many years, as discussed in Chapter 11, a wife was considered the property of her husband and it was legally permissible for him to beat her. Rape of a wife by her husband was considered a contradiction in terms: A husband had the right to have sex with his wife with or without her consent. The latter law has now been changed in many jurisdictions.

The assumption that a female rape victim had enticed her attacker, or had actually consented to have intercourse with him, was built into the rules of evidence for rape trials. Until the past decade, the victim's prior sexual history could be brought up in court to establish that she was promiscuous and therefore had probably consented to the intercourse. New laws made such evidence inadmissible in most American and Canadian jurisdictions; however, this legislation was struck down in Canada in 1991 on the grounds that it might deny a fair trial to the accused (Fulton, 1991). A new "rape-shield" law currently under consideration in Canada would place the burden of proof for the woman's consent to sexual relations on the man, rather than making it incumbent on the rape victim to prove that she did *not* consent. The so-called "no means no" legislation requires an explicit voluntary agreement, in words or action, by the woman to engage in sexual activity.

If a female victim kills her attacker while defending herself against rape, she is often regarded as having used unnecessary force and is sometimes jailed, whereas men who have killed while protecting themselves from rape by another man have generally been acquitted (Sapiro, 1986). One-half of this pattern may reflect a lack of understanding about how traumatic and dangerous rape can be for the female victim. As one person is reported to have commented during the 1977 trial of Inez Garcia, a woman who killed her rapist, "You can't kill someone for trying to give you a good time" (quoted in Sapiro, 1986). The other half of the pattern may relate to homophobia: A man defending himself against homosexual rape may be seen as defending himself from something unnatural, whereas heterosexual rape, in some people's perceptions, falls within the range of normal heterosexual experience.

A final twist on the gender bias that affects the treatment of victims is that on the relatively rare occasions when men find themselves the victims of sexual assault or physical abuse by women, they are likely to receive very unsympathetic treatment if they report the incident. A man who cannot successfully defend himself against a woman is not much of a man according to the prevailing norms of masculinity, and the male victim of female violence is more likely to be the target of jokes than sympathy.

In summary, gender ideology plays a large part in the justice system's treatment of victims, particularly when the crime is related to sexuality or male–female relationships. Some changes in the direction of increased sensitivity and fairness have begun to occur, such as better training for the police officers who must handle rape and spousal assault cases. However, it may be many years yet before the criminal justice system is equally responsive to the needs of female and male victims.

Social Change: Justice for All?

The Feminist Movement and Legislative Change

The past two and a half decades have seen the emergence of a strong movement for social change in the situation of women and the relations between women and men. The feminist movement has included small local groups of activists and broadly based national organizations such as the National Organization for Women (NOW) in the United States and the National Action Committee on the Status of Women (NAC) in Canada. Active women's caucuses have formed within most professional organizations and political parties. On university campuses, feminist students, faculty, and staff have pooled their efforts to establish women's resource centers and programs labeled "women's studies" or "feminist studies." This mobilization of energy into the feminist movement has generated the power to produce significant changes in the laws governing the treatment of the sexes in work, education, and the allocation of resources. In Canada, a national coalition of feminist groups lobbied successfully to have gender equality under the law built into the new Charter of Rights and Freedoms. Section 15 of the Charter, which took effect on April 17, 1985 (fondly referred to by Canadian feminists as "a date with equality") guarantees equality under the law to women and men and is currently providing the basis for challenging a number of discriminatory statutes and practices. In the United States, some important legislation has made sex discrimination more difficult in several areas. An example of the difference that such legislation can make can be seen in the impact of Title IX of the Education Amendments of 1972, which prohibited sex discrimination in federally funded educational institutions. Before this legislation came into effect, girls and women could routinely be excluded from certain educational programs on the basis of their gender, and there was no requirement that equal resources and facilities be available to both genders. Some of the most dramatic effects of Title IX are seen in the influx of girls and women into two previously male-dominated areas: sports and certain vocational education programs. Research by Carl Ojala shows that the number of American high school girls participating in sports rose from 300,000 participants in 14 sports in 1970–71, just before Title IX was passed, to more than 1.7 million participants in 33 sports in 1984 (Title IX cited, 1987). The unprecedented growth in girls' sports participation is attributable in large part to Title IX, which forced colleges to put more money into women's sports and thus made it possible for more high school girls to aspire to college sports scholarships.

Title IX also provided the impetus for large changes in vocational education. Females could no longer be excluded from particular vocational programs and, as provided by a later law (Title II of the Education Amendments of 1976), each state appointed a full-time sex equity coordinator to work on broadening the range of vocational education opportunities for women. In the ten years between 1972 and 1982, both the numbers and percentages of female students increased in the traditionally male programs of agriculture, technical, and trade and industry. Within programs training students for office occupations, women now constitute over half the students in the supervisory and management programs, whereas in 1971 only about one-quarter of these students were women (Vetter & Hickey, 1985). Women's share of the enrollment in the supervision and management sections of trade and industry programs has increased by more than 20 percent. At the same time, male student enrollment is up in two traditionally female programs: home economics and office occupations.

Although Title IX has had a large effect in promoting gender equity in education, its force was blunted considerably in 1984, when the Supreme Court ruled that the law applied only to the actual programs that were directly receiving federal money within an institution, and not to entire institutions (Supreme Court delivers mixed decisions, 1984). The lesson is clear: Although much positive change can be generated through good legislation, the legislation may not work well or even survive in a political climate that is unfavorable to equality between women and men.

Clearly, feminism as a social movement has already had a large impact on the way that females and males are treated in North America. Many instances of unfairness remain, however, and, as the following discussion will show, supporters of feminist social change do not always agree on the best way to rectify them.

How should the situation in which resources are distributed unfairly between the sexes, and in which the law often supports that unfairness, be rectified? How might we come up with a society that meets the ideals of justice held by both women and men? A variety of perspectives has been offered in response to such questions. Some have suggested that change will come faster if we recognize differences between women and men rather than denying them. Others have argued that what is needed is a deemphasis on gender as an organizing principle in society. Still others have stressed the importance of making people aware of the existence of sex discrimination and its impact on themselves. Finally, it has been argued that tinkering with the reward structure is not enough: There must be a transformation of social values and the institutions that represent them so that society's rewards are linked less strongly to competition and more strongly to behavior that emphasizes interpersonal harmony and cooperation. This section looks in turn at examples of each of these arguments.

Recognizing Differences

Alice Kessler-Harris (1985), in an examination of the historical failure to successfully achieve equality in the workplace for women, argues that the major reason why these attempts have failed is that they assume that women must adjust to the male-structured workplace. If women are to achieve equal status with men, the assumption has been, they must be prepared to make it in a man's world. Kessler-Harris suggests that, whether for reasons of preference or necessity, many women are not prepared to make this kind of adjustment in their priorities. If we want gender equality in the workplace, she says, we must make some accommodations in the workplace for women. Such accommodations may benefit both women and men by making the workplace more amenable to the special needs of all.

The following example is given by Kessler-Harris as a strategy that acknowledges gender-related differences but encompasses them in a policy that extends rights to all workers. In 1984, the Women's Rights Project of the American Civil Liberties Union (ACLU) filed a brief opposing Montana's Maternity Leave Act—an act that granted pregnant women the right to unpaid leave for a time before and after the birth of a child. The ACLU argued that such a law would place women in a special category, making them less attractive to employers as workers. The ACLU proposed instead that the law be extended to cover health-related unpaid leaves for all workers. In this way, an act that was potentially discriminatory could be turned into a gain for all workers, and the special needs of women with respect to pregnancy could still be met. (This example also fits the "sex-specific/gender-neutral" approach to equality under the law, discussed earlier in this chapter.) In 1987, in the *California Federal S. & L. v. Guerre* decision, the U.S. Supreme Court rejected the ACLU position in favor of a stance that it is permissible for states to treat women workers equally with men by establishing a maternity leave policy (an example of the "equality plus real differences" approach discussed earlier).

The main aspect of the approach advocated by Kessler-Harris is that the work that has traditionally been done by women—child care and the maintenance of home and family life—is important work that, in the quest for gender equality, must be publicly recognized and shared. Issues that have previously been considered private must be placed on the public stage. Family and relationship responsibilities are recognized as a necessary adjunct to the wage–work process, for men as well as women, so that it becomes important to consider family issues when designing the workplace:

> At its most optimistic, this approach is nothing less than
> a belief that gender equality will be achieved only when the
> values of the home (which have previously been assumed to
> keep women out of the workplace or to assign them to inferior
> places within it) are brought to the workplace where they can
> transform work itself. It opens the possibility that an ethic of

compassion or tolerance, a sense of group responsibility to the world at large (instead of to self) might in fact penetrate the workplace. (p. 157)

A Nongendered Social Order

Some people have argued that although it is currently necessary to draw attention to the issue of gender in order to combat it as a discriminative status, such strategies are likely to be effective only in the short term. At least one writer (Lorber, 1986) argues that the long-term goal of feminism should be to eradicate gender as an organizing principle in society, that as long as we continue to make gender an important category and to view women and men as essentially different, gender will be used to make distinctions—between workers, voters, political candidates, criminals, and so on.

Lorber tries to articulate what our society might be like if restructured to deemphasize gender. Policies regarding families would change, for instance. Each adult would be treated as a single unit for purposes of income, taxation, and legal responsibilities. Family and kinship would not be based on gender; groups of differing size and gender composition would make up households. Parenting would not be gender-linked: Women and men would be equally likely to take responsibility for dependent children. There would be no support for a division of labor along sexual lines within the family. The wage structure for workers would not discriminate on the basis of workers' gender or of the gender linkage of certain jobs; thus, the man would not automatically be the main financial support of the family. All adults would receive support allowances for themselves and their dependents, and professional caretaking of children would no longer be treated and paid as a low-status occupation but would be compensated according to its skill level. Women would no longer be kept out of positions of power and authority by a sex-stratified occupational structure or by powerful men's perception of them as "different."

Lorber argues that drastic steps to change the gender structuring of society are necessary because political and legal equality between women and men will not necessarily ensure social equality:

> In my mind, gender equality is too limited a goal. Unless women and men are seen as socially interchangeable, gender equality does not challenge the concept of sex differences that leads to separate spheres in the family and marketplace division of labor, which in turn results in women's lesser access to control of valued resources and positions of power. Scrupulous equality of categories of people considered essentially different needs constant monitoring. I would question the very concept of gender itself, and ask why, if women and men are social equals in all ways, there needs to be two encompassing social statuses at all. (p. 577)

Lorber's argument is based on the idea that our notions of gender are socially constructed and that the differences between women and men are largely a product of the emphasis that we as a society place on gender. Her proposal is not likely to be put into effect in the near future, so we cannot be sure of the extent to which her basic premise is correct. Yet, as discussed at many points in this book, research shows that social expectations about gender have a strong impact on male–female differences in many areas of behavior. Deemphasizing gender as a relevant category in the way society is structured is no doubt a necessary aspect of weakening those social expectations.

Raising Awareness of Discrimination

Lucy Stone, a nineteenth-century American suffragist and abolitionist, declared passionately in a speech delivered in 1885: "In education, in marriage, in religion, in everything disappointment is the lot of women. It shall be the business of my life to deepen this disappointment in every woman's heart until she bows down to it no longer."

Lucy Stone's recognition that a deep and clear awareness of injustice must precede action to correct the injustice is a well-accepted one. Before society can get very far with grand schemes for equality between women and men, individuals within society must be made aware of the fact that gender inequalities exist and affect them personally. People are simply more likely to mobilize for change if they feel that the current system is unjust, particularly if it is seen as disadvantageous to themselves. Yet researchers have found that people often do not recognize sex discrimination and that, even among women who recognize that discrimination against women in general exists, there is little recognition that they have personally been affected by it (Crosby, 1982; Unger & Sussman, 1986).

Some researchers have concentrated recently on the question of how best to raise awareness of discrimination (Crosby, Clayton, Alksnis, & Hemker, 1986). What they have found is that, at least some of the time, the failure to recognize discrimination is linked to the format in which information is presented. Crosby and her colleagues presented information about women and men in a fictitious corporation to male university students. Half of the time, the information was presented in aggregated form, providing subjects with an overall picture of the situation in the company; the rest of the time, subjects were shown case-by-case comparisons of women and men in particular departments. The researchers suggest that the first type of presentation is comparable to learning about discrimination through the media, while the second is more like what occurs when we hear of a particular case or consider our own situation relative to that of another person.

The results of this study confirmed the researchers' hypothesis that the perception of discrimination was influenced by information processing considerations. Apparently, it was easier to see patterns of discrimination when many cases were presented together, perhaps because the quantity of data was more compelling, or because, when information was aggregated, irrelevant differences among departments were averaged out, making the salary difference between women and men more obvious.

The results of this study indicate clearly that, when trying to demonstrate that sex discrimination exists in a particular setting, it is more effective to present an overall view than a trickle of case comparisons. The findings also demonstrate that cognitive factors, the way human beings process information, can have an impact above and beyond such attitudinal factors as prejudice or misogyny or the desire to see the world as a just place, on people's readiness to see discrimination. Attempts to rectify sex discrimination must take this factor into account.

Transformation of Institutions

Many feminists have argued that society's institutions must be fundamentally transformed rather than simply made more open to women's participation. They argue that the hierarchical, competitive, and individualistic values that permeate most institutions are fundamentally opposed to the designing of a system that would stress equality among groups. For instance, some groups of women have tried to challenge the male dominance of the health-care system, not by getting more women into medical school, but by a variety of tactics that question the doctor's place at the top of a medical hierarchy. Some groups have fought for the legalization of midwifery. Others have challenged traditional physician–nurse power relationships that make it impossible for a nurse to question a doctor's instructions with respect to a patient. Still others have started self-care clinics or information services to make people less dependent on medical experts for their health.

Other institutions have also felt the brunt of this approach. For example, in many universities, the introduction of women's studies courses has meant not just a new content area but a questioning of the way things are done in academia as well as in the outside world. As Hamilton (1985) notes, feminists in the academy tend to be political subversives: "They have challenged not only the structure of the university, and the limited place of women within it, but also the very parameters of what constitutes knowledge, and many of the assumptions underlying the traditional academic disciplines" (p. 3).

The transformational approach to social change is based on the idea that gender bias may be present even in areas where it has not yet been recognized: in the way we think about issues that have no obvious connection to gender. It thus forces a scrutiny of the status quo that goes even beyond that encouraged by the other approaches cited here. It is a difficult and often uncomfortable approach to social change, but, as Hamilton (1985) notes, "Students of society surely deserve challenge, not consolation, and this is especially true . . . in the questions that we pose about those aspects of human relationships that we have hitherto taken for granted" (p. 20).

Summary

We have seen that strong prescriptive stereotypes exist that women and men should rely on different standards of justice and morality, and that women's and men's experiences tend to push them in the direction of those stereotypes. For example, the power differences between women and men often mean that women have fewer resources than men, and the very prevalence of this situation may lead people to accept it as normal. As a result, women may come to believe that they *deserve* less, and men to believe that *they* deserve more. This difference in feelings of personal entitlement may cause what appears to be a gender difference in selfishness: Women stress equality, take less for themselves and give more to others, while men stress equity and are ready to reward themselves at the expense of others. Research indicates, however, that such differences are ephemeral. If the situation is changed by giving individuals an appropriate comparison group, if the situation is deliberately structured to emphasize either interpersonal concerns or task concerns, if individuals can reward their own superior performance without penalizing others—the traditional gender differences disappear.

It appears that, in the area of justice behavior, as in so many other areas discussed in this book, males and females are sensitive to situational cues about what behavior is appropriate, that these cues often differ for the two sexes, and that the difference relates back to the power difference between women and men.

Studies of the way that females and males actually think about justice and morality do not strongly support the idea that females emphasize equality and interpersonal concerns while males stress equity and rights. However, both the manner in which that field of inquiry has developed and the findings of the studies themselves indicate that there is a pervasive belief in the existence of the gender difference just described. Women are expected to emphasize care and interpersonal concerns, men to emphasize rights. A reading of the early psychological writings on justice and morality leaves no doubt that the stereotypically feminine morality of care and interpersonal responsibility has been devalued. Perhaps this devaluation has acted in a circular fashion to cause the dissociation of such an orientation from men, and thus to ensure that it would continue to be devalued in a society that assigns more status to men than to women.

The idea that women and men differ in their tendency to be emotional or rational with respect to justice has been reflected in the male dominance of the judicial system and is entrenched, along with other gender stereotypes, in the fabric of the law itself. For years, civil laws gave men authority over women, even within the family; some of these laws have yet to be changed. These laws have restricted women's legal and political rights and their access to economic resources, thus maintaining a power difference between women and men that, in turn, helped to maintain behavioral differences. In criminal law as well, gender stereotypes, particularly those concerning sexuality and marital roles, have made for inequities between women and men, both as criminals and as victims. The law itself, supposedly the embodiment of justice, sometimes perpetuates injustice on the basis of gender.

Many approaches have been offered as directions for social change that would redress the unbalanced distribution of resources and other injustices based on gender. These approaches range from practical suggestions about how to educate people with respect to sex discrimination, to attempts to develop the best possible vision of the ultimate goals of change. They include strategies for how to make the system work for women and strategies for a radical transformation of that system. All of them have in common a basis of passionate concern for gender justice. Although the debate goes on about the relative merits of these various approaches to social transformation, it advances, through a series of small changes, the notion that the real needs of both sexes must weigh equally in any consideration of justice.

For Additional Reading

Backhouse, C. (1991). *Petticoats and prejudice: Women and the law in nineteenth-century Canada*. Toronto, Ontario: The Women's Press. This legal history, filled with interesting vignettes, describes how Canadian law treated courtship and marriage, rape, abortion, infanticide, divorce, child custody, and prostitution.

Collins, P. H. (1990). *Black feminist thought: Consciousness and the politics of empowerment*. Cambridge, MA: Unwin Hyman. This book provides an analysis of the intellectual and social activism of black women as they have struggled to develop a perspective that is "both emancipatory and reflective."

Faludi, S. (1991). *Backlash: The undeclared war against American women*. New York: Crown Publishers. A journalist analyzes the anti-feminist social forces that American women currently face, particularly through the media.

Kimmel, M. S., & Mosmiller, T. E. (Eds.). (1992). *Against the tide: Pro-feminist men in the United States 1776–1990*. When the editors first mentioned the possibility of this book to their feminist women friends, one scoffed that a book about pro-feminist men would surely be the shortest book in history! Actually, this book provides over five hundred pages of information about, and statements by, men who made their voices heard on behalf of gender justice.

Epilogue

The Ties That Bind:
The Future of Sex & Gender

Sex and gender together have formed one of the most important distinctions that human beings have made about one another. The awareness of another person's femaleness or maleness shapes our reactions to that person from the moment she or he is born. We judge ourselves and others according to the degree to which we and they fit the expectations of femininity and masculinity; most of us cannot imagine what it would be like to have the body of the other sex or the role expectations and identity of the other gender.

As distinctions go, however, there is something unique about the one based on sex and gender. Although we insist on the division, on the importance of the distinction between female and male, feminine and masculine, we tend to argue not that the two genders should be kept separate, but that they should go together—that they complement and complete each other. We speak of situations needing a "woman's touch" or a "man's hand," and, as a society, we espouse an ideal of intimacy that involves a shared, lifelong commitment between a woman and a man. Despite the talk about how different men and women are and how little they understand each other, a large number of North American adults would count their closest, most important relationship as one with a spouse or partner of the other gender.

The gender division is somewhat unique, then, in that the two genders, though divided, are thought to "go together." But, both as individuals and as groups, women and men have tended to go together not as equal partners but as participants in a hierarchical arrangement, with men holding the top positions. Our culture's ideas about male–female differences reflect this hierarchy. Stereotypes of femininity and masculinity split up human qualities between females and males. The qualities that are assigned to females are devalued—a devaluation that is linked to females' subordinate position in the gender hierarchy. Interestingly, a quality that is stereotyped as feminine may in fact be equally prevalent in both women and men, but because it is associated with femininity it may be devalued and thus unacknowledged in men. A clear example of this phenomenon comes from the research on moral reasoning discussed in the last chapter. An ethic of care and responsibility, ignored in previous male-centered research on moral reasoning, was proposed as a principle that was especially characteristic of women's moral reasoning (Gilligan, 1982). However, as researchers began to include this hitherto ignored element of morality in their studies of moral reasoning, most found to their surprise that it was equally characteristic of women and men. Why had no one noticed it before? Perhaps because, since the tendency to base decisions on concern for relationships is stereotyped as feminine, male researchers and subjects were not noticing or acknowledging this tendency in themselves, and females were simply accepting men's definition of the situation. The hierarchical social context in which women and men perceive and relate to each other makes it impossible for us to be completely clear-eyed about what gender similarities and differences exist. The more carefully we do our research, however, the more it appears that women and men share, or have the potential to share under conditions of social equality, most qualities.

The realization that we need not be limited to present cultural definitions of femininity and masculinity can be an empowering one for both women and men. However, it can also be a frightening one. Social change is now occurring at such a rapid rate that individuals or whole societies may freeze in "future shock" rather than adapt comfortably to new possibilities. Part of this inability or refusal to adapt may well involve holding on with grim determination to traditional gender roles. And there are, of course, good reasons for not discarding the qualities that are associated with traditional gender roles. As Joan Rabin (1987) argues, under the current conditions of rapid social change, we human beings are especially in need of the communal qualities usually associated with women in order to maintain a sense of comfort and connection—in order to ensure our survival as a social species. Indeed, traditions form important anchors in a rapidly changing world, and they often help us to maintain our sense of meaning and connection with one another. Women, whose communal, family roles often implicate them as the guardians of tradition and social bonds, may feel especially guilty as they redefine their roles and cannot devote as much energy to things that bring family and friends together. Yet such feelings of guilt are based on the assumption that only women can fulfill these functions—an assumption that is simply wrong. As a society, we may finally come to the realization that the functions and qualities stereotypically associated with each gender are valuable and necessary—and much more interchangeable and shareable than we used to think.

References

Abbey, A. (1982). Sex differences in attributions for friendly behavior: Do males misperceive females' friendliness? *Journal of Personality and Social Psychology, 42*(5), 830–838.

Abbondanza, M. (1982, July). *Categorization, identification and feelings of deprivation: A multidimensional study of homemaker and employed mothers' social perceptions.* Paper presented at the Twentieth International Congress of Applied Psychology, Edinburgh.

Abbondanza, M. (1983, June). *Cognitive barriers to intergroup equality between the sexes.* Paper presented at the Section on Social Psychology graduate student awards session, forty-fourth annual convention of the Canadian Psychological Association, Winnipeg, Manitoba.

Abella, Judge R. S. (1984). *Equality in employment: A royal commission report.* Ottawa: Canadian Government Publishing Centre.

Abplanalp, J. M. (1983). Premenstrual syndrome: A selective review. *Women & Health, 8*(2/3), 107–123.

Abramowitz, S., & Herrera, H. R. (1981). On controlling for patient psychopathology in naturalistic studies of sex bias: A methodological demonstration. *Journal of Consulting and Clinical Psychology, 49,* 597–603.

Abu-Laban, S. M. (1981). Women and aging: A futurist perspective. *Psychology of Women Quarterly, 6*(1), 85–98.

Adair, J. G. (1973). *The human subject: The social psychology of the psychological experiment.* Boston: Little, Brown.

Adams, C. G., & Turner, B. F. (1985). Reported change in sexuality from young adulthood to old age. *Journal of Sex Research, 21*(2), 126–141.

Adams, D. B., Gold, A. R., & Burt, A. D. (1978). Cycles of sexual desire. *New England Journal of Medicine, 229,* 21.

Adams, G. R. (1982). Physical attractiveness. In A. G. Miller (Ed.), *In the eye of the beholder: Contemporary issues in stereotyping* (pp. 253–304). New York: Praeger.

Adams, K. A. (1980). Who has the final word? Sex, race and dominance behavior. *Journal of Personality and Social Psychology, 38,* 1–8.

Adams, K. A. (1983). Aspects of social context as determinants of black women's resistance to challenges. *Journal of Social Issues, 39,* 69–78.

Adler, N. E. (1975). Emotional responses of women following therapeutic abortion. *American Journal of Orthopsychiatry, 45*(3), 446–454.

Adler, N. E. (1984). Contraception and unwanted pregnancy. *Behavioral Medicine Update, 5*(4), 28–34.

Adler, T. (1990). NIH opens office on women's issues. *APA Monitor, 21*(12), 5.

Agate, C., & Meacham, C. (1977). Women's equality: Implications of the law. In A. Sargent (Ed.), *Beyond sex roles* (pp. 434–450). St. Paul: West.

Ahlgren, A. (1983). Sex differences in the correlates of cooperative and competitive school attitudes. *Developmental Psychology, 19*(6), 881–888.

Ahlgren, A., & Johnson, D. W. (1979). Sex differences in cooperative and competitive attitudes from the 2nd through the 12th grades. *Developmental Psychology, 15,* 45–49.

Albino, J. E., & Tedesco, L. A. (1984). Women's health issues. In A. U. Rickel, M. Gerrard, & I. Iscoe (Eds.), *Social and psychological problems of women* (pp. 157–172). Washington, DC: Hemisphere.

Allen, L. S., Richey, M. F., Chai, Y. M., & Gorski, R. A. (1991). Sex differences in the corpus callosum of the living human being. *Journal of Neuroscience, 11*(4), 933–942.

Allport, G. W. (1954). *The nature of prejudice.* Reading, MA: Addison-Wesley.

Almquist, E. M. (1989). The experiences of minority women in the United States: Intersections of race, gender, and class. In J. Freeman (Ed.), *Women: A feminist perspective* (4th ed., pp. 414–456). Mountain View, CA: Mayfield.

Alper, J. S. (1985). Sex differences in brain asymmetry: A critical analysis. *Feminist Studies, 11*(1), 7–38.

Amatea, E. S., & Fong, M. L. (1991). The impact of role stressors and personal resources on the stress experience of professional women. *Psychology of Women Quarterly, 15*(3), 419–430.

American Psychiatric Association. (1980). *Diagnostic and statistical manual of mental disorders* (3rd ed.). Washington, DC: Author.

American Psychological Association. (1975). Report of the Task Force on Sex Bias and Sex-role Stereotyping in Psychotherapeutic Practice. *American Psychologist, 30,* 1169–1175.

American Psychological Association. (1978). Guidelines for therapy with women. *American Psychologist, 13,* 1122–1123.

Amir, M. (1971). *Patterns in forcible rape.* Chicago: University of Chicago Press.

Anastasi, A. (1937/1958). *Differential psychology: Individual and group differences in behavior.* New York: Macmillan.

Anastasi, A. (1958). Heredity, environment, and the question "how?." *Psychological Review, 65,* 197–208.

Anastasi, A. (1981). Sex differences: Historical perspectives and methodological implications. *Developmental Review, 1,* 187–206.

Andersson, B. (1979). Developmental trends in reaction to social pressure from adults versus peers. *International Journal of Behavior Development, 2,* 269–286.

Andrew, W. K. (1985). The phenomenological foundations for empirical methodology I: The method of optional variations. *Journal of Phenomenological Psychology, 16*(2), 1–29.

Andrew, W. K. (1986). The phenomenological foundations for methodology II: Experimental phenomenological psychology. *Journal of Phenomenological Psychology, 17*(1), 77–97.

Antill, J. K., & Cunningham, J. D. (1982). Sex differences in performance on ability tests as a function of masculinity, femininity and androgyny. *Journal of Personality and Social Psychology, 42,* 718–728.

Arbeit, S. A. (1975). *A study of women during their first pregnancy.* Unpublished doctoral dissertation, Yale University.

Archer, C. (1984). Children's attitudes toward sex-role division in adult occupational roles. *Sex Roles, 10,* 1–10.

Archer, J. (1979). *Animals under stress.* London: Edward Arnold.

Archer, J. (1984). Gender roles as developmental pathways. *British Journal of Social Psychology, 23,* 245–256.

Archer, J., & Lloyd, B. (1985). *Sex and gender.* Cambridge: Cambridge University Press.

Archer, J., & Westeman, K. (1981). Sex differences in the aggressive behavior of schoolchildren. *British Journal of Social Psychology, 20,* 31–61.

Aries, E. (1976). Interaction patterns and themes of male, female, and mixed groups. *Small Group Behavior, 7*(1), 7–18.

Armitage, K. J., Schneiderman, L. J., & Bass, R. A. (1979). Response of physicians to medical complaints in men and women. *Journal of the American Medical Association, 241*(20), 2186–2187.

Ashmore, R. D., Del Boca, F. K., & Wohlers, A. J. (1986). Gender stereotypes. In R. D. Ashmore & F. K. Del Boca (Eds.), *The social psychology of female–male relations* (pp. 69–119). Orlando, FL: Academic Press.

Ashton, E. (1983). Measures of play behavior: The influence of sex-role stereotyped children's books. *Sex Roles, 9,* 43–47.

Association of MBA Executives, Inc. (1981). *AMBA's mba Employment Guide 1981.* New York: Alberta P. Hegyi.

Astin, A. W. (1985, January 16). Freshman characteristics and attitudes. *Chronicle of Higher Education,* pp. 15–16.

Astin, H. (1974). Sex differences in mathematical and scientific precocity. In J. C. Stanley, D. P. Keating, & L. H. Fox (Eds.), *Mathematical talent: Discovery, description and development.* Baltimore: Johns Hopkins University Press.

Astrachan, A. (1989). Dividing lines. In M. S. Kimmel & M. A. Messner (Eds.), *Men's lives* (pp. 63–73). New York: Macmillan.

Atkinson, J., & Huston, T. L. (1984). Sex role orientation and division of labor early in marriage. *Journal of Personality and Social Psychology, 46*(2), 330–345.

Atkinson, J. W. (Ed.). (1958). *Motives in fantasy, action and society.* Princeton, NJ: Van Nostrand.

Atkinson, J. W., & Feather, N. T. (1966). *A theory of achievement motivation.* New York: Wiley.

Atwood, R. A., Zahn, B., & Weber, G. (1986). Perceptions of the traits of women on television. *Journal of Broadcasting and Electronic Media, 30,* 95–101.

Aubry, T. (1986). *Marital relations in the context of the unemployment of the husband.* Unpublished master's thesis, University of Manitoba.

Aubuchon, P. G., & Calhoun, K. S. (1985). Menstrual cycle symptomatology: The role of social expectancy and experimental demand characteristics. *Psychosomatic Medicine, 47*(1), 35–45.

Baber, K. M., & Monaghan, P. (1988). College women's career and motherhood expectations: New options, old dilemmas. *Sex Roles, 19,* 189–203.

Baca Zinn, M. (1989). Chicano men and masculinity. In M. S. Kimmel & M. A. Messner (Eds.), *Men's lives* (pp. 87–97). New York: Macmillan.

Backhouse, C., & Cohen, L. (1978). *The secret oppression: Sexual harassment of working women.* Toronto: Macmillan of Canada.

Bacon, M. (1974). The dependency-conflict hypothesis and the frequency of drunkenness: Further evidence from a cross-cultural study. *Quarterly Journal of Studies on Alcohol, 35,* 863–876.

Baenninger, M., & Newcombe, N. (1989). The role of experience in spatial test performance: A meta-analysis. *Sex Roles, 20*(5/6), 327–344.

Bailey, D. A., Shephard, R. J., Mirwald, R. L., & McBride, G. A. (1974). A current view of Canadian cardiorespiratory fitness. *Canadian Medical Association Journal, 111*(1), 25–30.

Baker, M. (1985). *"What will tomorrow bring? . . ." A study of the aspirations of adolescent women.* Ottawa: Canadian Advisory Council on the Status of Women.

Baker, S. W. (1980). Biological influences on human sex and gender. *Signs: Journal of Women in Culture and Society, 6,* 80–96.

Bandura, A. (1973). *Aggression: A social learning analysis.* Englewood Cliffs, NJ: Prentice-Hall.

Bandura, A. (1977). *Social learning theory.* Englewood Cliffs, NJ: Prentice-Hall.

Bankart, B. (1989). Japanese perceptions of motherhood. *Psychology of Women Quarterly, 13,* 59–76.

Barash, D. (1979). *The whisperings within.* New York: Harper & Row.

Barbach, L. G. (1976). *For yourself: The fulfillment of female sexuality.* Garden City, NY: Anchor Books.

Barbarino, T. L. (1991). *Effects of viewing rock videos on women's acceptance of rape myths.* Unpublished master's thesis, Radford University.

Barclay, R. I., & Barclay, M. L. (1976). Aspects of the normal psychology of pregnancy: The midtrimester. *American Journal of Obstetrics and Gynecology, 125,* 207.

Barcus, F. E. (1978). *Commercial children's television on weekends and weekday afternoons.* Newtonville, MA: Action for Children's Television.

Bardwick, J. (1971). *The psychology of women: A study of bio-cultural conflicts.* New York: Harper & Row.

Barfield, A. (1976). Biological influences on sex differences in behavior. In M. S. Teitelbaum (Ed.), *Sex differences: Social and biological perspectives* (pp. 62–121). New York: Anchor Books.

Barglow, P., & Brown, E. (1972). Pseudocyesis. To be and not to be pregnant: A psychosomatic question. In J. G. Howells (Ed.), *Modern perspectives in psycho-obstetrics* (pp. 53–67). New York: Brunner/Mazel.

Baron, J. N., & Newman, A. E. (1990). For what it's worth: Organizations, occupations, and the value of work done by women and nonwhites. *American Sociological Review, 55*(2), 155–175.

Baron, R. A. (1977). *Human aggression.* New York: Plenum.

Bart, P. (1971). Depression in middle-aged women. In V. Gornick & B. Moran (Eds.), *Women in sexist society.* New York: Basic Books.

Bart, P. (1980, March). *Socialization and rape avoidance: How to say no to Storaska and survive.* Paper presented at the National Conference on Feminist Psychology, Santa Monica.

Bar-Tal, D., & Frieze, I. H. (1977). Achievement motivation for males and females as a determinant of attributions for success and failure. *Sex Roles, 3*(3), 310–314.

Baruch, G. K. (1972). Maternal influences upon college women's attitudes toward women and work. *Developmental Psychology, 6,* 32–37.

Baruch, G. K., Barnett, R., & Rivers, C. (1983). *Lifeprints: New patterns of love and work for today's women.* New York: McGraw-Hill.

Basketball star Magic Johnson retires with AIDS virus. (1991, November 8). *The Washington Post,* pp. A1, A14.

Basler, B. (1984, February 12). Study finds sex stereotypes affect voters at polls. *New York Times,* p. 4.

Basow, S. A. (1986). *Gender stereotypes: Traditions and alternatives.* Monterey, CA: Brooks/Cole.

Battle, E. (1965). Motivational determinants of academic task persistence. *Journal of Personality and Social Psychology, 2,* 209–218.

Baumgartner, A. (1983). *"My daddy might have loved me": Student perceptions of differences between being male and being female.* Denver: Institute for Equality in Education.

Baumrind, D. (1979, March). *Sex-related socialization effects.* Paper presented at the meeting of the Society for Research in Child Development, San Francisco.

Bayley, N., & Oden, M. (1955). The maintenance of intellectual ability in gifted adults. *Journal of Gerontology, 10,* 91–107.

Bayrd, E. (1978). *The thin game: Dieting scams and dietary sense.* New York: Avon.

Bazin, N. T., & Freeman, A. (1974). The androgynous vision. *Women's Studies, 2*(2), 185–215.

Beaman, A. L. (1991). An empirical comparison of meta-analytic and traditional reviews. *Personality and Social Psychology Bulletin, 17*(3), 252–257.

Beck, J. B., Ward-Hull, C. J., & McLear, P. M. (1976). Variables related to women's somatic preferences of the male and female body. *Journal of Personality and Social Psychology, 34,* 1200–1210.

Becker, B. J., & Hedges, L. N. (1984). Meta-analysis of cognitive gender differences: A comment on an analysis by Rosenthal and Rubin. *Journal of Educational Psychology, 76,* 583–587.

Becker, B. J., & Hedges, L. N. (1988). The effects of selection and variability in studies of gender differences. *Behavioral and Brain Sciences, 11*(2), 183–184.

Becker, J. R. (1981). Differential treatment of females and males in mathematics classes. *Journal for Research in Mathematics Education, 12,* 40–53.

Bee, H. L., Mitchell, S. K., Barnard, K. E., Eyres, S. J., & Hammond, M. A. (1984). Predicting intellectual outcomes: Sex differences in response to early environmental stimulation. *Sex Roles, 10,* 783–803.

Beer, W. (1982). *Househusbands: Men and housework in American families.* New York: Praeger.

Behr, A. N. (1973). Achievement, aptitude, and attitude in mathematics. *Two Year College Mathematics Journal, 4,* 72–74.

Belanger, S. (1984). Women and technology. *Canada's Mental Health, 32*(3), 17–18.

Bell, A. P., & Weinberg, M. S. (1978). *Homosexualities.* New York: Simon & Schuster.

Bell, A. P., Weinberg, M. S., & Hammersmith, S. K. (1981). *Sexual preference.* Bloomington: Indiana University Press.

Bell, I. P. (1989). The double standard: Age. In J. Freeman (Ed.), *Women: A feminist perspective* (4th ed., pp. 236–244). Mountain View, CA: Mayfield.

Bell, R. R. (1981). Friendships of women and men. *Psychology of Women Quarterly, 5,* 402–417.

Belle, D. (1984). Inequality and mental health: Low income and minority women. In L. Walker (Ed.), *Women and mental health policy* (pp. 135–150). Beverly Hills, CA: Sage.

Belle, D., & Goldman, N. (1980). Patterns of diagnoses received by men and women. In M. Guttentag, S. Salasin, & D. Belle (Eds.), *The mental health of women* (pp. 21–30). New York: Academic Press.

Bellinger, D. C., & Gleason, J. B. (1982). Sex differences in parental directives to young children. *Sex Roles, 8,* 1123–1139.

Belote, B. (1976). Masochistic syndrome, hysterical personality, and the illusion of a healthy woman. In S. Cox (Ed.), *Female psychology: The emerging self* (pp. 335–348). Chicago: Science Research Associates.

Bem, S. L. (1974). The measurement of psychological androgyny. *Journal of Consulting and Clinical Psychology, 42,* 155–162.

Bem, S. L. (1975). Sex-role adaptability: One consequence of psychological androgyny. *Journal of Personality and Social Psychology, 31,* 634–643.

Bem, S. L. (1981). Gender schema theory: A cognitive account of sex typing. *Psychological Review, 88,* 354–364.

Bem, S. L. (1985). Androgyny and gender schema theory: A conceptual and empirical integration. In T. B. Sonderegger (Ed.), *Nebraska Symposium on Motivation: Psychology of gender* (pp. 179–226). Lincoln: University of Nebraska Press.

Bem, S. L., & Lenney, E. (1976). Sex-typing and the avoidance of cross-sex behavior. *Journal of Personality and Social Psychology, 33*(1), 48–54.

Bem, S. L., Martyna, W., & Watson, C. (1976). Sex-typing and androgyny: Further exploration of the expressive domain. *Journal of Personality and Social Psychology, 34,* 1016–1023.

Benbow, C. P. (1986). Physiological correlates of extreme intellectual precocity. *Neuropsychologia, 24,* 719–725.

Benbow, C. P. (1988). Sex differences in mathematical reasoning ability in intellectually talented preadolescents: Their nature, effects, and possible causes. *Behavioral and Brain Sciences, 11*(2), 169–232.

Benbow, C. P., & Stanley, J. C. (1980). Sex differences in mathematical ability: Fact or artifact? *Science, 210,* 1262–1264.

Benbow, C. P., & Stanley, J. C. (1982). Consequences in high school and college of sex differences in mathematical reasoning ability: A longitudinal perspective. *American Educational Research Journal, 19,* 598–622.

Benbow, C. P., & Stanley, J. C. (1983). Sex differences in mathematical reasoning ability: More facts. *Science, 222,* 1029–1031.

Bennett, J. E., & Loewe, P. M. (1975). *Women in business: A shocking waste of human resources.* Toronto: Maclean-Hunter.

Berganza, C. E., Peyre, C. A., & Aguilar, G. (1989). Sexual attitudes and behavior of Guatemalan teenagers: Considerations for prevention of adolescent pregnancy. *Adolescence, 24,* 327–337.

Bergman, B. (1991, November 11). Women in fear. *Maclean's,* pp. 26–32.

Berman, P. W. (1976). Social context as a determinant of sex differences in adults' attraction to infants. *Developmental Psychology, 12,* 365–366.

Berman, P. W. (1980). Are women more responsive than men to the young? A review of developmental and situational variables. *Psychological Bulletin, 88,* 668–695.

Bernard, J. (1972). *The future of marriage.* New York: World.

Bernard, J. (1974). *The future of motherhood.* New York: The Dial Press.

Bernard, J. (1976). Where are we now? Some thoughts on the current scene. *Psychology of Women Quarterly, 1*(1), 21–37.

Bernat, F. P. (1984). Gender disparity in the setting of bail: Prostitution offenses in Buffalo, NY, 1977–1979. *Journal of Offender Counseling, Services and Rehabilitation, 9*(1/2), 21–47.

Berndt, T. J., & Hoyle, S. G. (1985). Stability and change in childhood and adolescent friendships. *Developmental Psychology, 21*(6), 1007–1015.

Berry, J. W. (1966). Temne and Eskimo perceptual skills. *International Journal of Psychology, 1,* 207–229.

Berzins, J., Welling, M., & Wetter, R. (1975). *The PRF Andro scale user's manual.* Unpublished manual, University of Kentucky.

Betz, N. E., & Hackett, G. (1983). The relationship of mathematics self-efficacy expectations to the selection of science-based college majors. *Journal of Vocational Behavior, 23,* 329–345.

Beuf, A. (1974). Doctor, lawyer, household drudge. *Journal of Communication, 24*(2), 142–145.

Beyer, S. (1990). Gender differences in the accuracy of self-evaluations of performance. *Journal of Personality and Social Psychology, 59*(5), 960–970.

Bianchi, S., & Spain, D. (1983). *Wives who earn more than their husbands.* Washington, DC: U.S. Government Printing Office.

Bibring, G. (1959). Some considerations of the psychological process of pregnancy. In *The psychoanalytic study of the child* (Vol. 14, pp. 113–121). New York: International Universities Press.

Bickman, L. (1974). Sex and helping behavior. *Journal of Social Psychology, 93*(1), 43–53.

Bielby, D. D., & Bielby, W. T. (1988). She works hard for the money: Household responsibilities and the allocation of work effort. *American Journal of Sociology, 83*(5), 1031–1059.

Binion, V. (1990). Psychological androgyny: A Black female perspective. *Sex Roles, 22,* 487–507.

Births to unmarried top 1 million in U.S. (1991, June 14). *Roanoke Times & World News,* p. A4.

Black, S. L., & Koulis-Chitwood, A. (1990). The menstrual cycle and typing skill: An ecologically-valid test of the "raging hormones" hypothesis. *Canadian Journal of Behavioural Science, 22*(4), 445–455.

Blackwell, J. E. (1985). *The black community* (2nd ed.). New York: Harper & Row.

Blanchard, R. (1985). Gender dysphoria and gender reorientation. In B. W. Steiner (Ed.), *Gender dysphoria: Development, research, management* (pp. 227–257). New York: Plenum Press.

Blanchard, R., Steiner, B. W., & Clemmensen, L. H. (1985). Gender dysphoria, gender reorientation, and the management of transsexualism. *Journal of Consulting and Clinical Psychology, 53*(3), 295–304.

Blanck, P. D., Rosenthal, R., Snodgrass, S. E., DePaulo, B. M., & Zuckerman, M. (1981). Sex differences in eavesdropping on nonverbal clues: Developmental changes. *Journal of Personality and Social Psychology, 41,* 391–396.

Bleier, R. (1984). *Science and gender: A critique of biology and its theories on women.* New York: Pergamon Press.

Block, J. H. (1973). Conceptions of sex roles: Some cross-cultural and longitudinal perspectives.

American Psychologist, 28, 512–526.

Block, J. H. (1984). *Sex role identity and ego development*. San Francisco: Jossey-Bass.

Block, W. (1984, November). Directions for future research. *Proceedings of Colloquium on the Economic Status of Women in the Labour Market*. Ottawa: The Economic Council of Canada.

Blood, R., & Wolfe, D. (1960). *Husbands and wives*. New York: Free Press.

Bloom, B. L., White, S. W., & Asher, S. J. (1979). Marital disruption as a stressful life event. In G. Levinger & O. C. Moels (Eds.), *Divorce and separation* (pp. 184–200). New York: Basic Books.

Blough, P. M., & Slavin, L. K. (1987). Reaction time assessments of gender differences in visual-spatial performance. *Perception and Psychophysics, 41*(3), 276–281.

Blumstein, P., & Schwartz, P. (1976). Bisexual women. In J. P. Wiseman (Ed.), *The social psychology of sex*. New York: Harper & Row.

Blumstein, P., & Schwartz, P. (1983). *American couples*. New York: William Morrow.

Bock, D. R., & Kolakowski, D. (1973). Further evidence of a sex-linked major-gene influence on human spatial visualizing ability. *American Journal of Human Genetics, 25*, 1–14.

Boring, E. (1929). *A history of experimental psychology* (Vol. 1). New York: Appleton-Century.

Bornstein, R. A. (1984). Unilateral lesions and the Wechsler Adult Intelligence Scale—Revised: No sex differences. *Journal of Consulting and Clinical Psychology, 52*, 604–608.

Borowy, T., & Goebel, R. (1976). Cerebral lateralization of speech: The effects of age, sex, race, and socioeconomic class. *Neuropsychologia, 14*, 363–370.

Borys, S., & Perlman, D. (1985). Gender differences in loneliness. *Personality and Social Psychology Bulletin, 11*(1), 63–74.

Boskind-White, M. (1985). Bulimarexia: A sociocultural perspective. In S. W. Emmett (Ed.), *Theory and treatment of anorexia nervosa and bulimia. Biomedical, sociocultural, and psychological perspectives* (pp. 113–126). New York: Brunner/Mazel.

Bouchard, T. J. (1983). Do environmental similarities explain the similarity in intelligence of identical twins reared apart? *Intelligence, 7*(2), 175–184.

Bowen, D. J., & Grunberg, N. E. (1990). Variations in food preference and consumption across the menstrual cycle. *Physiology and Behavior, 47*(2), 287–291.

Boy still meets girl—but not at the computer. (1987, January/February). *NEA Today, 5*(5), 17.

Boyd, N. (1979). Black families in therapy: A study of clinicians' perceptions. *Sandoz Psychiatric Spectator, 11*(7), 21–25.

Bozeman, S. T. (1989). Black women mathematicians: In short supply. *Sage: A Scholarly Journal on Black Women, 6*(2), 18–23.

Brabeck, M. (1983). Moral judgment: Theory and research on differences between males and females. *Developmental Review, 3*, 274–291.

Bradford, D. L., Sargent, A. G., & Sprague, M. S. (1975). The executive man and woman: The issue of sexuality. In F. E. Gordon & M. H. Strober (Eds.), *Bringing women into management*. New York: McGraw-Hill.

Bradley, C. F. (1983). Psychological consequences of intervention in the birth process. *Canadian Journal of Behavioral Science, 15*(4), 422–438.

Brannock, J. C., & Chapman, B. E. (1990). Negative sexual experiences with men among heterosexual women and lesbians. *Journal of Homosexuality, 19*(1), 105–110.

Brannon, R. (1976). The male sex role: Our culture's blueprint for manhood and what it's done for us lately. In D. David & R. Brannon (Eds.), *The forty-nine percent majority*. Reading, MA: Addison-Wesley.

Breathnach, C. S. (1990). The secondary sexual characteristics of the brain. *Irish Journal of Psychological Medicine, 7*(1), 59–63.

Brehm, J. W. (1966). *A theory of psychological reactance*. New York: Academic Press.

Brehony, A. (1982). Women and agoraphobia: A case for the etiological significance of the feminine sex role stereotype. In V. Franks & E. Rothblum (Eds.), *Sex role stereotypes and women's mental health*. New York: Springer.

Brehony, K. A., & Geller, E. S. (1981). Relationship between psychological androgyny, social conformity and perceived locus of control. *Psychology of Women Quarterly, 6*, 204–217.

Bretl, D. J., & Cantor, J. (1988). The portrayal of men and women in U.S. television commercials: A recent content analysis and trends over 15 years. *Sex Roles, 18*(9/10), 595–609.

Bridges, J. S. (1987). College females' perception of adult roles and occupational fields for women. *Sex Roles, 16,* 591–604.

Bridges, J. S. (1988). Sex differences in occupational performance expectations. *Psychology of Women Quarterly, 12*(1), 75–90.

Briere, J., Corne, S., Runta, M., & Malamuth, N. (1984, August). *The rape arousal inventory: Predicting actual and potential sexual aggression in a university population.* Paper presented at the meeting of the American Psychological Association, Toronto.

Briere, J., & Malamuth, N. (1983). Self-reported likelihood of sexually aggressive behavior: Attitudinal versus sexual explanations. *Journal of Research in Personality, 17,* 315–323.

Brockner, J., & Adsit, L. (1986). The moderating impact of sex on the equity-satisfaction relationship: A field study. *Journal of Applied Psychology, 71*(4), 585–590.

Brodie, M. J., & Vickers, J. M. (1982). *Canadian women in politics: An overview.* Ottawa: Canadian Research Institute for the Advancement of Women.

Brodsky, A. M. (1980). A decade of feminist influence on psychotherapy. *Psychology of Women Quarterly, 4,* 331–344.

Brodsky, G. (1986, Fall). LEAF's legal cases: an update. *LEAF Letter,* p. 4.

Brody, E. M. (1981). "Women in the middle" and family help to older people. *The Gerontologist, 21,* 471–479.

Bronstein, P. (1984). Differences in mothers' and fathers' behaviors toward children: A cross-cultural comparison. *Developmental Psychology, 20*(6), 995–1003.

Brooks, J., Ruble, D. N., & Clarke, A. E. (1977). College women's attitudes and expectations concerning menstrual-related changes. *Psychosomatic Medicine, 39*(5), 288–298.

Brooks, L., & Perot, A. R. (1991). Reporting sexual harassment: Exploring a predictive model. *Psychology of Women Quarterly, 15*(1), 31–48.

Brooks-Gunn, J., Burrow, C., & Warren, M. P. (1988). Attitudes toward eating and body weight in different groups of female adolescent athletes. *International Journal of Eating Disorders, 7,* 749–757.

Brooks-Gunn, J., & Ruble, D. (1980). Menarche. In A. J. Dan, E. A. Graham, & C. P. Beecher (Eds.), *The menstrual cycle* (Vol. 1). New York: Springer.

Broverman, I. K., Broverman, D. M., Clarkson, F. E., Rosenkrantz, P. S., & Vogel, S. R. (1970). Sex role stereotypes and clinical judgments of mental health. *Journal of Consulting and Clinical Psychology, 34*(1), 1–7.

Broverman, I. K., Vogel, S. R., Broverman, D. M., Clarkson, F. E., & Rosenkrantz, P. S. (1972). Sex-role stereotypes: A current appraisal. *Journal of Social Issues, 28*(2), 59–78.

Brown, A., Larsen, M. B., Rankin, S. A., & Ballard, R. A. (1980). Sex differences in information processing. *Sex Roles, 6,* 663–673.

Brown, D. (1992, May 22). Smoking deaths seen climbing. *The Washington Post,* pp. A1, A6.

Brown, D., Fulkerson, K. F., Furr, S., Ware, W. B., & Voight, N. L. (1984). Locus of control, sex role orientation, and self-concept in black and white third- and sixth-grade male and female leaders in a rural community. *Developmental Psychology, 20,* 717–721.

Brown, J. D. (1985). Race and gender in rock video. *Social Science Newsletter, 70*(2), 82–86.

Brown, J. D., Childers, K. W., & Waszak, C. S. (1990). Television and adolescent sexuality. *Journal of Adolescent Health Care, 11*(1), 62–70.

Brown, L. K. (1979). Women and business management. *Signs, 5*(2), 266–288.

Brown, L. S. (1989). New voices, new visions: Toward a lesbian/gay paradigm for psychology. *Psychology of Women Quarterly, 13*(4), 445–458.

Brown, M., Amoroso, D. M., & Ware, E. E. (1976). Behavioral effects of viewing pornography. *Journal of Social Psychology, 98,* 235–245.

Brown, W. B., Bhrolchain, M., & Harris, T. (1975). Social class and psychiatric disturbance among women in an urban population. *Sociology, 9*(2), 225–254.

Brownmiller, S. (1975). *Against our will: Men, women, and rape.* New York: Simon and Schuster.

Brownmiller, S. (1984). *Femininity.* New York: Fawcett Columbine.

Bruch, H. (1973). *Eating disorders: Obesity, anorexia nervosa and the person within.* New York: Basic Books.

Bruer, J. (1983, September). Women in science: Lack of full participation. *Science, 221,* 1339.

Bryden, M. P., & Vrbancic, M. I. (1988). Dichotic lateralization, cognitive ability, and age at puberty. *Developmental Neuropsychology, 4*(2), 169–180.

Buchanan, M., & Robbins, C. (1990). Early adult psychological consequences for males of adolescent pregnancy and its resolution. *Journal of Youth and Adolescence, 19*(4), 413–424.

Budoff, P. W. (1980). *No more menstrual cramps and other good news*. New York: Putnam.

Burchardt, C. J., & Serbin, L. A. (1982). Psychological androgyny and personality adjustment in college and psychiatric populations. *Sex Roles, 8*, 835–851.

Burger, J., & Gochfeld, M. (1989). Gender differences in smoking behavior in a university workplace. *Sex Roles, 20*(9/10), 523–533.

Burkhauser, R. V., & Duncan, G. J. (1989). Economic risks of gender roles: Income loss and life events over the life course. *Social Science Quarterly, 70*(1), 3–23.

Burlew, A. K. (1982). The experiences of black females in traditional and nontraditional professions. *Psychology of Women Quarterly, 6*(3), 312–326.

Burns, R. B. (1977). Male and female perceptions of their own and the other sex. *British Journal of Social and Clinical Psychology, 16*, 213–220.

Busby, L. (1974). Defining the sex-role standard in commercial network television programs directed toward children. *Journalism Quarterly, 51*, 690–696.

Buss, D. M., & Barnes, M. (1986). Preferences in human mate selection. *Journal of Personality and Social Psychology, 50*(3), 559–570.

Bussey, K., & Bandura, A. (1984). Influence of gender constancy and social power on sex-linked modeling. *Journal of Personality and Social Psychology, 47*, 1292–1302.

Bussey, K., & Perry, D. G. (1982). Same-sex imitation: The avoidance of cross-sex models or the acceptance of same-sex models? *Sex Roles, 8*, 773–784.

Butler, D., & Geis, F. L. (1990). Nonverbal affect responses to male and female leaders: Implications for leadership evaluations. *Journal of Personality and Social Psychology, 58*(1), 48–59.

Butler, E. (1985). The amenorrheic athlete. *The Melpomene Report, 4*(2), 7–12.

Byne, W., Bleier, R., & Houston, L. (1988). Variations in human corpus callosum do not predict gender: A study using magnetic resonance imaging. *Behavioral Neuroscience, 102*(2), 222–227.

Byrne, D. (1983). Sex without conception. In D. Byrne & W. A. Fisher (Eds.), *Adolescents, sex, and contraception*. Hillsdale, NJ: Lawrence Erlbaum.

Cafferata, G. L., & Meyers, S. M. (1990). Pathways to psychotropic drugs: Understanding the basis of gender differences. *Medical Care, 28*(4), 285–300.

Cahill, S. E. (1983). Reexamining the acquisition of sex roles: A social interactionist approach. *Sex Roles, 9*, 1–15.

Caldwell, M. A., & Peplau, L. A. (1982). Sex differences in same-sex friendships. *Sex Roles, 8*, 721–732.

Callahan-Levy, C. M., & Messe, L. A. (1979). Sex differences in the allocation of pay. *Journal of Personality and Social Psychology, 37*, 433–446.

Campaign for Women's Health. (1991). Fact sheet on women and health care in the U.S. (Available from O.W.L., 730 Eleventh Street, NW, Suite 300, Washington, DC 20001)

Canadian Advisory Council on the Status of Women. (1984). *Prostitution in Canada*. Ottawa: Author.

Canadian Advisory Council on the Status of Women. (1985). *Women and work*. Ottawa: Author.

Canadian Human Rights Commission. (1983). *Unwanted sexual attention and sexual harassment: Results of a survey of Canadians*. Ottawa: Author.

Canadian Mental Health Association. (1984). *Work and well-being: The changing realities of employment*. Toronto: Author.

Canadian Psychological Association. (1980). *Guidelines for therapy and counselling with women*. Ottawa: Author.

Canadian Psychological Association. (1982). *Therapy and counselling with women: A handbook on educational materials*. Ottawa: Author.

Cann, A., & Garnett, A. K. (1984). Sex stereotype impacts on competence ratings by children. *Sex Roles, 11*, 333–343.

Cannon, L. W., Higginbotham, E., & Leung, M. L. A. (1991). Race and class bias in qualitative research on women. In J. Lorber & S. A. Farrell (Eds.), *The social construction of gender* (pp. 237–248). Newbury Park, CA: Sage.

Cano, L., Solomon, S., & Holmes, D. S. (1984). Fear of success: The influence of sex, sex-role identity, and components of masculinity. *Sex Roles, 10*, 341–346.

Caplan, P. J., & Eichler, M. (1989). *A proposal for the Delusional Dominating Personality Disorder*. Toronto: Authors.

Caplan, P. J., MacPherson, G. M., & Tobin, P. (1985). Do sex-related differences in spatial ability exist? A multilevel critique with new data. *American Psychologist, 40*(7), 786–799.

Caputi, J., & Russell, D. E. H. (1990, September/October). "Femicide": Speaking the unspeakable. *Ms., 1*(2), 34–37.

Carbonell, J. L. (1984). Sex roles and leadership revisited. *Journal of Applied Psychology, 53,* 377–382.

Carli, L. L. (1990). Gender, language, and influence. *Journal of Personality and Social Psychology, 59*(5), 941–951.

Carlson, A. (1991, March). When is a woman not a woman? *Women's Sports & Fitness,* pp. 24–29.

Carlson, B. E., & Videka-Sherman, L. (1990). An empirical test of androgyny in the middle years: Evidence from a national survey. *Sex Roles, 23*(5/6), 305–324.

Carroll, J., Volk, K. D., & Hyde, J. S. (1985). Differences between males and females in motives for engaging in sexual intercourse. *Archives of Sexual Behavior, 14,* 131–139.

Carver, C. S., & de la Garza, N. H. (1984). Schema-guided information search in stereotyping of the elderly. *Journal of Applied Social Psychology, 14*(1), 69–81.

Cash, T. F., Gillen, B., & Burns, D. S. (1977). Sexism and "beautyism" in personnel consultant decision making. *Journal of Applied Psychology, 62,* 301–310.

Caspi, A., Bem, D., & Elder, G. H., Jr. (1989). Continuities and consequences of interactional styles across the life course. *Journal of Personality, 57*(2), 375–406.

Cass, V. C. (1979). Homosexual identity formation: A theoreti-

cal model. *Journal of Homosexuality, 4,* 219–235.

Cate, R., Henton, J., Koval, J., Christopher, F. S., & Lloyd, S. (1982). Premarital abuse: A social psychological perspective. *Journal of Family Issues, 3,* 79–90.

Cate, R. M., Lloyd, S., Henton, J. M., & Larson, J. (1982). Fairness and reward level as predictors of relationship satisfaction. *Social Psychology Quarterly, 45,* 177–181.

Cattell, J. M. (1903). A statistical study of eminent men. *Popular Science Monthly, 62,* 359–377.

Cazenave, N. A. (1984). Race, socioeconomic status, and age: The social context of American masculinity. *Sex Roles, 11*(7/8), 639–656.

Cazenave, N. A., & Leon, G. H. (1987). Men's work and family roles and characteristics: Race, gender, and class perceptions of college students. In M. S. Kimmel (Ed.), *Changing men: New directions in research on men and masculinity* (pp. 244–262). Newbury Park, CA: Sage.

Center for the American Woman and Politics. (1984). *Women holding elective office.* New Brunswick, NJ: Eagleton Institute of Politics, Rutgers University.

Central Statistics Office. (1984). *Social Trends* (No. 14). London: Her Majesty's Stationery Office.

Chaison, G. N., & Andrappan, P. (1982). Characteristics of female union officers in Canada. *Industrial Relations, 37*(4), 765–778.

Change over a decade. (1985, March 10). *New York Times,* p. 24E.

Chavez, D. (1985). Perpetuation of gender inequality: A content analysis of comic strips. *Sex Roles, 13*(1/2), 93–102.

Chernin, K. (1981). *The obsession: Reflections on the tyranny of slenderness.* New York: Harper & Row.

Cherry, F., & Deaux, K. (1978). Fear of success versus fear of gender-inappropriate behavior. *Sex Roles, 4,* 97–101.

Chertok, L. (1969). *Motherhood and personality.* London: Tavistock.

Chesler, P. (1971). Patient and patriarch: Women in the psychotherapeutic relationship. In V. Gornick & B. Moran (Eds.), *Women in sexist society: Studies in power and powerlessness* (pp. 251–275). New York: Basic Books.

Chesler, P. (1972). *Women and madness.* New York: Doubleday.

Chino, A. F., & Funabiki, D. (1984). A cross-validation of sex differences in the expression of depression. *Sex Roles, 11,* 175–187.

Chipman, S. F., Brush, L. R., & Wilson, D. M. (1985). *Women and mathematics: Balancing the equation.* Hillsdale, NJ: Lawrence Erlbaum.

Chodorow, N. (1978). *The reproduction of mothering: Psychoanalysis and the sociology of gender.* Berkeley: University of California Press.

Chodorow, N. (1989). *Feminism and psychoanalytic theory.* New Haven, CT: Yale University Press.

Chrisler, J. C., & Levy, K. B. (1990). The media construct a menstrual monster: A content analysis of PMS articles in the popular press. *Women and Health, 16*(2), 89–104.

Christensen, A., & Heavey, C. L. (1990). Gender and social structure in the demand/withdraw pattern of marital conflict. *Journal of Personality and Social Psychology, 59*(1), 73–81.

Christiansen, K., & Knussman, R. (1987). Androgen levels and components of aggressive behavior in men. *Hormones and Behavior, 21,* 170–180.

Chusmir, L. H., & Koberg, C. S. (1986). Creativity differences among managers. *Journal of Vocational Behavior, 29*(2), 240–253.

Cicone, M. V., & Ruble, D. N. (1978). Beliefs about males. *Journal of Social Issues, 34*(1), 5–16.

Clark, C. (1972). Race, identification, and television violence. In G. A. Comstock, E. A. Rubenstein, & J. P. Murray (Eds.), *Television and social behavior:* Vol. 5. *Television's effects: Further explorations.* Washington, DC: U.S. Government Printing Office.

Clark, L., & Lewis, D. (1977). *Rape: The price of coercive sexuality.* Toronto: Women's Press.

Clark, R., & Hatfield, E. (1989). Gender differences in receptivity to sexual offers. *Journal of Psychology and Human Sexuality, 2*(1), 39–55.

Clarke, E. (1873). *Sex in education; or, a fair chance for girls.* Boston: Osgood and Co.

Clarke-Stewart, K. A. (1991). A home is not a school: The effects of child care on children's development. *Journal of Social Issues, 47*(2), 105–124.

Clement, U., Schmidt, G., & Kruse, M. (1984). Changes in sex differences in behavior: A replication of a study on West German students (1966–1981). *Archives of Sexual Behavior, 13,* 99–120.

Clinton, J. F. (1987). Physical and emotional responses of expectant fathers throughout pregnancy and the early postpartum period. *International Journal of Nursing Studies, 24*(1), 59–68.

Cobb, N. J., Stevens-Long, J., & Goldstein, S. (1982). The influence of televised models on toy preference in children. *Sex Roles, 8,* 1075–1080.

Cochran, S. D., & Peplau, L. A. (1985). Value orientations in heterosexual relationships. *Psychology of Women Quarterly, 9*(4), 477–488.

Cochrane, J. (1977). *Women in Canadian politics.* Toronto: Fitzhenry & Whiteside.

Cody, M. J., McLaughlin, M. L., & Jordan, W. J. (1980). A multidimensional scaling of three sets of compliance-gaining strategies. *Communication Quarterly, 28,* 34–46.

Coe, R. M. (1978). *Sociology of medicine.* New York: McGraw-Hill.

Cohen, A. G., & Gutek, B. A. (1985). Dimensions of perceptions of social-sexual behavior in a work setting. *Sex Roles, 13*(5/6), 317–328.

Cohen, D., & Wilkie, F. (1979). Sex-related differences in cognition among the elderly. In M. A. Wittig & A. C. Petersen (Eds.), *Sex-related differences in cognitive functioning: Developmental issues* (pp. 145–159). New York: Academic Press.

Coker, D. R. (1984). The relationship among concepts and cognitive maturity in preschool children. *Sex Roles, 10,* 19–31.

Coleman, A., & Coleman, L. (1971). *Pregnancy: The psychological experience.* New York: Seabury.

Coleman, L. M., & Antonucci, T. C. (1983). Impact of work on women at midlife. *Developmental Psychology, 19*(2), 290–294.

Collins, E. G. C. (1983, September-October). Managers and lovers. *Harvard Business Review,* pp. 142–153.

Collis, B. (1985). Psychosocial implications of sex differences in attitudes toward computers: Results of a survey. *International Journal of Women's Studies, 8*(3), 207–213.

Colwill, N. L. (1984, November). Direction for future research. *Proceedings of Colloquium on the Economic Status of Women in the Labour Market.* Ottawa: The Economic Council of Canada.

Colwill, N. L. (1986). Men and women in organizations: Roles and status, stereotypes and power. In K. S. Koziara, M. H. Moskow, & L. D. Tanner (Eds.), *Working women: Past, present, future* (pp. 97–117). Washington, DC: The Bureau of National Affairs, Inc.

Colwill, N. L., & Colwill, H. D. (1985). Women with blue collars: The forgotten minority. *Business Quarterly, 50*(2), 15–17.

Colwill, N. L., & Josephson, W. L. (1983). Attitudes toward equal opportunity in employment: The case of one Canadian government department. *Business Quarterly, 48*(1), 87–93.

Colwill, N. L., & Lips, H. M. (1978). Masculinity, femininity, and androgyny: What have you done for us lately? In H. M. Lips & N. L. Colwill, *The psychology of sex differences* (pp. 125–144). Englewood Cliffs, NJ: Prentice-Hall.

Colwill, N. L., Perlman, D., & Spinner, B. (1982, June). *Effective power styles for women and men: A test of Johnson's model.* Paper presented at the forty-third annual convention of the

Canadian Psychological Association, Montreal.

Colwill, N. L., Perlman, D., & Spinner, B. (1983, June). *"Masculine" and "feminine" power styles of female secretaries and regional managers: An in-basket task.* Paper presented at the forty-fourth annual convention of the Canadian Psychological Association, Winnipeg.

Colwill, N. L., Pollock, M., & Sztaba, T. I. (1986). Power in home economics: An individual and personal issue. *Canadian Home Economics Journal, 36*(2), 59–61.

Colwill, N. L., & Roos, N. P. (1978). Debunking a stereotype: The female medical student. *Sex Roles, 4*(5), 717–722.

Colwill, N. L., & Sztaba, T. I. (1986). Organizational genderlect: The problem of two different languages. *Business Quarterly, 51*(2), 64–66.

Condon, J. T. (1987). Psychological and physical symptoms during pregnancy: A comparison of male and female expectant parents. *Journal of Reproductive and Infant Psychology, 5*(4), 207–219.

Condry, J., & Condry, S. (1976). Sex differences: A study of the eye of the beholder. *Child Development, 47,* 812–819.

Condry, J., & Ross, D. (1985). Sex and aggression: The influence of gender label on the perception of aggression in children. *Child Development, 56,* 225–233.

Condry, S. M., & Dyer, S. (1976). Fear of success: Attribution of cause to the victim. *Journal of Social Issues, 32*(3), 63–83.

Connor, J. M., & Serbin, L. A. (1985). Visual-spatial skill: Is it important for mathematics? Can it be taught? In S. Chipman, L. Brush, & D. Wilson (Eds.), *Women and mathematics: Balancing the equation* (pp. 151–174). Hillsdale, NJ: Lawrence Erlbaum Associates.

Connor-Greene, P. A. (1988). Gender differences in body weight perception and weight-loss strategies of college students. *Women and Health, 14*(2), 27–42.

Constantinople, A. (1973). Masculinity-femininity: An exception to a famous dictum? *Psychological Bulletin, 80*(3), 389–407.

Constantinople, A. (1979). Sex-role acquisition: In search of the elephant. *Sex Roles, 5,* 121–133.

Cook, E. P. (1985). *Psychological androgyny.* New York: Pergammon Press.

Cooper, K. L., & Guttmann, D. L. (1987). Gender identity and ego mastery style in middle-aged pre- and post-empty nest women. *The Gerontologist, 27,* 347–352.

Cornell, E. H., & Strauss, M. S. (1973). Infants' responsiveness to compounds of habituated visual stimuli. *Developmental Psychology, 2,* 73–78.

Cotton, N. S. (1979). The familial incidence of alcoholism: A review. *Journal of Studies on Alcohol, 40*(1), 89–116.

Cowan, C. P., Cowan, P. A., Coie, L., & Coie, J. D. (1978). Becoming a family: The impact of a first child's birth on the couple's relationship. In W. B. Miller & L. F. Newman (Eds.), *The first child and family formation.* Chapel Hill, NC: Carolina Population Center.

Cowan, G., Drinkard, J., & MacGavin, L. (1984). The effects of target, age, and gender in the use of power strategies. *Journal of Personality and Social Psychology, 47,* 1391–1398.

Cox, S., & Radloff, L. S. (1984). Depression in relation to sex roles: Differences in learned susceptibility and precipitating factors. In C. Widom (Ed.), *Sex roles and psychopathology* (pp. 123–144). New York: Plenum.

Craig, T. J., & Lin, S. P. (1984). Sex differences in mortality rate among long-stay psychiatric inpatients. *Sex Roles, 10,* 725–732.

Cramer, R. E., Dragna, M., Cupp, R. G., & Stewart, P. (1991). Contrast effects in the evaluation of the male sex role. *Sex roles, 24*(3/4), 181–193.

Crandall, V. C. (1963). Achievement. In H. W. Stevenson (Ed.), *Child psychology: Sixty-second yearbook of the National Society for the Study of Education.* Chicago: University of Chicago Press.

Crandall, V. C. (1969). Sex differences in expectancy of intellectual and academic reinforcement. In C. P. Smith (Ed.), *Achievement-related motives in children* (pp. 11–45). New York: Russell Sage Foundation.

Crandall, V. C., Katkovsky, W., & Preston, A. A. (1960). A conceptual foundation for some research on children's achievement development. *Child Development, 31,* 787–797.

Crino, M. D., White, M. C., & DeSanctis, G. L. (1983). Female participation rates and the occupational prestige of the professions: Are they inversely related? *Journal of Vocational Behavior, 22*(2), 243–255.

Crocker, L., Schmitt, A., & Tang, L. (1988, January). Test anxiety and standardized achievement test performance in the middle school years. *Measurement and Evaluation in Counseling and Development, 20*(4), 149–157.

Crohan, S. E., Antonucci, T. C., Adelmann, P. K., & Coleman, L. M. (1989). Job characteristics and well-being at midlife: Ethnic and gender comparisons. *Psychology of Women Quarterly, 13*(2), 223–236.

Crooks, R., & Bauer, K. (1987). *Our sexuality* (3rd ed.). Menlo Park, CA: Benjamin/Cummings.

Crosby, F. J. (1982). *Relative deprivation and working women.* New York: Oxford.

Crosby, F. J. (1984). The denial of personal discrimination. *American Behavioral Scientist, 27*(3), 371–386.

Crosby, F. J. (1990). Divorce and work life among women managers. In H. Y. Grossman & N. L. Chester (Eds.), *The experience and meaning of work in women's lives* (pp. 121–142). Hillsdale, NJ: Lawrence Erlbaum Associates.

Crosby, F. J., Clayton, S., Alksnis, O., & Hemker, K. (1986). Cognitive biases in the perception of discrimination: The importance of format. *Sex Roles, 14*(11/12), 637–646.

Crown, J., & Heatherington, L. (1989). The costs of winning? The role of gender in moral reasoning and judgments about competitive athletic encounters. *Journal of Sport and Exercise Psychology, 11*(3), 281–289.

Crull, P. (1980). The impact of sexual harassment on the job: A profile of the experiences of 92 women. In D. A. Neugarten & J. M. Shafritz (Eds.), *Sexuality in organizations: Romantic and coercive behaviors at work*

(pp. 67–71). Oak Park, IL: Moore.

Cunningham, J. D., & Antill, J. K. (1984). Changes in masculinity and femininity across the family life cycle: A reexamination. *Developmental Psychology, 20*(6), 1135–1141.

Cunningham, S. (1983, November). Women still do majority of childcare, housework. *APA Monitor,* p. 16.

Cutrona, C. E. (1982). Nonpsychotic postpartum depression: A review of recent research. *Clinical Psychology Review, 2,* 487–503.

Dabbs, J. M., Jr., de La Rue, D., & Williams, P. M. (1990). Testosterone and occupational choice: Actors, ministers, and other men. *Journal of Personality and Social Psychology, 39*(6), 1261–1265.

Dabbs, J. M., Jr., Frady, R. L., Carr, T. S., & Besch, N. F. (1987). Saliva testosterone and criminal violence in young adult prison inmates. *Psychosomatic Medicine, 49,* 174–182.

Dabbs, J. M., Jr., & Morris, R. (1990). Testosterone, social class, and antisocial behavior in a sample of 4,462 men. *Psychological Science, 1*(3), 209–211.

Dalton, D. R., & Todor, W. D. (1985). Gender and workplace justice: A field assessment. *Personnel Psychology, 38,* 133–151.

Dalton, K. (1964). *The premenstrual syndrome.* Springfield, IL: Thomas.

Daly, M. (1973). *Beyond God the Father..* Boston: Beacon Press.

Dan, A. J. (1976). Patterns of behavioral and mood variations in men and women: Variability and the menstrual cycle. *Dissertation Abstracts International, 37*(6-B), 3145–3146.

Dan, A. J. (1979). The menstrual cycle and sex-related differences in cognitive variability. In M. A. Wittig & A. C. Petersen (Eds.), *Sex-related differences in cognitive functioning: Developmental issues* (pp. 241–260). New York: Academic Press.

Darley, J. M., & Fazio, R. H. (1980). Expectancy confirmation processes arising in the social interaction sequence. *American Psychologist, 35,* 867–881.

Darwin, C. (1967). *The descent of man.* New York: Modern Library. (Original work published 1871)

Davidson, C. V., & Abramowitz, S. (1980). Sex bias in clinical judgement: Later empirical returns. *Psychology of Women Quarterly, 4,* 377–395.

Davidson, J. M. (1989). Sexual emotions, hormones, and behavior. *Advances, 6*(2), 56–58.

Davidson, L. R., & Duberman, L. (1982). Friendship: Communication and interactional patterns in same-sex dyads. *Sex Roles, 8,* 809–822.

Davies, M. (1975). Women's place is at the typewriter: The feminization of the clerical work force. In R. C. Edwards, M. Reich, & D. Gordon (Eds.), *Labor market segmentation* (pp. 279–296). Lexington, MA: Heath.

Davis, A. (1981). *Women, race and class.* New York: Random House.

Davis, A. J. (1984). Sex-differentiated behaviors in non-sexist picture books. *Sex Roles, 11,* 1–16.

Davis, C., & Cowles, M. (1985). Type A behaviour assessment: A critical comment. *Canadian Psychology, 26*(1), 39–42.

Davis, D. M. (1990). Portrayals of women in prime-time network television: Some demographic characteristics. *Sex Roles, 23*(5/6), 325–332.

Davis, J. A., & Smith, T. (1984). *General social surveys, 1972–1984: Cumulative data*. New Haven, CT: Yale University, Roper Center for Public Opinion Research.

Davis, M., & Weitz, S. (1981). Sex differences in body movements and positions. In C. Mayo & N. M. Henley (Eds.), *Gender and nonverbal behavior* (pp. 81–92). New York: Springer-Verlag.

Davis, M. D., & Kennedy, E. L. (1990). Oral history and the study of sexuality in the lesbian community: Buffalo, New York, 1940–1960. In E. C. DuBois & V. L. Ruiz (Eds.), *Unequal sisters: A multicultural reader in U. S. women's history* (pp. 387–399). New York: Routledge.

Davis, S. (1990). Men as success objects and women as sex objects: A study of personal advertisements. *Sex Roles, 23*(1/2), 43–50.

Deaux, K. (1977). Sex differences. In T. Blass (Ed.), *Personality variables in social behavior* (pp. 357–378). Hillsdale, NJ: Lawrence Erlbaum.

Deaux, K. (1984a). Blue-collar barriers. *American Behavioral Scientist, 27*(3), 287–300.

Deaux, K. (1984b). From individual differences to social categories: Analysis of a decade's research on gender. *American Psychologist, 39*(2), 105–116.

Deaux, K., & Emswiller, T. (1974). Explanations of successful performance on sex-linked tasks: What's skill for the male is luck for the female. *Journal of Personality and Social Psychology, 29*, 80–85.

Deaux, K., & Lewis, L. L. (1983). Components of gender stereotypes (Ms. no. 2583). *Psychological Documents, 13*, 25.

Deaux, K., & Lewis, L. L. (1984). Structure of gender stereotypes: Interrelationships among components and gender label. *Journal of Personality and Social Psychology, 46*(5), 991–1004.

Deaux, K., & Major, B. (1987). Putting gender into context: An interactive model of gender-related behavior. *Psychological Review, 94*(3), 369–389.

Deaux, K., & Ullman, J. C. (1983). *Women of steel: Female blue-collar workers in the basic steel industry*. New York: Praeger.

De Beauvoir, S. (1952). *The second sex*. New York: Alfred A. Knopf.

De Cecco, J. P., & Shively, M. G. (1983/1984). From sexual identity to sexual relationships: A contextual shift. *Journal of Homosexuality, 9*(2/3), 1–26.

Deckard, B. S. (1983). *The women's movement: Political, socioeconomic and psychological issues*. New York: Harper & Row.

DeGregorio, E., & Carver, C. S. (1980). Type A behavior pattern, sex role orientation, and psychological adjustment. *Journal of Personality and Social Psychology, 39*, 286–293.

de Koninck, M. (1984). Double work and women's health. *Canada's Mental Health, 32*(3), 28–31.

de Lacoste-Utamsing, C., & Holloway, R. L. (1982). Sexual dimorphism in the human corpus callosum. *Science, 216*, 1431–1432.

Delaney, J., Lupton, M. J., & Toth, E. (1976). *The curse*. New York: Dutton.

Del Boca, F. K., & Ashmore, R. D. (1980). Sex stereotypes through the life cycle. In L. Wheeler (Ed.), *Review of personal and social psychology* (Vol. 1, pp. 163–192). Beverly Hills, CA: Sage.

De Lisi, R., & Soundranayagam, L. (1990). The conceptual structure of sex role stereotypes in college students. *Sex Roles, 23*(11/12), 593–611.

De Luccie, M. F., & Davis, A. J. (1991). Do men's adult life concerns affect their fathering orientations? *The Journal of Psychology, 125*(2), 175–188.

Demaré, D. (1986). *The effects of erotic and sexually violent mass media on attitudes toward women and rape*. Unpublished manuscript, University of Winnipeg.

Demaré, D., Briere, J., & Lips, H. M. (1988). Violent pornography and self-reported likelihood of sexual aggression. *Journal of Research in Personality, 22*, 140–153.

Demaré, D., Lips, H., & Briere, J. (1991). *Pornography, anti-women attitudes, and sexual aggression*. Unpublished manuscript, University of Winnipeg.

Deutsch, H. (1945). *The psychology of women* (Vol. 2). New York: Grune & Stratton.

De Wolf, V. A. (1981). High school mathematics preparation and sex differences in quantitative abilities. *Psychology of Women Quarterly, 5*, 555–567.

Dexter, C. R. (1985). Women and the exercise of power in organizations: From ascribed to achieved status. In L. Larwood, A. H. Stromberg, & B. A. Gutek (Eds.), *Women and work: An annual review* (Vol. 1, pp. 239–258). Beverly Hills, CA: Sage.

Dickason, A. (1976). Anatomy and destiny: The role of biology in Plato's views of women. In C. C. Gould & M. W. Wartofsky (Eds.), *Women and philosophy: Toward a theory of liberation* (pp. 45–53). New York: G. P. Putnam's Sons.

Dickens, W. J., & Perlman, D. (1981). Friendship over the life cycle. In S. Duck & R. Gilmour (Eds.), *Personal relationships: Vol. 2. Developing personal relationships* (pp. 91–122). London: Academic Press.

Die, A. H., Debbs, T., Jr., & Walker, J. L., Jr. (1990). Managerial evaluations by men and women managers. *The Journal of Social Psychology, 130*(6), 763–769.

Dietz, P. E., & Evans, B. (1982). Pornographic imagery and prevalence of paraphilia. *American Journal of Psychiatry, 139,* 1493–1495.

Dinnerstein, D. (1976). *The mermaid and the minotaur: Sexual arrangements and human malaise.* New York: Harper Colophon.

Dipboye, R. L., Fromkin, H. L., & Wiback, K. (1975). Relative importance of applicant sex, attractiveness, and scholastic standing in evaluation of job applicant resumes. *Journal of Applied Psychology, 60,* 39–43.

DiPietro, J. A. (1981). Rough and tumble play: A function of gender. *Developmental Psychology, 17,* 50–58.

Dobash, R. E., & Dobash, R. P. (1984). The nature and antecedents of violent events. *British Journal of Criminology, 24,* 269–288.

Dobbins, G. H. (1986). Equity vs equality: Sex differences in leadership. *Sex Roles, 15*(9/10), 513–525.

Dodril, C. (1979). Sex differences on the Halsted-Reitan Neuropsychological Battery and on other neuropsychological measures. *Journal of Clinical Psychology, 35,* 236–241.

Dodson, B. (1974). *Liberating masturbation: A meditation on self love.* (Available from Body-sex Designs, P.O. Box 1933, New York, NY 10001)

Doering, C. H., Brodie, H. K. H., Kraemer, H. C., Becker, H. B., & Hamburg, D. A. (1974). Plasma testosterone levels and psychological measurements in men over a 2-month period. In R. C. Friedman, R. M. Richart, & R. L. Vande Wiele (Eds.), *Sex differences in behavior* (pp. 413–421). New York: Wiley.

Donnerstein, E. (1980). Aggressive-erotica and violence against women. *Journal of Personality and Social Psychology, 3,* 269–277.

Donnerstein, E. (1983). Erotica and human aggression. In R. Green & E. Donnerstein (Eds.), *Aggression: Theoretical and empirical reviews* (Vol. 2). New York: Academic Press.

Doty, R. L., & Silverthorne, C. (1975). Influence of the menstrual cycle on volunteering behavior. *Nature, 254,* 139–140.

Doucette, J. (1986). Violent acts against disabled women. In *The future is now* (Appendix A). Report of the conference of the Ontario Disabled Women's Network. (Available from D.A.W.N., 122 Galt Ave., Toronto, Ontario, Canada, M4M 2Z3)

Douvan, E., & Adelson, J. (1966). *The adolescent experience.* New York: Wiley.

Douvan, E., & Pleck, J. (1978). Separation as support. In R. Rapoport & R. N. Rapoport (Eds.), *Working couples* (pp. 138–146). New York: Harper Colophon.

Downs, A. C. (1983). Letters to Santa Claus: Elementary school-age children's sex-typed toy preferences in a natural setting. *Sex Roles, 9,* 159–163.

Downs, A. C., & Harrison, S. K. (1985). Embarrassing age spots or just plain ugly? Physical attractiveness stereotyping as an instrument of sexism on American television commercials. *Sex Roles, 13*(1/2), 9–19.

Doyle, J. A. (1983). *The male experience.* Dubuque, IA: Wm. C. Brown.

Doyle, J. A. (1985). *Sex and Gender: The human experience.* Dubuque, IA: Wm. C. Brown.

Driver, 65, beaten, slain. (1991, August 24). *The Washington Post,* pp. A1, A10.

Dubinsky, K. (1985). *Lament for a "patriarchy lost"? Anti-feminism, anti-abortion, and R.E.A.L. women in Canada.* Ottawa: Canadian Research Institute for the Advancement of Women.

Dubnos, P. (1985). Attitudes toward women executives: A longitudinal approach. *Academy of Management Journal, 28*(1), 235–239.

DuBrin, A. J. (1989). Sex differences in endorsement of influence tactics and political behavior tendencies. *Journal of Business and Psychology, 4*(1), 3–14.

Dugger, K. (1991). Social location and gender-role attitudes: A comparison of black and white women. In J. Lorber & S. A. Farrell (Eds.), *The social construction of gender* (pp. 38–59). Newbury Park, CA: Sage.

Duke, L. (1991, August 19). Military's last social taboo: Homosexuality. *The Washington Post,* pp. A1, A8.

Dumas, M. C., Calliet, L. L., Tumblin, I. G., & King, A. R. (1984). Menstrual cycle influence on alcohol consumption among Blacks. *Journal of Black Psychology, 11*(1), 9–18.

Dunkle, J. H., & Francis, P. L. (1990). The role of facial masculinity/femininity in the attribution of homosexuality. *Sex Roles, 23*(3/4), 157–167.

Dutton, D. G. (1986). Wife assaulters' explanations for assault: The neutralization of self-punishment. *Canadian Journal of Behavioural Science, 18*(4), 381–390.

Dutton, D. G. (1987a). The criminal justice response to wife assault. *Law and Human Behavior, 11*(3), 189–206.

Dutton, D. G. (1987b). Wife assault: Social psychological contributions to criminal justice policy. *Applied Social Psychology Annual, 7,* 238–261.

Dutton, D. G., & Browning, J. J. (1983). *Violence in intimate relationships.* Paper presented at the International Society for Research on Aggression, Victoria, British Columbia.

Dutton, D. G., & Strachan, C. E. (1987). Motivational needs for power and spouse-specific assertiveness in assaultive and nonassaultive men. *Violence and Victims 2*(3), 145–156.

Duxbury, L. E., & Higgins, C. A. (1991). Gender differences in work-family conflict. *Journal of Applied Psychology, 76*(1), 60–74.

Dweck, C. S. (1975). The role of expectations and attributions in the alleviation of learned helplessness. *Journal of Personality and Social Psychology, 31,* 674–685.

Dweck, C. S., Davidson, W., Nelson, S., & Enna, B. (1978). Sex differences in learned helplessness. II. The contingencies of evaluative feedback in the classroom. III. An experimental analysis. *Developmental Psychology, 14,* 268–276.

Dweck, C. S., Goetz, T. E., & Strauss, N. L. (1980). Sex differences in learned helplessness: IV. An experimental and naturalistic study of failure generalization and its mediators. *Journal of Personality and Social Psychology, 38,* 441–452.

Dye, E., & Roth, S. (1990). Psychotherapists' knowledge about and attitudes toward sexual assault victim clients. *Psychology of Women Quarterly, 14*(2), 191–212.

Eagly, A. H. (1983). Gender and social influence: A social psychological analysis. *American Psychologist, 38,* 971–981.

Eagly, A. H. (1987). *Sex differences in social behavior: A social-role interpretation.* Hillsdale, NJ: Lawrence Erlbaum.

Eagly, A. H., & Carli, L. L. (1981). Sex of researchers and sex-typed communications as determinants of sex differences in influenceability: A meta-analysis of social influence studies. *Psychological Bulletin, 90,* 1–20.

Eagly, A. H., & Crowley, M. (1986). Gender and helping behavior: A meta-analytic review of the social psychological literature. *Psychological Bulletin, 100,* 283–308.

Eagly, A. H., & Johnson, B. T. (1990). Gender and leadership style: A meta-analysis. *Psychological Bulletin, 108,* 233–256.

Eagly, A. H., & Karau, S. J. (1991). Gender and the emergence of leaders: A meta-analysis. *Journal of Personality and Social Psychology, 60*(5), 685–710.

Eagly, A. H., Mladinic, A., & Otto, S. (1991). Are women evaluated more favorably than men? An analysis of attitudes, beliefs, and emotions. *Psychology of Women Quarterly, 15,* 203–216.

Eagly, A. H., & Steffen, V. J. (1984). Gender stereotypes stem from the distribution of women and men into social roles. *Journal of Personality and Social Psychology, 46*(4), 735–754.

Eagly, A. H., & Steffen, V. J. (1986). Gender and aggressive behavior: A meta-analytic review of the social psychological literature. *Psychological Bulletin, 100,* 309–330.

Eagly, A. H., & Wood, W. (1982). Inferred sex differences in status as a determinant of gender stereotypes about social influence. *Journal of Personality and Social Psychology, 43,* 915–928.

Eagly, A. H., & Wood, W. (1985). Gender and influenceability: Stereotype versus behavior. In V. O'Leary, R. Unger, & B. Wallston (Eds.), *Women, gender, and social psychology* (pp. 225–256). Hillsdale, NJ: Lawrence Erlbaum Associates.

Eagly, A. H., & Wood, W. (1991). Explaining sex differences in social behavior: A meta-analytic perspective. *Personality and Social Psychology Bulletin, 17*(3), 306–315.

Eagly, A. H., Wood, W., & Fishbaugh, L. (1981). Sex differences in conformity: Surveillance by the group as a determinant of male nonconformity. *Journal of*

Personality and Social Psychology, 40, 384–394.

Eakins, B. W., & Eakins, R. G. (1978). *Sex differences in human communication*. Boston: Houghton Mifflin.

Eaton, W. O., & Enns, L. R. (1986). Sex differences in human motor activity level. *Psychological Bulletin, 100*(1), 19–28.

Eccles, J. (1985). Sex differences in achievement patterns. In T. B. Sonderegger (Ed.), *Psychology and gender. Nebraska Symposium on Motivation, 1984* (pp. 97–132). Lincoln: University of Nebraska Press.

Eccles, J. (1987). Gender roles and women's achievement-related decisions. *Psychology of Women Quarterly, 11*(2), 135–172.

Eccles (Parsons), J., Adler, T. F., Futterman, R., Goff, S. B., Kaczala, C. M., Meece, J. L., & Midgley, C. (1983). Expectations, values and academic behaviors. In J. T. Spence (Ed.), *Achievement and achievement motives* (pp. 75–146). San Francisco: W. H. Freeman.

Edwards, J. R., & Williams, J. E. (1980). Sex-trait stereotypes among young children and young adults: Canadian findings and cross-national comparisons. *Canadian Journal of Behavioural Science, 12*, 210–220.

Efron, R. (1990). *The decline and fall of hemispheric specialization*. Hillsdale, NJ: Lawrence Erlbaum Associates.

Ehrenreich, B. (1981). The woman's movement—feminist and anti-feminist. *Radical America, 15*(1 and 2), 43–101.

Ehrenreich, B. (1983). *The hearts of men: American dreams and the flight from commitment*. Garden City, NY: Anchor.

Ehrenreich, B., & English, D. (1979). *For her own good: 150 years of the experts' advice to women*. Garden City, NY: Anchor Books.

Ehrhardt, A. A. (1985). Gender differences: A biosocial perspective. In T. Sonderegger (Ed.), *Nebraska Symposium on Motivation: Psychology of gender* (pp. 37–57). Lincoln: University of Nebraska Press.

Ehrhardt, A. A., & Baker, S. W. (1974). Fetal androgens, human central nervous system differentiation, and behavior sex differences. In R. M. Richart, & R. L. Vande Wiele (Eds.), *Sex differences in behavior* (pp. 33–52). New York: Wiley.

Ehrhardt, A. A., & Baker, S. W. (1976). *Prenatal androgens and future adolescent behavior*. Paper presented at the International Conference of Sexology, Montreal.

Eichler, M. (1980). *The double standard*. London: Croon-Helm.

Eichler, M. (1983). *Sexism in research and its policy implications*. Ottawa: Canadian Research Institute for the Advancement of Women.

Eichler, M. (1986). *The pro-family movement: Are they for or against families?* Ottawa: Canadian Research Institute for the Advancement of Women.

Eichler, M., & Lapointe, J. (1985). *On the treatment of the sexes in research*. Ottawa: Social Sciences and Humanities Research Council of Canada.

Eisenberg, N., & Lennon, R. (1983). Sex differences in empathy and related capacities. *Psychological Bulletin, 94*(1), 100–131.

Eisenstock, B. (1984). Sex-role differences in children's identification with counterstereotypic televised portrayals. *Sex Roles, 10*, 417–430.

Elias, M. (1981). Serum cortisol, testosterone and testosterone-binding globulin responses to competitive fighting in human males. *Aggressive Behavior, 7*, 215–224.

Ellis, L. (1982). Developmental androgen fluctuations and the dimensions of mammalian sex (with emphasis upon the behavioral dimension and the human species). *Ethology and Sociobiology, 3*, 171–179.

Ellis, L., & Ames, M. A. (1987). Neurohormonal functioning and sexual orientation. *Psychological Bulletin, 101*(2), 233–258.

Ellis, L., Burke, D., & Ames, M. A. (1987). Sexual orientation as a continuous variable: A comparison between the sexes. *Archives of Sexual Behavior, 16*(6), 523–529.

Ellyson, S. L., Dovidio, J. F., & Fehr, B. J. (1981). Visual behavior and dominance in women and men. In C. Mayo & N. M. Henley (Eds.), *Gender and nonverbal behavior* (pp. 63–79). New York: Springer-Verlag.

Elsner, C. W., Buster, J. E., Schindler, R. A., Nessim, S. A., & Abraham, G. E. (1980). Bromocryptine in the treatment of premenstrual tension syndrome. *Obstetrics and Gynecology, 56*, 723–726.

Entwisle, D. R., & Baker, D. P. (1983). Gender and young children's expectations for performance in arithmetic. *Developmental Psychology, 19*(2), 200–209.

Epstein, C. (1973). The positive effects of multiple negatives: Explaining the success of black professional women. In J. Huber (Ed.), *Changing women in a changing society* (pp. 150–173). Chicago: University of Chicago Press.

Epstein, C. F. (1983, April). The new total woman. *Working Woman*, pp. 100–103.

Equal Employment Opportunity Commission. (1980). Guidelines on discrimination because of sex. *Federal Register, 45*(219), 74676–74677.

Erickson, B. E., Lund, E. A., Johnson, B. C., & O'Barr, W. M. (1978). Speech style and impression formation in a court setting: The effects of "powerful" and "powerless" speech. *Journal of Experimental Social Psychology, 14,* 266–279.

Erikson, E. (1950). *Childhood and society.* New York: Norton.

Erkut, S. (1983). Exploring sex differences in expectancy, attribution, and academic achievement. *Sex Roles, 9,* 217–231.

Erlick, A. C., & LeBold, W. K. (1975). *Factors influencing the science career plans of high school students.* West Lafayette, IN: Purdue University, Measurement and Research Center.

Eron, L. D., Huessman, L. R., Brice, P., Fischer, P., & Mermelstein, R. (1983). Age trends in the development of aggression, sex typing, and related television habits. *Sex Roles, 19*(1), 71–77.

Espín, O. M. (1987). Issues of identity in the psychology of Latina lesbians. In The Boston Lesbian Psychologies Collective (Eds.), *Lesbian Psychologies* (pp. 35–55). Urbana: University of Illinois Press.

Estimate of rape victims is quintupled (1992, April 24). *The Washington Post,* p. A11.

Etaugh, C. (1974). Effects of maternal employment on children: A review of recent research. *Merrill Palmer Quarterly, 20,* 71–98.

Etaugh, C., & Duits, T. (1990). Development of gender discrimination: Role of stereotypic and counterstereotypic gender cues. *Sex Roles, 23*(5/6), 215–222.

Etaugh, C., & Kasley, H. C. (1981). Evaluating competence: Effects of sex, marital status, and parental status. *Psychology of Women Quarterly, 6,* 196–203.

Etaugh, C., Levine, D., & Mennella, A. (1984). Development of sex biases in children: 40 years later. *Sex Roles, 10,* 913–924.

Ethington, C. A., & Wolfle, L. M. (1984). Sex differences in a causal model of mathematics achievement. *Journal for Research in Mathematics Education, 15,* 361–377.

Etzkowitz, H. (1971). The male sister: Sexual separation of labor in society. *Journal of Marriage and the Family, 33,* 431–434.

Ezell, H. F., Odewahn, C. A., & Sherman, J. D. (1981). The effects of having been supervised by a woman on perceptions of female managerial competence. *Personnel Psychology, 34*(2), 291–299.

Fagot, B. I. (1984). Teacher and peer reactions to boys' and girls' play styles. *Sex Roles, 11,* 691–702.

Fagot, B. I. (1985). Beyond the reinforcement principle: Another step toward understanding sex role development.

Developmental Psychology, 21(6), 1097–1104.

Fagot, B. I., & Hagan, R. (1985). Aggression in toddlers: Responses to the assertive acts of boys and girls. *Sex Roles, 12*(3/4), 341–351.

Fairhurst, G. T. (1985). Male-female communication on the job: Literature review and commentary. In M. McLaughlin (Ed.), *Communication Yearbook* (Vol. 9, pp. 83–115). Beverly Hills, CA: Sage.

Fairweather, H. (1976). Sex differences in cognition. *Cognition, 4,* 231–280.

Fairweather, H., & Hutt, S. J. (1972). Sex differences in a perceptual motor skill in children. In C. Ounsted & D. C. Taylor (Eds.), *Gender differences: Their ontogeny and significance.* Edinburgh: Churchill Livingstone.

Falbo, T. (1977). Multidimensional scaling of power strategies. *Journal of Personality and Social Psychology, 35,* 537–547.

Falbo, T., & Peplau, L. A. (1980). Power strategies in intimate relationships. *Journal of Personality and Social Psychology, 38,* 618–628.

Fallon, A. E., & Rozin, P. (1985). Sex differences in perceptions of desirable body shape. *Journal of Abnormal Psychology, 94*(1), 102–105.

Farley, J. (1980). Worklife problems for both women and men. In D. A. Neugarten & J. M. Shafritz (Eds.), *Sexuality in organizations: Romantic and coercive behaviors at work* (pp. 29–37). Oak Park, IL: Moore.

Farmer, H. S., & Vispoel, W. P. (1990). Attributions of female and male adolescents for real-life failure experiences. *Journal of Experimental Education, 58,* 127–140.

Farrell, M., & Rosenberg, S. (1981). *Men at midlife*. Boston: Auburn House.

Farris, A. (1978). Commuting. In R. Rapoport & R. N. Rapoport (Eds.), *Working couples* (pp. 100–107). New York: Harper Colophon.

Fasting, K., & Sisjord, K. (1985). Gender roles and barriers to participation in sports. *Sociology of Sport Journal, 2*(4), 345–351.

Fausto-Sterling, A. (1985). *Myths of gender: Biological theories about women and men*. New York: Basic Books.

Fausto-Sterling, A., & English, L. A. (1986, January). Women and minorities in science: An interdisciplinary course. *Radical Teacher*, pp. 16–20.

Favreau, O. E. (1977). Sex bias in psychological research. *Canadian Psychological Review, 18*(1), 56–65.

Favreau, O. E. (1991). *Do the Ns justify the means? Is the median the message?* Paper presented at the annual meeting of the Association for Women in Psychology, Hartford, CT.

Feather, N. T. (1966). Effects of prior success and failure on expectations of success and subsequent performance. *Journal of Personality and Social Psychology, 3*(3), 287–298.

Fedigan, L. M. (1982). *Primate paradigms: Sex roles and social bonds*. Montreal: Eden Press.

Fehr, S. C. (1992, January 14). Dramatic increase in traffic fatality rate for women puzzles analysts. *The Washington Post*, p. A7.

Fein, R. A. (1974). *Men's experiences before and after the birth of a first child: Dependence, marital sharing and anxiety*. Unpublished doctoral dissertation, Harvard University.

Feingold, A. (1988). Cognitive gender differences are disappearing. *American Psychologist, 43*(2), 95–103.

Feingold, A. (1990). Gender differences in effects of physical attractiveness on romantic attraction: A comparison across five research paradigms. *Journal of Personality and Social Psychology, 59*(5), 981–993.

Feldman, J. J. (1966). *The dissemination of health information*. Chicago: Aldine.

Feldman, N. S., & Brown, E. (1984, April). *Male vs. female differences in control strategies: What children learn from Saturday morning television*. Paper presented at the meeting of the Eastern Psychological Association, Baltimore, MD.

Feldman, S. S., Biringen, Z. C., & Nash, S. C. (1981). Fluctuations of sex-related self-attributions as a function of stage of family life-cycle. *Developmental Psychology, 17*, 24–35.

Feldman, S. S., & Nash, S. C. (1978). Interest in babies during young adulthood. *Child Development, 49*, 617–622.

Feldman, S. S., Nash, S. C., & Cutrona, C. (1977). The influence of age and sex on responsiveness to babies. *Developmental Psychology, 13*, 675–676.

Feldstein, J. H., & Feldstein, S. (1982). Sex differences on televised toy commercials. *Sex Roles, 8*, 581–587.

Female victims of crime. (1985). *Canadian Urban Victimization Survey Bulletin*, p. 4.

The feminization of the professional workforce. (1986, February 17). *Business Week*, p. 21.

Fenelon, J., & Megargee, E. (1971). Influence of race on the manifestation of leadership. *Journal of Applied Psychology, 55*, 353–358.

Fennema, E., & Sherman, J. (1977). Sex-related differences in mathematics achievement, spatial visualization and affective factors. *American Educational Research Journal, 14*, 51–71.

Fennema, E., & Tartre, L. A. (1985). The use of spatial visualization in mathematics by girls and boys. *Journal for Research in Mathematics Education, 16*(3), 184–206.

Feshbach, S. (1970). Aggression. In P. H. Mussen (Ed.), *Carmichael's manual of child psychology* (Vol. 2, pp. 159–260). New York: Wiley.

Fidell, L. S. (1970). Empirical verification of sex discrimination in hiring practices in psychology. *American Psychologist, 25*, 1094–1098.

Fidell, L. S. (1980). Sex role stereotypes and the American physician. *Psychology of Women Quarterly, 4*, 313–330.

Fidell, L. S. (1982). Gender and drug use and abuse. In I. Al-Issa (Ed.), *Gender and psychopathology* (pp. 221–236). New York: Academic Press.

Field, T., Sandberg, D., Garcia, R., Vega-Lahr, N., Goldstein, S., & Guy, L. (1985). Pregnancy problems, postpartum depression, and early mother-infant interaction. *Developmental Psychology, 21*(6), 1152–1156.

Figes, E. (1970). *Patriarchal attitudes*. New York: Stein and Day.

Figueira-McDonough, J. (1987). Discrimination or sex differences? Criteria for evaluating the juvenile justice system's handling of minor offenses. *Crime and Delinquency, 33*(3), 403–424.

Fine, M. (1991, March). *Women with disabilities*. Paper presented at the national conference of the Association for Women in Psychology, Hartford, CT.

Fine, M., & Asch, A. (1981). Disabled women: Sexism without the pedestal. *Journal of Sociology and Social Welfare, 8,* 233–248.

Fink, D. (1983, April 19). The sexes agree more about sex. *USA Today,* pp. 1D–2D.

Finkelhor, D. (1979). *Sexually victimized children*. New York: Free Press.

Finn, J. D. (1980). Sex differences in educational outcomes. A cross-national study. *Sex Roles, 6,* 9–26.

Fischbein, S. (1990). Biosocial influences on sex differences for ability and achievement test results as well as marks at school. *Intelligence, 14*(1), 127–139.

Fischer, C. T. (1984). A phenomenological study of being criminally victimized: Contributions and constraints of qualitative research. *Journal of Social Issues, 40*(1), 161–178.

Fish, M. C., Gross, A. L., & Sanders, J. S. (1986). The effect of equity strategies on girls' computer usage in school. *Computers in Human Behavior, 2*(2), 127–134.

Fishbein, J. (1988, December). Teenage girls know about AIDS, but don't act accordingly. *The Nation's Health, 18*(12).

Fisher, K. (1986, August). AIDS. Military testing documents virus in heterosexuals; privacy concerns growing. *APA Monitor, 17*(8), 19.

Fishman, P. M. (1978). Interaction: The work women do. *Social Problems, 25,* 397–406.

Fisk, N. (1973). Gender dysphoria syndrome (The how, what, and why of a disease). In D. Laub & P. Gandy (Eds.), *Proceedings of the second international symposium on gender dysphoria syndrome* (pp. 7–14). Palo Alto, CA: Stanford University Press.

Fisk, W. R. (1985). Responses to "neutral" pronoun presentations and the development of sex-biased responding. *Developmental Psychology, 21*(3), 481–485.

Fitzgerald, L. F. (1980). Nontraditional occupations: Not for women only. *Journal of Counseling Psychology, 27,* 252–259.

Fitzgerald, L. F., & Cherpas, C. C. (1985). On the reciprocal relationship between gender and occupation: Rethinking the assumptions concerning masculine career development. *Journal of Vocational Behavior, 27,* 109–122.

Fleischer, R. A., & Chertkoff, J. M. (1986). Effects of dominance and sex on leader selection in dyadic work groups. *Journal of Personality and Social Psychology, 50*(1), 94–99.

Fleming, J. (1982). Fear of success in black male and female graduate students: A pilot study. *Psychology of Women Quarterly, 6*(3), 327–341.

Fleming, J. (1983a). Black women in black and white college environments: The making of a matriarch. *Journal of Social Issues, 39*(3), 41–54.

Fleming, J. (1983b). Sex differences in the educational and occupational goals of black college students: Continued inquiry into the black matriarchy theory. In M. S. Horner, M. Notman, & C. Nadelson (Eds.), *The challenge of change.* New York: Plenum.

Flexner, A. (1914). *Prostitution in Europe*. New York: Century.

Fodor, I. G. (1982). Gender and phobia. In I. Al-Issa (Ed.), *Gender and psychopathology* (pp. 179–197). New York: Academic Press.

Fogel, R., & Paludi, M. A. (1984). Fear of success and failure, or norms for achievement? *Sex Roles, 10,* 431–443.

Foot, H. C., Chapman, A. J., & Smith, J. R. (1977). Friendship and social responsiveness in boys and girls. *Journal of Personality and Social Psychology, 35,* 401–411.

Ford, M. R., & Lowery, C. R. (1986). Gender differences in moral reasoning: A comparison of the use of justice and care orientations. *Journal of Personality and Social Psychology, 50*(4), 777–783.

Forrest, J. D., & Henshaw, S. K. (1983, August). What U.S. women think and do about contraception. *Family Planning Perspectives, 15*(4), 157–166.

Foushee, H. C., Davis, M. H., & Archer, R. L. (1979). Empathy, masculinity, and femininity. *JSAS Catalogue of Selected Documents in Psychology, 9,* 85. (Ms. no. 1974).

Foushee, H. C., Helmreich, R. L., & Spence, J. T. (1979). Implicit theories of masculinity and femininity: Dualistic or bipolar? *Psychology of Women Quarterly, 3,* 259–269.

Fox, L. H. (1976). Career education for gifted pre-adolescents. *The Gifted Child Quarterly, 20,* 262–273.

Fox, L. H. (1981). *The problem of women and mathematics*. New York: Ford Foundation.

Fox, L. H., & Cohn, J. J. (1980). Sex differences in the development of precocious mathematical talent. In L. H. Fox, L. Brody, & D. Tobin (Eds.), *Women and the mathematical mystique* (pp. 94–112). Baltimore: Johns Hopkins University Press.

Fox, M., Gibbs, M., & Auerbach, D. (1985). Age and gender dimensions of friendship. *Psychology of Women Quarterly, 9,* 489–502.

Fox, M. F., & Hesse-Biber, S. (1984). *Women at work.* Palo Alto, CA: Mayfield.

Frank, E. J. (1988). Business students' perceptions of women in management. *Sex Roles, 19*(1/2), 107–118.

Frank, R. H. (1978). Why women earn less: The theory and estimation of differential overqualification. *American Economic Review, 68,* 360–373.

Frank, R. T. (1931). The hormonal causes of premenstrual tension. *Archives of Neurological Psychiatry, 26,* 1053.

Frankel, M. T., & Rollins, H. A., Jr. (1983). Does mother know best? Mothers and fathers interacting with preschool sons and daughters. *Developmental Psychology, 19*(5), 694–702.

Franken, M. (1983). Sex role expectations in children's vocational aspirations and perceptions of occupations. *Psychology of Women Quarterly, 8,* 59–68.

Franklin, C. W., II (1984). *The changing definition of masculinity.* New York: Plenum.

Franklin, C. W., II (1988). *Men and society.* Chicago: Nelson-Hall.

Franklin, U. M. (1985). *Will women change technology or will technology change women?* Ottawa: Canadian Research Institute for the Advancement of Women.

Franzoi, S. L., Anderson, J., & Frommelt, S. (1990). Individual differences in men's perceptions of and reactions to thinning hair. *The Journal of Social Psychology, 130*(2), 209–218.

Freedman, R. R. (1989). Laboratory and ambulatory monitoring of menopausal hot flashes. *Psychophysiology, 26*(5), 573–579.

Freedman, S. A. (1991). *Triggering the gender schema.* Unpublished master's thesis, Radford University.

Freedman, S. A., & Lips, H. M. (1992). Articulating feminist identities against a backdrop of heterosexuality: Six voices. Unpublished manuscript, Center for Gender Studies, Radford University, Radford VA.

Freiberg, P. (1991a). Self-esteem gender gap widens in adolescence. *APA Monitor, 22*(4), 29.

Freiberg, P. (1991b). Women's health office in ADAMHA proposed. *APA Monitor, 22*(5), 39.

French, J. R. P., Jr., & Raven, B. H. (1959). The bases of social power. In D. Cartwright (Ed.), *Studies in social power* (pp. 150–167). Ann Arbor: University of Michigan Press.

Freud, S. (1960). *A general introduction to psychoanalysis.* (J. Riviere, Trans.). New York: Washington Square Press. (Original work published 1924)

Freud, S. (1961). *Letters of Sigmund Freud, 1873–1939.* (E. L. Freud, Ed.). London: Hogarth Press.

Freud, S. (1974). Some psychical consequences of the anatomical distinction between the sexes. In J. Strachey (Ed. and Trans.), *The standard edition of the complete psychological works of Sigmund Freud* (Vol. 19, pp.

241–260). London: Hogarth Press and the Institute of Psycho-Analysis. (Original work published 1925)

Frey, K. A. (1981). Middle-aged women's experience and perceptions of menopause. *Women & Health, 6*(1/2), 25–36.

Fried, R., & Major, B. (1980). *Self-presentation of sex-role attributes to attractive others.* Paper presented at the meeting of the Eastern Psychological Association, Hartford, CT.

Friedan, B. (1963). *The feminine mystique.* New York: Dell.

Friedan, B. (1981). *The second stage.* New York: Summit Books.

Friederich, M. A. (1983). Dysmenorrhea. *Women & Health, 8*(2/3), 91–106.

Friedman, A. (1987). Getting powerful with age: Changes in women over the life cycle. *Israel Social Science Research, 5,* 76–86.

Friedman, L. (1989). Mathematics and the gender gap: A meta-analysis of recent studies on sex differences in mathematical tasks. *Review of Educational Research, 59*(2), 185–213.

Friedman, M., & Rosenman, R. H. (1959). Association of specific overt behavior patterns with blood and cardiovascular findings. *Journal of the American Medical Association, 169,* 1286–1296.

Friedman, R. C., Hurt, S. W., Arnoff, M. S., & Clarkin, J. (1980). Behavior and the menstrual cycle. *Signs: Journal of Women in Culture and Society, 5,* 719–738.

Friedman, W. J., Robinson, A. B., & Friedman, B. L. (1987). Sex differences in moral judgments? A test of Gilligan's theory. *Psychology of Women Quarterly, 11*(1), 37–46.

Friend, T. (1990, January 26). Abuse in med school 'common'. *USA Today*, p. 1.

Frieze, I. H. (1975). Women's expectations for and causal attributions of success and failure. In M. Mednick, S. Tangri, & L. Hoffman (Eds.), *Women and achievement* (pp. 158–171). New York: Wiley.

Frieze, I. H. (1979). Perceptions of battered wives. In I. H. Frieze, D. Bar-Tal, & J. S. Carroll (Eds.), *New approaches to social problems: Applications of attribution theory* (pp. 79–108). San Francisco: Jossey-Bass.

Frieze, I. H. (1983). Causes and consequences of marital rape. *Signs, 8*, 532–553.

Frieze, I. H. (1986, August). *The female victim: Rape, wife battering, and incest*. American Psychological Association Master Lecture, presented at the annual meeting of the American Psychological Association, Washington, DC.

Frieze, I. H., Whiteley, B. E., Jr., Hanusa, B. H., & McHugh, M. C. (1982). Assessing the theoretical models for sex differences in causal attributions for success and failure. *Sex Roles, 8*, 333–343.

Frodi, A., & Lamb, M. (1978). Sex differences in responsiveness to infants: A developmental study of psychophysiological and behavioral responses. *Child Development, 49*, 1182–1188.

Frodi, A., Macaulay, J., & Thome, P. R. (1977). Are women always less aggressive than men? A review of the experimental literature. *Psychological Bulletin, 84*, 634–660.

Fromm, E. (1973). *The anatomy of human destructiveness*. Greenwich, CT: Fawcett.

Frueh, T., & McGhee, P. (1975). Traditional sex role development and amount of time spent watching television. *Developmental Psychology, 11*, 109.

Fujita, F., Diener, E., & Sandvik, E. (1991). Gender differences in negative affect and well-being: The case for emotional intensity. *Journal of Personality and Social Psychology, 61*(3), 427–434.

Fulkerson, K. F., Furr, S., & Brown, D. (1983). Expectations and achievement among third-, sixth-, and ninth-grade black and white males and females. *Developmental Psychology, 19*(2), 231–236.

Fulton, E. K. (1991, September 2). Rape and the court. *Maclean's*, p. 45.

Futuyma, D. J., & Risch, S. J. (1984). Sexual orientation, sociobiology, and evolution. *Journal of Homosexuality, 9*(2/3), 157–168.

Gaddis, A., & Brooks-Gunn, J. (1985). The male experience of pubertal change. *Journal of Youth and Adolescence, 14*(1), 61–69.

Gagnon, J., & Simon, W. (1973). *Sexual conduct*. Chicago: Aldine.

Gallaway, L. E. (1969). The effect of geographic labor mobility on income: A brief comment. *Journal of Human Resources, 4*, 103–109.

Gandelman, R. (1983). Gonadal hormones and sensory function. *Neuroscience and Biobehavioral Reviews, 7*, 1–17.

Garcia, A. M. (1991). The development of Chicana feminist discourse. In J. Lorber & S. A. Farrell (Eds.), *The social construction of gender* (pp. 269–287). Newbury Park, CA: Sage.

Garfinkle, E. M., & Morin, S. F. (1978). Psychotherapists' attitudes toward homosexual psychotherapy clients. *Journal of Social Issues, 34*(3), 101–112.

Garfinkel, P. E., & Garner, D. M. (1982). *Anorexia nervosa: A multidimensional perspective*. New York: Brunner/Mazel.

Garrison, D. (1981). Karen Horney and feminism. *Signs, 6*(4), 672–691.

Gary, L. E. (1981). *Black men*. Beverly Hills, CA: Sage.

Gaskell, J. (1981). Sex inequalities in education for work: The case of business education. *Canadian Journal of Education, 6*(2), 54–72.

Gaskell, J. (1985, November). *Young women choose paths to the future*. Paper presented at the annual meeting of the Canadian Research Institute for the Advancement of Women, Saskatoon.

Geffner, D. S., & Hochberg, I. (1971). Ear laterality performance of children from low and middle socioeconomic levels on a verbal dichotic listening task. *Cortex, 7*, 193–203.

Geis, F., Brown, V., Jennings (Walstedt), J., & Porter, N. (1984). TV commercials as achievement scripts for women. *Sex Roles, 10*, 513–525.

Geller, G. (1984). Aspirations of female high school students. *Resources for Feminist Research, 13*(1), 17–19.

Gerber, E. W., Felshin, J., Berlin, P., & Wyrick, W. (1974). *The American woman in sport*. Reading, MA: Addison-Wesley.

Gerber, G. L. (1984). Attribution of feminine and masculine traits to opposite-sex dyads. *Psychological Reports, 55*(3), 907–918.

Gerdes, E. P., & Garber, D. M. (1983). Sex bias in hiring: Effects of job demands and applicant competence. *Sex Roles, 9*(3), 307–319.

Gervasio, A. H., & Crawford, M. (1989). Social evaluations of assertiveness: A critique and speech act reformulation. *Psychology of Women Quarterly, 13*(1), 1–26.

Geschwind, N., & Behan, P. (1982). Left-handedness: Association with immune disease, migraine, and developmental learning disorder. *Proceedings of the National Academy of Sciences, 79,* 5097–5100.

Gibbs, M., Auerbach, D., & Fox, M. (1980). A comparison of male and female same-sex friendships. *International Journal of Women's Studies, 3*(3), 261–272.

Gilbert, L. A., Lee, R. N., & Chiddix, S. (1981). Influence of presenter's gender on students' evaluations of presenters discussing sex fairness in counseling: An analogue study. *Journal of Counseling Psychology, 28,* 258–264.

Gillen, B., & Sherman, R. C. (1980). Physical attractiveness and sex as determinants of trait attributions. *Multivariate Behavioral Research, 15,* 423–437.

Gillespie, M. A. (1991, January/February). HIV: The global crisis. *Ms., 1*(4), 17–22.

Gilligan, C. (1982). *In a different voice: Psychological theory and women's development.* Cambridge, MA: Harvard University Press.

Gilligan, C. (1990). Teaching Shakespeare's sister: Notes from the underground of female adolescence. In C. Gilligan, N. P. Lyons, & T. J. Hanmer (Eds.), *Making connections* (pp. 6–29). Cambridge, MA: Harvard University Press.

Gilligan, C., & Attanucci, J. (1988). Two moral orientations: Gender differences and similarities. *Merrill Palmer Quarterly, 34*(3), 223–237.

Ginsberg, G. L., Frosch, W. A., & Shapiro, T. (1972). The new impotence. *Archives of General Psychiatry, 26*(3), 218–220.

Gitter, A. G., Black, H., & Mostofsky, D. (1972). Race and sex in the communication of emotion. *Journal of Social Psychology, 88,* 273–276.

Gjerdingen, D. K., Froberg, D. G., & Kochevar, L. (1991). Changes in women's mental and physical health from pregnancy through six months postpartum. *Journal of Family Practice, 32*(2), 161–166.

Gladue, B. A., Boechler, M., & McCaul, K. D. (1989). Hormonal response to competition in human males. *Aggressive Behavior, 15,* 409–422.

Gladue, B. A., & Delaney, H. J. (1990). Gender differences in perception of attractiveness of men and women in bars. *Personality and Social Psychology Bulletin, 16*(2), 378–391.

Gladue, B. A., Green, R., & Hellman, R. E. (1984). Neuroendocrine response to estrogen and sexual orientation. *Science, 225,* 1469–1499.

Gladwell, M. (1990, November 26). Public health experts turn to economic ills. *The Washington Post,* p. A3.

Glassner, B. (1989). Men and muscles. In M. S. Kimmel & M. A. Messner (Eds.), *Men's lives* (pp. 310–320). New York: Macmillan.

Glenn, E. N., & Feldberg, R. L. (1989). Clerical work: The

female occupation. In J. Freeman (Ed.), *Women: A feminist perspective* (4th ed., pp. 287–311). Mountain View, CA: Mayfield.

Gold, A. R., & Adams, D. B. (1981). Motivational factors affecting fluctuations of female sexual activity at menstruation. *Psychology of Women Quarterly, 5,* 670–680.

Gold, D. P. (1969). Effect of experimenter in eyeblink conditioning. *Psychonomic Science, 17,* 232–233.

Gold, R. (1981). Women entering the labor force draw attention to reproductive hazards for both sexes. *Family Planning/Population Reporter, 10*(1), 10–13.

Goldberg, D. C., Wipple, B., Fishkin, R. E., Waxman, H., Fink, P. J., & Weisberg, M. (1983). The Grafenberg spot and female ejaculation: A review of initial hypotheses. *Journal of Sex and Marital Therapy, 9,* 27–37.

Goldberg, P. H. (1968). Are women prejudiced against women? *Trans-action, 5,* 28–30.

Golden, C. (1987). Diversity and variability in women's sexual identities. In The Boston Lesbian Psychologies Collective (Eds.), *Lesbian psychologies* (pp. 18–34). Urbana: University of Illinois Press.

Golding, J. M. (1988). Gender differences in depressive symptoms. *Psychology of Women Quarterly, 12*(1), 61–74.

Golding, J. M. (1990). Division of household labor, strain, and depressive symptoms among Mexican Americans and non-Hispanic whites. *Psychology of Women Quarterly, 14,* 103–117.

Goldman, N., & Ravid, R. (1980). Community surveys: Sex differences in mental illness.

In M. Guttentag, S. Salasin, & D. Belle (Eds.), *The mental health of women* (pp. 31–55). New York: Academic Press.

Goldsmith, R. E., & Matherly, T. A. (1988). Creativity and self-esteem: A multiple operationalization validity study. *Journal of Psychology, 122*(1), 47–56.

Golinkoff, R. M., & Ames, G. J. (1979). A comparison of fathers' and mothers' speech with their young children. *Child Development, 50,* 28–32.

Golub, S. (1976). The effect of premenstrual anxiety and depression on cognitive function. *Journal of Personality and Social Psychology, 34,* 99–104.

Golub, S. (1983). Menarche: The beginning of menstrual life. *Women & Health, 8*(2/3), 17–36.

Golub, S., & Catalano, J. (1983). Recollections of menarche and women's subsequent experiences with menstruation. *Women & Health, 8,* 49–61.

Golub, S., & Harrington, D. M. (1981). Premenstrual and menstrual mood changes in adolescent women. *Journal of Personality and Social Psychology, 41,* 961–965.

Gomberg, E. S. L. (1982). Historical and political perspective: Women and drug use. *Journal of Social Issues, 38*(2), 9–23.

Good, P. R., & Smith, B. D. (1980). Menstrual distress and sex-role attributes. *Psychology of Women Quarterly, 4,* 482–491.

Goodchilds, J. D. (1979). Power: A matter of mechanics? *Society for the Advancement of Social Psychology Newsletter, 5*(3), p. 3.

Gordon, H. W., & Lee, P. A. (1986). A relationship between gonadotropins and visuospatial function. *Neuropsychologia, 24*(4), 563–576.

Gordon, M., & Shankweller, P. J. (1971). Different equals less: Female sexuality in recent marriage manuals. *Journal of Marriage and the Family, 33,* 459–466.

Gornick, V. (1990). *Women in science.* New York: Simon & Schuster.

Gould, R. M. (1973). Measuring masculinity by the size of a paycheck. *Ms., 1*(12), 18–21.

Gould, S. (1981). *The mismeasure of man.* New York: W. W. Norton.

Gove, W. (1972). The relationship between sex roles, marital status, and mental illness. *Social Forces, 51,* 34–44.

Gove, W. (1979). Sex differences in the epidemiology of mental disorder: Evidence and explanations. In E. S. Gomberg & V. Franks (Eds.), *Gender and disordered behavior: Sex differences in psychopathology* (pp. 23–68). New York: Brunner/Mazel.

Gove, W. R. (1985). The effect of age and gender on deviant behavior: A biopsychosocial perspective. In A. Rossi (Ed.), *Gender and the life course* (pp. 115–144). New York: Aldine.

Gove, W., & Tudor, J. F. (1973). Adult sex roles and mental illness. *American Journal of Sociology, 78,* 812–832.

Goy, R. W. (1968). Organizing effects of androgen on the behavior of rhesus monkeys. In R. P. Michael (Ed.), *Endocrinology and human behaviour* (pp. 12–31). London: Oxford University Press.

Goy, R. W. (1970). Experimental control of psychosexuality. In G. W. Harris & R. G. Edwards (Eds.), *A discussion on the determination of sex.* London: Philosophical Transactions of the Royal Society.

Gralewski, C., & Rogdon, M. M. (1980). Effect of social and intellectual instruction on achievement motivation as a function of role orientation. *Sex Roles, 6,* 301–309.

Grant, L. (1984). Black females' "place" in desegregated classrooms. *Sociology of Education, 57,* 98–111.

Gravenkemper, S. A., & Paludi, M. A. (1983). Fear of success revisited: Introducing an ambiguous cue. *Sex Roles, 9,* 897–900.

Gray-Little, B., & Burks, N. (1983). Power and satisfaction in marriage: A review and critique. *Psychological Bulletin, 93,* 513–538.

Grayson, J. P. (1983). The effects of a plant closure on the stress levels and health of workers' wives—A preliminary analysis. *Journal of Business Ethics, 2,* 221–225.

Green, D. H., & Zenisek, T. J. (1983). Dual career couples: Individual and organizational implications. *Journal of Business Ethics, 2,* 171–184.

Green, R. (1974). *Sexual identity conflict in children and adults.* Baltimore: Penguin Books.

Greene, E. (1987, January 28). Too many women? That's the problem at Chapel Hill, say some trustees. *Chronicle of Higher Education,* pp. 27–28.

Greenglass, E. R. (1976). *After Abortion.* Toronto: Longman Canada.

Greenglass, E. R. (1985a). An interactional perspective on job-related stress in managerial women. *The Southern Psychologist, 2,* 42–48.

Greenglass, E. R. (1985b). Psychological implications of sex bias in the workplace. *Academic Psychology Bulletin, 1,* 227–240.

Greenglass, E. R. (1991). Burnout and gender: Theoretical and organizational implications. *Canadian Psychology, 32*(4), 562–572.

Grimm, J. (1978). Women in female-dominated professions. In A. H. Stromberg & S. Harkess (Eds.), *Women working: Theories and facts in perspective* (pp. 293–315). Palo Alto, CA: Mayfield.

Grimm, J., & Stern, R. N. (1974). Sex roles and the internal labor market structures: The "female" semi-professions. *Social Problems, 21,* 690–705.

Grimm, L., & Yarnold, P. R. (1985). Sex typing and the coronary-prone behavior pattern. *Sex Roles, 12,* 171–178.

Gross, H. E. (1980). Dual-career couples who live apart: Two types. *Journal of Marriage and the Family, 42,* 567–576.

Gross, L., & Jeffries-Fox, S. (1978). What do you want to be when you grow up, little girl? In G. Tuchman, A. Daniels, & J. Benet (Eds.), *Hearth and home* (pp. 240–265). New York: Oxford University Press.

Grossman, F. K., Eichler, L. S., & Winickoff, S. A. (1980). *Pregnancy, birth, and parenthood.* San Francisco: Jossey-Bass.

Gurwitz, S. B., & Dodge, K. A. (1975). Adults' evaluation of a child as a function of sex of adult and sex of child. *Journal of Personality and Social Psychology, 32,* 822–828.

Gutek, B., & Nakamura, C. (1983). Gender roles and sexuality in the world of work. In E. R. Allgeier & N. B. McCormick (Eds.), *Changing boundaries: Gender roles and sexual behavior* (pp. 182–201). Palo Alto, CA: Mayfield.

Guthrie, R. V. (1976). *Even the rat was white: An historical view of psychology.* New York: Harper & Row.

Gutierres, S. E., Kenrick, D. T., & Goldberg, L. (1983, August). *Adverse effect of popular erotica on judgments of one's mate.* Paper presented at the meeting of the American Psychological Association, Anaheim, CA.

Gutmann, D. (1972). Ego psychological and developmental approaches to the "retirement crisis" in men. In F. M. Carp (Ed.), *Retirement* (pp. 267–305). New York: Behavioral Publications.

Haefner, J. E. (1977). Sources of discrimination among employees: A survey investigation. *Journal of Applied Psychology, 62*(3), 265–270.

Hahn, C., & Blankenship, G. (1983). Women and economics textbooks. *Theory and Research in Social Education, 11*(3), 67–75.

Hall, A., Delahunt, J. W., & Ellis, P. M. (1985). Anorexia nervosa in the male: Clinical features and follow-up of nine patients. *Journal of Psychiatric Research, 19,* 315–321.

Hall, J. A. (1978). Gender effects in decoding nonverbal cues. *Psychological Bulletin, 85,* 845–875.

Hall, J. A. (1984). *Nonverbal sex differences: Communication accuracy and expressive style.* Baltimore: Johns Hopkins University Press.

Hamburg, D. A., & Lunde, D. T. (1966). Sex hormones in the development of sex differences in human behavior. In E. E. Maccoby (Ed.), *The development of sex differences* (pp. 1–24). Stanford, CA: Stanford University Press.

Hamburg, D. A., Moos, R. H., & Yalom, I. D. (1968). Studies of distress in the menstrual cycle and the postpartum period. In R. P. Michael (Ed.), *Endocrinology and human behaviour* (pp. 94–116). London: Oxford University Press.

Hamilton, D. L. (1979). A cognitive-attributional analysis of stereotyping. *Advances in Experimental Psychology, 12,* 53–81.

Hamilton, J. A., & Gallant, S. J. (1990). Problematic aspects of diagnosing premenstrual phase dysphoria: Recommendations for psychological research and practice. *Professional Psychology Research and Practice, 2*(1), 60–68.

Hamilton, J. A., Gallant, S. A., & Lloyd, C. (1989). Evidence for a menstrual-linked artifact in determining rates of depression. *Journal of Nervous and Mental Disease, 177*(6), 359–365.

Hamilton, R. (1985). Feminists in the academy: Intellectuals or political subversives? *Queens's Quarterly, 92*(1), 3–20.

Hammond, D., & Dingley, J. (1989). Sex differences in career preferences of lower sixth formers in Belfast grammar schools. *Journal of Occupational Psychology, 62,* 263–264.

Hampson, E. (1990a). Estrogen-related variations in human spatial and articulatory-motor skills. *Psychoneuroendocrinology, 15*(2), 97–111.

Hampson, E. (1990b). Variations in sex-related cognitive abilities across the menstrual cycle. *Brain and Cognition, 14*(1), 26–43.

Hampson, J. L., & Hampson, J. G. (1961). The ontogenesis of sexual behavior in man. In

W. C. Young (Ed.), *Sex and internal secretions* (Vol. 1, pp. 1401–1432). Baltimore, MD: Williams and Wilkins.

Hansen, C. H., & Hansen, R. D. (1988). How rock music videos can change what is seen when boy meets girl: Priming stereotypic appraisal of social interactions. *Sex Roles, 19,* 287–316.

Hanson, S. M. H. (1985). Fatherhood: Contextual variations. *American Behavioral Scientist, 29*(1), 55–77.

Harding, S. (1986). *The science question in feminism.* Ithaca, NY: Cornell University Press.

Hare-Mustin, R. (1983). An appraisal of the relationship between women and psychotherapy: 80 years after the case of Dora. *American Psychologist, 38,* 593–601.

Hargreaves, D. J., Bates, H. M., & Foot, J. M. C. (1985). Sex-typed labelling affects task performance. *British Journal of Social Psychology, 24,* 153–155.

Harrington, D. M., & Anderson, S. M. (1981). Creativity, masculinity, femininity, and three models of psychological androgyny. *Journal of Personality and Social Psychology, 41,* 744–757.

Harris, B. (1979). Careers, conflict, and children. In A. Roland & B. Harris (Eds.), *Career and motherhood* (pp. 55–86). New York: Human Sciences Press.

Harris, B. (1980). Prospective trial of L-tryptophan in maternity blues. *British Journal of Psychiatry, 137,* 233–235.

Harris, J. F. (1991, October 19). Va. to drop its ban on gay bars. *The Washington Post,* p. C1.

Harrison, J. (1978). Warning: The male sex role may be dangerous to your health. *Journal of Social Issues, 34*(1), 65–86.

Harry, B., & Balcer, C. M. (1987). Menstruation and crime: A critical review of the literature from the clinical criminology perspective. *Behavioral Sciences and the Law, 5*(3), 307–321.

Hartmann, H., & Spalter-Roth, R. (1991, February 27). *Improving employment opportunities for women.* Testimony concerning H.R.1 Civil Rights Act of 1991, before the U.S. House of Representatives Committee on Education and Labor.

Hartup, W. W. (1983). The peer system. In P. Mussen & E. Heatherington (Eds.), *Handbook of child psychology* (4th ed., Vol. 4, pp. 103–196). New York: Wiley.

Hasher, L., & Zacks, R. T. (1984). Automatic processing of fundamental information: The case of frequency of occurrence. *American Psychologist, 19,* 1372–1388.

Hatchett, S. J., & Quick, A. D. (1983). Correlates of sex-role attitudes among black men and women: Data from a national survey of black Americans. *Urban Research Review, 9*(2), 1–3, 11.

Hatfield, E. (1983). What do women and men want from love and sex? In E. R. Allgeier & N. B. McCormick (Eds.), *Changing boundaries: Gender roles and sexual behavior* (pp. 106–134). Palo Alto, CA: Mayfield.

Hatfield, E., & Sprecher, S. (1986). *Mirror, mirror: The importance of looks in everyday life.* New York: SUNY Press.

Hatfield, E., Sprecher, S., Pillemer, J. T., & Greenberger, D. (1988). Gender differences in what is desired in the sexual relationship. *Journal of Psychol-*

ogy and Human Sexuality, 1(2), 39–52.

Hatkoff, T. S., & Laswell, T. E. (1979). Male-female similarities and differences in conceptualizing love. In M. Cook & G. Wilson (Eds.), *Love and attraction: An international conference* (pp. 221–228). New York: Pergamon Press, 1979.

Haynes, S. G., & Feinleib, M. (1980). Women, work, and coronary heart disease: Prospective findings from the Framingham Heart Study. *American Journal of Public Health, 70,* 133–141.

Hazzard, W. R. (1986). Biological basis of the sex differential in longevity. *Journal of the American Geriatric Society, 34*(6), 455–471.

Heath, D. (1976). Competent fathers: Their personalities and marriages. *Human Development, 19,* 26–39.

Heilbrun, A. B., Jr. (1984). Sex-based models of androgyny: A further cognitive elaboration of competence differences. *Journal of Personality and Social Psychology, 46,* 216–229.

Heilbrun, A. B., & Heilbrun, M. R. (1986). The treatment of women within the criminal justice system: An inquiry into the social impact of the women's rights movement. *Psychology of Women Quarterly, 10*(3), 240–251.

Heilbrun, C. (1973). *Toward a recognition of androgyny.* New York: Harper & Row.

Heilman, M. E., Martell, R. F., & Simon, M. C. (1988). The vagaries of sex bias: Conditions regulating the undervaluation, equivaluation, and overvaluation of female job applicants. *Organizational Behavior and Human Decision Processes, 41,* 98–110.

Heiman, J. R. (1977). A psycho-physiological exploration of sexual arousal patterns in females and males. *Psychphysiology, 14,* 266–274.

Heiser, P., & Gannon, L. (1984). The relationship of sex-role stereotypes to anger expression and the report of psychosomatic symptoms. *Sex Roles, 10,* 601–611.

Helson, R., & Mitchell, V. (1990). Women's prime of life: Is it the fifties? *Psychology of Women Quarterly, 14,* 451–470.

Helson, R., & Picano, J. (1990). Is the traditional role bad for women? *Journal of Personality and Social Psychology, 59*(2), 311–320.

Henderson, N., & Baker, P. (1990, February 2). For VMI cadets, it's still 'better dead than coed'. *The Washington Post,* pp. B1, B7.

Hendrick, S., Hendrick, C., Slapion-Foote, M. J., & Foote, F. H. (1985). Gender differences in sexual attitudes. *Journal of Personality and Social Psychology, 48*(6), 1630–1642.

Heneman, H. G., III. (1977). Impact of test information and applicant sex on applicant evaluations in a selection simulation. *Journal of Applied Psychology, 62,* 524–526.

Henley, N. (1973). Power, sex and nonverbal communication. *Berkeley Journal of Sociology, 18,* 1–26.

Henley, N. (1977). *Body politics: Power, sex, and nonverbal communication.* Englewood Cliffs, NJ: Prentice-Hall.

Henley, N., & Freeman, J. (1989). The sexual politics of interpersonal behavior. In J. Freeman (Ed.), *Women: A feminist perspective* (4th ed., pp. 457–469). Mountain View, CA: Mayfield.

Henley, N., & LaFrance, M. (1984). Gender as culture: Difference and dominance in nonverbal behavior. In A. Wolfgang (Ed.), *Nonverbal behavior: Perspectives, applications, intercultural insights* (pp. 351–372). New York: C. J. Hogrefe.

Hennig, M., & Jardim, A. (1977). *The managerial woman.* New York: Doubleday.

Hepburn, C. (1985). Memory for the frequency of sex-typed versus neutral behaviors: Implications for the maintenance of sex stereotypes. *Sex Roles, 12*(7/8), 771–776.

Herbert, J. (1976). Hormonal basis of sex differences in rats, monkeys, and humans. *New Scientist, 70,* 284–286.

Herek, G. M. (1988). Heterosexuals' attitudes toward lesbians and gay men: Correlates and gender differences. *Journal of Sex Research, 25*(4), 451–477.

Herman, J. L. (1981). *Father-daughter incest.* Cambridge: Harvard University Press.

Herring, S., & Reitan, R. M. (1984, August). *Sex similarities in neuropsychological sequelae of lateralized cerebral lesions.* Paper presented at the meeting of the American Psychological Association, Toronto, Ontario.

Herz, E. J., & Reis, J. S. (1987). Family life education for young inner-city teens: Identifying needs. *Journal of Youth and Adolescence, 16*(4), 361–377.

Herzog, A., & Detre, T. (1976). Psychotic reactions associated with childbirth. *Diseases of the Nervous System, 37,* 229–235.

Hetherington, E. M., Cox, M., & Cox, R. (1976). Divorced fathers. *The Family Coordinator, 25,* 417–428.

Hill, C. E., Hobbs, M. A., & Verble, C. (1974). A developmental analysis of the sex-role identification of school-related objects. *Journal of Educational Research, 67,* 205–206.

Hill, C. T., Rubin, Z., & Peplau, L. A. (1976). Breakups before marriage: The end of 103 affairs. *Journal of Social Issues, 32,* 147–168.

Hilton, T. L., & Berglund, G. W. (1974). Sex differences in mathematics achievement: A longitudinal study. *Journal of Educational Research, 67,* 231–237.

Hines, M. (1982). Prenatal gonadal hormones and sex differences in human behavior. *Psychological Bulletin, 92,* 56–80.

Hines, M., & Shipley, C. (1984). Prenatal exposure to diethylstilbestrol (DES) and the development of sexually dimorphic cognitive abilities and cerebral lateralization. *Developmental Psychology, 20*(1), 81–94.

Hirsch, K. (1990, September/October). Fraternities of fear. *Ms., 1*(2), pp. 52–56.

Hite, S. (1976). *The Hite report.* New York: Macmillan.

Hite, S. (1981). *The Hite report on male sexuality.* New York: Alfred A. Knopf.

Ho, D. D., Schooley, R. T., Rota, T. R., Kaplan, J. C., Flynn, T., Salahuddin, S. Z., Gonda, M. A., & Hirsch, M. (1984). HTLV-III in the semen and blood of a healthy homosexual man. *Science, 226*(4673), 451–453.

Hodgins, D. C., & Kalin, R. (1985). Reducing sex bias in judgements of occupational suitability by the provision of sex-typed personality information. *Canadian Journal of Behavioural Science, 7,* 346–358.

Hodson, R. (1989). Gender differences in job satisfaction: Why aren't women more dissatisfied? *Sociological Quarterly, 30*(3), 385–399.

Hofferth, S. L., & Phillips, D. A. (1987). Child care in the United States: 1970 to 1995. *Journal of Marriage and the Family, 49*, 559–571.

Hoffman, J. C. (1982). Biorhythms in human reproduction: The not-so-steady states. *Signs, 7*(4), 829–844.

Hoffman, L. W. (1972). Early childhood experiences and women's achievement motives. *Journal of Social Issues, 29*(2), 120–155.

Hoffman, L. W. (1974). Effects of maternal employment on the child: A review of the research. *Developmental Psychology, 10*, 204–228.

Hoffnung, M. (1989). Motherhood: Contemporary conflict for women. In J. Freeman (Ed.), *Women: A feminist perspective* (4th ed., pp. 157–175). Palo Alto, CA: Mayfield.

Hokanson, J. E., & Edelman, R. (1966). Effects of three social responses on vascular processes. *Journal of Personality and Social Psychology, 3*, 442–447.

Hokanson, J. E., Willers, K. R., & Koropsak, E. (1968). The modification of autonomic responses during aggressive interchange. *Journal of Personality, 36*, 386–404.

Hollingworth, L. (1914). *Functional periodicity: An experimental study of the mental and motor abilities of women during menstruation.* New York: Teachers College, Columbia University.

Hollingworth, L. (1916). Sex differences in mental traits. *Psychological Bulletin, 13*, 377–385.

Hollingworth, L. (1918). Comparison of the sexes in mental traits. *Psychological Bulletin, 25*, 427–432.

Hollingworth, L. (1922). Differential action upon the sexes of forces which tend to segregate the feebleminded. *Journal of Abnormal Psychology and Social Psychology, 17*, 35–57.

Hollingworth, L., & Montague, H. (1914). The comparative variability of the sexes at birth. *American Journal of Sociology, 20*, 335–370.

Holms, V. (1985). *Factors related to career motivation among female adolescents.* Unpublished master's thesis, University of Manitoba.

Homans, G. C. (1974). *Social behavior: The elementary forms.* New York: Harcourt Brace Jovanovich.

Homicide among young black males—United States, 1978–1987. (1990, December 7). *MMWR, 39*, 48.

Hooker, E. (1957). The adjustment of the male overt homosexual. *Journal of Projective Techniques, 21*, 18–31.

Hooks, B. (1981). *Ain't I a woman?* Boston: South End Press.

Hopkins, J., Marcues, M., & Campbell, S. B. (1984). Postpartum depression: A critical review. *Psychological Bulletin, 95*, 498–515.

Hopkins, J. R. (1977). Sexual behavior in adolescence. *Journal of Social Issues, 33*(2), 67–85.

Horner, M. (1968). *Sex differences in achievement motivation and performance in competitive and noncompetitive situations.* Unpublished doctoral dissertation, University of Michigan.

Horner, M. (1970). Femininity and successful achievement: A basic inconsistency. In J. Bardwick, E. Douvan, M. Horner, & D. Guttman (Eds.), *Feminine personality and conflict* (pp. 45–76). Belmont, CA: Brooks/Cole.

Horney, K. (1939). *The neurotic personality of our time.* New York: W. W. Norton.

Horney, K. (1973). The flight from womanhood. In J. B. Miller (Ed.), *Psychoanalysis and women* (pp. 5–20). Baltimore, MD: Penguin Books. (Original work published 1926)

Horowitz, M. C. (1976). Aristotle and women. *Journal of the History of Biology, 9*, 183–213.

Horowitz, M. J., Schaefer, C., & Cooney, P. (1974). Life event scaling for recency of experience. In E. K. E. Gunderson & R. H. Rahe (Eds.), *Life stress and illness* (pp. 125–133). Springfield, IL: Charles C. Thomas.

Hort, B. E., Fagot, B. I., & Leinbach, M. D. (1990). Are people's notions of maleness more stereotypically framed than their notions of femaleness? *Sex Roles, 23*(3/4), 197–212.

Horwitz, E. L. (1990, October). For your health's sake. *AAUW Outlook*, p. 5.

Houston, M. (1991, May 7). Girls opt for pink ghetto. *Winnipeg Free Press*, pp. 1, 4.

Howard, J. A., Blumstein, P., & Schwartz, P. (1986). Sex, power, and influence tactics in intimate relationships. *Journal of Personality and Social Psychology, 51*(1), 102–109.

Hrdy, S. B. (1981). *The woman that never evolved.* Cambridge, MA: Harvard University Press.

Hubbard, R. (1990). *The politics of women's biology.* New Brunswick, NJ: Rutgers University Press.

Hudgens, G. A., Fatkin, L. T., Billingsley, P. A., & Mazurczak, J. (1988). Hand steadiness: Effects of sex, menstrual phase, oral contraceptives, practice, and handgun weight. *Human Factors, 30*(1), 51–60.

Hull, F. M., Mielke, P. W., Timmons, R. J., & Willeford, J. A. (1971). The national speech and hearing survey: Preliminary results. *ASHA, 3,* 501–509.

Humphreys, A. P., & Smith, P. K. (1987). Rough and tumble friendship and dominance in school children: Evidence for continuity and change with age in middle childhood. *Child Development, 58,* 201–212.

Hunt, M. (1974). *Sexual behavior in the 1970s.* Chicago: Playboy Press.

Huston, A. C., Greer, D., Wright, J. C., Welch, R., & Ross, R. (1984). Children's comprehension of televised formal features with masculine and feminine connotations. *Developmental Psychology, 20*(4), 707–716.

Huston, T. L., & Ashmore, R. D. (1986). Women and men in personal relationships. In R. D. Ashmore & F. K. Del Boca (Eds.), *The social psychology of female-male relations* (pp. 167–210). Orlando, FL: Academic Press.

Huston, T. L., McHale, S. M., & Crouter, A. C. (1986). When the honeymoon is over: Changes in the marriage relationship over the first year. In R. Gilmour & S. Duck (Eds.), *The emerging field of personal relationships* (pp. 109–132). Hillsdale, NJ: Lawrence Erlbaum.

Hyde, J. S. (1981). How large are cognitive gender differences? A meta-analysis using ω^2 and d. *American Psychologist, 36,* 892–901.

Hyde, J. S. (1984a). Children's understanding of sexist language. *Developmental Psychology, 20*(4), 697–706.

Hyde, J. S. (1984b). How large are gender differences in aggression? A developmental meta-analysis. *Developmental Psychology, 20,* 722–736.

Hyde, J. S. (1986). *Understanding human sexuality.* New York: McGraw-Hill.

Hyde, J. S., Fennema, E., & Lamon, S. J. (1990a). Gender differences in mathematics performance: A meta-analysis. *Psychological Bulletin, 107*(2), 139–155.

Hyde, J. S., Fennema, E., Ryan, M., Frost, L., & Hopp, C. (1990b). Gender comparisons of mathematics attitudes and affect. *Psychology of Women Quarterly, 14,* 299–324.

Hyde, J. S., & Linn, M. C. (1988). Gender differences in verbal ability: A meta-analysis. *Psychological Bulletin, 104*(1), 53–69.

Hyde, J. S., Rosenberg, B. G., & Behrman, J. (1974). *Tomboyism: Implications for theories of female development.* Paper presented at the annual convention of the Western Psychological Association, San Francisco.

Imperato-McGinley, J., Guerrero, L., Gautier, T., & Peterson, R. E. (1974). Steroid 5-Alpha-Reductase deficiency in man: An inherited form of male pseudohermaphroditism. *Science, 186,* 1213–1215.

Imperato-McGinley, J., Peterson, R. E., Gautier, T., & Sturla, E. (1979). Androgens and the evolution of male gender identity among male pseudohermaphrodites with a 5-Alpha-Reductase deficiency. *New England Journal of Medicine, 310,* 839–840.

Institute for Women's Policy Research. (1990). *Unnecessary losses* (Research-in-Brief fact sheet). Washington, DC: Author.

Institute for Women's Policy Research. (1991). The thirty-five million: The status of young women (Research-in-Brief fact sheet). Washington, DC: Author.

Instone, D., Major, B., & Bunker, B. B. (1983). Gender, self-confidence, and social influence strategies: An organizational simulation. *Journal of Personality and Social Psychology, 44,* 322–333.

International Labour Office. (1991). *Year book of labour statistics* (50th ed.). Geneva: Author.

Irvine, J. J. (1986). Teacher-student interactions: Effects of student race, sex, and grade level. *Journal of Educational Psychology, 78*(1), 14–21.

Jabes, J. (1980). Causal attributions and sex-role stereotypes in the perceptions of women managers. *Canadian Journal of Behavioural Science, 12*(1), 52–63.

Jacklin, C. N. (1985, June). *Stalking the development of sex differences.* Invited address to the Canadian Psychological Association, Halifax, Nova Scotia.

Jacklin, C. N., Maccoby, E. E., & Doering, C. H. (1983). Neonatal sex-steroid hormones and timidity in 6–18-month-old boys and girls. *Developmental Psychobiology, 16*(3), 163–168.

Jacklin, C. N., Maccoby, E. E., Doering, C. H., & King, D. R. (1984). Neonatal sex steroid hormones and muscular strength of boys and girls in the first three years. *Developmental Psychobiology, 17*(3), 301–310.

Jacklin, C. N., & McBride, C. (1991). *The effects of feminist scholarship on developmental psychology.* Paper presented at the annual meeting of the Association for Women in Psychology, Hartford, CT.

Jackson, L. A. (1989). Relative deprivation and the gender wage gap. *Journal of Social Issues, 45*(4), 117–133.

Jacobs, J. A. (1985). Sex segregation in American higher education. In L. Larwood, A. H. Stromberg, & B. A. Gutek (Eds.), *Women and work: An annual review* (Vol. 1, pp. 191–214). Beverly Hills, CA: Sage.

James, W. (1890). *The principles of psychology.* New York: Holt.

Jassin, S. A. (1980). *A comparison of agoraphobics, anxiety neurotics, and depressive neurotics using the MMPI and the Beck Depression Inventory.* Unpublished doctoral dissertation, Temple University, Philadelphia, PA.

Jazzman Billy Tipton revealed as a woman. (1989, February 1). *Tucson Citizen,* p. 3A.

Jedlicka, D., & Robinson, I. E. (1987). Fear of venereal disease and other perceived restraints on the occurrence of premarital coitus. *Journal of Sex Research, 23*(3), 391–396.

Jenkin, N., & Vroegh, K. (1969). Contemporary concepts of masculinity and femininity. *Psychological Reports, 25,* 679–697.

Jenkins, C. D., Rosenman, R. H., & Friedman, M. (1967). Development of an objective psychological test for the determination of the coronary-prone behavior pattern in employed men. *Journal of Chronic Disease, 20,* 371–379.

Jennings (Walstedt), J., Geis, F., & Brown, V. (1980). Influence of television commercials on women's self-confidence and independent judgment. *Journal of Personality and Social Psychology, 38,* 203–210.

Jensen, J. M. (1990). Native American women and agriculture: A Seneca case study. In E. C. DuBois & V. L. Ruiz (Eds.), *Unequal sisters: A multicultural reader in U.S. women's history* (pp. 51–65). New York: Routledge.

Jobson, S., & Watson, J. S. (1984). Sex and age differences in choice behaviour: the object-person dimension. *Perception, 13*(6), 719–724.

Johnson, C. A., Smith, D. E., Whatley, J. L., & DeVoge, T. (1973). The effects of sex and personalism factors on subjects' responses to hypnotic suggestions. *Proceedings of the 81st Annual Convention of the American Psychological Association* (pp. 1077–1078). Montreal.

Johnson, H. J. (1974). *Executive life styles: A life extension institute report on alcohol, sex and health.* New York: Crowell.

Johnson, P. (1974). *Social power and sex role stereotypes.* Paper presented at the meeting of the Western Psychological Association, San Francisco.

Johnson, P. (1976). Women and power: Toward a theory of effectiveness. *Journal of Social Issues, 32,* 99–110.

Johnson, P., & Goodchilds, J. D. (1976, October). How women get their way. *Psychology Today,* pp. 69–70.

Jones, J. C., & Barlow, D. H. (1990). Self-reported frequency of sexual urges, fantasies and masturbatory fantasies in heterosexual males and females. *Archives of Sexual Behavior, 19*(3), 269–279.

Jones, W. H., Chernovetz, M. E., & Hansson, R. O. (1978). The enigma of androgyny: Differential implications for males and females? *Journal of Consulting and Clinical Psychology, 46,* 298–313.

Jordan, M. (1992, February 12). Wide gender gap found in schools. *The Washington Post,* pp. A1, A8.

Jordan, P. L. (1990). Laboring for relevance: Expectant and new fatherhood. *Nursing Research, 39*(1), 11–16.

Joseph, C. A., McKay, T., & Joseph, C. R. (1982). Sex effects on free recall and recognition of orally presented nouns into imagery form. *Journal of General Psychology, 106,* 213–217.

Kaats, G., & Davis, K. (1971). Effects of volunteer biases in studies of sexual behavior and attitudes. *Journal of Sex Research, 7,* 26–34.

Kagan, J., & Lewis, M. (1965). Studies of attention in the human infant. *Merrill-Palmer Quarterly, 11,* 95–127.

Kahana, B., & Kahana, E. (1970). How different generations view each other. *Geriatric Focus, 9*(10), 1–13.

Kahn, A. S., O'Leary, V., Krulewitz, J. E., & Lamm, H. (1980). Equity and equality: Male and female means to a just end. *Basic and Applied Social Psychology, 1,* 173–197.

Kahn, A. S., & Yoder, J. D. (1989). The psychology of women and conservatism: Rediscovering social change. *Psychology of Women Quarterly, 13*(4), 417–432.

Kaij, L., & Nilsson, A. (1972). Emotional and psychotic illness following childbirth. In J. G. Howells (Ed.), *Modern Perspectives in psycho-obstetrics* (pp. 364–384). London: Oliver & Boyd.

Kalin, R., Stoppard, J. M., & Burt, B. (1980). Sex-role ideology and sex bias in judgements of occupational suitability. In C. Stark-Adamec (Ed.), *Sex roles: origins, influences, and implications for women* (pp. 89–99). Montreal: Eden Press Women's Publications.

Kandel, D. B. (1980). Drug and drinking behavior among youth. *Annual Review of Sociology, 6,* 235–285.

Kanter, R. M. (1975). Women and the structure of organizations: Explorations in theory and behavior. In M. Millman & R. M. Kanter (Eds.), *Another voice* (pp. 34–74). New York: Anchor Press.

Kanter, R. M. (1976). Why bosses turn bitchy. *Psychology Today, 9*(2), 56–59, 88–91.

Kanter, R. M. (1977). *Men and women of the corporation.* New York: Basic Books.

Kanter, R. M. (1979). Power failure in management circuits. *Harvard Business Review, 57,* 65–75.

Kantner, J. F., & Zelnick, M. (1972). Sexual experience of young unmarried women in the United States. *Family Planning Perspectives, 4*(4), 9–18.

Kaplan, A. G. (1980). Human sex-hormone abnormalities viewed from an androgynous perspective: A reconsideration of the work of John Money. In J. E. Parsons (Ed.), *The psychobiology of sex differences and sex roles* (pp. 81–94). Washington, DC: Hemisphere Publishing.

Kaplan, A. G., & Surrey, J. L. (1984). The relational self in women: Developmental theory and public policy. In L. E. Walker (Ed.), *Women and mental health policy* (pp. 79–94). Beverly Hills, CA: Sage.

Kaplan, H. S. (1974). *The new sex therapy.* New York: Brunner/Mazel.

Kaplan, H. S., & Sager, C. (1971, June). Sexual patterns at different ages. *Medical Aspects of Human Sexuality, 5,* 10–23.

Kaplan, M. (1983). A woman's view of the DSM-III. *American Psychologist, 38*(7), 786–792.

Karabenick, S. A. (1983). Sex-relevance of content and influenceability: Sistrunk & McDavid revisited. *Personality and Social Psychology Bulletin, 9,* 243–252.

Kasl, S., & Cobb, S. (1979). Some mental health consequences of plant closing and job loss. In L. Ferman & J. Gordus (Eds.), *Mental health and the economy.* Kalamazoo, MI: Upjohn Institute.

Katz, J. B. (1977). *I am the fire of time: The voices of Native American women.* New York: E. P. Dutton.

Katz, P. A. (1979). The development of female identity. In C. B. Kopp (Ed.), *Becoming female* (pp. 3–28). New York: Plenum.

Katz, P. A. (1986). Gender identity: Development and consequences. In R. D. Ashmore & F. K. Del Boca (Eds.), *The social psychology of female-male relations* (pp. 21–67). Orlando, FL: Academic Press.

Katz, P. A., & Boswell, S. L. (1984). Sex-role development and the one-child family. In T. Falbo (Ed.), *The single-child family* (pp. 63–116). New York: The Guilford Press.

Kaufman, D. R. (1989). Professional women: How real are the recent gains? In J. Freeman (Ed.), *Women: A feminist perspective* (4th ed., pp. 329–346). Mountain View, CA: Mayfield.

Kay, B., & Neelley, J. N. (1982). Sexuality and aging: A review of current literature. *Sexuality and Disability, 5*(1), 38–46.

Kelgeri, Khadi, P. B., & Phadnis (1989). Creativity among urban and rural boys and girls. *Indian Journal of Behaviour, 13*(4), 10–14.

Keller, E. F. (1985). *Reflections on gender and science.* New Haven, CT: Yale University Press.

Kelly, C., Huston, T. L., & Cate, R. M. (1985). Premarital relationships correlates of the erosion of satisfaction in marriage. *Journal of Social and Personal Relationships, 2*(2), 167–178.

Keltikangas-Jarvinen, L. (1990). The stability of self-concept during adolescence and early adulthood: A six-year follow-up study. *Journal of General Psychology, 117*(4), 361–368.

Kennedy, F. (1970). Institutionalized oppression vs. the female. In R. Morgan (Ed.), *Sisterhood is powerful* (pp. 438–446). New York: Vintage Books.

Kershner, J. R., & Ledger, G. (1985). Effect of sex, intelligence, and style of thinking on creativity: A comparison of gifted and average IQ children. *Journal of Personality and Social Psychology, 48,* 1033–1040.

Kessler, S. J. (1990). The medical construction of gender: Case management of intersexed infants. *Signs, 16*(1), 3–26.

Kessler-Harris, A. (1985). The debate over equality for women in the workplace: Recognizing differences. In L. Larwood, A. H. Stromberg, & B. Gutek

(Eds.), *Women and work: An annual review* (Vol. 1, pp. 141–161). Beverly Hills, CA: Sage.

Key, M. (1975). The role of male and female in children's books—Dispelling all doubt. In R. Unger & F. Denmark (Eds.), *Woman—Dependent or independent variable?* (pp. 56–70). New York: Psychological Dimensions.

Khosroshahi, F. (1989). Penguins don't care, but women do: A social identity analysis of a Whorfian problem. *Language in Society, 18*(4), 505–525.

Kiechel, W., III. (1983, December 14). Beyond the liberated secretary. *Fortune*, pp. 173–174.

Kim, J. (1981). *The process of Asian-American identity development: A study of Japanese American women's perceptions of their struggle to achieve positive identities.* Unpublished doctoral dissertation, University of Massachusetts.

Kimball, M. (1989). A new perspective on women's math achievement. *Psychological Bulletin, 105*, 198–214.

Kimball, M. (1991). *Feminist politics and theories of gender.* Paper presented at the annual meeting of the Association of Women in Psychology, Hartford, CT.

Kimble, C. E., Yoshikawa, J. C., & Zehr, H. D. (1981). Vocal and verbal assertiveness in same-sex and mixed-sex groups. *Journal of Personality and Social Psychology, 40*, 1047–1054.

Kimura, D. (1985, November). Male brain, female brain: The hidden difference. *Psychology Today*, pp. 50–52, 54, 56–58.

Kimura, D. (1987). Are men's and women's brains really different? *Canadian Psychology, 28*(2), 133–147.

King, F. (1985). *Confessions of a failed southern lady.* New York: St. Martin's Press.

King, K., Balswick, J. O., & Robinson, I. E. (1977). The continuing premarital sexual revolution among college females. *Journal of Marriage and the Family, 39*, 455–459.

Kinsey, A. C., Pomeroy, W. B., & Martin, C. E. (1948). *Sexual behavior in the human male.* Philadelphia: Saunders.

Kinsey, A. C., Pomeroy, W. B., Martin, C. E., & Gebhard, P. H. (1953). *Sexual behavior in the human female.* Philadelphia: Saunders.

Kipnis, D. (1972). Does power corrupt? *Journal of Personality and Social Psychology, 24*, 33–41.

Kipnis, D. (1984). The use of power in organizations and in interpersonal settings. In S. Oskamp (Ed.), *Applied social psychology annual* (Vol. 5, pp. 179–210). Beverly Hills, CA: Sage.

Kipnis, D., Castell, P. J., Gergen, M., & Mauch, D. (1976). Metamorphic effects of power. *Journal of Applied Psychology, 61*, 127–135.

Kipnis, D., Schmidt, S. M., & Wilkinson, I. (1980). Intraorganizational influence tactics: Explorations in getting one's way. *Journal of Applied Psychology, 65*, 440–452.

Kirkpatrick, J. J. (1973). Occupational aspirations, opportunities, and barriers. In K. S. Miller & R. M. Dreger (Eds.), *Comparative studies of blacks and whites in the United States.* New York: Seminar Press.

Kisker, E. (1985). Teenagers talk about sex, pregnancy and contraception. *Family Planning Perspectives, 17*, 83–90.

Kleiman, C. (1991, August 18).

Female and unemployed in recession: Stormy seas ahead. *The Washington Post*, p. H2.

Kleiman, C. (1992, January 12). 'All the right stuff' often goes wrong for female managers. *The Washington Post*, p. H2.

Klein, E. (1984). *Gender politics.* Cambridge, MA: Harvard University Press.

Klein, M. (1960). *The psychoanalysis of children.* New York: Grove Press. (Original work published 1932)

Klerman, G. L., & Weissman, M. M. (1980). Depressions among women: Their nature and causes. In M. Guttentag, S. Salasin, & D. Belle (Eds.), *The mental health of women* (pp. 57–92). New York: Academic Press.

Kling, A. (1975). Testosterone and aggressive behavior in men and non-human primates. In B. Eleftheriou & R. Spott (Eds.), *Hormonal correlates of behavior* (pp. 305–323). New York: Plenum.

Knussman, R., Christiansen, K., & Couwenbergs, C. (1986). Relations between sex hormone levels and sexual behavior in men. *Archives of Sexual Behavior, 15*(5), 429–445.

Koberg, C. S., & Chusmir, L. H. (1989). Relationship between sex role conflict and work-related variables: Gender and hierarchical differences. *The Journal of Social Psychology, 129*(6), 779–791.

Kobrin, F. E., & Hendershot, G. E. (1977). Do family ties reduce mortality—evidence from United States, 1966–1968. *Journal of Marriage, 39*, 737–745.

Koehler, M. C. S. (1986). Effective mathematics teaching and sex-related difference in algebra one classes (Doctoral dissertation, University of Wisconsin, 1985). *Dissertation Abstracts International, 46,* 2953A.

Koeske, R. K., & Koeske, G. F. (1975). An attributional approach to moods and the menstrual cycle. *Journal of Personality and Social Psychology, 31,* 474–478.

Koff, E., Rierdan, J., & Stubbs, M. L. (1990). Conceptions and misconceptions of the menstrual cycle. *Women and Health, 16*(3/4), 119–136.

Kohlberg, L. (1964). Development of moral character and moral ideology. In M. Hoffman & L. Hoffman (Eds.), *Review of child development research* (Vol. 1, pp. 383–431). New York: Russell Sage Foundation.

Kohlberg, L. (1966). A cognitive-developmental analysis of children's sex-role concepts and attitudes. In E. E. Maccoby (Ed.), *The development of sex differences* (pp. 82–173). Stanford, CA: Stanford University Press.

Kohlberg, L. (1984). *The psychology of moral development.* San Francisco: Harper & Row.

Kohlberg, L., & Kramer, R. (1969). Continuities and discontinuities in childhood and adult moral development. *Human Development, 12,* 93–120.

Kohlberg, L., & Ullian, D. Z. (1974). Stages in the development of psychosexual concepts and attitudes. In R. C. Friedman, R. M. Richart, & R. L. Vande Wiele (Eds.), *Sex differences in behavior* (pp. 209–222). New York: Wiley.

Kolbe, R., & LaVoie, J. (1981). Sex-role stereotyping in preschool children's picture books.

Social Psychology Quarterly, 44(4), 369–374.

Komarovsky, M. (1974). Patterns of self-disclosure of male undergraduates. *Journal of Marriage and the Family, 36,* 677–686.

Komarovsky, M. (1976). *Dilemmas of masculinity: A study of college youth.* New York: Norton.

Kome, P. (1986, July 24). Feminism in the home [Letter to the editor]. *Globe & Mail,* p. A6.

Kotelchuk, M. (1976). The infant's relationship to the father: Experimental evidence. In M. E. Lamb (Ed.), *The role of the father in child development* (pp. 329–344). New York: Wiley.

Kramer, C. (1974). Women's speech: Separate but unequal? *Quarterly Journal of Speech, 60,* 14–24.

Krasner, L., & Houts, A. C. (1984). A study of the "value" systems of behavioral scientists. *American Psychologist, 39,* 840–850.

Kreuz, L. E., & Rose, R. M. (1972). Assessment of aggressive behavior and plasma testosterone in a young criminal population. *Psychosomatic Medicine, 34,* 321.

Kreuz, L. E., Rose, R. M., & Jennings, J. R. (1972). Suppression of plasma testosterone levels and psychological stress. *Archives of General Psychiatry, 26,* 479–482.

Kristiansen, C. M. (1984, August). *Women and health behavior: For ourselves or others?* Paper presented at the annual convention of the American Psychological Association, Toronto.

Krupnick, C. G. (1985, May). Women and men in the class-

room: Inequality and its remedies. *On Teaching and Learning. The Journal of the Harvard-Danforth Center,* 18–25.

Kuhn, D., Nash, S. C., & Brucken, L. (1978). Sex-role concepts of two- and three-year olds. *Child Development, 49,* 445–451.

Kurdek, L. A., & Schmitt, J. P. (1986a). Interaction of sex role self-concept with relationship quality and relationship beliefs in married, heterosexual cohabiting, gay, and lesbian couples. *Journal of Personality and Social Psychology, 51*(2), 365–370.

Kurdek, L. A., & Schmitt, J. P. (1986b). Relationship quality of partners in heterosexual married, heterosexual cohabiting, and gay and lesbian relationships. *Journal of Personality and Social Psychology, 51*(4), 711–720.

Lacoursiere, R. (1972). Fatherhood and mental illness: A review and new material. *Psychiatric Quarterly, 46,* 105–124.

Ladner, J. A. (1987). Black teenage pregnancy: A challenge for educators. *Journal of Negro Education, 56*(1), 53–63.

Laessle, R. G., Tuschl, R. J., Schweiger, U., & Pirke, K. M. (1990). Mood changes and physical complaints during the normal menstrual cycle in healthy young women. *Psychoneuroendocrinology, 15*(2), 131–138.

Lahey, K. (1984). *Equality and specificity in feminist thought.* Paper presented to the Charter of Rights Educational Fund Statute Audit Project of Ontario. (Summarized in the *Newsletter of the National Association of Women and the Law, 5*(8), 24–25)

Lamb, M. E., Owen, M. T., & Chase-Lansdale, L. (1979). The father-daughter relationship: Past, present, and future. In C. B. Kopp (Ed.), *Becoming female: Perspectives on development* (pp. 89–112). New York: Plenum.

Lancaster, J. B. (1975). *Primate behavior and the emergence of human culture.* New York: Holt, Rinehart & Winston.

Landers, A. D. (1977). The menstrual experience. In E. Donelson & J. Gullahorn (Eds.), *Women: A psychological perspective* (pp. 65–78). New York: Wiley.

Landrine, H. (1985). Race x class stereotypes of women. *Sex Roles, 13*(1/2), 65–75.

Landrine, H. (1987). On the politics of madness: A preliminary analysis of the relationship between social roles and psychopathology. *Psychology Monographs, 113,* 341–406.

Landrine, H. (1989). The politics of personality disorder. *Psychology of Women Quarterly, 13*(3), 325–340.

Lane, M. J. (1988, May). The current status of women and minorities in engineering and science. *Engineering Education,* pp. 750–755.

Langlie, J. K. (1979). Interrelationships among preventive health behaviors: A test of competing hypotheses. *Public Health Reports, 94,* 216–225.

Laqueur, T. (1990). *Making sex: Body and gender from the Greeks to Freud.* Cambridge, MA: Harvard University Press.

Larwood, L., & Wood, M. (1977). *Women in management.* Lexington, MA: Lexington Books.

Latane, B., & Darley, J. M. (1970). *The unresponsive bystander: Why doesn't he help?.* New York: Appleton-Century-Crofts.

Leacock, E. (1983). Ideologies of male dominance as divide and rule politics: An anthropologist's view. In M. Lowe & R. Hubbard (Eds.), *Woman's nature: Rationalizations of inequality* (pp. 111–122). New York: Pergamon Press.

Leahy, R. L., & Shirk, S. R. (1984). The development of classificatory skills and sex-trait stereotypes in children. *Sex Roles, 10,* 281–292.

Lee, E., & Ames, M. A. (1987). Neurohormonal functioning and sexual orientation: A theory of homosexuality-heterosexuality. *Psychological Bulletin, 101*(2), 233–258.

Lehne, G. K. (1976). Homophobia among men. In D. S. David & R. Brannon (Eds.), *The forty-nine percent majority* (pp. 66–88). Reading, MA: Addison-Wesley.

Lehrke, R. G. (1972). A theory of X-linkage of major intellectual traits. *American Journal of Mental Deficiency, 76,* 611–619.

Leifer, M. (1980). *Psychological effects of motherhood: A study of first pregnancy.* New York: Praeger.

Leinhardt, G., Seewald, A. M., & Engel, M. (1979). Learning what's taught: Sex differences in instruction. *Journal of Educational Psychology, 71,* 432–439.

Leiss, W. (1974). *The domination of nature.* Boston: Beacon Press.

Leland, J. (1982). Gender, drinking, and alcohol abuse. In I. Al-Issa (Ed.), *Gender and psychopathology* (pp. 201–220). New York: Academic Press.

Lennane, K. J., & Lennane, R. J. (1973). Alleged psychogenic disorders in women—a possible manifestation of sexual prejudice. *New England Journal of Medicine, 288,* 288–292.

Lenney, E. (1977). Women's self-confidence in achievement settings. *Psychological Bulletin, 84,* 1–13.

Lennon, M. C. (1987). Is menopause depressing? An investigation of three perspectives. *Sex Roles, 17*(1/2), 1–16.

Lerner, M. J. (1970). The desire for justice and reactions to victims. In J. Macaulay & L. Berkowitz (Eds.), *Altruism and helping behavior* (pp. 205–230). New York: Academic Press.

Lerner, M. J. (1974). Social psychology of justice and interpersonal attraction. In T. L. Huston (Ed.), *Foundations of interpersonal attraction* (pp. 331–351). New York: Academic Press.

Lerner, R. M., & Karabenick, S. A. (1974). Physical attractiveness, body attitudes and self-concept in late adolescents. *Journal of Youth and Adolescence, 3,* 307–316.

Lerner, R. M., Orlos, J. B., & Knapp, J. R. (1976). Physical attractiveness, physical effectiveness and self-concept in late adolescents. *Adolescence, 11,* 313–326.

LeVay, S. (1991). A difference in hypothalamic structure between heterosexual and homosexual men. *Science, 253,* 1034–1037.

Levin, R. J., & Levin, A. (1975, October). The *Redbook* report on premarital and extramarital sex. *Redbook,* p. 38.

Levine, M. (1976). *Identification of reasons why qualified women do not pursue mathematical careers* (NSF Grant No. GY-11411). Report to the National Science Foundation.

Levine, S. (1966). Sex differences in the brain. *Scientific American, 214*(4), 84–90.

Levinson, D. J. (1978). *The seasons of a man's life*. New York: Ballantine.

Levinson, R. M. (1975). Sex discrimination and employment practices: An experiment with unconventional job inquiries. *Social Problems, 22*(4), 533–543.

Levy, J. (1972). Lateral specialization of the human brain: Behavioral manifestations and possible evolutionary basis. In J. A. Kiger (Ed.), *The biology of behavior* (pp. 159–180). Corvallis: Oregon State University Press.

Levy-Shiff, R., & Israelashvili, R. (1988). Antecedents of fathering: Some further exploration. *Developmental Psychology, 24*(3), 434–440.

Lewin, M. (1984). "Rather worse than folly?" Psychology measures femininity and masculinity, 1: From Terman and Miles to the Guilfords. In M. Lewin (Ed.), *In the shadow of the past: Psychology portrays the sexes* (pp. 155–178). New York: Columbia University Press.

Lewis, M. (1969). Infants' response to facial stimuli during the first year of life. *Developmental Psychology, 1*, 75–86.

Lewis, M., & Rosenblum, L. A. (1974). *The effect of the infant on its caregiver*. New York: Wiley.

Lewis, M., & Weinraub, M. (1974). Sex of parent x sex of child: Socioemotional development. In R. Richart, R. Friedman, & R. Vande Wiele (Eds.), *Sex differences in behavior* (pp. 165–190). New York: Wiley.

Lewis, M., & Weinraub, M. (1976). The father's role in the child's social network. In M. E. Lamb (Ed.), *The role of the father in child development*

(pp. 157–184). New York: Wiley.

Lewis, M., & Weinraub, M. (1979). Origins of early sex-role development. *Sex Roles, 5*, 135–153.

Lewis, R. A. (1978). Emotional intimacy among men. *Journal of Social Issues, 34*(1), 108–121.

Lewis, R. J., Winstead, B. A., & Derlega, V. J. (1989). Gender differences in volunteering for friendship research. *Journal of Social Behavior and Personality, 4*(5), 623–632.

Lewis, S. N., & Cooper, C. L. (1988). The transition to parenthood in dual-earner couples. *Psychological Medicine, 18*(2), 477–486.

Libby, M. N., & Aries, E. (1989). Gender differences in preschool children's narrative fantasy. *Psychology of Women Quarterly, 13*, 293–306.

Liebenberg, B. (1969). Expectant fathers. *Child and Family, 8*(3), 265–277.

Liem, R., & Rayman, P. (1982). Health and social costs of unemployment: Research and policy considerations. *American Psychologist, 37*, 1116–1123.

Lifton, P. D. (1985). Individual differences in moral development: The relation of sex, gender, and personality to morality. *Journal of Personality, 53*(2), 306–334.

Light, B., Staton, P., & Bourne, P. (1989). Sex equity content in history textbooks. *History and Social Science Teacher, 25*(1), 18–20.

Lii, S., & Wong, S. (1982). A cross-cultural study on sex-role stereotypes and social desirability. *Sex Roles, 8*(5), 481–491.

Linn, M. C. (1985). Gender equity in computer learning

environments. *Computers and the Social Sciences, 1*(1), 19–27.

Linn, M. C., & Petersen, A. C. (1985). Emergence and characterization of gender differences in spatial ability: A meta-analysis. *Child Development, 56*, 1479–1498.

Linton, S. (1971). Primate studies and sex differences. In A. S. Skolnick & J. H. Skolnick (Eds.), *Families in transition* (pp. 194–197). Boston: Little, Brown.

Linz, D., Donnerstein, E., & Penrod, S. (1984). The effects of multiple exposure to filmed violence against women. *Journal of Communications, 34*(3), 130–147.

Lipman-Blumen, J. (1984). *Gender roles and power*. Englewood Cliffs, NJ: Prentice-Hall.

Lipman-Blumen, J., & Leavitt, H. (1976). Vicarious and direct achievement patterns in adulthood. *The Counseling Psychologist, 6*, 26–32.

Lipovenko, D. (1985, April 11). Compensation decision sets precedent: Sexual harassment ruled work injury. *Globe and Mail*, pp. 1–2.

Lippa, R., & Beauvais, C. (1983). Gender jeopardy: The effects of gender, assessed femininity and masculinity and false success/failure feedback on performance in an experimental quiz game. *Journal of Personality and Social Psychology, 44*, 344–353.

Lips, H. M. (1980, March). *Pregnancy as a stimulus factor in the perception of women's moods and their causal attribution*. Paper presented at the Seventh Annual Conference on Feminist Psychology, Santa Monica, CA.

Lips, H. M. (1982a). Somatic and emotional aspects of the normal pregnancy experience: The first five months. *American Journal of Obstetrics and Gynecology, 142*(5), 524–529.

Lips, H. M. (1982b, June). *Symptom-reporting among expectant fathers: A new look at the couvade syndrome.* Paper presented at the annual meeting of the Association for Birth Psychology, Halifax, Nova Scotia.

Lips, H. M. (1982c, June). *Themes of the pregnancy experience: A content analysis of personal reports.* Paper presented at the Institute of the Section on Women and Psychology, Canadian Psychological Association meeting, Montreal.

Lips, H. M. (1983). Attitudes toward childbearing among women and men expecting their first child. *International Journal of Women's Studies, 6*(2), 119–129.

Lips, H. M. (1984, September). *University women's causal attributions for participation in math and science.* Paper presented at the annual meeting of the American Psychological Association, Toronto.

Lips, H. M. (1985a). Gender and the sense of power: Where are we and where are we going? *International Journal of Women's Studies, 8*(5), 483–489.

Lips, H. M. (1985b). A longitudinal study of the reporting of emotional and somatic symptoms during and after pregnancy. *Social Science and Medicine, 21*(6), 631–640.

Lips, H. M. (1986a). *Self-schema theory and gender-related behaviours: Research on some correlates of university women's participation in mathematics, sci-* ence and athletic activities. (ERIC Document ED 263517, ERIC Clearinghouse on Counselling and Personnel Services)

Lips, H. M. (1986b). Women and power in the workplace. In G. Hoffman Nemiroff (Ed.), *Interdisciplinary readings on gender* (pp. 403–415). Toronto: Fitzhenry & Whiteside.

Lips, H. M. (1991). *Women, men and power.* Mountain View, CA: Mayfield.

Lips, H. M. (1992). Gender and science-related attitudes as predictors of college students' academic choices. *Journal of Vocational Behavior, 40,* 62–81.

Lips, H. M., & Freedman, S. A. (in press). Heterosexual feminist identities: Private boundaries and shifting centers. *Feminism & Psychology.*

Lips, H. M., & Mayo, L. L. (1978, March). *Causal attributions for male and female career success as a function of job status and sex role appropriateness.* Paper presented at the Fifth Annual Conference on Feminist Psychology, Pittsburgh.

Lips, H. M., & Morrison, A. (1986). Changes in the sense of family among couples expecting their first child. *Journal of Social and Personal Relationships, 3*(3), 393–400.

Lips, H. M., & Temple, L. (1990). Majoring in computer science: Causal models for women and men. *Research in Higher Education, 31*(1), 99–113.

Lockheed, M. E. (1985). Sex and social influence: A meta-analysis guided by theory. In J. Berger & M. Zelditch, Jr. (Eds.), *Status, rewards, and influence: How expectations organize behavior* (pp. 406–429). San Francisco: Jossey-Bass.

Lockheed, M. E., & Hall, K. P. (1976). Conceptualizing sex as a status characteristic: Applications to leadership training strategies. *Journal of Social Issues, 32*(3), 111–124.

Lockwood, D. (1980). *Prison sexual violence.* New York: Elsevier.

Long, B. (1989). Sex-role orientation, coping strategies, and self-efficacy of women in traditional and nontraditional occupations. *Psychology of Women Quarterly, 13,* 307–324.

Long, L. S., & Simon, R. J. (1974). The roles and statuses of women on children's and family programs. *Journalism Quarterly, 51,* 107–110.

Long, P. (1991, March/April). A woman's heart. *In Health, 5*(2), 53–58.

Long, V. O. (1991). Masculinity, femininity, and women scientists' self-esteem and self-acceptance. *The Journal of Psychology, 125*(3), 263–270.

Lorber, J. (1986). Dismantling Noah's Ark. *Sex Roles, 14*(11/12), 567–580.

Lord, C. G., & Saenz, D. S. (1985). Memory deficits and memory surfeits: Differential cognitive consequences of tokenism for tokens and observers. *Journal of Personality and Social Psychology, 49*(4), 918–926.

Lott, B. (1985). The devaluation of women's competence. *Journal of Social Issues, 41*(4), 43–60.

Lott, B. (1989). Sexist discrimination as distancing behavior: II. Primetime television. *Psychology of Women Quarterly, 13*(3), 341–355.

Lowe, M. (1983). The dialectic of biology and culture. In M. Lowe & R. Hubbard (Eds.), *Woman's nature: Rationalizations of inequality* (pp. 39–62). New York: Pergamon Press.

Lowenthal, M. F., Thurner, M., Chiriboga, D., & Associates (1975). *Four stages of life: A comparative study of women and men facing transitions.* San Francisco: Jossey-Bass.

Lubinski, D., Tellegen, A., & Butcher, J. N. (1981). The relationship between androgyny and subjective indicators of emotional well-being. *Journal of Personality and Social Psychology, 40,* 722–730.

Luker, K. (1984). *Abortion and the politics of motherhood.* Berkeley: University of California Press.

Lummis, M., & Stevenson, H. W. (1990). Gender differences in beliefs and achievement: A cross-cultural study. *Developmental Psychology, 26*(2), 254–263.

Lutter, J. M., Lee, V., & Cushman, S. (1984). Fetal outcomes of women who ran while pregnant: A preliminary report. *The Melpomene Report, 3*(3), 6–8.

Lutwin, D. R., & Siperstein, G. N. (1985). Househusband fathers. In S. M. H. Hanson & F. W. Bozett (Eds.), *Dimensions of fatherhood* (pp. 269–287). Beverly Hills, CA: Sage.

Luxton, M. (1980). *More than a labour of love: Three generations of women's work in the home.* Toronto: The Women's Press.

Lynn, D. B. (1966). The process of learning parental and sex-role identification. *Journal of Marriage and the Family, 28,* 466–470.

Lynn, D. B. (1979). *Daughters and parents: Past, present, and future.* Monterey, CA: Brooks/Cole.

Lyons, R. D. (1983, October 4). Sex in America. *New York Times,* p. C1.

Lytton, H., & Romney, D. M. (1991). Parents' differential socialization of boys and girls: A meta-analysis. *Psychological Bulletin, 109*(2), 267–296.

Maas, H. S., & Kuypers, J. A. (1974). *From thirty to seventy: A forty-year longitudinal study of changing life styles and personal development.* San Francisco: Jossey-Bass.

Maccoby, E. E. (1966). Sex differences in intellectual functioning. In E. E. Maccoby (Ed.), *The development of sex differences* (pp. 25–55). Stanford, CA: Stanford University Press.

Maccoby, E. E. (1990). Gender and relationships: A developmental account. *American Psychologist, 45*(4), 513–520.

Maccoby, E. E., Doering, C. H., Jacklin, C. N., & Kraemer, H. (1979). Concentrations of sex hormones in umbilical cord blood: Their relation to sex and birth order. *Child Development, 50*(3), 632–642.

Maccoby, E. E., & Jacklin, C. N. (1974). *The psychology of sex differences.* Stanford, CA: Stanford University Press.

Maccoby, E. E., & Jacklin, C. N. (1980). Sex differences in aggression: A rejoinder and reprise. *Child Development, 51,* 964–980.

Maccoby, E. E., Snow, M. E., & Jacklin, C. N. (1984). Children's dispositions and mother-child interaction at 12 and 18 months: A short-term longitudinal study. *Developmental Psychology, 20*(3), 459–472.

Macfarlane, J., Allen, L., & Honzik, M. A. (1974). *Developmental study of the behavioral problems of normal children.* Berkeley: University of California Press.

MacLean, P. A. (1991, April). Tee'd off. *Women's Sports & Fitness, 13*(3), 40, 44–46, 48.

MacLeod, L. (1980). *Wife battering in Canada: The vicious circle.* Hull, Quebec: Canadian Government Publishing Centre.

Macy, C. (1986). Psychological factors in nausea and vomiting in pregnancy: A review. *Journal of Reproductive and Infant Psychology, 4*(1/2), 23–55.

Maffeo, P. A., Ford, T. W., & Lavin, P. F. (1990). Gender differences in depression in an employment setting. *Journal of Personality Assessment, 55*(1/2), 249–262.

Magazanik, M. (1991, August 9). Rape trauma less for prostitute, says judge. *The Age* (Melbourne, Australia), p. 1.

Mainardi, P. (1970). The politics of housework. In R. Morgan (Ed.), *Sisterhood is powerful* (pp. 447–454). New York: Vintage Books.

Mainiero, L. A. (1986). A review and analysis of power dynamics in organizational romances. *Academy of Management Review, 11*(4), 750–762.

Major, B. (1981). Gender patterns in touching behavior. In C. Mayo & N. Henley (Eds.), *Gender and nonverbal behavior* (pp. 15–38). New York: Springer-Verlag.

Major, B. (1987). Women and entitlement. *Women and Therapy, 6*(3), 3–19.

Major, B., & Adams, J. B. (1983). The role of gender, interpersonal orientation and self-presentation in distributive justice behavior. *Journal of Personality and Social Psychology, 45,* 598–608.

Major, B., & Adams, J. B. (1984). Situational moderators of gender differences in reward allocations. *Sex Roles, 11*(9/10), 869–880.

Major, B., & Deaux, K. (1982). Individual differences in justice behavior. In J. Greenberg & R. L. Cohen (Eds.), *Equity and justice in social behavior* (pp. 43–76). New York: Academic Press.

Major, B., & Forcey, B. (1985). Social comparisons and pay evaluations: Preferences for same-sex and same-job wage comparisons. *Journal of Experimental Social Psychology*, 21, 393–405.

Major, B., McFarlin, D. B., & Gagnon, D. (1984). Overworked and underpaid: On the nature of gender differences in personal entitlement. *Journal of Personality and Social Psychology*, 47(6), 1399–1412.

Major, B., Vanderslice, V., & McFarlin, D. B. (1984). Effects of pay expected on pay received: The confirmatory nature of initial expectations. *Journal of Applied Social Psychology*, 14(5), 399–412.

Majors, R. (1989). Cool pose: The proud signature of black survival. In M. S. Kimmel & M. A. Messner (Eds.), *Men's Lives* (pp. 83–87). New York: Macmillan.

Makepeace, J. M. (1981). Courtship violence among college students. *Family Relations*, 30, 97–102.

Makihara, K. (1991, May/June). Death of a salaryman. *In Health*, 5(3), 40–50.

Makin, K. (1986, February 1). Media image of women is under fire in report. *Globe and Mail*, pp. A1–A2.

Makosky, V. P. (1980). Stress and the mental health of women: A discussion of research and issues. In M. Guttentag, S. Salasin, & D. Belle (Eds.), *The mental health of women* (pp.

111–128). New York: Academic Press.

Malamuth, N. M. (1981). Rape proclivity among males. *Journal of Social Issues*, 37(4), 138–157.

Malamuth, N. M. (1984). Aggression against women: Cultural and individual causes. In N. Malamuth & E. Donnerstein (Eds.), *Pornography and sexual aggression* (pp. 19–52). New York: Academic Press.

Malamuth, N. M., & Check, J. V. P. (1981). The effects of mass media exposure on acceptance of violence against women: A field experiment. *Journal of Research in Personality*, 15, 436–446.

Malamuth, N. M., Haber, S., & Feshbach, S. (1980). Testing hypotheses regarding rape: Exposure and sexual violence, sex differences and the "normality" of rapists. *Journal of Research in Personality*, 14(1), 121–137.

Male hormones key to math. (1986, May 28). *Winnipeg Free Press*, p. 38.

Maloiy, G. M. O., Heglund, N. C., Prager, L. M., Cavagna, G. A., & Taylor, C. R. (1986, February). Energetic costs of carrying loads: Have African women discovered an economic way? *Nature*, 319(6055), 668–669.

Maltz, D. N., & Borker, R. A. (1983). A cultural approach to male-female miscommunication. In J. A. Gumperz (Ed.), *Language and social identity* (pp. 195–216). New York: Cambridge University Press.

Mamiya, T. (1984). Aging and sex. *Japanese Psychological Review*, 27(3), 295–306.

Mancini, J. A., & Orthner, D. K. (1978). Recreational sexuality preferences among middle-class

husbands and wives. *Journal of Sex Research*, 14(2), 96–106.

Manley, R. O. (1977). Parental warmth and hostility as related to sex differences in children's achievement orientation. *Psychology of Women Quarterly*, 1(3), 229–246.

Mann, C. R. (1984). *Female crime and delinquency*. University: University of Alabama Press.

Mann, V. A., Sasanuma, S., Sakuma, N., & Masaki, S. (1990). Sex differences in cognitive abilities: A cross-cultural perspective. *Neuropsychologia*, 28(10), 1063–1077.

Mansfield, P. K., Hood, K. E., & Henderson, J. (1989). Women and their husbands: Mood and arousal fluctuations across the menstrual cycle and days of the week. *Psychosomatic Medicine*, 51(1), 66–80.

Manstead, A. S. R., & McCulloch, C. (1981). Sex-role stereotyping in British television advertisements. *British Journal of Social Psychology*, 20, 171–180.

Maracek, J. (1978). Psychological disorders in women: Indices of role strain. In I. Frieze, J. Parsons, P. Johnson, D. Ruble, & G. Zellman (Eds.), *Women and sex roles* (pp. 255–276). New York: Norton.

Marcus, R. (1991, March 21). 'Fetal protection' plan ruled biased. *The Washington Post*, pp. A1, A14, A15.

Markides, K. S. (1989). Consequences of gender differentials in life expectancy for Black and Hispanic Americans. *International Journal of Aging and Human Development*, 29(2), 95–102.

Markus, H., Crane, M., Bernstein, S., & Siladi, M. (1982). Self-schemas and gender. *Journal of*

Personality and Social Psychology, *42,* 38–50.

Markush, R., & Favero, R. (1974). Epidemiologic assessment of stressful life events, depressed mood, and psychophysiological symptoms—A preliminary report. In B. P. Dohrenwend & B. S. Dohrenwend (Eds.), *Stressful life-events: Their nature and effects* (pp. 171–190). New York: Wiley.

Marshall, D. S. (1971). Sexual behavior on Mangaia. In D. S. Marshall & R. C. Suggs (Eds.), *Human sexual behavior* (pp. 103–162). New York: Basic Books.

Marshall, L. L., & Rose, P. (1990). Premarital violence: The impact of family of origin on violence, stress, and reciprocity. *Violence and Victimology, 5*(1), 51–64.

Martin, C. L., & Halverson, C. F., Jr. (1983). Gender constancy: A methodological and theoretical analysis. *Sex Roles, 9,* 775–790.

Martin, D., & Lyon, P. (1984). Lesbian women and mental health policy. In L. E. Walker (Ed.), *Women and mental health policy* (pp. 151–180). Beverly Hills, CA: Sage.

Martin, D. S., & Huang, M. (1984). Effects of time and perceptual orientation on actors' and observers' attributions. *Perceptual and Motor Skills, 58,* 23–30.

Martin, J. A., Maccoby, E. E., & Jacklin, C. N. (1981). Mothers' responsiveness to interactive bidding and nonbidding in boys and girls. *Child Development, 52*(3), 1064–1067.

Mashal, M. M. S., & Kalin, R. (1985, June). *The development of an interrole strain measure for dual-worker couples.* Paper presented at the Forty-sixth Annual Convention of the Canadian Psychological Association, Halifax, Nova Scotia.

Masica, D., Money, J., & Ehrhardt, A. A. (1971). Fetal feminization and female gender identity in the testicular feminizing syndrome of androgen insensitivity. *Archives of Sexual Behavior, 1*(2), 131–142.

Maslow, A., & Sakoda, J. (1952). Volunteer-error in the Kinsey study. *Journal of Abnormal and Social Psychology, 47,* 259–267.

Mason, A., & Blankenship, V. (1987). Power and affiliation motivation, stress, and abuse in intimate relationships. *Journal of Personality and Social Psychology, 52*(1), 203–210.

Mason, T. (1980). Symbolic strategies for change: A discussion of the Chicana women's movement. In M. B. Melville (Ed.), *Twice a minority: Mexican American women* (pp. 95–108). St. Louis: C. V. Mosby.

Masson, J. (1984, December). The persecution and expulsion of Jeffrey Masson. *Mother Jones,* pp. 34–37, 42–47.

Masters, B. A. (1991, May 18). A rite of passage, a matter of rights. *The Washington Post,* pp. B1, B7.

Masters, W. H., & Johnson, V. (1966). *Human sexual response.* Boston: Little, Brown.

Masters, W. H., & Johnson, V. (1970). *Human sexual inadequacy.* Boston: Little, Brown.

Mathes, E. W., Brennan, S. M., Haugen, P. M., & Rice, H. B. (1985). Ratings of physical attractiveness as a function of age. *Journal of Social Psychology, 125*(2), 157–168.

Matthews, G. F. (1985). Mirror, mirror: Self-image and disabled women. *Resources for Feminist Research, 14*(1), 47–50.

Mayes, S., & Valentine, K. (1979). Sex-role stereotyping in Saturday morning cartoon shows. *Journal of Broadcasting, 23,* 41–50.

Mayo, C., & Henley, N. M. (1981). Nonverbal behavior: Barrier or agent for sex role change? In C. Mayo & N. M. Henley (Eds.), *Gender and nonverbal behavior* (pp. 3–13). New York: Springer-Verlag.

Mazur, A., & Lamb, T. A. (1980). Testosterone, status, and mood in human males. *Hormones and Behavior, 14,* 236–246.

Mazur, E. (1989). Predicting gender differences in same-sex friendships from affiliation motive and value. *Psychology of Women Quarterly, 13,* 277–291.

McArthur, L. Z. (1982). Judging a book by its cover: A cognitive analysis of the relationship between physical appearance and stereotyping. In A. Hastorf & A. M. Isen (Eds.), *Cognitive social psychology.* New York: Elsevier.

McArthur, L. Z., & Eisen, S. V. (1976). Achievements of male and female storybook characters as determinants of achieving behavior by boys and girls. *Journal of Personality and Social Psychology, 33,* 467–473.

McBroom, W. H. (1981). Parental relationships, socioeconomic status, and sex role expectations. *Sex Roles, 7,* 1027–1033.

McCall, R. B., & Kagan, J. (1970). Individual differences in the infant's distribution of attention to stimulus discrepancy. *Developmental Psychology, 2,* 90–98.

McClelland, D. C. (1961). *The achieving society.* Princeton, NJ: Van Nostrand.

McClelland, D. C. (1975). *Power: The inner experience.* New York: Irvington.

McClelland, D. C., Atkinson, J. W., Clark, R. A., & Lowell, E. L. (1953). *The achievement motive.* New York: Appleton.

McClelland, D. C., Davis, W. N., Kalin, R., & Wanner, E. (1972). *The drinking man.* New York: Free Press.

McCormack, A. (1985). The sexual harassment of students by teachers: The case of students in science. *Sex Roles, 13*(1/2), 21–32.

McCray, C. A. (1980). The black woman and family roles. In L. Rodgers-Rose (Ed.), *The black woman* (pp. 67–78). Beverly Hills, CA: Sage.

McDonnell, K. (1984). *Not an easy choice. A feminist re-examines abortion.* Toronto: The Women's Press.

McEwan, C. (1985). Crying the blues. Male postpartum depression explained. *Great Expectations, 14*(3), 56, 59.

McFarland, C., Ross, M., & DeCourville, N. (1989). Women's theories of menstruation and biases in recall of menstrual symptoms. *Journal of Personality and Social Psychology, 57*(3), 522–531.

McFarlane, J., Martin, C. L., & Williams, T. M. (1988). Mood fluctuations: Women versus men and menstrual versus other cycles. *Psychology of Women Quarterly, 12*(2), 201–223.

McGhee, P. E., & Frueh, T. (1980). Television viewing and the learning of sex-role stereotypes. *Sex Roles, 6,* 179–188.

McGlone, J. (1980). Sex differences in human brain asymmetry: A critical survey. *Behavioral and Brain Sciences, 3,* 215–263.

McGuinness, D. (1972). Hearing: Individual differences in perceiving. *Perception, 1,* 465–473.

McGuinness, D. (1976). Away from a unisex psychology: Individual differences in visual perception. *Perception, 5,* 279–294.

McGuinness, D. (1988). Socialization versus biology: Time to move on. *Behavioral and Brain Sciences, 11*(2), 203–204.

McGuinness, D., & Courtney, A. (1983). Sex differences in visual and phonetic search. *Journal of Mental Imagery, 7*(1), 95–104.

McGuinness, D., & McLaughlin, L. (1982). An investigation of sex differences in visual recognition and recall. *Journal of Mental Imagery, 6*(1), 203–212.

McGuinness, D., & Pribram, K. (1979). The origins of sensory bias in the development of gender differences in perception and cognition. In M. Bortner (Ed.), *Cognitive growth and development—Essays in honor of Herbert G. Birch* (pp. 3–56). New York: Brunner/Mazel.

McGuinness, D., & Symonds, J. (1977). Sex differences in choice behaviour: The object-person dimension. *Perception, 6,* 691–694.

McHale, S. M., & Huston, T. L. (1984). Men and women as parents: Sex role orientations, employment, and parental roles with infants. *Child Development, 55,* 1349–1361.

McHugh, M. C., Koeske, R. D., & Frieze, I. H. (Co-Chairs). (1981). *Guidelines for nonsexist research.* Washington, DC: American Psychological Association.

McIntyre, S. (1987). Gender bias in a Canadian law school. *Canadian Association of University Teachers Bulletin, 34*(1), 7–11.

McKee, J. P., & Sherriffs, A. C. (1957). The differential evaluation of males and females. *Journal of Personality, 25,* 356–371.

McKinlay, J. B., McKinlay, S. M., & Brambilla, D. (1987). The relative contributions of endocrine changes and social circumstances to depression in mid-aged women. *Journal of Health and Social Behavior, 28*(4), 345–363.

McLanahan, S. S., Sorensen, A., & Watson, D. (1989). Sex differences in poverty, 1950–1980. *Signs, 15*(1), 102–122.

Mead, M. (1935). *Sex and temperament in three primitive societies.* New York: Morrow.

Mead, M. (1980). A proposal: We need taboos on sex at work. In D. A. Neugarten & J. M. Shafritz (Eds.), *Sexuality in organizations: Romantic and coercive behaviors at work* (pp. 53–56). Oak Park, IL: Moore.

Megargee, E. (1969). Influence of sex roles on the manifestation of leadership. *Journal of Applied Psychology, 53,* 377–382.

Melges, F. T. (1968). Postpartum psychiatric syndromes. *Psychosomatic Medicine, 30,* 95–108.

Meredith, N. (1984, January). The gay dilemma. *Psychology Today,* pp. 56–62.

Messenger, J. C. (1971). Sex and repression in an Irish folk community. In D. S. Marshall & R. C. Suggs (Eds.), *Human sexual behavior* (pp. 3–37). New York: Basic Books.

Messing, K. (1983). The scientific mystique: Can a white lab coat guarantee purity in the search for knowledge about the nature of women? In M. Lowe & R. Hubbard (Eds.), *Woman's nature: Rationalizations of inequality* (pp. 75–88). New York: Pergamon Press.

Meyer-Bahlburg, H. F. L. (1980). Homosexual orientation in women and men: A hormonal basis? In J. Eccles Parsons (Ed.), *The psychobiology of sex differences and sex roles* (pp. 105–130). Washington, DC: Hemisphere.

Meyer-Bahlburg, H. F. L., Boon, D. A., Sharma, M., & Edwards, J. A. (1974). Aggressiveness and testosterone measures in man. *Psychosomatic Medicine, 36*, 267–274.

Micciolo, R., Zimmerman-Tansella, C., Williams, P., & Tansella, M. (1989). Seasonal variation in suicide: Is there a sex difference? *Psychological Medicine, 19*(1), 199–203.

Mikalachki, D., & Mikalachki, A. (1984). MBA women: The new pioneers. *Business Quarterly, 49*(1), 110–115.

Miles, R. (1988). *The women's history of the world.* New York: Harper & Row.

Miller, G. H., & Pyke, S. W. (1973). Sex, matrix variations, and perceived personality effects in mixed-motive games. *Journal of Conflict Resolution, 17*, 335–349.

Miller, J. B. (1977). *Toward a new psychology of women.* Boston: Beacon Press.

Miller, M. M., & Reeves, B. (1976). Dramatic TV content and children's sex-role stereotypes. *Journal of Broadcasting, 20*(1), 35–50.

Miller, W. E., & Friedman, S. (1988). Male and female sexuality during pregnancy: Behavior and attitudes. *Journal of Psychology and Human Sexuality, 1*(2), 17–37.

Mirande, A., & Enriquez, E. (1979). *La Chicana: The Mexican-American woman.* Chicago: University of Chicago Press.

Mischel, W. (1970). Sex-typing and socialization. In P. H.

Mussen (Ed.), *Carmichael's manual of child psychology* (Vol. 2, pp. 3–72). New York: Wiley.

Mishkind, M. E., Rodin, J., Silberstein, L. R., & Striegel-Moore, R. H. (1987). The embodiment of masculinity: Cultural, psychological, and behavioral dimensions. In M. S. Kimmel (Ed.), *Changing men: New directions in research on men and masculinity* (pp. 37–52). Newbury Park, CA: Sage.

Mitchell, J. (1974). *Psychoanalysis and feminism.* New York: Pantheon.

Moglia, R. (1986, March). Sexual abuse and disability. *SIECUS Report*, pp. 9–10.

Moir, A., & Jessel, D. (1991, May 5). A test: How female is your brain? *The Washington Post*, p. K3.

Monahan, L., Kuhn, D., & Shaver, P. (1974). Intrapsychic versus cultural explanations for the "Fear of Success" motive. *Journal of Personality and Social Psychology, 29*, 60–64.

Money, J., & Daley, J. (1977). Hyperadrenocortical 46 XX hermaphroditism with penile urethra: Psychological studies in seven cases, three reared as boys, four as girls. In P. A. Lee et al. (Eds.), *Congenital adrenal hyperplasia* (pp. 433–446). Baltimore, MD: University Park Press.

Money, J., & Ehrhardt, A. A. (1972). *Man and woman, boy and girl.* Baltimore: Johns Hopkins University Press.

Money, J., & Ogunro, B. (1974). Behavioral sexology: Ten cases of genetic male intersexuality with impaired prenatal and pubertal androgenization. *Archives of Sexual Behavior, 3*(3), 181–205.

Money, J., & Schwartz, M. (1977). Dating, romantic and nonromantic friendships, and sexuality in 17 early-treated adrenogenital females, aged 16–25. In P. A. Lee et al. (Eds.), *Congenital adrenal hyperplasia* (pp. 419–431). Baltimore, MD: University Park Press.

Money, J., Schwartz, M., & Lewis, V. G. (1984). Adult erotosexual status and fetal hormonal masculinization and demasculinization: 46,XX congenital virilizing adrenal hyperplasia and 46,XX androgen-insensitivity syndrome compared. *Psychoneuroendocrinology, 9*, 405–414.

Monk, T. H., Moline, M. L., Fookson, J. E., & Peetz, S. M. (1989). Circadian determinants of subjective alertness. *Journal of Biological Rhythms, 4*(4), 393–404.

Montagu, A. (1952). *The natural superiority of women.* New York: Macmillan.

Montaigne, M. de (1580). *Essays* I. Chapter 27—Of friendship. Quoted in M. Gibbs, D. Auerbach, & M. Fox, A comparison of male and female same-sex friendships. *International Journal of Women's Studies, 3*(3), 270.

Montemayor, R. (1974). Children's performance in a game and their attraction to it as a function of sex-typed labels. *Child Development, 45*, 152–156.

Moore, L. M., & Rickel, A. U. (1980). Characteristics of women in traditional and non-traditional managerial roles. *Personnel Psychology, 33*, 317–322.

Moreland, J. (1980). Age and change in the adult male sex role. *Sex Roles, 6*, 807–818.

Moreland, R. L. (1985). Social categorization and the assimilation of "new" group members. *Journal of Personality and Social Psychology, 48*(5), 1173–1190.

Morgan, M. (1982). Television and adolescents' sex role stereotypes: A longitudinal study. *Journal of Personality and Social Psychology, 43*, 947–955.

Morin, S. F., & Garfinkle, E. M. (1978). Male homophobia. *Journal of Social Issues, 34*(1), 29–47.

Morokoff, P. J. (1985). Effects of sex guilt, repression, sexual "arousability," and sexual experience on female sexual arousal during erotica and fantasy. *Journal of Personality and Social Psychology, 49*(1), 177–187.

Morris, J. (1974). *Conundrum*. Scarborough, Ontario: New American Library of Canada.

Morris, S. (1978, May). Do men *need* to cheat on their women? A new science says YES: Darwin and the double standard. *Playboy*, pp. 109ff.

Moss, P., Bolland, G., Foxman, R., & Owen, C. (1987). The division of household work during the transition to parenthood. *Journal of Reproductive and Infant Psychology, 5*(2), 71–86.

Mott, F. L. (1991). Developmental effects of infant care: The mediating role of gender and health. *Journal of Social Issues, 47*(2), 139–158.

Moyer, K. E. (1974). Sex differences in aggression. In R. C. Friedman, R. M. Richart, & R. L. Vande Wiele (Eds.), *Sex differences in behavior* (pp. 149–163). New York: Wiley.

Moynihan, D. (1967). The Negro family: The case for national action (1965). In L. Rainwater & W. Yancey (Eds.), *The Moy-nihan report and the politics of controversy* (pp. 39–124). Cambridge, MA: MIT Press.

Mulig, J. C., Haggerty, M. E., Carballosa, A. B., Cinnick, W. J., & Madden, J. M. (1985). Relationships among fear of success, fear of failure, and androgyny. *Psychology of Women Quarterly, 9*(2), 284–287.

Mulvey, A., & Dohrenwend, B. S. (1984). The relation of stressful life events to gender. In A. U. Rickel, M. Gerrard, & I. Iscoe (Eds.), *Social and psychological problems of women*. Washington, DC: Hemisphere.

Munroe, R. H., Shimmin, H. S., & Munroe, R. L. (1984). Gender understanding and sex role preference in four cultures. *Developmental Psychology, 20*, 673–682.

Murray, H. A. (1937). Techniques for a systematic investigation of fantasy. *Journal of Psychology, 3*, 115–143.

Murray, S. R., & Mednick, M. T. S. (1977). Black women's achievement orientation: Motivational and cognitive factors. *Psychology of Women Quarterly, 1*, 247–259.

Murrell, A. J., Frieze, I. H., & Frost, J. L. (1991). Aspiring to careers in male- and female-dominated professions: A study of Black and White college women. *Psychology of Women Quarterly, 15*(1), 103–126.

Myers, A. M., & Gonda, G. (1982). Utility of the masculinity-femininity construct: Comparison of traditional and androgyny approaches. *Journal of Personality and Social Psychology, 43*, 514–523.

Narrow, W. E., Rae, D. S., Moscicki, E. K., Locke, B. Z., & Regier, D. A. (1990). Depression among Cuban Americans. The Hispanic Health and Nutrition Examination Survey. *Social Psychiatry and Psychiatric Epidemiology, 25*(5), 260–268.

Nash, S. C. (1979). Sex role as a mediator of intellectual functioning. In M. A. Wittig & A. C. Petersen (Eds.), *Sex-related differences in cognitive functioning: Developmental issues* (pp. 263–302). New York: Academic Press.

Nash, S. C., & Feldman, S. S. (1981). Sex-role and sex-related attributions: Constancy and change across the family life cycle. In M. E. Lamb & A. L. Brown (Eds.), *Advances in developmental psychology* (Vol. 1, pp. 1–36). Hillsdale, NJ: Lawrence Erlbaum.

National Center for Education Statistics. (1989). *Digest of Education Statistics, 1989*. Washington, DC: U.S. Department of Education, Office of Educational Research and Improvement.

National Science Foundation. (1990). *Women and minorities in science and engineering*. Washington, DC: Author.

Neugarten, B. L., & Kraines, R. J. (1965). "Menopausal symptoms" in women of various ages. *Psychosomatic Medicine, 27*, 266.

Nevill, D. D., & Schlecker, D. I. (1988). The relation of self-efficacy and assertiveness to willingness to engage in traditional/nontraditional career activities. *Psychology of Women Quarterly, 12*(1), 91–98.

New Webster encyclopedia dictionary of the English language. (1971). Chicago: Consolidated Book Publisher.

Newcomb, M. D. (1984, August). *Notches on the bedpost: Correlates of sexual experience*. Paper presented at the annual convention of the American Psychological Association, Toronto.

Newcombe, N. (1987, April). *A longitudinal study of predictors of spatial ability in adolescent females*. Paper presented at the meeting of the Society for Research in Child Development, Baltimore, MD.

Newcombe, N., & Bandura, M. M. (1983). Effect of age at puberty on spatial ability in girls: A question of mechanism. *Developmental Psychology, 19*(2), 213–224.

Newcombe, N., Bandura, M. M., & Taylor, D. G. (1983). Sex differences in spatial ability and spatial activities. *Sex Roles, 9*, 377–386.

Newton, E. (1984). The mythic mannish lesbian: Radclyffe Hall and the new woman. *Signs, 9*, 557–575.

Newton, N. (1971). Trebly sensuous woman. *Psychology Today, 5*, 68–71, 98–99.

Nicholson, J. (1984). *Men & women: How different are they?* Oxford: Oxford University Press.

Nieva, V. F. (1985). Work and family linkages. In L. Larwood, A. H. Stromberg, & B. Gutek (Eds.), *Women and work: An annual review* (Vol. 1). Beverly Hills, CA: Sage.

Nolan, J. D., Galst, J. P., & White, M.A. (1977). Sex bias on children's television programs. *Journal of Psychology, 96*, 197–204.

Nolen-Hoeksema, S. (1987). Sex differences in unipolar depression: Evidence and theory. *Psychological Bulletin, 101*(2), 259–282.

Noller, P. (1980). Misunderstandings in marital communication: A study of couples' nonverbal communication. *Journal of Personality and Social Psychology, 39*, 1135–1148.

Nunes, M., & White, D. (1973). *The lace ghetto*. Toronto: New Press.

Nyborg, H. (1983). Spatial ability in men and women: Review and a new theory. *Advances in Behaviour Research and Therapy, 5*, 89–140.

Nye, F. I. (1976). *Role structure and analysis of the family*. Beverly Hills, CA: Sage.

Nyquist, L., & Spence, J. (1986). Effects of dispositional dominance and sex role expectations on leadership behaviors. *Journal of Personality and Social Psychology, 50*(1), 377–382.

Oakes, R. (1984). Sex patterns in DSM III: Bias or basis for theory development [Letter to the editor]. *American Psychologist, 39*, 1320–1322.

Oakley, A. (1980). *Women confined: Toward a sociology of childbirth*. New York: Schocken.

Oden, M. H. (1968). The fulfillment of promise: 40-year follow-up of the Terman gifted group. *Genetic Psychology Monographs, 77*, 3–93.

O'Farrell, B. (1982). Women and nontraditional blue collar jobs in the 1980s: An overview. In P. A. Wallace (Ed.), *Women in the workplace* (pp. 135–165). Boston: Auburn House.

O'Hara, M. W. (1985). Depression and marital adjustment during pregnancy and after delivery. *American Journal of Family Therapy, 13*(4), 49–55.

O'Heron, C. A., & Orlofsky, J. L. (1990). Stereotypic and non-stereotypic sex role trait and behavior orientations, gender identity, and psychological adjustment. *Journal of Personality and Social Psychology, 58*(1), 134–143.

O'Keefe, E. S. C., & Hyde, J. S. (1983). The development of occupational sex-role stereotypes: The effects of gender stability and age. *Sex Roles, 39*, 481–492.

O'Kelly, C. G., & Carney, L. S. (1986). *Women and men in society. Cross-cultural perspectives on gender stratification*. Belmont, CA: Wadsworth.

O'Leary, V. E. (1977). *Toward understanding women*. Monterey, CA: Brooks/Cole.

O'Leary, V. E., & Harrison, A. O. (1975, September). *Sex role stereotypes as a function of race and sex*. Paper presented at the annual convention of the American Psychological Association, Chicago.

Olian, J. D., Schwab, D. P., & Haberfeld, Y. (1988). The impact of applicant gender compared to qualifications on hiring recommendations: A meta-analysis of experimental studies. *Organizational Behavior and Human Decision Processes, 41*, 180–195.

Olstad, K. (1975). Brave new men: A basis for discussion. In J. Petras (Ed.), *Sex: Male/Gender: Masculine* (pp. 160–178). Port Washington, NY: Alfred.

On the legislative front (1990, September/October). *Ms., 1*(2), 45.

Oppenheimer, V. K. (1970). *The female labor force in the United States: Demographic and economic factors governing its growth and changing composition* (Population Monograph Series No. 5). Berkeley: University of California.

Ortmeyer, L. E. (1979). The female's natural advantage? Or, the unhealthy environment of males?: The status of sex mortality differentials. *Women and Health, 4*(2), 121–133.

Ostertag, P. A., & McNamara, J. R. (1991). "Feminization" of psychology: The changing sex ratio and its implications for the profession. *Psychology of Women Quarterly, 15*(3), 349–370.

Ott, E. M. (1989). Effects of the male-female ratio at work: Policewomen and male nurses. *Psychology of Women Quarterly, 13*(1), 41–58.

Padian, N. S., Shiboski, S. C., & Jewell, N. P. (1991). Female-to-male transmission of human immunodeficiency virus. *Journal of the American Medical Association, 266*(12), 1664–1667.

Pagelow, M. D. (1984). *Family violence.* New York: Praeger.

Paige, K. E. (1971). The effects of oral contraceptives on affective fluctuations associated with the menstrual cycle. *Psychosomatic Medicine, 33,* 515–537.

Paige, K. E. (1973). Women learn to sing the menstrual blues. *Psychology Today, 7*(4), 41–46.

Paikoff, R. L., & Savin-Williams, R. C. (1983). An exploratory study of dominance interactions among adolescent females at a summer camp. *Journal of Youth and Adolescence, 12,* 419–433.

Pajntar, M. (1972). Obstetrical complications—Personality changes and emotional tension during pregnancy. In N. Morris (Ed.), *Psychosomatic medicine in obstetrics and gynecology* (Third International Congress, London, 1971). Basel: Karger.

Paludi, M. A. (1984). Psychometric properties and underlying assumptions of four objective measures of fear of success. *Sex Roles, 10,* 765–781.

Paludi, M. A., & Strayer, L. A. (1985). What's in an author's name? Differential evaluations of performance as a function of author's name. *Sex Roles, 12*(3/4), 353–362.

Pantony, K., & Caplan, P. J. (1991). Delusional dominating personality disorder: A modest proposal for identifying some consequences of rigid masculine socialization. *Canadian Psychology, 32*(2), 120–135.

Papini, D. R., Farmer, F. F., Clark, S. M., Micka, J. C., & Barnett, J. K. (1990). Early adolescent age and gender differences in patterns of emotional self-disclosure to parents and friends. *Adolescence, 25,* 959–976.

Paralyzed woman in beauty pageant. (1987, January 17). *Winnipeg Free Press,* p. 73.

Parisi, N. (1982). Are females treated differently? A review of the theories and evidence on sentencing and parole decisions. In N. H. Rafter & E. A. Stanko (Eds.), *Judge, lawyer, victim, thief: Women, gender roles, and criminal justice* (pp. 205–229). Boston: Northeastern University Press.

Parke, R. D. (1981). *Fathers.* Cambridge, MA: Harvard University Press.

Parke, R. D., & Sawin, D. B. (1976). The father's role in infancy: A reevaluation. *The Family Coordinator, 25,* 365–371.

Parlee, M. B. (1972). Comments on D. M. Broverman, E. L. Klaiber, Y. Kobayashi, and W. Vogel: Roles of activation and inhibition in sex differences in cognitive abilities. *Psychological Review, 79,* 180–184.

Parlee, M. B. (1973). The premenstrual syndrome. *Psychological Bulletin, 80,* 454–465.

Parlee, M. B. (1974). Stereotypic beliefs about menstruation: A methodological note on the Moos menstrual distress questionnaire and some new data. *Psychosomatic Medicine, 36,* 229–240.

Parlee, M. B. (1975). Psychology. *Signs, 1,* 119–138.

Parlee, M. B. (1982). Changes in moods and activation levels during the menstrual cycle in experimentally naive subjects. *Psychology of Women Quarterly, 7,* 119–131.

Parlee, M. B. (1983). Menstrual rhythms in sensory processes: A review of fluctuations in vision, olfaction, audition, taste, and touch. *Psychological Bulletin, 93,* 539–548.

Parsons, J. E., Adler, T. F., & Kaczala, C. M. (1982). Socialization of achievement attitudes and beliefs: Parental influences. *Child Development, 53,* 310–321.

Parsons, T., & Bales, R. F. (1955). *Family, socialization, and interaction process.* Glencoe, IL: Free Press.

Paul, J. P. (1985). Bisexuality: Reassessing our paradigms of sexuality. *Journal of Homosexuality, 10*(3/4), 21–34.

Paulsen, K., & Johnson, M. (1983). Sex role attitudes and mathematical ability in 4th-, 8th-, and 11th-grade students from a high socioeconomic area. *Developmental Psychology, 19*(2), 210–214.

Pauly, I. (1968). The current status of the change of sex operation. *Journal of Nervous and Mental Disorders, 147,* 460–471.

Pearlin, L. (1975). Sex roles and depression. In N. Datan & L. Ginsberg (Eds.), *Life-span developmental psychology: Normative life crises* (pp. 191–207). New York: Academic Press.

Pearlin, L., & Johnson, J. (1977). Marital status, life-strains and depression. *American Sociological Review, 42*, 704–715.

Pedersen, D. M., Shinedling, M. M., & Johnson, D. L. (1975). Effects of examiner and subject on children's quantitative test performance. In R. K. Unger & F. L. Denmark (Eds.), *Woman: Dependent or independent variable* (pp. 409–416). New York: Psychological Dimensions.

Pennebaker, J. W. (1982). *The psychology of physical symptoms*. New York: Springer-Verlag.

Peplau, L. A. (1981, March). What homosexuals want in relationships. *Psychology Today, 15*(3), 28–38.

Peplau, L. A. (1983). Roles and gender. In H. H. Kelley, E. Berscheid, A. Christensen, J. H. Harvey, T. L. Huston, G. Levinger, E. McClintock, L. A. Peplau, & D. R. Peterson (Eds.), *Close Relationships* (pp. 221–264). New York: W. H. Freeman.

Peplau, L. A., & Amaro, H. (1982). Understanding lesbian relationships. In W. Paul, J. D. Weinrich, J. C. Gonsiorek, & M. E. Hotvedt (Eds.), *Homosexuality: Social, psychological, and biological issues* (pp. 233–247). Beverly Hills, CA: Sage.

Peplau, L. A., & Cochran, S. D. (1981). Value orientations in the intimate relationships of gay men. *Journal of Homosexuality, 6*(3), 1–19.

Peplau, L. A., Cochran, S., Rook, K., & Padesky, C. (1978). Loving women: Attach-ment and autonomy in lesbian relationships. *Journal of Social Issues, 34*(3), 7–27.

Peplau, L. A., & Conrad, E. (1989). Beyond nonsexist research: The perils of feminist methods in psychology. *Psychology of Women Quarterly, 13*(4), 379–400.

Percival, E. (1991). *Thinking about gender similarities and differences: A discussion paper.* Paper presented at the annual meeting of the Association for Women in Psychology, Hartford, CT.

Perlman, D. (1974). Self-esteem and sexual permissiveness. *Journal of Marriage and the Family, 36*, 470–473.

Perry, D. G., & Bussey, K. (1979). The social learning theory of sex differences: Imitation is alive and well. *Journal of Personality and Social Psychology, 37*, 1699–1712.

Perry, J. D., & Whipple, B. (1981). Pelvic muscle strength of female ejaculators: Evidence in support of a new theory of orgasm. *Journal of Sex Research, 17*, 22–39.

Pesmen, C. (1991, November). Love and sex in the '90s: Our national survey. *Seventeen*, pp. 63–68.

Peters, M., Servos, P., & Day, R. (1990). Marked sex differences on a fine motor skill task disappear when finger size is used as covariate. *Journal of Applied Psychology, 75*(1), 87–90.

Petersen, A. C. (1976). Physical androgyny and cognitive functioning in adolescence. *Developmental Psychology, 12*, 524–533.

Petersen, A. C., & Wittig, M. A. (1979). Sex-related differences in cognitive functioning: An overview. In M. A. Wittig & A. C. Petersen (Eds.), *Sex-related differences in cognitive func-tion: Developmental issues* (pp. 1–17). New York: Academic Press.

Petersen, A. E. (1983). Menarche: Meaning of measures and measuring meaning. In S. Golub (Ed.), *Menarche.* Lexington, MA: D. C. Heath.

Peterson, D. L., & Pfost, K. S. (1989). Influence of rock videos on attitudes to violence against women. *Psychological Reports, 64*, 319–322.

Peterson, G. H., Mehl, L. E., & Leiderman, P. H. (1979). The role of some birth related variables in father attachment. *American Journal of Orthopsychiatry, 40*, 330–338.

Pettigrew, T. (1964). *A profile of the Negro American.* Princeton, NJ: Van Nostrand.

Phillips, D., & Segal, B. (1969). Sexual status and psychiatric symptoms. *American Sociology Review, 34*, 58–72.

Phillis, D. E., & Gromko, M. H. (1985). Sex differences in sexual activity: Reality or illusion? *The Journal of Sex Research, 21*(4), 437–448.

Phillips, R. D., & Gilroy, F. D. (1985). Sex-role stereotypes and clinical judgements of mental health: The Broverman's findings reexamined. *Sex Roles, 12*, 179–193.

Phinney, J. S. (1989). Stages of ethnic identity in minority group adolescents. *Journal of Early Adolescence, 9*, 34–49.

Phinney, J. S. (1990). Ethnic identity in adolescents and adults: Review of research. *Psychological Bulletin, 108*(3), 499–514.

Phoenix, C., Goy, R., & Resko, J. A. (1968). Psychosexual differentiation as a function of androgenic stimulation. In M. Diamond (Ed.), *Reproduction and sexual behavior.* Bloomington: Indiana University Press.

Piaget, J. (1954). *The construction of reality in the child.* New York: Basic Books.

Piaget, J. (1965). *The moral judgment of the child.* New York: Free Press. (Original work published 1932)

Pidano, A. E., & Tennen, H. (1985). Transient depressive experiences and their relationship to gender and sex-role orientation. *Sex Roles, 12,* 97–110.

Piliavin, J. A., & Unger, R. K. (1985). The helpful but helpless female: Myth or reality? In V. O'Leary, R. Unger, & B. Wallston (Eds.), *Women, gender, and social psychology* (pp. 149–189). Hillsdale, NJ: Lawrence Erlbaum Associates.

Pillard, R. C., & Weinrich, J. D. (1986). Evidence of familial nature of male homosexuality. *Archives of General Psychiatry, 43*(8), 800–812.

Pingree, S. (1978). The effects of nonsexist TV commercials and perceptions of reality on children's attitudes about women. *Psychology of Women Quarterly, 2,* 262–277.

Pleck, J. (1981). *The myth of masculinity.* Cambridge, MA: The MIT Press.

Pleck, J. (1983). Husbands' paid work and family roles: Current research issues. In H. Lopata & J. Pleck (Eds.), *Research in the interweave of social roles: Vol. 3. Families and jobs* (pp. 251–333). Greenwich, CT: JAI Press.

Pleck, J. (1984). The theory of male sex role identity: Its rise and fall, 1936 to the present. In M. Lewin (Ed.), *In the shadow of the past: Psychology portrays the sexes* (pp. 205–225). New York: Columbia University Press.

Pleck, J. H., & Rustad, M. (1980). *Husbands' and wives' time in family work and paid work in the 1975–76 study of time use* (Working Paper No. 63). Wellesley, MA: Wellesley College, Center for Research on Women.

Plomin, R., & Foch, T. (1981). Sex differences and individual differences. *Child Development, 52,* 383–385.

PMS defense successful in Va. drunken driving case. (1991, June 7). *The Washington Post,* p. A1.

Poewe, K. O. (1980). Universal male dominance: An ethnological illusion. *Dialectical Anthropology, 5,* 111–125.

Polk, B. B. (1974). Male power and the women's movement. *The Journal of Applied Behavioral Science, 10*(3), 415–431.

Porter, N., & Geis, F. (1981). Women and nonverbal leadership cues: When seeing is not believing. In C. Mayo & N. Henley (Eds.), *Gender and nonverbal behavior* (pp. 39–59). New York: Springer-Verlag.

Poussaint, A. F. (1982, August). What every black woman should know about black men. *Ebony,* pp. 36–40.

Powers, E., & Bultena, G. (1976). Sex differences in intimate friendships of old age. *Journal of Marriage and the Family, 38,* 739–747.

Prather, J. E. (1971). When the girls move in: A sociological analysis of the feminization of the bank teller's job. *Journal of Marriage and the Family, 33*(4), 777–782.

Prather, J. E., & Fidell, L. S. (1978). Drug use and abuse among women: An overview. *The International Journal for the Addictions, 13,* 863–885.

Pratt, M. W., Pancer, M., & Hunsberger, B. (1990). Reasoning about the self and relationships in maturity: An integrative complexity analysis of individual differences. *Journal of Personality and Social Psychology, 59*(3), 575–581.

Price, W. H., & Whatmore, P. B. (1967a). Behavior disorders and pattern of crime among XYY males identified at a maximum security prison. *British Medical Journal, 1,* 533–536.

Price, W. H., & Whatmore, P. B. (1967b). Criminal behavior and the XYY male. *Nature, 213,* 815.

Pryor, J. B. (1985). The lay person's understanding of sexual harassment. *Sex Roles, 13*(5/6), 273–286.

Pursell, P., & Stewart, L. (1990). Dick and Jane in 1989. *Sex Roles, 22*(3/4), 177–185.

Pyke, S. (1979). Cognitive templating: A technique for feminist (and other) counselors. *The Personnel and Guidance Journal, 57*(6), 315–318.

Pyke, S. W. (1980). Androgyny: A dead end or a promise? In C. Stark-Adamec (Ed.), *Sex roles: Origins, influences, and implications for women* (pp. 20–32). Montreal: Eden Press Women's Publications.

Quill, T. E., Lipkin, M., & Lamb, G. S. (1984). Health-care seeking by men in their spouse's pregnancy. *Psychosomatic Medicine, 46*(3), 277–283.

Quinn, R. E. (1977). Coping with cupid: The formation, impact, and management of romantic relationships in organizations. *Administrative Science Quarterly, 22,* 30–45.

Rabin, J. S. (1987, March). *Adaptation across the lifespan: Evolution, sex roles, and social change.* Paper presented at the Conference of the Association for Women in Psychology, Denver, CO.

Radin, N. (1982). Primary caregiving and role-sharing fathers. In M. E. Lamb (Ed.), *Nontraditional families: Parenting and child development* (pp. 173–204). Hillsdale, NJ: Lawrence Erlbaum Associates.

Radloff, L. S. (1980). Risk factors for depression: What do we learn from them? In M. Guttentag, S. Salasin, & D. Belle (Eds.), *The mental health of women* (pp. 93–109). New York: Academic Press.

Ragins, B. R., & Sundstrom, E. (1989). Gender and power in organizations: A longitudinal perspective. *Psychological Bulletin, 105*(1), 51–88.

Ramey, E. (1972). Men's cycles. *Ms., 1*(8), 8, 11–12, 14–15.

Randall, D. M. (1985). Women in toxic work environments. A case study and examination of policy impact. In L. Larwood, A. H. Stromberg, & B. A. Gutek (Eds.), *Women and work: An annual review* (Vol. 1, pp. 259–281). Beverly Hills, CA: Sage.

Rapist husband (1991, September 14). *The Times*, p. 14.

Raskin, P. A., & Israel, A. C. (1981). Sex-role imitation in children: Effects of sex of child, sex of model, and sex-role appropriateness of modeled behavior. *Sex Roles, 7*, 1067–1077.

Rasmussen, L., Rasmussen, L., Savage, C., & Wheeler, A. (1976). *A harvest yet to reap: A history of prairie women.* Toronto: The Women's Press.

Rauhala, A. (1987, April 2). Religion is key for anti-abortionists, study finds. *Globe and Mail*, pp. A1, A5.

Ravelli, G., Stein, Z., & Susser, M. (1976). Obesity in young men after famine exposure *in utero* and early infancy. *New England Journal of Medicine, 295*, 349–353.

Raven, B. H. (1965). Social influence and power. In I. D. Steiner & M. Fishbein (Eds.), *Current studies in social psychology* (pp. 371–381). New York: Holt, Rinehart & Winston.

Rawlings, E. I., & Carter, D. K. (1977). *Psychotherapy for women: Treatment toward equality.* Springfield, IL: Charles C. Thomas.

Raymond, J. (1979). *The transsexual empire: The making of the she-male.* Boston: Beacon Press.

RCMP accused of sexual abuses. (1986, January 20). *Winnipeg Free Press*, p. 20.

Rebelsky, F., & Hanks, C. (1971). Fathers' verbal interaction with infants in the first three months of life. *Child Development, 43*, 63–68.

Reinisch, J. (1981). Prenatal exposure to synthetic progestins increases potential for aggression in humans. *Science, 211*, 1171–1173.

Reis, H. T., Wheeler, L., Spiegel, N., Kernis, M. H., Nezlek, J., & Perri, M. (1982). Physical attractiveness in social interaction: II. Why does appearance affect social experience? *Journal of Personality and Social Psychology, 43*, 979–996.

Reis, H. T., & Wright, S. (1982). Knowledge of sex-role stereotypes in children aged 3 to 5. *Sex Roles, 8*, 1049–1056.

Remple, J. K., Holmes, J. G., & Zanna, M. P. (1985). Trust in close relationships. *Journal of Personality and Social Psychology, 49*(1), 95–112.

Rendina, I., & Dickerscheid, J. D. (1976). Father involve-ment with first-born infants. *Family Coordinator, 25*, 373–379.

Rheingold, H., & Cook, K. (1975). The contents of boys' and girls' rooms as an index of parents' behaviors. *Child Development, 46*, 459–463.

Rich, A. (1976). *Of woman born.* New York: W. W. Norton.

Richards, M. H., Gitelson, I. B., Petersen, A. C., & Hurtig, A. L. (1991). Adolescent personality in girls and boys: The role of mothers and fathers. *Psychology of Women Quarterly, 15*, 65–81.

Richards, M. P. M., Dunn, J. F., & Antonis, B. (1977). Caretaking in the first year of life: The role of fathers' and mothers' social isolation. *Child: Care, Health and Development, 3*, 23–26.

Richardson, D., Leonard, K., Taylor, S., & Hammock, G. (1985). Male violence toward females: Victim and aggressor variables. *The Journal of Psychology, 119*(2), 129–135.

Richardson, J. T. (1989). Student learning and the menstrual cycle: Premenstrual symptoms and approaches to studying. *Educational Psychology, 9*(3), 215–238.

Richman, J. A., Raskin, V. D., & Gaines, C. (1991). Gender roles, social support, and post-partum depressive symptomatology. The benefits of caring. *Journal of Nervous and Mental Disorders, 179*(3), 139–147.

Ricketts, M. (1989). Epistemological values of feminists in psychology. *Psychology of Women Quarterly, 13*(4), 401–416.

Ricks, F. A., Pyke, S. W., Ames, E. W., Parry, P., & Duncan, P. (1980). The status of women and men in Canadian psychology academia. *Canadian Psychology, 21*(3), 109–115.

Riddle, D. I., & Sang, B. (1978). Psychotherapy with lesbians. *Journal of Social Issues, 34*(3), 84–100.

Robbins, M. B., & Jensen, G. D. (1977). Multiple orgasm in males. In R. Gemme & C. C. Wheeler (Eds.), *Progress in sexology* (pp. 323–334). New York: Plenum.

Roberto, K. A., & Scott, J. P. (1986). Friendships of older men and women: Exchange patterns and satisfaction. *Psychology and Aging, 1*(2), 103–109.

Roberts, T. (1991). Gender and the influence of evaluations on self-assessments in achievement settings. *Psychological Bulletin, 109*(2), 297–308.

Robinson, G. E., & Garfinkel, P. E. (1990). Problems in the treatment of premenstrual symptoms. *Canadian Journal of Psychiatry, 35*(3), 199–206.

Robinson, J. P., Yerby, J., Fieweger, M., & Somerick, N. (1977). Sex-role differences in time use. *Sex Roles, 3*(3), 443–458.

Rodin, J., & Janis, I. (1979). The social power of health-care practitioners as agents of change. *Journal of Social Issues, 35*(1), 60–81.

Rodin, J., Silberstein, L., & Striegel-Moore, R. (1985). Women and weight: A normative discontent. In T. B. Sonderegger (Ed.), *Psychology and gender: Proceedings of the Nebraska Symposium on Motivation, 1984* (pp. 267–307). Lincoln: University of Nebraska Press.

Rodin, J., & Striegel-Moore, R. H. (1984, September). *Predicting attitudes toward body weight and food intake in women.* Paper presented at the 14th Congress of the European Association of Behavior Therapy, Brussels.

Roe, K. V., Drivas, A., Karagellis, A., & Roe, A. (1985). Sex differences in vocal interaction with mother and stranger in Greek infants: Some cognitive implications. *Developmental Psychology, 21*(2), 373–377.

Romer, N. (1990). Is political activism still a "masculine" endeavor? Gender comparisons among high school political activists. *Psychology of Women Quarterly, 14*(2), 229–244.

Romer, N., & Cherry, D. (1980). Ethnic and social class differences in children's sex-role concepts. *Sex Roles, 6*(2), 245–263.

Rosaldo, M. Z. (1974). Woman, culture and society: A theoretical overview. In M. Z. Rosaldo & L. Lamphere (Eds.), *Woman, culture and society* (pp. 1–16). Stanford, CA: Stanford University Press.

Rose, R. M. (1969). Androgen excretion in stress. In P. G. Bourne (Ed.), *The psychology and physiology of stress* (pp. 117–147). New York: Academic Press.

Rose, S. M. (1985). Same-sex and cross-sex friendships and the psychology of homosociality. *Sex Roles, 12*, 63–74.

Rosen, B., & Jerdee, T. H. (1973). The influence of sex-role stereotypes on evaluations of male and female supervisory behavior. *Journal of Applied Psychology, 57*(1), 44–48.

Rosen, B., & Jerdee, T. H. (1974). Influence of sex role stereotypes on personnel decisions. *Journal of Applied Psychology, 59*, 9–14.

Rosenberg, R. (1982). *Beyond separate spheres: Intellectual origins of modern feminism.* New Haven, CT: Yale University Press.

Rosenkrantz, P. S., Vogel, S. R., Bee, H., Broverman, I. K., & Broverman, D. M. (1968). Sex-role stereotypes and self-concepts in college students. *Journal of Consulting and Clinical Psychology, 32*, 287–295.

Rosenthal, R. (1966). *Experimental effects in behavioral research.* New York: Appleton-Century-Crofts.

Rosenthal, R., Archer, D., DiMatteo, M. R., Kowumaki, J. H., & Rogers, P. O. (1974, September). Body talk and tone of voice: The language without words. *Psychology Today, 8*, 64–68.

Rosenthal, R., & DePaulo, B. M. (1979). Sex differences in eavesdropping on nonverbal cues. *Journal of Personality and Social Psychology, 37*, 273–285.

Rosenthal, R., Persinger, G. W., Mulry, R. C., Vikan-Kline, L., & Grothe, M. (1964). Changes in experimental hypotheses as determinants of experimental results. *Journal of Projective Techniques and Personality Assessment, 28*, 465–469.

Rosenthal, R., & Rubin, D. B. (1982). Further meta-analytic procedures for assessing cognitive gender differences. *Journal of Educational Psychology, 74*, 708–712.

Rosenwasser, S. M., & Dean, N. G. (1989). Gender role and political office: Effects of perceived masculinity/femininity of candidate and political office. *Psychology of Women Quarterly, 13*(1), 77–86.

Rosenweig, S. (1933). The experimental situation as a psychological problem. *Psychological Review, 40*, 337–354.

Rosewater, L. B. (1984). Feminist therapy: Implications for practitioners. In L. Walker (Ed.),

Women and mental health policy (pp. 267–280). Beverly Hills, CA: Sage.

Rosewater, L. B., & Walker, L. E. (Eds.). (1985). *Handbook of feminist therapy: Women's issues in psychotherapy*. New York: Springer.

Ross, S. I., & Jackson, J. M. (1991). Teachers' expectations for Black males' and Black females' academic achievement. *Personality and Social Psychology Bulletin, 17*(1), 78–82.

Rosser, P. (1982, December). Do schools teach computer anxiety? *Ms.*, p. 15.

Rossi, A. S., & Rossi, P. E. (1977). Body time and social time: Mood patterns by menstrual cycle phase and day of week. *Social Science Research, 6,* 273–308.

Rossi, J. D. (1983). Ratios exaggerate gender differences in mathematical ability. *American Psychologist, 38,* 348.

Rothman, B. K. (1982). *In labor: Women and power in the birthplace*. New York: Norton.

Rotkin, K. F. (1972). The phallacy of our sexual norm. *RT: A Journal of Radical Therapy, 3*(11). Reprinted in A. G. Kaplan & J. D. Bean (Eds.), (1976), *Beyond sex-role stereotypes: Readings toward a psychology of androgyny* (pp. 154–162), Boston: Little, Brown.

Rousso, H. (1986, March). Confronting the myth of asexuality: The networking project for disabled women and girls. *SIECUS Report,* pp. 4–6.

Rubenstein, C. (1983). The modern art of courtly love. *Psychology Today, 17*(2), 40–41, 44–49.

Rubin, I. (1965). *Sexual life after sixty*. New York: Basic Books.

Rubin, J., Provenzano, F., & Luria, Z. (1974). The eye of the beholder: Parents' views on sex of newborns. *American Journal of Orthopsychiatry, 44,* 512–519.

Rubin, L. (1976). *Worlds of pain*. New York: Basic Books.

Rubin, L. (1979). *Women of a certain age: The mid-life search for self*. New York: Harper & Row.

Rubin, R. T., Reinisch, J. M., & Haskett, R. F. (1981). Postnatal gonadal steroid effects on human behavior. *Science, 211,* 1318–1324.

Rubin, Z., Peplau, L. A., & Hill, C. T. (1981). Loving and leaving: Sex differences in romantic attachments. *Sex Roles, 7,* 821–835.

Ruble, D. N. (1977). Premenstrual symptoms: A reinterpretation. *Science, 197,* 291–292.

Ruddick, S. (1989). *Maternal thinking: Toward a politics of peace*. New York: Ballantine.

Ruether, R. R. (1983). *Sexism and god-talk. Toward a feminist theology*. Boston: Beacon Press.

Rush, F. (1980). *The best kept secret: Sexual abuse of children*. New York: McGraw-Hill.

Rushton, J. P., Russell, R. J. H., & Wells, P. A. (1984). Genetic similarity theory: Beyond kin selection. *Behavior Genetics, 14*(3), 179–193.

Russell, D. (1975). *The politics of rape: The victim's perspective*. New York: Stein and Day.

Russell, D. (1983a). The incidence and prevalence of intrafamilial and extrafamilial sexual abuse of female children. *Child Abuse and Neglect, 7,* 133–146.

Russell, D. (1983b). *Rape in marriage*. New York: Macmillan.

Russell, D. (1984). *Sexual exploitation: Rape, child sexual abuse and workplace harassment*. Beverly Hills, CA: Sage.

Russell, D., & Howell, N. (1983). The prevalence of rape in the United States revisited. *Signs, 8,* 688–695.

Russell, D., Peplau, L. A., & Cutrona, C. E. (1980). The revised UCLA loneliness scale: Concurrent and discriminant validity evidence. *Journal of Personality and Social Psychology, 39,* 472–480.

Russell, G. (1982). Shared-caregiving families: An Australian study. In M. E. Lamb (Ed.), *Nontraditional families: Parenting and child development*. Hillsdale, NJ: Lawrence Erlbaum Associates.

Russell, S. (1985). Social dimensions of disability: Women with MS. *Resources for Feminist Research, 14*(1), 56–58.

Russo, N. F., Amaro, H., & Winter, M. (1987). The use of inpatient mental health services by Hispanic women. *Psychology of Women Quarterly, 11*(4), 427–441.

Russo, N. F., & Sobel, S. B. (1981). Sex differences in the utilization of mental health facilities. *Professional Psychology, 12,* 7–19.

Ryan, M. (1992, January 5). Don't quit on us. *Parade,* pp. 8–9.

Saal, F. E., Johnson, C. B., & Weber, N. (1989). Friendly or sexy? It may depend on whom you ask. *Psychology of Women Quarterly, 13,* 263–276.

Sadker, M., & Sadker, D. (1985, March). Sexism in the schoolroom of the '80s. *Psychology Today,* pp. 54–57.

Saghir, M. T., & Robins, E. (1973). *Male and female homosexuality*. Baltimore, MD: Williams & Wilkins.

Sales, E., & Frieze, I. H. (1984). Women and work: Implications for mental health policy. In L. E. Walker (Ed.), *Women and mental health policy* (pp. 229–246). Beverly Hills, CA: Sage.

Sampson, G. A. (1979). Premenstrual syndrome: A double-blind controlled trial of progesterone and placebo. *British Journal of Psychiatry, 135,* 209–215.

Sampson, G. A. (1981). An appraisal of the role of progesterone in the therapy of premenstrual syndrome. In P. A. vanKeep & W. H. Utian (Eds.), *The premenstrual syndrome* (pp. 51–69). Lancaster, England: MTP Press.

Sanday, P. R. (1981a). *Female power and male dominance: On the origins of sexual inequality.* Cambridge: Cambridge University Press.

Sanday, P. R. (1981b). The sociocultural context of rape: A cross-cultural study. *Journal of Social Issues, 37,* 5–27.

Sanders, B., & Soares, M. P. (1986). Sexual maturation and spatial ability in college students. *Developmental Psychology, 22*(2), 199–203.

Sanger, M. (1938). *Margaret Sanger: An autobiography.* New York: Dover.

Sapiro, V. (1983). *The political integration of women: Roles, socialization, and politics.* Urbana: University of Illinois Press.

Sapiro, V. (1986). *Women in American society.* Palo Alto, CA: Mayfield.

Sarrel, P., & Masters, W. (1982). Sexual molestation of men by women. *Archives of Sexual Behavior, 11,* 117–132.

Saunders, D. G. (1986). When battered women use violence: Husband-abuse or self-defense? *Victims and Violence, 1,* 47–60.

Scamarella, T. J., & Brown, W. A. (1978). Serum testosterone and aggressiveness in hockey players. *Psychosomatic Medicine, 40,* 262–265.

Scanzoni, J. (1972). *Sexual bargaining: Power politics in the American marriage.* Englewood Cliffs, NJ: Prentice-Hall.

Scarf, M. A. (1979). The more sorrowful sex. *Psychology Today, 12*(11), 44–52, 89–90.

Scarr, S. (1988). How genotypes and environments combine: Development and individual differences. In N. Bolger, A. Caspi, G. Downey, & M. Moorhouse (Eds.), *Persons in context: Developmental processes* (pp. 217–244). Cambridge: Cambridge University Press.

Scarr, S. (1991, February 25). *How genes and environments work together.* Colloquium presentation at Radford University, Radford, VA.

Schacter, S., & Singer, J. E. (1962). Cognitive, social, and physiological determinants of emotional state. *Psychological Review, 69,* 379–399.

Schein, E. H. (1968). Organizational socialization and the profession of management. *Industrial Management Review, 9,* 1–15.

Schmid, R. E. (1984, April 11). Gains seen for women on the job. *Philadelphia Inquirer,* p. 3A.

Schmidt, G., & Sigusch, V. (1970). Sex differences in response to psychosexual stimulation by films and slides. *Journal of Sex Research, 6,* 268–283.

Schneider, F. W., & Coutts, L. M. (1985). Person orientation of male and female high school students: To the educational disadvantage of males? *Sex Roles, 13*(1/2), 47–63.

Schneider, M. S. (1986). The relationships of cohabiting lesbian and heterosexual couples: A comparison. *Psychology of Women Quarterly, 10*(3), 234–239.

Schnellmann, J., & Gibbons, J. L. (1984, August). *The perception by women and minorities of trivial discriminatory actions in the classroom.* Paper presented at the annual meeting of the American Psychological Association, Toronto.

Schofield, M. G. (1965). *Sociological aspects of homosexuality.* London: Longmans, Green.

School rapes common: Head. (1991, July 25). *The News,* (Adelaide, Australia), p. 8.

Schoonmaker, M. E. (1986). The "experts" who want to turn back the clock. *Working Mother, 9*(4), 78–80.

Schubert, J. B., Bradley-Johnson, S., & Nuttal, J. (1980). Mother-infant communication and maternal employment. *Child Development, 51*(1), 246–249.

Schultz, N. R., & Moore, D. (1986). The loneliness experience of college students: Sex differences. *Personality and Social Psychology Bulletin, 12*(1), 111–119.

Schwartz, E., Kofie, V. Y., Rivo, M., & Tuckson, R. V. (1990). Black/white comparisons of deaths preventable by medical intervention: United States and District of Columbia 1980–1986. *International Journal of Epidemiology, 19*(3), 591–598.

Schwartz, J. M., & Abramowitz, S. I. (1975). Value-related effects on psychiatric judgment. *Archives of General Psychiatry, 32*(2), 1525–1529.

Scientists identify sex of 3-day-old embryos. (1990, April 19). *New York Times*, p. B7.

Scott, W. B., & Webster, S. K. (1984, August). *Gender differences in the attributional effect of videotape self-observation.* Paper presented at the annual meeting of the American Psychological Association, Toronto.

Seifert, K. H. (1979). The attitudes of working people toward disabled persons, especially in regard to vocational rehabilitation. *International Journal of Rehabilitation Research*, 2(1), 79–94.

Selgado de Snyder, V. N., Cervantes, R. C., Padilla, A. M. (1990). Gender and ethnic differences in psychosocial stress and generalized distress among Hispanics. *Sex Roles*, 22(7/8), 441–453.

Selkow, P. (1984, August). *Maternal employment: Effects on daughters' and sons' early career aspirations.* Paper presented at the annual meeting of the American Psychological Association, Toronto.

Serbin, L., & O'Leary, K. (1975). How nursery schools teach girls to shut up. *Psychology Today*, 9(7), 56–58ff.

Sewell, W. H., Hauser, R. M., & Wolf, W. C. (1980). Sex, schooling, and occupational success. *American Journal of Sociology*, 86, 551–583.

Shaffer, D. R., Gresham, A., Clary, E. G., & Thielman, T. J. (1986). Sex-ratios as a basis for occupational evaluations: A contemporary view. *Social Behavior and Personality*, 14(1), 77–83.

Shapiro, J. L. (1987, January). The expectant father. *Psychology Today*, 21(1), 36–42.

Sharabany, R., Gershoni, R., & Hofman, J. E. (1981). Girl friend, boy friend: Age and sex differences in development of intimate friendships. *Developmental Psychology*, 17, 800–808.

Sharpe, R. (1992, January/February). Capitol Hill's worst kept secret: Sexual harassment. *Ms.*, 2(4), 28–31.

Sherfey, M. J. (1966). The evolution and nature of female sexuality in relation to psychoanalytic theory. *Journal of the American Psychoanalytic Association*, 14, 28–128.

Sherif, C. W. (1980). A social psychological perspective on the menstrual cycle. In J. E. Parsons (Ed.), *The psychobiology of sex differences and sex roles* (pp. 245–268). Washington, DC: Hemisphere.

Sherman, B. L., & Dominick, J. R. (1986). Violence and sex in music videos: TV and rock'n roll. *Journal of Communication*, 36(1), 79–93.

Sherman, J. A. (1982). Mathematics, the critical filter: A look at some residues. *Psychology of Women Quarterly*, 6, 428–444.

Sherman, J. A., & Fennema, E. (1977). The study of mathematics by high school girls and boys: Related variables. *American Educational Research Journal*, 14, 159–168.

Sherman, J. A., Koufacos, C., & Kenworthy, J. A. (1978). Therapists: Their attitudes and information about women. *Psychology of Women Quarterly*, 2, 299–313.

Sherwin, B. B. (1988). A comparative analysis of the role of androgen in human male and female sexual behavior: Behavioral specificity, critical thresholds, and sensitivity. *Psychobiology*, 16(4), 416–425.

Shields, N. M., & Hanneke, C. R. (1983). Attribution processes in violent relationships: Perceptions of violent husbands and their wives. *Journal of Applied Social Psychology*, 13, 515–527.

Shields, S. A. (1975). Functionalism, Darwinism and the psychology of women: A study in social myth. *American Psychologist*, 30(7), 739–754.

Shields, S. A. (1984). "To pet, coddle, and 'do for'": Caretaking and the concept of maternal instinct. In M. Lewin (Ed.), *In the shadow of the past: Psychology portrays the sexes* (pp. 256–273). New York: Columbia University Press.

Shigetomi, C. C., Hartmann, D. P., & Gilford, D. M. (1981). Sex differences in children's altruistic behavior and reputations for helpfulness. *Developmental Psychology*, 17(4), 434–437.

Shively, M. G., Jones, C., & De Cecco, J. P. (1983/1984). Research on sexual orientation: Definitions and methods. *Journal of Homosexuality*, 9(2/3), 127–136.

Shomer, R. W., & Centers, R. (1970). Differences in attitudinal responses under conditions of implicitly manipulated group salience. *Journal of Personality and Social Psychology*, 15(2), 125–132.

Shortridge, K. (1989). Poverty is a woman's problem. In J. Freeman (Ed.), *Women: A feminist perspective* (pp. 422–501). Palo Alto, CA: Mayfield.

Shusterman, L. R. (1976). The psychosocial factors of the abortion experience: A critical review. *Psychology of Women Quarterly*, 1(1), 79–106.

Sigelman, C. K., Thomas, D. B., Sigelman, L., & Ribich, F. D.

(1986). Gender, physical attractiveness and electability: An experimental investigation of voter bias. *Journal of Applied Social Psychology, 16*(3), 229–248.

Signorella, M. L., & Frieze, I. H. (1989). Gender schemas in college students. *Psychology, 26*(4), 16–23.

Silverman, I. (1979). The experimenter, a (still) neglected stimulus object. *Canadian Psychologist, 15*(3), 257–270.

Silverman, L. K. (1989). It all began with Leta Hollingworth: The story of giftedness in women. *Journal for the Education of the Gifted, 12*(2), 86–98.

Simmons, R. G., Blyth, D. A., Van Cleave, E. F., & Bush, D. M. (1979). Entry into early adolescence: The impact of school structure, puberty, and early dating on self esteem. *American Sociological Review, 44,* 948–967.

Simpson, J. A., Gangestead, S. W., & Lerma, M. (1990). Perception of physical attractiveness: Mechanisms involved in the maintenance of romantic relationships. *Journal of Personality and Social Psychology, 59*(6), 1192–1201.

Sistrunk, F., & McDavid, J. W. (1971). Sex variables in conforming behavior. *Journal of Personality and Social Psychology, 17,* 200–207.

Sivard, R. L. (1985). *Women . . . a world survey.* Washington, DC: World Priorities.

Six, B., & Eckes, T. (1991). A closer look at the complex structure of sex stereotypes. *Sex Roles, 24*(1/2), 57–71.

Skrypnek, B. J., & Snyder, M. (1982). On the self-perpetuating nature of the stereotypes about women and men. *Journal of Experimental Social Psychology, 18,* 277–291.

Slaby, R. G., & Frey, K. S. (1975). Development of gender constancy and selective attention to same-sex models. *Child Development, 46,* 849–856.

Sloane, B. K. (1983, November). In brief. *National NOW Times,* p. 16.

Slocum, W., & Nye, F. (1976). Provider and housekeeper roles. In F. Nye (Ed.), *Role structure and analysis of the family* (pp. 81–100). Beverly Hills, CA: Sage.

Smith, A., & Stewart, A. J. (1983). Approaches to studying racism and sexism in black women's lives. *Journal of Social Issues, 39*(3), 1–15.

Smith, E. J. (1982). The black female adolescent: A review of the educational, career, and psychological literature. *Psychology of Women Quarterly, 6*(3), 261–288.

Smith, J. E., Waldorf, V. A., & Trembath, D. L. (1990). "Single white male looking for thin, very attractive . . . " *Sex Roles, 23*(11/12), 675–685.

Smith, L. (1987, January). *A feminist approach to legal research.* Paper presented at the conference on The Effects of Feminist Approaches on Research Methodologies, Calgary Institute for the Humanities, Calgary, Alberta.

Smith, M. (1980). Sex bias in counseling and psychotherapy. *Psychological Bulletin, 87,* 392–407.

Smith, P. B., Chacko, M. R., & Bermudez, A. (1989). Contraceptive and sexuality knowledge among inner-city middle school students from minority groups. *School Counselor, 37*(2), 103–108.

Smith, P. K., & Daglish, L. (1977). Sex differences in parent and infant behavior in the home. *Child Development, 48,* 1250–1254.

Smith-Rosenberg, C., & Rosenberg, C. (1976). The female animal: Medical and biological views of women. In C. Rosenberg, *No other gods: On science and American social thought* (pp. 54–70). Baltimore, MD: The Johns Hopkins University Press.

Smye, M. D., Wine, J. D., & Moses, B. (1980). Sex differences in assertiveness: Implications for research and treatment. In C. Stark-Adamec (Ed.). *Sex roles: Origins, influences, and implications for women* (pp. 165–175). Montreal: Eden Press Women's Publications.

Snodgrass, S. E. (1985). Women's intuition: The effect of subordinate role upon interpersonal sensitivity. *Journal of Personality and Social Psychology, 49,* 146–155.

Snow, M. E., Jacklin, C. N., & Maccoby, E. E. (1981). Birth-order differences in peer sociability at thirty-three months. *Child Development, 52*(2), 589–595.

Snow, W. G., & Sheese, S. (1985). Lateralized brain damage, intelligence, and memory: A failure to find sex differences. *Journal of Consulting and Clinical Psychology, 33*(6), 940–941.

Sohn, D. (1982). Sex differences in achievement self-attributions: An effect-size analysis. *Sex Roles, 8,* 345–357.

Sommer, B. (1973). The effect of menstruation on cognitive and perceptual-motor behavior: A review. *Psychosomatic Medicine, 35,* 515–534.

Sommer, B. (1975). *Mood and the menstrual cycle*. Paper presented at the annual meeting of the American Psychological Association, Chicago.

Sommer, B. (1983). How does menstruation affect cognitive competence and psychophysiological response? *Women & Health, 8*(2/3), 53–90.

Sommer, B. (1984, August). PMS in the courts: Are all women on trial? *Psychology Today*, pp. 36–38.

Sonkin, D. J., Martin, D., & Walker, L. E. A. (1986). *The male batterer: A treatment approach*. New York: Springer.

Sorenson, R. C. (1973). *Adolescent sexuality in contemporary America*. New York: World.

Spalter-Roth, R., & Hartmann, H. (1990). *Raises and recognition: Secretaries, clerical workers and the union wage premium*. Washington, DC: Institute for Women's Policy Research.

Spence, J. T., & Helmreich, R. L. (1978). *Masculinity and femininity: The psychological dimensions, correlates and antecedents*. Austin: University of Texas Press.

Spence, J. T., Helmreich, R., & Stapp, J. (1974). The personal attributes questionnaire: A measure of sex-role stereotypes and masculinity-femininity (Ms. no. 617). JSAS *Catalog of Selected Documents in Psychology, 4*, 43.

Spence, J. T., & Sawin, L. L. (1985). Images of masculinity and femininity: A reconceptualization. In V. E. O'Leary, R. K. Unger, & B. S. Wallston (Eds.), *Women, gender, and social psychology* (pp. 35–66). Hillsdale, NJ: Lawrence Erlbaum.

Spender, D. (1980). *Man made language*. London: Routledge & Kegan Paul.

Sperling, M. B., & Berman, W. H. (1991). An attachment classification of desperate love. *Journal of Personality Assessment, 56*(1), 45–55.

Sperry, R. (1982). Some effects of disconnecting the cerebral hemispheres. *Science, 217*, 1223–1226.

Spigelman, M., & Schultz, K. (1981, June). *Attitudes toward obesity*. Paper presented at the annual convention of the Canadian Psychological Association, Toronto.

Springer, S. P., & Deutsch, G. (1981). *Left brain, right brain*. San Francisco: W. H. Freeman.

St. Lawrence, J. S., & Joyner, D. J. (1991). The effects of sexually violent rock music on males' acceptance of violence against women. *Psychology of Women Quarterly, 15*(1), 49–64.

Stafford, R. E. (1961). Sex differences in spatial visualization as evidence of sex-linked inheritance. *Perceptual and Motor Skills, 13*, 428.

Stake, J. E. (1985). Exploring the basis of sex differences in third-party allocations. *Journal of Personality and Social Psychology, 48*(6), 1621–1629.

Stallings, J. (1985). School, classroom, and home influences on women's decisions to enroll in advanced mathematics courses. In S. F. Chipman, L. R. Brush, & D. M. Wilson (Eds.), *Women and mathematics: Balancing the equation* (pp. 199–223). Hillsdale, NJ: Lawrence Erlbaum.

Staples, R. (1978). Masculinity and race: The dual dilemma of black men. *Journal of Social Issues, 34*(1), 169–183.

Starhawk. (1979). *The Spiral Dance*. New York: Harper & Row.

Stark, R., & McEvoy, J. (1970). Middle class violence. *Psychology Today, 4*, 107–112.

Stark-Adamec, C., & Kimball, M. (1984). Science free of sexism: A guide to the conduct of non-sexist research. *Canadian Psychology, 25*(1), 23–34.

Stead, B. A. (1983, February). The national secretarial shortage: A management concern. *MSU Business Topics*, pp. 43–47.

Steel, B. S., & Lovrich, N. P. (1987). Comparable worth: The problematic politicization of a public personnel issue. *Public Personnel Management, 16*(1), 23–36.

Stein, A. H. (1971). The effects of sex-role standards for achievement and sex-role preference on three determinants of achievement motivation. *Developmental Psychology, 4*, 219–231.

Stein, A. H., & Bailey, M. M. (1973). The socialization of achievement orientation in females. *Psychological Bulletin, 80*(5), 345–366.

Stein, A. H., Pohly, S. R., & Mueller, E. (1971). The influence of masculine, feminine, and neutral tasks on children's achievement behavior, expectancies of success, and attainment value. *Child Development, 42*, 195–207.

Steinbacher, R., & Gilroy, F. (1990). Sex selection technology: A prediction of its use and effect. *The Journal of Psychology, 124*(3), 283–288.

Steinem, G. (1983). *Outrageous acts and everyday rebellions*. New York: Holt, Rinehart and Winston.

Steiner, M., & Carroll, B. J. (1977). The psychobiology of premenstrual dysphoria: Review of theories and treatments. *Psychoneuroendocrinologica, 2*, 321–335.

Stellman, J. M. (1977). *Women's work, women's health*. New York: Pantheon.

Stellman, J. M. (1978). Forum on women's occupational health: Medical, social and legal implications. Occupational health hazards of women: An overview. *Preventive Medicine*, 7, 281–293.

Sternberg, R. J. (1986). A triangular theory of love. *Psychological Review*, 93, 119–135.

Sternglanz, S. H., & Serbin, L. A. (1974). Sex-role stereotyping in children's television programs. *Developmental Psychology*, 10, 710–715.

Stevens, G. E., & DeNisi, A. S. (1980). Women as managers: Attitudes and attributions for performance by men and women. *Academy of Management Journal*, 23(2), 355–360.

Stevenson, H. W., Lee, S., & Stigler, J. (1986, February 14). Mathematics achievement of Chinese, Japanese, and American children. *Science*, pp. 693–699.

Stewart, A., & Salt, P. (1981). Life stress, life-styles, depression and illness in adult women. *Journal of Personality and Social Psychology*, 40(6), 1063–1069.

Stewart, A. J., & Winter, D. G. (1976). Arousal of the power motive in women. *Journal of Consulting and Clinical Psychology*, 44(3), 495–496.

Stewart, D. E. (1989). Positive changes in the premenstrual period. *Acta Psychiatrica Scandinavica*, 79(4), 400–405.

Stigma of unmarried mother fading fast, figures reveal. (1991, September 18). *The Guardian*, p. 4.

Stiller, N. J., & Forrest, L. (1990). An extension of Gilligan and Lyon's investigation of morality: Gender differences in college students. *Journal of College Student Development*, 31(1), 54–63.

Stockard, J., & Johnson, M. (1979). The social origins of male dominance. *Sex Roles*, 5(2), 199–218.

Stockard, J., Schmuck, P. A., Kempner, K., Williams, P., Edson, S. K., & Smith, M. A. (1980). *Sex equity in education*. New York: Academic Press.

Stone, L. (1885, October 17–18). Disappointment is the lot of women [Speech]. Quoted in E. Parnow (Ed.), *The quotable woman* (Vol. 1, p. 84), Los Angeles: Pinnacle Books.

Storms, M. D. (1973). Videotape and the attribution process: Reversing actors' and observers' points of view. *Journal of Personality and Social Psychology*, 27, 165–175.

Storms, M. D. (1980). Theories of sexual orientation. *Journal of Personality and Social Psychology*, 38, 783–792.

Straus, M. A., Gelles, R. J., & Steinmetz, S. K. (1980). *Behind closed doors: Violence in the American family*. Garden City NY: Doubleday.

Streicher, H. W. (1974). The girls in the cartoons. *Journal of Communications*, 24(2), 125–129.

Strommen, E. A. (1977). Friendship. In E. Donelson & J. Gullahorn (Eds.), *Women: A psychological perspective* (pp. 154–167). New York: Wiley.

Stuenkel, C. A. (1989). Menopause and estrogen replacement therapy. *Psychiatric Clinics of North America*, 12(1), 133–152.

Stuntzner, G. D. (1991). Women and HIV disease: An emerging social crisis. *Social Work*, 36(1), 22–28.

Sulloway, F. J. (1979). *Freud, biologist of the mind*. New York: Basic Books.

Summers, T. P. (1988). Examination of sex differences in expectations of pay and perceptions of equity in pay. *Psychological Reports*, 62(2), 491–496.

Sun, S. W., & Lull, J. (1986). The adolescent audience for music videos and why they watch. *Journal of Communication*, 29(1), 116–124.

Super, C. M. (1976). Environmental effects on motor development: The case of "African infant precocity." *Developmental and Medical Child Neurology*, 18, 561–567.

Super, D. L. (1951). Vocational adjustment: Implementing a self concept. *Occupations*, 30, 88–92.

Suplee, C. (1991, August 30). Brain may dictate sexuality. *The Washington Post*, pp. A1, A13.

Supreme Court delivers mixed decisions on key cases. (1984, May). *NEA Today*, 2(7), 23.

A surgeon cuts to the heart of the matter. (1991, October 28). *People*, p. 50.

Surrey, J. L., Scott, L., & Phillips, E. L. (1975). Menstrual cycle and the decision to seek psychological services. *Perceptual and Motor Skills*, 40, 886.

Susman, E. J., Inoff-Germain, G., Nottlemann, E. D., Loriaux, D. L., Cutler, G. B., & Chrousos, G. P. (1987). Hormones, emotional dispositions, and aggressive attributes in young adolescents. *Child Development*, 58, 1114–1134.

Swaab, D. F., & Hofman, M. A. (1988). Sexual differentiation of the human hypothalamus: Ontogeny of the sexually dimorphic nucleus of the preoptic area. *Developmental Brain Research*, 44(2), 314–318.

Swardson, A. (1991, June 18). Women and the sporting life. *The Washington Post*, p. D3.

Swartzman, L. C., Edelberg, R., & Kemmann, E. (1990). The menopausal hot flush: Symptom reports and concomitant physiological changes. *Journal of Behavioral Medicine*, 13(1), 15–30.

Sweeney, J., & Bradbard, M. R. (1989). Mothers' and fathers' changing perceptions of their male and female infants over the course of pregnancy. *Journal of Genetic Psychology*, 149(3), 393–404.

Symons, D. (1979). *The evolution of human sexuality*. Oxford: Oxford University Press.

Szymanski, L. A., & Chrisler, J. C. (1990/1991). Eating disorders, gender-role, and athletic activity. *Psychology*, 27(4) & 28(1), 20–29.

Tamir, L. M. (1982). *Men in their forties: The transition to middle age*. New York: Springer.

The Tampax Report. (1981). (Available from Ruder, Finn & Rotman, 110 E. 59th Street, New York, NY 10022)

Tangri, S., Burt, M. R., & Johnson, L. B. (1982). Sexual harassment at work: Three explanatory models. *Journal of Social Issues*, 38(4), 33–54.

Tauber, M. A. (1979). Parental socialization techniques and sex differences in children's play. *Child Development*, 50, 225–234.

Taylor, S. E., & Langer, E. J. (1977). Pregnancy: A social stigma? *Sex Roles*, 3, 27–35.

Teahan, J. E. (1974). The effect of sex and predominant socioeconomic class school climate on expectations of success among black students. *Journal of Negro Education*, 43, 245–255.

Tennov, D. (1975). *Psychotherapy: The hazardous cure*. New York: Abelard-Schuman.

Teri, L. (1982). Effects of sex and sex-role style on clinical judgement. *Sex Roles*, 8, 639–649.

Terman, L. M. (1925). *Genetic studies of genius: Vol. 1. Mental and physical traits of a thousand gifted children*. Stanford, CA: Stanford University Press.

Terman, L. M. (1951). Correlates of orgasm adequacy in a group of 556 wives. *Journal of Psychology*, 32, 115–172.

Terman, L. M., & Miles, C. C. (1936). *Sex and personality, Studies in masculinity and femininity*. New York: McGraw-Hill.

Terman, L. M., & Oden, M. (1947). *The gifted child grows up*. Stanford, CA: Stanford University Press.

Terman, L. M., & Oden, M. (1959). *The gifted group at midlife*. Stanford, CA: Stanford University Press.

Terrelonge, P. (1989). Feminist consciousness and Black women. In J. Freeman (Ed.), *Women: A feminist perspective* (4th ed., pp. 556–566). Mountain View, CA: Mayfield.

Tersman, Z., Collins, A., & Eneroth, P. (1991). Cardiovascular responses to psychological and physiological stressors during the menstrual cycle. *Psychosomatic Medicine*, 53(2), 185–197.

Testa, R. J., Kinder, B. N., & Ironson, G. (1987). Homosexual bias in the perception of loving relationships of gay males and lesbians. *Journal of Sex Research*, 23(2), 163–172.

Thibaut, J., & Kelley, H. (1959). *The social psychology of groups*. New York: Wiley.

Thoma, S. J. (1986). Estimating gender differences in the comprehension and preference of moral issues. *Developmental Review*, 6(2), 165–180.

Thomas, J. R., & French, K. E. (1985). Gender differences across age in motor performance: A meta-analysis. *Psychological Bulletin*, 98, 260–282.

Thomas, V. G. (1989). Body-image satisfaction among black women. *The Journal of Social Psychology*, 129(1), 107–112.

Thomas, V. L. (1989). Black women engineers and technologists. *Sage: A Scholarly Journal on Black Women*, 6(2), 24–32.

Thompson, A. P. (1983). Extramarital sex: A review of the research literature. *Journal of Sex Research*, 19, 1–22.

Thompson (Woolley), H. B. (1903). *The mental traits of sex: An experimental investigation of the normal mind in men and women*. Chicago: University of Chicago Press.

Thompson, T. (1985, November). Advertising's not-so-subtle sexism. *Report on Business Magazine*, pp. 106–108.

Thorndike, E. L. (1910). *Educational psychology* (2d ed.). New York: Columbia University, Teacher's College.

Thurer, S. L. (1982). Women and rehabilitation. *Rehabilitation Literature*, 43(7–8), 194–197, 207.

Tieger, T. (1980). On the biological basis of sex differences in aggression. *Child Development*, 51, 943–963.

Tiger, L. (1969). *Men in groups*. New York: Random House.

Tinsley, E. G., Sullivan-Guest, S., & McGuire, J. (1984). Feminine sex role and depression in middle-aged women. *Sex Roles*, 11, 25–32.

Title IX cited for fivefold increase in girls playing high school sports. (1987, June 17). *Arizona Daily Star*, p. 9C.

Tobias, S. (1982, January). Sexist equations. *Psychology Today*, pp. 14–17.

Tobin, S. M. (1957). Emotional depression during pregnancy. *Obstetrics & Gynecology, 10,* 677.

Tomlinson-Keasey, C. (1990). The working lives of Terman's gifted women. In H. Y. Grossman & N. L. Chester (Eds.), *The experience and meaning of work in women's lives* (pp. 213–240). Hillsdale, NJ: Lawrence Erlbaum Associates.

Tonkinson, R. (1974). *The Jigalong Mob: Aboriginal victors of the desert crusade*. Menlo Park, CA: Cummings.

Top, T. J. (1991). Sex bias in the evaluation of performance in the scientific, artistic, and literary professions: A review. *Sex Roles, 24*(1/2), 73–106.

Tosi, H. L., & Einbender, S. W. (1985). The effects of the type and amount of information in sex discrimination research: A meta-analysis. *Academy of Management Journal, 28,* 712–723.

Touhey, J. C. (1974). Effects of additional women professionals on ratings of occupational prestige and desirability. *Journal of Personality and Social Psychology, 29,* 86–89.

Towson, S. M. J., MacDonald, G., & Zanna, M. P. (1981, June). *Confirming sex-role stereotypes in the job interview: Payoffs and pitfalls*. Paper presented at the annual convention of the Canadian Psychological Association, Montreal.

Trahan, D. E., & Quintana, J. W. (1990). Analysis of gender effects upon verbal and visual memory performance in adults.

Archives of Clinical Neuropsychology, 5, 325–334.

Travis, C. B., Phillippi, R. H., & Henley, T. B. (1991). Gender and causal attributions for mastery, personal, and interpersonal events. *Psychology of Women Quarterly, 15,* 233–249.

Treiman, D. J. (1985). The work histories of women and men: What we know and what we need to find out. In A. S. Rossi (Ed.), *Gender and the life course* (pp. 213–232). New York: Aldine.

Trepanier, M. L., & Romatowski, J. A. (1985). Attributes and roles assigned to characters in children's writing: Sex differences and sex-role perceptions. *Sex Roles, 13*(5/6), 263–272.

Trescott, J. (1991, August 17). Anthology of a mother's grief. *The Washington Post*, pp. C1, C5.

Tresmer, D. (1976). Do women fear success? *Signs, 1*(4), 863–874.

Trethowan, W. H. (1972). The Couvade syndrome. In J. G. Howells (Ed.), *Modern perspectives in psycho-obstetrics* (pp. 68–93). New York: Brunner/Mazel.

Trotter, R. J. (1987). Mathematics: A male advantage? *Psychology Today, 21*(1), 66–67.

Tuck, R. (1975). The relationship between a mother's menstrual status and her response to illness in her child. *Psychosomatic Medicine, 37,* 388–394.

Tucker, L. A. (1982). Relationship between perceived somatotype and body cathexis of college males. *Psychological Reports, 50,* 1055–1061.

Tuli, M. R. (1982). Sex and regional differences in mathematical creativity. *Indian Educational Review, 17*(3), 128–134.

Turell, S. C., Armsworth, M. W., & Gaa, J. P. (1990). Emotional responses to abortion: A critical review of the literature. *Women and Therapy, 9*(4), 49–68.

Tyler, L. (1965). *The psychology of human differences*. New York: Appleton-Century-Crofts. (Original work published 1947)

Tyler, L., & Phillips, S. (1984, November). *Women and sports*. Presentation at the annual conference of the Canadian Research Institute for the Advancement of Women, Montreal.

Unger, R. (1979). Toward a redefinition of sex and gender. *American Psychologist, 34,* 1085–1094.

Unger, R. K., & Sussman, L. E. (1986). "I and thou": Another barrier to societal change? *Sex Roles, 14*(11/12), 629–636.

U.S. Department of Commerce, Bureau of the Census. (1982). *Statistical abstract of the United States, 1982–1983* (103rd ed.). Washington, DC: U.S. Government Printing Office.

U.S. Department of Commerce, Bureau of the Census. (1984). *Statistical abstract of the United States, 1984*. Washington, DC: U.S. Government Printing Office.

U.S. Department of Commerce, Bureau of the Census. (1990). *Statistical abstract of the United States, 1990*. Washington, DC: U.S. Government Printing Office.

U.S. Department of Commerce, Bureau of the Census. (1991). *Statistical abstract of the United States, 1991*. Washington DC: U.S. Government Printing Office.

U.S. Department of Health and Human Services. (1987). *1986 annual cancer statistics review.* Bethesda, MD: National Institutes of Health.

U.S. Department of Health and Human Services. (1988). *National household survey on drug abuse: Main findings 1988.* Bethesda, MD: Alcohol, Drug Abuse and Mental Health Administration.

U.S. Equal Opportunity Commission. (1980). Guidelines on discrimination because of sex. *Federal Register, 45*(219), 74676–74677.

U.S. Merit Systems Protection Board. (1981). *Sexual harassment in the federal workplace: Is it a problem?*, Washington, DC: U. S. Government Printing Office.

Urberg, K. A. (1982). The development of the concepts of masculinity and femininity in young children. *Sex Roles, 8,* 659–668.

Utne, M. K., Hatfield, E., Traupmann, J., & Greenberger, D. (1984). Equity, marital satisfaction, and stability. *Journal of Social and Personal Relationships, 1,* 323–332.

Valois, R. F., & Waring, K. A. (1991). An analysis of college students' anonymous questions about human sexuality. *Journal of American College Health, 39*(6), 263–268.

Vance, E. B., & Wagner, N. N. (1976). Written descriptions of orgasm: A study of sex differences. *Archives of Sexual Behavior, 5,* 87–98.

Van Gelder, L. (1985). The strange case of the electronic lover: A real-life story of deception, seduction, and technology. *Ms., 14*(4), 94–95, 99, 101–104, 117, 123–124.

Van Gelder, L. (1991, March/April). A lesbian family revisited. *Ms., 1*(5), 44–47.

Van Preagh, P. (1982). The Hamilton birth control clinic: In response to need. *News/Nouvelles, Journal of the Planned Parenthood Federation of Canada, 3*(1), 2.

Ventura, S. J., Taffel, S., & Mosher, W. D. (1985). Estimates of pregnancies and pregnancy rates for the U.S., 1976–1981. *Public Health Reports, 100*(1), 31–34.

Verbrugge, L. (1979). Female illness rates and illness behavior: Testing hypotheses about sex differences in health. *Women & Health, 4,* 61–79.

Verbrugge, L. (1982a). Sex differences in legal drug use. *Journal of Social Issues, 38*(2), 59–76.

Verbrugge, L. (1982b). Work satisfaction and physical health. *Journal of Community Health, 7*(4), 262–282.

Verbrugge, L. (1983, March). Multiple roles and physical health of women and men. *Journal of Health and Social Behavior, 24,* 16–30.

Verbrugge, L., & Madans, J. H. (1985, March). Women's roles and health. *American Demographics, 7*(3), 36–39.

Veroff, J., Douvan, E., & Kulka, A. (1981). *The inner American: A self-portrait from 1957–1976.* New York: Basic Books.

Vetter, B. M., & Babco, E. L. (1984). Women and minorities continue to grow in workplace. *Science, 226*(4671), 159.

Vetter, L., & Hickey, D. R. (1985, October). Women in vocational education: Changes since Title IX. *Vocational Education Journal, 60,* 26–29.

Villardita, C., Smirni, P., LePira, F., & Zappala, G. (1981). Verbal, visual, and spatial learning in adolescence: Sex differences. *Italian Journal of Psychology, 8,* 81–85.

Voda, A. M., & Eliasson, M. (1983). Menopause: The closure of menstrual life. *Women & Health, 8*(2/3), 137–156.

Vollmer, F. (1984). Sex differences in personality and expectancy. *Sex Roles, 11,* 1121–1139.

von Baeyer, C. L., Sherk, D. L., & Zanna, M. P. (1981). Impression management in the job interview. When the female applicant meets the male "chauvinist" interviewer. *Personality and Social Psychology Bulletin, 7,* 45–51.

Vrbancic, M. I., & Mosley, J. L. (1988). Sex-related differences in hemispheric lateralization: A function of physical maturation. *Developmental Neuropsychology, 4*(2), 151–167.

Waber, D. (1977). Sex differences in mental abilities, hemispheric lateralization, and rate of physical growth at adolescence. *Developmental Psychology, 13,* 29–38.

Waber, D. P., Bauermeister, M., Cohen, C., Ferber, R., & Wolff, P. H. (1981). Behavioral correlates of physical and neuromotor maturity in adolescents from different environments. *Developmental Psychobiology, 14,* 513–522.

Waber, D. P., Mann, M. B., Merola, J., & Moylan, P. M. (1985). Physical maturation rate and cognitive performance in early adolescence: A longitudinal examination. *Developmental Psychology, 21*(4), 666–681.

Wada, J. A., Clark, R., & Hamm, A. (1975). Cerebral hemisphere asymmetry in humans. *Archives of Neurology, 32,* 239–246.

Wade, R. (1978). *For men, about abortion.* (Available from Roger C. Wade, P.O. Box 4748, Boulder, CO, 80306)

Waldron, I. (1976). Why do women live longer than men? *Social Science and Medicine, 10,* 349–362.

Waldron, I. (1978). Type A behavior pattern and coronary heart disease in men and women. *Social Science and Medicine, 12,* 167–170.

Waldron, I. (1983). Employment and women's health: An analysis of causal relationships. In E. Fee (Ed.), *Women and health: The politics of sex and medicine* (pp. 119–138). Farmingdale, NY: Baywood.

Waldron, I., & Herold, J. (1984, May). *Employment, attitudes toward employment, and women's health.* Paper presented at the meeting of the Society for Behavioral Medicine, Philadelphia.

Walker, E., Bettes, B. A., Kain, E. L., & Harvey, P. (1985). Relationship of gender and marital status with symptomatology in psychotic patients. *Journal of Abnormal Psychology, 94,* 42–50.

Walker, L. E. (1979). *The battered woman.* New York: Harper & Row.

Walker, L. E. (1984a). *The battered woman syndrome.* New York: Springer.

Walker, L. E. (1984b). Introduction. In L. E. Walker (Ed.), *Women and mental health policy* (pp. 7–19). Beverly Hills, CA: Sage.

Walker, L. J. (1984). Sex differences in the development of moral reasoning: A critical review. *Child Development, 55,* 677–691.

Walker, L. J. (1989). A longitudinal study of moral reasoning. *Child Development, 60,* 157–166.

Walker, L. O., & Best, M. A. (1991). Well-being of mothers with infant children: A preliminary comparison of employed women and homemakers. *Women & Health, 17*(1), 71–89.

Wallen, J., Waitzkin, H., & Stoeckle, J. D. (1979). Physician stereotypes about female health and illness: A study of patients' sex and the informative process during medical interviews. *Women & Health, 4,* 135–146.

Wallston, B. S., DeVellis, B. M., & Wallston, K. (1983). Licensed practical nurses' sex role stereotypes. *Psychology of Women Quarterly, 7,* 199–208.

Walsh, R. H., Ferrell, M. L., & Tolone, W. L. (1976). Selection of reference groups, perceived reference group permissiveness, and personal permissiveness attitudes and behavior: A study of two consecutive panels (1967–1971; 1970–1974). *Journal of Marriage and the Family, 38,* 495–507.

Walshok, M. L. (1981). *Blue-collar women: Pioneers on the male frontiers.* Garden City, NY: Doubleday.

Walster, E. (1974). Passionate love. In Z. Rubin (Ed.), *Doing unto others* (pp. 150–162). Englewood Cliffs, NJ: Prentice-Hall.

Walster, E., Berscheid, E., & Walster, G. W. (1973). New directions in equity research. *Journal of Personality and Social Psychology, 25,* 151–176.

Walster, E., & Walster, G. W. (1975). Equity and social justice. *Journal of Social Issues, 31*(3), 21–43.

Wand, B. (Ed.). (1977). Report of the task force on the status of women in Canadian psychology [entire issue]. *Canadian Psychological Review, 18*(1).

Wardle, M. G. (1976). Women's physiological reactions to physically demanding work. *Psychology of Women Quarterly, 1*(2), 151–159.

Washington, V. (1982). Racial differences in teacher perceptions of first and fourth grade pupils on selected characteristics. *Journal of Negro Education, 51,* 60–72.

Watts-Jones, D. (1990). Toward a stress scale for African-American women. *Psychology of Women Quarterly, 14*(2), 271–276.

Webb, N. M., & Kenderski, C. M. (1985). Gender differences in small-group interaction and achievement in high- and low-achieving classes. In L. C. Wilkinson & C. B. Marrett (Eds.), *Gender influences in classroom interactions* (pp. 209–236). Orlando, FL: Academic Press.

Weber, M. (1965). *The protestant ethic and the spirit of capitalism.* London: Unwin.

Weber, R., & Crocker, J. (1983). Cognitive processes in the revision of stereotypic beliefs. *Journal of Personality and Social Psychology, 45,* 961–977.

Weideger, P. (1977). *Menstruation and menopause.* New York: Dell.

Weidner, G., & Helmig, L. (1990). Cardiovascular stress reactivity and mood during the menstrual cycle. *Women and Health, 16*(3/4), 5–21.

Weiner, B., Frieze, I. H., Kukla, A., Reed, L., Rest, S., & Rosenbaum, R. M. (1971). *Perceiving the causes of success and failure.* Morristown, NJ: General Learning.

Weinstein, S., & Sersen, E. A. (1961). Tactual sensitivity as a function of handedness and laterality. *Journal of Comparative and Physiological Psychology, 54,* 665–669.

Weis, D. L. (1983). Affective reactions of women to their initial experiences of coitus. *Journal of Sex Research, 19,* 209–237.

Weisberg, D. K. (Ed.). (1982). *Women and the law: The social historical perspective: Vol. 1. Women and the criminal law.* Cambridge, MA: Schenkman.

Weiss, R. S. (1973). *Loneliness: The experience of emotional and social isolation.* Cambridge, MA: MIT Press.

Weissman, M., & Klerman, G. (1977). Sex differences and the epidemiology of depression. *Archives of General Psychiatry, 34,* 98–111.

Weisstein, N. (1971). *Psychology constructs the female or, the fantasy life of the male psychologist.* Boston: New England Free Press.

Weitz, R. (1989). What price independence? Social reactions to lesbians, spinsters, widows, and nuns. In J. Freeman (Ed.), *Women: A feminist perspective* (pp. 446–456). Mountain View, CA: Mayfield.

Weitz, S. (1976). Sex differences in nonverbal communication. *Sex Roles, 2*(2), 175–184.

Weitzman, L. (1975). Sex-role socialization. In J. Freeman (Ed.), *Women: A feminist perspective* (pp. 105–144). Palo Alto, CA: Mayfield.

Weitzman, L., Eifler, D., Hokada, E., & Ross, C. (1972). Sex role socialization in picture books for preschool children. *American Journal of Sociology, 77,* 1125–1150.

Weitzman, N., Birns, B., & Friend, R. (1985). Traditional and nontraditional mothers' communication with their daughters and sons. *Child Development, 56,* 894–898.

Welch, R., Huston-Stein, A. C., Wright, J. C., & Plehal, R. (1979). Subtle sex-role cues in children's commercials. *Journal of Communication, 29,* 202–209.

Welch, S., & Sigelman, L. (1982). Changes in public attitudes toward women and politics. *Social Science Quarterly, 63,* 312–322.

Wentworth, D. K., & Anderson, L. R. (1984). Emergent leadership as a function of sex and task type. *Sex Roles, 11,* 513–524.

Wergers, R. M., & Frieze, I. H. (1977). Gender, female traditionality, achievement level and cognitions of success and failure. *Psychology of Women Quarterly, 2,* 125–137.

Westkott, M. (1986). *The feminist legacy of Karen Horney.* New Haven, CT: Yale University Press.

Westoff, C. (1974). Coital frequency and contraception. *Family Planning Perspectives, 6*(3), 136–141.

Weston, J. (1986). Incentive program gives equity a boost. *University Affairs, 27*(6), 3–4, 12.

Weyant, R. G. (1979). The relationship between psychology and women. *International Journal of Women's Studies, 2*(4), 358–385.

Wheeler, A., Lee, E. S., & Loe, H. (1983). Employment, sense of well-being, and use of professional services among women. *American Journal of Public Health, 73*(8), 908–911.

Wheeless, V. E., & Berryman-Fink, C. (1985). Perceptions of women managers and their communicator competencies. *Communication Quarterly, 33*(2), 137–148.

Whitbeck, C. (1976). Theories of sex difference. In C. C. Gould & M. W. Wartofsky (Eds.), *Women and philosophy: Toward a theory of liberation* (pp. 54–80). New York: G. P. Putnam's Sons.

White, J. (1980). *Women and unions.* Ottawa: Canadian Advisory Council on the Status of Women.

White, J. W. (1983). Sex and gender issues in aggression research. In R. G. Geen & E. I. Donnerstein (Eds.), *Aggression: Theoretical and empirical reviews: Vol. 2. Issues in research.* New York: Academic Press.

White, J. W. (1988). Influence tactics as a function of gender, insult, and goal. *Sex Roles, 18,* 433–448.

White, J. W., & Roufail, M. (1989). Gender and influence strategies of first choice and last resort. *Psychology of Women Quarterly, 13*(2), 175–189.

White, K. M., Speisman, J. C., Jackson, D., Bartis, S., & Costos, D. (1986). Intimacy maturity and its correlates in young married couples. *Journal of Personality and Social Psychology, 50*(1), 152–162.

White, L., & Brinkerhoff, D. (1981). The sexual division of labor: Evidence from childhood. *Social Forces, 60,* 170–181.

Whitehead, T. (1981). Sex hormone treatment of prisoners. In P. Brain & D. Benton (Eds.), *Multidisciplinary approaches to aggression research* (pp. 503–511). Amsterdam: Elsevier.

Whiting, B., & Edwards, C. P. (1973). A cross-cultural analysis of sex differences in the behavior of children aged three through eleven. *Journal of Social Psychology, 91* (second half), 171–188.

Wiersma, U. J. (1990). Gender differences in job attribute preferences: Work-home role conflict and job level as mediating variables. *Journal of Occupational Psychology, 63,* 231–243.

Wiggins, J. S., & Holzmuller, A. (1981). Further evidence on androgyny and interpersonal flexibility. *Journal of Research in Personality, 15,* 67–80.

Wikan, U. (1977). Man becomes woman: Transsexualism in Oman as a key to gender roles. *Man, 12,* 304–319.

Wilbur, J., Dan, A., Hedricks, C., & Holm, K. (1990). The relationship among menopausal status, menopausal symptoms, and physical activity in midlife women. *Family and Community Health, 13*(3), 67–78.

Wilder, G., Mackie, D., & Cooper, J. (1985). Gender and computers: Two surveys of computer-related attitudes. *Sex Roles, 13*(3/4) 215–228.

Wiley, M. G., & Eskilson, A. (1990). What price success? Evaluations of male and female managers. *Sociological Focus, 23*(2), 115–127.

Wilkinson, D. Y. (1984). Afro-American women and their families. *Marriage and Family Review, 7*(3/4), 125–142.

Wilkinson, L. C., Lindow, J., & Chiang, C. P. (1985). Sex differences and sex segregation in students' small-group communication. In L. C. Wilkinson & C. B. Marrett (Eds.), *Gender influences in classroom interaction* (pp. 185–207). Orlando, FL: Academic Press.

Will, J., Self, P., & Datan, N. (1976). Maternal behavior and perceived sex of infant. *Ameri-*

can *Journal of Orthopsychiatry, 46,* 135–139.

Williams, D. A., & King, P. (1980, December 15). Do males have a math gene? *Newsweek,* p. 73.

Williams, J. B., & Spitzer, R. L. (1983). The issue of sex bias in DSM-III. *American Psychologist, 38,* 793–798.

Williams, J. E., & Bennett, S. M. (1975). The definition of sex stereotypes via the adjective check list. *Sex Roles, 1,* 327–337.

Williams, J. E., & Best, D. L. (1982). *Measuring sex stereotypes: A thirty nation study.* Beverly Hills, CA: Sage.

Williams, L. R. (1983). Beliefs and attitudes of young girls regarding menstruation. In S. Golub (Ed.), *Menarche.* Lexington, MA: D. C. Heath.

Willis, S. L., & Schaie, K. W. (1988). Gender differences in spatial ability in old age: Longitudinal and intervention findings. *Sex Roles, 18*(3/4), 189–203.

Wilmore, J. H. (1974). Alterations in strength, body composition and anthropometric measurements consequent to a 10-week weight training program. *Medicine and Science in Sports, 6,* 133–138.

Wilmore, J. H. (1975). Inferiority of female athletes, myth or reality? *Journal of Sports Medicine, 3,* 1–6.

Wilson, E. O. (1975). *Sociobiology: The new synthesis.* Cambridge, MA: Harvard University Press.

Win-O'Brien, M. (1980). Law in conflict: Another view. *Journal of Occupational Medicine, 22*(8), 509–510.

Winter, D. G. (1973). *The power motive.* New York: Free Press.

Winter, D. G., & Barenbaum,

N. B. (1985). Responsibility and the power motive in women and men. *Journal of Personality, 53*(2), 335–355.

Winter, D. G., & Stewart, A. J. (1978). Power motivation. In H. London & J. Exner (Eds.), *Dimensions of personality* (pp. 391–448). New York: Wiley.

Witkin, H. A., Mednick, S. A., Schulsinger, F., Bakkestrom, E., Christiansen, K. O., Goodenough, D. R., Hirschhorn, K., Lundsteen, C., Owen, D. R., Philip, J., Rubin, D. B., & Stocking, M. (1976). Criminality in XYY and XXY men. *Science, 193,* 547–555.

Wittig, M. A. (1979). Genetic influences of sex-related differences in intellectual performance: Theoretical and methodological issues. In M. A. Wittig & A. C. Petersen (Eds.), *Sex-related differences in cognitive functioning: Developmental issues* (pp. 21–66). New York: Academic Press.

Wittig, M. A. (1985). Metatheoretical dilemmas in the psychology of gender. *American Psychologist, 40*(7), 800–811.

Wolfson, S. L. (1981). Sex, dependency and volunteering. *British Journal of Social Psychology, 20,* 293–294.

Women and minorities continue to grow in workplace. (1984). *Science, 266*(4671), 159.

Women clerics find sexual harassment (1990, December 1). *The Washington Post,* p. C12.

Women on Words and Images. (1975). *Dick and Jane as victims: Sex stereotyping in children's readers* (expanded ed.) Princeton, NJ: Author.

Women's intuition linked to thicker nerves in brain. (1986, July 24). *Winnipeg Free Press,* p. 34.

Wong, M. W., & Csikszentmi-halyi, M. (1991). Affiliation motivation and daily experience: Some issues on gender differences. *Journal of Personality and Social Psychology, 60*(1), 154–164.

Wong, P. T. P., Kettlewell, G., & Sproule, C. F. (1985). On the importance of being masculine: Sex role, attribution, and women's career achievement. *Sex Roles, 12,* 757–769.

Wood, W., Rhodes, N., & Whelan, M. (1989). Sex differences in positive well-being: A consideration of emotional style and marital status. *Psychological Bulletin, 106*(2), 249–264.

Woods, N. F. (1981). Women and their health. In C. I. Fogel & N. F. Woods (Eds.), *Health care of women: A nursing perspective* (pp. 3–26). St Louis: C. V. Mosby.

Wooley, S. C., & Wooley, O. W. (1985). Intensive outpatient and residential treatment for bulimia. In D. M. Garner & P. E. Garfinkel (Eds.), *Handbook of psychotherapy for anorexia and bulimia* (pp. 391–430). New York: Guilford.

Woolf, V. (1929/1957). *A room of one's own.* New York: Harcourt, Brace & World.

Wu, J. H., & Eichmann, M. A. (1988). Fetal sex identification and prenatal bonding. *Psychological Reports, 63*(1), 199–202.

Yalom, I., Green, R., & Fisk, N. (1973). Prenatal exposures to female hormones: Effect on psychosexual development in boys. *Archives of General Psychiatry, 28,* 554–561.

Yanico, B. J. (1978). Sex bias in career information: Effects of language on attitudes. *Journal of Vocational Behavior, 13,* 26–37.

Yankelovich, D. (1974). The meaning of work. In J. Rosow (Ed.), *The worker and the job* (pp. 19–48). Englewood Cliffs, NJ: Prentice-Hall.

Yee, D. K., & Eccles, J. S. (1988). Parent perceptions and attributions for children's math achievement. *Sex Roles, 19*(5/6), 317–333.

Yengoyan, A. (1982, Spring). Transvestitism and the ideology of gender. *Newsletter of the Committee for Gender Research* (no. 1), pp. 1, 3, 6–7.

Yoder, J. D., & Sinnett, L. M. (1985). Is it all in the numbers? A case study of tokenism. *Psychology of Women Quarterly, 9*(3), 413–418.

Zaner, A. R., Levee, R. F., & Gunta, R. R. (1968). The development of auditory perceptual skills as a function of maturation. *Journal of Auditory Research, 8,* 313–322.

Zanna, M., & Bowden, M. (1977, June). *Influence of interpersonal relationships on justice.* Paper presented at the annual convention of the Canadian Psychological Association, Vancouver.

Zanna, M., Crosby, F., & Loewenstein, G. (1987). Male reference groups and discontent among female professionals. In B. A. Gutek & L. Larwood (Eds.), *Women's career development* (pp. 18–41). Beverly Hills, CA: Sage.

Zanna, M. P., & Pack, S. J. (1975). On the self-fulfilling nature of apparent sex differences in behavior. *Journal of Experimental Social Psychology, 11,* 583–591.

Zarbatany, L., Hartmann, D. P., Gelfand, D. M., & Vinciguerra, P. (1985). Gender differences in altruistic reputation: Are they artifactual? *Developmental Psychology, 21,* 97–101.

Zaslow, M. J. (1991). Variation in child care quality and its implications for children. *Journal of Social Issues, 47*(2), 125–138.

Zellman, G. L., & Goodchilds, J. D. (1983). Becoming sexual in adolescence. In E. R. Allgeier & N. B. McCormick (Eds.), *Changing boundaries: Gender roles and sexual behavior* (pp. 49–63). Palo Alto, CA: Mayfield.

Zelnick, M., & Kantner, J. (1977). Sexual and contraceptive experiences of young unmarried women in the United States, 1976 and 1971. *Family Planning Perspectives, 9,* 55–71.

Zelnick, M., & Kantner, J. (1980). Sexual activity, contraceptive use, and pregnancy among metropolitan-area teenagers: 1971–1979. *Family Planning Perspectives, 12,* 230–237.

Zern, D. S. (1984). Relationships among selected child-rearing variables in a cross-cultural sample of 110 societies. *Developmental Psychology, 20*(4), 683–690.

Zickmund, W. G., Hitt, M. A., & Pickens, B. A. (1978). Influence of sex and scholastic performance on reactions to job applicant resumes. *Journal of Applied Psychology, 63,* 252–254.

Zilbergeld, B. (1978). *Male sexuality.* Boston: Little, Brown.

Zimmerman, D. H., & West, C. (1975). Sex roles, interruptions and silence in conversation. In B. Thorne & N. Henley (Eds.), *Language and sex: Difference and dominance* (pp. 105–129). Rowley, MA: Newbury House.

Zorza, V. (1986, September 1). Wife-sharing works in the remote Himalayas. *Globe and Mail,* p. A7.

Zuckerman, D. (1981). Family background, sex-role attitudes, and life goals of technical college and university students. *Sex Roles, 7,* 1109–1126.

Zuckerman, D. M., Singer, D. S., & Singer, J. L. (1980). Children's television viewing, racial and sex-role attitudes. *Journal of Applied Social Psychology, 10,* 281–294.

Zussman, J. U., Zussman, P. P., & Dalton, K. (1975). *Postpubertal effects of prenatal administration of progesterone.* Paper presented at the meeting of the Society for Research in Child Development, Denver.

Subject Index

Author Index

Credits, continued from copyright page

Page 126, Fig. 5.1 Copyright © 1965 CIBA-GEIGY Corporation. Reproduced with permission from THE CIBA COLLECTION OF MEDICAL ILLUSTRATIONS by Fred H. Netter, MD. All rights reserved.

Page 158, Fig. 6.2 From Richard Restak, *The Brain: The Last Frontier* (New York: Warner, 1979), p. 190. Copyright © 1979 by Richard Restal. Reproduced by permission of Doubleday & Company, Inc.

Pages 179, 180, Figs. 7.1, 7.2 From J. S. Hyde, *Understanding Human Sexuality,* pp. 200, 201. Copyright © 1986 by J. S. Hyde. Reproduced by permission of McGraw-Hill Book Company.

Page 155, Fig. 6.1 From J. S. Hyde, E. Fennema, and S. J. Lamon, "Gender Differences in Mathematics Performance: A Meta-Analysis," *Psychological Bulletin, 107* (2), p. 149.

Photographs: Chapter 1, © Bob Kalman/The Image Works; Chapter 2, © Suzanne Arms Wimberley; Chapter 3, © Zefa/H. Armstrong Roberts; Chapter 4, © H. Armstrong Roberts; Chapter 5, © Suzanne Arms Wimberley; Chapter 6, © Suzanne Arms Wimberley; Chapter 7; © M. B. Duda/Photo Researchers, Inc.; Chapter 8, © Rapho/Photo Researchers, Inc.; Chapter 9, © Bonnie Freer/Photo Researchers, Inc.; Chapter 10, © David S. Strickler/Monkmeyer Press Photo Service; Chapter 11, © 1986 Rona Beame/Photo Researchers, Inc.; Chapter 12, © Alan Carey/The Image Works; Chapter 13, © Suzanne Arms Wimberley; Chapter 14, © Bettye Lane/Photo Researchers, Inc.